W9-AED-353

ABOUT THE COVER IMAGE

Hebrew Astrolabe An astrolabe is an astronomical instrument that enables the user to determine time and position during the day with the help of the sun, and at night with the help of the stars. It can also be used in the preparation of horoscopes and for surveying purposes—to name but a few of its functions. Although familiar to ancient Greeks, the astrolabe was particularly important for the Islamic world, as it allowed the faithful to find the direction of the holy city of Mecca. The astrolabe pictured here, however, is a Jewish one made in Spain around 1350. Inscribed with Hebrew lettering, it contains as well Arabic and Spanish words and combines both Islamic and European decorative elements. It is not just an advanced scientific instrument but also an emblem of the peaceful exchange of knowledge and ideas among Christian, Jewish, and Muslim scholars in medieval Spain before 1492—when this intellectual alliance would be swept away by a militant Spanish monarchy intent on asserting Christian dominance.

Cultures of the West

A History

Volume 1: To 1750

Second Edition

Cultures of the West

A History

Volume 1: To 1750

Second Edition

Clifford R. Backman
Boston University

New York   Oxford
OXFORD UNIVERSITY PRESS

Oxford University Press is a department of the University of Oxford.
It furthers the University's objective of excellence in research,
scholarship, and education by publishing worldwide.

Oxford   New York
Auckland   Cape Town   Dar es Salaam   Hong Kong   Karachi
Kuala Lumpur   Madrid   Melbourne   Mexico City   Nairobi
New Delhi   Shanghai   Taipei   Toronto

With offices in
Argentina   Austria   Brazil   Chile   Czech Republic   France   Greece
Guatemala   Hungary   Italy   Japan   Poland   Portugal   Singapore
South Korea   Switzerland   Thailand   Turkey   Ukraine   Vietnam

Copyright © 2016, 2013 by Oxford University Press

For titles covered by Section 112 of the US Higher Education
Opportunity Act, please visit www.oup.com/us/he for the
latest information about pricing and alternate formats.

Published by Oxford University Press
198 Madison Avenue, New York, New York 10016
http://www.oup.com

Oxford is a registered trademark of Oxford University Press

All rights reserved. No part of this publication may be reproduced,
stored in a retrieval system, or transmitted, in any form or by any means,
electronic, mechanical, photocopying, recording, or otherwise,
without the prior permission of Oxford University Press.

Cataloging-in-Publication data is on file with the Library of Congress.

ISBN 978-0-19-024046-2

Printing number: 9 8 7 6 5 4 3 2 1

Printed in the United States of America
on acid-free paper

This book is for
Graham Charles Backman
Puero praeclaro, Scourge of Nations

and for my mother
Mary Lou Betker
with my best love

and in memory of my brother
Neil Howard Backman, U.S.N. (ret.)
(1956–2011)
who found his happiness just in time

BRIEF CONTENTS

CONTENTS

The interaction of the Indo-European groups and the primarily Semitic-speaking peoples of the Fertile Crescent opened the way for the development of the Greater West—a civilization that bridged Europe and western Asia.

The romanticization of David and Solomon introduced an entirely new element into Greater Western culture, or at least one for which no earlier evidence survives—namely, the popular belief in a past paradise, a lost era of former glory, when humanity had attained a perfection of happiness.

The Greeks, especially the Athenians, came to regard the mid-5th century bce with a determined awe, recalling it as a lost halcyon era that outshone anything that came before it or since. Through the centuries, much of Western culture has continued the love affair and has extolled "the glory that was Greece" as a pinnacle of human achievement.

7. The Rise of Christianity in a Roman World . . . 209

40 BCE–300 CE

8. The Early Middle Ages 241

300–750

9. The Expansive Realm of Islam. 277

30–900

The story fascinates, thrills, comforts, angers, and embarrasses at every turn, often all at once. It has touched everything from Western political ideas to sexual mores. Christianity began as an obscure reformist sect within Palestinian Judaism, at one time numbering no more than fifty or so believers. It went on, after three centuries of persecution by the Roman Empire, to become the world's most dominant faith.

The Western world had never seen a military juggernaut like this: in 622 Muhammad and his small group of followers had been forced from their home in Mecca, yet within a hundred years those followers had conquered an empire that stretched from Spain to India, an area twice the size of that conquered by Alexander the Great.

Latin Europe's history had been shaped by two opposed waves of development. The dual economic and cultural engine of the Mediterranean region spread its influence northward, bringing elements of cosmopolitan urban life, intellectual innovation, and cultural vibrancy into the European heartlands. Political leadership, however, came from the north, as the monarchies of England and France and the Holy Roman Empire pushed their boundaries southward, drawn by Mediterranean commerce and the gravitational pull of the papal court. The cross-fertilization of north and south benefited each and fostered Europe's ability to reform and revitalize itself.

The three elements most characteristically associated with the Renaissance—classicism, humanism, and modern statecraft—represent no essential break with medieval life at all. They may in fact be thought of as the culmination of medieval strivings.

Though often referred to as the "wars of religion," the wars that wracked the Greater West in the sixteenth and seventeenth centuries enmeshed religious antagonisms with economic, social, and political conflict. A more accurate term might come from English philosopher Thomas Hobbes (1588–1679): "the war of all against all."

Maps

Preface

I wrote this book with a simple goal in mind: to produce the kind of survey text I wished I had read in college. As a latecomer to history, I wondered why I so enjoyed studying a subject whose textbooks I found dry and lifeless. People, after all, are enormously interesting; and history is the story of people. So why were so many of the books I was assigned to read tedious?

Part of the problem lay in method. Teaching and writing history is difficult, in large part because of the sheer scope of the enterprise. Most history survey books stress their factual comprehensiveness and strict objectivity of tone. The trouble with this approach is that it too often works only for those few who are already true believers in history's importance and leaves most students yawning in their wake. I chose a different option—to teach and write history by emphasizing ideas and trends and the values behind them; to engage in the debates of each age rather than to narrate who won them. Students who are eagerly engaged in a subject, and who understand its significance, can then appreciate and remember the details. Moreover, twenty-five years of experience has taught me that they will do so.

This book adopts a thematic approach, but a theme seldom utilized in contemporary histories. While paying due attention to other aspects of Western development, it focuses on what might be called the *history of values*—that is, on the assumptions that lie behind political and economic developments, behind intellectual and artistic ventures, and behind social trends and countertrends. Consider, for example, the achievements of the Scientific Revolution. The advances made in fields like astronomy, chemistry, and medicine did not occur simply because individuals smart enough to figure out new truths happened to come along. William Harvey's discovery of the circulatory system was possible only because the culture in which he lived had begun, albeit hesitantly, to allow the dissection of human corpses for scientific research. For many centuries, even millennia, before Harvey's time, cultural and religious taboos had forbidden the desecration of bodies. But the era of the Scientific Revolution was also the era of political absolutism in Europe, a time when prevailing sentiment held that the king should hold all power and authority. Any enemy of the king—for example, anyone convicted of a felony—therefore deserved the ultimate penalty of execution and dissection. No king worship, no discovery of the circulation of the blood. At least not at that time.

A history that emphasizes the development of values runs the risk of distorting the record to some extent, because obviously not every person living at a given time held those values. Medieval Christians did not uniformly hate Jews and Muslims, believe the world was about to end, support the Inquisition, and blindly follow the dictates of the pope. Not every learned man and woman in the 18th century was "enlightened" or even wanted to be. The young generation of the 1960s was not composed solely of war protesters, feminist reformers, and rock-music lovers. With this important caveat in mind, however, it remains possible to offer general observations about the ideas and values that predominated in any era. This book privileges those ideas and sensibilities and views the events of each era in relation to them.

And it does so with a certain amount of opinion. To discuss value judgments without ever judging some of those values seems cowardly and is probably impossible anyway. Most large-scale histories mask their subjectivity simply by deciding which topics to discuss and which ones to pass over; I prefer to argue my positions explicitly, in the belief that to have a point of view is not the same thing as to be unfair. Education is as much about teaching students to evaluate arguments as it is about passing on knowledge to them, and students cannot learn to evaluate arguments if they are not presented with any.

In a second departure from tradition (which in this case is really just habit), this book interprets Western history on a broad geographic and cultural scale. All full-scale histories of Western civilization begin in the ancient Near East, but after making a quick nod to the origins of Islam in the 7th century, most of them focus almost exclusively on western Europe. The Muslim world thereafter enters the discussion only when it impinges on European actions. This book overtly rejects that view and insists on including the region of the Middle East in the general narrative, as a permanently constitutive element of the Greater West. For all its current global appeal, Islam is essentially a Western religion, after all, one that has its spiritual roots in the Jewish and Christian traditions and the bulk of whose intellectual foundations are in the classical Greco-Roman canon. To treat the Muslim world as an occasional sideshow on the long march to western European and American world leadership is, I believe, to falsify the record and to get the history wrong. The "European world" and the "Middle Eastern world" have been in a continuous relationship for millennia, buying and selling goods, sharing technologies, studying each other's political ideas, influencing each other's religious beliefs, learning from each other's medicine, facing the same challenges from scientific advances and changing economies. We cannot explain who we are if we limit ourselves to the traditional scope of Western history; we need a Greater Western perspective, one that includes and incorporates the whole of the monotheistic world.

Because religious belief has traditionally shaped so much of Greater Western culture—whether for good or ill is every reader's responsibility to determine—I have placed it at the center of my narrative. Even for the most unshakeable of modern agnostics and atheists, the values upheld by the three great monotheisms have had, and continue to have, a profound effect on the development of our social mores, intellectual pursuits, and artistic endeavors as well as on our politics and international relations.

In another break with convention, the book incorporates an abundance of primary sources into the narrative. I have always disliked the boxed and high-lighted source snippets that pockmark so many of today's textbooks. It seems to me that any passage worth quoting is worth working into the text itself—and I have happily done so. But a word about them is necessary. For the first three chapters I have needed considerable help. I am ignorant of the ancient Middle Eastern languages and have relied on the current version of a respected and well-loved anthology.[1] When discussing the sacred texts of Judaism, Christianity, and Islam, I have used their own authorized translations. Simple courtesy, it seems to me, calls for quoting a Jewish translation of the Bible when discussing Judaism; a Catholic, Orthodox, or Protestant Bible whenever discussing those main branches of Christianity; and the English version of the Qur'an prepared by the royal publishing house in Saudi Arabia when discussing Islam.[2] Last, some of the political records I cite (for example, the Cairo Declaration of Human Rights) are quoted from their official English versions. But apart from these special cases—all duly noted—every translation in this book, from chapter 4 onward, is my own.

CHANGES TO THE SECOND EDITION

Since the publication of the first edition of *Cultures of the West*, I have received, thankfully, a great number of notes and e-mails from teachers and students who appreciated the book, as well as dozens of formal critiques commissioned by the press. A textbook, unlike most scholarly works, affords historians the rare chance to revise the original work and to make it better. This second edition gave me the opportunity to realize my vision of the book, and I am pleased and grateful to point to the following main changes, all intended to make *Cultures of the West* a text that will engage students and teachers alike:

---

[1] Nels M. Bailkey and Richard Lim, *Readings in Ancient History: Thought and Experience from Gilgamesh to St. Augustine*, 7th ed. (Wadsworth, 2011).

[2] *Tanakh: The Holy Scriptures*, by the Jewish Publication Society; *New American Bible*, published by the U.S. Conference of Catholic Bishops; *New Revised Standard Version*, published by Oxford University Press; and *The Orthodox Study Bible*. For the Qur'an I have used *The Holy Qur'an: English Translations of the Meanings, with Commentary*, published by the King Fahd Holy Qur'an Printing Complex (A.H 1410).

- *Consistent reinforcement of the history of values*—as evidenced most easily by new chapter introductions and conclusions, but I highlighted the book's central theme throughout the narrative.
- *A more comprehensive treatment of Western Europe to ground students' exploration of the Greater West*—as evidenced, for example, by fuller coverage of the Middle Ages, the French Revolution, and the world wars. To keep the length of the book manageable for readers, I compensated for these additions by streamlining or excising outright subjects and passages that instructors found too advanced for the survey course.
- *A new chapter in Volume 1 and two fewer chapters in Volume 2* for a more course-friendly periodization. The new chapter (9), *The Expansive Realm of Islam, 30–900*, parallels the chapters on early Judaism (3) and Christianity (7) for a full treatment of the monotheistic cultures that gave rise to the Greater West. Basically a reworking of materials previously scattered among different chapters, I am especially proud of this newcomer to the Western civilization textbook literature. To reduce the number of chapters in Volume 2, I combined directly related first-edition chapters 20 and 23 into the new chapter 22, *The Challenge of Secularism*, and the final two first-edition chapters into chapter 29, *Global Warmings: Since 1989*.
- *Consistent treatment of women and gender in the central narrative.* The warm reception to a chapter devoted to the modern woman encouraged me to keep a carefully revised version of this chapter (21) in the new edition, but elsewhere I worked hard to integrate women's history and gender issues into the main story of events.
- *New marginal headings that identify key events and developments* to supplement the book's well-received single-heading structure of the narrative.
- *Expanded map program.* The second edition includes twenty-four new maps. All of the maps have been corrected and redesigned for improved clarity.
- *New Prologue: Before History*, for readers of Volume 1 and the combined edition. Because the first edition neglected the Paleolithic and Neolithic eras, I was especially happy to add this illustrated discussion.

- *Updated scholarship.* The research that goes into revision of a single-authored textbook is as rewarding as it is time consuming. I am pleased to include many new titles in the chapter bibliographies that inform the narrative.

ACKNOWLEDGMENTS

Working with Oxford University Press has been a delight. Charles Cavaliere has served as point man, guiding me through the entire project with grace and kindness. His cheery enthusiasm kept me going through many a difficult hour. If the prose in this book has any merit, please direct your compliments to John Haber and Elizabeth Welch, the talented editors who guided me through, respectively, the first and second editions. Beth did more than edit; she reenvisioned and gave new life to the book (and its author) by her enthusiasm, rigor, and good humor. Christi Sheehan, Debbie Needleman, Theresa Stockton, Lisa Grzan, Eden Kram-Gingold, Kateri Woody, Meg Botteon, and Michele Laseau shepherded me through the production and marketing phases and deserve all the credit for the wonderful physical design of the book and its handsome map and art programs.

I am also deeply grateful to the many talented historians and teachers who offered critical readings of the first edition. My sincere thanks to the following instructors, whose comments often challenged me to rethink or justify my interpretations and provided a check on accuracy down to the smallest detail:

Robert Brennan, Cape Fear Community College
Lee L. Brice, Western Illinois University
Keith Chu, Bergen Community College
Jason Coy, College of Charleston
Marc Eagle, Western Kentucky University
Christine Eubank, Bergen Community College
Jennifer L. Foray, Purdue University
Edith Foster, Case Western Reserve University
Matthew Gerber, University of Colorado at Boulder
David M. Head, John Tyler Community College
Brian Hilly, Suffolk County Community College
Christopher Howell, Red Rocks Community College
Andrew Keitt, University of Alabama at Birmingham
Christina Bosco Langert, Suffolk County Community College
Ryan Messenger, Monroe Community College
Alexander Mikaberidze, Louisiana State University–Shreveport
Kathryn Ordway, Colorado Community College Online

Jennifer Popiel, Saint Louis University
Matthew Ruane, Florida Institute of Technology
Nicholas L. Rummell, Trident Technical College
Robert Rusnak, Trident Technical College
Sarah Shurts, Bergen Community College

I thank as well the good folks at Trident Tech Community College in Charleston, South Carolina, who hosted a workshop in June 2014 that provided a forum for me to sound out the revision plan. Professors Donald West, Barbara Tucker, Robert Rusnak, Nicholas Rummell, and several other History TTCC faculty members were kind enough to spend a morning with me sharing their experiences using *Cultures of the West* and offering suggestions for how it could be improved. I hope they are pleased with the result. I especially want to thank Katherine Jenkins of Trident Tech Community College, who prepared many of the excellent supplementary materials for the second edition and saved me from several embarrassing errors.

My former student at Boston University, Christine Axen (PhD, 2015), has been a support from the start. She has taught with me, and occasionally for me, through the past three years, and I appreciate the time she took away from her own dissertation research to assist me on this project—pulling books from the library, running down citations, suggesting ideas. When Oxford asked me to prepare a companion volume of primary texts for this book, Christine proved to be such an immense help that she deserves to share the title page with me. The sourcebook too is appearing in a second edition.

To my wife, Nelina, and our sons, Scott and Graham, this book has been an uninvited houseguest at times, pulling me away from too many family hours. They have put up with it, and with me, with patience and generosity that I shall always be thankful for. Their love defines them and sustains me.

SUPPORT MATERIALS FOR *CULTURES OF THE WEST*

Cultures of the West comes with an extensive package of support materials for both instructors and students.

- **Dashboard** Dashboard delivers quality content, tools and assessments to track student progress in an intuitive, web-based learning environment. Assessments are designed to accompany *Cultures of the west*, and automatically graded so instructors can easily check students' progress as they complete their assignments. The color-coded gradebook illustrates at a glance where students are succeeding and where they can improve so busy instructors can adapt lectures to student needs. Dashboard features a streamlined interface that connects instructors and students with the functions they perform most, and simplifies the learning experience by putting student progress first. All Dashboard content is engineered to work on mobile devices, including the iOS platform. Our goal is to create a platform that is simple, informative, and mobile. Please contact your local Oxford University Press representative for a demonstration of Dashboard.

- **Oxford First Source** (www.oup.com/us/firstsource) Oxford First Source is an online database, with custom print capability, of primary source documents in World History. The continuously updated collection consists of approximately 300 documents for European and World History, both textual and visual, selected and organized to complement any World History survey text. These documents cover a broad range of political, social, and cultural topics. The documents are indexed by date, title, subject, and region and are fully searchable. Each is accompanied by a headnote and study questions. Six-month access to Oxford First Source is $10.00 when bundled with *Cultures of the West*, or can be purchased standalone for $19.95. Please contact your local Oxford University Press representative for details.

- *Sources for Cultures of the West, Volume 1: To 1750* and *Sources for Cultures of the West, Volume 2: Since 1350*. Edited by Clifford R. Backman and Christine Axen, it includes approximately 175 primary sources, organized to match the chapter organization of *Cultures of the West*. Forty-one of the sources are new to the second edition. Each source is accompanied by a headnote and reading questions. The sourcebooks are significantly discounted when bundled with the text.

    - **Companion Website (http://www.oup.com/us/ backman/**): For students, the open-access site includes quizzes, flashcards, documents, interactive maps, and links to YouTube videos. Access to the student site is unrestricted.

    - **Ancillary Resource Center** (ARC): Includes PowerPoint slides and JPEG and PDF files for all the maps and photos in the text; an additional four hundred map files, in PowerPoint format, from *The Oxford Atlas of World History*; and approximately 250 additional PowerPoint-based slides organized by theme and topic. The ARC also includes an Instructor's Resource Manual, which includes, for each chapter, a detailed chapter outline, suggested lecture topics, learning objectives, suggested Web resources, and digital media files. It also includes, for each chapter, approximately thirty multiple-choice, short-answer, true-or-false, and fill-in-the-blank questions as well as numerous essay questions. The test questions are available in a computerized test bank that can be customized by the instructor.

- **Mapping the Cultures of the West, Volume 1: To 1750:** Includes approximately forty full-color maps, each accompanied by a brief headnote. Free when bundled with the text.

- **Mapping the Cultures of the West, Volume 2: Since 1350:** Includes approximately forty full-color maps, each accompanied by a brief headnote. Free when bundled with the text.

- **Now Playing: Studying Western Civilization through Film** (available in both student and instructor editions) is a concise print supplement that provides synopses, recommended scenes, and discussion questions for thirty of the most commonly assigned films in Western Civilization classes. Qualified adopters can receive a Netflix subscription with their adoption. *Now Playing* can be bundled with *Cultures of the West* at no additional cost.

- **E-book for *Cultures of the West* (both volumes):** An e-book is available for purchase at **http://www.course smart.com.**

BUNDLING OPTIONS

Cultures of the West can be bundled at a significant discount with any of the titles in the popular Very Short Introductions or Oxford World's Classics series, as well as other titles from the Higher Education division world history catalog (**http://www.oup.com/us/catalog/he/**). Please contact your OUP representative for details.

About the Author

Clifford Backman has been a member of the History Department at Boston University since 1989. In addition to the two-semester Western Civilization course, he teaches several courses on medieval Europe, the Mediterranean, the Crusades, piracy, and the history of sexual morality. He also teaches in the university's Core Curriculum, a four-semester sequence in the humanities and the social sciences. He is currently at work on a book that traces the development of toleration and interpersonal forgiveness in medieval Christianity, Judaism, and Islam.

Note on Dates

I follow a few basic conventions. Instead of the old BC ("before Christ") and AD (*anno Domini*, "in the year of the Lord") designations for centuries, I use the new norms of BCE ("before the common era") and CE ("common era"). Dates are given, whenever possible, for every figure mentioned in the book. Political leaders are identified by the years they were in power. All other personal dates, unless otherwise noted, are birth and death dates.

Prologue: Before History

Strictly speaking, history is a textual discipline: When human beings developed writing, they started to create written records, the foundation of history (from the Greek word *historia*, meaning "inquiry"). Study of the human world before the advent of writing is the domain of archeology and anthropology. All three disciplines share the same aim—to understand how human life, in all its variety, has developed over time—but they use different tools and methods. Apart from a handful of early markings found in southeastern Europe, dating to the 6th century BCE, which may or may not be examples of writing (scholars have been debating them since they were discovered), the first definite use of writing appeared around the year 3200 BCE in the ancient Near East.

Although it was a long time ago, 3200 BCE should be considered the end, even the culmination, of a story that began much, much earlier.

Archeology and anthropology tell us that human beings (the species *Homo sapiens sapiens*) appeared in eastern Africa approximately 200,000 years ago.[3] Other humanlike (hominid) species still existed in far greater numbers across Africa, Europe, and Asia—species like *Homo neanderthalensis* and *Homo erectus*—but *Homo sapiens sapiens* had several advantages over their distant relatives, the most important being the large forebrain that rests above, rather than behind, the eyes. Increased brain capacity contributed to the use of stone tools and the development of fire, and the raised forehead that accompanied it made possible more subtle communicative abilities. The appearance of human beings marks the beginning of the Paleolithic (or "Old Stone") Age, which lasted until approximately 10,000 BCE.

Two broad hypotheses dominate research into the Paleolithic Age. First, the long-standard "Out of Africa" hypothesis maintains that soon after their appearance in today's country of Ethiopia, humans branched out across Africa. Crossing Egypt's Sinai Peninsula sometime around 125,000 BCE, they settled in the Near East before fanning out in all directions (see Map P.1). Those who ventured westward crossed Anatolia (modern Turkey) and moved on into Europe by 40,000 BCE. Those who migrated eastward reached India as early as 60,000 BCE and advanced as far as southeast Asia and Australia by 50,000 BCE. At still

---

[3] Why *sapiens sapiens*? Because it turns out that we humans are a subspecies rather than a species proper. Also known to specialists as AMH, or Anatomically Modern Humans, we are an offshoot of the *Homo sapiens* species. Fossils of another offshoot, *Homo sapiens idaltu*, now extinct, were discovered by archeologists in Ethiopia in 1997.

another turn of direction, groups of humans moved northward through China, crossed the Siberian–Alaskan ice bridge around 15,000 BCE, and between three and five thousand years later migrated southward into the Americas. By 10,000 BCE, in other words, humans had expanded throughout the entire world. Around that same time, human beings began to practice agriculture—the stage of development at which the Paleolithic Age ends and the Neolithic ("New Stone") Age begins.

The Out of Africa thesis makes geographical and chronological sense, insofar as it places humans at sites and times around the globe that correspond with the fossil record—and this is why it has dominated the thinking about human development and the Paleolithic Age for the past two centuries. But in the past few decades, a second hypothesis has emerged that utilizes previously unknown evidence. The discovery of DNA and genetic coding has made it possible to analyze the Paleolithic remains in greater detail and has revealed a problem with the Out of Africa model—namely, that there should be vastly greater genetic diversity

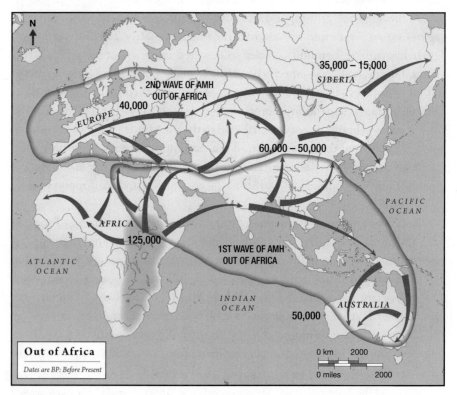

MAP P.1   The map shows the general chronology and migration patterns of anatomically modern humans (AMH) out of Africa. The migrations occurred in two waves: the first directed primarily to the east, and a second, later wave that moved into Europe.

among human beings than there is, given the age of our species. At some point, therefore, something must have happened to decrease dramatically the gene pool. Some researchers have argued that the entire human population must have been reduced to as few as five thousand people to account for the smallness of the genetic variation observable. What could such an event have been? Around 70,000 BCE there was a catastrophic explosion of the supervolcano at Lake Toba, in Indonesia, which scientists reckon (by analyzing ash deposits) was the most violent event on earth in the past 25 million years. So enormous was the blast that it spewed enough ash and sulfur dioxide into the air to alter dramatically the earth's climate, dropping global average temperatures as much as 5°C (41°F) for a decade and triggering a mini ice age that lasted for a thousand years. This "Toba Event" happened early enough in the process of human expansion (when human beings coming out of Africa had made it only as far as Anatolia and India) to nearly eradicate the entire species, thus accounting for the diminished gene pool of the survivors.

The Toba Event hypothesis thus fine-tunes, rather than contradicts, the Out of Africa hypothesis. Researchers still debate the details, but the modified model of human migration in the Paleolithic Age has won broad acceptance. It also helps to explain the abrupt disappearance of the other hominids. Only *Homo sapiens sapiens* had the ability to recover from the biological apocalypse and adapt to the new environment. Peoples' ability to use tools for hunting, building shelter, producing fire, constructing watercraft, and self-defense enabled them to survive when other species could not. For tens of thousands of years they survived as hunter–gatherers, people literally traveling through the earth in search of food.

In the Neolithic Age (10,000–3000 BCE) people everywhere gradually learned agriculture, and populations consequently began to concentrate in areas where the soil and climate were amenable to producing food. The earliest sites of farming discovered by archeologists appear in the region known as the Fertile Crescent, the broad arc of land that stretches from Mesopotamia, in today's southern Iraq, skirts the highlands of northern Syria, and passes along the eastern Mediterranean into Egypt. The domestication of cattle, goats, pigs, and sheep followed soon after; fossils reflecting the domestication of goats date as early as 8900 BCE, and pig domestication dates to roughly 7000 BCE. Most people lived in rural communities made up of various clans, with some of these villages holding several hundred people. The men plowed the fields and harvested, spending the months in between hunting and gathering. Women and children tended to growing crops and the farm animals. Most homes were simple constructions of stone or clay brick—because the region is not rich in timber, most of the wood available was used for cooking.

Archeologists in 1958 discovered a site of unusual size and development in southern Anatolia at a place called Catalhüyük, which was settled around 7500 BCE, where Neolithic peoples lived for two thousand years. As its height, Catalhüyük had as many as six thousand inhabitants, possibly even more, living

A "Mother Goddess"?   This figurine from Catalhüyük is generally thought to depict a corpulent and fertile Mother Goddess in the process of giving birth while seated on her throne. Because no contemporary texts exist to explain the significance of the figurine's obesity and pronounced sexual characteristics, however, we can only speculate about the complex meanings that prehistoric peoples extracted from them.

in a nest of connected mud houses that the people entered through holes in their roofs. (Since no footpaths existed between the buildings, the contiguous rooftops served as an open-air market square.) The interior walls of each house were covered in plaster. No buildings have been identified as anything other than homes and storage units. There were no temples, no ruler's court. This fact suggests that social stratification had not yet developed, nor had any organized political life. Some individual rooms have been identified as shrines, but little is known of the people's religion. People appear to have buried their dead in pits beneath their homes, and surviving artifacts suggest they may have practiced a form of ancestor worship. Hundreds of figurines survive, as do examples of their textiles, tools, and pottery.

Although writing was unknown to them, the inhabitants of Catalhüyük showed considerable artistic skill. Murals covered many walls, and surviving figurines are beautifully made. Obviously people were seeking ways to express themselves through art well before the development of "civilization," the subject of chapter 1. Three concerns seem to have been predominant: death, reproduction, and survival. Numerous mural paintings at Catalhüyük depict vultures pecking at human corpses (the people seem to have left their dead exposed until nothing remained but the bones, which they buried beneath their homes), whereas others portray large-breasted women, who may or may not have served as fertility symbols, either copulating with, or giving birth to, bulls—presumably images of virility. Hunting scenes featuring large wild cattle are another common motif.

The people who settled in Europe lived in more difficult circumstances because the dense woodlands and heavy soil were difficult to work with stone tools. Hunting and gathering remained the mode of existence, and agriculture hence did not begin until at least a thousand years after it appeared in the Fertile Crescent. The first sites of settled agriculture did not appear until sometime around 2500 BCE, in the Balkans. The earliest Europeans are known above all for the giant stone structures they erected. Called megaliths, these structures were raised all across western Europe, from Scandinavia to the Mediterranean. The best-known of these is Stonehenge, on the Salisbury plain in southern England. Initially a ring of pits dug into the ground, it developed around 2300 BCE into a circle of tall standing stones. The stones were quarried far away, in Wales. No one knows precisely what the purpose or function of Stonehenge was, but its mere existence is evidence of a high degree of social organization, skilled labor, and engineering proficiency.

It is a long story, from the emergence of *Homo sapiens sapiens* in Ethiopia to the start of civilization in the Fertile Crescent. Humankind showed its

Stonehenge   Possibly Britain's greatest national icon, Stonehenge symbolizes mystery, power, and endurance. Its original purpose is unclear, but some scholars speculate that it was a temple made for the worship of ancient earth deities.

remarkable adaptability to circumstances, and life progressed from a mere struggle for daily survival to a continuous search for more than that—a search for meaning. The murals and figurines of Catalhüyük and the mysterious grandeur of Stonehenge, whatever their precise interpretation, bear witness to the human desire to make sense out of life's struggle and to find value and purpose in it.

Cultures of the West

A History

Volume 1: to 1750

Second Edition

CHAPTER 1

Water and Soil, Stone and Metal: The First Civilizations

10,000–2100 BCE

The origins of Western civilization lie in southern Iraq. The region was called Sumer five thousand years ago, and it was the first site of the features that historians associate with civilization: consistent use of agriculture, the domestication of animals that made farming possible, the construction of cities, and the invention of writing. At first glance it seems an unlikely place for civilization to begin. The soil is sandy, summertime temperatures regularly surpass 110°F (43°C), and the dull flatland receives a scant 8 inches of annual rainfall. (By comparison, most of the Mediterranean basin receives nearly four times as much.) There is no stone to quarry, no metal ores to mine, and little timber with which to build. Bordered by the relatively low-lying Zagros Mountains of Iran to the east, Sumer nevertheless lay exposed to raiding groups from the Iranian steppe.

THE ANCIENT NEAR EAST

The Invention of Writing
Unassuming clay objects such as this one from Sumer, in the south of modern Iraq, reveal human beings' earliest ability to record information for the future. Dating to 3300–3100 BCE, this tablet is impressed with cuneiform signs that represent a grain (barley) inventory.

But it was in Sumer that Greater Western civilization began. Many nomadic groups had passed through the region as early as 7000 BCE, following their herds, pursuing prey, or fleeing from rivals. The appearance of the Sumerians around four thousand years later, however, marks the start of **civilization**. *Civilization*, of course, is an expansive term; it is also value laden. After all, its alternative—to be *uncivilized*—implies barbarism. But historians use it in a nonjudgmental sense to designate a society that has advanced beyond a basic search for sustenance. Agriculture, specialization of labor, and trade, under the right conditions, produce surpluses that release people from the daily struggle for survival and allow them to pursue other endeavors like investigating the physical world and the heavens (the seed of science); creating images, objects, and sounds for pleasure (the origin of art); and wondering where human life came from and what, if anything, it is for (the root of religion and philosophy). These are the elements that make up civilization, and in the case of Sumer they appeared around 3000 BCE. Under different circumstances, they appeared more or less contemporaneously in Egypt's Nile River valley.

Civilization, because it involves the desire for something beyond mere survival, entails the search for values—the ideas, assumptions, and hopes on which human beings rely to give their lives meaning. As the examples of ancient Sumer and Egypt show, the earliest values that emerged in what became the Greater West ranged widely, from a resigned acceptance of life's inherent purposelessness to a conviction in the perfect and eternal order of the world.

CHAPTER TIMELINE

9000 BCE	8500 BCE	7000 BCE	5500 BCE	4500 BCE

- ca. 9000 BCE Evidence of grain storage, Jericho

- ca. 7000 BCE Earliest evidence of farming, Sumer

- ca. 5500 BCE Appearance of cities in Eridu and Ur, Sumer

THE TIGRIS, THE EUPHRATES, AND THE LAND BETWEEN THE RIVERS

Sumer lay in the narrowing plain between the lower reaches of the Tigris and Euphrates rivers. Indeed, the region is also known as Mesopotamia ("between the rivers"), which derives from the ancient Greek name for the area (see Map 1.1). The Sumerians had access to the Persian Gulf, whose headlands reached about 100 miles farther inland in ancient times than they do today. Yet they never developed a maritime tradition and remained resolutely bound to the soil. Sandy though that soil was, it was made fertile by the flooding of the two great rivers, as the winter rains of Syria and the spring thaws of the snows of the Taurus Mountains to the far north brought layer upon layer of silt to fertilize the land. Twisting slowly eastward through narrow gorges until they reached the high plains of Syria and Kurdistan, the rivers then plunged dramatically southward, picking up speed as they approached the site of today's city of Baghdad in Iraq. The Tigris River, with its deep bed, flooded less widely but with a strong current. The Euphrates, on the other hand, was broad and shallow, overran its banks easily, and scattered highland silt over a wide expanse. The faster-flowing Tigris usually reached its high-water mark in April, whereas the Euphrates generally reached full flood about a month later. By managing this water via an elaborate network of levees, reservoirs, and irrigation canals, the Sumerians were able to produce abundant

4000 BCE	3500 BCE	3000 BCE	2500 BCE	1500 BCE

- ca. 4000–1500 BCE **Bronze Age**
- ca. 3500 BCE **Earliest evidence of writing, Sumer**
- ca. 3150 BCE **Egypt united under a single ruler, Menes/Narmer**
- ca. 2686–2134 BCE **Old Kingdom Egypt**
- ca. 2600 BCE **Rule of Gilgamesh in Uruk**
- ca. 2350–2200 BCE **Akkadian Empire founded by Sargon I**
- ca. 2100–2000 BCE **Third Dynasty of Ur**

yields of summer grains for themselves and prairie grasses for their herds. Crop yields may have reached ratios as high as 30:1—that is, 30 bushels of grain harvested for every bushel of seeds planted.

Spread of Agriculture   Archeological evidence suggests that the Ubaids—the first identifiable group to settle in the region—began farming in Sumer perhaps as early as 7000 BCE. Remnants of irrigation tunnels, built of stone, date to at least 5900 BCE and possibly earlier. Archeologists have discovered even older settlements involving agriculture in other sites throughout the Middle East. At Jericho in Palestine, for example, evidence of grain storage—although not necessarily of grain production—reaches back to 9000 BCE. Agriculture also developed in northern Mesopotamia only two hundred years later, then on the south-central Anatolian plateau around 7500 BCE, and finally in southern Russia and along the banks of the Black Sea about 7000 BCE, after the geological shifting of continental plates opened the Dardanelles and let the saltwater of the Mediterranean pour in, to create the Black Sea out of what used to be a freshwater lake. But only Sumer gives evidence of continuous settlement, systematic agriculture, developed urban life, and the use of writing. From its location in the **Fertile Crescent**—the belt of rich farmland that extends from Mesopotamia in the east through Syria in the north and down to Egypt in the west—the techniques of agriculture spread eastward into India, westward

At Home in Çatalhöyük   This reconstruction shows a typical village home, ca. 6000 BCE, at Çatalhöyük, in modern central Turkey. The entrance to the house was through the roof. The opening in the floor led to the underground graves of the family's dead.

to the coastal plains of the eastern Mediterranean, and even as far as western Europe (see Map 1.1).

Early agriculture depended on collective labor, and lots of it: until native animals such as oxen were domesticated, the brutal work of cutting open the soil, planting seeds, weeding, pruning vines, cutting stalks, and grinding grains had to be done by hand. Skeletal remains of early agriculturalists—chiefly women—display agonizingly curved spines. Men, on the other hand, hunted, gathered, and ruled. Villages began to appear, some of them rather large; for safety, the people at most sites constructed stone or earthen walls to protect them from attack. The early settlement at Jericho had a population of roughly two thousand people by 7000 BCE and a fortification wall that may have reached 30 feet in height. In west-central Anatolia, at about the time Jericho was completing its wall, cattle breeders settled at Çatalhöyük, where their population swelled to between eight and ten thousand. They built a village of closely placed mud-brick houses without streets in between; roofs served as walkways, and residents entered their homes through holes in their roofs.

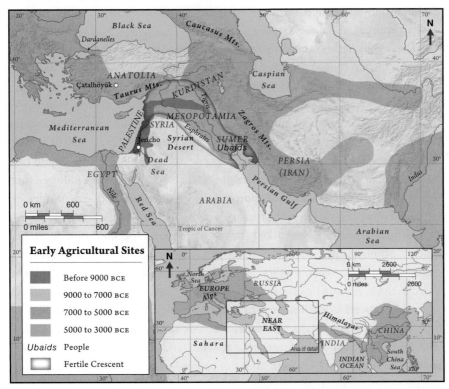

MAP 1.1   Early Agricultural Sites   The earliest agricultural societies appeared in northern Syria and Palestine, where archeological evidence survives from before 9000 BCE. These areas benefited from the higher rainfall of the Mediterranean basin.

Start of the Bronze Age

Primitive metal tools appeared around 7000 BCE as well, when small bits of raw copper were hammered into shape with stones. By 5000 BCE early settlers had learned how to smelt copper ore into the pure metal, which they then either cast into molds or, by 4000 BCE, mixed with tin to produce bronze. Bronze was significantly stronger than its component parts, and its use in weaponry and farm implements spread throughout the Near East quickly—inaugurating the **Bronze Age** (ca. 4000–1500 BCE).

EARLY MESOPOTAMIA: KINGS AND PRIESTS

Rich in potential for grain producing but lacking the stone and metal needed to bring it about, the Sumerians had to develop trade relations. These reached to the ore-rich but grain-poor settlements along the upper Tigris River and westward into Palestine and lower Anatolia. Sumerian grain traveled well in the arid atmosphere of the Near East, and the masses of heavy stone and metal they needed to produce it were easily transported down the strong current of the Tigris. But maintaining these important commercial ties over such long distances compelled the Sumerians to develop writing. With it they could keep records of orders, shipments, revenues, and obligations.

The origins of the Sumerians are unknown since their language is unrelated to any other known tongue, whether ancient or later. It is likely that they entered the Tigris–Euphrates plain, as did most of their subsequent invaders, from the Zagros Mountains in Iran. Sumerians were not the only inhabitants of Mesopotamia, of course, but they were the dominant group until their conquest by the Akkadians around 2500 BCE. Their founding myths identify Eridu and Ur as their first cities; archeological evidence confirms that these appeared as early as 5500 BCE and contained as many as fifty thousand inhabitants at their peak. They were followed soon by settlements at Uruk, Lagash, Nippur, and Kish; Sumerian cities were considerably larger and more complex than the rural villages in Palestine, Syria, and Anatolia.[1]

Although most people worked the land, economic specialization developed quickly. Stonemasons, merchants, rivermen, weavers, dyers, civil and hydraulic engineers, metalworkers, potters, and scribes—all emerged as distinct occupations. In the first centuries, these cities were governed by clan elders, who perhaps worked in concert as a primitive form of municipal council. They could not, however, defend the Sumerians against invaders or satisfy the whims of the deities who controlled the natural forces of heat, wind, and water. These constant needs resulted in the rise of new twin nodes of power—militarily backed monarchies and divinely appointed priesthoods.

---

[1]   Settlements were also heavily fortified. Uruk had a full 6 miles of battlements surrounding it.

Kingship and priesthood commonly emerged together in Western societies, sometimes in contest with each other and sometimes elided into a single office. Military action was most efficiently directed by a single commander to whom everyone owed obedience—the king, whose formal title was **lugal**. Protection against the gods, especially the unpredictable deities that the Sumerians believed in, required the priests. This large and permanent caste was charged with anticipating the gods' desires, interpreting their actions, and above all placating their wrath through prayer and sacrifice. Given their joint responsibility for protecting the people from harm, kings and priests have traditionally worked together: kings stand as bulwarks and standard-bearers of the priests' institutionalized religion, whereas priests serve to consecrate kings and bless their actions. In the ancient Near East, and well into Europe's own history, the worst crises frequently occurred when the secular and religious powers were at cross-purposes.

Secular and Religious Power

The Sumerians' own king list, written around 2100 BCE but reflecting a much older oral tradition, fancifully boasted that an unbroken string of monarchs had governed Sumer for well over 200,000 years. This tradition reached back even before the worst crisis of all: a mythical Great Flood sent by capricious gods that covered the entire earth and all but annihilated mankind. Much like the biblical tale of Noah and the ark, for which it served as a model, the Great Flood never happened but retained its psychological power because of the people's genuine fear of actual flooding. The Tigris and Euphrates occasionally swelled to unusual size and covered farms, fields, and flocks.[2] This legend, told in the great Mesopotamian poem the *Epic of Gilgamesh* (discussed in chapter 2), served to remind the people of the unpredictability of the gods while creating a reference point for the start of their own history.

Sumer consisted of a sprawl of independent city-states, each governed by a lugal, a priestly caste, or an uneasy combination of the two (see Map 1.2). The earliest king we can identify with any certainty was En-Mebaragesi, who ruled over Kish, near the site of the later city of Babylon, around 2600 BCE. His most significant achievement was the construction of the temple in Nippur, dedicated to the great sky god Enlil. En-Mebaragesi ruled during the so-called Early Dynastic Period, which lasted from about 2900 to 2350 BCE. By far the most famous of the Early Dynasts was **Gilgamesh**, who ruled Uruk around 2600 BCE. Tradition credits him with building the battlements surrounding that city and claims that after his death the grateful people of Uruk gave him a magnificent burial: they diverted the Euphrates River, buried his body in the exposed riverbed, and then released the waters once again into their original channel so their ruler would lie

The Early Dynasts

---

[2]   It seems likely that the legend of the Great Flood, if it had any basis in historical fact at all, originated with the creation of the Black Sea, described above.

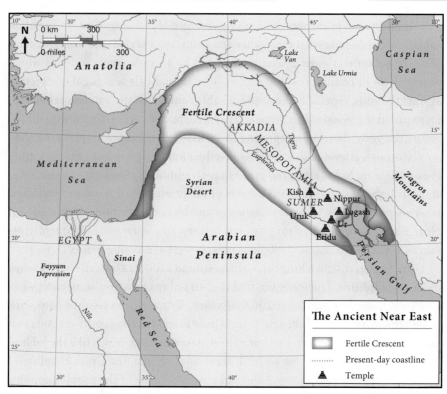

MAP 1.2   The Ancient Near East   Agriculture formed the foundation of civilization, but other necessary components were cities, literacy, and organized religion. Shown here are the major temple sites in Sumer.

forever beneath the great river.[3] But Gilgamesh is best known as a literary figure, the hero of the later Babylonian epic that bears his name.

The Akkadian Conquest

A Semitic-speaking people called the Akkadians overwhelmed the Sumerian city-states around 2350 BCE, thus establishing what historians call the Akkadian Period, which lasted until about 2100. They had lived for several centuries along the upper Tigris, trading with the Sumerians and the peoples of Syria. Although they were foreigners, the Akkadians respected Sumerian culture and adopted its language, institutions, and religion. The most successful of the Akkadian kings was the first, **Sargon I**, who conquered everything from lower Sumer to northern Syria, all the way to the Mediterranean. This fierce conqueror boasted constantly of his cruelty as a matter of policy, making him perhaps the first ruler who found that simply maintaining a reputation for savagery can hold a large population in check as effectively as actual savagery can.

---

3   In 2003 a team of German archeologists discovered what they believe to be the ancient city of Uruk. The excavation is still underway; Gilgamesh's grave has yet to be located.

THE IDEA OF EMPIRE

Sargon placed family members in control of the territories he conquered, thereby governing a knitted-together **empire** (see Map 1.3). This was a surprisingly new idea. The Sumerians had fought plenty of wars over the centuries, but their custom had always been to defeat a neighbor and then to withdraw and receive annual tribute from the conquered. The notion of actually governing the lands they conquered seems never to have occurred to them. Sargon, however, saw that a hitherto unimagined level of wealth and power could result not only from controlling grain-rich Sumer but also from commanding the trade routes of upper Mesopotamia. Through this region Sumerian grain traveled northward, while textiles, metalwork, and animal products of the northern portions of the Fertile Crescent moved south. His empire far exceeded any earlier kingdom in its magnificence, but its real significance lay in the model of strategic authority that it established. By recognizing the Fertile Crescent's connective role—that is, its status as a commercial center or meeting point for the central Asian and eastern Mediterranean economies—he highlighted what was to become perhaps the dominant trait of

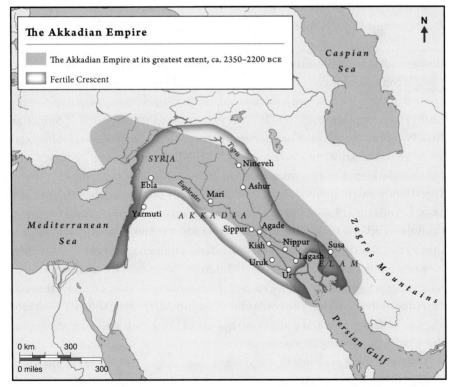

MAP 1.3   The Akkadian Empire, ca. 2350–2200 BCE   The Akkadian ruler Sargon was the first political figure to envision a state that united the territories of the Fertile Crescent under a single government.

Middle Eastern history, its strategic significance as the connection point between East and West.

The Sumerians had commonly referred to their rulers as shepherds of the people. The Akkadians, however, would have none of that. The *Babylonian Chronicle of Early Kings* declares, "Sargon, King of Agade, came to power during the reign of Ishtar and had neither rival nor equal. His splendor spread over the land and crossed over the sea to the east. And in the eleventh year he conquered to the west as far as it went." An inscription from the reign of one of Sargon's successors—his grandson Naram-Sin—describes him as "the Strong, the Ruler of Akkad" and claims his own share of his grandfather's glory:

> Even when the four corners of the earth were united in opposition to him, [Naram-Sin] emerged victorious . . . and took captive all the kings who had united against him. Because he had saved Akkad in time of crisis, all the people of the city begged of the gods—of Ishtar, in Eanna; of Enlil, in Nippur; of Dagan, in Tuttel; of Ninhursaga, in Kesh; of Enki, in Eridu; of Sin, in Ur; of Shamash, in Sippur; and of Nergal, in Kutha—that Naram-Sin might be worshipped as a god in Akkad. Accordingly, they built a temple for him in the center of the city.

The Akkadians thus appear to have introduced the cult of king worship.

Sargon's empire collapsed roughly one hundred years after his death, and control of the region passed to a series of native kings known collectively as the Third Dynasty of Ur (ca. 2100–2000 BCE). This was the last period of Sumerian history, since new waves of invaders who poured over Mesopotamia (sometimes en route to Palestine) ultimately displaced the Ur dynasts after 2000 BCE: the Semitic-speaking Amorites from southern Iran (2000–1600 BCE); the Hittites, an Indo-European group from central Anatolia (1600–1400 BCE); the Mitanni, also Indo-Europeans (1500–1300 BCE); and the Assyrians, a Semitic-speaking group from the northernmost reaches of the Tigris River (1500–600 BCE). There were others, too. But these groups generally disdained Sumerian culture and did their best to suppress or supplant it. Their interests lay more in the northern and western reaches of the Fertile Crescent, from Syria and Anatolia down through Palestine and approaching Egypt. As Sumer declined, the priestly caste went into elegiac mode, writing and preserving hymns to their gods and laments for the lost glories of the early city-states.

There is some evidence that economic decline contributed to the invaders' disdain for the Sumerian way of life. Centuries of flooding and irrigation had left high quotients of mineral salts in the farm fields. Since these salts rose to the surface as the water was absorbed into the land, the quality of the soil deteriorated, reducing productivity. Local farmers attempted to stop the decline by introducing new grains, but it seems clear that the gradual corrosion of the alluvial plain, which worsened the farther south one went toward the confluence of the two great rivers, brought an end to Sumerian life. It was no coincidence that the Amorites, the group to succeed the Akkadians, built a new capital for themselves considerably farther to the north, a city that remained the dominant Mesopotamian city for many centuries thereafter: Babylon.

MESOPOTAMIAN LIFE: FARMS AND CITIES, LETTERS AND NUMBERS

So much for the political framework. But what do we know about how people in early Mesopotamia lived, what they valued and believed, and how they understood the world?

Since agriculture is what brought them there in the first place, it is fitting to start with their working of the land. Farming occupied probably 90 percent of the *Farmers* population, who used wooden plows, bronze-tipped seed drills, and stone-bladed hoes. Mesopotamia comprised roughly 8,000 square miles of land fed by a network of major stone canal ways and an elaborate sprawl of subsidiary smaller channels, which divided the land into relatively regularly spaced and equally sized plots. Whereas the largest estates belonged to the kings and temple priests, most farmland was held privately. Whole clans, rather than individuals, owned each plot of land, and they worked out for themselves the distribution of tasks and profits. In most cases the consent of the whole clan was needed before any parcel of land could be sold. Yet it remains unclear how that consent was achieved—whether by all the adults equally, solely by the men, under the leadership of the clan elders, or by some other means. Clans who wanted to relinquish their land-ownership, perhaps to migrate northward into Syria or into Palestine, resorted to adopting would-be buyers into their clan to facilitate the sale of their property. Inheritance practices were **patrilinear**, through male heirs, although in the absence of one, women could own property and give evidence in courts.

A barter economy predominated, with farmers giving grain portions to the various craftsmen—carpenters, smiths, potters, and weavers—who produced the tools they needed to work the land. Payments in kind were likewise made to the priests in the local temples. Commoners also owed a certain amount of labor to their communities, usually for the all-important tasks of maintaining the irrigation canals and urban fortifications. All adult men fought to defend the city-state from attack and were responsible for supplying their own weapons and equipment. Law allowed for divorce and remarriage, although women were not considered equal partners of their husbands.

City Life   The cities that dominated Sumer were built of sunbaked brick and surrounded by deep moats and fortified battlements. The major streets within each
city ran from the gates to the market squares and then to the temples and the
royal palace. These streets could accommodate two-way traffic of chariots and
ass-drawn wagons and carts; branching off these were tangles of narrow byways
and alleys where the bulk of the people lived in cramped, low-roofed huts. Open
space came at a premium; the wealthy displayed their status and good fortune
by building interior courtyards in their palaces. Larger towns like Ur, Uruk,
Lagash, Kish, and Nippur held populations as large as forty or fifty thousand,
but five to ten thousand was more common. Rank and filthy, these towns had no
sewers; human waste was simply dumped into the unpaved streets, where it was
foraged (and added to) by crowds of swine, goats, oxen, and dogs. Clean water
to drink was a luxury, which accounts for the Sumerians' early invention of
beer—the alcohol in it forestalled the proliferation of pathogens. A Sumerian
drinking song of the mid-2nd millennium BCE bears witness to the importance
of beer:

> Fellow, I will teach you truly who your god is:
> Cast down unhappiness in triumph, forget the silence of death!
> Let one day of happiness make up for 36,000 years of the silence of death!
> Let the Beer Goddess rejoice over you as if you were her own child!
> That is the destiny of humankind.

The practice of slavery appeared early in Sumer; it was a decidedly urban phenomenon. Two principle sources of slaves existed: debt bondage and the taking of
captives in war. People who owed money to landlords or merchants seldom sold
themselves into slavery; instead, they sold their family members. The practice
may have begun as the offering of a child as collateral for a loan or as a ransom
against a promise to repay a debt. Failure to pay resulted in the child's permanent
loss of freedom. War captives and their descendants, however, probably represented the larger portion of the slave population. The frequent warring between
the city-states, and between the Sumerians and their invaders, resulted in a steady
supply of new slaves—which was a necessity in ancient times, since the harshness
of slave life meant that slave populations were seldom self-sustaining. Their mortality rates almost always exceeded their birth rates. Given the vulnerability of
this population, therefore, the Sumerians kept their slaves from the backbreaking
work of tilling the land and maintaining the irrigation canals. Too, the Sumerians
generally avoided using slave labor in the fields because the opportunities for
escape were too great. Instead, slaves remained in the cities, working as domestic
servants, laborers in workshops, and concubines.

Ziggurat at Ur   Built in honor of the moon god Nanna/Sin, the patron deity of the city of Ur, this great temple was constructed in the reign of Ur-Nammu, ca. 2000 BCE.

Temples dotted the cityscape. Sumerians believed in and sacrificed to hosts of deities, but each city observed the formal recognition of a particular patron god, for whom they erected vast terraced, pyramid-like mounds called **ziggurats**, atop which stood lavishly decorated temples that served as the earthly home of the god or goddess. Sumerian religion maintained that the gods had invented humans to serve them and perform the labor that they would otherwise have to do for themselves; hence temple worship involved prayer, the singing of hymns, and the offering to deities of an array of gifts. Priests received a percentage of every farmer's produce and of every manufacturer's wares. In return, they presided over the temples' rites and sought to keep the gods appeased. Human life was subject to the whims of the gods. The Sumerians believed that their deities commanded the forces of nature, and although the deities were generally benevolent (hence Sumerian prosperity), they could nevertheless act capriciously and were easily roused to anger.

Priests often worked alongside the king to govern the city-state, creating a de facto theocracy. To aid in that work, and to keep a careful tally of payments made *Invention* or yet owed to the deities, the priestly caste invented writing—Mesopotamia's *of Writing* greatest single contribution to the world. The earliest surviving documents (records of payments received from temple worshippers, primarily) come from Uruk and Kish around 3500 BCE. Sumerian scribes wrote by pressing figures into mud or clay tablets that were then either sun dried or baked until hardened. They started with pictograms, or drawn representations of objects. These gave way to a script that is called **cuneiform**—a sophisticated system of ideograms, which

Cuneiform Writing   This clay receipt from about 2300 BCE tallies the number of sheep and goats in a particular herd. Perhaps part of a bill of sale, it may also be a record for taxation purposes.

represent concepts, and phonograms, or marks indicating syllabic phonetic values.[4] The latter are similar to the shortcuts used by today's text messagers. Sumerian writing used nearly two thousand symbols, which meant that literacy remained a tightly held monopoly of professional scribes, who consequently enjoyed positions of great significance in society. Without them, kings and priests could not compile records, issue decrees, or establish legal or liturgical canons.

Once the script had become established, Sumerian scribes set to work recording economic transactions, astronomical charts, religious poems and prayers, medical regimens, legal decrees, arithmetical calculations—all manner of things. Among the most interesting writings are early word lists. These lists were not dictionaries, but rather groups of related nouns—four-legged animals, birds of various sizes, types of flowers and other plants, species of fish, and varieties of precious stones and metals. Such lists probably originated as study guides for learning the cuneiform script. Yet they also represent human beings' first documented efforts to make sense of the world by classifying its components and seeking order among its bewildering variety.

The first author in the Greater Western tradition whose name is known was **En-Heduanna** (2285–2250 BCE), the daughter of Sargon. En-Heduanna served as the high priestess of the Akkadian moon goddess Nanna and left behind a sizable collection of religious poetry. Among her best-known works is a hymn in honor of the love goddess Inanna, who, as the protectress of the city of Uruk, often doubled as a war goddess. En-Heduanna extols Inanna as much for her ferocity on the battlefield as for her beauty and power at inspiring love:

> Great queen of queens, issue of a holy womb for righteous divine powers,
> More holy even than your own mother, wise and sage,
> Lady of all the foreign lands, life-force of the teeming people—
> I will recite your holy song!
> True goddess fit for divine powers, your splendid utterances are
>   magnificent.
> Deep-hearted, good woman with a radiant heart,
> I will enumerate your divine powers!
> . . .

---

4   Cuneiform literally means "wedge shape" in Latin, after the indentation made into the clay by a reed stylus.

Be it known that you are lofty as the heavens!
Be it known that you are broad as the earth!
Be it known that you destroy the rebel lands!
Be it known that you roar at the foreign lands!
Be it known that you crush heads!
Be it known that you devour corpses like a dog!

. . .

You have become the greatest!
My lady, beloved by [the sky god] An, I shall tell
Of all your rages. I have heaped up coals in the censer,
And prepared the purification rites. The shrine awaits you.
Might your heart not be appeased towards me?

A second set of markings depicted numbers. Sumerian mathematics used place-value numerals, with both base-ten and base-sixty notations. (The latter *Mathematics* survives in our division of time into sixty-minute hours and sixty-second minutes.) By 2300 BCE they had either invented or imported the abacus, a manual computing device. They used arithmetic to keep financial accounts and to study the constellations and the movement of the planets in the night sky. Since their survival depended on knowing when to expect the spring floods, the Sumerians paid close attention to measuring time. They followed a solar calendar but divided it into twelve lunar months, which necessitated the insertion of a thirteenth month every third year. The flooding of the rivers eroded the Sumerians' mud-brick buildings and boundary markers, so they quickly became adept at basic geometry to re-create their washed-away property lines.

Oral custom and written law structured Sumerian life, and as early as 2300 BCE at least one ruler, Ur-Ukagina of Lagash, had brought these laws *Written* into a single, published code that articulated the pursuit of justice, not the *Law* preservation of inherited right, as the aim of government. Economic specialization in the cities had created a degree of social stratification that ancient custom could neither address nor restrain, leaving thousands vulnerable to exploitation in every city. Written law emerged from this as an effort to reform society by restricting the rights of the powerful. Ur-Ukagina's law code survives only in fragments and in references found in later texts. The portions that survive limit the rights of the priestly caste and wealthy landowners to evict tenants and seize their property, exempt widows and orphans from paying taxes, and oblige the government to meet the funeral expenses of the poor. One inscription reads, "[Ur-Ukagina] freed the people of Lagash from usury, burdensome controls, hunger, theft, murder, and seizure of their property. He established freedom. Widows and orphans were no longer at the mercy of powerful individuals."[5] This effort to relieve oppression did not last long, however: the Akkadians conquered Sumer shortly after Ur-Ukagina's reign. Subsequent rulers, however, continued to produce reformist codes, the most famous of all being that instituted around 1700 BCE by the Babylonian ruler Hammurabi (discussed in chapter 2).

RELIGION AND MYTH: THE GREAT ABOVE AND GREAT BELOW

Sumerian religion, as reconstructed from myths and ritual prayers written in Babylonian times, consisted of a complex web of relations. It encompassed at least three strata of existence: Heaven, the Great Above, and the Great Below.

Major Gods and Goddesses

The Sumerians regarded the day and night sky as the high overarching bowl of Heaven, a fixed semisphere where dwelt Anu (meaning "sky" literally but representing the divine force itself) and a group of spirits known as the Igigi. The Great Above consisted of the space from the dome of the sky down to the surface of the earth; this was the dwelling of the Annunaki—the assemblage of gods and goddesses to whom the people of Sumer sacrificed and offered prayers and whose aid they invoked. Enlil, the god of the air, reigned supreme here. Other chief gods were Utu, the sun god (called Shamash by the Akkadians); Nanna Suen, the moon god (Sin to the Akkadians); Nin-Khursaga, the earth goddess (Akkadian Ishtar); and Enki, the god of waters (later identified with the Babylonian god Ea), but the names of at least fifty other Annunaki survive. Humanity was the creation of Enki, who had made human beings specifically to provide food and comfort for the gods. People, in other words, were the servants of the gods in the most literal sense. Interestingly, the Annunaki—all forces of nature—did not create the world but were in fact created by it.

The world itself came about through the movement of two primordial forces—the male and female principles (Abzu and Tiamat, respectively)—which resulted in the creation of the physical world and then of the gods themselves. But the Annunaki feared the creation of even more gods, who presumably might have supplanted them, and so Enlil killed their mother, Tiamat, and Enki slew Abzu. The murdered parents thus descended into the Great Below, the world beneath the surface of the earth. Also beneath the earth was Kur (Ersetu to the Akkadians), which was the Land of No Return, the place to which all humans went after death. The Sumerians believed there existed two separate entrances to the world of the dead, one in the caves of the Zagros Mountains and another in a secret staircase hidden in the city of Uruk. After dying, all Sumerians entered Kur by one

---

5   This inscription contains the first known use of the word for "freedom" in any Western language: *ama-gi*.

of these portals, whereupon they received judgment from a council of six hundred gods. It is hard to say what the purpose of such judgment was, however, since all the dead—kings and commoners alike—were consigned to spending eternity wandering naked and exposed through an endless expanse of darkness, dust, and heat.

Each city-state possessed its own unique patron deities, and it was the joint responsibility of the lugal and his corps of priests to lead their societies in ritual worship. Sumerian gods numbered more than three thousand, but most of them remained unknown outside their local cult centers. Only the major deities like Enlil, Enki, and Nin-Khursaga enjoyed wide recognition, through the stories that made up Sumerian mythology. Anthropomorphic in form and all too humanlike in behavior, the gods nonetheless stood well beyond human understanding. A crude barter characterized human–divine relations: the Sumerians courted favor from the gods by offering them prayers and appeasing them with gifts, and the gods blessed the people (when it suited them) by sending favorable conditions for the growing of abundant food.

Local Deities

The gods were capricious, however, and could lash out in anger by sending a burning drought, a devastating flood, a plague of crop-eating insects, or a wave of foreign invaders. Sumerian priests guarded against such divine fickleness by reading omens in the organs of animals sacrificed in the temple, by interpreting dreams, or by seeing coded messages in the flight patterns of birds. Religious life in Sumer thus consisted largely of maintaining favorable but distant relations with the gods and goddesses. Heavenly interaction with humans spelled doom as often as it brought delight.

The Standard of Ur   Excavated in the 1920s, the "Standard of Ur" of about 2500 BCE is actually a wooden box, about 8-1/2 × 20 inches, with an inlaid mosaic of lapis lazuli, limestone, and shells. This panel portrays farmers, carters, scribes, merchants, and priests en route to offer their sacrifices to the deities.

In earliest times Sumerian myths lacked a strong moral element: the gods exhibited the same self-interest that humans did and pursued their pleasures and whims accordingly. By the start of the 2nd millennium BCE, however, as urban culture developed and social stratification increased, myths appeared that bore witness to a heightened interest in justice and a sense of rational moral order. A hymn to the goddess Nanshe of Lagash, for example, lauds her as the deity who "sees the oppression of man over man, who is the guardian of orphans, . . . the caregiver of widows, who seeks justice for the poor, . . . who comforts the homeless and shelters the weak."

The best known of the moralized Sumerian hymns is called the Shamash Hymn after the Babylonian name for the sun god Utu. The hymn offers praise for the god's relentless protection of the weak and troubled:

> You care for all the peoples of the lands,
> And everything that Enlil/Ea . . . has created is entrusted to you.
> All that draws breath you shepherd without exception. . . .
> The whole of mankind bows to you,
> Shamash, the universe longs for your light. . . .
> You stand by the traveler whose road is difficult,
> To the seafarer in dread of the waves you give [comfort]. . . .
> You save from the storm the merchant carrying his capital;
> The [boatman] who sinks in the ocean you equip with wings;
> You point out settling places to refugees and fugitives, and
> To the captive you point out [escape] routes known only to you.

The hymn goes on to praise Utu/Shamash for punishing corrupt judges and dishonest merchants, for granting long life to those who work for justice, and for rewarding the honest and kindly. The lugals, too, came to be valued for the extent to which they provided justice, since their temple duties of leading sacrifices and observing the chief festivals of the religious year gained in significance.

A contrary tradition in Sumerian myth laments the unpredictability of the gods' affections and care to protect the righteous. "The Poem of the Righteous Sufferer" expresses the agonies of an unnamed Sumerian who, despite his strict ritual observance, has nevertheless suffered the loss of his wealth and social position:

> Who knows the will of the gods in heaven?
> Who understands the plans of the underworld gods?
> Where have mortals learnt the way of a god?
> He who was alive yesterday is dead today.
> For a minute he was dejected, suddenly he is exuberant.
> One moment people are singing in exaltation,

Another they groan like professional mourners.
Their condition changes like the opening and shutting of the legs,
When starving they become like corpses,
When replete they vie with the gods.
In prosperity they speak of scaling heaven,
Under adversity they complain of going down to hell.
I am appalled at these things; I do not understand their significance.

A later Babylonian writer reworked this poem into a song of praise for the god Marduk. This patron deity of Babylon comes to the sufferer's aid and restores him to happiness, ending with a paean to traditional teaching and ritual.[6] In the original tale, however, the dominant tone is despair. The narrator seeks not an end to human suffering but merely an explanation for it. Why do the wicked prosper? Why are the lives of the righteous filled with want, fear, violence, and confusion? Why will the gods not spare humans from the pain of life?

To judge from their literary remains, the people of Mesopotamia thought long and deeply about these matters. The precarious nature of life almost demanded it. *Search for* After all, the land they inhabited had many natural blessings but was vulnerable to *Meaning* invasion by raiders seeking to snatch away the very blessings the Sumerians worked so hard to procure. Moreover, the rivers that gave such abundant life to the region also destroyed it by unpredictable and uncontrollable flash flooding. The more the Sumerians prospered, the more likely they were to be attacked. These were ironies of a most soul-searching kind. If the gods could alternately bless and batter humans so capriciously, is it vain to regard the world as being in any way ethically ordered? And if life lacks moral sense, is it worth the agony of living it? Can we have trust in heaven? Attitudes shifted with time and fortune, but the Sumerians recognized that life is serious business. Among their many important contributions to Western culture was the invention of the conscious search for meaning in life. And that may be their most fundamental contribution of all.

ANCIENT EGYPT, GIFT OF THE NILE

Southwest of the Fertile Crescent, along the banks of the Nile River in Africa, lay the second cradle of Western civilization. The Nile originates in two sub-Saharan tributaries—one in northern Ethiopia, fed by Lake Tana, and the other stretching all the way south to Lake Victoria in Uganda. They meet near today's Sudanese capital city of Khartoum. From there the Nile flows northward, dropping through

---

[6] The Babylonian tale may have provided a model for the Hebrew author of the biblical Book of Job, in which the unmerited sufferings of an upright man are also discussed in detail.

a series of dramatic cataracts, or waterfalls, before reaching the gentle sloping plane of Egypt itself.

For 600 miles it meanders slowly northward, cutting a green swath of fertile land on either side of the riverbed, until about 100 miles shy of the Mediterranean it branches out in a delta with no fewer than seven major openings to the sea, spread over nearly 250 miles of coastline. This delta region forms "Lower Egypt," and the 600-mile-long river valley directly south of it comprises "Upper Egypt" (see Map 1.4). Ancient Egypt thus consisted of two extremely long strips of land on either side of the Nile, between 4 and 12 miles across, and a vast triangular delta. The waters of the Nile swelled annually, beginning in August. At their peak in September, they reached nearly 20 feet above their low ebb in April and May, bringing more than 100 million tons of rich sediment to replenish the banks. Spring planting thus began when the greatest amount of land was exposed, and the harvest was brought in just before the next replenishing flood began. People lived in small communities along the river's edge as early as 5000 BCE but did not begin to farm the land until approximately 3500 BCE. Until then, they tended their flocks, living off the plants and trees that grew naturally along the shores.

Egyptian ships moved constantly on the great river, bringing foodstuffs, building materials, and laborers to wherever they were needed. Given the Nile's gentle flow, most boats were open and flat bottomed, which made it easy to load and unload cargo. Rowers propelled the boats downstream—that is, from south to north—because the prevailing winds blew southward; boats heading upriver therefore were sail driven. The "Hymn to the Nile," one of ancient Egypt's key religious texts, bears witness to the importance of the river to daily life:

> [The Nile] shines when he issues forth from the darkness
> To cause his flocks to prosper.
> It is his force that gives existence to all things;
> Nothing remains hidden from him.
> Let men clothe themselves to fill his gardens.
> He watches over his works,
> Producing the inundation during the night. . . .
> A festal song is raised for thee on the harp,
> With the accompaniment of the hand.
> The young men and children acclaim thee
> And prepare their long exercises.
> Thou art the august ornament of the earth,
> Letting thy bark advance before men,
> Lifting up the heart of women in labor,
> And loving the multitude of the flocks.

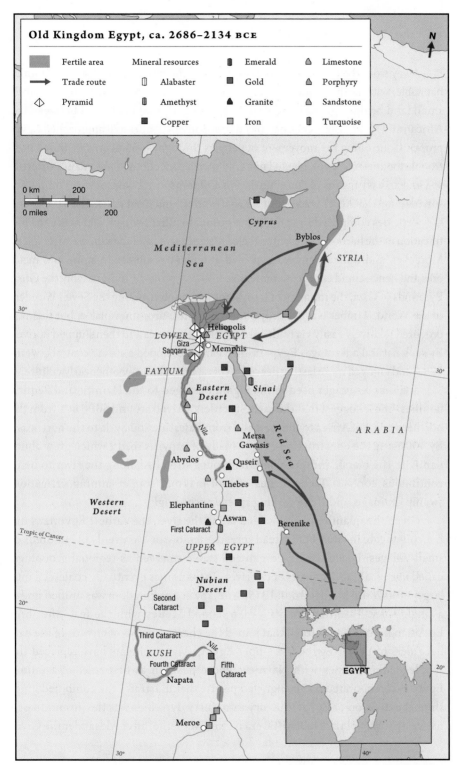

Old Kingdom Egypt, ca. 2686–2134 BCE

▨ Fertile area	Mineral resources	▯ Emerald	△ Limestone
➔ Trade route	▯ Alabaster	▪ Gold	◭ Porphyry
◁▷ Pyramid	▯ Amethyst	▲ Granite	◭ Sandstone
	▪ Copper	◻ Iron	▯ Turquoise

N

Cyprus

Mediterranean
Sea

Byblos

SYRIA

30°

Heliopolis
LOWER EGYPT
Giza
Saqqara Memphis

FAYYUM

30°

Eastern
Desert *Sinai*

Nile

Mersa
Gawasis

Red Sea

ARABIA

Abydos

Quseir

Thebes

Western
Desert

Elephantine

Tropic of Cancer

Aswan
First Cataract

Berenike

UPPER EGYPT

Nubian
Desert

20°

Second
Cataract

Third Cataract

KUSH
Fourth Cataract Fifth
Nile Cataract

Napata

EGYPT

20°

Meroe

30° 40°

MAP 1.4 Old Kingdom Egypt, ca. 2686–2134 BCE   The banks of the Nile grew more fertile
the farther downstream (that is, to the north) one traveled, as shown here. But most of Egypt's
mineral wealth lay along the upper reaches of the river (to the south).

Away from the cultivated shores of the Nile, the rest of Egypt was all but uninhabitable, with nothing but arid desert to the east, west, and south. The relatively small land bridge of the Sinai Peninsula, the only point of contact between the African and Asian continents, narrowed to a span of 40 miles as it approached Egypt proper. Controlling the movement of peoples through so small an area posed little trouble for ancient Egypt, blessed not only with a concentrated abundance of fertile soil and an easy means of communication and transport, but also with a protective surrounding that kept invaders out for nearly fifteen hundred years. The marshy delta's port cities comprised Egypt's only exposure to other peoples, and hence the fortification of the harbors represented the only significant military expense of its rulers. Moreover, and unlike Sumer, Egypt had abundant resources in stone and metal ores and hence could engage in impressive building projects, most notably the Great Pyramids of Giza, the monumental royal tombs counted among the Seven Wonders of the World. Timber was the only vital natural resource unavailable, but this was procured relatively easily via trade through the delta cities and then shipped upriver. By such natural advantages Egypt unified early, developed a strong central government, and enjoyed more lasting peace and prosperity than any other early culture.

The first languages used in the region belonged to the Hamitic and Semitic families. These suggest that the earliest settlers arrived around 5000 BCE from the northern coast of Africa to the west and from Palestine and Syria to the northeast. By 4000 BCE the construction of rafts made of papyrus reeds, which grew abundantly in the marshlands, enabled the groups stretched along the river to be in continuous contact. Technologies of tool making, copper mining, irrigation, swamp drainage, and stone carving spread accordingly.

Unification of Egypt

Given the quantity of arable land along the river, the earliest Egyptians did not congregate in cities but instead spread out more or less evenly in hundreds of small villages; hence the first organized states emerged as regional groupings, called *nomes*, along segments of the river. These nomes eventually coalesced into larger units, until finally, around 3150 BCE, the entire kingdom was unified under a single ruler. Tradition credits a man named **Menes** with the feat; after him Egyptian kings wore a crown that joined the characteristics of crowns of the earlier rulers of Lower Egypt and Upper Egypt.[7] Many scholars have replaced the semilegendary Menes with **Narmer**, whose position as first ruler of a united Egypt is corroborated by an engraved palette that illustrates the combined kingship. The division of Egypt's history into thirty dynasties was the invention of a native historian of the Hellenistic era named Manetho, after Alexander the Great

---

[7]   The word *pharaoh*, which means "palace" or "great house," did not come into general use until the period of the New Kingdom, discussed in chapter 2. Since the Egyptians believed their ruler to be a god, to speak his name aloud was blasphemy.

(discussed in chapter 5) had conquered the kingdom in 332 BCE. Manetho divided Egyptian history into the periods of the Old, Middle, and New Kingdoms, with so-called Intermediate Periods separating them. The thirty dynasties were then parceled out between the kingdoms and periods. Scholars have since tinkered with the details but have kept Manetho's general scheme (see Table 1.1).

TABLE 1.1 **Ancient Egypt**

Archaic Period: ca. 3150–2686 BCE (Dynasties 1–2)

Old Kingdom: ca. 2686–2134 BCE (Dynasties 3–6)

First Intermediate Period: ca. 2134–2035 BCE (Dynasties 7–10)

Middle Kingdom: ca. 2035–1640 BCE (Dynasties 11–12)

Second Intermediate Period: ca. 1640–1570 BCE (Dynasties 13–17)

New Kingdom: ca. 1570–1070 BCE (Dynasties 18–20)

Third Intermediate Period: ca. 1070–664 BCE (Dynasties 21–26)

Late Period: ca. 664–332 BCE (Dynasties 27–30)

Narmer Palette This plaque commemorates King Narmer (a.k.a. Menes—Old Kingdom rulers had as many as five names each), the king who united Lower and Upper Egypt. The front image (left) portrays Narmer as he prepares to smash the skull of a rival with a mace. To the right the god Horus, in the shape of a falcon, brings him captives. Narmer wears a kilt, with the tail of a bull (symbol of strength) attached to his backside. The reverse side of the plaque (right) shows another bull, at the bottom, breaking through the fortifications of a city and trampling a victim, while above, servants attend to two great beasts whose long necks are entwined, a scene that presumably represents the union of the Lower and Upper Kingdoms. On top, a ruler with his servants carries banners and the spoils of war.

An identifiable Egyptian civilization thus took shape at roughly the same time that organized Sumerian society began—around the start of the 3rd millennium BCE. This corresponds with the appearance of writing in both societies. The Egyptians—who had established trade relations with the Sumerians by that early time—may have acquired the idea of writing from Mesopotamia. Unlike the Sumerian cuneiform, however, the Egyptians developed a system of **hieroglyphs** (literally, "sacred carving"), based on a combination of pictograms and phonetic signs. The Egyptians wrote on a kind of paper made of woven strips of papyrus reed that was much easier to use than the Sumerians' clay tablets and that made it possible for Egyptian scribes to devise two cursive scripts (known as demotic and hieratic scripts) that made record keeping considerably easier. As a result, the written records of Egypt vastly exceed those of Mesopotamia in both number and variety, and the arid condition of the local environment enabled them to survive the long centuries more or less intact. For the first four dynasties, in fact, more of their writings survive than the buildings they lived in because the latter were made of baked mud-brick, which

Egyptian Hieroglyphs   In this paint-on-plaster portrait dating from around 2550 BCE, Nefertiabet, the daughter of the pharaoh Cheops (or Khufu), is shown wearing a leopard skin. Surrounding the table at which she sits are a variety of tribute-gifts: linens, loaves of bread, and offerings of beer or wine.

erodes rapidly even in Egypt's dry climate. They reserved expensive stone for the palaces and tombs of the wealthy and for the temples presided over by the influential priestly caste.

LIFE AND RULE IN OLD KINGDOM EGYPT

As in Mesopotamia, most Egyptians worked the land. Slavery existed but was not as widespread as in Mesopotamia. Egypt's relative insulation from outsiders de- *Social* prived it of the main source of slaves: prisoners of war. Besides, the king had an *Strata and* unquestioned right to force his subjects to join labor crews for public-works proj- *Daily Life* ects. Society was strictly stratified, with social distinctions expressed by dress codes. Slightly above the farmers in social status were the simple artisans: brewers, weavers, stonemasons, bricklayers. Higher were the makers of luxury items for the elites: goldsmiths, jewelry makers, perfumers. A smaller corps of professionals stood above these: physicians, scribes, architects, priests, and civic officials. In theory, all Egyptians were equal under the law regardless of class or sex, and even the lowliest farmer could hope to petition for redress of a legal complaint—but that was theory, not reality.

Monogamous marriage was the norm for Egyptians, although law did not require it, and men of all classes frequently took additional wives or concubines. Women, however, were subject to harsh legal punishment and social ostracism for engaging in sex outside of marriage to a single husband. Both sexes, however, could own property, enter contracts, and settle disputes in court.

The basic Egyptian diet consisted of varieties of grain—whether as bread, gruel, or beer—supplemented with a few vegetables (leeks, garlic, squash, and lettuce, especially), along with figs, dates, and fish. Meat was a rare treat for commoners, as was wine. Two other food practices date back to the Old Kingdom: the keeping of bee colonies, for honey and wax, and the netting of wild geese as they followed their own food trail along the river's edges.[8] June to September was the flooding season, October to February saw the growing of the grain fields, and March to May was the harvest. Given the often extreme heat, most Egyptians wore little clothing. Children, in fact, generally went naked until they entered puberty, and it was common for men to shave and oil their entire body. Most people's homes, too, were designed to offset the heat: simple mud-brick, often painted white, remained relatively cool throughout the day, and all cooking was done in small open-air patios. They covered their homes' packed-earth floors with reed mats. The Egyptians followed a solar calendar but never felt compelled to develop the technological tools or scientific expertise of

---

[8]   The Egyptians learned early the trick of fattening the geese by feeding them large quantities of raw bread dough.

the Sumerians. Remarkably, the monumental architectural marvels for which the Old Kingdom is known were created without the wheel.

Agricultural abundance was the hallmark of Old Kingdom life. Papyrus texts, wall paintings, and tomb inscriptions describe masses of men and women at work in every aspect of food production—little other industry receives much attention—and preserve hundreds of popular songs that the farmers reportedly sang as they toiled. The composers of the songs clearly either came from or consciously extolled the upper classes.

> A good day—it is cool.
> The cattle are pulling
> And the sky does according to our desire.
> Let us work for the noble!

Another song was apparently a favorite of the grain-threshers:

> Thresh ye for yourselves, O cattle!
> Straw to eat, and barley for your masters.
> Let not your hearts be weary, for it is cool.

A last song expressed the joy of the slaves who carried their masters on palanquins, seats held aloft on poles:

> Go down into the palanquin—it is sound and it is well!
> The carrying poles are on the shoulders of the carriers.
> O palanquin of Ipi, be as heavy as you wish.
> It is pleasanter full than when empty!

Ideology of Kingship

Ruler worship dominated Old Egyptian life—or at least it was the dominant characteristic of the regimes that produced the evidentiary record. The king presented himself as a living god, the source of justice and stability, the munificent owner of the whole of Egypt and its people, and the embodiment of the people's hopes and love. Officials who wanted to remain in the king's good graces took great care to reinforce the royal self-image:

> To the great King, my Lord, the Sun-God from Heaven, thus I, Prince Zatatna of Acre, Your servant, the most humble servant of the Great King—indeed, the very dirt beneath Your feet, the ground upon which You tread—sends greeting. Seven times, O Great King, seven times, O Sun-God from Heaven, I fall, prostrate and helpless, at Your feet.

So began a typical piece of provincial administration. The glorification given to the king in the 3rd and 2nd millennia BCE, much of it on a colossal scale, would have brought an envious tear to the eye of many a 20th-century dictator. The **Great Pyramids** at Giza, massive royal tombs built by moving huge stones from a quarry and dragging and lifting them into place, tell only part of the tale. Statues of the kings adorned every temple; inscriptions praising their magnificence appeared in every city; hymns in their honor rang out in every religious service.

From their palace at the capital city of Memphis, strategically and symbolically located at the meeting point of Lower and Upper Egypt, the kings controlled every aspect of public life through cults of personality backed up by armies of bureaucratic and military officials. Each nome was administered by a nomarch appointed by

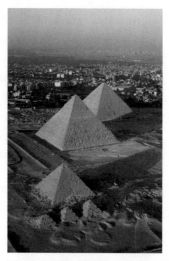

The Pyramids of Giza   This striking photograph shows the proximity of the vast structures to the present city of Cairo. There is still no general agreement on how the pyramids were constructed. Most archeologists follow the idea that long ramps were constructed, up which the quarried stones were transported.

the king, and they all reported to a central official called a vizier. The nomarchs oversaw all public-works projects, coordinated food distribution, heard appeals, and dispensed justice. Assisting all these was an army of scribes who kept census records, tallied tax revenues, noted expenditures, and issued the government's decrees. Members of the royal family held many of these posts.

Few states in Western history have experienced such completely centralized rule. As evidence, despite its invention and wide use of writing, Egypt never created a law code. Since the king, a living god, walked the earth, whatever he said at any moment was, in effect, the law. When the king, who was identified as the sun god Horus, died, he became an even greater deity by being absorbed into Osiris, an amalgam of all kings merged into one, the ruler of the underworld, where his supreme authority never ended. Royal officials received estates from the king in return for their service, rather than salaries. The kings likewise endowed mortuary cults and temples to promote the worship of themselves after their deaths on earth.

It was an efficient way to govern, to be sure, and under benevolent rulers and judicious officials ancient Egypt enjoyed a material standard of living that vastly exceeded that of any contemporary society until the end of the Old Kingdom. By then, the pharaohs had transferred so much of their land that they began to have trouble meeting their enormous administrative costs, prompting the nomarchs to challenge royal power for the first time and thereby inaugurating the First

Intermediate Period. In the early centuries, however, safe from foreign aggression because of the surrounding deserts, easily unified by the quiet-flowing Nile, and fed by the abundance of grain and fruit sprouting along its banks, Egypt had only not to disturb nature's rhythms to reap its rewards.

Commitment to Ma'at   Accordingly, the supreme virtue of Egyptian culture was **ma'at**—a recognition of the world's ordering and a commitment to preserve it. Scholars commonly translate ma'at as "justice," which is too generous. Ma'at, in practice, was an acceptance of the world as it is, a reluctance to change anything for fear that the result might be worse than the (often beneficent) reality.

Prominent among the remains of Old Kingdom literature are "Instructions," or self-help guides written by fathers for their heirs, texts that repeatedly emphasize the message not to disturb ma'at. For example, the Instructions written for his son by Ptah-hotep, a royal official during the Fifth Dynasty, begin with the pronouncement that "a great thing is ma'at, enduring and surviving; it has not been upset since the time of Osiris. He who departs from its laws is punished." What actions maintain ma'at? Above all, never to question any established social custom or institution. Married life, for example, is valuable for the stability it brings. "If you are prosperous you should establish a household and love your wife as is fitting. Fill her belly and clothe her back. . . . Make her heart glad as long as you live. She is a profitable field for her lord." Loyal service to one's patron or employer is essential as well. "If you are a worthy man sitting in the council of your lord, confine your attention to excellence. Silence is more valuable than chatter. Speak only when you can resolve difficulties. . . . Bend your back to him who is over you, your superior in the administration; then your house will endure by reason of its prosperity, and your reward will come in due season. Wretched is he who opposes his superior, for one lives only so long as he is gracious."

Above all, Ptah-hotep writes, one must know the limits established by tradition and do nothing to challenge them. Ma'at must be preserved from generation to generation:

> If the son of a man accepts what his father says, no plan of his will fail. . . . Failure follows him who does not listen. A son who hears is a follower of Horus; there is good for him who listens. When he reaches old age and attains honor, he tells the like to his children, renewing the teaching of his father. Every man teaches as he has acted. He speaks to his children so that they may speak to their children.

The cultural contrasts between ancient Egypt and Mesopotamia are striking. The separate city-states of Mesopotamia were in perennial conflict—challenging, experimenting, wondering, often failing, but always adapting to new circumstances and searching for meaning in the apparent jumble of it all. Unified nearly from the start, ancient Egypt created a wealthy, profoundly religious, and strongly centralized society that revolved around the king—and a worldview intended to preserve this social order. Thus it embodied a conservative principle that may be ancient Egypt's most significant legacy to Western culture.

THE KINGDOM OF THE DEAD

Although king worship was a key part of religious life, ancient Egyptian religion was a mix of local myths and traditions that defies easy description. Each nome revered a specific local deity, most of them animal shaped, and a statue of whom stood in the local temple and whose cults formed the center of village religious life. The temple statue was believed to be the god or goddess, not merely to represent him or her; individual homes often would have small statuettes to the deity in a corner, to whom the people offered small gifts of grain, oil, or wine at mealtimes.

A company of major deities ruled over the local gods and probably served to create a sense of shared culture among the peoples of Lower and Upper Egypt. One *Gods and* of these major gods, named Ptah, was credited with creating the world, but beyond *Kings* this he played little role in Egyptian mythology. The most important deities by far were the incestuous brother and sister Osiris and Isis, whose love for each other set the whole cosmology in motion. Osiris became the first god-king of the earth that Ptah had created, but his brother Seth, jealous of Osiris's kingship and possibly of his relations with Isis, killed Osiris, chopped him up, and scattered bits of his body all along the length of the Nile. Distraught, Isis searched out every piece and with the help of Anubis, the god of mummification, reassembled Osiris's body, bringing it miraculously back to life just long enough for Isis to enjoy one last sexual union with her brother, who promptly died again after completing the deed. But the job was done: Isis became pregnant and in time gave birth to the god Horus—who eventually grew to manhood, avenged his father by killing Seth, and took over the rulership of the world. Every king was thus believed to be a new incarnation of Horus, the god himself walking the earth. And on his death every king transformed into Osiris, who ruled over the realm of the dead for eternity.

The Isis–Osiris myth remained central to Egyptian culture for thousands of years, until it was supplanted by Christianity in the early centuries CE—which was itself largely succeeded by Islam in the 7th and 8th centuries CE. Rather than a tale of resurrection, of life defeating death—Osiris, after all, was revived only briefly—his tale expresses the notion of life's renewal, a cycle of generation, death, and regeneration that paralleled the rhythm of flood, planting, and harvest along the great Nile's banks. Temples and statues to Isis and Osiris were erected all

A Tomb with a View   Archeologists have unearthed several hundred ancient Egyptian aristocratic tombs called *mastabas* ("houses for eternity"). These were raised structures, 20 to 30 feet tall, made of mud-brick, with inward-slanting walls. This detail of an inscription on one mastaba (belonging to the head butcher for the royal court) shows part of an invocation to the god Osiris.

throughout the kingdom and reminded people everywhere of the universality of the king's authority. In the afterworld Osiris judged the souls of the dead kings before admitting them to his realm—a realm that was remarkably similar to life along the Nile: not a better life but simply *more* life, which the Egyptians seem to have regarded as blessing enough. Common people in the Old Kingdom received vastly simpler burials, the arable land on the bank being too precious to use for commoners' graves. Buried well away from the great pyramid valleys and far from the Nile itself, they were assumed to move easily into the afterworld—where they continued to farm, mine, and manufacture, in service to the redeemed kings forever.

Admission to the afterworld was not automatic for a king, yet neither was it tied closely to ethical behavior in his lifetime. Ancient Egyptian religion held that the soul of the deceased wandered through a dim wasteland, beset by various demon-spirits, in search of the House of Judgment where Osiris, along with forty-two other judges, would decide whether the dead soul could enter. One could in theory remain lost in the wasteland for eternity, but the ancient Egyptians created a canon of texts intended to lead the king to paradise. These incantations, magic spells, proclamations, and hymns were inscribed on the walls of the royal tombs—hence their collective name of Pyramid Texts. They guided the dead through the wasteland and provided sets of prayers and incantations to deploy against the demons. Moreover, they supplied the answers needed to satisfy the questions posed by Osiris and the other judges. With such scripted clues, the king's eternal reward was assured. After passing the examination, the dead ruler then made a final solemn declaration:

> I have not done evil to mankind.
> I have not oppressed the members of my family. . . .
> I have not brought forward my name for exaltation to honors.
> I have not ill-treated servants.
> I have not belittled a god.
> I have not defrauded the oppressed of their property.
> I have not done that which is an abomination to the gods. . . .
> I have made no man to suffer hunger.
> I have made no one to weep.
> I have done no murder.
> I have not given an order for murder to be done for me.
> I have not inflicted pain. . . .
> I have not committed fornication. . . .
> I have not encroached on the fields of others. . . .
> I have not cut into a canal of running water. . . .
> I have not obstructed a god in his procession
> *I am pure! I am pure! I am pure! I am pure!*

After the declaration the god Anubis weighed the dead king's heart on a scale, and if the purified heart weighed no more than a feather, the soul was admitted to the eternal presence of Osiris.

Note that the departed king's confession before Osiris lacks a positive spirit of morality: virtue consists of not performing evil rather than actively doing good. Just as ma'at did not equal justice, neither did the spiritual purity that entitled one to enter paradise imply anything more than correct behavior. In the earliest centuries only members of the royal family could receive the supreme reward, but the privilege of salvation was extended to the nobles in the Middle Kingdom period and to all Egyptians eventually—although only in the New Kingdom many centuries later. This is not to say that the ancient Egyptians were immoral or amoral. Rather, as with their contemporaries in Mesopotamia, their sense of moral values was distinct from the tenets and practices of their religion.

◆

Although it lacked the emotional complexity of Sumerian religion, Egyptian religion possessed an attractively hopeful belief in the unstoppable resilience of life.

Death, although not exactly a thing to be yearned for, did not need to be feared. It represented only a rite of passage—back to the shores of the Nile, where time would run as endlessly as the great river itself. The tumultuous history of ancient Egypt after the end of the Old Kingdom would test that faith.

WHO, WHAT, WHERE

Bronze Age	Fertile Crescent	ma'at
civilization	Gilgamesh	Menes/Narmer
cuneiform	Great Pyramids	patrilinear
empire	hieroglyphs	Sargon I
En-Heduanna	lugal	ziggurats

SUGGESTED READINGS

Primary Sources

Instructions of Ptah-hotep

Laws of Ur-Ukagina

Poem of the Righteous Sufferer

Shamash Hymn

Anthologies

Bailkey, Nels, and Richard Lim, eds. *Readings in Ancient History: Thought and Experience from Gilgamesh to St. Augustine* (2011, orig. 1987).

Bryce, Trevor. *Letters of the Great Kings of the Ancient Near East: The Royal Correspondence of the Late Bronze Age* (2014, orig. 2003).

Coogan, Michael D. *A Reader of Ancient Near Eastern Texts: Sources for the Study of the Old Testament* (2013).

Foster, John L., trans. *Ancient Egyptian Literature: An Anthology* (2001).

Glassner, Jean-Jacques. *Mesopotamian Chronicles* (2004).

Lichtheim, Miriam. *Ancient Egyptian Literature: A Book of Readings*, 3 vols. (2006, orig. 1973).

Vanstiphout, Herman, and Jerrold S. Cooper. *Epics of Sumerian Kings: The Matter of Aratta* (2004).

Studies

Anthony, David W. *The Horse, the Wheel, and Language: How Bronze-Age Riders from the Eurasian Steppes Shaped the Modern World* (2010, orig. 2007).

Aruz, Joan. *Art of the First Cities: The Third Millennium BC from the Mediterranean to the Indus* (2003).

Assmann, Jan. *The Mind of Egypt: History and Meaning in the Time of the Pharaohs* (2003).

Assmann, Jan. *The Search for God in Ancient Egypt* (2001).

Bottéro, Jean. *Everyday Life in Ancient Mesopotamia* (2001).

Bottéro, Jean. *Religion in Ancient Mesopotamia* (2001).

Brewer, Douglas J., and Emily Teeter. *Egypt and the Egyptians* (2007).

Charvát, Petr. *Mesopotamia before History* (2008).

Crawford, Harriet. *Sumer and the Sumerians* (2004).

Foster, Benjamin R., and Karen Polinger Foster. *Civilizations of Ancient Iraq* (2011).

Germonde, Philippe. *An Egyptian Bestiary: Animals in Life and Religion in the Land of the Pharaohs* (2001).

Glassner, Jean-Jacques. *The Invention of Cuneiform: Writing in Sumer* (2007).

Harris, David R. *Origins of Agriculture in West Central Asia: An Environmental–Archaeological Study* (2010).

Hodder, Ian. *The Leopard's Tale: Revealing the Mysteries of Çatalhöyük* (2011).

Kemp, Barry J. *Ancient Egypt: Anatomy of a Civilization* (2005, orig. 1992).

Leick, Gwendolyn. *Mesopotamia: The Invention of the City* (2003).

Leick, Gwendolyn. *Sex and Eroticism in Mesopotamian Literature* (2003, orig. 1994).

Liverani, Mario. *Uruk: The First City* (2006).

Maynes, Mary Jo, and Ann Waltner. *The Family: A World History* (2012).

O'Brien, Cormac. *The Fall of Empires: From Glory to Ruin, an Epic Account of History's Ancient Civilizations* (2009).

Robins, Gay. *The Art of Ancient Egypt* (2008, orig. 1997).

Romer, John. *A History of Ancient Egypt: From the First Farmers to the Great Pyramid* (2013).

Silverman, David P., ed. *Ancient Egypt* (2003).

Wilkinson, Toby. *The Rise and Fall of Ancient Egypt: The History of a Civilization from 3000 BC to Cleopatra* (2013).

For additional resources, including maps, primary sources, visuals, web links, and quizzes, please go to **www.oup.com/us/backman**.

CHAPTER 2

Law Givers, Emperors, and Gods: The Ancient Near East

2100–486 BCE

THE MIDDLE EAST AND
THE EASTERN MEDITERRANEAN

The second millennium BCE can hardly be topped for drama. Droughts, famines, civil wars, foreign invasions, deadly new weapons, and powerful empires—all these characterized the age and marked its major turning points. Four empires dominated the era: Egypt's Middle and New Kingdoms, the Babylonian (and later Persian) Empire in southern Mesopotamia, the Assyrian Empire of northern Mesopotamia, and the Hittite Empire in Anatolia (modern Turkey). Between them lay a sprawl of smaller states along the eastern Mediterranean coastline and skirting the southern edges of the Anatolian mountains. Once established, this patchwork of big and small states lived in relative harmony, in a dense web of commercial, cultural, and diplomatic connections that inspired some remarkable advances in each society.

Hatshepsut as Pharaoh This sculpture of the New Kingdom Egyptian ruler Hatshepsut (r. 1479–1458 BCE) depicts her as a male, with ceremonial beard. A prolific builder, Hatshepsut oversaw hundreds of construction projects, but her greatest achievement may have been the reestablishment and expansion of Egyptian trading networks.

Around 1200 BCE, however, newcomers appeared—groups of outsiders who operated separately but were loosely related by their dialects of a language family known as Indo-European. Little is known about these mysterious bands, but their waves of invasion set off a chain reaction of political collapse and economic ruin that wiped out nearly every state in the Near East. It left the peoples adrift and unsure, vulnerable to new regimes and exposed to new ideas about values such as human fate, man's relationship with the divine, the purpose of government, and the essence of morality. By 1000 BCE, or thereabouts, Western history had taken on a radical realignment that would have been unthinkable only two hundred years earlier. This realignment led to the birth of Western culture's first two great religions, Judaism and Zoroastrianism.

Moreover, the interaction of the Indo-European groups and the primarily Semitic-speaking peoples of the Fertile Crescent opened the way for the development of the Greater West—a civilization that bridged Europe and western Asia. This Greater West was composed not of a single hybrid culture but rather of the sense of a shared destiny in a large matrix of individual cultures. Europe and the Middle East have remained connected ever since by bonds of trade, intellectual cross-fertilization, cultural overlap, and religious rivalry.

OLD BABYLON

The city of Babylon was founded around 1950 BCE by the Semitic-speaking Amorites, who seized control of Sumer soon after the turn of the second millennium. Its location at the nexus of several trade routes through the Mesopotamian plain made it a strategic base for extending power out of Sumer itself and northward toward Syria, from which the Amorites themselves had come. The most famous of the early Babylonian rulers was **Hammurabi** (r. 1792–1750 BCE). A large archive of his diplomatic records survive, which document his crafty rise

CHAPTER TIMELINE

2250 BCE	2000 BCE	1750 BCE	1500 BCE	1250 BCE

- ca. 2035–1640 BCE Middle Kingdom Egypt
- ca. 2000 BCE Beginning of Indo-European migrations
- ca. 1950 BCE Amorites seize control of Sumer
- 1792–1750 BCE Reign of Hammurabi of Babylon
- ca. 1640–1570 BCE Hyksos ascendancy in Egypt
- ca. 1570–1070 BCE New Kingdom Egypt
- ca. 1478–1458 BCE Reign of Egyptian queen Hatshepsut
- ca. 1200 BCE Appearance of invaders known as the Sea Peoples

to power. At the start of his reign Babylon was simply one among many Amorite *Law Code of* kingdoms and was by no means the largest or strongest. Unable or unwilling *Hammurabi* to challenge his neighbors on the battlefield, Hammurabi instead managed to convince all of them of the existence of numerous conspiracies against their

crowns. He passed endless false rumors, usually of his own making and reiterated in person by his many ambassadors. Believing the lies, the other Amorite kings continually attacked one another for nearly twenty years and exhausted themselves in the process. Hammurabi then went on the offensive and in less than a decade conquered them all. He emerged as the sole ruler of virtually the entire Tigris–Euphrates region; thus was built the great Babylonian Empire (see Map 2.1).

Shortly thereafter, he issued a set of laws known as the Code of Hammurabi, texts of which presumably were distributed throughout the empire. He also had the entire Code engraved upon an 8-foot column of basalt as a permanent record of his greatness as a ruler. As propaganda, the Code could hardly have been

Propaganda Device   Hammurabi set up several tall stone pillars (steles) throughout his kingdom to proclaim his laws. The top portion shown here depicts the king receiving symbols of justice from the seated god Marduk.

1100 BCE	750 BCE	500 BCE	250 BCE	O

▪ ca. 1100 BCE **Iron weapons proliferate throughout ancient Near East**

▪ 669–627 BCE **Reign of Assyrian ruler Ashurbanipal**

▪ 559–530 BCE **Reign of Persian emperor Cyrus the Great**

▪ 521-486 BCE **Reign of Persian emperor Darius**

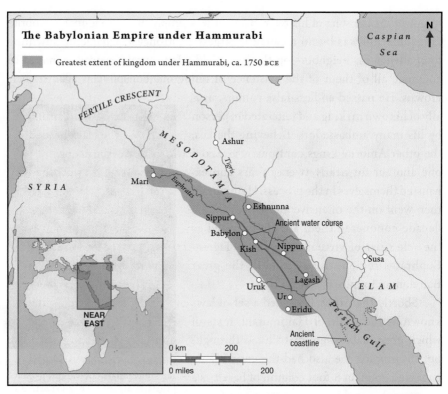

MAP 2.1   The Babylonian Empire under Hammurabi   Hammurabi's conquests rivaled those of Sargon the Great in their extent (see Map 1.3). Best known for the law code he implemented, Hammurabi should be remembered also for his introduction of religious imperialism, as he made worship of the Babylonian deity Marduk mandatory for all his subjects.

more successful, since scholars have credited Hammurabi as the first great law giver in Western history ever since. In fact, however, the Code is only a partial law code: although it addresses issues like property rights, water rights, marriage, violent crime, and wage regulations, it neglects to mention many equally vital aspects of Babylonian life, such as the commercial marketplace that formed the lifeblood of the economy. More significantly, the Code is never mentioned in the actual judicial records that survive from Hammurabi's reign or from those of later Babylonian kings. Its statutes may simply represent new laws added to an already-existing body of legislation.

The prologue and epilogue together make up half of the Code's text and proclaim the king's magnificence in glowing terms:

> When the lofty Anu, king of the Anunnaki gods, and Enlil, lord of
> heaven and earth, he who determines the destiny of the land, committed
> the rule of all mankind to Marduk, the chief son of Ea; when they made

him great among the Igigi gods; when they pronounced the lofty name of
Babylon; when they made it famous among the quarters of the world and
in its midst established an everlasting kingdom whose foundations were
firm as heaven and earth—at that time, Anu and Enlil appointed me,
Hammurabi, the exalted prince, the worshiper of the gods, to cause justice
to prevail in the land, to destroy the wicked and evil, to prevent the strong
from oppressing the weak, to go forth like the sun over the black-headed
people, to enlighten the land and to further the welfare of the people. . . .

These are the just laws which Hammurabi, the wise king, established
and by which he gave the land stable support and good government. Hammurabi, the perfect king, am I. . . . The great gods called me, and I am the
guardian shepherd whose scepter is just and whose beneficent shadow is
spread over my city. In my bosom I carried the people of the land of Sumer
and Addad; under my protection they prospered; I governed them in
peace; in my wisdom I sheltered them. . . . The king who is pre-eminent
among kings am I. My words are precious, my wisdom is unrivaled. By the
command of Shamash, the great judge of heaven and earth, I make justice
to shine forth on the land. By the order of Marduk, my lord, no one may
scorn my statutes, and my name shall be remembered with favor in Esagila
forever. . . . In the days that are yet to come, for all future time, may the king
who is in the land observe the words of justice which I have written upon
my monument! . . . My words are weighty; my deeds are unrivalled; only to
the fool are they vain; to the wise they are worthy of every praise.

The actual statutes of the Code seem an afterthought in comparison.

Nonetheless, the Code tells us much about how Babylonian society differed
from the Sumerian one it supplanted. As we saw in chapter 1, the Sumerian chief *Babylonian*
military executive (or lugal), assisted by scribes and priests, had supervised a bat- *Society and*
tery of local officials—with a complex web of traders, craftsmen, and farmers. The *Culture*
Babylonians replaced this norm with a top-heavy and decidedly heavy-handed
plutocracy, a governing class composed of the wealthy. Hammurabi's conquests
resulted in the monopolization of wealth by his royal court and armed supporters. Vast estates and commercial concerns controlled by the Babylonian elites
took the place of the more diverse economy of the Sumerians. Most of Babylonia's
inhabitants remained legally free but were nevertheless land tenants or commercial dependents of the nobles who dominated the palaces and temples. The Babylonians also expanded the use of slave labor on their estates and began to buy and
sell slaves on the international market.

Social stratification increased as well, and the penalties for offenses against
one's superiors were severe. Women of all classes, except for slaves, had the right

to divorce abusive husbands and to receive financial support from husbands who divorced them without good cause. Capital punishment was meted out unhesitatingly for any number of crimes—murder, assault, rape, theft, and adultery (applicable to women only) were the most common—but the means varied according to sex: men were killed by the blade, women by drowning.

Hammurabi also introduced a form of religious imperialism that both paralleled and legitimated his political oppression. The worship of Marduk, the patron god of the city of Babylon, became required throughout the empire; Hammurabi's subjects could continue to worship their old gods only if they accepted Marduk as the supreme Babylonian deity. Interpreting his military conquests as the worldly enactment of Marduk's spiritual victory over all other gods and goddesses, Hammurabi stands at the beginning of a long Greater Western tradition of justifying warfare as a religious duty. If the Divine Authority demands that His followers engage in warfare to fulfill His own cosmic aims, then what else can pious followers do? Such warfare is not only morally justifiable, because it is divinely sanctioned, but also in fact an act of religious devotion itself.

It is striking how frequently religious warfare, such as Hammurabi's conquests, occurs throughout Greater Western history. We shall see it again and again in later chapters: the *milhemet mitzvah* ("war of religious obligation") that inspired the Hebrews to seize their Promised Land from the Canaanites, Philistines, and Amalikites; the *jihad*-stoked conquests and the Crusades of medieval Muslims and Christians; the Wars of Religion of early modern Europe; the efforts to tame the "Godless heathen" of the New World or "to bring Christianity to the savages" of Africa in the 18th and 19th centuries; and the battles waged against "infidels" by extremist sects in 21st-century Islam. Western culture is not unique in this regard, of course, and wars without an explicitly religious motive have been equally numerous, but religiously based conflict is a notably recurring element in Greater Western history. Hammurabi is our first religious zealot, and the society he created, although it lasted only two centuries after his death, left a bitter legacy of lies, greed, and brutality. Few people mourned the passing of the Old Babylonian Empire.

It did produce a literary masterpiece, however. An anonymous Babylonian scribe gathered a number of folktales about the legendary Sumerian king Gilgamesh—ruler of Uruk some eight hundred years before the Babylonian conquest—and wove them together into an epic of remarkable sophistication.

Epic of Gilgamesh   The **Epic of Gilgamesh** relates the adventures of a powerful but egotistical king whose arrogance leads him to offend the gods. Unexpectedly, the gods' subsequent plot to kill him fails when Gilgamesh tames the savage half-man half-beast Enkidu, whom they had sent to destroy him, and the two become friends and pursue a series of heroic adventures. When the gods strike again by slaying his beloved new friend, Gilgamesh is filled with panic at the inevitability of death. He spends the rest of the story on a doomed quest for enlightenment and the secret to eternal life.

The poem notably credits women for their civilizing influence on men. Enkidu, for example, is tamed by an encounter with a temple priestess:

> The lass beheld him, the savage man,
> The barbarous fellow from the depths of the steppe....
> [She] freed her breasts, bared her bosom,
> and he possessed her ripeness.
> She was not bashful as she welcomed his ardor.

They spend six days and seven nights in nonstop passion; then Enkidu undergoes a transformation that estranges him from the other animals of the steppe:

> After he had had his fill of her charms,
> He set his face toward his wild beasts.
> On seeing him, the gazelles ran off,
> The wild beasts of the steppe drew away from [him]....
> His [legs] became motionless.... Things were not as they were before.
> Now he had wisdom, broader understanding.
> Returning he sat at the feet of the [priestess].... She says to him,
> "Thou art wise now, Enkidu; thou art become like a god."

Gilgamesh himself, seeking to drown his sorrows after Enkidu's death, receives some sensible advice from a kindly barmaid who is actually the grain goddess Sippur in human form:

> Gilgamesh, ... the life thou pursueth, thou shalt not find.
> When the gods created mankind,
> Death for mankind they set aside,
> Life in their own hands retaining.
> Thou, Gilgamesh, let full be thy belly,
> Make thou merry by day and by night.
> Of each day make thou a feast of rejoicing,
> Day and night dance thou and play!
> Let thy garments be sparkling fresh,
> Thy head be washed; bathe thou in water.
> Pay heed to the little one that holds on to thy hand,
> Let thy spouse delight in thy bosom!
> For this is the task of mankind!

Gilgamesh, however, obsessively continues his quest and learns of a magic plant growing on the floor of the sea. Whoever pulls the plant from its root and eats it will in fact gain eternal life. Eventually Gilgamesh locates the plant by tying heavy stones to his feet and walking the ocean floor. When he arrives back on shore and is about to eat the plant, however, a giant serpent emerges from the sea, snatches the plant from his hand, and pulls it back to the depths. Gilgamesh is left alone and hopeless on the shore, doomed to the death he could not avoid.

The poem depicts old Sumerian culture but was written down, in the full version in which it survives, in Babylonian times and in the Babylonian dialect. Little seems added to the original Sumerian folktales. The Babylonian compiler merely changed the names of several of the characters and of the gods into Babylonian ones. Thus the figure who tells Gilgamesh about the Plant of Life is named Ziusudra in the Sumerian fragments that survive but is called Utnapishtim, a Babylonian name, in the full compiled version. Was the compiler merely trying to make the text more appealing to a Babylonian audience?

A more subversive aim is possible too: perhaps the compiler hoped the epic could inspire the Babylonians to strive after something more than the wealth and power they hoarded so single-mindedly. Gilgamesh at the beginning of the poem is arrogant, self-centered, and boastful. He sounds more than a bit like Hammurabi in the bombastic claims of the Code. At the end he is broken, fearful, and sad beyond expression, but he has grown into spiritual maturity. He has become deserving of pity and even forgiveness.

MIDDLE KINGDOM EGYPT

The erosion of royal authority, beginning in the Fifth Dynasty of the Old Kingdom, brought about the First Intermediate Period in Egypt (ca. 2134–2035 BCE). In this relatively brief but turbulent period, the local nomarchs usurped royal power, plundered farmers' property, and engaged in widespread lawlessness. Mentuhotep II, the first king of the Eleventh Dynasty, however, was able to subdue the nomarchs and restore central authority from Thebes. It was the start of several periods of empire, including the reigns of the most active and powerful kings and the origins of a new religious tradition, monotheism.

Restoration of Royal Control   Mentuhotep II's reign ushered in the Middle Kingdom (ca. 2035–1640 BCE). Thebes lay in Upper Egypt, roughly 300 miles south of the traditional capital at Memphis (see Map 2.2). Moving the capital there allowed for closer oversight of the nomarchs. It also provided a base for launching new military expeditions southward, up the great river, into Nubia, to secure control of the strategic cataracts (high waterfalls) and to acquire the vast stone quarries and gold deposits found there.

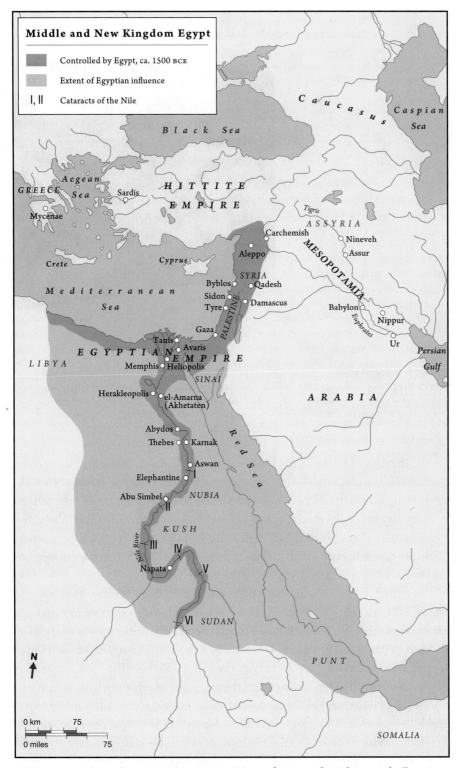

Middle and New Kingdom Egypt

- Controlled by Egypt, ca. 1500 BCE
- Extent of Egyptian influence
- I, II Cataracts of the Nile

Black Sea

Caspian Sea

Caucasus

GREECE

Aegean Sea

Sardis

Mycenae

HITTITE EMPIRE

Tigris

Crete

Cyprus

Carchemish

ASSYRIA

Nineveh

Aleppo

Assur

MESOPOTAMIA

Mediterranean Sea

Byblos

SYRIA

Qadesh

Sidon

Tyre

Damascus

PALESTINE

Babylon

Euphrates

Nippur

Gaza

Ur

Persian Gulf

Tanis

Avaris

LIBYA

EGYPTIAN EMPIRE

Memphis

Heliopolis

SINAI

ARABIA

Herakleopolis

el-Amarna (Akhetaten)

Abydos

Red Sea

Thebes

Karnak

Aswan

Elephantine

I

Abu Simbel

II

NUBIA

KUSH

III

IV

Napata

V

Nile River

VI

SUDAN

PUNT

N

0 km 75

0 miles 75

SOMALIA

MAP 2.2   Middle and New Kingdom Egypt   Waves of invasion drove home to the Egyptians that they could no longer rely on geographical barriers to preserve them from attack, and hence they went on the offensive. As shown here, by 1500 BCE they had extended their control as far north as the southern reaches of the Hittite Empire in Anatolia.

Voyage to the Next World   This wonderfully preserved wooden coffin held the remains of a
Middle Kingdom priest named Nekhtankh. The hieroglyphs invoke the gods Osiris, Isis, Nephthys,
and others to provide Nekhtankh with all the food and comforts he will need in the afterlife.
The vivid eyes represent the priest's soul looking expectantly to the voyage into the next world.

With restored fortunes, the kings of the Middle Kingdom were able to renew
public building programs—such as land reclamation in the delta and the extension of irrigation networks and reservoirs along the river. They could even pursue
military expansion beyond Egypt's natural borders, into Sinai and along the
Syrian coast. These projects required more laborers than the local population
could provide, however, which may have led the kings to recruit groups of foreigners (*hyksos* in Egyptian) to work in the mines and fields.

Developments in Egyptian Culture and Society   Egyptian religion continued to be a myriad of local cults rather than a single
organized faith. The cults remained *henotheistic*: although they recognized the
existence of other deities, each locale proclaimed allegiance to a particular god or
goddess as its special protector. In the case of the king's court, new prominence
was won by Amon-Ra, patron deity of the city of Thebes. The most significant
development in religion, however, was the extension of salvation (that is, entry to
the House of Judgment) to the nomarchs, other nobles, and wealthy commoners.
The heavenly reward was no longer a monopoly of the kings. The cause of this
development is unknown, but the means of it is clear: the contents of the Pyramid
Texts (formerly confined to the walls of royal tombs, as we saw in chapter 1)
began to circulate among the well-to-do. They were also inscribed into papyrus
books, or coffin texts, placed alongside the bodies in their tombs.

By the end of this period, the various coffin texts had been consolidated into the ***Book of the Dead***, an anthology of incantations, magical spells, boilerplate praise poems, and cribbed solutions to the riddles put to souls by Osiris at the entrance to the House of Judgment. This book, when placed in a casket, theoretically opened the gates of paradise, such as it was, to anyone who died with it in his or her possession. Ma'at, acceptance of the world's right ordering, remained the dominant focus and the supreme virtue. To the extent that Osiris and his council truly judged anyone's ethical behavior in life, they did so according to the dead soul's record of sustaining ma'at, which in most cases meant not performing injustice.

The Middle Kingdom did produce an exceptionally large body of writing—mythological stories, folktales, handbooks of practical advice, medical regimens, travelogues, love poetry, personal letters, and professional treatises (on being a successful merchant, civil administrator, estate manager, or whatever). The mix suggests that the intellectual tenor of the age was above all else pragmatic and industrious. The popular father-to-son advice handbooks—the "Instructions"—urge the recipient to work hard at his trade, to obey his superiors, and to cultivate a modest demeanor; they praise charitable acts and denounce corruption and exploitation of the poor. Should one fall short of the moral standard, the *Book of the Dead* was there to help.

The Instructions left behind by several Middle Kingdom kings have an altogether different tenor, one that reflects the less elevated general position these rulers held in comparison to their godlike Old Kingdom predecessors. In Amenemhet I's (r. 1991–1962 BCE) Instruction to his son, for example, he urges, "Hold yourself apart from those subordinate to you . . . and be on guard even when you

Ushabti Funerary figures who accompanied the new dead on their journey were called *ushabtis*. They were the servants of the dead, charged with providing food and water, performing physical labor, and in some cases providing sexual amusement. The hieroglyphs found most frequently on ushabtis quote a passage from the sixth chapter of the *Book of the Dead*: "Hail, ushabti! If [the deceased] be decreed to do any work in the afterlife, let every task that stands in his way be removed—whether plowing fields, tending the water channels, or carrying sand."

are asleep." Trust no one, neither family nor friend, and be especially watchful of the treacherous nomarchs, he warns. The advice, in this case, was sound: Amenemhet left his Instruction unfinished, and a later scribe completed it with a wry note that the great king had been assassinated by one of the officials in the royal court before he could finish the memo.

Middle Egypt's most renowned arts were architecture and sculpture—practical arts both, since most of the works produced served the purpose of promoting or extending the might of the king. Painting and sculpture followed stylistic and iconographic norms that dated to the Old Kingdom, with simple lines, flat surfaces, and a modest palette of colors. Funerary figurines made of clay or wood were exceedingly common. Although simple in design, these figures (called *ushabti*, or "those who respond") represented the servants who continued to work for souls in the afterlife. Science and technology mattered little, since Egypt's technological needs were amply met by the might of the river and the availability of the virtual slave labor of the masses. Mathematical knowledge was not widespread. Government officials probably understood and used all four computational operations—addition, subtraction, multiplication, and division. They employed fractions and discovered how to estimate the area of a circle by measuring the diameter, subtracting one-ninth of its value, and squaring the result. Egypt also did not develop wheeled vehicles until the New Kingdom and relied on oxen and donkeys (for plowing and carting, respectively) long after the Babylonians had already domesticated horses for farming and for pulling wheeled chariots.

The Hyksos Ascendancy   The modest stability of the Middle Kingdom collapsed quickly when the Semitic-speaking foreigners admitted to the realm suddenly rose in revolt and took control of most of the delta region around 1700 BCE. The precise identity of this group is still debated, and Egyptian sources refer to them only as the Hyksos ("foreigners"), but it seems likely that they were the Amorites from Palestine or a group closely related to them. Armed with recurve bows, long lances, and swords made of bronze, the Hyksos quickly seized control of the Nile Delta and forced the rulers in far-southern Thebes to recognize their overlordship. The Hyksos style of warfare unnerved the Egyptians, who used neither cavalry nor archers (since trees to make bows were relatively rare) and had traditionally relied on swarms of infantrymen armed with spears and stone-headed clubs.

For seventy years, from 1640 to 1570 BCE (the Second Intermediate Period), the Hyksos dominated Egypt; thus this period is also known as the **Hyksos ascendancy**. The Hyksos forged extensive commercial and diplomatic links with Palestine, Syria, and the islands of the Aegean Sea. During this time the Nubians to the far south broke away from the rulers in Thebes and established an independent kingdom called Kush. The Theban rulers thus found themselves trapped between foreigners at each end of the Nile, but they capitalized on the direness of the situation by inspiring their soldiers to pursue the noble cause of national liberation—which they promptly did, after quickly studying the new techniques of war. With their modernized army, they drove the Hyksos from Egypt around 1570 BCE and pursued them all the way to Palestine, a campaign that inaugurated Egypt's golden age—that of the New Kingdom (ca. 1570–1070 BCE).

THE NEW KINGDOM EMPIRE

The years of rule by the Hyksos proved to the Egyptians that the defense provided by their surrounding deserts no longer sufficed. Realizing that Egypt's relative isolation was at an end, the kings of the New Kingdom—now called **pharaohs**—decided to seize the initiative by extending their might to other lands. They subdued the Nubians to the south, which guaranteed Egypt's access to the gold mines of the region—a necessity now that gold had been established as the international standard for commerce throughout the Near East. From this vantage point they opened new trade routes down the western shores of the Red Sea and as far away as present day-Sudan and Somalia (see Map 2.2).

Militarily, the reinvigorated army—now led on the battlefield by the chariot-mounted pharaoh himself—conquered all of Palestine and advanced into Syria *Egyptian* as far north as the city of Aleppo. The most aggressive of the New Kingdom pha- *Expansion* raohs was Thutmose I (r. 1504–1492 BCE), who led his army into Syria until he reached the banks of the upper Euphrates, where he erected a victory plaque and proclaimed himself the greatest of Egypt's rulers. He had "surpassed the achievements of all the kings who lived before me. . . . The gods have delighted in my reign, and their temples have been filled with celebration. . . . I have pushed the boundaries of Egypt as far as the sun shines, . . . and I have made her triumphant over every land." His victories consisted more of looting raids than true conquests; nevertheless, his reign marked Egypt's transition into a fully militarized society in which army officers replaced civil officials as the backbone of the administration. Booty and tribute poured into the royal coffers, as did Nubian gold, and the increased wealth allowed him to construct scores of luxurious palaces for the high military caste and a network of new temples to gods both old and new. The god of military victory, named Amen, predictably rose in religious

Valley of the Kings   Though grander than most, the temple complex of Queen Hatshepsut is characteristic of the New Kingdom period. Instead of remote pyramids, notable Egyptians constructed elaborate malls with administrative offices, altar rooms, libraries, treasuries, and living quarters.

prominence during this period. His main temple at Karnak, just across the river from Thebes, received a series of massive additions and embellishments until it became a vast complex of halls, temples, administrative buildings, and storehouses, making it by far the largest religious compound in the ancient world.

The reign of Queen **Hatshepsut** (r. ca. 1478–1458 BCE) was notable for its prosperity and peace, evident from the spectacular mortuary temple she had constructed at Deir el-Bahri, near Thebes—a series of terraced gardens and broad colonnades carved into the high cliffs of the river valley. All the pharaohs of the New Kingdom after Thutmose I chose to be buried in this Valley of the Kings, their answer to the Great Pyramids at Giza. The burial sites were separate from the mortuary temples themselves. They hoped that this manner of entombment—in deep caves whose entrances were then concealed—would foil grave robbers.

Pharaonic Rule   The royal family practiced traditional brother–sister marriage, the idea behind it being that only the daughter of a pharaoh was sufficiently exalted to be the queen of another pharaoh. These marriages were usually but not always asexual. Every pharaoh, however, had dozens if not hundreds of wives in his harem, by whom he produced his heirs. Hatshepsut was the daughter of Thutmose I, the queen of Thutmose II (r. 1492–1478 BCE), and the bane of her stepson Thutmose III (r. 1458–1425 BCE). Egyptian law allowed for a woman to rule in her own right, although the occurrence was rare enough that royal monuments sometimes portrayed Hatshepsut with a fake beard. During her rule Hatshepsut extended her realm's commercial contacts as far as the lower reaches of the Red Sea and used much of the improved revenue to undertake ambitious building programs. According to some sources, she also led a military expedition or two.

Although Thutmose III officially began his reign upon his father's death in 1478 BCE, he was a child and lived for twenty tense years under the firm control of his stepmother. Once he took power for himself, he ordered his stonemasons to deface Hatshepsut's images and erase her name from all monuments. He dedicated his reign to extending Egypt's might even farther into Palestine and Syria, personally leading as many as sixteen campaigns. He left a network of client kings to do the actual work of governing the empire, taking their sons with him back to Thebes to be indoctrinated in Egyptian law and custom. In this way, when these children grew to maturity, they could govern their lands in a reliably Egyptian context. Diplomatic marriages between the daughters of the client kings and the Egyptian royal sons were also common. No Egyptian princess was ever wedded to a foreign king, however. Instead, princesses were either dedicated as temple priestesses or given a ceremonial marriage to a male family member.

In 1887 a treasure-trove of cuneiform tablets was discovered at Amarna, in Upper Egypt, that provide an intriguing view of Egyptian governance in the 14th century BCE. Known now as the Amarna Letters, the archive consists of 382 clay tablets, written in Akkadian (the language of international diplomacy at the time), containing letters between the pharaohs from Amenhotep III (r. 1388–1351) to Tutankhamen (r. 1332–1323) and their regional administrators. Several letters mention a group of people called the Apiru or Habiru—which some historians believe to be the first external reference to the Hebrews. In this example, the Egyptian governor of Jerusalem asks for additional military assistance against some rebels:

> They seized Rubutu. The land of the king deserted to the Apiru. And now, besides this, a town belonging to Jerusalem, Bit-Ninurta by name, a city of the king, has gone over to the side of the men of Qiltu. May the lord king give heed to Abdi-Heba [the governor writing this letter], your servant. And send archers to restore the land of the king to the king. If there are no archers, the land of the king will desert to the Apiru.

The goal of bringing the broader Near East under Egyptian influence had less to do with extending values and culture than with simply bringing more people, whether slave or free, into the service of the pharaoh. If Egypt could no longer retain its splendid isolation, then the rest of the world should at least recognize the need to sustain the ma'at that only acceptance of pharaonic rule could effect. Driving the point home were the huge reliefs of Egyptian armies and their

Family Hour at the Pharaoh's   This bas relief from about 1350 BCE portrays Akhenaten and Nefertiti along with three of their six daughters. Akhenaten is best remembered for his effort to replace traditional Egyptian religion with a new cult devoted to a single god called Aten. In this scene, the royal family offers prayers to this sun deity. The image continues a little-understood artistic tradition that portrays Akhenaten in androgynous fashion. Note that his body is curvier than that of his queen, a famous beauty.

victorious generals that bedecked palace and temple walls everywhere they went. Additions to the temple complexes at Karnak and Luxor further attest to the grandeur of imperial Egypt at its height.

The reigns of Amenhotep III (r. 1390–1352 BCE) and his son Amenhotep IV (r. 1352–1338 BCE) mark both the pinnacle of the New Kingdom and the start of its decline. The priests who presided over the temples now controlled roughly a quarter of the empire's land. Concerned about their growing power—especially that of the priests at Karnak, home of the sun god Amon-Ra—Amenhotep IV instituted a radical change: renaming himself **Akhenaten**, he elevated a minor solar deity called Aten to supreme status among the gods. The pharaoh's new name meant, literally, "the one devoted to Aten." Egyptian mythology in fact maintained separate cults for different phases and aspects of the sun. The god of the sunrise was different from the god of the sun at noontime, for example, and the god of sunset was yet another distinct entity. Amon-Ra was thought of principally as the heat energy of the

Akhenaten's Religious Reforms

sun.[1] Akhenaten closed the temples to Amon-Ra, violently suppressed their cults, and, with his queen Nefertiti, promoted Aten as the sole true and universal deity. He even had Amon-Ra's name chiseled out of royal inscriptions. He hoped to forestall popular protest by emphasizing that it was the royal family's obligation to worship Aten, whereas the obligation of the Egyptian people was to continue worshipping the pharaoh as always. He abandoned the palace at Thebes and erected a new capital some 300 miles to the north at a place called Akhetaten ("the horizon of the Aten"), now known as el-Amarna (see Map 2.2).

The belief in a single, supreme deity—or **monotheism**—was a novelty, and it did not go over easily with the people. They still craved the consolation of their all but certain eternal blessedness in the old faith. Akhenaten and Nefertiti, however, although undoubtedly motivated in part by a desire to break the power of the

---

[1]   The new god Aten was originally the physical sphere comprising the sun. Under Akhenaten's imposed monotheism, however, Aten incorporated all the many aspects of the sun.

priests, were genuine enthusiasts for the new religion. Tradition credits the pharaoh with composing the heartfelt Hymn to Aten:

> Thou appearest beautifully on the horizon of heaven,
> Thou living Aten, the beginning of life!
> When thou art arisen on the eastern horizon,
> Thou hast filled every land with thy beauty.

Central to the hymn is Aten's provision for the human world. All good things are connected with the life-giving sun.

Akhenaten's plans went awry, however, because he underestimated both the *Reign of* popularity of Amon-Ra and the priests' determination to hold onto their lofty po- *Ramses* sition. Akhenaten gradually became something of a religious recluse, isolated in *the Great* his palace and ignoring the needs of the empire. His successors on the throne—Tutankhamen, Ay, and Horemheb—quickly suppressed the new cult and restored the old faith. Eventually, a new pharaoh arose from the ranks of the military and restored the empire's fortunes. **Ramses II** (r. 1279–1212 BCE), Egypt's only ruler known as "the Great," built temples, palaces, and statues on a colossal scale. Perhaps one-half of all the Egyptian monuments that survive today belong to Ramses II's reign. Nevertheless, the reign of Ramses II was a last gasp of glory before Egypt once again fell to outsiders. Peoples from far away swept through the Aegean Sea and over Egypt, and rampaged through the rest of the Near East around 1200 BCE.

THE INDO-EUROPEAN ARRIVAL

The newcomers were a motley crew, related to one another by language: each group spoke one of a family of languages known today as **Indo-European.** In 1786 an English philologist named Sir William Jones, then serving as a judge in colonial India, delivered a paper to the Asiatic Society in which he observed that ancient Sanskrit (the tongue from which the major languages spoken in northern India are derived) shared an exceptional number of word roots and grammatical forms with Greek, Latin, and the Gothic and Celtic languages; from this he argued that ancient Indian and European languages must therefore be related. This common ancestor eventually came to be called Proto-Indo-European and is now believed to have originated somewhere north of the Black Sea. The idea of a single source for the family of languages from Ireland to India had been put forth in a more general way a hundred years earlier by a Dutch philologist. But Jones (who spoke thirteen languages fluently and could read another fifteen) produced enough data to make the theory rightly his own.

MOVEMENT OF
INDO-EUROPEAN PEOPLES

▮ Indo-European homeland, ca. 2000 BCE
→ Spread of Indo-Europeans, 2nd millennium BCE

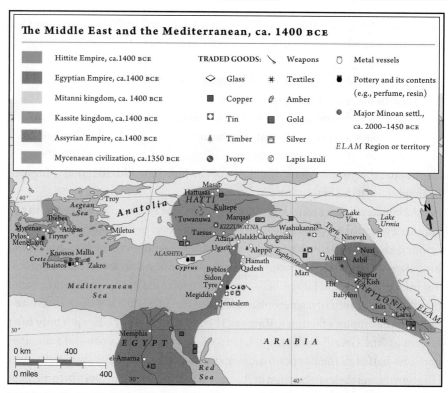

The Middle East and the Mediterranean, ca. 1400 BCE

Hittite Empire, ca.1400 BCE		
Egyptian Empire, ca.1400 BCE		
Mitanni kingdom, ca. 1400 BCE		
Kassite kingdom, ca.1400 BCE		
Assyrian Empire, ca.1400 BCE		
Mycenaean civilization, ca.1350 BCE		

TRADED GOODS:

Weapons   Metal vessels
Glass   Textiles   Pottery and its contents (e.g., perfume, resin)
Copper   Amber
Tin   Gold   Major Minoan settl., ca. 2000–1450 BCE
Timber   Silver   *ELAM* Region or territory
Ivory   Lapis lazuli

MAP 2.3   The Middle East and the Mediterranean, ca. 1400 BCE   By 1400 BCE the political composition of the Western world consisted of a half-dozen well-defined states—Mycenaean Greece, the Hittite Empire, and New Kingdom Egypt along the Mediterranean coast and the Mitanni kingdom, the Kassite kingdom, and the Assyrian Empire dividing the Mesopotamian lands.

The Indo-European peoples, a collection of nomadic shepherding populations, began to radiate from their homeland near the Black Sea as early as 2000 BCE. Several groups moved into western Europe, the forerunners of the Goths and the Celts. One strain migrated into the Aegean Sea, where they established the base for what was to become the Greek-speaking world. Many other groups—most notably the Hittites and the Mitanni—settled throughout Anatolia and the Iranian plain.

The Hittites   The Hittites initially settled in north-central Anatolia in a sprawl of small states, but by 1700 BCE they had united into a single kingdom (see Map 2.3). From the time they appeared on the scene, archeology reveals an aggressive warrior society. Although they raided Mesopotamia regularly (even sacking Babylon in 1595 BCE), the Hittites focused their military efforts on the Egyptian-held portions of Syria and Palestine. They advanced slowly. Although superior in arms, the Hittites could not put as many soldiers on the field as the Egyptian army could. The turning point came in 1286–1285 BCE, when Egypt, under Ramses II, and the Hittites, under their king Hattusilis III, declared a truce after an inconclusive battle at the Syrian city of Qadesh and established the first written peace treaty in Western history:

> Behold: Hattusilis, the great chief [of the Hittites], has made a treaty with [Ramses], the great ruler of Egypt, beginning this day, to establish good peace and brotherhood between us forever. . . . And the children of the children of the great ruler of the Hittites shall live in brotherhood and peace with the children of the children of Ramses, . . . and hostilities between them shall cease forever.

The peace did not last long. The Hittites, it turned out, had a gift for conquest but little for government, and their unified kingdom faced continual challenges from regional warlords who preferred their own local despotism to the national brand. When yet another wave of Indo-European invaders swept through the area, the Hittite Empire collapsed.

Before it fell, however, the Hittite Empire acquired literacy. The Hittites adopted a version of Mesopotamian cuneiform script and left behind a large archive of government records, including the peace treaty quoted above. Two features stand out in these documents. First, government actions were prefaced by a summary of the events that had led up to them; thus the Hittites contributed to the development of historical writing as a way not only to preserve but also to shape the memory of past events. Second, by presenting the historical context for their actions, the Hittites showed a unique willingness to recognize the failures and mistakes of their rulers. Such a willingness was unthinkable in Egypt or Babylon. In fact, the Hittites likely pioneered the use of critical history as a means of undercutting monarchical pretensions and ambitions.

Another new Indo-European arrival was the mysterious group labeled by the Egyptians as the Sea Peoples, who ran over much of the Aegean and the eastern Mediterranean between 1300 and 1200 BCE. Little is known of them, but they were probably a loose confederation of tribes, clans, and warrior-pirate crews. They moved first into Greece before branching farther south and east; by 1200 BCE they controlled most of the Nile Delta, a move that effectively ended Egyptian rule in Palestine, since the pharaohs no longer had direct access to the sea. *The "Sea Peoples"*

The Sea Peoples fought on land as an infantry, wielding bronze double-edged swords and spears. They also brought to the battlefield an innovation: bronze plate armor, which protected their soldiers far more reliably than any earlier type of protective covering. The Hittites and the Egyptians who slowly learned from them had relied on lightly clad archers who rode lightweight chariots; their greater speed and agility could wreak havoc on most ancient infantries, armed as they mostly were with clubs and spears. But the bronze armor of the Sea Peoples gave them enough protection against archers that they could hold their formations and defeat the Egyptian and Hittite forces.

No one knows precisely who the Sea Peoples were, although theories abound. Were they the Philistines described in the Hebrew Bible? A rival tribe of the Mycenaean Greeks? Or the Trojans, the Hebrews, the Siculi (the indigenous people of Sicily)? Egyptian records occasionally identify specific subgroups among the Sea Peoples, which suggests that they used the name as a catchall for a whole swarm of different ethnic groups.[2] Whoever they were, and wherever they came from, the invaders left behind a trail of annihilation so great that virtually no records survive to describe the wreckage until they reached Egypt. In Greece alone, 90 percent of the population was obliterated.

In Egypt, our first written and pictorial evidence of the Sea Peoples comes from an inscription set up by Ramses III (r. 1186–1155 BCE) to commemorate a rare (for him) victory around 1176 BCE over the intruders. The carved relief shows attackers of many varieties, wearing distinctive clothing and headdresses and carrying an assortment of weapons. The text of the inscription clearly was intended to revive flagging hopes. One portion depicts Ramses in his war chariot, leading his brave troops to battle. Its caption reads in part,

> The king, rich in strength as he rides forth, filling the hearts of the [Sea Peoples] with fear and awe; sole lord, whose hand is capable, conscious of his strength, like a valiant lion lying in wait for wild cattle, freely going forward, his heart confident, smashing thousands into heaps in the space of a moment. His power in the fray is like a fire, making all who assail him to collapse in ashes.

The inscription goes on to depict Ramses in the midst of the battle, scattering an army of terrified Sea Peoples:

> Behold him, as when Set rages, overthrowing the enemy, . . . trampling down the plains and hill-countries; the enemy lies prostrate, beaten from head to tail before his horse. His heat burns up their bodies like a flame. Hacked to pieces are their bodies, throughout eternity.[3]

The destruction caused by the Sea Peoples was vast. In southern and southeastern Europe, they annihilated whole cities. Few ancient Near Eastern cities

---

2   Among the specific peoples named by the Egyptians were the "Habiru," whom some believe to have been the Hebrews. This seems unlikely, however. The Habiru spoke an Indo-European, not a Semitic, tongue, and several centuries separate the Habiru and the Hebrews—if, indeed, the Hebrews ever were present in Egypt (see chapter 3).

3   Set (also spelled Seth) was the wrathful war god of the desert.

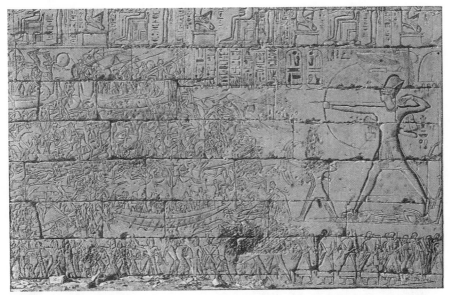

The Sea Peoples Defeated   This wall engraving from the mortuary temple of Ramses III at Medinet Habu in the western district of Thebes shows the pharaoh, at right, leading an ambush of the Sea Peoples. Ramses had blocked the channels of the Nile Delta, which prevented the Sea Peoples' advance, and then unleashed an archery assault on the ships as they struggled to turn course and escape to the sea.

disappeared altogether, but the invaders smashed old trade routes and splintered the diplomatic connections that had kept the region relatively stable from 1500 to 1200 BCE. The three major states of the era—New Kingdom Egypt, Hittite Anatolia, and Babylonian Mesopotamia—had generally managed to keep the wider region peaceful and had kept commerce moving. Even the smaller states that provided a sort of buffer zone among the major empires had thrived for those three centuries. But the advance of the Indo-Europeans sent shockwaves of displacement and despair through all three empires

The disappearance of the Sea Peoples is as much a mystery as is their origin. Despite Ramses III's fanciful inscriptions, no evidence exists of an annihilating defeat of them or of their continued horrific progress. Hence it is likely that they were absorbed into the indigenous populations. This assumption helps to explain the unusual degree of cultural innovation, economic realignment, political reconfiguration, and religious change that occurred in their wake. And an important part of that change was the perfecting of an old technology: the refining of iron.

THE AGE OF IRON BEGINS

Iron ore was plentiful in the ancient Near East, and people had been mining it for a long time. Objects made of iron have been dated to as early as 5000 BCE. By 1200 BCE, metalworkers had begun to perfect their methods. By repeating the

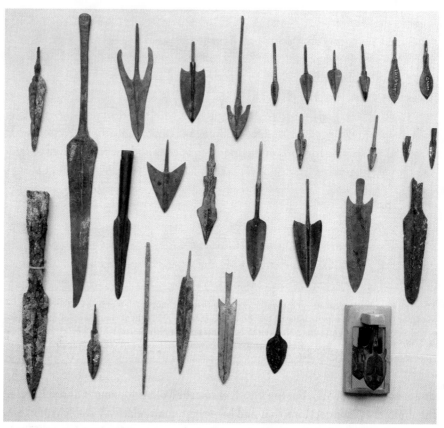

Iron Weapons   Armies in the ancient Near East fought primarily with spears, arrows, and knives, rather than swords. Swords did not become common until the arrival of the Indo-European peoples.

process of heating, quenching, and hammering, they could produce iron objects of ever-greater strength. With new weapons and new trading goods, power shifted again and again. The changes culminated in a new model of statecraft under the Persians and a new religion of fire, Zoroastrianism.

Iron ore was not an obvious choice, however. It is brittle and will produce a usable metal only after it is melted and its impurities burned away. The process, although simple to describe, is difficult to master. Iron melts at a much higher temperature than copper (the main constituent element in bronze) and must remain in its melted state for a considerably longer time to fashion into objects. The constant temperature needed is difficult to achieve with primitive wood fires. Moreover, iron is a weaker metal than bronze and is more susceptible to deterioration by moisture. Even in the dry climate of the Near East, iron can easily oxidize (that is, rust). A clash between an iron sword and a bronze sword would invariably end with the iron sword shattered.

Given these disadvantages, what was gained by producing iron weapons and tools? Simply put, mass production. Iron ore is abundant throughout the region, and, consequently, once the production process was perfected, people of all walks of life could afford iron implements.[4] By 1100 BCE iron weapons began to proliferate; by 800 BCE most common homes were well supplied with iron pots, tools, and utensils. The problem with bronze was that its two constituent parts—copper and tin—are both considerably rarer than iron ore and are seldom found in the same region. To maintain a constant supply of bronze, the Near East had to maintain steady commercial relations; any disruption in the long-distance movement of these metals, and the available supply of bronze disappeared. This is precisely what happened with the incursions of the Indo-Europeans and the mass waves of refugees they set in motion. Trade networks that had proliferated during the centuries from 1600 to 1200 BCE simply disintegrated. The abrupt decline in the availability of copper and tin gave the advantage to the iron-brandishing newcomers.

With the Hittite Empire destroyed, Babylon set reeling, and Egypt sent into yet another Intermediate Period (the Third, ca. 1070–664 BCE), the political map of the ancient Near East changed dramatically. New peoples and states arose, some of them of old provenance, others of newcomers. The region resembled a busy intersection whose traffic lights have gone out at rush hour. Groups like the Phoenicians, the Philistines, the Kassites, the Amorites, the Mitanni, and the Hurrians—to name only some of the best known—appeared on the scene in a bewildering tangle.

The Phoenicians were particularly successful, since they took to the sea from their home base (roughly today's Lebanon) to establish a network of trading colonies that stretched across the major Mediterranean islands (Cyprus, Sicily, Sardinia, the Balearics) and along the northern coast of Africa. Their name, which the ancient Greeks translated from a West Semitic dialect as "the purple people," refers to their expertise in dyeing. (The waters off the shore of Phoenicia had large populations of murex snails, from whose shells a distinctive reddish-purple dye was made.) Later writers like the Greek historian Herodotus reported that Phoenician sailors claimed to have circumnavigated Africa, although this is doubtful. The Phoenicians' most important contribution to Western culture was the dissemination of their alphabet, which simplified the task of writing. Among the first alphabets in Western history, it provided the model for the alphabet later adopted by the Greeks and hence led directly to the development of the alphabet used in the Western world today. The most famous of Phoenician cities was Carthage, founded sometime in the 9th century BCE in present-day Tunisia, which later challenged Rome for mastery of the entire Mediterranean.

The Phoenicians

The Philistines, by contrast, settled in the territory just south of the Phoenician homeland. They are best known as the villains of the Hebrew scriptures (discussed in chapter 3). Possibly an offshoot of the Peleset (one of the groups singled out by the Egyptians as being among the Sea Peoples), the Philistines in fact were an urban,

The Philistines

---

4   Iron is actually the sixth most abundant element in the universe. It makes up roughly 5 percent of the earth's crust.

commercial people who practiced little agriculture—just enough to put them at odds with pastoralist groups like their Hebrew neighbors.[5] Little is known of their language, but archeological remains link them with ancient Greek culture. The Philistines introduced to the Levant grape and olive vines, which are indigenous to the Greek archipelago, for example. Their architectural styles—as exemplified by the great citadels at Ashdod, Ashkelon, and Gaza—likewise resemble the fortified palaces of the Mycenaeans. The Philistines lived in the cities but controlled the agricultural hinterland and the regional trade routes. Most important, the Philistines occupied the region of Palestine that provided much of the copper and tin needed to produce bronze. Their control of such strategic sites and their access to superior weaponry, while making it impossible for their foes to forge similar weapons of their own, is what made the Philistines so substantial a foe to the advancing Hebrews.

The Assyrians

The Assyrians, who lived along the upper reaches of the Tigris, created one of the most feared of the new kingdoms. Caught between strangers to the west and unsure of the Hittites and Babylonians to their north and south, respectively, Assyrian culture turned militant and relied overtly on the use of violence and terror to maintain order. Their political fortunes rose and fell, depending on the relative ruthlessness of subsequent rulers, but from the mid-12th century BCE Assyria earned a well-deserved reputation for savagery that lasted for at least six centuries. From their imposing capital at Nineveh, the Assyrians maintained a large standing army of more than 100,000 soldiers divided into specialized units (infantry, cavalry, archers, engineers, and so on) that, uniquely among ancient armies, trained to work in concert (see Map 2.4).

The Assyrians were the first army to use iron weapons extensively and may also have pioneered another technological advance: the addition of carbon and nickel to refined iron to produce steel. Steel blades were significantly stronger than both iron and bronze blades and resisted decomposition. Producing it was expensive, however, which meant that many centuries would pass before steel production became widespread. The Assyrians knew the value of broadcasting their fearsome strength at arms, however. The victory monuments they erected depicted brutal scenes of slaughter, decapitation, rape, and torture, often in chilling detail. Their goal was to frighten people into submission, and it usually worked. When warnings failed, the army did its dirty work with gusto—going so far on occasion as to annihilate entire populations. This was the fate of the "ten lost tribes of Israel," who fell to the Assyrians in 722 BCE. Assyrian law dictated corporal punishments for hosts of crimes, resulting in thousands of publicly performed mutilations a year. On the other hand, at least one Assyrian ruler (Ashurbanipal, r. 669–627 BCE) built the first known library in Western

---

[5]   Traditionally, societies based on permanent settlement do not get along well with nomadic groups. Think of the conflicts between the cattle ranchers and farmers of the American West in the 19th century.

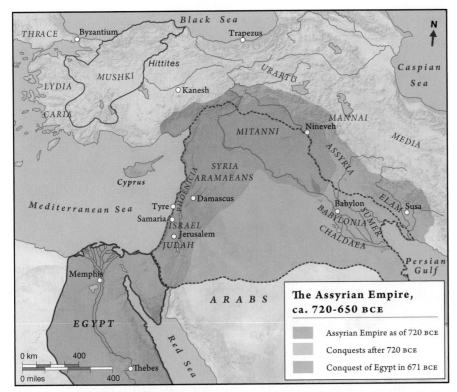

MAP 2.4   The Assyrian Empire, ca. 720–650 BCE   At its height, the Assyrian Empire united the whole of the ancient Near East. Renowned for their military might, the Assyrians were also the first Greater Western people to engage in the large-scale resettlement of populations. The practice aimed to weaken subject peoples' attachment to their homelands (thereby hopefully increasing their sense of identity as members of the Assyrian realm in general) and to maximize agricultural and manufacturing output by bringing manpower to areas with insufficient supplies of labor.

history. Archeologists have recovered thirty thousand clay tablets from its ruins in Nineveh. Most of this treasure store consisted of foreign literary works preserved in Assyrian cuneiform. For example, many modern editions of the *Epic of Gilgamesh* are based on Assyrian redactions unearthed at Nineveh.

Assyria's cruelty earned it the furious hatred of its neighbors. In 612 BCE an alliance led by the Medes, an Indo-European people, and the Chaldeans, the Semitic-speaking residents of southern Babylonia—known also as neo-Babylonians—stormed into Nineveh and reduced it to ashes and dust. Within another decade all vestiges of Assyrian might were destroyed. The new victors did not introduce an era of good feeling, however. The Medes were happy to return to Iran, knowing that the Assyrians were gone once and for all. That left the neo-Babylonians in control of all of Mesopotamia and much of the Levant, where they adopted Assyrian methods and ruled by brute force. One of the neo-Babylonian kings, Nebuchadnezzar II (r. 605–562 BCE), led his army into

The Neo-Babylonians

Ashurbanipal's Library at Nineveh   This cuneiform fragment contains a passage from the *Epic of Gilgamesh*. The remnants of Ashurbanipal's library are now housed in the British Museum.

Jerusalem, destroyed the Hebrew Temple, and carried tens of thousands of Hebrews into slavery back east, in Babylon.

PERSIA AND THE RELIGION OF FIRE

Still another group arose in the middle of the 6th century BCE, a people who toppled the neo-Babylonians and brought some stability to this near-hopeless situation that had continued, off and on, since 1200 BCE. These were the Persians, an Indo-European people whose origins are unknown. Led by an energetic and charismatic ruler named **Cyrus the Great** (r. 559–530 BCE), they lived near the midpoint of the eastern shore of the Persian Gulf. Suddenly and unexpectedly, the Persians united their various tribes, freed themselves from the overlordship of the Medes, and defeated their next neighbor, the Lydians. They then invaded Mesopotamia so quickly that Babylon surrendered without a fight.

Persia's Multi-cultural Empire

Cyrus was the undisputed master of the east, the largest empire the Western world had yet seen. He freed the Hebrews and allowed them to return to Jerusalem, where they quickly established a semiautonomous vassal state. Such largess was

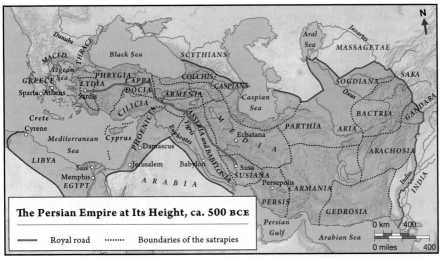

MAP 2.5   The Persian Empire at Its Height, ca. 500 BCE   Cyrus the Great (r. 559–530 BCE) founded the Persian Empire, which his successors expanded to be even larger than the Assyrian Empire that it replaced. The Persians were notably tolerant of local customs, religions, and social norms. What they provided was a single legal and administrative system that aimed above all to increase trade.

typical of Persian rule, but it resulted from strategic, not altruistic, thinking. The Persian Empire was simply too large for a central government to administer effectively. It was a land empire that, in contrast to Egypt, did not have a grand reliable waterway running through its center to allow easy unification. Cyrus thus portioned out his empire with care and forethought. Why govern a group like the Hebrews, when they could do so themselves? So long as they recognized Persian overlordship, caused no trouble, and sent payments of tax and tribute on time, Cyrus was wisely content to let them go their own way. The Hebrews were not the only people treated in this manner.

Cyrus's son and heir, Cambyses (r. 530–522 BCE), conquered Egypt itself and advanced far into Anatolia, uniting the entire Near East for the first time. The great Persian Empire ultimately stretched from the Aegean coast in the west to the Indus River in the east, from the upper Nile in the south to the middle reaches of the Black, Caspian, and Aral seas in the north. It covered well over 2,000 miles on an east–west axis and more than 1,000 miles from north to south. The ancient world had seen nothing like it (see Map 2.5). The Persians instituted a single currency and a standardized system of weights and measures, but otherwise allowed their subject peoples to govern themselves according to their own traditions. After centuries of Babylonian, Egyptian, Hittite, and Assyrian brutality and control, the light-handed imperial approach of the Persians was a welcome relief—which explains the relative absence of rebellion against the new rulers. The conquered could consider, and perhaps even admire, Persian culture, science, and religion.

The death of Cambyses triggered a dynastic crisis, since he died young and without an heir. Eventually a cousin named Darius carried the day. His reign lasted from 521 to 486 BCE, during which time he reformed the administration and undertook an extensive campaign to improve the empire's infrastructure. His projects included an unprecedented 1,600-mile roadway from Sardis (near the Aegean coast, in Asia Minor) to Susa (near the Persian Gulf, in modern-day Iran) that became the main artery for moving goods, capital, services, information, and soldiers through the heart of the empire (see Map 2.5). Darius also cut a canal that connected the Nile to the Red Sea, to facilitate trade with Egypt, and brought systematic irrigation to the Iranian plateau for the first time, which dramatically increased the agricultural production of the land. Last, he built a vast new capital in Persepolis, 200 miles east of Babylon. The move calmed people's concerns about having an emperor breathing down their necks and brought the eastern half of his empire, which extended to India, within his gaze.

With a calm and peaceful interior at last, with a single currency, and with physical barriers to efficient interaction removed, the economy of the Near East roared

Bringing Tribute to the Emperor   This relief from the Apadana (a high-columned open-air royal hall) in Persepolis shows the various peoples of the Persian Empire bringing tribute to the ruler, Darius I (r. 550–486 BCE). In the upper level, Babylonians bring amphorae filled with wine and oil, linens, and a hump-backed bull; in the lower level, Phoenicians bring gifts of bracelets, bowls, and a two-horse chariot.

to new life. The material standard of life improved for most people, and for most of those it improved dramatically. The Persians had created not just a new state but also a new model of statecraft: imperialism via accommodation and tolerance.

The stunning political and social success of the Persians paved the way for a revolution in religious life because they brought with them a new religion that spread rapidly throughout the Near East and remained the dominant faith of that part of the world until the rise of Islam in the 7th century CE.

The Persians originally had a polytheistic religion not unlike the ancient Sumerian faith, with deities of various types representing natural ele- *Zoroastrianism* ments and forces. In what may have been a self-conscious effort at reform, a man named Zoroaster began to preach the supremacy of a single god and the requirement of an ethical basis of life as the proper way of worshipping him. It was the beginning of **Zoroastrianism**, the first transnational Western religion.

We know little of Zoroaster (the Greek version of his Persian name, Zarathustra); he lived sometime around 1300 BCE and claimed to have received a vision of this "Wise Lord," Ahura Mazda. Ahura Mazda, he preached, was the one true and eternal God, altogether wise, just, and good; significantly, however, Ahura Mazda was not all-powerful—because he had an adversary named Angra Mainyu, later known as Ahriman. "Truly there are two primal spirits, twins renowned to be in conflict. In thought, word, and act they are two: the Good and the Bad," as one of Zoroaster's holy texts attests. It was to defeat Ahriman, Zoroaster taught, that Ahura Mazda created the world and all living things, to provide a battleground for the cosmic struggle between the forces of good and evil.

Zoroaster composed a sequence of hymns to Ahura Mazda. These seventeen poems—known as the Gathas—were passed on orally for many centuries until the Persians acquired writing. By the time the Gathas were written down in the 3rd century CE, a great number of other holy texts had been produced by Zoroastrian priests. These were combined with the original Gathas, and the result was the **Avesta**—the holy book of the Zoroastrians.[6]

The creation myth of this new faith maintained that Ahura Mazda disseminated his spirit to form seven principal elements: Sky, Water, Earth, Plants, Cattle, Man, and Fire. Ahriman brought death into the world, but Ahura Mazda so ordained that the first five elements would be self-regenerating, always bringing more life and therefore more good into the world. Man alone bears the responsibility of choice. The ethical quality of our lives determines not only our own fates but also the fate of the world.

---

[6]   The Avesta consisted of twenty-one books, but only fragments remain, since the Muslim conquerors of the Middle Ages searched out every copy they could and destroyed them.

Keeping the Flame Alive A ring of Zoroastrian priests celebrate their New Year festival with a ritual dance around the sacred flame. Once the most widespread religion in the ancient world, Zoroastrianism today has only about 200,000 followers worldwide. Low birth rates and high rates of conversion to more mainstream religions are contributing to their rapid decline.

Zoroaster wanted to emphasize the unity of mankind, the fact that all peoples regardless of ethnicity are linked by moral necessity and that all lives have value. In his teachings, our lives have a vast purpose—not merely, as in the Sumerian and Egyptian religions, an obligation to serve—that ennobles us and gives meaning to our suffering. God's final element, Fire, exists to inspire and assist us. It represents God's righteousness and truth, his purifying strength, and our hope. Living righteously meant regular prayer (five times daily), always in the presence of fire; performing various temple rituals; and following a high ethical standard of honesty, charity, cleanliness, and respect for nature. In this way, Zoroastrians had every hope of personal salvation, which meant joyous reunion with Ahura Mazda in paradise and the satisfaction of playing a role in God's ultimate victory over Evil. The Gathas enjoined believers to love all peoples, to aid the poor, to practice generous hospitality. They showed respect for nature by not eating animals before the animals had attained maturity and could reproduce. Persian temples drew freely on Sumerian, Akkadian, Babylonian, Assyrian, and Egyptian architectural styles to emphasize that Ahura Mazda was the god of all peoples.

Zoroastrian priests were called **magi**. Their primary responsibility was to tend the sacred fires in the temples, where various rituals central to Zoroastrian life were conducted: marriage, initiation rites, burial rites. Special study was required to become a magus, mostly involving study of the fast-multiplying Avesta texts and memorization of liturgical prayers, but the magi, although highly respected, were not regarded as possessing supernatural powers. Priests and laity remained distinct, but they interacted socially and even intermarried. Priests wore white garments that represented purity; initiated laity were identified primarily by wearing a lengthy cord called a kusti. Zoroastrianism recognized differences between the sexes. It had special temple rites, for example, to help women conceive and to purify them after childbirth. But it allowed all men and women, boys and girls, equal access to the temples and performed the same initiation rites for them all. Away from the temple, female believers could lead the family in prayers and even perform certain rituals.

Zoroastrian belief spread rapidly. The state did not forbid other religions or attempt to suppress them, which may have been the key to Zoroastrianism's success. For many subjects of the empire, Ahura Mazda became a kind of benevolent overlord, whereas their traditional deities were left as immortal spirits in service to the great God. But the ethical element of the faith needs emphasizing. Before Zoroaster, early religions posited no connection between religion and morality. The Sumerian gods, for example, cared only how people treated them, not how they treated each other. The Egyptians were required to obey the divine pharaoh and never upset the order of ma'at—but the only moral expectation placed on them by their religion was not to do harm. Zoroastrian faith gave people the deep satisfaction of feeling that their actions mattered: the way they treated each other helped to create a better world. It appealed to the millions who wanted meaning in life. It assured them that they were good, that their deeds and strivings had purpose, and that a higher ethical standard made life more tolerable for everyone.

◆

The 2nd millennium BCE, for all its political drama and military conflict, marks an important stage in the development of Greater Western values: the rise of pluralistic empires. Whether under the leadership of the New Kingdom Egyptians, the Hittites, the Assyrians, or the Persians, previously independent and ethnically based states were united under a strong central authority. The degree to which subject peoples assimilated and the sources of the most influential traditions varied enormously, but the emergence of pluralistic empires marked the recognition that, despite its cultural diversity, the Greater West was—or at least could be—a single civilization.

WHO, WHAT, WHERE

Akhenaten	Hammurabi	monotheism
Avesta	Hatshepsut	pharaohs
Book of the Dead	Hyksos ascendancy	plutocracy
Cyrus the Great	Indo-European	Ramses II
Epic of Gilgamesh	magi	Zoroastrianism

SUGGESTED READINGS

Primary Sources

Avesta

Book of the Dead

Epic of Gilgamesh

Source Anthologies

Black, Jeremy, trans. *The Literature of Ancient Sumer* (2004).

Chavalas, Mark W., ed. *The Ancient Near East: Historical Sources in Translation* (2006).

Hoffner, Harry A., Jr., trans. *Letters from the Hittite Kingdom* (2009).

Luckenbill, Daniel David, ed. *Annals of Sennacherib* (2005).

Moran, William L., ed. and trans. *The Amarna Letters* (2000).

Simpson, William Kelley. *The Literature of Ancient Egypt: An Anthology of Stories, Instructions, Stelae, Autobiographies, and Poetry* (2003).

Studies

Akkermans, Peter M. M. G., and Glenn Martin Schwartz. *The Archaeology of Syria: From Complex Hunter-Gatherers to Early Urban Societies, ca. 16,000–300 BC* (2004).

Aubet, Maria Eugenia. *The Phoenicians and the West: Politics, Colonies, and Trade* (2001).

Boardman, John. *Persia and the West: An Archaeological Investigation of the Genesis of Achaemenid Persian Art* (2000).

Briant, Pierre. *From Cyrus to Alexander: A History of the Persian Empire* (2006).

Brosius, Maria, ed. *Ancient Archives and Archival Traditions: Concepts of Record-Keeping in the Ancient World* (2003).

Brosius, Maria, ed. *The Persians: An Introduction* (2006).

Bryce, Trevor. *The Kingdom of the Hittites* (2005).

Bryce, Trevor. *Life and Society in the Hittite World* (2004).

Curtis, John E., and Nigel Tallis. *Forgotten Empire: The World of Ancient Persia* (2005).

Day, John V. *Indo-European Origins: The Anthropological Evidence* (2001).

Fleming, Daniel E. *Democracy's Ancient Ancestors: Mari and Early Collective Governance* (2004).

Galil, Gershon. *The Lower Stratum Families in the Neo-Assyrian Period* (2007).

Grajetzki, Wolfram. *The Middle Kingdom of Ancient Egypt: History, Archaeology, and Society* (2006).

Holloway, Steven W. *Aššur Is King! Aššur Is King!: Religion in the Exercise of Power in the Neo-Assyrian Empire* (2002).

Joannès, Francis. *The Age of Empires: Mesopotamia in the First Millennium BC* (2005).

Killebrew, Ann E., and Gunnar Lehmann. *The Philistines and Other Sea Peoples in Text and Archeology* (2013).

Leick, Gwendolyn. *The Babylonians: An Introduction* (2002).

Meskell, Lynn. *Private Life in New Kingdom Egypt* (2004).

Morris, Ian, and Walter Scheidel, eds. *The Dynamics of Ancient Empires: State Power from Assyria to Byzantium* (2009).

Oates, Joan, and David Oates. *Nimrud: An Assyrian Imperial City Revealed* (2001).

O'Brien, Cormac. *The Fall of Empires: From Glory to Ruin—An Epic Account of History's Ancient Civilizations* (2009).

Oren, Eliezer D. *The Sea Peoples and Their World: A Reassessment* (2000).

Ray, John. *Reflections of Osiris: Lives from Ancient Egypt* (2001).

Roehrig, Catharine H., ed. *Hatshepsut: From Queen to Pharaoh* (2005).

Silverman, David P., Josef W. Wegner, and Jennifer Houser Wegner. *Akhenaten and Tutankhamun: Revolution and Restoration* (2006).

Tyldesley, Joyce A. *Ramesses: Egypt's Greatest Pharaoh* (2001).

Van de Mieroop, Marc. *A History of Ancient Egypt* (2010).

Van de Mieroop, Marc. *A History of the Ancient Near East, ca. 3000–323 BC* (2007).

Van de Mieroop, Marc. *King Hammurabi of Babylon: A Biography* (2005).

Wiesehöfer, Josef. *Ancient Persia from 550 BC to 650 AD* (2001).

Yasur-Landau, Assaf. *The Philistines and Aegean Migration at the End of the Late Bronze Age* (2010).

For additional resources, including maps, primary sources, visuals, web links, and quizzes, please go to **www.oup.com/us/backman.**

בְּרֵאשִׁית

א אֱלֹהִים אֵת הַשָּׁמַיִם וְאֵת הָאָרֶץ: וְהָאָרֶץ הָיְתָה תֹהוּ וָבֹהוּ
שֶׁךְ עַל־פְּנֵי תְהוֹם וְרוּחַ אֱלֹהִים מְרַחֶפֶת עַל־פְּנֵי הַמָּיִם: וַיֹּאמֶ
לֹהִים יְהִי אוֹר וַיְהִי־אוֹר: וַיַּרְא אֱלֹהִים אֶת־הָאוֹר כִּי־טוֹב וַיַּבְדֵּ
לֹהִים בֵּין הָאוֹר וּבֵין הַחֹשֶׁךְ: וַיִּקְרָא אֱלֹהִים ׀ לָאוֹר יוֹם וְלַחֹשֶׁ
א לַיְלָה וַיְהִי־עֶרֶב וַיְהִי־בֹקֶר יוֹם אֶחָד: פ וַיֹּאמֶר אֱלֹהִי
רָקִיעַ בְּתוֹךְ הַמָּיִם וִיהִי מַבְדִּיל בֵּין מַיִם לָמָיִם: וַיַּעַשׂ אֱלֹהִי
דְהָרָקִיעַ וַיַּבְדֵּל בֵּין הַמַּיִם אֲשֶׁר מִתַּחַת לָרָקִיעַ וּבֵין הַמַּיִם אֲשֶׁ
עַל לָרָקִיעַ וַיְהִי־כֵן: וַיִּקְרָא אֱלֹהִים לָרָקִיעַ שָׁמָיִם וַיְהִי־עֶרֶב וַיְהִ
ֵל יוֹם שֵׁנִי: פ וַיֹּאמֶר אֱלֹהִים יִקָּווּ הַמַּיִם מִתַּחַת הַשָּׁמַיִם אֶל
ד אֶחָד וְתֵרָאֶה הַיַּבָּשָׁה וַיְהִי־כֵן: וַיִּקְרָא אֱלֹהִים ׀ לַיַּבָּשָׁה אֶר
מִקְוֵה הַמַּיִם קָרָא יַמִּים וַיַּרְא אֱלֹהִים כִּי־טוֹב: וַיֹּאמֶר אֱלֹהִי

CHAPTER 3

The People of the Covenant

1200–350 BCE

Sometime between 1800 and 1700 BCE, according to the Biblical story, a tired old man in the city of Ur, near the confluence of the Tigris and Euphrates rivers, began to hear a voice in his head. His name was Abram, and according to the legends passed on about him he was then seventy-five years old, poor, and childless. The voice came from heaven, and it told Abram to take his family—which consisted of his wife Sarai, his nephew Lot, and their servants—and to leave Ur and go where God would lead him. "The LORD said to Abram, 'Go forth from your native land and from your father's house to the land that I will show you. I will make you a great nation, and I will bless you; I will make your name great, and you shall be a blessing. I will bless those who bless you and curse him that curses you; and all the families of the earth shall bless themselves by you'" (Genesis 12.1–3).

It is a tale filled with complex meanings. Part of the collection of books now called the Hebrew Bible (or, to use the Christian term, the Old Testament), it is also a tale of the origins of two peoples—the Jews and the Arabs—and three world religions—Judaism, Christianity, and Islam. Before entering the debate over the tale's factual accuracy, let us follow the narrative a bit further.

In the Beginning This page of the opening of the book of Genesis—here showing its Hebrew name *Bereshit* ("in the beginning") in enlarged letters—comes from a multivolume edition of the Bible planned for publication in Germany in the 1930s. This first volume appeared just before Hitler's rise to power in 1933; the rest of the project was never completed. By long-standing Jewish tradition the text of the scriptures is never adorned with representational imagery, in order to maintain attention on the holy word. Decorative elements consist almost entirely of the beautiful presentation of the script itself.

Being pious, Abram and his family obeyed the call without hesitation. Their trek followed the course of the Fertile Crescent. God led them northward through the Mesopotamian plain, westward across Syria, then southward into the land of the Canaanites in Palestine. At Shechem, which was roughly in the center of Canaan, the Lord appeared to Abram and promised to give all the surrounding land to his offspring. That promise is only the beginning of the tale's complex relationship to history.

Abram built the Lord an altar as a way of giving thanks, but he may have wondered whether the gift was such a blessing. The land was then suffering from a horrific famine, which forced Abram and his family to continue traveling southward in search of food, past the Negev desert, then westward across Sinai and into Egypt. This was a dangerous move, because Abram's wife was an exceptionally beautiful woman, and he believed the Egyptians to be so lecherous that someone might kill him to capture her. Pleading his self-concern, he persuaded Sarai to pose as his (presumably unmarried) sister. Pharaoh's agents saw her beauty and sent her to the royal palace as a new addition to his harem. "And because of her, it went well with Abram; he acquired sheep, oxen, asses, male and female slaves, she-asses, and camels" (Genesis 12.16). But the Lord sent a plague upon the pharaoh because of the wrong done to Sarai, and so the pharaoh sent her and Abram packing. They returned to Palestine, where the Lord repeated his promise of dominion over the land and descendants as numberless as the stars in the night sky.

CHAPTER TIMELINE

1300 BCE	1200 BCE	1100 BCE	1000 BCE	900 BCE

- ca. 1200 BCE **Hebrews move into Palestine**

- ca. 1005–965 BCE **Creation of a unified monarchy under King David**

- ca. 965–928 BCE **Reign of King Solomon; construction of First Temple at Jerusalem**

Yet a decade passed without either promise fulfilled. When Abram was eighty-six, Sarai sent her own servant, an Egyptian maiden named Hagar, into his bed so that he might produce a child by her. Hagar became pregnant, and Sarai, embarrassed at the ease with which Hagar had achieved what she herself had never been able to accomplish, beat her harshly. Hagar eventually gave birth to a son to whom Abram gave the name Ishmael. Another dozen years passed. The Lord appeared to Abram again and repeated his promises yet again, but this time he told Abram to change his name to Abraham (meaning "father of a multitude"), whereas Sarai was henceforth to be called Sarah ("noble-woman"). The new names signaled a sort of spiritual promotion in their relationship with God. Moreover, God ordered Abraham to circumcise himself and Ishmael and to promise to circumcise all their male offspring henceforth on the eighth day after their birth. Abraham did indeed cut off his own foreskin, and some short time later, remarkably, the ninety-nine-year-old Abraham and the ninety-year-old Sarah did conceive a child—a son. They named him Isaac and duly circumcised him on the eighth day. Sarah was joyful to have a child at last but could not help resenting the continued presence of Ishmael and his mother, Hagar, so she ordered them to leave the household. The story takes a bittersweet turn when the Lord, speaking to Hagar for the first time, assures her that he has a plan for Ishmael as well: "I will make a great nation of him" (Genesis 21.18).

950 BCE	800 BCE	700 BCE	600 BCE	500 BCE

- ca. 950 BCE **Composition of first biblical texts**
- ca. 937 BCE **Kingdom splits into Israel (north) and Judah (south)**
- ca. 721 BCE **Assyrians conquer Israel**
- ca. 587 BCE **Neo-Babylonians conquer Judah and destroy Temple**
- 586–539 BCE **Babylonian Captivity**
- ca. 538 BCE **Persian emperor Cyrus the Great allows exiles to return to Judah**
- ca. 515 BCE **Second Temple is dedicated**

Whether or not it accords with historical truth, the story reflects a tradition that this one man, Abram/Abraham, was the patriarch of two great peoples. Through Sarai/Sarah he fathered the nation of the Hebrews, out of which developed the religion of Judaism, and with his Egyptian concubine Hagar he produced the line that resulted in the nation of the Arabs and their faith of Islam.

The tale bristles with difficulties: Why was Abram/Abraham chosen? Why was his family led to the land promised to them at a time of famine, when they could not live there? How could Abram/Abraham justify handing his beloved wife over to the pharaoh's lust? After their release from Egypt, why did God repeat his promise to Abram/Abraham's family, only to let another ten years go by before fulfilling it? After Hagar produced Ishmael, why did he let another twelve years pass before allowing Isaac to be born? And why he did make Hagar endure twelve years of Sarai/Sarah's bullying before extending any consoling promise to her?

But even this is only the beginning of the complexities that frustrate the effort to know the origins of the Hebrews. Political and religious ideologies play an important role in this problem, of course, but even more fundamental is the vexing question of the Bible itself and its usefulness as a historical source. The debate is as old as the Bible itself.

THE BIBLE AND HISTORY

To begin, the Bible is not a book but a library. The Hebrew Bible consists of twenty-four books written over a period of nearly one thousand years. According to Jewish tradition, the entire set of books was finally established, ordered, and canonized around 450 BCE by a group remembered as the "Men of the Great Assembly." Most scholars, however, would regard that as too early a date and prefer something around 250 or 200 BCE—and they place the composition of the first biblical texts around 950 BCE.

Approaching the Hebrew Bible   Many Christians will be surprised by a first look at the Hebrew Bible, since it organizes the books in a way unfamiliar to Christian tradition. The Hebrew Bible is commonly known as the **Tanakh**—an acronym based on the letters T (for *Torah*, meaning "Instructions"), N (for *Nevi'im*, or "Prophets"), and K (for *Ketuvim*, or "Writings")—and it groups its books accordingly. Moreover, there are two distinct versions of the Hebrew Bible: the Masoretic text compiled in Hebrew in the 2nd century CE and the Greek text, the Septuagint, compiled around 200 BCE for the Greek-speaking Jews of the Hellenistic era (discussed in chapter 5). Jewish tradition, supported by textual evidence, regards the Masoretic text as a definitive re-creation of the lost version put together by the Men of the Great Assembly. It thus has priority over the Greek version, which is actually five hundred years older. The Septuagint text varies from the Masoretic in some significant ways,

The Dead Sea Scrolls   The scrolls are a collection of 972 ancient texts found in caves near the west bank of the Dead Sea beginning in the late 1940s. They consist largely of Hebrew biblical texts like the ones shown here (roughly 40 percent of the total), with a somewhat smaller number of apocryphal biblical writings. The rest of the collection consists of legal and devotional texts. Most of the scrolls are on parchment and are written in Hebrew, Aramaic, Greek, and Nabataean.

most especially in its acceptance of certain additional books that do not appear in the Hebrew tradition.[1] The variations in the canon are important: the Hebrew scriptures did not emerge fully formed at a single moment in history but rather evolved over centuries.

The problems are obvious. For one, the Bible ascribes impossibly long lives to the early leaders of the Hebrews. Abraham, we are assured, died in his 175th year, and his son Isaac died at the age of 180. We are told that Isaac's son Jacob died when he was very old, although a precise age is never given, but Jacob's son Joseph reportedly lived to be 110. A second problem is that the scriptures coopt stories from other ancient Near Eastern cultures as if they had occurred uniquely to the Hebrews. The biblical legend of Noah and the ark clearly echoes the Sumerian tale of the Great Flood, to pick the most obvious example. Even the single most important episode in defining the Hebrews as a people presents a problem. Here, Moses is chosen by God to lead the Hebrews out of Egyptian bondage, receives the **Torah** (laws for righteous living, collected in the first five books of the Hebrew Bible) on Mount Sinai in the desert northeast of Egypt, and—in return for

---

[1]   The Roman Catholic and the Orthodox churches regard the Septuagint version as normative. Protestant churches usually print the Septuagint's extra books (which they call the *Apocrypha*) as a type of appendix.

agreeing to worship God exclusively and to live by his laws—guides the Hebrews to a promised land of safety and prosperity. The escape from Egypt establishes the Hebrews' special **covenant**, or contract, with God, and yet there is virtually no archeological or documentary evidence for it outside of the Bible itself.

These difficulties hardly negate the Bible's value as a historical source. Rather, we must read the texts on their own terms. They portray not human history in the usual sense but the development of a relationship—the growth of a people's understanding of their connection to a transcendent deity (see Table 3.1).

Whatever the Hebrew Bible lacks in historical accuracy, it makes up for with a searing depiction of a difficult, demanding, and inscrutable God. He places extraordinary obligations on a small, persecuted minority from whom he expects the highest degree of ethical behavior. And their failures to live up to that standard are narrated again and again. The Hebrews are depicted as the Chosen People—but that status confers more obligations than rewards. They are chosen, but not in the sense of favored. Rather, they are held responsible for maintaining a standard of moral behavior and pursuing justice on earth. How else can one interpret the travails of Abraham? Along with the repeated promises and the constant requirement of waiting for fulfillment, he must undergo tension and division within his own household. God tests Abraham far more frequently than he rewards him, and those tests are severe.

Debate over Authorship

The origins of the Bible remain subject to debate even after three thousand years of intense study. The first texts to be composed, scholars agree, were the five books of the Torah, which began to appear, in various forms, around 950 BCE and perhaps a bit later than that. What makes dating the texts so challenging is that several authors and editors had a hand in the process. Most biblical scholars hold

TABLE 3.1   **The Central Tenets of Judaism**

Although Judaism does not have an official statement on doctrine, most Jews accept the statement of "The Thirteen Essential Beliefs" as summarized by the great medieval scholar R. Moses ben Maimon (d. 1204):

1. God will reward the good and punish the wicked.
2. The messiah will come.
3. The dead will be resurrected.
4. God exists.
5. God is one and unique.
6. God is incorporeal.
7. God is eternal.
8. Prayer is to be directed to God alone.
9. The words of the prophets are true.
10. The prophecies of Moses are true, and Moses was the greatest of the prophets.
11. The written Torah and the oral Torah were both given to Moses.
12. There will be no other Torah.
13. God knows the thoughts and deeds of all people.

to the so-called **Documentary Hypothesis**, which posits that the texts as they survive result from the intertwining of several writers' work, writers known by the initials J, E, D, and P. These indicate, respectively, the Yahwist author (ca. 950 BCE), the Elohist author (ca. 750 BCE), the Deuteronomist author (ca. 650 BCE), and the Priestly author (ca. 550 BCE). Some scholars add a still later figure known as R, for the Redactor.

The Yahwist (J) is believed to have been the first, and his writings can be identified by his use of the term **YHWH** to stand for God. J is presumed to have written most of the biblical book of Genesis and certainly those parts of it that relate the stories of Abraham and his descendants.[2] J's God is always YHWH in Hebrew (which English-language Bibles represent by the all-capitals word LORD), and as we have seen, YHWH frequently intervenes directly in his human characters' lives.

The Elohist (E), by contrast, uses a different word—Elohim, meaning simply "god" or "deity"—and never depicts any direct human encounters with him. In Genesis, the long final section telling the tale of Joseph and his brothers comes from E. (Joseph is the first human being in the Bible who never sees or hears God personally, yet still believes.) E's handiwork is the patchiest, with few long passages apart from the Joseph story, which suggests that it reflects an oral as opposed to a written tradition, something interwoven here and there throughout the J narrative. Around 750 BCE, the argument goes, as the Assyrian armies drew nearer to the Hebrew lands, E set to work, trying to preserve the tales handed down among those who settled in the northern part of Palestine as a counterbalance to J's heavy emphasis on the Hebrews in southern Palestine. This desire to preserve the traditions of the northern Hebrews may explain why E so frequently tells stories of sibling rivalry, such as that between Jacob and Esau (Isaac's sons) and between Joseph and his brothers.

The Deuteronomist (D) is the most controversial of the purported authors. Some scholars consider him the author of the book of Deuteronomy but of little else, whereas others regard him as the most critical figure in biblical transmission. D insists on the absolute centrality of allegiance to Torah and worship in the Jerusalem Temple, but also relentlessly describes the crisis of the Assyrian conquest and the approach of the neo-Babylonians as the result of the Hebrews' failure of morals and observance.

Finally, the Priestly author (P), or more likely authors, set to work after the fall of Jerusalem to the neo-Babylonians around 587 BCE and inserted a vast body of

---

[2]   The Hebrew letter *yod* can be transliterated as either the English J or Y. The name of God is not to be spoken—hence the use of the abbreviation YHWH. Christians, not being subject to the traditional restriction, expand the abbreviation as Yahweh or Jehovah.

priestly ordinances from the time of the First Temple into the traditional material of the Torah. P's handiwork is woven throughout the first books of the Bible but is especially evident in the book of Leviticus and in the first ten chapters of Numbers. P is also responsible for the first chapter of Genesis (J's version of creation had begun with chapter 2), a priestly version of Abraham's covenant with God.

Not all biblical scholars adhere to the Documentary Hypothesis. Some prefer other explanations for the Bible's abrupt shifts, numerous repetitions, and frequent contradictions. Everyone agrees, however, that the Bible is a patchwork of many writers' contributions—as well as the product of considerable revision, expansion, editing, and rearrangement. It is above all a testament to the Hebrews' perseverance, their determination to make sense of their experience, and their faith in God. As we shall see, much of that experience consisted of repeated persecution and oppression.

THE LAND OF CANAAN

Whatever their legendary origins, the Hebrews moved into Palestine sometime around 1200 BCE. This is a long time after their biblical arrival under Abraham in 1800 BCE. The Bible tells of four hundred years of enslavement in Egypt, followed by a heroic march of liberation and the conquest of Canaan (Palestine), also referred to as the Promised Land.

In the Bible the march of liberation was led by Moses, to whom was given the first elements of the Torah. As mentioned before, however, no nonbiblical evidence exists for a large Hebrew presence in Egypt at any time during the New Kingdom. Nor is there evidence for a dramatic Hebrew rebellion and subsequent release from bondage. It seems unlikely that events of such magnitude would leave no trace in the hundreds of thousands of Egyptian records that survive from the New Kingdom era. Yet it seems equally unlikely that a people would invent a legend of their own humiliating enslavement if it had no basis in fact. All that can be said with certainty is that when the Hebrews moved into Palestine, they brought with them an unshakeable conviction: God, they believed, had vouchsafed the land to them. In return, they felt a special obligation to live according to an exacting ethical and ritual code, to care for the poor and downtrodden, and to serve the cause of justice.

Tribal Organization

They were not necessarily a single people and may instead have been a loose assemblage of speakers of related dialect groups. Ancient sources describe the Hebrews' division into twelve tribes. Figures known as **judges** held a combination of religious and political authority over each tribe, together with military leadership in times of war. The Hebrews communicated with the other groups who had already settled the land—the Amalekites, Amorites, Aramaeans, Philistines, and Phoenicians—but the Hebrews were overwhelmingly a pastoral people. Their movement over the land with their herds put them at odds with the other groups, who were chiefly farmers and town dwellers. Although they remained seminomadic, the Hebrew tribes had carved out certain zones for themselves by 1000 BCE. Those in the hilly south called themselves the people of **Judah**, whereas the northern-based tribes took the name of **Israel** (see Map 3.1).

Religious life centered on the family, with daily prayers and rituals to observe the emerging body of Torah. The judges and a caste of priests led communal services that frequently involved some form of animal sacrifice (the "burnt offerings" referred to in the Bible). The Hebrews did not proselytize to non-Hebrews and focused instead on broadening the acceptance of YHWH among their own people. For a long time even after the YHWH cult was established, the Hebrews practiced a henotheistic religion—that is, a religion that recognizes the existence of other gods but insists on the supremacy of its one individual god.

The Hebrews preserved the political autonomy of each tribe for as long as they could, but when the Philistines conquered the southern coastal plain of the *Philistine* Levant, they were forced to mount a united defense against annihilation. They *Conquest*

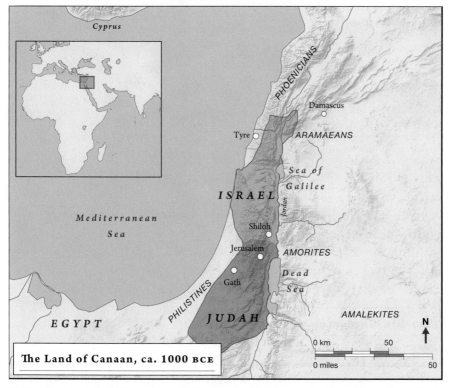

MAP 3.1 The Land of Canaan, ca. 1000 BCE   Originally organized by tribes under the leadership of religious judges, the Hebrews may have contended with one another as bitterly as they did with the peoples they displaced. The Hebrew Bible's book of Judges tells much of this story.

entered the alliance thinking it would be temporary, and internal bickering made concerted action difficult. In 1050 BCE, or thereabouts, the Philistines demolished the main Hebrew sanctuary at Shiloh and carted off the **Ark of the Covenant**—the chest that held the stone tablets of the Torah as received by Moses—as a war trophy. After that military catastrophe, the bulk of the people called out for the creation of a Hebrew monarchy. Only a clear central command under a charismatic figure with military skill, they argued, could hold the confederation together and destroy the Philistines.

DREAMS OF A GOLDEN AGE

Their choice fell ultimately upon David, a low-born but ambitious soldier. **David** (r. ca. 1005–965 BCE) united the kingdoms of Judah and Israel and pushed the borders of the newly unified Israelite kingdom to their greatest expanse, from the Gulf of Aqaba in the south to 50 miles north of the Sea of Galilee (see Map 3.2).

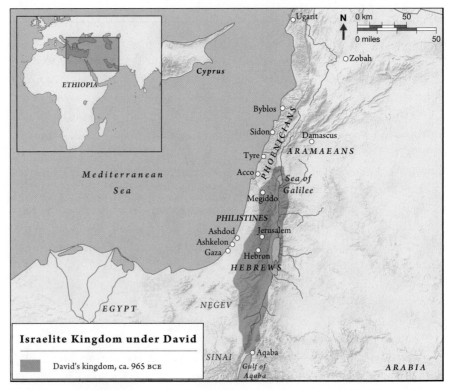

MAP 3.2   Israelite Kingdom under David   The unified kingdom established by King David had its capital at Jerusalem. The choice of city was strategic: Jerusalem had no special significance for any of the Hebrew tribes, so there was no worry about any particular tribe holding pre-eminence over the others.

Politically, the Israelites under David were among the most powerful peoples in the Near East. The choice of Jerusalem for the new capital of his kingdom showed David's shrewdness because its central location made it well placed to watch over both the northern and the southern tribes. Even more important, the city, which had been founded centuries earlier by the Canaanites, had no prior religious significance for the Hebrews and hence was unlikely to fuel tribal competition for privilege. David brought the Ark of the Covenant into the city and began to construct a magnificent palace for himself (which he financed with a combination of heavy taxation, forced loans, and slave labor). Of the 150 prayer-songs that make up the Bible's book of Psalms, tradition ascribes most of them to David's own pen, although modern scholars generally believe that if he did in fact compose any of them, these were most likely Psalms 1 through 41.

Unification under David

David's son **Solomon** (r. ca. 965–928 BCE) succeeded him and threw his considerable energy into enlarging his father's palace complex. He also began construction of a temple to house the Ark of the Covenant. The Bible devotes three entire chapters to describing the Temple (1 Kings 6–8). Everything about it deserved mention, starting with its size—30 feet wide, 90 feet long, three stories tall. It had latticed windows, inlaid wood paneling, carved cherubim, chains that secured double doors leading into the inner sanctuary where the Ark was placed, and statuary embossed with gold leaf. This was, the Bible assures us, a house fit for the Lord. Solomon also expanded the royal palace until it formed a vast complex with the Temple.

Reign of Solomon

Moreover, he built the Israelites' first commercial fleet, which sailed out of the Gulf of Aqaba at the kingdom's far southern tip on the Red Sea (see Map 3.2). It put Israel in direct contact with Upper Egypt, Ethiopia, and the coastal peoples of the Arabian peninsula. The Israelites sold the copper that they—or their slaves, actually—mined from the rich veins found in the southern Negev desert. This trade was highly lucrative and helped to finance the palace and Temple projects. Records survive that indicate commercial ties as far as southern India—the source of the incense and spices used in Temple rites and of the sandalwood used to decorate the sacred space.

Solomon, like his father, survives in Hebrew tradition as a wise and great ruler who championed the causes of justice and piety.[3] Solomon wrote psalms, too, and is credited with writing the book of Proverbs and the Song of Songs. Both men, however, could be selfish and despotic and were nowhere near as popular in their lifetimes as in later centuries. Their sexual appetites were tireless: David pursued married women as well as servant girls, and Solomon, we are told, had

---

[3] "King Solomon excelled all the kings on earth in wealth and in wisdom. All the world came to pay homage to Solomon and to listen to the wisdom with which God had endowed him" (1 Kings 10.23–24).

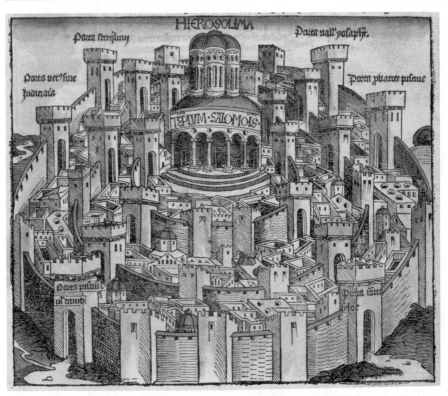

The Temple in Jerusalem   No one knows exactly what the Temple built by King Solomon looked like, despite the detailed description of it given in the Bible. This representation comes from the Nuremberg Chronicle by Hartmann Schedel, which appeared in 1493.

seven hundred wives and three hundred concubines, including "the daughter of Pharaoh, women of the Moabites, Ammonites, Edomites, Zidonians, and Hittites" (1 Kings 11.1). Solomon's consorts were of an exceptionally large number, but his bed-hopping was not regarded as intrinsically wrong. Polygamy was common among the early Israelites, especially among the elites. Both men had cruel streaks, too. In the story of the beautiful Bathsheba, David intentionally ordered her husband into a ferocious battle so that he could then claim his widow for himself. After a victory over the people of Zobah, David took more than twenty thousand Canaanite soldiers captive as slaves and had all their horses hamstrung.

Most likely, the overwhelmingly flattering nature of the Bible's portrayal of these men resulted from the role they played in strengthening the cult of YHWH. All their conquests, their building projects, their artistic endeavors, their efforts to provide justice for the people—everything was done in service to the God whose great Temple they had raised in Jerusalem. Compared to this, what did some sexual peccadilloes matter? The Bible's compilers gladly held up the David–Solomon era as the golden age of ancient Israel, and the tales of these two kings entered Jewish folklore.

The romanticization of David and Solomon introduced an entirely new element into Greater Western culture, or at least one for which no earlier evidence survives—namely, the popular belief in a past paradise, a lost era of former glory, when humanity had attained a perfection of happiness. This is more than mere nostalgia, and it has been a hallmark of Greater Western life ever since. Throughout the centuries societies have attempted to evoke or re-create a golden age—a past from which we have declined and to which we hope to return. Our reformations therefore tend to be *re*formations, efforts to restore past glories rather than to create new ones. It might be the Jews' struggle to reestablish themselves in the Promised Land. It might be American mythmaking about the Founding Fathers or the old West. It might be modern Muslims' longing for the fabled tolerance and high culture of the classical Islamic world. In each case, Greater Western culture has sought to return to a perfection we have lost.

The northern tribes refused to accept Solomon's son Rehoboam as their king and broke away to form a separate realm. Hence from 937 to 721 BCE there were *Conquest* two Hebrew kingdoms—the kingdom of Israel in the north and the kingdom of *of Israel* Judah in the south, still centered on Jerusalem (see again Map 3.1). Judah, al- *and Judah* though smaller, had the advantage of its relatively isolated position in the hills. As a state and, more importantly, as a people, Israel disappeared with its fall to the Assyrians around 721 BCE. These brutal conquerors annihilated tens of thousands and sent the rest off into slavery throughout the Assyrian Empire, where they eventually vanished—the famed ten lost tribes of Israel.

The people of Judah held out until they themselves were overwhelmed by the neo-Babylonians, or Chaldeans, under their ruler Nebuchadnezzar, around 587 BCE. Thus began the **Diaspora** ("exile" or "scattering"). The neo-Babylonians destroyed the Temple at Jerusalem and drove the Judaeans eastward into the **Babylonian Captivity** (ca. 586–539 BCE). Exile and enslavement forced the people to redefine, or at least to reinterpret, their religious identity. Did their defeat by the Chaldeans mean that the Hebrews had lost their status of YHWH's Chosen People? If not, how were they to understand their enslavement—as a punishment for their failings or as a challenge to be overcome? More specifically, how could they observe their laws now that they lived in exile from the Holy Land and the Temple? With the Temple in ruins, was the authority of the priests rendered null and void? And what of the demands of Torah? For example, the Torah instructed that no Hebrew should eat a meal under the roof of a non-Hebrew (to ensure adherence to biblical dietary restrictions)—but as slaves in Babylon they had no option but to live and eat under their masters' roofs. Was the Law therefore temporarily suspended?

Ten Lost Tribes of Israel   The Assyrians invaded the northern Hebrew kingdom of Israel around 732 BCE and completed its conquest of the land by about 721 BCE. Campaigns against towns along the former border with the kingdom of Judah continued for another quarter century. This relief depicts Israelite captives loading provisions onto a cart, in preparation for their long trek into enslavement in the east. An Assyrian soldier stands guard in the center. One entire room in the Assyrian palace at Nineveh was devoted to depicting this particular campaign of the ruler Sennacherib (r. 705–681 BCE) against the Israelite city of Lachish. This relief forms just one small component of the larger pictorial narrative.

Questions like these demanded a new reckoning of the identity, values, and traditions of YHWH's people. The question immediately facing them was: Who had the right to decide, and on what basis? The problem touched every aspect of their culture, from the Torah itself, to the status of traditional priestly leadership, to the mundane details of daily life—and it raised particularly important questions about the status and role of women in Hebrew life.

WOMEN AND THE LAW

Fixing the status of women in ancient Jewish society is no easy task, but not, as with other Near Eastern peoples, because of a dearth of evidence. The Bible devotes hundreds of pages to describing, praising, criticizing, legislating, berating, lamenting, and thanking the women of the Hebrew world. The image that emerges is complex and sometimes self-contradictory, and yet it is clear that the

Hebrews gave their women more social autonomy, legal rights, education, and respect than any other ancient group, with the possible exception of the Persian Zoroastrians—whose treatment of women remains far less understood because of the paucity of sources. (As noted in chapter 2, most of the archives and libraries of the Zoroastrians were destroyed, often intentionally, during the Islamic conquests of the 7th and 8th centuries CE.)

The biblical passages depicting the pre-Mosaic era invariably describe women as having been created to help, if not to serve, men. From Sarai/Sarah on, *Women's* Hebrew women appear overwhelmingly in the roles of dutiful daughters, obedient *Expansion of* wives, and loving mothers. Enough exceptions to the pattern exist, however, to *Proscribed* suggest that many women did carve out different paths for themselves. Moses's *Roles*

own sister, the prophetess Miriam, helped to guide the Hebrews across the Red Sea and led their celebration of thanksgiving once they had reached the other side. Another prophetess, Deborah, actually governed one of the twelve tribes, according to the book of Judges. And a married woman named Huldah was so respected for her knowledge of Hebrew law that King Josiah of Judah (r. 641–609 BCE) entrusted her with validating a newly discovered Torah-scroll fragment found in Jerusalem. Two other women, whether historical or not, were deemed significant enough to deserve entire biblical books devoted to their stories: Esther, a young Jewish girl who becomes queen of Persia and uses her position to forestall a plot to annihilate the Jews within the empire, and Ruth, the main character (and a convert to Judaism) in a charming story about long-suffering love, faithful friendship, and fulfillment.[4]

Story of Ruth   The tale of Ruth, the widowed daughter-in-law of the widowed Naomi, is among the best-loved of biblical stories. Ruth's tender loyalty to Naomi is rewarded, ultimately, when Naomi arranges a new marriage for her. This painting by Julius Huebner (1806–1882) was long believed to have been destroyed in World War II but was rediscovered and restored in 2005.

---

4   To this day, Jews in Iran are referred to colloquially as *Esther's children*.

Rules for
Women

The Torah established the framework for women's roles in Jewish society. As usual, the discrepancies between male and female prerogatives are first to draw one's attention. The Law strictly demands virginity of girls before marriage but lays no comparable burden on boys; women cannot give testimony in civil or criminal cases; a husband can divorce his wife for cause, but not vice versa unless the husband agrees to the split. On the other hand, tradition gave girls the right to a basic education (usually enough to allow them to read the scriptures and guide their own children's early religious education), guaranteed their entitlement to inherit property, allowed them limited economic autonomy, and accorded protection to widows. The bans on women entering the Temple or performing other liturgical rites during menstruation or immediately after giving birth, times when they are labeled "impure" or "unclean" (Hebrew *tumeh*), may seem misogynistic but appear less so when one considers the more numerous conditions that rendered a man *tumeh*—such as touching the carcasses of proscribed animals, experiencing nocturnal emissions, developing a rash or sore on his skin, or even just acquiring a bald patch in his beard. To be *tumeh* did not denote sinfulness or a loss of self-worth; it meant only that one was not ceremonially fit for certain religious rites and needed to undergo a ritual purification or cleansing. Nevertheless, women of all ages were generally regarded as individuals needing higher degrees of protection and guidance.

The fifth commandment given to Moses on Mount Sinai enjoined all Hebrews to honor their mothers and fathers equally, and a later rabbinical judgment declared—rhetorically, not legally—"Death to him who strikes or curses his own mother." But the tenth commandment forbade men from coveting their neighbors' wives, houses, work animals, "or any other thing belonging to your neighbor," a command that would seem to regard wives as possessions rather than people. Within marriage, the Law required husbands to honor, support, and work on behalf of their wives at least to an extent that matched the value of the property a woman brought into the marriage by her dowry. Wives who brought no domestic servants into their marriage were expected to perform six specific household tasks for their husbands: grinding grain, cooking, cleaning, spinning and weaving, bed preparation, and child nursing. A Jewish wife was entitled to relinquish one of these essential labors for every servant provided by her dowry. Wives were exempt from performing fieldwork. The Law expected women as well as men to make annual visits to the Temple in Jerusalem, especially for their most important holy days, and provided special bathing spaces for women to prepare themselves for entering the House of the Lord. Mothers led the prayers that preceded the main daily meal, and in pre-Temple times they participated in performing ritual sacrifices.

One of the biblical books, the Song of Songs (also known as the Song of Solomon), consists of a poetic dialogue between a bride and bridegroom that celebrates married love in all its emotional and physical intimacy. Centuries of religious commentary have interpreted the text as an allegory of the covenant between God and his people, but a simpler reading sees in it a hymn to the joy that married union brings in equal measure to man and wife. The bride speaks first:

> Oh, give me the kisses of your mouth,
> For your love is more delightful than wine.
> Your ointments yield a sweet fragrance,
> Your name is like finest oil—
> Therefore do maidens love you.
> Draw me after you, let us run!
> The king has brought me to his chambers.
> Let us delight and rejoice in your love,
> Savoring it more than wine. (Song of Songs 1.2–4)

To which the bridegroom sings in reply:

> You have captured my heart,
> My own, my bride,
> You have captured my heart
> With one glance of your eyes,
> With one coil of your necklace.
> How sweet is your love,
> My own, my bride!
> How much more delightful your love than wine,
> Your ointments more fragrant
> Than any spice!
> Sweetness drops
> From your lips, O bride;
> Honey and milk
> Are under your tongue;
> And the scent of your robes
> Is like the scent of Lebanon. (4.9–11)

Sexual delight is an intrinsic element of married love, and the Law recognizes a wife's right to full enjoyment of it. But pleasure is not the only reason for marriage. God's first instruction to Adam and Eve—the first man and woman, according to the book of Genesis—was to reproduce: "Be fertile and increase, fill the earth and master it." Every Jewish man was expected to marry as early as possible, which most priests and rabbis interpreted to mean the onset of puberty. The Torah not only declines to praise celibacy, it never even mentions it.[5] A girl could not be forced into marriage before puberty and retained a limited right to refuse a marriage partner proposed by her father after she had reached it. The Law does not demand marriage of all females as it does of males, but rabbinical tradition advises women not to remain single, lest they come under suspicion by their neighbors as sexual adventuresses.

Women in ancient Israel and Judah, on the whole, were better off than most of their contemporaries. They could own and inherit property, received at least a basic education, enjoyed legal rights in marriage, participated actively in the religious life of the community, and received the respect of their peers and the veneration of their families. So long, that is, as they obeyed the Law.

PROPHETS AND PROPHECY

In Jewish tradition, the splitting of the Israelite kingdom and the subsequent disappearance of successor states prompted the arrival of the age of the great prophets, messengers of God. Samuel, last of the Judges, was the first of the great prophets. After him came Elijah and Elisha (both mid- to late 9th century BCE), Amos and Hosea (mid-8th century BCE), Isaiah and Micah (late 8th century BCE), Jeremiah (late 7th to early 6th centuries BCE), and Ezekiel (early 6th century BCE). The minor prophets—so called for the length, not the significance, of their prophetic books—came too. Allowing for differences among them as individuals, the **prophets** as a group shared a calling to warn the Hebrews of the approaching Assyrian and Babylonian dangers and to interpret those dangers as signs of YHWH's growing displeasure. By failing to uphold standards of justice, decency, and observance of the Torah, they cautioned, the people had placed themselves in both mortal and spiritual peril. As Jeremiah put it in his Temple sermon,

> Thus said the LORD of Hosts, the God of Israel: "Mend your ways and your actions, and I will let you dwell in this place. Don't put your trust in illusions and say, 'The Temple of the LORD, the Temple of the LORD, the Temple of the LORD are the [buildings].' No, if you really mend your ways and your actions; if you execute justice between one man and another; if you do not oppress the stranger, the orphan, and the

---

[5] The prophet Jeremiah is the only Jewish figure in the Hebrew Bible known to have been celibate (see Jeremiah 16.2).

widow; if you do not shed the blood of the innocent in this place; if you do not follow other gods, to your own hurt—then only will I let you dwell in this place, in this land that I gave to your fathers for all time." (Jeremiah 7.3–7)

In casting the blame for their misfortunes on themselves, the Hebrews introduced the essential notions of self-criticism and moral responsibility into Western culture. It hardly seems possible to imagine a Sumerian interpreting a calamity like the Hittite invasion as anything other than divine whim or to picture an Egyptian interpreting the Hyksos catastrophe as the consequence of a moral failing on Egypt's part. Earlier societies had senses of morality, but those morals usually existed alongside their religions. The Jews, however, conflated faith and morals to a degree that they could not be separated or distinguished. She'ol was the biblical underworld, and yet the Hebrews did not believe in separate places of reward and punishment in the afterlife. A good life of devotion to YHWH, ethical behavior, and commitment to justice was desirable for its own sake, not as a means to a heavenly end. Ethic and action were necessary components of each other, intrinsic and inextricable.

The Value of Moral Responsibility

This was a revolutionary development in Western life, but one that hardly made the Jews any happier a people. Joy and agony are both present on every page of the Bible, and indeed the scriptures are often at their greatest expressive power when crying out in pain. Among the psalms attributed to David, one that has entered Jewish liturgy as a daily prayer for supplication is the following:

> O LORD, do not punish me in anger,
>> do not chastise me in fury.
>> Have mercy on me, O LORD, for I languish;
>> heal me, O LORD, for my bones shake with terror.
>> My whole being is stricken with terror,
>> while You, LORD—O, how long!
> O LORD, turn! Rescue me!
>> Deliver me as befits Your faithfulness.
>> For there is no praise of You among the dead;
>>> in Sheol, who can acclaim You?
>>> I am weary with groaning;
>>> every night I drench my bed.
>>> I melt my couch in tears.
>> My eyes are wasted by vexation,
>>> worn out because of all my foes.
>>> Away from me, all you evildoers,

> for the LORD heeds the sound of my weeping.
> The LORD heeds my plea,
>   the LORD accepts my prayer.
> All my enemies will be frustrated and stricken with terror;
>   they will turn back in an instant, frustrated. (Psalm 6)

Few ancient texts expressed comparable sentiments. Only the Sumerian "Song of the Righteous Sufferer" (excerpted in chapter 1) comes close to such power.

THE STRUGGLE FOR JEWISH IDENTITY

The loss of Jerusalem, the Temple, and the land of their fathers as well as captivity in Babylon represented crises of the highest order. Had YHWH abandoned the Hebrews, revoking the promises he had made to Abraham and Moses? These concerns had inspired the prophets to call the Hebrews to stricter observance of Torah, to stamp out immoral behavior, and to turn their hearts and minds to YHWH. But how was stricter observance of Torah possible when the Hebrews no longer lived in their own society?

For nearly five hundred years Hebrew religious life had been centered on the home and the Temple. To live an observant life, although ethically challenging, was logistically simple in a homogeneous Hebrew society: the distances involved were, after all, not so great. The daily disciplines of prayer, charity, fair dealing, and hospitality were practiced in the home. The ritual demands of communal worship could be observed by intermittent journeys to the Temple in Jerusalem. The high priests controlled Temple life, performed the rituals, resolved disputes, and represented the community of the Chosen. The king administered the realm, defended the people, and worked to keep the economy afloat.

Now the Hebrews were shorn of centuries of tradition—exiled from their Temple, the ritual prayers, ceremonies, and sacrifices that provided spiritual sustenance and communal identity. They were in captivity and in the minority, facing day-to-day situations that had never occurred in their own kingdom. In these times, established law no longer clearly applied. Might a Hebrew slave indentured to a Persian obey his boss's commands on the Sabbath? Should he risk death by refusing to work? Under what conditions might a Hebrew enter a business partnership with a nonbeliever? Such problems had been addressed to some extent in the past, but usually in the abstract. These questions, and others like them, were now urgent.

Origins of Rabbinical Judaism   Compounding the difficulties, the priestly caste had been largely eradicated or marginalized. To whom, then, could the Hebrews turn for answers? During the nearly fifty years of their Babylonian Captivity, they turned increasingly to their rabbis. The status of **rabbi** had a long lineage going back centuries. Originally an honorific term, the word meant something like "master," in the sense of a person of skill: a man who learned a craft from an expert might call that expert his rabbi, just as a person might honor a special tutor. By the 6th century BCE, however, a rabbi was specifically a teacher of Hebrew Law. Shorn of their Temple lives, the Hebrews in exile turned to the rabbis, who became their de facto leaders. Rabbis continued to teach Torah but also increasingly became religious judges. Their role was to extrapolate from the principles of Torah, so as to redefine an authentic Hebrew life in radically changed circumstances. The incremental growth of a body of rabbinical law—analogous to the tort law of modern societies—came to heavily influence Hebrew life and identity, even to the point where legal scholars started to refer to rabbinical judgments as the expression of an oral Torah that supplemented the written Law. In response, groups of exiled priests began to revise the codified Torah, inserting laws and rituals associated with the P author and re-emphasizing the centrality of priestly worship in Hebrew life.

In 538 BCE the Persian emperor Cyrus the Great released the Hebrews and allowed them to return to Judah. His decision triggered a predictable conflict. Should *Return* the new generations of Hebrews—now known as Jews from the name of their *to Judah* homeland—who had never known Temple worship or the authority of the priests relinquish rabbinical teaching and leadership? Was rabbinical Judaism merely a temporary measure in an emergency, or was it a new and authentic way of being a Jew? Moreover, who would decide—the priests? The rabbis? The people themselves?

Ezra and Nehemiah, the two most prominent prophets of the mid-5th century BCE and ardent champions of Temple worship, leapt into the debate and railed against Jews who had married outside the faith and those who undeservingly claimed the traditional self-identification of "children of Israel" and "children of Abraham." Ezra condemned all mixed marriages and declared them formally dissolved. (The Jews who accepted Ezra's judgments simply dismissed their wives and renounced any children they might have produced.) In Jewish tradition Ezra is a figure of immense stature, a second Moses in his authority, for his dual role of rebuilding the Temple and purifying the community, thus giving his people a religious rebirth.

The prophets Haggai and Zechariah, who appeared next, likewise urged the rebuilding of the Temple and the reestablishment of priestly authority. Did the construction of a Second Temple on the ruins of the First mean the restoration of the old order, or could rabbinical tradition somehow embrace and even subsume the traditions of the past? This debate motivated much of the compiling, editing, and rewriting of the Bible described earlier in this chapter. The territory of Judah would continue under Persia's political control for another two hundred years, but the social and cultural situation remained in flux.

Factions of Jews debated not only the proper ways of worshipping YHWH and adhering to his laws but also even the fundamental issue of who exactly was a Jew. The neo-Babylonians had not forcibly relocated every single Jew to the east. They had carted off primarily the elite members of Hebrew society, along with professionals and artisans, in an effort to decapitate Jewish society and render it more pliant. The numbers involved were small. The population of Judah before the Exile had been perhaps as low as thirty thousand, one-quarter of whom were sent into captivity. Certainly that was enough to end Judean life as it had existed. The economy of the fifty-year Persian era declined to mere subsistence level; effective government ended and was replaced by Persian overseers whose chief interest was the collection of tribute. The biblical book of Lamentations vividly depicts the despair felt by the people who interpreted Judah's fall as a sign of God's rejection of them:

> The Lord has laid waste without pity
> All the habitations of Jacob;
> He has razed in His anger
> Fair Judah's strongholds.
> He has brought low in dishonor
> The kingdom and its leaders.
> In blazing anger He has cut down
> All the might of Israel;
> He has withdrawn His right hand
> In the presence of the foe;
> He has ravaged Jacob like flaming fire,
> Consuming on all sides. (Lamentations 2.2–3)

Adding to the biblical portrayal of misery, many Hebrews decided to abandon the YHWH cult altogether and assimilated into the culture and religion of their captors. Jeremiah, who was among the Hebrews deported to Egypt, prophesied YHWH's further wrath upon the apostates who gave themselves over to foreign gods:

> And now, thus said the LORD, the God of hosts, the God of Israel: "Why are you doing such great harm to yourselves, so that every man and woman, child and infant of yours shall be cut off from the midst of Judah, and no remnant shall be left of you? For you vex me by your deeds, making offerings to other gods in the land of Egypt where you have come to sojourn, so that you shall be cut off and become a curse and a mockery among all the nations of earth. . . . I am going to set my face against you for punishment, to cut off all of Judah. I will take the remnant of Judah

who turned their faces toward the land of Egypt, to go and sojourn there, and they shall be utterly consumed in the land of Egypt. They shall fall by the sword, they shall be consumed by famine; great and small alike shall die by the sword and by famine, and they shall become an execration and a desolation, a curse and a mockery. I will punish those who live in the land of Egypt as I punished Jerusalem, with the sword, with famine, and with pestilence. Of the remnant of Judah who came to sojourn here in the land of Egypt, no survivor or fugitive shall be left to return to the land of Judah. Though they all long to return and dwell there, none shall return except [a few] survivors." (Jeremiah 44.7–8, 11–14)

Few of the Jews who had remained behind in Judah welcomed the idea of reinstalling the old hierarchy, so relations between the population and the returnees remained tense. The elites, widely suspected of collusion with the Persian over-lords, made matters worse by referring to themselves as the "children of the Exile" while dismissing the rest of the population as the "people of the land." Intention-ally or not, the Temple faction, with Ezra and Nehemiah its leaders, implied that they alone were the true bearers of Jewish tradition. Economic factors played a role in this conflict too. Many of the returnees had put up their old properties as collateral for loans: they needed cash to recapitalize their business concerns. When some of those concerns failed, their property was often seized.

With so much at stake, it hardly comes as a surprise that a great amount of recording, revising, expanding, editing, and reinterpreting of the scriptures took place in this era. The Jews of the 6th and 5th centuries BCE were in a crucible of intense political and economic heat that compounded and aggravated the painful struggle to define Jewish identity. YHWH was proving to be a harsh taskmaster, and his people were learning that to be chosen was not necessarily to win.

SECOND TEMPLE JUDAISM

Inspired by their prophets, the Jews rebuilt their Temple in about twenty years; the new building was dedicated around 515 BCE. Tested by exile and enslave-ment, and purified by their prophets, the Jews were determined to reestablish their authority over the Holy Land that had been promised them by YHWH and to maintain themselves as a people set apart. An inscription from the new Temple (a fragment now on display in the Istanbul Archeological Museum) reads, "Let no foreigner pass beyond the balustrade that surrounds the sanctuary and its court-yard. Any [foreigner] who is caught doing so shall have only himself to blame for [his] death that will surely follow." Conflicts over Jewish identity persisted for centuries, however. The traces of these conflicts are evident in the numerous

The "Wailing Wall"   The Western Wall in Jerusalem is the holiest of Jewish sites, sacred because it is a remnant of the retaining wall that once enclosed and supported the Second Temple. European observers named it the "Wailing Wall" because for centuries Jews have gathered here to lament the loss of their Temple.

efforts to expand, rewrite, and edit the canon of holy books that had sustained the people through the centuries.

The Jews entered the fourth century BCE engaged in intense debate about their communal identity. The two principal factions—the "children of the Exile" and the "people of the land"—soon divided into a multiplicity of sects, distinguished by doctrinal divisions, tribal and political loyalties, class distinctions, and linguistic identities. Opposing notions of political overlordship played a role, too. The Hellenistic kingdoms of Ptolemaic Egypt and Seleucid Asia (discussed in chapter 5) both claimed jurisdiction over Judea until 198 BCE, forcing the multiple Jewish factions to perform a careful balancing act between the two foreign powers.[6] Judea held no interest for either power, so long as the Jews paid the taxes levied upon them. Yet the rival imperial claims on the land led to the development of large Jewish communities within both Egypt and Anatolia.

In Alexandria alone, as many as fifty thousand Jews resided. These Jews retained their religious identity but became so assimilated into Hellenistic culture that by around 260 BCE they needed to have the Bible translated into Greek, since they no longer understood Hebrew sufficiently. According to a text known as the *Letter of Aristeas*, a group of seventy-two biblical scholars gathered in Alexandria and carried out the task, thus producing the version of scripture called the Septuagint (that being the Latin word for "seventy"). The *Letter of Aristeas* further reports, delightfully, that the seventy-two translators miraculously spoke as

---

[6]   The parade of similar-sounding (and imprecise) place-names can be confusing. The *Holy Land* or the *Land of Israel* consists of the territory believed by the ancient Hebrews to have been given them by YHWH. The specific borders of this territory, however, are unclear since the various biblical passages that describe them are inconsistent. The term *Kingdom of Israel* denotes both the kingdom established under King David and passed on to his son King Solomon, and the smaller northern splinter kingdom that resulted from the splitting of the Davidic–Solomonic realm into two states. The southern state that resulted from the split is the *Kingdom of Judah*, and *Judah* (minus the *Kingdom of* portion) is likewise the name given to the restored realm after the Hebrews' return from Babylonian enslavement. *Judea*, by contrast, is the name used by the Greeks for the kingdom of Judah after it had been made into a province of Alexander the Great's empire. When the Roman Empire supplanted the Greeks, they retained the name *Judea* for the now-Roman province. In the ancient world the word *Palestine* was a geographical term only; it denoted an area, but not a specific state or institutional province.

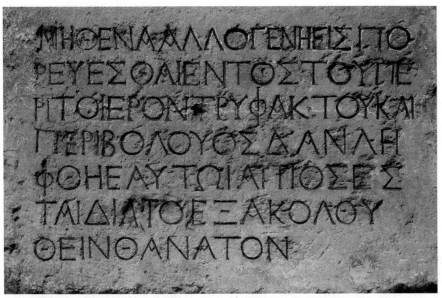

Inscription from the Ruins of the Second Temple   Written in Greek, the inscription (preserved here in a plastic cast) stood outside the outermost wall of the Temple grounds. It states that only Jews may enter the Temple precinct itself. Non-Jews found within the walls potentially faced the penalty of death.

one throughout the entire project, agreeing on each and every word of the translation. Aristeas was a Greek-speaking Jewish historian who lived roughly one hundred years after the Septuagint was completed.

Jewish Hellenization involved more than adoption of the Greek language. A partial religious **syncretism**, or union of doctrines, occurred as well, as Judaism made contact with and adopted certain characteristics of the dominant Zoroastrian faith. This is most apparent in the development of an apocalyptic tradition (with its tenets regarding the approach of a messiah) within mainstream Judaism and among some lesser strands such as the Gnostic sects. YHWH's justice shall come upon earth, scatter and destroy His enemies, and reward faithful Israel:

Influence of Zoroastrianism

> Behold the LORD Himself
> Comes from afar
> In blazing wrath,
> With a heavy burden—
> His lips full of fury,
> His tongue like devouring fire,
> And His breath like a raging torrent
> Reaching halfway up the neck—
> To set a misguiding yoke upon nations

And make a misleading bridle upon the jaws of peoples,
For you, there shall be singing
As on a night when a festival is hallowed;
There shall be rejoicing as when they march
With flute, with timbrels, and with lyres
To the Rock of Israel on the Mount of the LORD.
For the LORD will make His majestic voice heard
And display the sweep of His arm
In raging wrath,
In a devouring blaze of fire,
In tempest, and rainstorm, and hailstones. (Isaiah 30.27–30)

Some of the intense moralism of Zoroastrianism can be detected in a passage like this, showing the two faiths as complementary. Persian generosity had allowed the Jews to return to the homeland, and Persian money had even financed the start of the construction of the new Temple. If the Persians' faith had injected a note of moral earnestness in Judaism, the Jews' faith had inspired a concern for justice for all peoples in Zoroastrianism. After such cross-fertilization, and having endured so many travails, the Jews of the Second Temple era had learned an important lesson: to expect more trouble.

◆

Judaism's genius for reinvention helped it to survive tumultuous changes in its social and political fortunes. Whatever their earliest origins, the Hebrews had entered Palestine with a developing understanding of their uniqueness. Rare monotheists in an overwhelmingly polytheistic world, they sustained a faith in their responsibility to God and in their exclusive rights to a particular homeland. Its dissolution and loss were only the first of many catastrophes that prompted them to reengage with their tradition, to reinterpret their past and present lives, and to chart new paths for their future.

WHO, WHAT, WHERE

Ark of the Covenant	Documentary	rabbi
Babylonian	Hypothesis	Solomon
Captivity	Israel	syncretism
covenant	Judah	Tanakh
David	judges	Torah
Diaspora	prophets	YHWH

SUGGESTED READINGS

Primary Sources

Berlin, Adele, and Marc Zvi Brettler, eds. *The Jewish Study Bible: Jewish Publication Society Tanakh Translation* (2004).

Friedman, Richard Elliott. *The Bible with Sources Revealed: A New View into the Five Books of Moses* (2005).

Anthologies

Arnold, Bill T., and Bryan E. Beyer, eds. *Readings from the Ancient Near East: Primary Sources for Old Testament Study* (2002).

Hallo, William W., ed. *The Context of Scripture* (2002).

Studies

Bartor, Assnat. *Reading Law as Narrative: A Study in the Casuistic Laws of the Pentateuch* (2010).

Esler, Philip F. *Ancient Israel: The Old Testament in Its Social Context* (2006).

Finkelstein, Israel, and Neil Asher Silberman. *The Bible Unearthed: Archaeology's New Vision of Ancient Israel and the Origin of Its Sacred Texts* (2002).

Finkelstein, Israel, and Neil Asher Silberman. *David and Solomon: In Search of the Bible's Sacred Kings and the Roots of the Western Tradition* (2007).

Flusser, David. *Judaism of the Second Temple Period.* Vol. 1, *Qumran and Apocalypticism* (2007).

Flusser, David. *Judaism of the Second Temple Period.* Vol. 2, *The Jewish Sages and Their Literature* (2009).

Golden, Jonathan M. *Ancient Canaan and Israel: An Introduction* (2004).

Halpern, Baruch. *The First Historians: The Hebrew Bible and History* (2003).

Hays, J. Daniel, and Tremper Longman. *The Message of the Prophets: A Survey of the Prophetic and Apocalyptic Books of the Old Testament* (2010).

Hendel, Ronald. *Remembering Abraham: Culture, Memory, and History in the Hebrew Bible* (2005).

King, Philip J., and Lawrence E. Stager. *Life in Biblical Israel* (2002).

Liverani, Mario. *Israel's History and the History of Israel* (2007).

Pardes, Ilana. *The Biography of Ancient Israel: National Narratives in the Bible* (2002).

Person, Raymond F., Jr. *The Deuteronomic History and the Book of Chronicles: Scribal Works in an Oral World* (2010).

Schiffman, Lawrence H. *Qumran and Jerusalem: Studies in the Dead Sea Scrolls and the History of Judaism* (2010).

Schiffman, Lawrence H. *Understanding Second Temple and Rabbinic Judaism* (2003).

Smith, Mark S. *The Memoirs of God: History, Memory, and the Experience of the Divine in Ancient Israel* (2004).

Stavrakopoulou, Francesca, and John Barton. *Religious Diversity in Ancient Israel and Judah* (2010).

Van der Toorn, Karel. *Scribal Culture and the Making of the Hebrew Bible* (2009).

Vaughn, Andrew G., and Ann E. Killebrew. *Jerusalem in Bible and Archeology: The First Temple Period* (2003).

Weinfeld, Moshe. *Normative and Sectarian Judaism in the Second Temple Period* (2010).

Weinfeld, Moshe. *The Place of the Law in the Religion of Ancient Israel* (2004).

For additional resources, including maps, primary sources, visuals, web links, and quizzes, please go to **www.oup.com/us/backman.**

CHAPTER 4

Greeks and Persians

2000–479 BCE

Origin myths are rarely pretty. According to the ancient Greeks, the cosmos began with primordial Chaos, out of which emerged the elemental forces of Gaia (Earth), Eros (Love), Tartarus (Abyss), and Erebus (Darkness). Earth brought forth

GREECE AND PERSIA

Uranus (Sky)—which is when the trouble began. Uranus took his own mother, Gaia, as his wife, and they produced the twelve Titans.

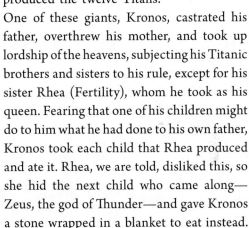

Koure Starting in the Archaic Age, Greek sculptors popularized the use of figures called *kouros* ("youth") and *koure* ("maiden"). The purpose of the statues is still debated, though the frequent discovery of them in temples dedicated to Apollo suggest worship of the Greek sun god. Male kouroi are usually nude, beardless, and standing erect in a posture reminiscent of Egyptian statuary. This statue of a *koure* dates from about 550 BCE and was used to mark the grave of the woman who modeled for it. The artist's inscription at the base gives her name, Phrasikleia. It reads: "The grave marker of Phrasikleia. I shall be called a maiden *[koure]* forever, since the gods allotted me this identity instead of a marriage. Aristion of Paros carved me."

One of these giants, Kronos, castrated his father, overthrew his mother, and took up lordship of the heavens, subjecting his Titanic brothers and sisters to his rule, except for his sister Rhea (Fertility), whom he took as his queen. Fearing that one of his children might do to him what he had done to his own father, Kronos took each child that Rhea produced and ate it. Rhea, we are told, disliked this, so she hid the next child who came along— Zeus, the god of Thunder—and gave Kronos a stone wrapped in a blanket to eat instead. When Zeus grew to manhood, he drugged his father with a potion that made him vomit all the children he had eaten. Zeus then rallied his revived siblings to join him in killing Kronos and seizing control of heaven.

All this is just the beginning of the story. Greek mythology consists of hundreds of tales regarding the great Olympian deities (Zeus and his siblings, who lived on the mythical Mount Olympus), demigods, and heroes, whose adventures display astonishing creative power and vitality. Themes of incest, patricide, and rebellion occur with unnerving frequency. Like some of their Near Eastern peers, Greek gods and goddesses can be petulant, vain, and full of self-importance, but they also embody virtues of honor, justice, and love. They do not always act admirably, but they do not act without reason. If anything, the myths portray life as an intricate web of passionate feeling and reaction. Each myth leads into and influences the next. A spurned wife here emerges as a wrathful lover there. A proud king in one story becomes the humbled fallen in another. Greek mythology presents a universe of emotion, ambition, and a search for justice—but it also portrays, often with horrifying effect, the unexpected consequences of every action. Life began with Chaos, as the Greeks saw it, and it usually ends in tragedy.

THE FIRST GREEKS

Ancestors of the Greeks had moved into the mainland region of Greece by perhaps 8000 BCE, but the first culture definitely identified as Greek (because of its Indo-European language) arose only around 1600 BCE. We know these people as

CHAPTER TIMELINE

2000 BCE	1800 BCE	1600 BCE	1400 BCE	1200 BCE

▪ ca. 2000–1500 BCE Height of Minoan culture on Crete

▪ ca. 1600–1200 BCE Mycenaean Age in Greece; use of Linear B script

▪ ca. 1500 BCE Mycenaeans destroy and/or take over most cities in Crete

▪ ca. 1200–750 BCE
Greece experiences
Dark Age

the Mycenaeans, a name derived from the hilltop site of Mycenae. Although the Mycenaean settlers may have been of diverse origins, they quickly developed a sense of cultural unity and began to refer to themselves by another name—as a single people, the Hellenes (Greeks). They inhabited a larger territory than the Greek mainland itself. In ancient times, the term for Greece meant the rough circle of land consisting of the Greek peninsula to the west, the coasts of Macedonia and Thrace to the north, coastal Anatolia to the east, and the island of Crete to the south, plus the scores of smaller islands throughout the Aegean Sea (see Map 4.1). The climate is magnificent, with year-round sun and modest rainfall, but the land itself is harsh. Greece proper has a wild, jagged coastline with few harbors broad and deep enough for mooring large vessels. Inland the countryside is mountainous and irregular: less than 20 percent of the land is arable. The land was covered with forests in the Neolithic Age, but by the time the Mycenaeans arrived most of the trees had long since disappeared. Complicating matters, mineral ores were scarce, rivers even scarcer, and the waters of the Aegean Sea not particularly well stocked with fish.

What made the Aegean rim so attractive was the sea: sailing through the calm waters was easy at any time of the year. Distances were short, and the sheer abundance of islands meant that one never risked getting lost. (Ancient mariners navigated more by landmarks than by the stars.) Hundreds of coastal communities could thus be in constant contact with one another. The Hellenes may have settled in a vast sprawl of isolated sites, but by devoting themselves to trade they

1000 BCE	800 BCE	600 BCE	400 BCE	200 BCE

- ca. 776 BCE First Olympic Games held
- ca. 750 BCE Greeks begin to create the polis; Homeric epics transcribed
- 750–500 BCE Archaic Age in Greece
- ca. 630 BCE Lyric poet Sappho is born
- ca. 594 BCE Solon's reforms promote early democracy in Athens
- ca. 546 BCE Pisistratos becomes Athens's first tyrant
- ca. 508 BCE Cleisthenes's reforms extend democracy in Athens
- 499–494 BCE Ionian cities revolt against Persian Empire
- 494–479 BCE Persian Wars

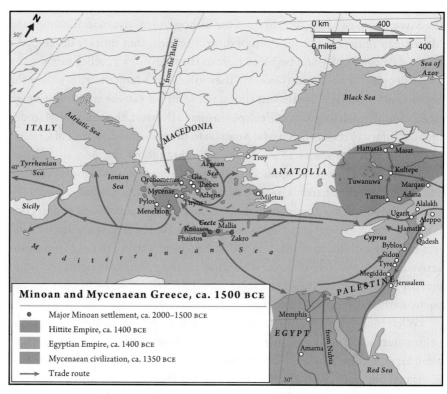

MAP 4.1   Minoan and Mycenean Greece, ca. 1500 BCE   With a dearth of natural resources to support manufacturing, and with only one-tenth of its land suitable for agriculture, Greece became a distributive economy. Its position in the eastern Mediterranean (especially with its links to Crete) gave it an advantage in transporting goods throughout the eastern sea basin.

could prosper. Although they were generally able to feed and clothe themselves, the ancient Greeks never developed much of a manufacturing base; they shipped goods from one site to another rather than producing goods of their own. Transport, not industry, made their fortunes. Their high degree of contact with other cultures meant more than an active economy; it also exposed them to ideas, technologies, value systems, political institutions, artistic styles, and religious practices. The result was an exhilarating cultural adaptivity—a willingness to criticize old ideas and to experiment with new ones.

Minoan Culture

The first signs of Aegean prosperity and creative energy emerged in Crete. In 1899 a British archeologist, Sir Arthur Evans (1851–1941), unearthed a magnificent palace complex at Knossos—with three stories and nearly thirteen hundred rooms. Evans mistakenly identified it as the palace of the Greeks' legendary king Minos and gave the name Minoan to a culture that had its heyday from 2000 to 1500 BCE (see Map 4.1). Subsequent excavations have found numerous other palaces, although none quite so splendid. Vibrant decoration—murals, statuary,

Palace at Knossos   The palace complex on Crete was brightly colored, with scenes of real and imaginary creatures, people, flowers, rocks, and geometric patterns. Shown here is a school of dolphins (common to the Mediterranean) decorating a wall of what scholars surmise to be the queen's private room.

frescos, tiling, pottery, textiles, and metalwork—characterized them all, which suggests that Minoan wealth was widely spread. Moreover, none of the palaces had fortifications of any kind, which likely means that naval defenses were sufficient to keep marauders away. Homes of town dwellers have been found, too—more modest, but still more attractive and comfortable than common urban homes in Middle Kingdom Egypt or Hittite Anatolia. Minoan ships carried tons of Egyptian wheat, Greek olive oil and wine, Palestinian metalwork, Anatolian textiles, and Babylonian spices.

Like the other great commercial cultures of ancient times, the Minoans invented a system of writing to keep records of their activities. Two distinct scripts have survived, which are known as **Linear A** (in use by 1800 BCE) and **Linear B** (which appeared about three hundred years later, after the island was overrun by the Mycenaean Greeks). Linear A remains a mystery, although most scholars agree that the language it records is not Indo-European. Linear B, however, records an early form of Greek. Apparently the trader culture on Crete predated the arrival of the Mycenaeans, and the success of that earlier culture may have been what attracted them into the Aegean in the first place. Numerous legends, after all, describe the ancient Greeks' enduring fascination with Minoan life and magnificence. The stories about the Greek hero Theseus are among the best known. Theseus, a prince from the city of Athens, traveled to Crete to pay tribute to King

The Phaistos Disk   This disk was found in 1908
by archeologists working at the Minoan palace of
Phaistos on the island of Crete. Nearly six inches
in diameter, it has a spiral of various symbols
stamped into the clay on each side. All efforts to
decipher the code have failed, leading some
historians to suggest that the disk is a hoax.
Others argue that it is a calendar, an astronomical
chart, or even a game board.

Minos, who sent the hero into his famed Labyrinth, built to hold the monstrous Minotaur
(a freakish beast created when Minos's lecherous wife mated with a bull). Theseus, keen to
prove his heroism, finds the Minotaur, slays it,
and retraces his path out of the maze and into
the arms of Minos's daughter. Legend also has it
that the god Zeus, seeking to evade his cannibal-
istic father, went to Crete and hid inside another
labyrinth until he was ready to rebel against
Kronos.

Minoan Crete taught the Mycenaeans sea-
faring, commerce, writing, and the rudiments of
government. In short, the Minoans deeply influenced ancient Greek culture. By 1400 BCE, however, disaster struck Crete. Whether it was an
invasion or a natural calamity like an earthquake,
the island was devastated, and the Minoans' vibrant culture and economy—now
in the hands of the Hellenes—began to fade.

The Mycenaean Age

The Hellenes living on the Greek mainland then began to dominate the
Aegean. The years from roughly 1600 to 1200 BCE are known as the Mycenaean
Age, after the city of Mycenae, which according to tradition was ruled by the legendary king Agamemnon. Like their mythical king, the Mycenaeans were haughty
and militaristic.[1] What kept them from becoming a powerful empire was their internal division. The Greek mainland consists of hundreds of highland valleys and
plains separated by irregular mountains and deep gorges; by controlling a handful
of mountain passes, a tribal leader could effectively seal off an entire plateau area
and create an autonomous, if isolated, miniature kingdom for himself. Once in control, these leaders governed through a tightly centralized royal court made up of
military officers and bureaucrats, who lived and worked in enormous citadel-pal-
aces constructed from large stone blocks. Common peasants, nominally free but
little better off because of it, and slave teams worked the land and tended the herds.

---

[1]   Archeological records are fairly abundant for parts of Mycenaean history. A wealthy (and somewhat shady)
businessman and amateur archeologist from Germany named Heinrich Schliemann (1822–1890) dedicated three decades to the search for the palace of King Agamemnon and the ancient city of Troy. His methods were not exactly state-of-the-art (he liked to use dynamite), but he did unearth the cities of Mycenae in
Greece and Troy in Anatolia. He built himself a mansion in Athens, where he kept much of his stolen booty;
the building is today a museum. So great was his passion for the Mycenaeans that he named his son and
daughter (by his second wife) Agamemnon and Andromache, and he "baptized" them by placing a copy of
Homer's *Iliad* on each child's head while reciting from memory one hundred lines from the text. Agamemnon
Schliemann (1878–1954) in adulthood became the Greek ambassador to the United States.

Peasant women wove fabric, minded children, and prepared food. Handfuls of artisans engaged in leatherwork, winemaking, and metalsmithing.

Virtually all of the surviving Linear B tablets consist of supply lists for the kings' armies. They detail grain rations, wine allowances, clothing, and armor allotments. Larger kingdoms engaged in mass manufacture. The palace at Pylos, for example, maintained more than four hundred bronzesmiths on site. Since this number of smiths would produce vastly more armor and weapons than their king needed, it seems clear that Mycenaean Pylos specialized as an arms manufacturer.

The intense competition for raw materials, markets, and control of trade routes kept the Mycenaeans in more or less constant conflict with one another—which, in turn, validated their militarism. A king kept his position of dominance by acquiring the things his people needed, which he did by trade when possible but by force when necessary. Royal tombs, shaped like inverted beehives, dotted the landscape, and they and the royal palaces were veritable display-houses of weaponry and armor, all surrounded by wall drawings of war scenes and the slaughtering of captives.

Little is known of Mycenaean religion. Various texts mention the names of several gods—most notably Zeus, Poseidon (the god of the sea), and Demeter (the goddess of grain). Since the Mycenaeans built no temples, which might have left some record of their activities, however, we know nothing about communal religious life, or indeed whether any existed at all. Homes had individual shrines within them, either for the worship of ancestors or for petitioning the few gods whose names have survived. Yet no prayers or inscriptions survive to describe the content of their faith. The beehive tombs and their militaristic contents tell us more about Mycenaean life than any afterlife they might have believed in.

The "Lion Gate"   This gate formed the main entrance to the citadel at Mycenae and is the only surviving piece of monumental architecture from the Mycenaean age. The lionesses carved at the top symbolize the power of the Mycenaean kings and may also represent the goddess Hera. The gate was constructed in the 13th century BCE.

THE SEARCH FOR MYTHIC ANCESTORS IN ARCHAIC AGE GREECE

The later Greeks insisted on claiming the Mycenaeans as their ancestors, ascribing to them the epic adventures of their mythical heroes. When the poet or poets known as **Homer** composed the *Iliad* and the *Odyssey*, sometime around 750 BCE, he chose a subject set in Mycenaean times—the events of the Trojan War. In reality, the war, named for Troy, an important trading city in northwestern Asia Minor, was one of many struggles by the newcomer Greeks to seize part of the Aegean rim, but in Homer's reimagining, the tale becomes one of Greek honor and military destiny. Paris, son of King Priam of Troy, has been appointed the judge of a beauty contest among three goddesses. Each goddess bribes Paris, who ultimately selects the goddess (Aphrodite) who offers him the most beautiful mortal woman on earth. That woman is Helen, wife of King Menelaus of Sparta (also brother of Agamemnon), who is promptly delivered to Troy as Paris's prize. The war then begins when all the Mycenaean kings join forces to avenge the injury done to Menelaus's honor. Homer assuredly based his epic on ancient oral traditions, but the *Iliad* can hardly be taken to represent Mycenaean culture accurately. If anything, it describes aspects of the era known as Greece's "Dark Age" (ca. 1200–750 BCE), which separated Homer's world from Agamemnon's. But telling tales of Mycenaean heroes, powerful rulers, and their origins in a murky distant era of violently contending gods gave the Greeks a sense of rootedness. It tied them to their new Aegean home and helped them to make sense out of the chaos of their lives.

The Aegean Dark Age

The Mycenaean age ended abruptly with the invasion, around 1200 BCE, of one or more of the unidentified Indo-European groups who caused so much damage in Egypt and the Levant, as we saw in chapter 2. The newcomers spoke a dialect of early Greek and may well have been present already in the Aegean rim for some time. The Mycenaeans had thrown up a considerable number of new fortifications (and reinforced existing ones) around 1250 BCE, which suggests they saw trouble coming. But the invaders, by themselves, could hardly have brought about the decline of the Mycenaeans and the start of Greece's Dark Age, because the calamity that hit the ancient Mediterranean and Near East proved so monumental that it must have resulted from other factors as well—whether plague, famine, civil strife, emigration, or a combination of them all.

A single, astonishing fact drives the point home: between 1200 and 800 BCE Greece lost 90 percent of its population. The agrarian peasants in Greece were the least well-off farmers of the ancient Mediterranean and Near East, given the harshness of their land, and were therefore least able to survive the catastrophe. The town dwellers of the Aegean cities were in a better position, but once the demographic hemorrhage interrupted the trade cycle, there was little they could do to compensate. Hence everyone presumably fled or was cut down by war, famine, or disease before they could flee. By the time the Dark Age ended, around 750 BCE, the Greeks had not only declined dramatically in numbers but also shifted tenancy. A majority of those who survived had moved from the inland plateaus to the coastal towns, where they attempted to take up new trades. The days of isolated rural kingdoms were over.

And that is precisely what Homer mourns in the *Iliad* and *Odyssey*. These epic poems, like all great art, work on many levels; on the political level, they are conservative, romanticized nostalgia, another instance of lament for a lost, idealized past. The *Iliad*'s heroes are all kings, and the conflicts dramatized by the poem center on the issue of the honor due to them. In an early scene in the *Iliad*, as the Greeks take the field to prepare for yet another battle, Priam leads Helen to the ramparts that surround Troy so that she can identify the Greek leaders for him:

Homer and the Heroic Tradition

> "Come, Helen," said Priam, "and tell me who is that great and powerful
> man over there? Others are taller than he, but never have I seen a warrior
> more finely formed, more noble in bearing; surely he is a king."
> Beautiful Helen replied, . . . "That is Agamemnon, the son of Atreus,
>   the lord
> of the Argos plain, a noble ruler and dread warrior." . . .
> Then old Priam looked out again, and this time he beheld Odysseus,
>   and asked,
> "And who is that one? He is a head shorter than Atreus's son, but has
> broader shoulders and a more powerful chest. He has laid his armor and
> weapons on the ground, and strides commandingly up and down
>   the ranks
> like a burly ram keeping a flock of silver-fleeced sheep in line."
> And Helen, the heavenly beauty, answered him, "That is Odysseus,
>   the son
> of Laertes, the skillful mastermind, Ithaca-born (that raw, stony island!),
> who knows every trick and stratagem of war." (*Iliad* 3.150–220)

Thus Homer lauds the heroic age of landed kings.

The *Odyssey* treats the same theme. With the end of the Trojan War, wily Odysseus, the king of Ithaca, spends ten years struggling to get home to his devoted wife, Penelope, and his loving son, Telemachus.[2] In the meantime, his royal palace has been taken over by Penelope's suitors—young upstarts from the town who try to persuade the queen that Odysseus is dead and to choose one of them as a new husband. Hence we have the noble king's adventure, in which he proves his

---

2 Odysseus battles giant beasts, survives shipwrecks, is seduced by a goddess, visits the underworld, taunts the sea god Poseidon, encounters witches, and outwits one foe after another.

The Trojan Horse   This is one of the earliest representations (ca. 670 BCE) of the stratagem that supposedly ended the Trojan War. Greek soldiers hid inside the wooden sculpture that was offered as a parting gift to the victorious Trojans and emerged from it at night and opened the city gates to the entire Greek army. The story does not appear in the *Iliad* but is mentioned in the *Odyssey*. In this image, taken from an amphora (a large storage vessel for wine, oil, or water) found at Mykonos, the Greeks are shown as though peering through windows.

superiority to every challenge, and a society, Ithaca, paralyzed with self-doubt. The suitors represent the "new" society of Homer's own time—brash, pushy, and self-interested. The Ithacans ask, "When, oh when, will our king come back? Oh, if only our king were here, we would then see justice and right order restored!"

Rise of the Polis

The Dark Age obviously had its share of calamities. Still, once the demographic collapse had occurred and the migration of the survivors to the coasts had taken place, Greece was not a place of unrelenting misery. The decreased population meant that the amount of food needed to maintain it also declined, to the point where the mainland was able to feed itself unaided by imports from the Near East. Since the foodstuffs produced in Greece—grain, oil, wine, and meat—were difficult to preserve in the bright heat, the rulers of Homer's time tended to distribute surpluses among the people, thus ensuring at least an absence of famine. The upland villages and coastal towns were small enough to be self-governing, which inspired a sense of independence among the people. Identifying themselves as the sustainers of their own communal lives, they gradually coined a new word—**polis** (plural poleis)—for their communities. The polis, or Greek city-state, referred to the physical town and its agrarian hinterland, the people who resided in them, and the group identity they shared. To belong to a polis meant more than to reside in a particular locale. It meant being a constituent element of something larger than oneself, participating in a web of mutual obligations, responsibilities, and rights.

COLONISTS, HOPLITES, AND THE PATH TOWARD CITIZENSHIP

As the Homeric era gave way to the Archaic period (ca. 750–500 BCE), the poleis of Greece began to extend their reach by following the example of the Phoenicians and establishing networks of colonies. These networks extended around the Aegean rim, then into the Black Sea, and ultimately westward into the Mediterranean. With the expanded reach of the poleis came other changes as well— including a society built for war.

The colonies were not military expansions, however. The Greeks generally searched out uninhabited harbors, established small coastal settlements around them, and then *Greek* opened trade relations with inland populations. Inheritance practices lay behind this *Colonization* growth. Greek custom dictated that a man's estate be divided by his legitimate heirs— an easy enough matter when it came to cash, flocks and herds, and portable property. But what about a man's farmland? A farm might be large enough to survive subdivision among a man's sons, but what happened to those subdivisions when the next generation came along? At a certain point (and usually an early one), the portions of land received by individual heirs could not support a family. This forced many heirs to sell their land, usually to a sibling but in theory to anyone with available funds. With the money, they would then relocate to a colony and set up anew.

The colonists, in other words, were neither military adventurers nor impoverished exiles but landholders—specifically, landholders who had cashed out their equity and were looking for new investments. Groups of these entrepreneurs would set out together from a polis in search of new settlement. Personal connections and a sense of shared identity also caused them to establish commercial ties with the polis from which they had come. In this way, the Greek colonies established were not just dependencies of the home city-state, to be exploited for domestic gain. Rather, they took on the character of smaller reproductions of the home city. They were independent and self-governing, yet united in identity with the original polis.

Between 750 and 500 BCE, the Greeks established hundreds of colonies around the Mediterranean and Near East (see Map 4.2). A handful of colonies appeared along the North African coast as well.[3] This explosive growth coincided

---

[3]   There were two types of colonies: *apoidikiai* and *empora;* the first were self-governing, and the second were governed from the mainland as trading outposts.

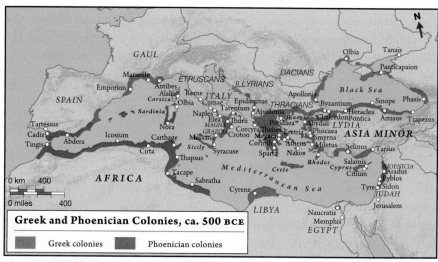

MAP 4.2   Greek and Phoenician Colonies, ca. 500 BCE   Between them, the Greeks and Phoenicians established colonies around the perimeters of both the Mediterranean and the Black seas.

almost exactly with the collapse of Israel under the Assyrians (ca. 722 BCE) and the conquest of Judah by the neo-Babylonians (ca. 587 BCE). And for a reason: the turmoil in the Holy Land interrupted the commercial activity of the Phoenicians, who had previously been the main actors on the sea-lanes. The Greeks thus had few competitors for control of the sea-lanes, and certainly none with the geographical advantages they had. Because of the opportunities abroad, most Greek cities maintained fairly stable population levels in the Archaic period, and many colonies outstripped their home cities in size.

The colonists actively sought out contact with their neighboring or host populations, but were careful not to assimilate. Ethnic pride forbade that—because the Greeks, like many ancient cultures, regarded themselves as superior to other peoples, whom they called "barbarians," peoples whose speech, to Greek ears, sounded like nonsense ("bar-bar-bar"). Moreover, the ease and speed of contact with the mainland kept the colonists' cultural identity as Greeks strong. **Panhellenic** ("all-Greek") religious festivals and competitions like the Olympic Games (the first of which took place in 776 BCE) helped to keep the scattered Greek colonists in close contact with one another.[4] But because the overseas

---

[4]   Several mythical tales give different stories behind the start of the Games. Most likely, they began as annual foot-races of girls to determine who would become that year's priestess of the goddess Hera at a sacred site outside the town of Olympia. The idea of regular competitions among male athletes soon won out. The Panhellenic Games consisted of four separate tournaments (held in sequence, one per year)— the Olympic, Isthmian, Nemean, and Pythian Games. The Olympic Games were held in the highest regard. By 720 BCE, if not earlier, the tradition had developed of staging all athletic contests in the nude. The Games continued until 394 CE, when the Roman emperor Theodosius I, a Christian, banned all pagan religious festivals.

Greeks encouraged contact with their non-Greek neighbors, a steady exposure to new ideas, technologies, and practices helped promote innovation. It is no accident that many of ancient Greece's greatest thinkers and artists came from the colonies rather than the mainland.

One did not have to be a prominent merchant, civic official, or intellectual to serve one's polis. During the Archaic Age, the effective defense of a polis increasingly required a standing militia. Accordingly, every male between the ages of eighteen and sixty served in the polis's military force. The use of trained infantry did not originate with the Greeks, but with the Assyrians—although there is no clear evidence that the Greeks learned the technique from them. Earlier military strategy, if it can be called that, consisted of mass swarmings of foot soldiers under the leadership of chariot-riding kings or generals. Once the battle lines were drawn up, the fighting quickly devolved into a free-for-all. The Greeks, however, perfected fighting in trained units. What they came up with was the notion of groups of foot soldiers holding tight formation as a block, eight horizontal lines of ten to twenty men each, who stood shoulder to shoulder and moved as a single unit. Called a **phalanx**, such a unit rushed at the enemy and smashed through them, like a kind of foot-powered armored tank. Each of these soldiers, known as **hoplites**, wore a breastplate and helmet, had a short sword at his belt, and carried a round shield and a thrusting spear. By combining their weight and momentum, they made up a powerful force.[5]

The Hoplite Army

It required long hours of training to develop an effective phalanx because each soldier had to overcome the instinct to fend for himself by thrusting his spear or stabbing his sword at everything that moved. Instead, the hoplites had to hold formation and fight as a single unit. This had two important consequences. First, since all men fought in their polis's army, all had to attain a degree of physical conditioning—and hence the Greek emphasis on exercise. Athletic competitions (such as the Olympics), public training facilities, sporting events, and the like all played important roles in Archaic Age culture, a fact we can see in the artwork of the time. Greek painting, sculpture, and poetry emphasize the beauty of a fit male physique more so than any other ancient culture. To be fit and strong, the Greeks believed, was more than to be beautiful: it was freedom itself. Second, the hoplite army underscored and confirmed the interdependence of the polis. It was the body politic, the community that literally stood together as one or perished. A phalanx was living proof that people are stronger together than apart.

And this led to trouble. The more the Greek cities relied on the new armies, the more important the commoners who made up their ranks became. These

---

[5]   The name for these soldiers, *hoplites*, derives from the shields they carried.

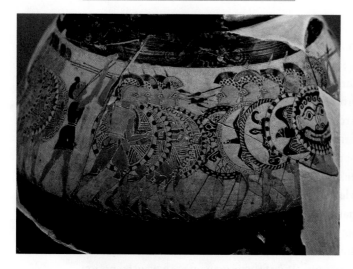

Hoplites (left)   This Greek vase painting from around 650 BCE is the earliest known depiction of hoplites fighting in phalanx formation. The phalanx's discipline and group-mindedness are evident here in the uniformly faceless soldiers, the perfect alignment of their marching feet, and the parallel lines formed by their spears.

Athletes (right)   Scenes of wrestling, boxing, and racing were common decorations on Greek vases in the Archaic Age. As shown here, athletic contests were performed in the nude, the better to appreciate the beauty of the human form.

Challenges to the Social Order soldiers paid for their own equipment and took battlefield instructions from one another through a combination of verbal and manual signals. The aristocrats who made up the charioted officer class declined in importance accordingly, which had important repercussions for political life. A city that depends on its common men for survival cannot long deny them political power. This is why the Archaic Age was filled with social strife—and why Homer's great epics are politically significant. Under pressure from hoplites, colonists, merchants, and workers, the stratified society ruled by noble kings and aristocratic heroes was giving way to a nascent egalitarian order.

A CULT OF MASCULINITY

Archaic Greece developed a cult of masculinity that distinguished it from other ancient cultures. Their's was a society built for war, in which every able-bodied man eighteen to sixty was expected to serve in the hoplite army. Girls received little or no education and were raised with the idea that their sole function in life was to marry, produce children, and care for their household. At marriage a young woman became the legal dependent of her husband, having the same (and no more) rights as the children she would produce. Apart from going to the market or the public well, visiting family members, and attending funerals and a handful of religious ceremonies, women seldom appeared alone in public. Doing so would bring shame on the household and give the father or husband leave to punish her severely. Most homes in fact were physically divided into male and female zones, often with the female rooms enclosed behind a locked door to which the husband kept the key.

Citizenship in a polis, like ownership of property, was hereditary and a right so precious as to inspire an obsession with legitimate birth. Maintaining a *Roles for* woman's seclusion was the best way, men determined, to ensure her chastity *Women* before marriage and fidelity within it. Female virginity was an absolute require- ment for marriage, except for cases of a man wedding a widow. Before the cere- mony, young brides typically offered special prayers and presented gifts at a temple to the virgin goddess Artemis; these gifts often consisted of the toys en- joyed by the bride in her girlhood. As a sexually experienced wife, she would no longer have need of them.

Marriages were arranged, and a woman's guardian would often engage her to another man's son while she was still a child. The wedding usually took place when the girl was in her early teens and the groom ten to fifteen years older. In most poleis monogamy was the rule, as was a nuclear family (parents and chil- dren living together without other relatives in the same house). Although male citizens were free to have sexual relations with slaves, prostitutes, or willing males, female citizens had no such freedom. Sex between a wife and anyone other than her husband carried harsh penalties for both parties. Street prostitutes worked in most cities, but for wealthier patrons a caste of women known as cour- tesans emerged as a semirespectable profession. Called *hetairai* in Greek ("com- panions," literally), these women were professional hostesses, usually foreigners, who offered meals and music in addition to sex. They received customers in their own residences, for the most part, but higher-priced hetairai also offered a kind of catering service, attending aristocratic symposia (drinking parties) and enter- taining guests with music, dancing, and witty banter, in addition to the expected sexual couplings.

Homosexual contact was accepted, and even approved of, by society so long as *Attitudes* certain norms were followed. Generally it was a unique privilege of the aristocracy, *toward* who did not regard wives as intellectual partners. Older men took noble youths, usu- *Homo-* ally aged twelve to fifteen, under their protection, to guide them in the ways of soci- *sexuality* ety, government, and elite culture. Sexual relations were understood to be a part of this tutoring. In Sparta same-sex activity also existed, although, given Sparta's proud tradition of egalitarianism among its people, the relationships usually involved indi- viduals of equal age. The city-state of Thebes, in the 4th century BCE, famously pos- sessed an elite military unit composed solely of 150 pairs of lovers—the so-called

Sacred Band, which won every battle it engaged in until defeat finally came in 338 BCE at the hands of Philip of Macedonia (discussed in the next chapter).

CIVILIZED PURSUITS: LYRIC POETRY

Archaic Age aristocrats were deeply invested in the heroic ideal enshrined in the Homeric epics. But they also strove to express their unique culture in newer poetic forms like lyric and elegy—the first sung to accompaniment on a lyre, the second to the music of a flute. The range of Greek lyric is impressive, from songs in praise of war, of love, of justice, and of sensual delights to bawdy invectives against real or imagined enemies. An early poet named Tyrtaeus lived in Sparta in the 7th century BCE and composed patriotic songs:

> March forward, sons of men of Sparta,
> the land of brave men!
> With your shields in your left hands
> and your spears in your right,
> march bravely forward with no fear for your lives!
> For the fear of death is unbecoming to a Spartan.

Bacchylides, from the Aegean island of Ceos, in the 5th century BCE sang in praise of peace:

> Great gifts, Peace brings to mortals:
> Wealth; the bursting forth of sweet-sounding music;
> in bright flames atop carved altars
> choice pieces of cattle and woolly sheep roasting
> in honor of the gods; and beautiful youths keen
> for sports, and the arts, and revelry.

The two greatest lyric poets were Pindar (ca. 522–443 BCE) and Sappho (ca. 620–570 BCE). Pindar, who lived and worked in Thebes, made his name by composing odes for special occasions. Among his most popular verses were a series of odes in honor of victors in athletic contests like the Olympic Games. His poetry is notoriously difficult to translate since he delights in sophisticated meters and rhetorical flourishes.

Sappho   **Sappho**, however, invites translation. Her poetry depends less on technical tricks, more on acute observation and emotional directness. According to tradition she wrote some nine volumes of poetry, although only one poem survives in its entirety, a hymn to Aphrodite. Many of the surviving fragments express homoerotic love, and Sappho's homeland of the island of Lesbos has given its name to lesbianism. Here she describes her feelings at a dinner party with her beloved at the table:

> That man seems to me equal to the gods,
> the one who sits opposite you
> and listens so closely
> to your sweet voice
> and your beguiling laughter—
> oh, how the heart in my chest is stirred!
> For whenever I look at you, even for a moment,
> to speak is beyond me—not one single word;
> my tongue freezes in silence;
> a lick of flame runs beneath my skin;
> my eyes can see nothing;
> my ears hear only a din;
> a cold sweat covers me;
> my body trembles—and I sigh
> and turn greener than grass
> and think I might die.

The only surviving complete poem from Sappho, it leaves one wishing for more— the case, indeed, for most of Greek imaginative literature. As a culture that cherished physical beauty, intellectual engagement, and civic vitality, ancient Greece has never ceased to fascinate. One special element of that fascination was the Greeks' adaptive capacity—their ability and willingness to try different means to a particular end—as we see in the varieties of political and social organization they employed.

SPARTA: THE MILITARIZATION OF THE CITIZENRY

Evidence attests to roughly nine hundred poleis in the Archaic period, and about most of them we know very little. To appreciate the variety of forms political life could take in Archaic Greece, we will examine three particularly well-documented poleis. Sparta, Miletus, and Athens were the most powerful city-states of the age. And each was powerful in a different way.

Sparta boasted the most impressive military. Governed since the 7th century BCE by a council of elders known as the *gerousia* (literally, "group of old men"), it *The Helots* was a brutally efficient city—a large community in which an exceptionally sizable slave population (as much as three-quarters of the city's inhabitants) performed the labor of producing food, building homes, tending animals, weaving cloth, and doing basic craftwork. The slaves' labor freed the Spartan citizens to pursue the solitary goal of preparing for war. They did so neither to repel foreign invasion nor to seek overseas conquests of their own but simply to keep their economic foundation—the enormous state-owned slave population—in check. A revolt by these state-owned slaves, called **helots**, in the mid-7th century BCE had nearly toppled the Spartans and persuaded them to stay on their guard.

Education and Training   The militarization of the citizenry in the mid-7th century was nearly absolute and began at childbirth. City officials examined every infant born to judge whether he or she was healthy enough to keep; those who failed to pass muster were abandoned in the nearby mountains. Military training began at age seven for boys, with group exercise, marching drills, and athletic competitions, especially wrestling and javelin hurling. Girls, also starting at age seven, received group exercise and athletic training. The sexes separated at age twelve, with girls taught elementary reading and writing and domestic economy, whereas boys were handed over to live in military barracks and instructed in fighting with weapons.

A Spartan Youth   This handle from a water jug (ca. 540 BCE) depicts a young Spartan boy—identifiable by the long braids of his hair—holding the tails of two young lions.

Diets were sharply restricted—not to combat obesity, but to inspire the boys to become effective thieves. Food thieves were punished harshly for the crime of getting caught. The food they stole was from their own farms. When training began at age seven, each boy was awarded a farm by the state. This farm was run for him by helots. A hungry Spartan lad was expected to sneak from his barracks, dash to his own farm, steal his own food, and make it back without being caught or observed at either end. The idea was to acquire real-life experience of enduring the pains of hunger, of learning to move about without being seen, and of becoming self-reliant.

Boys were taught basic literacy, but the bulk of their training was military. At age twenty they began active service in the hoplite army. If they served ten straight years, they were granted full Spartan citizenship, which involved the right to speak in the assembly and to hold leadership positions in the polis. If a Spartan married while in his twenties, he still lived in his barracks—and had to sneak out at night to visit his wife. He was then punished, if he was caught, for the crime of being caught.

The superhuman rigor of Spartan training is easily overstated, and it is significant that the only detailed contemporary description of Spartan life comes from Xenophon (427–354 BCE), an Athenian who witnessed the humiliating defeat of his city by the Spartans in the Peloponnesian War (431–404 BCE), as we will see in chapter 5. He dramatizes Spartan life in his book *Hellenica* ("Greek History"), in which he narrates the failure of Athenian democracy and his own disillusionment with his city. A later work, *The Constitution of the Lacedaemonians*, written in 388 BCE, provides the colorful detail. And the better-known *Life of Lycurgus* by Plutarch (ca. 50–120 CE) draws heavily on Xenophon's treatise but adds considerable amounts of gossip and hearsay.[6] Plutarch relates a popular story in which a young Spartan, having gone off in search of food, caught a fox. On the way back to his barracks, some older Spartans came upon him in the dark. Rather than face the humiliation of being caught, the young man hid the live fox under his cloak and never gave a hint of it to the elders, even as the fox bit and clawed its way into his entrails.

Xenophon blames Athens's defeat on its lack of order and discipline, the very traits he proclaims of his adopted Sparta. All Spartan men, he insists, had the right to beat any Spartan youth for misbehavior, and the father of that youth, after learning of the beating, would beat the child again to show his solidarity with his peers. To discourage materialism and greed, he reports, Sparta forbade the use of gold and silver and instituted a new coinage made of iron—which was so valueless that it would require a wagonload of cash to make even a modest purchase. A Spartan man who was too old to satisfy his wife's sexual longings and produce children, he says, was required by law to appoint a young stud to be his wife's lover—which the elder Spartan always did with equanimity, knowing that he was doing what was best for the polis. Xenophon's description of the relentless rigor of Spartan life can hardly be believed, but it began a tradition that the Spartans were keen to propagate. It was also a tradition that the Athenians wished to elaborate, since it lessened the embarrassment of their defeat in the Peloponnesian War. Who could blame them for falling to such superhumans?

Despite such exaggerations, Sparta was a notably disciplined and austere place. Spartan life aimed at a central goal—keeping its citizens strong and resolute enough to keep the helots in place. The deadening effect on the society of this narrowness of vision might well have been the undoing of Sparta, had it not been

---

[6]   When the war ended, Xenophon went into voluntary exile and ultimately ended up in Sparta, where he lived for twenty years before finally returning to Athens in 366 BCE.

for a slow-gathering threat—a Persian invasion of Greece. Military dangers justify military precautions and give their founders an aura of foresight. The enormity of the Persian danger enhanced the perceived wisdom of Sparta's military reformers and added to their reputation for superhuman fortitude.

MILETUS: THE BIRTHPLACE OF PHILOSOPHY

Miletus offered a sharp contrast to Sparta. Located on the western coast of Asia Minor, it was a commercial and cultural hub, involved equally in mainland Greek and Anatolian affairs. Miletus (modern Milet) originated in the Mycenaean period, declined during the Dark Age, and then reemerged as one of the Archaic Age's most vibrant cities. It had as many as a hundred colonies, most of these in the Black Sea region, like Sinope and Trapezus, its two most important colonies and the Turkish cities of Sinop and Trabzon today (see Map 4.2).[7]

A Cosmopolitan Crossroads   Located on a small but strategic peninsula, Miletus was one of the principal way stations for Greek goods entering Asia Minor. There was also a fair-sized harbor, although accumulating sediment from the Maeander River has since filled it, and it now lies roughly 3 miles from the sea. It was also close to the inland city of Sardis, the western terminus of the Royal Highway built by the Persians as the main thoroughfare running through the heart of their empire. This made it a natural distribution point for Persian goods throughout the eastern Mediterranean. In constant contact with the Greek, Hittite, Phoenician, and Egyptian worlds in addition to the Lydian and Persian ones, Miletus was among the most cosmopolitan of cities in the 7th and 6th centuries BCE. It acquired a reputation for producing both high-quality ceramics and remarkable intellectuals—like the philosophers Thales (ca. 624–546 BCE), Anaximander (ca. 610–546 BCE), and Anaximenes (ca. 585–528 BCE) and the early historian Hecataeus (ca. 550–476 BCE).

Governed by a merchant council, the people of Miletus saw greater potential for growth in the Mediterranean than in the land trade with Persia, and so they organized the other coastal cities of Anatolia into an alliance called the **Ionian League**, a confederation of poleis pledged to support one another. This was the first such organization in the Greek world.

The First Philosophers   Miletus's greatest claim to fame, however, is as the birthplace of philosophy ("love of wisdom"). The first three true philosophers in Western history— Thales, Anaximander, and Anaximenes—all appeared there. The city's essence as a cultural crossroads no doubt contributed much to this development,

---

7   Miletus's colonies focused on shipping slaves, timber, and wheat from the region of southern Russia. All were in short supply in the Aegean.

although evidence of a heightened appreciation for **rationalism** is present in Greek culture going back to Mycenaean times. What Thales and his followers began was the effort to systematize the observations one draws from everyday experience. Cause and effect surround us at all times, of course, and to notice that fact does not take genius. We observe the world's workings every day: seeds buried in soil grow into plants; wood placed in fire is itself inflamed, whereas metal or stone is not; wine, when drunk, produces lightheadedness; the shadow produced by a stick placed vertically in the ground lengthens, shortens, and changes direction as the sun moves through the sky. To explain the relation of cause and effect, when discussing details of the natural word, is the realm of science. Thales and his followers, however, tried to ascertain whether all of nature follows a rational order. Is nature in fact a system? Is there a set of universal truths that hold together the material world—and if so, how can we learn them? Does human life exist within an eternal code of truths larger than anything our cultural traditions or religions teach us? This is the realm of philosophy.

Thales, the first philosopher, never wrote a word. Philosophy, he believed, is best explored in conversation. The answer to every question, after all, raises another question (at least if the answer is interesting). A written text, however, is finite and fixed and therefore cannot possibly be completely right. Anaximander, his student, disagreed on that point and wrote reams, although only a few fragments survive. Consciously or not, they and Anaximenes all began with an assumption that provides the foundation of all of modern physics—the conservation of matter. Everything came from somewhere, and since the complexity and variety of the world is obviously increasing as we move forward in time, then everything must be traceable to a single point, a single element, if we move backward through time.

What was this universal source? For Thales it was water, the primordial substance from which everything derives. Anaximander posited the existence of a single infinite ether, a malleable goo that took different forms when subjected to opposing forces of heat and cold, wetness and dryness. Anaximenes went even further and added the complicating factor of air, which affects the shape-shifting of the ether by its relative density or lightness. What is interesting about these speculations is the way they hint at a theory of evolution. If the entire physical cosmos has a common beginning, and if the world we observe is still constantly changing, then surely we ourselves came to be through a process of change in the past.[8]

Nothing quite like this had ever been attempted before. The mutability of the physical world has always been known. The Sumerians complained about it

---

[8]   Anaximenes even asserted that humans must have been at one time fish.

incessantly, and the Egyptians saw it as a deviation from the stability offered by obedience to the pharaoh. The Hebrews initially regarded it as the fulfillment of YHWH's design, then later feared that he had turned his back on them and his plan. The Ionian Greeks, however, were the first to approach the mutability of the physical world as a rational problem and to test their interpretations of it with logical arguments. This was to be one of the ancient world's greatest legacies for Greater Western culture—a sense of order, a search for meaning, and a tradition of submitting one's ideas to critical inspection.

The Ionian thinkers even submitted religion to critical analysis. The boldest figure of all was Xenophanes of Colophon (ca. 570–480 BCE), who noted that deities in every culture tend to have the physical characteristics of the culture: thus Ethiopian gods and goddesses have black skin and curly hair, whereas Greek artists portray their divinities with olive skin and dark wavy hair, and the barbarians of Thrace (a region well to the north of Greece) worship deities with fair skin, reddish hair, and blue eyes. His conclusion? Humans make gods in their own image—not, as the Hebrew Bible says, the other way around. If cattle could speak, Xenophanes quips, they would pray to gods who looked like cattle. His main concern was to turn people away from the Olympian-deity cults, which he regarded as poetic nonsense, and to examine life through critical reason. Although it is impossible to know the truth with absolute certainty, the point, Xenophanes insists, is to make the effort.

Radical speculation like this declined in Ionia after the Persians conquered Lydia in 494 BCE and acquired control of Miletus, as we will see. The philosophers either fled or joined the resistance. The mode of critical thinking begun in Miletus spread quickly to the Greek mainland, however, where it took root especially in the city of Athens.

ATHENS: HOME TO DEMOCRACY

Athens is older than Jerusalem, older than Nineveh, older than Sparta or Miletus. Perhaps only Jericho, of all the cities of the Greater Western world, has a longer history of continuous human settlement. As early as 3000 BCE, Neolithic tribesmen built a fort atop the rocky hill known as the Acropolis ("high-point of the city"), and people have lived there ever since. Geography favors it: the hilltop provides a natural defensive position from which to control the nearby plains, which provide farmland and pasturage. The Eridanus River flowed through the center of the town (it has long since dried up), and the port of Piraeus lies only 6 miles away. Athens thus had ready access to natural resources and communication links but was also sufficiently isolated to enjoy natural protection. Already a leading city in Mycenaean times, Athens was able to hold out against the so-called

Sea Peoples, although it then went into the same sharp decline as the other cities of the Dark Age.

As the clouds cleared by 700 BCE, Athens stood ready to take advantage once again of its uniquely strong position, and under the leadership of the landholding aristocracy the city slowly seized control of the entire region of Attica.[9] By the mid-600s BCE, however, so many new people had been added to the roster of Athenians that they began to challenge the authority of the nobles and wealthy merchants who ran the polis as an oligarchy. The clash between the privileges of the few and the demands of the many is what would ultimately lead to the invention of Athenian democracy.

An early effort at social revolution occurred at Athens in 632 BCE, when a popular athlete named Cylon tried unsuccessfully to rouse the masses against the aristocrats. Forty years later, in 594 BCE, the city council gave extraordinary authority to a fellow aristocrat named Solon, who instituted widespread reforms to free the city from class strife. Specifically, **Solon** made all adult (male) citizens members of the Athenian Assembly—which was the group that elected the city's governing officials; he also lowered the social and financial qualifications an individual had to have before being elected to office. On the economic front, Solon permitted foreign tradesmen who settled in Athens to become citizens, so long as they brought their families with them. This maneuver helped to bring skilled craftsmen into the city and increase foreign trade. His most celebrated reform, however, was the cancellation of all agrarian debts and the manumission of all poor farmers who had fallen into debt-slavery.

Solon's Reforms

Solon's efforts ultimately failed, however, which resulted in a more populist figure named Pisistratos seizing power around 560 BCE. Pisistratos (d. 527 BCE) was Athens's first **tyrant**. The word *tyrant* carries a pejorative meaning in English, but in ancient Greek a tyrant (*tyrannos*) was simply a person who wielded power temporarily to bring about dramatic reform in a politically deadlocked state. Tyranny was thus a kind of administrative receivership. In terms of social class, the tyrants were aristocrats but were usually allied with the masses. Tyrannies seldom lasted longer than a decade or two, by which time the reasons for the tyranny had either been achieved or were deemed hopeless. In either case the tyrant lost the popular support of the hoplites, which put an end to his power.

Greek Tyranny

Tyrants were installed to reform the state and were judged good or ill according to that standard alone. The methods they employed were of less significance. Pisistratos went so far as to wound himself with a spear so that he could ride his chariot into the Athenian marketplace, blood dripping from his injury, and claim to

---

[9]   Athens grew by bringing smaller neighboring towns into its jurisdiction—what classical historians call *synoikismos* ("gathering together in a single home"). "Urban sprawl" works just fine.

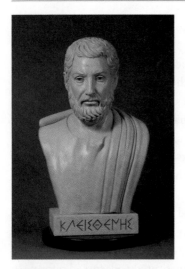

Cleisthenes   This modern bust of the founder of Athenian democracy stands in the Ohio Statehouse. Photograph © 2015 Museum of Fine Arts, Boston

have survived an assassination attempt from his rivals. All this was to whip the crowd of his supporters into a frenzy and quiet his rivals. Pisistratos ruled Athens three times, from 561 to perhaps 557 BCE, again from 556 to 555 BCE, and finally again from 546 to 527 BCE. Each time, Pisistratos saw to it that municipal offices were parceled out more equitably among the social classes, lowered taxes, and increased the number of judges to break up a backlog of criminal and civil cases. (Pisistratos also deserves credit for ordering the permanent archiving of the texts of Homer's *Iliad* and *Odyssey*.) He was succeeded in power by his two sons, Hippias and Hipparchus, who followed their father's policies, but when rivals murdered Hipparchus in 514 BCE, Hippias grew increasingly bitter, suspicious, and vindictive. He was thrown out of office in 510 BCE and eventually replaced by **Cleisthenes**, whom tradition regales as "the father of Athenian democracy."

The system as established under Cleisthenes remained more or less in place until Alexander the Great conquered Athens in 338 BCE, and it provides the model for our understanding of Athenian **democracy**.

Cleisthenes's Reforms   Cleisthenes's most important reform involved changing the political organization from a reliance on clans and clients to a new structure organized around urban precincts called *demes* (the origin of the English word *democracy*). Representatives in council thus represented whole neighborhoods rather than individual families and alliances.

The main body of the government was the citizens' Assembly (*ekklesia* in Greek), which met to consider new legislation, adjudicate trials, and set policies. As many as five to six thousand men comprised the assembly at any one time, which was obviously too cumbersome a group for any effective governance; hence most day-to-day government was performed by a smaller group called the council (*boule*). Chosen by lots and serving for only one day, the members of the council selected the leading magistrates; these were not elections in the modern sense, but an actual lottery. Elections were reserved for the positions of *strategoi*— the military commanders in charge of the citizen army. Magistracies and command positions were for one-year terms, and whereas popular strategoi could serve an unlimited number of consecutive terms, all magistrates were removed from office after a single term.

Full participatory citizenship was restricted to somewhere between 5 and 10 percent of the population: slaves, women, the working poor, and most lesser craftsmen and artisans were denied the right to vote in the assembly and to hold municipal office. The numbers come from the Athenian historian Thucydides (ca. 455–399 BCE), who reckoned the number of citizens at forty thousand. He put the number of slaves in Athens as high as 400,000 and the number of nonciti-zen residents at seventy thousand. Called *metics*, these resident aliens had no democratic rights and had to pay for the privilege of residing in the city.

Still, no other ancient society placed power in the hands of so many of its people. Further, the real accomplishment of the constitution lay not in the size of the electorate, but in its strict definition and supervision of the powers of civic officials. In other ancient societies, officeholders served a king or regarded their own will as the constitution. In Athens, officeholders served the city and its con-stitution. In the context of its time, Athens's experiment with government by (some of) the people was a rare and beautiful thing.

THE PERSIAN WARS

By the 490s BCE Sparta, not Athens, was the strongest polis in Greece, however. Most other cities of the time would have named it as their leader, if asked. As ten-sions rose with the advancing Persian Empire, more and more poleis turned to the Spartans for guidance. Not only was their army the strongest in Greece, but also Sparta—alone among Greek cities—did not have overseas colonies. This assured people that Sparta's leadership in a Panhellenic military force would play no favorites. Few people trusted the Athenians to be so selfless.

The Persian Wars (494–479 BCE) did not have to happen. Persia had been eager enough to conquer all of the Near East, but the empire initially showed no signs of determination, or even desire, to add Greece to its dominion. Doing so, after all, would require the Persians to develop maritime skills that they neither had nor needed. The Greeks controlled the sea-lanes throughout the eastern Mediterranean and the Black Sea. Since the Persians controlled everything else, the Greeks had no one else with whom to trade. Conquering the people would have been a waste of resources.

Revolt by the Ionian Greeks, aided by sympathetic rebels from the island of Naxos, changed all of that. The trouble started in Miletus, which had been gov- *Ionian* erned by a brief series of Persian-affiliated tyrants. The Ionian Greek colonies *Revolt* tired of sending their taxes and tribute eastward and waited only for a leader to organize them into a full-scale rebellion. The rebels' chance came when the tyrant of Miletus, Aristagoras, turned on the Persians. Apparently convinced that he had lost the emperor Darius's favor, Aristagoras roused the Milesians and the rest of Ionia to revolt against Persian rule. He gambled that the Greek mainland would come to the Ionians' assistance and that the Persians, lacking a navy, would let the Ionian colonies go. He was right and wrong in equal measure. The coastal colonies did unite in seceding from Persia, and the mainland Greeks did come to their aid. But Persia refused to let the challenge to their authority go unanswered.

Athens Takes Command   When Sparta—ever concerned over the threat to national security that the helots presented—balked at sending its troops to Miletus, the Athenians, sensing an opportunity, leaped in. In 499 BCE they led a force that sacked the Persians' provincial capital at Sardis (modern Sart). But then the Athenians declared victory and went home, leaving the Ionian cities to face the Persian emperor's wrath alone. Darius decided to teach the Athenians a lesson, and in 490 BCE he sent an army of twenty thousand to thirty thousand elite troops across the Aegean with orders to land on the mainland and to march on Athens and destroy it. The armies met on the plain at Marathon, where the Athenian phalanxes routed the Persian forces. The Greek historian Herodotus records that 6,400 Persians were killed, whereas the Athenians lost only 192. Darius, humiliated, withdrew.[10] Athens rejoiced in its victory and its new standing as the champion of all of Greece (see Map 4.3).

One of the city's leading politicians, Themistocles (ca. 524–459 BCE), advised the polis that the Persians would undoubtedly come back and that the Athenians should therefore prepare. They did so by investing in a fleet of two hundred new warships called **triremes**, thereby turning Athens into a major naval power. Invented by the Phoenicians in the 8th century BCE and introduced in Greece, according to Thucydides, in the 5th century, triremes were oared warships, with three tiers of rowers. Constructed of pine or fir, they were relatively light ships that, with a well-trained crew, could attain high speed. With a bronze-tipped hardwood prow, they were extremely effective at ramming into the hulls of opposing ships.[11]

---

[10]   The Athenians took the field in a long horizontal line, hoping to appear more numerous than they were, but with their middle ranks intentionally shallow, only a few ranks deep, and their forces bulked up on either flank. When the Persians charged, the Athenian line quickly broke in the center, as planned, and the strong flanks then wheeled inward in a pincer movement and trapped the Persians between them. Herodotus's casualty numbers cannot be believed but have entered tradition. The battle later lent its name to the "Marathon" foot-race—supposedly a messenger ran the 26 miles from Marathon to Athens, bringing the news of the great Athenian victory. Herodotus mentions no such messenger but does relates the story of Pheidippides running from Athens to Sparta to ask for help. In the lead-up to the battle he ran all the way to Sparta—a distance of 150 miles—to request reinforcements, only to race back again with the news that the Spartans' arrival was going to be delayed and that the Athenians were on their own. A later writer, Lucian of Samosata (125–180 CE), was the first to describe the supposed Marathon-to-Athens run, with the melodramatic conclusion of Pheidippides crying out, "Victory is ours!" before collapsing in death.

[11]   Another favorite tactic was to build up speed, approach alongside an enemy ship, withdraw the oars, and let the momentum of the trireme shear away the oars of the foe, leaving him helplessly adrift.

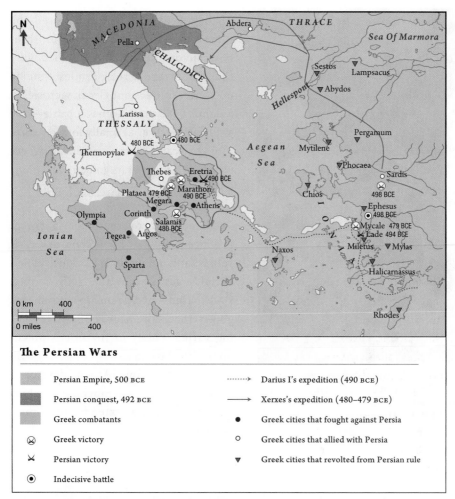

The Persian Wars

▨	Persian Empire, 500 BCE	┄┄┄➤	Darius I's expedition (490 BCE)
▨	Persian conquest, 492 BCE	⟶	Xerxes's expedition (480–479 BCE)
▨	Greek combatants	●	Greek cities that fought against Persia
⊗	Greek victory	○	Greek cities that allied with Persia
⋊	Persian victory	▼	Greek cities that revolted from Persian rule
◉	Indecisive battle		

MAP 4.3   The Persian Wars   The Greeks defeated the Persians in nearly every confrontation. Shown here are the most important battle sites: Marathon, Thermopylae, Salamis, and Plataea.

The empire did strike back, in 480 BCE. Darius's son Xerxes (r. 486–465 BCE) was then in charge, and he assembled the largest army in ancient history for a land assault. Herodotus reckoned it at 1.7 million soldiers, but most historians estimate the real figure was about one-tenth of that. The Persians marched north from Sardis, crossed the Hellespont, moved westward across Thrace and Macedonia, and prepared to invade Greece from the north. The Persian threat finally persuaded most of the rebel Greeks to unite in defense. Sparta fought a heroic frontline action at the battle of Thermopylae (480 BCE), while the Athenians harried the Persians, supply ships. Spartan bravery at Thermopylae has long been remembered, deservedly, as one of the greatest military feats of Western

The Battle of Salamis   This is a modern rendering of the decisive naval battle that culminated in the defeat of Xerxes's army. Note the ramming prow (complete with smiley face) on the Athenian trireme.

history. With only three hundred soldiers they held off the Persians for three days before succumbing, which gave the rest of the Greek armies time to muster.[12] Subsequent Greek victories at Salamis (480 BCE)—a naval battle—and at Plataea (479 BCE) finally forced Xerxes to give up and return to Persia. Greece was poised to enter its golden age.

◆

Greece's recovery from its Dark Age produced a new set of personal and civic values, and a new form of political and social organization: the polis, a city-state based on citizenship and shared governance. The degree of power sharing varied widely in the Greek poleis. Some, like Sparta and Miletus, were oligarchies. Over time, Athens developed the most extensive democracy, in which political power was extended to all male citizens.

WHO, WHAT, WHERE

Cleisthenes	Linear A	Sappho
democracy	Linear B	Solon
helots	Panhellenic	triremes
Homer	phalanx	tyrant
hoplites	polis	
Ionian League	rationalism	

---

12   Thermopylae ("Hot Springs," literally—so named because of sulfurous hot springs nearby) is a coastal floodplain and the only place where an ancient army could pass from Thessaly into Greece. The plain is considerably wider now than in ancient times, because of sedimentary deposition; in fact, a modern highway now passes through the site.

SUGGESTED READINGS

Primary Sources

Herodotus. *The Persian Wars.*

Hesiod. *Theogony.*

Hesiod. *Works and Days.*

Homer. *The Iliad.*

Homer. *The Odyssey.*

Thucydides. *The Peloponnesian War.*

Xenophon. *Hellenica.*

Xenophon. *Constitution of the Lacedaemonians.*

Anthologies

Buckley, Terry. *Aspects of Greek History, 750–323 BC: A Source-Based Approach* (2010).

Lefkowitz, Mary R., and Maureen B. Fant, comps. *Women's Life in Greece and Rome: A Source Book in Translation* (2005).

Nagle, D. Brendan, and Stanley M. Burstein. *Readings in Greek History: Sources and Interpretations* (2006).

Rice, David G., and John E. Stambaugh. *Sources for the Study of Greek Religion* (2000).

Studies

Bagnall, Nigel. *The Peloponnesian War: Athens, Sparta, and the Struggle for Greece* (2006).

Brunschwig, Jacques, and Geoffrey E. R. Lloyd, eds. *Greek Thought: A Guide to Classical Knowledge* (2000).

Camp, John M. *The Archaeology of Athens* (2002).

Cartledge, Paul A. *The Spartans: An Epic History* (2003).

Cawkwell, George. *The Greek Wars: The Failure of Persia* (2005).

Davidson, James. *The Greeks and Greek Love: A Bold New Exploration of the Ancient World* (2009).

De Souza, Philip. *The Greek and Persian Wars, 499–386 BC* (2003).

Dickinson, Oliver. *The Aegean from Bronze Age to Iron Age: Continuity and Change between the Twelfth and Eighth Centuries BC* (2007).

Ducat, Jean. *Spartan Education: Youth and Society in the Classical Period* (2006).

Gere, Cathy. *Knossos and the Prophets of Modernism* (2009).

Graham, Daniel W. *Explaining the Cosmos: The Ionian Tradition of Scientific Philosophy* (2006).

Hall, Jonathan M. *A History of the Archaic Greek World, ca. 1200–479 BCE* (2006).

Hughes, Bettany. *Helen of Troy: The Story Behind the Most Beautiful Woman in the World* (2007).

Langdon, Susan. *Art and Identity in Dark Age Greece, 1100–700 BCE* (2010).

Morris, Ian, and Barry B. Powell. *The Greeks: History, Culture, and Society* (2009).

Osborne, Robin. *Athens and Athenian Democracy* (2014).

Osborne, Robin. *Greece in the Making, 1200–479 BC* (2009).

Pedley, John. *Sanctuaries and the Sacred in the Ancient Greek World* (2005).

Pomeroy, Sarah B. *Spartan Women* (2002).

Pomeroy, Sarah B., Stanley M. Burstein, Walter Donlan, Jennifer Tolbert Roberts, and David Tandy. *Ancient Greece: A Political, Social, and Cultural History Third Edition* (2012).

Schofield, Louise. *The Mycenaeans* (2007).

Snodgrass, Anthony M. *The Dark Age of Greece: An Archaeological Survey of the Eleventh to Eighth Centuries BC* (2000).

Thomas, Rosalind. *Herodotus in Context: Ethnography, Science, and the Art of Persuasion* (2002).

Waterfield, Robin. *The First Philosophers: The Presocratics and the Sophists* (2009).

For additional resources, including maps, primary sources, visuals, web links, and quizzes, please go to **www.oup.com/us/backman.**

CHAPTER 5

Classical Greece and the Hellenistic World

479–30 BCE

The Classical and Hellenistic ages witnessed all the best and worst of ancient Greek life. The first, the Classical Age, dates from the successful defense of Greece against Persia to the conquest of Persia by the Greeks under Alexander the Great (479–323 BCE). The Hellenistic Age that followed ran from Alexander's death to the conquest of the East by the Romans (323–30 BCE). A sense of euphoria swept through the Greek people after their victory over Xerxes, and the Athenians felt more euphoric than any. Their bravery at Marathon and their decision to build a fleet of triremes had led directly to the Persians' defeat. Now, with the exception of Sparta and a few outliers, every polis in Greece recognized Athens's new position of leadership.

THE CLASSICAL AND HELLENISTIC AGES

Its leadership involved more than military achievements. Mid-5th-century BCE Greece, especially Athens, witnessed a remarkable vitality in civic life, economic prosperity, artistic expression, and literary and scientific achievement. Yet it seems

The Discus Thrower Carved around 450 BCE, the original *Diskobolos* ("discus thrower") of Myron is lost, but this classical Greek masterpiece is known through numerous Roman copies, such as this marble sculpture. The discus throw was one of the events in the ancient pentathlon: discus, javelin, long jump, sprint, and wrestling. All five events took place in one day.

only right that one of its greatest achievements was tragedy, because its Golden Age ended with the disastrous war between Athens and Sparta known as the Peloponnesian War (431–404 BCE), which lasted twenty-seven years and consumed much of the Greek peninsula. As it happened, of the period's greatest philosophers—Socrates, Plato, and Aristotle—the last taught the military heir to the disaster, Alexander the Great. Alexander's conquests had far-reaching consequences. By defeating Persia, he brought the entire Near East and the eastern Mediterranean under a single command for the first time, an achievement that confirmed and highlighted the ties that held together the Greater West as a single, although pluralistic, civilization. The intentional cross-fertilization of Greek and Persian cultures that followed, atop the traditional values of the indigenous Semitic-speaking societies across the region, catalyzed the development of a cosmopolitan culture that defined the Hellenistic Age and laid the foundations for the development of Christianity and eventually of Islam.

ATHENS'S GOLDEN AGE

Despite their victory in 479 BCE, none of the Greeks believed they had seen the end of the Persian threat. Athens argued successfully for the creation of a military alliance among all the poleis, one dedicated to maintaining a strong defense and,

CHAPTER TIMELINE

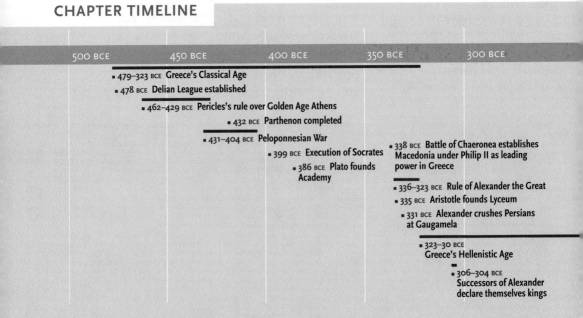

if possible, even pressing the offensive into Persian territory. The alliance was called the **Delian League**, named for the Aegean island of Delos where the group's treasury was kept. By 470 BCE, in other words, Greece was victorious, independent, organized, self-confident, and quickly amassing wealth. The Greeks could be forgiven if they felt a bit of pride. They could be forgiven, too, if they did not foresee that the next great conquests, following their downfall, were to come from peoples they knew as little more than barbarians. They could have noticed even earlier the return of the Jews, freed by the Persians, to Judea.

Golden ages seldom last long, and the Greek one was no different. They also are seldom as golden as people believe them to have been. The Greeks, especially the Athenians, came to regard the mid-5th century BCE with a determined awe, recalling it as a lost halcyon era that outshone anything that came before it or since. Through the centuries, much of Western culture has continued the love affair and has extolled "the glory that was Greece" as a pinnacle of human achievement. A more sober viewer can admire the brilliance of the time without overlooking its less praiseworthy elements.

Most of the great achievements of the age were connected in some fashion to Athens. That city, in the heady atmosphere of patriotic victory over Persia and its newfound prosperity, had ample material and spiritual resources to devote to education, urban development, artistic expression, and religious ritual. Moreover, Athenian ties to the Ionian cities grew closer with the creation of the Delian

250 BCE   200 BCE   150 BCE   100 BCE   50 BCE

■ 167–142 BCE **Maccabean Revolt**

■ 30 BCE
**Rome
completes
conquest of
Hellenistic
East**

League, which brought an injection of the vigorous intellectualism of the Near East into Athenian life. The stimulus was significant.

The greatest of the Athenian leaders, **Pericles** (495–429 BCE), lavished money on building temples, theaters, schools, and public meeting houses. He held the office of *strategos* ("general") from 462 to 429 BCE. This was an elected office with a one-year term, but the Athenian constitution placed no limit on the number of terms a strategos could serve; Pericles won reelection thirty-two times. Although he himself had a high aristocratic lineage, he had an ardent populist streak, as a result of which he broadened the scope of Athenian democracy to include all free-born (male) citizens. Poor Athenian free men, if they could afford the time away from their work, could attend the assembly and vote on legislation. Pericles made it easier for them to participate in civic life by offering to reimburse their lost day wages if they wished to attend the municipal council meeting.

Athens's gain was the rest of Greece's loss—because no other city had anything like the cultural flowering of Periclean Athens, many of the best architects, sculptors, playwrights, scholars, scientists, and poets across Greece rushed to partake of Pericles's patronage. But even with all its advantages, Golden Age Athens was possible only because Athens controlled the treasury of the whole Delian League and appropriated its funds.

Periclean Athens

The Parthenon   The chief temple of ancient Athens, dedicated to the city's patron goddess Athena, the Parthenon was built when the city was at the height of its power. The temple also doubled as the Athenian treasury.

THE POLIS: RITUAL AND RESTRAINT

Although prosperous, Greek life in the Classical Era was surprisingly modest. Most homes were comfortable but simple; no palaces were built, not even by those few who did achieve great wealth. Personal luxuries were spurned. Instead, prosperous Greeks spent their money on commercial investment, public building projects, and supporting arts and education. Temples, public halls, amphitheaters, baths, and athletic fields all benefited from private largess.

Each polis administered its major religious celebrations, which naturally differed from one another depending on the particular deities associated with each *Public* city. In Athens itself, the two most significant festivals were the Panathenaia, a *Religion* celebration held every May in honor of the goddess Athena, and the Great Dionysia, a festival honoring Dionysius. Religion was ritualistic, and it neither asserted a creed nor promoted an ethical code.[1] People presented offerings, performed their prayers, consulted their oracles (priests or priestesses through whom the gods spoke directly to people), and honored the gods in song. No uniformity of opinion existed regarding the afterlife, although the great majority of Greeks believed in Hades, a shadowy afterworld to which all who received funeral rites went, regardless of the morality or immorality of their earthly lives. Those who did not receive a proper funeral were thought to wander the world as ghosts.

The Panathenaia?   This scene was long thought to depict the preparations for the opening ceremony of the Panathenaia, the high point of which was the solemn procession of Athena's sacred robes to the Acropolis. Recent scholarship suggests a different interpretation, however, arguing that the scene illustrates the preparations for the sacrificial slaying of Chthonia, the daughter of an Archaic Age king named Erechtheus. An oracle demanded the sacrifice as the price for Athens's victory in a war against Eleusis.

---

[1]   The ancient Greek language had no word corresponding to the English word "belief" or "beliefs" in its religious sense.

Daily Life   The Greeks disdained the luxurious diets of the Persians, which they considered a sign of the Persians' supposed decadence, and most ate simple meals. In his *History of the Persian Wars*, Herodotus is bemused by Persian eating and drinking habits:

> The day they value most of all is a birthday; on one of those they think it right to set up a greater banquet than usual—for wealthier Persians will arrange to have an ox, horse, camel, or ass roasted whole and set out before them (the less well-to-do use smaller beasts). They eat only a little of their main course but an abundance of desserts; moreover, they never use salt. This is why the Persians say that we Greeks are still hungry when we finish eating, for there is nothing worth having after we finish our main course—but if some delicacies were given us, we would eat our fill. The Persians are very devoted to wine (but they never vomit or piss in front of one another). Such are their customs. They will get drunk even when discussing the most important matters. The following day the host of the house they are in will ask them—now that they are sober—to reconsider their decisions of the night before. If they are still so inclined, the matter is settled; if not, not. If it happens that they deliberate an issue when sober, they reconsider it later when they are drunk. (1.133)

For the Greeks, grains, olive oil, and wine formed the basis of all meals. Breakfast commonly consisted of barley bread dipped in wine. Lunch was usually a form of soup or stew (made chiefly of lentils, onions, and beans, since fresh vegetables were hard to come by in the cities), accompanied by cheese and honey. Dinner was eaten at nightfall and was the largest meal of the day. For most people this was the only meal at which meat was served. Pork was the cheapest meat, and each city had its own favorite preparation.[2] Fish was relatively rare inland; the coastal cities and the Aegean islanders had little success transporting it inland without spoiling. Men and women always ate separately; in a small house with limited dining area the men ate first, then the women, then the male servants, and finally the female servants. Most Greek houses did not have stone ovens; instead, women cooked by heaping red-hot coals on a flat stone and setting an inverted clay bowl over the pile. Once the stone was hot, they scraped away the coals, placed the food on the heated stone, covered it with the hot bowl, and surrounded the bowl with the coals again. Holding little regard for such artful food preparation, however, the Greeks tended to devalue the role that women played in it. Food was fuel, not pleasure.

---

2   The Spartans' signature dish was *melas zomos*, a dark, thick stew made of pork, vinegar, and pigs' blood. In Aristophanes's play *Peace* (1.374), a small piglet is said to cost three days' wages for a civil servant.

Drinking, however, was another matter. The Greeks developed the first vintage wines, and among the many civic officials in local government was the person responsible for affixing the municipal seal to wines for export. By reputation, the best wines came from three Aegean islands: Chios, Lesbos, and Thasos; the wine produced in Achaea, the mainland district surrounding Athens, was among the worst. Claudius Aelianus (d. 235 CE), a Roman historian who wrote in Greek, records that Achaean wine was reputed to induce miscarriages in pregnant women.

Wine was drunk throughout the day, always cut (diluted) with water. Drinking uncut wine was considered barbarous, as was the drinking of wine by women, except in Sparta, where moderate wine drinking was thought to increase a woman's fertility. Drinking to excess was also looked down upon, except at symposia, the all-male drinking parties where testing one's limits was the whole point—to drink as much as possible without getting drunk, as a sign of one's manliness.

Divine Wine   A 5th-century BCE drinking cup depicting the goddess Athena pouring wine for the famous hero Herakles.

Plato's dialogue *The Symposium* is the most famous depiction of one of these parties, although it is not characteristic. Few people can drink that much and still engage in such intelligent discussion. Still, some Greeks, like the philosopher Socrates, earned renown for their ability to imbibe.[3]

THE EXCLUDED: WOMEN, CHILDREN, AND SLAVES

Pericles's democratic reforms extended only to poor free men: Athenian women, children, and slaves remained without political rights, and women remained largely out of public view. Every polis had its own standards. Corinth, for instance, was renowned for the number, beauty, and prominence of its temple priestesses (hetairai) dedicated to the goddess Aphrodite. (According to the Roman poet Horace, they were also famously expensive to hire.) Women in the polis of Ephesus, on the Anatolian coast, enjoyed considerable liberality of social movement and economic rights; under the protection of the goddess Artemis, the polis produced several female artists of high repute. Women in Delphi, Megara, and Sparta were able to own land independently. Athens, it turns out, was unique (or nearly so) in the low value it placed on women. But certain customs were widely recognized. Every home had a specially designated "woman's zone" (*gynaeceum*), in which women passed the time with their children and servants. A woman never entered the public area of her house, where visitors might appear, without the permission of her husband. Children started their education at home, learning their letters and numbers and some music from their mothers. Boys usually began attending schools at age seven. These were private institutions that included rigorous physical education, since at age eighteen all boys began military service in the hoplite infantry.

Girls began another kind of service even earlier. From the time of her first menstruation a girl was considered marriageable; arranged marriages frequently happened as early as age fourteen, the idea being to take maximum advantage of her fertile years. "We have prostitutes for pleasure," wrote one Athenian, "concubines for company, and wives for producing heirs and maintaining the household." But even if few Greeks wedded for love, affectionate marriages certainly existed. Take two representative gravestone inscriptions:

> Here by this busy road lies Aspasia, a worthy wife now dead. Her husband Euopides put up this monument for her in memory of her good disposition; she was his consort. (Chios, 5th century BCE)

---

[3]   Socrates never went drink-for-drink against Milo of Croton, a 6th-century BCE Olympic athlete who reportedly ate twenty pounds of meat daily—which he washed down with two gallons of wine.

> The woman buried here cared neither for clothes nor money in her lifetime, but only for her husband and for maintaining an upright reputation. Dionysia, your husband Antiphilus inscribes your tomb in return for the youthful years you shared with him. (Athens, 4th century BCE)

From the time of her wedding, a woman all but disappeared into her husband's house, seldom going into public, and devoting her days to childrearing and weaving. Greek culture abhorred idleness, and since most households—even relatively poor ones—had slaves to do the bulk of domestic labor, married women traditionally kept busy at the loom.[4] A healthy wife might expect to have ten pregnancies in her lifetime, although it remains unclear how many miscarriages she might suffer or how many of her children might die in infancy.

Wives governed their households—watching over their children, planning menus, caring for household items—but slaves performed most of the domestic chores. Classical Greece lived off slave labor, but slave populations in the ancient

Penelope and Telemachus   While seated at her ever-present loom, Penelope and her son ponder the whereabouts of the long-absent Odysseus.

---

[4]   Odysseus's wife, Penelope, who spent twenty years at her loom while patiently waiting for her husband to return from his wanderings, was an iconic image.

world were not self-perpetuating. The conditions of their lives were so harsh that their mortality rates exceeded their birth rates. The Greeks thus constantly needed fresh supplies of slaves to continue their lives of democratic freedom. Apart from domestic work, most slaves were used in farm labor and menial shopwork. The least fortunate of the male slaves were put to work mining or as oarsmen in Greek ships; the least fortunate of the females were the forced sexual partners of their male owners.

Two groups of women formed important exceptions to these constraints. Rural women regularly appeared in the towns, where they sold their produce in open-air markets. And companies of priestesses were important figures in various religious rites and festivals—especially the women known as *maenads*, the ecstatic followers of the god Dionysius, whose cult figured large in the development of Greek tragedy.

THE INVENTION OF DRAMA

What epic and lyric poetry were to the Archaic Age, stage drama was to the Classical—its characteristic and most powerful expression. Theater was more than an art form; it was a public rite and a civic obligation. Athens led the way, although the other major cities soon staged tragedy festivals as well.

Tragedy

Tragedy was the most distinctive form of public theater. The first tragedies we know of were staged in the time of Cleisthenes in the 6th century BCE—indeed, it is possible that the development of tragedy was one of Cleisthenes's civic reforms discussed in chapter 4—but the genre possibly dates to even earlier. The earliest complete plays that have come down to us are seven dramas by Aeschylus (525–456 BCE), often described as the father of tragedy. Although tragedy's actual origins are uncertain, it likely began with the choral odes sung by crowds to Dionysius—the god of wine, of passionate feeling, of life force—at the spring festival held in his honor in Athens. A latecomer to the Greek pantheon, Dionysius was a potent but disruptive force, one who promised his followers a transformative experience, a sense of moving out of oneself (ecstasy—from Greek *ek stasis*, meaning "out of nonmovement").

This was an unnerving development. Greek religion had always been passionately adhered to without ever being essentially emotive. Gods and goddesses often had, and played, favorites among human beings. Athena's protection of Odysseus comes to mind, as does Hera's guardianship over women in childbirth. Yet they seldom felt or showed any actual emotion toward humans except for episodic wrath. People offered prayers and sacrifices to the Olympian deities, but the relationship between the faithful and the deities was more contractual than intimate. Wanting a good grain crop, they prayed to Demeter, who granted the wish or not depending on whether she liked their offerings. Wanting safe passage at sea, they prayed to Poseidon. The cult of Dionysius was different. People turned to him not for favors but for spiritual elation and passionate release. His most passionate followers were the maenads, women who wore animal skins and brandished torches while celebrating the god's power in dance and song. At the peak of their frenzy, groups of maenads would sometimes attack wild animals with their bare hands and tear them apart. At the climax of *The Bacchae* by Euripides (d. 406 BCE) a group of them claw and tear apart a man before eating his flesh.

The German philosopher Friedrich Nietzsche (1844–1900) famously attributed tragedy to the Greek world's efforts to rein in the raw emotional power of the Dionysian cult. By sublimating these choral celebrations into a carefully managed public theatrical rite, he argued, the leaders of Athens created tragedy, a genre that provides a cathartic release of elemental passions within a strictly controlled setting. Nietzsche got many details wrong in his analysis, but his *Birth of Tragedy out of the Spirit of Music* (originally published in 1872 and revised in 1886) remains one of the most stimulating books ever written about ancient Greece.

Certain norms governed the practice, one of the most important being that tragic playwrights were expected not to compose original stories but to draw from a store of well-established popular legends and folktales. Sophocles (ca. 496–406 BCE) was not the only playwright to write a tragedy about Oedipus; rather, his great work is simply the best-known version. To the Greeks, it simply

The Amphitheater at Delphi   Ancient Greek amphitheaters were very large, open-air structures that took advantage of hillsides for their terraced seating. This example dates to the 4th century and is set on the slopes of Mount Parnassus—sacred to the gods in Greek mythology—above the temple of Apollo at Delphi.

required more artistry to captivate an audience with a story they already knew than to rely on an original plot—the ancient stage equivalent of a computer-generated special effect in today's movies. One can be startled by such a thing, even impressed, but not emotionally moved. Euripides (ca. 485–406 BCE) was often criticized for his use of innovations—original or little-known stories, unexpected plot twists, surprise endings—although most people granted his brilliance with language and characterization. (Socrates reportedly once asserted that Euripides was the only playwright whose works were worth the walk to the theater.) Every major polis staged tragedies as a ritual of religious observance. Athens was the center of theatrical culture, with its annual festival called the Dionysia, for which playwrights submitted trilogies of new tragic plays, plus a burlesque piece called a satyr play and a comedy, usually political in nature. A civic council selected the most promising plays and produced them for the festival, at which attendance was required of all adult male citizens. At the end of the festival, the audience selected the best tragic trilogy of the year, and its author was granted awards and high honor.

Tragedy aimed to inspire both fear and empathy, which it accomplished by showing the relentless nature of fate and exploiting the paradox that people take pleasure in observing the suffering of others—a paradox made doubly ironic by the world's indifference to human pain. To the Greeks the cardinal sin was **hubris**—the excessive pride that leads people to think that they are in control of their own lives—because the hard reality is that our fates are fixed. Greek morality consisted of recognitions: of our obligations, our limitations, the futility of our aspirations, and our helplessness against the world's indifference. For the Greeks, we cannot alter what the world does to us, but we can control how we respond and adapt to our fates.

In the tales of the Theban ruler Oedipus, for example, the hero believes he has escaped the fate decreed for him at birth—namely, that he would kill his father and marry his mother. Then he discovers that he has done precisely that. Horrified by the revelation, he blinds himself and spends the rest of his life as a wandering beggar. In *Oedipus at Colonnus* the playwright Sophocles has the chorus sing a sorrowful ode as the blind beggar sits in despair:

> What foolishness it is to desire more life, after one has tasted
> A bit of it and seen the world; for each day, after each endless day,
> Piles up ever more misery into a mound. As for pleasures: once we
> Have passed youth they vanish away, never again to be seen.
>
> Death is the end of all.
> Never to be born is the best thing. To have seen the daylight
> And be swept instantly back into dark oblivion comes second. *(lines 1211–1238)*

Such misery is not a matter of life being fair or unfair; life is simply life, and we ought not to resist or bemoan it. "Let weeping cease, then," sings the chorus in *Oedipus at Colonnus*'s last lines, "and let there be no mourning. These things are in the hands of the gods." Happiness in life is possible, but it is not a birthright. A gloomy outlook, but a necessary one, to the Greeks: only by facing this hard reality can we truly have courage, and only thus can we accept both the good that happens and the evil that comes to us. Tragedy humbles us and reminds us to be thankful for small blessings.

Comedy, on the other hand, indulged not only the desire for merriment but also the urge to make fun of someone. We know of comic playwrights from many poleis, but the overwhelming number of surviving plays and fragments come from Athens. The earliest comedy writers, like Aristophanes (ca. 446–386 BCE), emphasized political satire. Eleven plays of his survive (of thirty that we know of), most of which skewer Athens's leading politicians, generals, and social leaders. Poets, playwrights, and philosophers receive their share of ridicule too. Much of the humor is coarse. In *The Acharnians*, for example, Aristophanes makes fun of two poets he disliked by staging a scene in which they both appear on a dark street one night. The first fellow, fearing that he is going to be mugged by an attacker, defends himself by hurling a rock—but he misses his attacker and hits the other poet in the face, and it turns out that what he threw was not a rock but a large turd. *Comedy*

Aristophanes's most famous play is perhaps *Lysistrata*, which is a bitingly satirical piece about the conduct of the Peloponnesian War. The title character stages her own form of protest against the never-ending war by persuading the Athenian women (wives and hetairai) to join in a sexual boycott until the men come to their senses and negotiate an end to the conflict. The play abounds in rapid-fire, crisp dialogue and clever sexual puns. It also includes crude but funny set-pieces that portray the increasingly frustrated men as they stagger across the stage, groaning with gigantic prosthetic erections and begging their wives to come back to bed.

Comedy after Aristophanes became somewhat tamer, in that it aimed its barbs less at specific real individuals and more at generic personality types—the braggart soldier, the clever servant, the shrewish wife, the coquettish maid. Few of these plays survive, and we owe most of what we know of them to later Greek writers who made reference to them.

THE PELOPONNESIAN DISASTER

A war with Sparta ended Athens's Golden Age. Lasting longer than any previous war in Greek history, this twenty-seven-year conflict is called the **Peloponnesian War** (431–404 BCE) because it matched Sparta's Peloponnese-based alliance against Athens and the Delian League. The result would leave Greece in ruins.

Trying to make sense of the war, in turn, would inspire new Athenian contributions to history, medicine, mathematics, and philosophy. Like the figures in the great tragedies for which they were famous, the Athenians brought their misfortune on themselves—and indeed on all of Greece—by their hubris. The most famed democracy of the ancient world turned itself into a grasping despotism and in effect willed its own demise. In the contest between values and greed, values lost.

Origins of the War

Athens had learned neither humility nor gratitude after the Persian Wars. Heady with pride and headstrong with determination to retain leadership in Greece, the Athenians spent most of the 5th century BCE bullying the city-states they had helped to defend against Darius and Xerxes. At first, no one dared to question them. When the Athenians began to withdraw funds from the Delian treasury to build up and beautify their own city, only Sparta (and its closest ally, Corinth) complained about Athenian hypocrisy. Through the 470s and 460s BCE, however, several cities grumbled openly about Athens treating them like colonies—to which Athens responded by attacking and colonizing them outright (see Map 5.1).

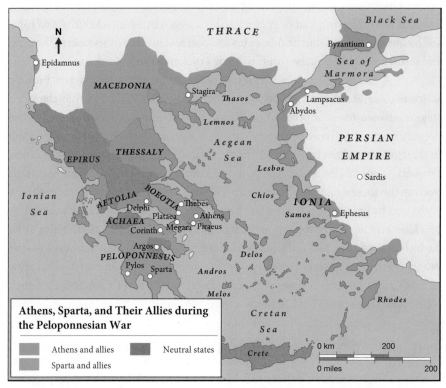

MAP 5.1   Athens, Sparta, and Their Allies during the Peloponnesian War   It took some time for the alliances to take shape, and many diplomatic shifts and adjustments occurred during the two decades before the start of the war in 431 BCE. Directly or indirectly, the war affected every polis in Greece.

Athenian garrisons were established across Greece, and corps of Athenian officials were set in charge of polis after polis. If they ever questioned their entitlement to an empire, no evidence of it survives. By 440 BCE Pericles had established a peace treaty with Persia so that he could set his sights on Sparta and Corinth, the last barriers to Athenian control of all of Greece. After several more years of provocations and last-minute resolutions, open war between Athens and Sparta erupted in 431 BCE.

Sparta's hoplite army was superior to that of Athens, but the Athenian navy ruled the sea. There were surprisingly few pitched battles in the first years of the war; instead, the Spartans laid a protracted siege of Athens by land, while the Athenian ships established a blockade that kept food and goods from reaching Sparta by sea. The stalemate favored Athens until an epidemic of typhus struck the city in 429 BCE and killed roughly one-third of the population, including the aged Pericles. *Course of the War*

Military command in Athens was henceforth contested by a series of ambitious figures, none of whom was more devious and brilliant than Alcibiades (ca. 450–404 BCE), one of the last members of an ancient aristocratic family. In a game of brinksmanship with a political rival, Alcibiades urged Athens to send an army to Sicily to help a colony that had requested aid against a local rival of its own. This campaign, known as the Sicilian Expedition (415 BCE), turned out to be a military disaster for Athens, which prompted Alcibiades to flee the city and join Sparta. For three years he led Sparta's forces effectively against his old polis, turning the tide of the war, until rumors that he had an affair with another Spartan leader's wife forced him to flee again (412 BCE)—this time to Persian-controlled Anatolia. According to Thucydides, Alcibiades advised the Persians to focus their efforts on weakening both Athens and Sparta, rather than aiming at one or the other. Sound advice, but Thucydides goes on to insist that Alcibiades was actually using his influence at the Persian court to plot his own return to Athens's good graces, which he achieved the following year—although he took care not to press his luck by entering the city and wisely joined Athenian troops stationed afield instead.

Meanwhile the Spartans struck a deal with the Persians, who agreed to provide them with a fleet of their own triremes. The Spartans themselves knew little of sailing, but there were enough enemies of Athens around by now to fit out a navy. In 411 BCE Alcibiades led an Athenian naval force to two quick victories over the Spartans. At this point, Athens seemed poised to bring the war to a successful conclusion, but the Persians, irked by Alcibiades's connivances, replenished Sparta with money, men, and ships, and by 407 BCE the new naval force challenged Athenian invincibility, which effectively assured a Spartan victory. In 404 BCE the Spartan army entered Athens itself, and the war was over. Alcibiades fled once more to Anatolia, hoping to persuade the Persians to equip him with an army he could use to drive the Spartans out—but he was quickly murdered under circumstances that are not entirely clear.

With the long Greek catastrophe finally over, Corinth and Thebes both demanded that the Spartans level the city of Athens and enslave its entire population. But the Spartans demurred. Instead, they pulled down Athens's fortifications, scuttled its fleet, installed a committee of thirty antidemocratic Athenians—the Thirty Tyrants—to govern the defeated city, and, ever concerned about another helot uprising, returned to Sparta as fast as they could. In their brief time in power (eight months over 404–403 BCE), the Thirty Tyrants reportedly exiled or killed more than fifteen hundred Athenians whom they deemed political enemies and confiscated their money and property. Outraged at the Tyrants' violence and greed, citizens who wanted to restore democracy banded together to regain control of Athens, which they accomplished with the help of the Spartan leader Pausanias (d. 395 BCE). (Sparta's clemency arose from the conviction that despite the sorrows caused by Athenian hubris, the city's democratic principles should be restored in honor of Athens's role in winning the Persian Wars.) The democratic rebels defeated the forces of the Thirty Tyrants in a series of bloody street fights.

Consequences of the War   Athens never recovered from its defeat, however, nor did Greece from the general ruin. A pallid democracy was restored in 401 BCE, but with its imperial revenues lost and most of its territories scorched, the Athenian economy remained constricted. Sparta shied away from playing any larger role in Greek affairs and focused on suppressing any helots who may have been encouraged by the disaster to attempt rebellion. This made Greece a tempting target for a resurgent Persia, which soon began to ponder another invasion. As it happened, someone else beat them to the punch.

Catastrophes can have beneficial effects. By their very completeness, catastrophes inspire a willingness to rethink old assumptions. The collapse of Greece in the Peloponnesian War led a number of brave individuals to make deep and serious inquiries into the nature of politics, the weakness of human will, the causes of greed, the quest for justice, and the desire to believe that the world makes sense. These issues had long been essential concerns of Greek cultural and intellectual life but had been examined and explored more in artistic genres such as poetry and tragedy. The intellectual life of post–Peloponnesian War Greece had a more analytical and scientific quality.

ADVANCES IN HISTORICAL INQUIRY

Herodotus (ca. 484–425 BCE), we saw earlier, had given an exciting new direction to this inquiry when he all but invented historical writing with his *History of the Persian Wars.* Previous historical writing—with the partial exception of the historical books in the Hebrew Bible—had consisted largely of propagandistic narratives, lists of deeds, blowhard memorials, and the occasional funerary inscription. Herodotus was the first to gather information firsthand, to organize it systematically, and to present it critically. His successor Thucydides (ca. 460–395 BCE) extended Herodotus's methods and created something entirely original.

Thucydides's *History of the Peloponnesian War* is an astonishing achievement in many ways. Recognizing, as he writes in the book's stately preface, that "the war, when it began, would be great and important beyond any previous war," Thucydides dedicates himself to following it in detail. Before writing, he conducted interviews, reviewed documents, and checked contradictory accounts, paying attention to technological and logistical details with the thoroughness of a general preparing for battle. For Thucydides, the Peloponnesian War was the first ideological war in Western history—a conflict not merely between political states but between states of being. Athenian greed and hubris, and Spartan envy and suspicion, tell only part of the tale. Thucydides digs deeper and presents both sides as acting out of different conceptions of freedom.

Thucydides

Freedom, of course, is a relative quality; one defines it in terms of what one is free *from*. To militaristic Sparta, freedom meant freedom from chaos and unpredictability; to hyperambitious Athens it meant freedom from restraint in the pursuit of its desires and perceived rights. Thucydides sees a measure of truth in each point of view but is too committed to political realism to cast his vote entirely for one side or the other. In fact, the casting of votes is itself something Thucydides believes little in. Rather, he identifies as Athens's greatest weakness not its selfishness and hypocrisy but its commitment to democracy. Thucydides argues that democracy, despite its theoretical appeal, is doomed to fail because it is based on a lie—namely, the notion of human equality. To drive his point home, Thucydides composes a handful of brilliant set-pieces, either wholly fictitious events or highly imaginative reconstructions of speeches, dialogues, and debates. One of the best known is "Pericles's Funeral Oration" of 429 BCE, which Pericles delivered at Athens's annual public funeral for their war dead. He opens with praise for the city's forefathers:

> It is a good and proper thing, as we gather to lament those who have died, to begin by speaking of our ancestors and paying tribute to their memory. They inhabited this land from time immemorial, and as a result of their valor it has been handed from generation to generation, to this present day, leaving us the possessors of a free state. But as deserving of praise as those ancestors are, how much more so our own fathers whose

struggles added so greatly to this inheritance, leaving us, their sons, in possession of a great empire!

Then Pericles moves on to praise the glories of Athens's government:

> Our form of government is without parallel or peer in the institutions of others. We do not copy our neighbors but serve as an example to them. We are a democracy, it is true, since the power to govern is in the hands of the many rather than of the few; but while we maintain equal justice for all in private matters, we recognize the claims of excellence. When one of our citizens distinguishes himself in some way, we raise him to public service—not as a matter of privilege but as a reward for his merit. Poverty is no obstacle; any man, no matter how obscure his condition, can render his polis good service.

After praising Athenian cultural attainment, military might, and hospitality, Pericles sums up by declaring:

> Athens is the school of all Greece, and every Athenian, it seems to me, is alone equal to any challenge in any sphere of action, so happily versatile is he. This is no simple boast, thrown out for this special occasion. It is simple fact, as proven by the power of the great society created by those abilities. . . . These men whom we commemorate today died in a manner fitting for Athenians. We, their descendants, must resolve to be as steadfast in the field as they were. . . . Heroes have the whole earth for a tomb. Even in far-distant lands where columns bear inscriptions [of their deeds], there lives enshrined in every heart a record that needs no epitaph to preserve it. So let us take these heroes as our models, and, knowing that happiness comes from freedom and that freedom comes from valor, let us never shrink from the dangers of war.

Thucydides's history breaks off suddenly, in Book 8, with the battle of Cynossema in 411 BCE, a minor victory for Athens over the new Spartan naval force, leaving the last seven years of the war untreated. The work is clearly unfinished, although historians disagree about why the book was never completed. (Fortunately, the last years of the war are fully detailed in the *Hellenica* of Xenophon, a later Athenian historian, ca. 430–356 BCE.) It seems certain that a ninth book was intended, to reflect the nine-book structure of Herodotus's *Persian Wars*, but Thucydides completed enough of his masterpiece to leave the Greek tragedy dissected and exposed with unmatched and gimlet-eyed skill.

MEDICINE AS NATURAL LAW

Just as Thucydides gave clear-eyed diagnoses of Greek political decline, Hippocrates of Kos (ca. 460–370 BCE) divorced illness and disease from superstitions and religious beliefs. In the process, he made human suffering—or, at least, one type of human suffering—a feature of the natural world. His separation of physical health from religious issues also makes him the founder of Western medicine.

Earlier traditions, as in Egypt and Babylon, had built up an understanding of how to treat various maladies, but knowledge of how the body works, how *Hippocrates* diseases function, and why any given remedy works (or does not) remained mysteries. Such things were attributed to astral influences, spells cast by demons, and the whims of the gods. Hippocrates was the first to study medicine systematically to work out the processes by which various herbs and treatments produced their effects. He and his successors compiled the *Hippocratic Corpus*, seventy volumes that discuss maladies (such as epilepsy, the "sacred disease") as natural phenomena rather than divine curses. He was the first to categorize diseases and therefore to produce a preliminary sketch of a natural structure. Acute, chronic, endemic, and epidemic were the first categories, followed by subcategories according to organs and bodily systems.

One of the best-known parts of the *Hippocratic Corpus* is the oath to be sworn by all physicians, marking the official start of their careers. The original form of the **Hippocratic oath** goes as follows:

> I swear by Apollo, Asclepius, Hygeia, and Panacea, and do bear witness before all gods and goddesses that I will remain true to the following oath, to the best of my ability and judgment:
>
> that I will hold as dear to me as my own parents the man who taught me this art [of medicine], will live with him, and if necessary will share my possessions with him;
>
> that I will regard his children as my own brothers, and will teach them this same art;
> that I will prescribe health regimens for the good of my patients to the very best of my ability and will never intentionally do harm to anyone; . . .

that I will preserve the purity of my life and my practice; . . .

and that I will always preserve the confidentiality of anything I learn about my patients and their households in the practice of my profession, not permitting anything to be spread about.

To the extent that I faithfully keep this oath, may I live my life and practice my art enjoying always the respect of all men; but if I fail to do so, and if I violate this oath, may the opposite be the case.

The Hippocratic oath has been modified numerous times, but it remains a rite of passage for most practitioners of medicine in the Greater West.

The significance of Hippocrates's work lay not only in its contributions to medical science. He also regarded human beings as part of the natural landscape—capable of, and responsive to, rational analysis. He severed medicine from religion and allied it with philosophy.

THE FLOWERING OF GREEK PHILOSOPHY

Philosophy was the area of the Greeks' greatest and most enduring achievement. Much had happened in this field since the Milesians discussed in chapter 4.

The Pythagoreans

A group of philosophers known as the **Pythagoreans**—named after their founder, the Ionian Greek thinker and mathematician Pythagoras (570–495 BCE)—had directed philosophy away from the early Milesian focus on primal essences. The Pythagoreans sought instead to identify the rational ordering of those essences, the laws that governed their interaction; hence their focus on mathematics. Heraclitus of Ephesus (mid-5th century BCE), for example, tried to explain the world's obvious diversity and changeability as a rational patterning and repatterning of opposing forces (hot/cold, light/dark, wet/dry, etc.). If closely observed, even the infinite progressions of a child's kaleidoscope follow a rational pattern. Hence such conclusions as: "We step and yet we do not step into the same river twice; we are and we are not." "A road goes uphill and downhill at once—it is the same road." "No god or man made the world. It is the same for all, always was, is, and will be, an eternal fire eternally kindled and extinguished in equal measures."

Zeno of Elea (ca. 490–420 BCE) introduced a number of mathematical paradoxes that seem to presage Einstein's theories about time–space continuums. Imagine, for example, that an archer unleashes an arrow at a target. In any one instant of time, the arrow is moving neither to where it is nor to where it is not. It cannot move to where it is not because no time elapses for it to move there; it cannot move to where it was because it is already there. In other words, at every instant of time there is no motion occurring. If everything is motionless at every instant and time is composed of instants, then motion is impossible. Another Pythagorean, Empedocles of Acragas (ca. 490–430 BCE), undercut Heraclitus's argument about the interplay of opposing forces. Empedocles observed that such coming into existence and passing from existence of new substances makes no sense, since it would necessarily mean the coming into existence and passing from existence of nonexistence itself. Instead, Empedocles posited not one all-encompassing element of nature but four: fire, air, earth, and water. This theory of the four elements would become standard philosophical thought for the next two thousand years.

A second group of thinkers called the **Sophists** also had their day. Few of their names have come down to us, but in any case the Sophists specialized in *The Sophists* packaging ideas rather than in producing anything original. Their emphasis lay in rhetorical skill rather than in genuine investigation: in the bustling economic scene of classical Athens, they aimed to help enterprising people to prosper. The Sophists' closest modern-day analog would be the motivational speakers, investment gurus, and leadership coaches of cable-television specials and expensive weekend seminars. They traveled from city to city, offering paid instruction in everything from public speaking and career guidance to introductory surveys of exciting "useful knowledge" from around the world. These activities are easily mocked as derivative and shallow, and the Sophists have come in for more than their fair share of criticism over the centuries. (Indeed, the modern meaning of "sophistry" is plausible but deceptive argumentation.)

In the wake of the Peloponnesian War arose a trio of the most influential and impressive philosophers in history, whose lives, written works, and the schools they established changed Western intellectual culture forever. These three individuals—Socrates (469–399 BCE), Plato (ca. 427–347 BCE), and Aristotle (384–322 BCE)—permanently altered the direction and scope of philosophy. For the subsequent fifteen hundred years, Western science, religion, and politics, as well as philosophy itself, followed the intellectual trajectories they established.

Socrates, who left no writing of his own, is the most enigmatic of the three. At *Socrates* least partially trained in the Sophist tradition, he pulled philosophical inspection *and the* away from the theoretical model making of the Milesians and Pythagoreans and *Meaningful* insisted that it pursue questions that actually matter to any thinking individual *Life* who wants to live meaningfully. Geometrical schema are fine, Socrates felt—but what good are they for answering questions like What is the right way to live?, How can one know anything for certain?, What is love?, or What is justice? Socrates's signal achievement was to make philosophy a practical urgency—"to pull philosophy back down from the sky," as the 1st-century BCE Roman writer Cicero put it. Ethics and politics (by which he meant communal ethics), not cosmology and natural science, should be the essential concerns of philosophical inquiry, he insisted, or else why bother?

Reputedly the ugliest but most charming man in Athens, he married a woman named Xanthippe, had a family, worked as a stonemason, fought in the Athenian army, and participated in municipal government. At the age of seventy he was arrested on charges of impiety and corrupting the youth of the city; after an eventful trial he was convicted and sentenced to death by poison—a fate he reportedly accepted with calmness and grace. The charges against him may well have been politically motivated, or at least partly so. Like Thucydides, Socrates criticized democracy as an irrational political system based on the mistaken concept of human equality, and he had close friends among leading antidemocratic figures in Athens. The charge of impiety rested on his claim to be inspired by a "divine spirit" (*daimonion*). The corruption charge asserted that he intentionally urged his pupils to question the values handed to them by society.

Socrates founded no formal school but inspired so many later thinkers that he may be the single most influential figure in Greater Western philosophy. Certainly he set the terms of debate, for from his own time until the 19th century ethics and politics remained the central topics of inquiry. Only with the work of Karl Marx and Georg Friedrich Hegel—both mid-19th-century writers—did

The Death of Socrates   Jacques-Louis David (1748–1825) was the chief proponent of French classicism. This 1787 painting shows Socrates—arguing to the very end—as he prepares to drink a cup of poison while his friends and disciples mourn. The seated figure with his hand on Socrates's knee is Plato.

philosophy turn from these concerns toward the kind of philosophy dominant today. They helped make philosophy the study of the systems (economic, ideological, and linguistic) that restrain, shape, and perhaps control our thinking and lives.

Almost all that we know of Socrates's life and thought comes from four sources: the dialogues of his greatest pupil, Plato; the essays of another pupil, the historian Xenophon mentioned earlier; a few scraps of commentary by Aristotle (Plato's student); and a hilarious caricature of him in Aristophanes's comedy *The Clouds*. Together, they present a coherent although not conclusive portrait of the man whose misfortune was to reach his greatest fame when a sore and humiliated Athens was least inclined to tolerate criticism of its democratic greatness.

Socrates is associated more with a method than with a set of ideas. The **Socratic method** consisted of patient and thorough questioning, rather than the assertion of observations or deductions. A consistent pattern emerges in all his appearances in his pupil's dialogues. When asked, for example, to describe the best political system, he begins by asking what we mean by Justice—the quality that all political life aims to supply. Only by understanding the terms we use, Socrates insists, can we begin a proper inquiry. Nothing can be assumed if we wish to seek true understanding. Usually his interlocutors, turned in every direction by his clever questioning, end up admitting that they have no idea how to define anything, and Socrates declares that true philosophical inquiry can therefore at last begin. What the prosecutors at his trial failed to grasp was that Socrates did not doubt that Justice (or Love, or Being, or Truth, or Goodness) exists. He was merely willing to entertain such a doubt as a stimulus to thinking about it.

Despite his charisma and brilliance, or perhaps because of them, he was a terribly annoying man. Think of a conversational bully who delightedly dismantles the ideas of others but never fully offers ideas of his own to replace them. In *The Republic*, Plato's longest and most intricate dialogue, Plato presents Socrates tearing to shreds the ideas of four different characters regarding the nature of Justice. Then, when asked to offer his own definition, Socrates spends the next six books of the dialogue discussing the ideal form of government—but without ever offering his own convincing definition of what Justice actually is. In the end he wins by exhausting his opponents, not by defeating them. Nevertheless, Socrates set philosophy on a new course, one pursued avidly by his most brilliant student, Plato.

Plato came from a wealthy, aristocratic family. Brothers, half-brothers, and cousins populate many of his dialogues—presumably an indication of his pride in his kin. He received an excellent education in mathematics, music, literature, gymnastics, and philosophy, all of which are discussed and cited extensively in his writings. He seems, unlike his teacher, never to have had a profession apart

Plato and Ideal Forms

from teaching in the **Academy**, the school he founded when he reached the age of forty. As the Peloponnesian War drew to its close, he thought of taking an active role in politics, but he was enraged at the ham-fisted rule of the Thirty Tyrants. When the restored but nearly impotent democracy sentenced Socrates to death, Plato all but washed his hands of active public life. He took refuge at Megara for a while and traveled to Sicily and southern Italy. Returning to Athens around 385 BCE, he established the Academy, took on pupils, and began to lecture and compose his dialogues.

The period from 385 to 360 BCE were the years of his greatest productivity and originality. He peopled his dialogues with artists, politicians, poets, Sophists, and orators from the Athenian scene. References to poets and playwrights, often

Plato's Academy   This Roman mosaic from Pompeii (ca. 100 BCE) imagines a scene at Plato's Academy. A half-dozen philosophers, including Socrates (shown rubbing his chin), gather around Plato. Unlike his student Aristotle, who famously paced constantly while lecturing, Plato, a high aristocrat, enjoyed his leisure. Here he rests against a tree while examining a scroll.

including quotations, appear in almost every dialogue, as do many of the writers themselves. In the last dozen years of his life, 360–347 BCE, perhaps tiring after long labor, he began to outline and dictate in rough form his dialogues to his students, who then fleshed them out in a more turgid, "academic" style. The extraordinary literary polish of the middle years gradually disappeared, although his mind remained as sharp as ever. He became increasingly conservative as he aged, however, and by the time he wrote *The Laws*, one of his last works, he was deeply embittered by the world's foolishness.

Most of Plato's dialogues repeat a pattern. Socrates encounters a group somewhere in or near Athens and joins their conversation. It might be at an evening entertainment, along a road to a temple, sitting in a town square, or chatting in a portico. Picking up on an apparently offhand comment by one of the group, Socrates begins to probe his fellows' attitudes, language, convictions, and assumptions until they admit hopeless befuddlement and beg Socrates to set them aright. Socrates sometimes obliges but just as often demurs: the dialogue functions not as a means to a dogmatic conclusion but as an invitation to the reader to continue the discussion. Plato's earliest dialogues, most historians agree, present a historically accurate portrait of Socrates's own philosophy. As the years went on, however, he increasingly used Socrates as a literary device, a mouthpiece for his own ideas.

Plato begins with an observation: the world we observe with our senses is pale and imperfect—defective, jumbled, and filled with apparent contradictions. And yet we intuit order within it. We see parts of things; we intuit whole things. We observe, for example, two chairs. They may vary widely in size, shape, color, and material, and yet we know that they are both indeed chairs. They possess some quality, an ineffable "chairness," that determines their identity. Plato's philosophy argues that "chairness" really and truly exists; it is an example of what he terms the **Ideal Forms**. Where does it exist? Perhaps in a parallel universe or as an idea in the mind of God. Who can say? The point is that it does exist and that everything we perceive as a chair possesses it. Thus to Plato our world should be thought of as a pallid reflection of the world of Ideal Forms, a corrupt descendant filled with flawed and partial representations of the Forms. Plato's dialogues can be thought of as a series of discussions, each about a particular abstract Form—Love, Beauty, Goodness, Art, or Justice—because we can only understand our world in relation to the Forms it so imperfectly represents.

Plato insists that we can in fact understand the Ideal Forms because of the dual nature of human beings: we are not merely animated flesh but eternal souls temporarily housed in physical bodies. Each soul carries deep within itself an instinctive knowledge of the Ideal Forms, a memory of ultimate reality as yet lacking a clear shape. That is why we feel we know what chairness is, although we struggle to express it in words. Plato's philosophy is essentially romantic and mystical. It yearns for and aspires to an ineluctable perfect state of existence that seems as though it should be within our grasp. If only we can keep talking, if only we can remain willing to strip away untested assumptions, if only we can help one another along the way, we will eventually attain the true meaning of the Ideal Forms that constitute ultimate reality.

No other writer comes close to Plato's skill at portraying philosophy as a kind of pilgrimage, a journey toward a salvation that can be attained only with other people. There are no solitary revelers in Plato's world. Each of his dialogues ends differently, in terms of whether a true understanding of any particular Form is attained. Yet they all end with a warm feeling of community, of something special having been shared. It is the process of philosophy as much as the ideas attained by it that Plato portrays so lovingly and unforgettably.

Aristotle and the Pursuit of Happiness

Aristotle was Plato's most distinguished pupil and has a good claim to be among the most influential thinkers in Greater Western history. A tireless worker, he threw himself into the study of everything from ethics and metaphysics to botany and poetics. Ancient sources credit him with as many as two hundred separate treatises, some of great length. Roughly thirty treatises survive, perhaps more and perhaps fewer, depending on the debated authenticity of a handful of texts.

Two 4th-Century BCE Busts Portraying Plato and Aristotle   By tradition, Aristotle is always shown with a shorter beard than his teacher's.

Despite their unflagging brilliance, however, most of the texts consist not of Aristotle's own writing but of lecture notes later collated and stitched together (according to tradition by his son, Nicomachus). If his lectures were in fact like these composite transcripts, Aristotle was a remarkable but dull teacher. The contrast with Plato's dialogues could hardly be any stronger. Plato was an artist of the highest order; his dialogues have polish, wit, sharp characterization, and narrative drive. They manage the neat trick of expressing complex ideas with such clarity that anyone can grasp them. Aristotle, by contrast, comes across as an astonishing but long-winded teacher struggling to convey an enormous, unwieldy body of knowledge.

The ideas that come through are vital, however, although his range makes it difficult to present them in a systematic way. The key to Aristotle lies in his method: unlike his teacher (but much like his own father, a physician), Aristotle begins not with the theoretical examination of the Ideal Forms but with intense scrutiny of the tangible natural world. He accepts the notion of the Ideal Forms, or claims to, but he believes that their essential elements appear physically within each object. Existence consists of the continual interplay of Ideal Form and earthly matter—rather like the way our genetic coding continues to affect our physical development throughout our lives. Aristotle, then, offers a compromise between Plato's idealism and the rough materialism of the Milesians.

Moreover, Aristotle asserts that the continuous nature of the interplay of forces drives the universe forward toward a goal. Everything is in a state of becoming. A seed is on its way to becoming a seedling, then a plant in full flower, then a withering husk, then a decayed nutrient for another seed. Each existing thing, whether animate or not, plays a role in the unstoppable push forward to new life. Since we ourselves are part of this impetus of birth, life, and decay, we can take solace in knowing that our existence is ennobled with purpose. Every existing thing, he says, has a **telos**—an intrinsic purpose, a necessary role in the cosmic drama. The telos of an animal embryo is to become that animal; that of teeth is to chew food. For Plato, the physical world is a flaw and a hindrance to our understanding. Aristotle instead sees the world as a process—a march forward into ever new being (and hopefully, but not necessarily, ever better being).

But do human beings have a telos? If so, is it a general telos applicable to the whole species, or is it unique to each nation or even each individual? Aristotle wrestled with these questions over and over. If human life is teleological, is that not the same as saying it is fated or even predetermined? Are we in control of our own destinies, and if not, then what sound basis can there be for morality? Aristotle's answer is characteristically complex. He begins with the observation that ethics is a practical science, not a theoretical one. The point of it is to learn how to act and live a well-ordered life, not to gain some abstract knowledge about the nature of goodness for its own sake.

Most people, he says, would agree on most ethical propositions: that happiness is better than sadness, that pleasure is preferable to pain, that courage is superior to fearfulness. We all might disagree on specifics regarding those virtues; some of us, for example, might take greater pleasure in being renowned for beauty than for intelligence. What interests Aristotle is the relationship between ethical values. Is courage of greater or lesser value than loyalty? Is it more important to be temperate in one's desires or to be well liked? Whatever their relative standings, he insists that happiness (*eudaimonia* in Greek—meaning "being in accordance with the spirits," literally, or "living well," colloquially) is the supreme virtue, toward which all other virtues point. To Aristotle happiness must entail something intrinsic to human beings as a species. This something that we possess or experience that no other creatures can, he says, is our capacity for rational thought. If we follow the use of reason, if we cultivate it as a means of life, we can and will attain happiness. Whether we are happy has little to do with the contingency of world events and is the product of our own choices—choices in our actions and in how we react to the world. In this way, individual free will is preserved, as is the notion of a human telos. In other words, our telos is to pursue happiness, but whether we achieve it, or the way in which we achieve it, is up to us.

Plato and Aristotle were both interested in politics, although only at a distance. Two of Plato's dialogues—*The Republic* and *The Laws*—describe a vision of an ideal society, one in which an oligarchy of highly educated guardians or a monarchy led by an enlightened philosopher-king would oversee the day-to-day governance of society. Most people are neither capable of nor interested in governing their own affairs and are happy to leave the work of running the world to their superiors. This ideal system is clearly a response to the failures of Athenian democracy. But whether Plato himself believed in it is unlikely, because such a system assumes that properly educated rulers will never be corrupted by power, an assumption that cannot be made of the imperfect world in which we live.

Like Plato, Aristotle thought that democracy was a bad system because it did not restrict decision making to the most educated citizens. Unlike his great teacher, however, Aristotle believed in the implementation of good government—even to the point of writing constitutions for various poleis—although he had no direct involvement in political life that we know of. After Plato's death around 347 BCE, Aristotle left Greece altogether and lived in Asia Minor for four years. In 343 BCE King Philip II of Macedonia (r. 359–336 BCE) invited Aristotle to come to Pella, the capital of Macedonia, and tutor his teenage son. Aristotle took the job, in a kingdom to the north of Greece inhabited by a tribe who spoke a language of disputed relation to Greek. There he spent eight years teaching the lad, and then in 335 BCE he returned to Athens and established his own school, the **Lyceum**, where he spent the rest of his life teaching his empirically based, life-guiding philosophy.

The lad he tutored in Pella most definitely took an interest in politics. His name was Alexander.

THE RISE OF MACEDONIA AND THE CONQUESTS OF ALEXANDER THE GREAT

In its bloody, insurrection-filled past, Macedonia also had suffered in the invasions by Darius and Xerxes. The Greeks themselves regarded the Macedonians as barbarians—or at the very best as poor backward cousins. Whereas Greece prospered during the Periclean age, Macedonia remained ignored and reviled. But the self-destruction of Greece during the Peloponnesian War gave Philip II (r. 359–336 BCE), and then his son, dreams of glory.

Alexander the Great (r. 336–323 BCE) was the greatest conqueror of the ancient world. He took over from his father, Philip II, rule of a semi-Hellenized *Macedonian* kingdom when Philip was assassinated in 336 BCE. Philip had been an ambitious *Power* commander and seems to have had designs on conquering Greece from early on; he also pushed northward into the central Balkans. The strength of the Macedonian forces owed much to the extensive gold mines discovered in the Pangaion Hills in the southern Balkans, which enabled Philip and Alexander to raise, train, and equip an exceptionally effective army. In 347 BCE, when he was ready to make his attempt on Greece, Philip reportedly sent a herald to Sparta with a warning: "If I win this war, you will be my slaves forever." According to the legend, the Spartans sent back a terse one-word reply: "If." Philip never made it to Sparta or Athens, but he did advance as far as Thebes and Corinth before being murdered by one of his bodyguards (whose motives remain unclear).

By 334 BCE, two years after Philip's death, Alexander was firmly in control of all of Greece and had already determined to advance eastward against the Persian Empire. And that was just the start.

When Alexander succeeded to the Macedonian throne in 336 BCE, Greece could not stand in the way of his territorial ambitions, since all the poleis were in *The Rule of* such weak condition. In turning his sights to Persia, Alexander's thinking was *Alexander* sound. The conflict between Greece and Persia had never been settled definitively. Internal discord and political strife had followed the defeat of Xerxes's forces in 479 BCE, but by the time of the Peloponnesian conflict Persia was already trying to manipulate the outcome in Greece to prepare the way for another attempt. Alexander simply recognized, correctly, that Greece would never be free of the

Alexander the Great   This detail from a large floor mosaic in Pompeii depicts Alexander at the battle of Issus (333 BCE). He appears in the thick of the fighting, eyes fixed on the Persian emperor Darius. Alexander frequently went into battle without a helmet, confident in his destiny to conquer the whole of Persia. He is clean-shaven, a relative rarity for his time, and wears an image of the monster Medusa on his breastplate—the better to frighten his foes.

Persian threat. He decided to settle the matter once and for all by reversing the scales and sending his Greek army to topple the throne in faraway Persepolis.

The narrative of Alexander's campaigns is well documented (see Map 5.2). In 334 BCE he took Asia Minor; within two more years he had conquered the Holy Land and Egypt. By 331 BCE he had advanced through Syria and met the main Persian army at Gaugamela, not far from the ancient Assyrian city of Nineveh along the upper Tigris, and slaughtered it.[5] He then marched to Persepolis, deep into today's Iran, and in 330 BCE he destroyed the capital. Determined to press on until every last vestige of Persian power was defeated, Alexander spent five more years on campaign through the territories of Parthia and Bactria (today's eastern Iran and Afghanistan) and then down the Indus River valley, where his astonished men encountered Indian war elephants. Alexander still wanted to press on and take India, but his exhausted men threatened to mutiny, and so in 325–324 BCE he reluctantly led his forces back west to

---

5   After the battle of Gaugamela, the Persian emperor Darius III fled into the nearby hills, where a local tribal chieftain murdered him. This ended the empire founded in the 6th century BCE by Cyrus the Great.

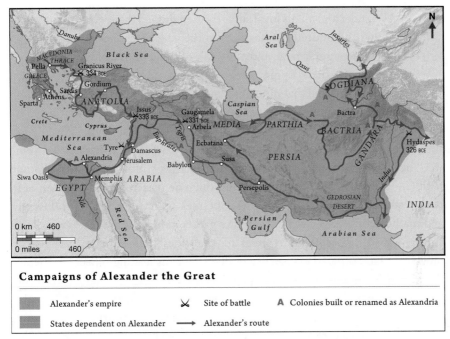

Campaigns of Alexander the Great

▨ Alexander's empire	✕ Site of battle	A Colonies built or renamed as Alexandria
▨ States dependent on Alexander	→ Alexander's route	

MAP 5.2 Campaigns of Alexander the Great Alexander's stunning conquest was mostly complete by 330 BCE.

the city of Babylon. It was the most stunning military adventure of the ancient world, an unparalleled feat.

But it is one thing to conquer vast territory and quite another to create an empire. Alexander's long-term plans are unknown, because in 323 BCE he took ill and died at the age of thirty-three. By the time he was halfway through his conquests, however, he had already instituted a profound change in his army by admitting large numbers of Persian soldiers and officers, who underwent training in Hellenic tactics, learned a simplified version of the Greek language (called *koiné*, or "common speech"), and wore Greek dress. Alexander's kinsmen nearly revolted at what they regarded as a treacherous "Persianization" of their ranks, but in a dramatic showdown at Opis, an ancient Babylonian city near the Tigris, Alexander regained their trust. As described later by the writer Arrian of Nicomedia (d. 160 CE) in his *History of Alexander*,

> To commemorate the restored harmony of his troops, Alexander offered sacrifice to all the gods he customarily honored, and hosted a great banquet, at which he made a point of sitting among his Macedonian contingent. The Persians, though, were placed immediately beside them, and right next to the Persians were the officer of other conquered peoples.

Alexander and all his loyal subjects then dipped their wine from the same bowl and poured out libations to the gods, each group following the lead of its augurs, magi, and priests. Alexander prayed aloud that the Greeks and Persians might rule together harmoniously in a single empire. It is reported that nine thousand men attended this banquet, and that every one of them repeated his prayer.

He had taken care to establish in his wake a sprawl of Greek-style cities. Some were newly built, most notably Alexandria in Egypt; others were refashioned with Greek institutions and laws. Within them he placed a loose network of libraries stocked with copies of the best of Greek literature, science, philosophy, and mathematics. He added to these the gathered manuscripts of Persian high culture—many translated into Greek for the widest dissemination. He also arranged (in fact, ordered on penalty of death) for his leading officers to divorce their Greek wives and to take Persian ones instead. It is unclear whether Alexander consciously intended by this to create a pluralistic society. Perhaps he intended simply to develop a new aristocracy, one that identified itself with a new race of his own manufacture. He certainly was impressed by, and attuned to, the eastern custom of deifying kings. In either case, he was developing a cosmopolitan social order.

THE HELLENISTIC WORLD

The eastern Mediterranean traditions had included the Greek, Egyptian, and Hebrew traditions. The Persian and Babylonian traditions had included those of the Mesopotamian valley and the eastern lands that had absorbed and assimilated them. As Alexander's vast battlefield settled into relative peace, a single Hellenistic civilization embraced and absorbed them all. This was the Hellenistic Age (323–30 BCE), and it lasted until the Romans came in the 1st century BCE and instigated a new era.

The Hellenistic Kingdoms

The political narrative of the time is not particularly enlightening. Many wars and palace coups came and went, but none in service of a significant new idea. In general terms, Alexander's enormous war zone split quickly into a quartet of separate kingdoms, each governed originally by one of his leading generals: Ptolemaic Egypt, Seleucid Asia, Attalid Anatolia, and Antigonid Greece.[6] Because the new rulers and settlers came from throughout Greece and not simply from a single city like Athens, the Hellenistic world had a broad degree of cul-

---

[6]   Take the -ic and -id endings off the dynastic adjectives, add -us (or -os, if you are a Hellenic purist), and you will have the names of the first succeeding generals.

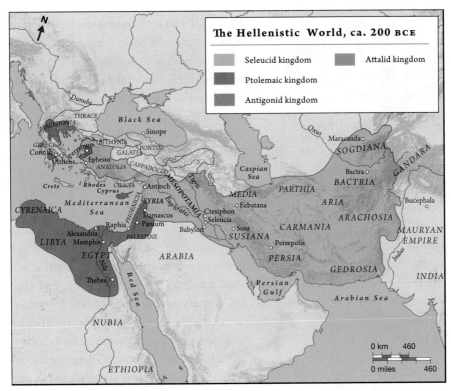

MAP 5.3 The Hellenistic World, ca. 200 BCE   Divided into four separate kingdoms, the Hellenistic world was noteworthy for its vibrant urban life, its dissemination of Greek culture and values, and its splendid libraries. Rural life remained impoverished, however, and court life seethed with conspiracies and betrayals.

tural cohesion. The single dialect of koiné Greek came into general usage throughout the territories—this was the Greek in which, ultimately, most of the Christian New Testament was written. In all four kingdoms the governments were tightly centralized, and efficient tax collection led to the building up of vast treasuries (see Map 5.3).

Urban Expansion

Apart from supporting their armies, the main expenditure of the governments was the construction of more and more cities and their supporting infrastructures. Manufacturing and commerce were the hallmarks of Hellenistic life, and these required a solid and expansive urban base. At least three hundred new cities were founded in this era, and hundreds more received huge injections of money to improve their infrastructures. Within a century of its construction, the city of Alexandria had a half-million inhabitants; Seleucia had a quarter million. The Seleucids poured money into refurbishing their Mediterranean harbors and extending their roadways into India. The Ptolemies in Egypt hired geographers and cartographers to search out and map new overland trade routes into Arabia, Ethiopia, and Nubia. The Antigonids invested in canals and a vastly

Cleopatra Cleopatra VII Thea Philopator (r. 51–30 BCE) was the last pharaoh to rule ancient Egypt. Renowned for her youthful beauty, she dazzled more with her charisma and wit. According to the much later Greek philosopher and biographer Plutarch (46–120 CE), she could speak nine languages. She presented herself to the Egyptians as the reincarnation of the goddess Isis.

expanded fleet of ships that was able to trade with Spain and Britain (important sources of silver and tin, respectively). The Attalids, who ruled the smallest of the successor-states, made a strategic alliance with the Roman republic to check the expansionist aims of the Antigonids. Their capital, Pergamum, had an amphitheater that could seat ten thousand and a library that contained 200,000 volumes.

Not everyone prospered. Farming remained the occupation of the great bulk of the population, and farmers generally lived in poverty throughout the Hellenistic years. Poor crop yields were not the cause. Farmers steadily produced abundant quantities of foodstuffs, and the proliferation of cities meant the increased, and increasingly easy, availability of markets. Rather, intentionally harsh tax policies in all the Hellenistic kingdoms kept small farmers poor. Two motives prompted such exploitation: a desire to promote the development of the urban economies and a perverse belief that abject poverty would keep the agrarian population incapable of rebellion. Hellenistic splendor thus resulted less from a general prosperity than from the intentionally inequitable distribution of wealth.

The Arts under Royal Support   Among those who benefited, at least financially, were writers and artists. Hellenistic monarchs became the supporters of scholarship and the arts on a vast scale, competing with one another to lure the best and the brightest to their capitals. Scholars and artists focused on gathering and assimilating the intellectual and cultural traditions of their various populations. The promotion of libraries was key here. Translations, commentaries, histories, and encyclopedias were the most characteristic cultural productions of the age. Explorers sent out by the four monarchies traveled to the Caspian, Black, and Red seas and came back with exciting travelogues describing new geographies, cultures, and technologies. The most adventurous Hellenistic Greek explorer of all was Pytheas (d. ca. 306 BCE), who ventured as far as central Norway. He was the first writer to describe the phenomena of the northern lights and the Arctic snow cap.

Non-Greeks who also ventured far and related their discoveries in koiné Greek included a Babylonian priest named Berosus (d. ca. 270 BCE), who wrote a history of his people and translated several astronomical works into the new common tongue. Manetho (d. ca. 270 BCE), an Egyptian, wrote a comprehensive history of his homeland too, in which he created the system of periodization still used today regarding Egypt's Old, Middle, and New Kingdoms, with their various Intermediary Periods. Others explored as far south as today's Ethiopia and Kenya and as far east as India.

The fortunes acquired by those in trade and industry, as well as in government, meant a widespread demand for decorative arts—statuary, jewelry, frescos and mosaics, tapestries—to adorn the homes and villas of the well-to-do. The preferred styles were more ornate, as with the exaggerated naturalism of statues like that pictured here of Laocoön and his sons.

In drama, playwrights turned to lighter fare than the Classical tragedians had produced. Working in politically repressive regimes, they aimed simply to entertain the masses with escapist comedies featuring stock characters—shrewish wives, clever slaves, braggart soldiers, and the like. The best of the writers of this so-called New Comedy was Menander of Athens (ca. 341–290 BCE), who wrote more than one hundred comedies, only one of which survives whole. He holds the distinction of being the only Greek playwright to be quoted in the Christian New Testament, when St. Paul warns his newly converted companions to avoid socializing with sinful people: "Bad company corrupts good morals."[7]

Laocoön and His Sons   In mythology, Laocoön was a priest in the cult of Poseidon who offended the sea god by marrying and, according to rumor, daring to make love to his bride in a temple dedicated to the deity. This sculpture shows Laocoön and his sons being attacked by two sea serpents sent by Poseidon. It was carved in the 1st century BCE, probably on the island of Rhodes, and housed in Rome. After going missing for many centuries, it was excavated in 1506. It now stands in the Vatican Museum as an iconic example of Hellenistic sculpture's emphasis on movement and gesture.

But it was in the sciences that Hellenistic intellectual life really shone. *Scientific* Scholars were able to bring together the Greek, Egyptian, and Persian traditions in *Innovation* everything from astronomy and geometry to mathematics, medicine, and physics. The wide availability of libraries and laboratories—both of which were considered "must-have" accessories of the well-to-do—sparked many new abstract and practical advances, word of which spread rapidly. Aristarchus of Samos (ca. 310–230 BCE) and Eratosthenes of Cyrene (ca. 285–194 BCE) were the preeminent

---

[7]   1 Corinthians 15.33.

astronomers. Between them, they proved, by applying Greek mathematics to Babylonian astronomical tables, that the earth and other planets revolved around the sun, and they calculated the circumference of the earth to within 200 miles.

In geometry, Euclid (ca. 330–270 BCE) led the way. *The Elements of Geometry* became the basic textbook for teaching the subject for fifteen hundred years. In medicine, figures like Herophilus of Chalcedon (ca. 335–280 BCE) introduced (briefly and on the sly) the practice of human dissection, from which he determined the role of the heart in transmitting blood through the arteries—a bit of knowledge quickly lost until it was rediscovered by the English physician William Harvey in the 17th century CE. Archimedes of Syracuse (287–212 BCE)—the physicist famous for shouting "Eureka!" ("I've got it!") and running naked through the street—determined the law of specific gravity, devised the first compound pulley, and invented the hydraulic screw propeller.

Philosophy for a New Age

In philosophy, thinkers turned away from both the abstract idealism of Plato and the empiricist realism of Aristotle. Instead, their works assumed that the human quest to understand the meaning of life and the nature of reality was pointless, either because no such meaning or reality exists or because human intellect is powerless to comprehend them. Four major schools of philosophy predominated: **Skepticism, Cynicism, Epicureanism,** and **Stoicism.** The first two differed from one another mostly in matter of degree. Skeptics like Pyrrho of Elis (ca. 360–270 BCE), Arcesilaus (ca. 315–241 BCE), and Carneades (ca. 214–128 BCE) emphasized the flaws inherent in human intellect. Since all our knowledge of the world derives from our senses and all of our senses can be deceived (as in optical illusions), then it is impossible for our minds to attain 100 percent certainty about anything. Cynics went even further to assert that only our natural instincts can possibly be deemed right and true—and thus the laws, morals, and customs that organize civil society must be rejected as shams. They made a point, therefore, of exposing what they regarded as the hypocrisy of civic life: by arguments when possible and by crude actions when necessary. The most famous early Cynic, Diogenes of Sinope (d. 323 BCE), at least once expressed his rejection of social conformity by defecating and masturbating in public. When asked why he customarily carried a lamp everywhere he went, even in the daylight, he would respond that he was seeking a single honest man. "Man has misconstrued every gift bestowed on him by the gods" was one of his maxims.

The Epicureans and Stoics, by contrast, were more moderate, disciplined, and pragmatic. *Of course* the world is beyond human comprehension, they asserted, but that is exactly where we need to start thinking the hardest, not stop in despair. "Any philosophy that does not relieve human suffering is worthless," according to

Zeno of Citium (d. 262 BCE), the founder of Stoicism. Relief from suffering was the central thrust of these two schools. The Epicureans' philosophy was not, as is widely assumed, to devote themselves to simple hedonism—to wine, women, and song, as the phrase goes—but rather to devote themselves to the avoidance of suffering. As Epicurus himself (d. 270 BCE, after whom the school is named) wrote to a friend,

> When we say that pleasure is the goal of life, we do not mean excess or sensuality; that is what others think about us, out of sheer ignorance, prejudice, or deceit. By pleasure we mean simply the absence of suffering in the body and of anguish in the soul. A pleasurable life comes not through endless bouts of drinking and revelry, not through sexual delight or the enjoyment of fine fish and other delicacies at the table. No, it comes from sober reasoning, from seeking out the true principles behind every choice and selection, and from rejecting every false belief that brings agony to the mind.

This "scaling down" of philosophical aims from Plato's search for Ideal Forms can be viewed as a decline, but as an expression of concern for the everyday human struggle to survive in a harsh world, the pragmatic turn of Hellenistic philosophy is deeply humane.

THE MACCABEAN REVOLT

In the second century BCE the Hellenistic monarchies grew increasingly unstable, which inspired a wave of palace coups and popular uprisings. The most significant of the latter was the rebellion of the Jews in Seleucid Palestine. The relative atmosphere of tolerance in Hellenistic times might have provided the Jews a respite from oppression, but the eastern-inspired custom of deifying monarchs—which Alexander the Great had originally encouraged—meant that the Jews would never be docile subjects.

The Revolt of the Maccabees (167–142 BCE) originated with a contested succession to the Jerusalem high priesthood during the reign of the Seleucid king Antiochus IV (r. 175–164 BCE). Two main contestants emerged: Jason and Menelaus, whose very names suggest the degree of Hellenization that took place even in the Holy City. Neither was a paragon of virtue.

Jason paid Antiochus a large bribe to win the post, which left Menelaus with no choice but to offer an even larger one, but Menelaus did not have enough cash on hand, so he broke into the Temple treasury and stole some golden vessels. Although it assured him the high priesthood, Menelaus's theft outraged the people, and the city erupted in riot. Antiochus invaded the city and established a garrison of his Syrian soldiers on the Temple Mount. These soldiers, consisting of followers of both the Greek and the Zoroastrian religions, demanded some sort of accommodation for their religious rites—and Antiochus (with Menelaus's consent as high priest) allowed pagan altars to be set up within the Temple.

Maccabean Triumph

This perceived act of profanity triggered a full-scale Jewish rebellion against Seleucid rule. The leaders of the rebellion were a family called the Hasmoneans, but the rebellion itself took its name from that of the eldest Hasmonean son, Judas Maccabeus. The revolt is a great heroic episode in the history of the Jews and their most significant military victory until the establishment of the modern state of Israel in 1948.

The odds were certainly against them, given the size and strength of the Seleucid forces, but the Jewish rebels showed remarkable tenacity. (A story from their retaking of the Temple itself, in 164 BCE, is the origin of the celebration of Hanukkah.) The surprised and exhausted Seleucids gave up the fight in 142 BCE and granted Judea independence. The Hasmoneans would remain in power until they were replaced by the Herodians in 40 BCE, a dynasty of puppet-kings under Roman control.

Changes in the Hebrew Canon

Despite the heroic nature of the revolt, however, the main Jewish texts that record its history, the books known as 1–2 Maccabees, were not admitted into the Hebrew canon. The ostensible reason for this—that they may have been written directly in Greek and hence lacked a Hebrew source/counterpart—only partially explains their omission. The Greek Septuagint Bible, including 1–2 Maccabees, remained in widespread use in the Jewish world for three hundred years: Jewish communities from North Africa to Mesopotamia used it, as did numerous communities within Palestine itself. The great Jewish philosopher Philo of Alexandria (d. 50 CE) used it. Rabbinical scholars drew on it in establishing new legislation. Syrian Jews used it to prepare their own translation of the Bible into vernacular Syriac (the Peshitta). For the rest of the Hellenistic period, and for at least two hundred years beyond, the Greek Septuagint was widely accepted canon in the Jewish world. The spread of Christianity in the first two centuries CE, however, altered Jewish attitudes toward their Greek Bible. Because Christians also used the Septuagint, it became tainted in Jewish eyes.

Returning to the Hebrew canon was a way of asserting the Jews' difference from the Christians, indeed, their independence from them. Hence they began to reconstitute the Hebrew text. The process of producing this version—by compiling old manuscripts, collating excerpts from older liturgical material, and at times even reconstructing the text from memory—resulted in the Masoretic text, the definitive Hebrew-language canon still in use today. Although still revered as part of the Jewish literary tradition, 1–2 Maccabees lost its canonical status. To disassociate themselves from the upstart new sect, the Jews cut themselves off from the biblical version that most of them used. In the process, they decanonized the books that record the last great triumph of their ancient era.

◆

The Hellenistic period was one of stark contrasts, when economic instability, extensive poverty, and authoritarian rule existed alongside great prosperity, astonishing scientific advances, and flourishing cosmopolitan culture. It bridged the gap between the tastes, customs, and values of Classical Greece and those that would be more characteristic of Rome. It was Hellenistic art and architecture, Hellenistic city planning and civic culture that the Romans strove to emulate, not those of Periclean Athens. The example set by Alexander, in particular, was one that the Romans would model, and the economic and political infrastructures that were put in place after his conquests would form the framework of Roman imperial government.

WHO, WHAT, WHERE

Academy	hubris	Skepticism
Alexander the Great	Ideal Forms	Socratic method
Cynicism	Lyceum	Sophists
Delian League	Peloponnesian War	Stoicism
Epicureanism	Pericles	telos
Hippocratic oath	Pythagoreans	tragedy

SUGGESTED READINGS

Primary Sources

Arrian. *The History of Alexander.*

Thucydides. *The Peloponnesian War.*

Xenophon. *Hellenica.*

Anthologies

Cohen, S. Marc, Patricia Curd, and C. D. C. Reeve. *Readings in Greek Philosophy: From Thales to Aristotle* (2011).

Irby-Massie, Georgia, and Paul T. Keyser. *Greek Science of the Hellenistic Era: A Sourcebook* (2002).

Lefkowitz, Mary R., and Maureen B. Fant. *Women's Life in Greece and Rome: A Source Book in Translation* (2005).

Tracy, Stephen V. *Pericles: A Sourcebook and Reader* (2009).

Studies

Bagnall, Nigel. *The Peloponnesian War: Athens, Sparta, and the Struggle for Greece* (2006).

Beard, Mary. *The Parthenon* (2010).

Bosworth, A. B. *The Legacy of Alexander: Politics, Warfare, and Propaganda under the Successors* (2005).

Briant, Pierre. *Alexander the Great and His Empire: A Short Introduction* (2010).

Briant, Pierre. *From Cyrus to Alexander: A History of the Persian Empire* (2002).

Burn, Lucilla. *Hellenistic Art from Alexander the Great to Augustus* (2005).

Connelly, Joan Breton. *Portrait of a Priestess: Women and Ritual in Ancient Greece* (2009).

Connelly, Joan Breton. *The Parthenon Enigma* (2014).

De Ste. Croix, G. E. M. *Athenian Democratic Origins, and Other Essays* (2005).

De Ste. Croix, G. E. M. *The Origins of the Peloponnesian War* (2002).

Dillon, Matthew. *Girls and Women in Classical Greek Religion* (2002).

Grabbe, Lester L. *A History of the Jews and Judaism in the Second Temple Period* (2006–2008).

Green, Peter, and Eugene N. Borza. *Alexander of Macedon, 356–323 BC: A Historical Biography* (2013).

Hanson, Victor David. *A War Like No Other: How the Athenians and Spartans Fought the Peloponnesian War* (2006).

Hanson, Victor David, and John Keegan. *The Western Way of War: Infantry Battle in Classical Greece* (2009).

Hölbl, Günther. *A History of the Ptolemaic Empire* (2001).

Humphreys, S. C. *The Strangeness of Gods: Historical Perspectives on the Interpretation of Athenian Religion* (2004).

Jonker, Louis. *Historiography and Identity (Re) Formulation in Second Temple Historiographical Literature* (2010).

Kagan, Donald. *The Peloponnesian War* (2003).

Navia, Luis E. *Socrates: A Life Examined* (2007).

Neils, Jenifer, and John H. Oakley. *Coming of Age in Ancient Greece: Images of Childhood from the Classical Past* (2003).

Reeve, C. D. C. *Philosopher-Kings: The Argument of Plato's "Republic"* (2006).

Romm, James. *Ghost on the Throne: The Death of Alexander the Great and the War for Crown and Empire* (2011).

Roochnik, David. *Beautiful City: The Dialectical Character of Plato's "Republic"* (2008).

Roochnik, David. *Retrieving the Ancients: An Introduction to Greek Philosophy* (2004).

Saxonhouse, Arlene W. *Free Speech and Democracy in Ancient Athens* (2008).

Shanske, Darien. *Thucydides and the Philosophical Origins of History* (2009).

Sourvinou-Inwood, Christiane. *Tragedy and Athenian Religion* (2003).

Thomas, Carol G. *Alexander the Great in His World* (2007).

Warren, James. *Presocratics: Natural Philosophers before Socrates* (2007).

Weinfeld, Moshe. *Normative and Sectarian Judaism in the Second Temple Period* (2005).

Weinfeld, Moshe. *The Place of the Law in the Religion of Ancient Israel* (2004).

Weinfeld, Moshe. *Social Justice in Ancient Israel and in the Ancient Near East* (2000).

Zuckert, Catherine H. *Plato's Philosophers: The Coherence of the Dialogues* (2009).

For additional resources, including maps, primary sources, visuals, web links, and quizzes, please go to **www.oup.com/us/backman.**

CHAPTER 6

Empire of the Sea: Rome

753 BCE–212 CE

The Romans believed themselves descended from the noble Trojans who had lost their city to Homer's Greeks. They may not have known their own true origin or they may simply have desired a better one. According to their legend, Aphrodite, the Greek goddess of love, fell head over heels for Anchises, a member of the younger branch of the Trojan royal family. Two things resulted from their tryst: a son named Aeneas, and the infliction of blindness on Anchises when he was caught boasting of his sexual escapade to some other soldiers. (Aphrodite's father, Zeus, hurled a lightning bolt from atop Mount Olympus and hit him in the eyes.) After the Greeks had set Troy ablaze, the story went on, Aeneas carried his blind old father on his back through crumbling ruins and flaming timbers to safety. Aeneas's postwar travels then took him into the central Mediterranean, where he learned of a prophecy that he would found a great new kingdom in central Italy, at a place called Latium.

ROME AND THE MEDITERRANEAN

After a series of adventures Aeneas did indeed reach Latium and brought the region under his control. But he did not found the city of Rome itself. That was the work of two much later descendants of Aeneas, the twin brothers Romulus and Remus, who, also according to the legend, laid the city's foundations in 753 BCE and established a dynasty. Its kings ruled until a rebellion in 509 BCE overthrew the monarchy and established a republic.

The Roman Forum A forum was a marketplace or town square, and every Roman city had one. As a natural meeting place, a forum was frequently a site of popular political gatherings. The great forum in Rome was the venue of speeches and rallies, triumphal processions, criminal trials, and, occasionally, gladiatorial contests.

Whatever the story or precise date of Rome's founding, Romans themselves valued practicality and dutifulness above all other virtues. But even pragmatists sometimes like to fantasize about noble ancestors and destined greatness. These spoke, too, to Rome's image as a republic of virtue, even as internal struggles put in doubt the Republic's very survival. And indeed, Rome achieved its golden age under an emperor, Augustus, and as an empire linked by the Mediterranean Sea.

ANCIENT ITALY AND THE RISE OF ROME

Links to Ancient Heroes

Their imagined link with Greece's heroic age mattered much to the Romans. On the practical level, an illustrious genealogy and a prophetic fate helped to legitimate, in their own eyes at least, the Romans' lording it over the other tribal and ethnic groups of central Italy. Surrounded by aggressive societies like the Etruscans and Sabines to the north and east and the Aurunces, Hernici, Marses, and Volscii to the south, the Romans were a warlike people from the first, continually forced to defend their own territory and conquests against other invaders.

Rule by Kings

On a deeper level, the Romans craved a linkage with ancient heroes because their early history boasted none of their own. Tradition told of seven monarchs who began Rome's rise in the world. These kings, who supposedly ruled from the founding of the city to the founding of the Republic (753–509 BCE), were for the

CHAPTER TIMELINE

750 BCE	650 BCE	550 BCE	450 BCE	350 BCE

- 753 BCE **Legendary foundation of Rome**
- ca. 753–509 BCE **Roman monarchy**
- 509–31 BCE **Roman Republic**
- ca. 450 BCE **First Roman law code (Twelve Tables)**
- 387 BCE **Gauls sack Rome**
- 367 BCE **Election of the first plebeian consul**

most part a competent group, but none of them would have made a suitable hero in an epic poem. (The regnal dates given in Table 6.1 are traditional but should not be regarded as factual because our knowledge of early Rome derives from archeological remains and sources that date to centuries later. In 387 BCE a Gaul army sacked Rome and burned down the municipal archives.)

Despite the individual kings' variable accomplishments, the period of monarchy did produce Rome's most famous and enduring government body: the **Senate**, a group of distinguished men chosen as the king's personal council. The Senate played the same role—advising government leaders—for a thousand years as Rome changed from a monarchy to a republic and back to a monarchy (the empire). It was always a Roman value that one should make important decisions only after consulting with advisors, never on one's own.

The early Greeks had the stimulus of continual contact with the other peoples of the eastern Mediterranean, but the Romans were in a different situation altogether: Italy, geographically speaking, faces westward (see Map 6.1). The Apennine mountain chain runs down the eastern edge of the peninsula, forming an imperfect but still significant natural barrier to approach from the Adriatic Sea. Moreover, most of Italy's abundant and fertile agricultural plains, as well as most of its natural harbors, stretch down the western coast. And apart from the great Po River complex that runs eastward across the northernmost part of the

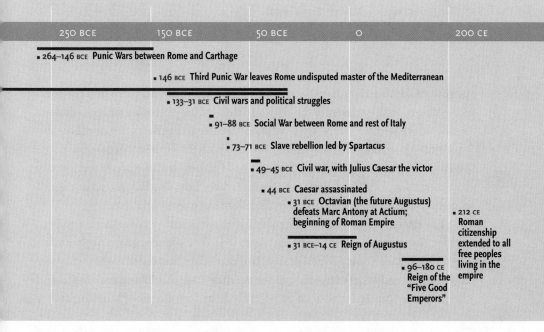

250 BCE   150 BCE   50 BCE   O   200 CE

- 264–146 BCE Punic Wars between Rome and Carthage

- 146 BCE Third Punic War leaves Rome undisputed master of the Mediterranean

- 133–31 BCE Civil wars and political struggles

- 91–88 BCE Social War between Rome and rest of Italy

- 73–71 BCE Slave rebellion led by Spartacus

- 49–45 BCE Civil war, with Julius Caesar the victor

- 44 BCE Caesar assassinated
- 31 BCE Octavian (the future Augustus) defeats Marc Antony at Actium; beginning of Roman Empire

- 212 CE Roman citizenship extended to all free peoples living in the empire

- 31 BCE–14 CE Reign of Augustus

- 96–180 CE Reign of the "Five Good Emperors"

TABLE 6.1 **Rome's Kings**

Romulus (r. ca. 753–715 BCE)	Formed the Roman army into its distinctive shape of individual legions, each composed of six thousand infantry and six hundred cavalry. But he is perhaps best remembered for the mass kidnapping of thousands of Sabine women to provide wives for his troops.
Numa Pompilius (r. ca. 715–673 BCE)	Established the priestesshood of the Vestal Virgins and abandoned the old lunar calendar for a solar one.
Tullus Hostilius (r. ca. 673–642 BCE)	A bloodthirsty warrior who, according to legend, so neglected the gods that on his deathbed, when he cried out to be saved, Zeus blasted him with a thunderbolt that turned his palace and his body instantly to ashes.
Ancus Marcius (r. ca. 640–616 BCE)	Built the first bridge across the Tiber River and founded the port at Ostia, thus connecting Rome to the sea. Also established Rome first's saltworks.
Tarquinius Priscus (r. ca. 616–579 BCE)	An Etruscan, he doubled Rome's size by conquering the Etruscans and used the booty he won to finance construction of the Roman Forum and the Circus Maximus. He also built Rome's sewer system.
Servius Tullius (r. ca. 579–535 BCE)	The second king of the Etruscan dynasty, he made socioeconomic status the determinant for voting rights, built the great Temple to Diana, and was murdered by his daughter and her husband, Tarquinius Superbus.
Tarquinius Superbus (Tarquin the Arrogant) (r. ca. 539–509 BCE)	A violent, loutish Etruscan dynast whose excesses led to his expulsion from Rome and the permanent overthrow of monarchy in 509 BCE.

peninsula, almost all of Italy's rivers flow westward. The only parts of Italy easily accessible to the Greeks were the southern third of the peninsula and the island of Sicily, where we find Greek settlements established as early as the mid-8th century BCE—the time of Homer. For these reasons the earliest **Latins** (the name given to the people who settled the region of Latium) had the greatest degree of commercial and cultural contact not with Greece but with Etruria, an advanced society to the north with whom they had close but uneasy relations.

The **Etruscans** were a literate people who left behind a considerable body of writing (especially inscriptions). However, since their language is poorly understood, all that we know of them derives from archeological remains plus whatever the Romans and others wrote about them. They were excellent metalsmiths and builders; the Romans appear to have learned the techniques of building arches

The Etruscans

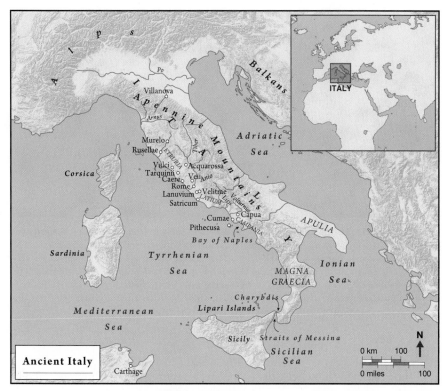

MAP 6.1   Ancient Italy   Italy's Apennine Mountains and the westward-flowing rivers that emerged from them shaped much of the peninsula's early history. Most towns and villages were oriented to the west, into the Tyrrhenian Sea, and to the south, into the central Mediterranean. Only a few towns faced east, into the Adriatic.

from them. The Etruscans also introduced the Romans to the blood sport of gladiatorial contests. Such contests originated as an aspect of funeral observances, an offering made in honor of the deceased, and were extremely popular. The Roman historian Livy (Titus Livius, 59 BCE–17 CE) describes a plethora of such games in 174 BCE. Titus Flamininus was a Roman general who would later play a big role in the conquest of Greece:

> Many gladiatorial games were held in that year; most of them were unremarkable, but one really stood out from the rest—namely, the games staged by Titus Flamininus to commemorate the death of his father. These games lasted four days, including the public food distribution, the general banquet, and the handful of theatrical performances that accompanied them. The high point of the festivity, of course, was the three-day contest in which seventy-four gladiators (a high number, in those times) fought.

Wrestling Match   In this Etruscan fresco from around 500 BCE from the Tomb of the Augurs at Tarquinii, two men wrestle over three metal cauldrons, which are probably the prizes of their contest. The cloaked figure to the left carries a curved staff known as a *lituus*, which was a mark of the priests known as *augurs*, or diviners. One of the chief ways to prophesize the future was to define a field of vision with a lituus and then observe within it the behavior of birds. Here, the cloaked figure seems to be supervising the contest, while the lituus and the birds flying over the combatants may indicate that he was seeking to foretell the result.

The Etruscans influenced the Latins in two profound ways: morals and religion. If we can credit the stories told about them by the Romans and Greeks, the Etruscans were well off and enjoyed their prosperity to the hilt. They held sumptuous feasts twice daily—with both male and female guests reclining on pillowed couches, in richly decorated homes, and imbibing flowing rivers of wine. Descriptions of these feasts fill many disapproving Latin and Greek pages—because the Romans, making a virtue of their own relative want, disdained luxury as self-indulgence. They never aspired to Spartan levels of austerity, but they placed a high value on frugality and self-discipline. Moral strength demanded sacrifice, as they saw it, and the placing of the common good before individual desire. In this way, the Etruscans taught the Romans by negative example.

In religion, however, their influence was direct and positive. The Etruscans practiced divination, or the reading of prophetic signs in certain natural phenomena—the shape of a slaughtered animal's liver, the blood splatter of a beheaded chicken, the rumbling sound of thunder or the groaning of a volcano, or the flight pattern of a group of birds. Divination was common throughout early Italy, but the Etruscan diviners (*haruspices*, in Latin) were considered the best.[1] The Romans adopted their practice and remained dedicated believers in it for many

---

[1]   Livy wrote, "When it came to signs and omens regarding public life, Roman custom was to consult nobody except Etruscan haruspices" (*History* 1.56).

centuries. Roman religion never fully recognized the haruspices as priests, but Roman society turned to them before any undertaking and took their warnings with the utmost seriousness.

FROM MONARCHY TO REPUBLIC

The Roman social elite's hatred of its Etruscan king motivated the creation of the Republic. In 509 BCE, the son of Tarquin the Arrogant raped a virtuous Roman matron Lucretia, who committed suicide to preserve her honor. Lucretia's kinsmen and friends overthrew Tarquin and established a form of government so new that they could label it only vaguely: **res publica**, "the public thing." Its constitution—mostly unwritten—changed numerous times over the centuries but remained based on the crucial idea of the separation of powers. In contrast to the ancient Athenians, who placed legislative authority in the single body of the popular assembly, the Romans erected an elaborate system of checks and balances between distinct institutions that prevented any single individual or group from amassing too much power. The Senate was the dominant body, composed of members of Rome's leading noble families, but its work was complemented by a number of legislative assemblies and executive magistracies. Most magistrates served one-year terms, so campaigning and deal making were more or less constant. Since different social groups were involved in the different offices, prudence dictated that families and classes would form alliances that would compete for choice political positions and to pass legislation.

In all, the early Republic functioned much in the spirit of Aristotle's ideal city-state, a smallish, organic society whose government involved all the leading figures of the city in a constantly changing network of mutually dependent relationships. Roman social hierarchy divided the population into three groups: the **patricians**, aristocrats who could trace their lineage to the members of the first Republican Senate established in 509 BCE; the **equestrians,** aristocrats of a lesser order who according to tradition originated as the earliest Roman cavalry; and the **plebeians**, all other free citizens. Initially, the patricians held the upper hand against the plebeians, but within two generations the so-called Struggle of the Orders had progressed to the extent that the Republic promulgated—sometime around 450 BCE—its first written law code. Known as the **Twelve Tables** (the name derives from the original dozen wooden slabs on which the code was written and set in public), it formed the basis for all subsequent Roman jurisprudence. It survives only in fragments, but the outline of its contents provides a good sense of its scope (see Table 6.2). The Tables marked the first significant concession to the plebeians; others would be demanded and gradually won over the next two centuries.

The Tables regarded property rights as the paramount concern of society. Indeed, the internal struggles of the first hundred years of the Republic centered on opening more avenues of government to the enterprising plebeian class, whose strength came from their prosperity rather than noble lineage. In part, property issues featured so prominently in the laws because a debtor's creditor could legally sell him into slavery, under certain circumstances. The Tables, therefore, defined those circumstances. What mattered in this regard were the size and length of the debt and the social status of the people involved. Roman law ultimately recognized a hierarchy of six distinct social classes. Interestingly, these distinctions originated as a means of determining the amount and type of military service owed by each citizen; military needs, not economic roles, shaped the foundational social structure.

The Twelve Tables

TABLE 6.2 **The Twelve Tables**

	Table Topic	Number of Laws	Sample Laws
I	On summonses to court	10	When anyone summons anyone to appear before a judge's tribunal, the latter must appear immediately and without delay. [No. 1]
II	On judgments and thefts	11	If anyone commits a theft during daytime and is caught in the act, he is to be scourged and handed over as a slave to the person from whom he stole. If the thief is [already] a slave, he shall be beaten with rods and hurled from the Tarpeian Rock. If he has not yet reached puberty, the praetor shall decide whether he should be scourged and released, as reparation for the theft. [No. 5]
III	On property that is lent	10	Anyone who charges more than [10 percent] interest per year on a loan shall pay quadruple the amount [of the loan] as a penalty. [No. 2]
IV	On the rights of fathers, and of marriage	4	A father shall instantly put to death any newborn son who is a monster or is born with a nonhuman form. [No. 3]
V	On estates and guardianships	7	When no legal guardian has been appointed for an insane person or a spendthrift, his nearest male relative shall take charge of his [inherited] property. [No. 7]
VI	On ownership of property	10	A woman who has lived for an entire year with a man, provided that she has never stayed away from him for three successive nights, shall pass into his control as his legal wife. [No. 5]
VII	On crimes	17	Anyone who commits perjury shall be hurled from the Tarpeian Rock. [No. 12]

VIII	On the laws of real property	9	A space of two and one-half feet must be left between neighboring buildings. [No. 1]
IX	On public law	7	Anyone who organizes a nighttime assembly within the city of Rome shall be put to death. [No. 6]
X	On religious law	18	An oath shall have the greatest possible legal force and effect for the purpose of maintaining good faith. [No. 1]
XI	Supplement to Tables I–V	2	No widowed member of the senatorial order, if he is a father, shall contract a [second] marriage with a member of the plebeian order. [No. 1]
XII	Supplement to Tables VI–XII	3	If a slave should commit theft or vandalism, with the foreknowledge of his master, then the master shall be handed over to the victim [of the crime] in reparation for the harm done by the slave. [No. 3]

At each level of the hierarchy the essential social unit was the *familia*, a broader institution than "family." A familia consisted of an entire household and included the various aunts, uncles, nephews, nieces, cousins, close friends, clients, concubines, attendants, and house servants who lived under the same roof. It was firmly patriarchal, like the society as a whole. The male head of the household—the **pater familias**—held complete authority over the entire familia and was, legally speaking, the sole possessor of its property. Moreover, the pater familias possessed a legal right known as *patria potestas* ("paternal power," the subject of the fourth of the Twelve Tables), which gave him the right of life and death over his family. Several passages in the Twelve Tables delineate the extent of paternal power:

Paternal Power

> To any father is given the power of life and death over his children. . . . A father has the power to sell any child of his into slavery, but if a child is sold three times by his father, he shall be free of his father after the third time. . . . In order to repudiate a wife, a husband shall simply say to her, "Manage your [dowry] property for yourself," take away her keys to the house, and expel her.

The father's authority was absolute and not to be questioned. Women were not property (except for slaves, of course) but had restrictions on their social actions. Roman law required a woman to have a legal guardian—usually her father or husband, but another male relative was possible—to conduct important public business like selling a property. Upper-class women often played influential roles in society; frequently well educated and socially connected, aristocratic women

Roles for Women

hosted formal dinners at which senatorial business was discussed, political allies and clients were courted, and prominent poets and scholars were patronized.

A unique subset of prominent women in Roman life was the tiny company of Vestal Virgins—six priestesses who presided over the cult of Vesta, the Roman goddess of the hearth. The Vestal Virgins were selected at a young age (usually between the ages of six and ten) and served terms of thirty years. Provided that they performed their temple duties unfailingly, they had complete legal independence, could own property, and received considerable honor. They were present at most public celebrations and at the dedication ceremonies of new public buildings. The Vestals's most important task was to preserve the Sacred Fire in the temple, which provided the source for all hearth fires in the city. As ritual guardians of the hearth the Vestals therefore served as the protectors of the Roman familia itself. After completing her service, a Vestal Virgin could marry if she wished, although if she did she then fell under the guardianship of her husband, who gained enormous prestige from having so renowned a wife.[2]

Pater Familias   An upper-class Roman, identifiable by the robe he wears, is shown holding the busts of his ancestors, probably his father and grandfather. Deceased parents became the household gods of Roman families, and processions with these busts were a common ritual at festivals.

Among the plebeians, a woman's status and activity depended in large part on the kind of marriage she had, since Roman customs recognized different types of marriages. In one type, a wife remained under the patria potestas of her father even after her wedding, which meant that (with her father's permission) she could control her own property within the marriage independent of her husband. More frequently, a wife was under the patria potestas of her spouse. Another form of bond was concubinage, in which a man had a publicly recognized

---

[2]   If a Vestal Virgin made the grave mistake of losing her virginity while serving the cult, she was punished by being buried alive in a chamber stocked with two or three days' provisions. As described by the Roman author Plutarch (ca. 50–120 CE), "There is no sight more dreadful than this. Indeed, Rome never experiences a day more filled with gloom. When the litter [carrying the offending priestess] arrives at the spot . . . the *pontifex maximus* [head priest] murmurs some obscure prayers, stretching out his hands to the gods. Then, the awful moment having arrived, he takes the priestess, who is completely shrouded [like a corpse], and guides her to the ladder that leads down to the chamber, before himself turning away from her, along with the other priests present. When she has descended the ladder, it is drawn up. The chamber is then quickly buried with an enormous quantity of dirt thrown down from above, until the earth is level with the rest of the embankment. Such is the punishment for those Vestals who forsake their chastity."

relationship with another woman (his concubine). Legally speaking, concubines were not regarded as wives but as socially acceptable partners to a married man, entitled to polite treatment in society. A woman could not be married to one man while being a concubine to another because that would constitute adultery. A Roman man, in contrast, could have sexual relationships with any female slave in his familia.

The Romans saw justice in these arrangements, since it was the fathers' and husbands' responsibility, ultimately, to preserve the honor of the familia. Without it, a family could not hold its place in society.

THE REPUBLIC OF VIRTUE

Honor means different things to different people. Etymologically, it derives from the Latin word for "burden" (*onus, oneris*), reflecting the toil and struggle one must maintain to achieve it. To the Romans, honor consisted of playing one's appointed role in the familia and in the Republic. A father's honor lay in preserving his family's economic, social, and moral well-being. The Republic helped by implementing the office of **censor**, one that quickly became the most prestigious and feared of all the Roman magistracies.

The best-known censor is Cato (234–149 BCE), the subject of one of the pop- *Censoring* ular biographies written by Plutarch (c. 50–120 CE), a Roman author and philoso- *the Public* pher working centuries after Cato's censorship. According to Plutarch's *Life of Cato the Elder,*

> The office of censor, one might say, towered above every other civic honor and was in fact a perfect climax to a political career. Its powers were many and widespread, and included the authority to inspect the lives and morals of the citizens. The people who created the censorship believed it right not to leave people free to act as they wished without others' seeing and judging them—not in marriage, the begetting of children, the workings of everyday life, or socializing with one's friends. In fact, they deemed these to be the very aspects of a man's life where he shows his truest character. (ch. 16)

Plutarch then goes on to describe Cato's most famous exercise of censorial power. A prominent senator named Lucius Quinctius had conducted an unseemly relationship with a handsome young lad. Once, when the two were reclining together after a dinner that included too much wine, the young lad declared that he loved Lucius so much that he had run to his house when summoned, although he had been watching his first gladiatorial combat ever and had been looking forward to seeing a man slaughtered. Lucius, ever the attentive lover, then ordered a convicted criminal beheaded in front of his beloved to make up for what the lad had missed. Cato, horrified, stripped Lucius of his senatorial rank.

The censor had three specific duties: to maintain the census (the official list of all citizens of Rome, their property, and their legal class), to administer the finances of the state for all public works, and, most ominously, to preserve public morals. The censors could reward or punish an individual, or even an entire familia, by entering notations in the official census about the person's moral health. A black mark in the census imposed a moral stain called infamy (*infamia*), which meant the loss of the right to vote or participate in public life, the loss of admission into proper society, the ruin of any hopes to establish suitable marriages for one's children, and a permanent demotion in social status. Hence Romans considered it essential to observe, and to be seen to observe, the moral standards demanded by society.

What ethical crimes earned the censor's black mark? Most had to do with a failure to exercise proper leadership of the familia: a lifestyle of excessive luxury; neglect of one's crops; overindulgence of one's wife and children; failure to observe norms regarding marriage, inheritance, or divorce; cruelty to slaves; failure to take care of one's clients; commercial fraud; or participation in disreputable trades like acting or prostitution.

Daily Life and Religion

The Romans valued simplicity. Clothing, although coded to distinguish social classes, was unelaborate. Diets consisted of bread, simple vegetable dishes, fruits, and roasted meat, plus wine, invariably cut with water. Houses were simple structures turned inward to face a central open courtyard; poorer families resided in multiunit apartments that were based on the same design. Education in the early Republic was minimal except for those of senatorial or equestrian rank, and it took place entirely in the home. Boys received the basics of reading, writing, and arithmetic; were filled with moral tales of figures from Roman history; and began physical training as a preparation for military service. Girls, on the other hand, were instructed in home crafts like spinning, weaving, and sewing. Economic life centered on farming and local handcrafts, and much of the trade was by barter; in fact, the Republic did not even have a standard coinage until the early 3rd century BCE, when the geographic expansion of the Republic made a single coinage necessary.

Roman religion was polytheistic and animistic, focusing on a multitude of gods and spirits. The well-known deities of Jupiter, Venus, Mars, and the rest bore close resemblance to the Olympian gods and goddesses of the Greeks, and in later centuries the Romans emphasized the union of their mythologies. But for most Romans the smaller local divinities took precedence, especially the spirits of family ancestors known as the "household gods" (*lares familiares*), the daily worship of whom was the responsibility of the pater familias. These spirits watched over the household and the family property. Family ancestors continued to care for their descendants, and so prayers of dedication, thanksgiving, and respect were given to them always.

Religious life demanded constant, dutiful observance, following precise formulas of wording, gesture, and offering. Any mistake or omission rendered the ritual null and void. Since the Romans believed their well-being depended on the care of their spirit gods, observation of proper ritual was a matter of crucial significance. Religion was not a source of joy or spiritual exaltation but rather a moral responsibility. It is not accidental that the characteristic descriptor of Rome's legendary ancestor, Aeneas, was the Latin adjective *pius*—not "pious," but "dutiful."

SIZE MATTERS

The institutions, practices, and civic values established by the early Republic faced a dramatic challenge when the Republic began to expand. By 387 BCE the Roman Republic's might had extended only through a sweep of territory roughly 30 miles from the city. The increased area brought with it an increased population, which Rome incorporated under its constitution. Conquered landowners and shopkeepers kept their property and legal rights, but now, as Roman plebeians, they paid taxes to the Republic. The Republic in turn used the additional revenues to connect towns with networks of roads and to bring freshwater into them with systems of aqueducts.

Territorial Expansion and Social Conflict

The larger the Republic grew, the more concessions it had to make to the plebeians who made up the bulk of the population. Two **consuls** served each year, sharing executive power. As early as 400 BCE plebeians had won the right of eligibility to the lower magistracies, and by 367 BCE the plebeians had forced passage of a law requiring that one of the two consuls be a plebeian. Soon the plebeians demanded a greater voice of their own in government, and the Republic responded by creating a plebeian council (*concilium plebis*) that played an advisory role. After the next wave of conquests, however, which extended the Republic's power through all of central Italy, the decisions of the plebeian council were made binding even if disapproved by the Senate.

The rise in power of the lower orders appeared to increase the representative nature of the Republic, but the patricians offset this by strengthening their ties with individual clients among the plebeian leaders. Moreover, the complex series of checks and balances among the various assemblies and magistracies prevented any single group from monopolizing power. The Greek historian Polybius (ca. 200–117 BCE) was a great admirer of the Republic and among the first to

Roman Aqueduct   The Romans excelled in building aqueducts—complex delivery systems of tunnels, channels, bridges, and fountains to transport freshwater from remote sources. Shown here is one of the best-preserved examples, the Pont du Gard near Nimes (ancient Nemausus) in France, constructed in the late 1st century BCE. Built of stones fitted together without clamps or mortar, the span soars 160 feet high and 875 feet long, carrying water in a channel along its topmost level from 35 miles away.

champion Rome as the natural successor to the Hellenistic world. He wrote, "The result of this ability the various classes have to help or hinder each other mutually is to create in effect a unified government that can respond to any emergency; it is impossible to find a constitution better than this" (*Histories* 6.18).

The conquest of territory gained momentum throughout the 3rd century BCE. It is not clear how much of this resulted from intentional expansionism and how much from successful defensive strategies. However it occurred, by 265 BCE the Romans were in control of nearly the whole of the Italian peninsula and with their command of the westward-facing harbors were poised to move out into the sea-lanes. But there was a problem, because most of the western Mediterranean then lay under the control of Carthage. This wealthy North African city had been founded as a Phoenician colony in the 9th century BCE and came to oversee a vast commercial empire. Carthage had more money, more military power, and more naval experience than Rome. Carthage was also closer to the island of Sicily than Rome was, and Sicily, much of it held by Carthage, mattered enormously: it was one of the three greatest grain-producing regions in the ancient world, the other two being Egypt and Anatolia. If all of Sicily fell into Carthaginian hands, Roman Italy would be hard-pressed to feed itself (see Map 6.2).

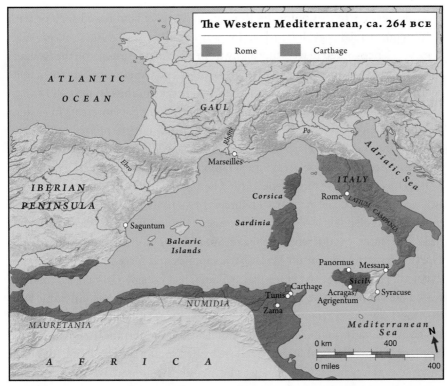

MAP 6.2   The Western Mediterranean in the 3rd Century BCE   The foundations for the later Roman Empire were laid in the western Mediterranean, where Roman forces defeated and supplanted the Carthaginians in the three Punic Wars.

Neither Rome nor Carthage saw any workable way for them to share control of the Mediterranean, and consequently they never really tried. Rome had two factors in its favor: the solid loyalty of the peoples they had incorporated into the Republic and its mastery of a new technique of naval warfare. By dropping a series of large spiked planks onto the deck of an opposing ship, they could affix it to the Roman vessel, which allowed their soldiers to cross over and fight an infantry battle on the high seas. Between 264 and 146 BCE Rome fought three bloody wars with Carthage, won each time, and ended up as the master of the entire western Mediterranean basin. These became known as the **Punic Wars** (the name coming from the Latin word for the Carthaginians—*Poeni*—that is, Phoenicians): the first being a war for Sicily (264–241 BCE); the second being a war for control of Spain (218–201 BCE); and the last being an assault directly on North Africa (149–146 BCE), which ended with the complete destruction of Carthage and the sale into slavery of every Carthaginian who survived the carnage.

The Punic Wars

The Punic Wars marked a crucial turning point in Roman history. The first war, fought for control of grain-rich Sicily, required the Republic to develop naval forces. Up to this point the Romans had been a land-based society, with ample commercial fleets but little in the way of military capabilities at sea. With the experience gained in wresting Sicily from Carthaginian control, the Romans quickly moved around 240 BCE to seize Sardinia and Corsica and add them to its realm. With the struggle to control the Mediterranean thus leaning in favor of Rome, Carthage spent the next two decades developing its interests in eastern Spain; Rome countered by extending its reach into northern Italy and coastal France. The inevitable clash came in 218 BCE when hostilities with Carthage were renewed. This second war's most famous chapter was the surprise invasion of Italy by Carthage's young general (and heir to the throne) Hannibal (247–182 BCE), who crossed the Alps with a force of twenty-five thousand infantry and eighteen war elephants. A Roman force under the command of Scipio Africanus (237–187 BCE) conquered Carthage's Spanish territories and advanced into North Africa, which cut off Hannibal's supplies and forced his withdrawal in 204 BCE. In battle against Hannibal at Zama, just outside Carthage, Scipio defeated the young general, who fled into exile, thus ending the Second Punic War. The third war arose from Rome's desire simply to complete the vanquishing of its rival. Already in possession of Carthage's Mediterranean holdings, the Romans chose to bring matters to a close by destroying the city that had caused them so much trouble. Carthage was burned to the ground and all its inhabitants enslaved.[3]

But that hardly ended matters. Off in the east, King Philip V of Macedonia (r. 221–179 BCE) had supported Carthage in its second war with Rome, which prompted the Republic to declare war on him in 200 BCE. Philip surrendered in 197 BCE, and Rome freed the Greek poleis that had been under Philip's control and then withdrew. But when the Seleucid emperor Antiochus III (r. 223–187 BCE) moved his army into newly liberated Greece, the Romans returned (191 BCE), drove him out, and pursued him across Anatolia. Ironically, the Romans' decisive victory over Antiochus took place at Thermopylae, the site of the heroic stand of the Spartan forces against the victorious Persian army of Darius. According to the Greek historian Appian (95–165 CE), the Romans lost only two hundred men at Thermopylae, compared to the Seleucids, who lost ten thousand. So began Rome's expansion into the eastern Mediterranean. By the end of the Third Punic War Rome had seized all of Greece and most of Anatolia. In 146 BCE Rome stood as the undisputed master of the whole sea (see Map 6.3).

The problem was that the Romans had not exactly planned for their success. Their political system, designed to govern a compact land-based republic,

---

[3] The oft-told tale of the Romans' plowing the Carthaginian fields with salt to ruin the soil and prevent anyone from resurrecting the city is untrue.

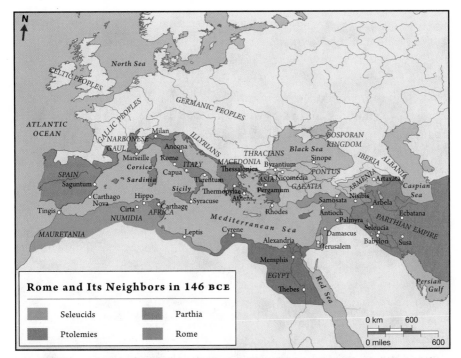

MAP 6.3   Rome and Its Neighbors in 146 BCE   The end of the Punic Wars in 146 BCE left Rome as the dominant force in the Mediterranean world.

unexpectedly found itself in awkward possession of a vast, scattered, sea-based empire. What to do? In the absence of an imperial plan, the Republic simply handed over the conquered lands to the generals who had taken them, thus outsourcing the expense of maintaining the armies and running the provinces.[4] These generals were thus able to amass vast personal fortunes, and they promptly used these to fund further campaigns and to buy influence with the various councils, assemblies, and magistrates back in Rome. To prevent civil servants from being corrupted by bribes, the Republic developed the tradition of assigning the leading magistrates, after their terms of office were complete, to provincial governorships. This got them out of the city and away from the avenues of power, but it also gave them the means to raise fortunes of their own so that they could reenter Republican politics with full coffers.

Stresses on the Republic

In other words, the Republic tried to combat corruption by spreading the corruption around. This revolving-door movement from central government to provincial leadership and back again proved immensely profitable to the forty or

---

[4]   Roman armies were organized into units called legions, which were in turn composed of three forces: cavalry, heavy infantry, and light infantry (auxiliaries). The size of legions varied considerably over time. Through most of the Republican period, a typical legion had three hundred cavalry and forty-two hundred heavy infantry, with highly changeable numbers of auxiliaries.

Bread and Circuses   The Circus Maximus ("Giant Track," literally) in Rome was, like the forum, a site for popular gatherings. Athletic contests of all sorts (especially chariot races) took place here, and the Circus also was a venue for food distributions. Most of the public games held here were associated with religious festivals.

fifty families who monopolized the process. It also caused terrible hardship and turmoil for the bulk of the people.

The Punic Wars had left many of Italy's farms physically and financially ruined, the victims of rampaging soldiers, neglect, or cheap imports of grain that knocked Italy's farmers out of the market. Many thousands of small landholders therefore sold their lands to the rich, who established vast plantations—known by the Latin term of **latifundia**—that specialized in commercial crops like olives and grapes. With so many slaves available because of the wars, there were few employment opportunities for the displaced rural classes, who flooded into towns and cities.

The population of Rome itself increased to unheard-of levels: from somewhere around 100,000 before the First Punic War (264–241 BCE) to easily five times that figure a little more than a century later. By the beginning of the Common Era, the city held well more than a million people within its borders. The government distributed "bread and circuses"—that is, food and entertainment—to keep the crowds quiet, but clearly something needed to be done. By the mid-2nd century BCE, voices in government were crying out for dramatic reform of the constitution as the only way to prevent the Republic from collapse. But what form would such reforms take?

CAN THE REPUBLIC BE SAVED?

From 133 to 31 BCE the Roman world suffered through a brutal series of internal wars and political struggles. Although the names kept changing, the basic issues at stake and the remedies proposed for them did not. The fundamental issue was whether the Republic could, or even should, be saved. Did an empire require a different form of government altogether, and if so, then what form should that government take? But other issues loomed large too. Should the military be reformed to allow broader participation by the people? What, if anything, should be done about the enormous inequities in wealth (and therefore in social and political power) that had resulted from Rome's rapid acquisition of so many new territories? Should a path to citizenship be opened to the newly conquered peoples at both ends of the Mediterranean—and if so, how broad and level should that path be? Conservative politicians wanted to preserve the constitution at any cost; they believed that traditional Roman values and virtues, if earnestly retained, could make the Republican framework work for the whole Mediterranean sprawl. Reformers, on the other hand, were convinced that the Republic was dead, or dying, and that hard-headed realism demanded sweeping change—although not increasing democracy. Calls to alter the constitution in favor of one social class or another met with fervent opposition from those demanding a different change or no change at all. The conflicts were fought in stages: between the Gracchi brothers and the Senate (133–122 BCE); between parties led by Marius and Sulla (86–82 BCE); then again by groups loyal to Julius Caesar and Pompey (52–44 BCE); and finally between the factions led by Octavian and Marc Antony (42–27 BCE).

With the Gracchi, the specific issue was economic: What should be done about displaced poor farmers? The Gracchi brothers, Tiberius (162–133 BCE) and *The* Gaius (152–121 BCE), championed a land redistribution plan that most in the *Gracchi* Senate—wealthy landowners who stood to lose from this legislation—would not tolerate. When efforts at a political resolution failed, the elder brother Tiberius was assassinated in 133 BCE. Gaius took up his brother's cause, but he too lost to his opponents—and committed suicide in 122 BCE. Gaius had proposed granting Roman citizenship to all of the Republic's Italian allies, which would have blocked the patricians' efforts to confiscate their landholdings.

Marius (157–86 BCE), a war hero who had served several terms as consul, al- *Marius* tered a long-standing policy regarding military recruitment. Admission to the *and Sulla* army had earlier required the ownership of land—the idea being that those with a vested interest in the Republic would make the most loyal and effective fighters.

But Marius saw how the vast numbers of displaced farmers, and their replacement with large slave-driven latifundia, meant that there were fewer landholders from whom to draw the number of soldiers needed to defend the state. After all, Rome now controlled an empire 3,000 miles from end to end. So he dropped the land-ownership requirement altogether and opened the ranks to anyone who was capable, interested in serving, and willing to swear loyalty to him as commander in chief. Other generals, in that age of semiprivatized armies, were free to follow suit. Those opposed to him, led by a patrician named Sulla (138–78 BCE), feared that admitting the lowest orders into public life would weaken the Republican spirit of the army.

The Republic dispatched Marius and his new army to North Africa in 107 BCE, where a local ruler named Jugurtha was stirring up opposition to Rome, and in 102 BCE sent him against a marauding group of Germans bent on invading Italy. Two years later, in 100 BCE, Marius retired from politics and moved to the east, hoping to spend his last years in peace. So much for planning. Throughout the 90s BCE Rome's Italian allies pressed their demands for citizenship in the Republic and their fair share in its seized lands and booty. These allies (*socii*, in Latin) finally formed an army of their own and decided to march on Rome, which triggered what is called the Social War (91–88 BCE). Marius was soon called out of retirement to help put down the rebels—after which he again withdrew.

At this point the patrician Sulla, elected consul in 88 BCE, was commissioned by the Senate to lead an army against a provincial rebellion in Anatolia, but the Plebeian Assembly appointed Marius to the post instead, which turned the two rivals (and their respective supporting factions) directly against one another. Sulla's forces purged both the Senate and the Assembly of his opponents, then marched off to Anatolia; Marius then entered Rome while Sulla was away and regained control, taking up his seventh term as consul—only to die soon thereafter. After Marius's death and his own victories in the east, Sulla seized control of Rome (82 BCE), had himself appointed dictator, and spent three years restoring the Senate's supreme position over the Plebeian Assembly—largely by proscribing anyone who opposed him.[5] The Republic lurched from one political extreme to another.

Caesar and Pompey

The effect of Sulla's dictatorship was to empower the aristocracy and weaken the power of the plebeians. Soon, however, new leaders emerged to espouse the people's cause, once again using the army as their tool of influence. The most prominent of these military men were **Julius Caesar** (100–44 BCE) and Pompey (106–48 BCE, called "the Great" after his service to Sulla in 82 BCE).

---

[5] Proscription was the formal proclamation, as well as condemnation of "enemies of the state." Individuals whose names appeared on proscription lists could be killed by any citizen—who could then confiscate the victim's wealth and property. Sulla proscribed three thousand individuals during his dictatorship.

Initially they cooperated on a plan to "restore the Republic" by forming an alliance with Marcus Crassus (ca. 115–53 BCE), but this alliance—a *triumvirate*, meaning "rule of three men"—soon dissolved into open rivalry between Caesar and Pompey, both headstrong, powerful egoists. Ostensibly, Caesar was the radical reformer, whereas Pompey was supported by the conservatives in the Senate. In reality they both probably wanted the same thing—namely, to run the empire as an empire. The centuries-old system of checks and balances among governmental assemblies and offices made efficient administration impossible. And Caesar and Pompey (whose backgrounds were as decidedly undemocratic military commanders) each wanted to institute a streamlined single-command administration. Caesar's power base was in the west; he had conquered Gaul. Pompey had made his name and fortune fighting in the east. Matters came to a head in 52 BCE when the Senate appointed Pompey as sole consul and declared Caesar an enemy of the state. War ensued.

In 49 BCE Caesar drove Pompey from Rome; Pompey fled east to raise more troops. Caesar caught up with him in Greece the following year and, in a battle at Pharsalus, defeated him. Pompey escaped from the battle but was later captured and assassinated by the Egyptian queen, Cleopatra (r. 51–30 BCE, the last active pharaoh Egypt ever had), who was allied with Caesar and in fact later became his lover and bore him a son. Caesar returned to Rome and became sole ruler. In 46 BCE he took the title of dictator. Two years later, after he had declared himself dictator for life, he was murdered by a group of nobles who feared that he was going to institute a monarchy. The Republic was essentially over (see Map 6.4).

Dreams of keeping a workable Republic died hard, however. When the civil struggle entered its final phase, between rival politicians and generals Marc Antony (83–30 BCE) and Octavian (63 BCE–14 CE), many still thought the old constitution could be restored. Antony soon left for Egypt to get support from Cleopatra, with whom he was in love. When Octavian—who was both Julius Caesar's grandnephew and his adopted son—finally defeated Marc Antony at the battle of Actium in 31 BCE, Octavian not only put an end to the strife but also added Egypt to the empire. After more than three thousand years of self-rule, Egypt was now another province in Rome's empire. Octavian's power was consolidated.

Octavian and Marc Antony

Taking the title **Princeps Augustus** (meaning "first in honor"—his name being the first one on the list of Roman citizens kept by the censors), Octavian instituted a new chapter in Rome's history, the principate, and inadvertently gave himself a new name: **Augustus**. Recognizing the utility of maintaining a Republican image, Augustus ruled the empire as an emperor but steadfastly maintained the fiction of representative government, portraying himself merely as the person who put into action the decrees made by the Senate. By appearing to play by the old rules

The Principate

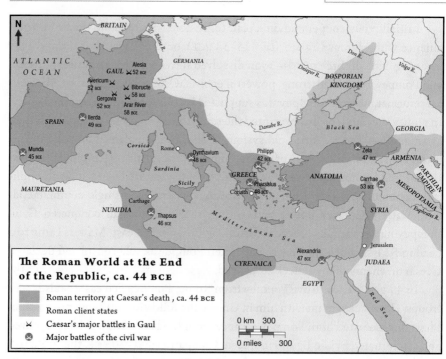

MAP 6.4   The Roman World at the End of the Republic, 44 BCE   By the time of Julius Caesar's assassination in 44 BCE, the territory that would be the Roman Empire was almost complete.

and to uphold traditional values, Augustus reinvented the political system. His reign (31 BCE–14 CE) was unusually successful. The Roman Empire had begun.

ROME'S GOLDEN AGE: THE AUGUSTAN ERA

Augustus and all his successors as rulers of Rome held the title of **imperator**, usually translated as "emperor" but which in Republican times was the term for a victorious general, especially one granted the right to a triumph.[6] This was an official recognition of exceptional military achievement, in which the triumphant general was allowed to parade his troops within the city limits amid songs, prayers, speeches, and festivities. At all other times the army was forbidden to cross the city limits (a line called the *pomerium*) and enter Rome itself. The only organized fighting force permitted within the pomerium was the imperator's personal bodyguard corps—the Praetorian Guard, which also functioned as a police force.

---

[6]   *Imperium* ("command") was the constitutional authority to command obedience—specifically from the military. Different magistracies held different degrees of imperium. All consuls held imperium during their term of office. But the Republic could assign *imperium maius* ("superior command") to individuals on a case-by-case basis.

The early emperors scrupulously avoided anything that smacked of monarchy: their homes were comfortable but not palatial; they wore simple dress; they walked the streets of Rome, took part in public debates, and attended religious services. Even their constitutional and honorific titles had Republican roots. With the exception of aberrant moral monsters like Caligula (r. 37–41 CE) and Nero (r. 54–68 CE), the early emperors cultivated auras of humility, honoring Republican traditions even while exercising central command. Caligula and Nero have been accused of nearly every imaginable vice: incest, theft, graft, torture, murder, prostitution. Caligula reportedly grew insane in office, insisting, for example, on his favorite horse's ordination as a priest, which he then tried to appoint to a consulship. Nero famously allowed the Great Fire of Rome to blaze for days without doing anything about it, then blamed the Christians for it and staged a bloody persecution of them that resulted in thousands more deaths. After nearly two hundred years of civil strife, most Romans were willing to accept autocracy so long as the autocrats kept the peace, promoted prosperity, and did not flaunt their power.[7]

To accomplish those goals, the emperors needed to control the army, facilitate urban growth, and help to integrate the hundreds of ethnic groups who lived within the empire. First, the army needed to be professionalized. In Republic times, soldiers had been essentially the paid employees of the generals who commanded them. Caesar had conquered Gaul, for example, largely to acquire a fortune. Later, when Caesar clashed with Pompey for control of the government, he used a portion of his vast wealth to lure many of Pompey's defeated soldiers to join his army; when Octavian/Augustus defeated Marc Antony at Actium, the same held true for him. Augustus's immediate concern on starting his reign as imperator was to shrink the gargantuan army he had inherited. Hence he commandeered all of Egypt as his personal domain and used the money available through it to offer pensions and award estates to more than a quarter-million soldiers. This action reduced the army to a manageable twenty-eight legions. Soldiers henceforth received their pay, according to a set scale, directly from Rome itself instead of from the generals.

Professionalization of the Army

Given the size of the empire, most government had to be local—which meant that western Europe had to be urbanized. Municipal traditions in the east were widespread and strong, but the west (meaning North Africa, the Spanish peninsula, and virtually all of Europe north of the Alps) remained overwhelmingly rural. Most of Europe itself, moreover, consisted of a vast, dense forest in which the tribal inhabitants had established a sprawl of occasional clearings. To bring order to this world, the Romans began to build cities and a network of roads to

Urban Growth

---

7   Caligula was murdered by members of his own bodyguard. Nero, who fancied himself a great artist and athlete, was politically inept as well as a murderous brute. He committed suicide before the group of soldiers planning to kill him could reach him.

connect them. Most inland cities began as military encampments that settlers refilled after the soldiers had moved on. The officials placed over these new settlements administered their surrounding districts, maintained the roads, and established all the public buildings needed to foster Roman civilization: temples, theaters, bathhouses, market squares, courts. So long as they maintained order, kept the population reasonably peaceful, and avoided blatant corruption, most municipal leaders, and later the provincial governors who represented the next higher stage of the imperial bureaucracy, enjoyed considerable freedom of action. In this way the empire operated more as a confederation of semi-independent city-states and provinces than as a monolithic empire taking orders from an autocratic central regime.

Social Integration   Many elements of Roman life contributed to social integration. The twin religious policies of toleration and syncretism played particularly important roles. Polytheisms, generally speaking, accommodate one another easily. My belief in one river god does not necessarily threaten your belief in another: two different rivers, two different deities—and hence there is no need for one religion to challenge or usurp the other. It is even possible that the two are the same god manifested and understood differently in different places. When the Romans absorbed first Greece and then the rest of the Hellenistic lands, they identified similarities between their faiths. The Greek thunder god Zeus approximated the Roman sky god Jupiter; Aphrodite paired with Venus; Athena resembled Artemis. Such parallels were not coincidental. As we have seen, polytheisms originate as attempts to explain natural phenomena: storms at sea happen because the sea god is angry about something, for example. And since Mediterranean societies confronted the same major phenomena, the divine powers they used to explain them bore certain similarities. By encouraging the Mediterranean peoples to recognize the same gods and goddesses, the Romans fostered a single, multiethnic civilization.

However, only the higher Greek divinities—the gods and goddesses of Mount Olympus—were merged in this way. Daily religious observances for most Roman people still focused on local deities and ancestral worship. This led the emperors to inaugurate communal ruler worship. The custom began as a civil recognition of the deification of late rulers; thus Augustus promoted the deification of the assassinated Julius Caesar, and his successor Tiberius (r. 14–37 CE) championed the deification of Augustus. Deceased rulers were to be regarded as universal "household gods"—symbolically, a pater familias to the entire empire. Soon enough, however, the notion arose of recognizing the divinity of the living emperor. By encouraging, and then by requiring, subjects to worship emperors (past or present) as divinities, the Romans tried to keep a degree of common religious practice among the people so as to counteract the forces that pulled them apart. It did not matter whether anyone actually believed in the emperor-god. It

The Ara Pacis   This procession of senators and high priests appears on a side wall of the Ara Pacis, the "Altar of Peace" in Rome, commissioned by the Senate to honor Augustus and consecrated in 9 CE. As a whole, the Ara Pacis reflects the Augustan vision of Roman civil religion.

mattered only that they were willing to participate in a public, communal ritual once a year in which thanks were given to the divine ruler for his guidance. Dutiful observance, not sincere conviction, was both the goal and the spirit of the requirement. A cohesive civil society, not spiritual enlightenment, was the aim.

THE SEA, THE SEA

The Mediterranean Sea—"Our Sea" (*Mare nostrum*) to the Romans—was the essential infrastructure holding the empire together (see Map 6.5). Physically, the sea consists of two deep basins separated by an underwater ridge between Sicily and Tunisia, with narrow straits at either end. (The Strait of Gibraltar connects it with the Atlantic Ocean to the west, and the Dardanelles links it to the Black Sea to the northeast.) With a surface area of nearly a million square miles, it stretches 2,200 miles from west to east and nearly 1,000 miles at its greatest north–south expanse. Water enters the sea through the two straits and from a handful of rivers—the Nile in Egypt, the Ebro in Spain, the Rhône in France, and the Po in Italy. However, the warm climate causes faster than usual evaporation, which in turn causes the Mediterranean's relatively high salinity—hence the proliferation of salt deposits around the coastline.

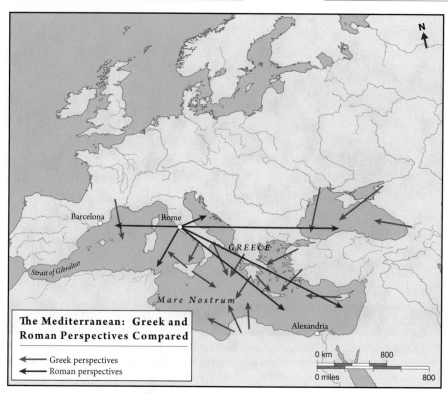

MAP 6.5   The Mediterranean: Greek and Roman Perspectives Compared   Whereas the Greeks established hundreds of colonies abroad, the Romans recognized that their central position in the Mediterranean was an ideal site from which to create a network of links with all the peoples of the sea. Adapted from Malkin, Irad, *A Small Greek World: Networks in the Ancient Mediterranean* (2011).

Despite those million square miles of surface area, however, the Mediterranean is not large enough to have a significant tide. Ships can thus set sail at almost any hour of any day, a significant advantage for the trading cities that surround it. The Mediterranean's temperate climate results from its fortunate geography, and its smooth waters are a consequence of the relative narrowness of the Strait of Gibraltar: most North Atlantic storms cannot pass through the strait and instead are diverted up the western coastline of Europe. (This is one reason why it rains so much in England.)

Given these inviting conditions, ancient sailors had a relatively easy time crossing the Mediterranean. Moreover, the many islands and jutting prom-

Mediterranean ontories like the Italian and Greek peninsulas meant that sailors could ply
Trade Routes   the sea-lanes without ever losing sight of land, which helped them to reach faraway ports without getting lost. The ancients steered by landmarks rather than by the stars. Peoples as far apart as eastern Spain and the Holy Land could be in

regular and reliable contact with one another, buying and selling wares, sharing ideas, and establishing permanent relationships. And in fact they needed such contact, because none of the coastal societies was economically self-sufficient. Mountains ring most of the eastern Mediterranean basin, and the Sahara Desert stretches along its southern expanse. In many places the mountains reach almost to the coast. Cut off from their agricultural hinterlands, coastal societies could not produce all the foodstuffs and material goods they needed to survive, and therefore they needed to trade with one another to stay alive. The natural qualities of the sea made this trade possible virtually year-round—even for bulky, heavy commodities.

The Romans recognized that their central position in the Mediterranean was an ideal site from which to create a network of links among all the peoples of the sea. With Carthage in ruins, no rival stood in Rome's way. But lust for power was not the only motive behind Rome's expansion—and may not even have been the most prominent one. Rather, the Roman value of practicality likely played an important role. The Mediterranean linked hundreds of coastal societies; a ship sent out from Rome could reach Barcelona in only three days, Alexandria in ten. And these societies shared similar agricultural methods (the terracing of arid hinterlands, widespread use of irrigation systems), similar diets (grains, fish, olive oil, and wine), and similar social organizations (tradesmen and merchants playing the lead, rather than large landholders). If we think of the Mediterranean as a single entity, then the attraction of uniting them under a single administration becomes clear: with a single currency, single law, single tariff code, and single system of weights and measures in place, goods, capital, and services will move with optimal efficiency, raising everyone's standard of living.

Rome Takes Charge

Experience within Italy had convinced the Romans that people will put up with the loss of political freedom if they can still prosper economically, whereas policies of inclusion of subjected peoples within the dominant society will go far to relieve civil unrest. When attempting to secure a new territory, the regime begun by Augustus therefore took care to "Romanize" its institutions and trade, reinstall local rulers as representatives of the empire, and then withdraw. Since travel by sea was so quick by ancient standards, the Romans seldom had to occupy the lands they conquered. Word of any rebellion would reach the imperial court quickly, and a fleet could be dispatched long before the rebellion had a chance to take root. In other words, a town or district newly added to the Roman Empire could conceivably never see a Roman soldier again, as long as the laws were obeyed, the taxes paid, and things kept quiet.

Romanization

Loading Grain on a Transport Ship   A worker here pours grain into a barrel; once full, the barrel would be rolled into the cargo area below deck. The name of the ship—*Isis Giminiana*—is given at the far left. The ship's master (*magister*) is Faurales, and the merchant is Abscanius. Two other workers haul sacks of grain up the gangplank at the right. This ca. 200 CE fresco comes from Ostia, a port city at the mouth of the Tiber River in central Italy.

While adding territories to its empire, Rome's army also provided a tool for social engineering. Taking further Alexander the Great's policy of cultural integration, the Romans opened the army to recruits from every part of the empire—enrolling Celts, Dacians, Illyrians, Libyans, Phoenicians, and Syrians alike, plus many others. In turn, their combined military experience helped bring Roman culture to the provinces. Non-Roman recruits received three meals a day and a regular salary, traveled from one end of the empire to another, and helped to keep the peace and serve the common cause. Along the way they learned Latin, acquired the basics of Roman law and morals, and practiced Roman civic religion. The empire's goal was to break down each soldier's sense of particular ethnic affiliation and replace it with a new identity, one based on membership in a larger, interconnected society. After twenty years of service, each soldier received either a cash pension or the grant of an estate and could enjoy all the fruits of citizenship.[8] The estates awarded were large, prosperous, and never in the individual soldier's original homeland. Having created a "Roman"—that is, someone whose self-identity and personal allegiance went beyond mere ethnicity, someone who participated in an idea of human unity—the last thing the government wanted was to restore him to his place of birth. In this way, the army used to fullest effect the Mediterranean, Mare Nostrum, to integrate the peoples of the empire, redistribute them, and cement the idea of "Romanness."

---

[8]   Citizenship was a prerequisite for joining the army. But noncitizens could enlist in the auxiliary forces and earn citizenship after retirement—to be passed on to their sons.

The emperor was the commander in chief of all the legions. In practice, however, the regular command of each legion was given to an imperial representative known as a **legate** (*legatus*), whom the emperor selected from the members in the Senate. In smaller provinces that required the presence of only one legion, the legate also served as the provincial governor. In larger provinces, two or more legions were assigned; a separate legate was assigned to each legion, but the provincial governor served as a superior commander to each legate. In this way, senators endorsed imperial power, while the throne made a point of recognizing senatorial privilege. Even more important, Rome placed senators in positions in which their status was publicly seen. The fiction of Republicanism was thus given continual attention, even as true control of the army remained centralized in the emperor's hands.

ROMAN LIVES AND VALUES

The first two centuries CE are known as the era of the Roman Peace, or **Pax Romana**. Like all historical labels it represents only a partial truth, and although most of the *Pax Romana* empire experienced a sustained tranquility, there was more than enough discontent around to keep the soldiers busy. Consider the rebellion in England in 60 CE led by Boudicca, the widow of a Briton tribal king. Some Roman soldiers had plundered the dead king's home, tied up and flogged Boudicca, and made her watch as they raped her daughters. After the attack, Boudicca rallied the Britons to drive the Romans from England. As the senator and historian Tacitus (ca. 56–120 CE) narrates it:

> Then a horde of Britons surrounded [the Roman garrison at Camulodunum—modern Colchester] and ransacked and set the town all ablaze, forcing the garrison to take refuge in the temple [to the divine emperor Claudius]; this temple was stormed after a two days' siege. Rome's ninth legion, under the command of Quintus Petulius Cerialis Caesius Rufus, tried to relieve the town but was first stopped, then routed, by the victorious Britons, who massacred the entire infantry. . . . [Boudicca's troops] delighted in plunder and scarcely gave a thought to anything else, for they continually passed right by Roman encampments and garrisons and headed straight for whatever targets had the most loot and the least protection. The Roman and provincial dead in those places is reckoned at seventy thousand, for the Britons had no interest in taking or ransoming prisoners or exchanging prisoners. All they wanted was to slit Roman throats or put nooses around them, to put Romans to the torch or to crucify them. . . . Boudicca circled her soldiers in a chariot in which her daughters rode with her, and cried out: "Britons! You are accustomed to female commanders in wartime. I am the daughter of accomplished warriors, but

I am not now fighting for wealth or for a realm. Rather, I fight simply as an ordinary woman who has lost her freedom; I fight for the wounds done to my body and for the outrage done to my daughters. Roman malice knows no bounds—they murder old men and rape young girls. May our gods grant us the revenge we deserve!" (*Annals* 14.32–35)

It took eleven years for the Roman army to put down Boudicca's revolt—although they never managed to capture Boudicca herself. Following the defeat of her army, Boudicca killed herself by drinking poison.

Even so, for all the signs of discontent, no ancient society experienced anything close to the prosperity and social stability of the empire during the two centuries of the Pax Romana. Cities multiplied and grew, rights of citizenship were continually extended to more and more people, and piracy in the Mediterranean—which had been widespread throughout the Hellenistic Age—came to an end. Literacy spread, and something close to a regular system of justice ordered everyone's lives. In 212 CE, under Emperor Caracalla (r. 198–217 CE), every person in the empire who was not a slave was declared a citizen. The elaborate commercial networks allowed each region of the empire to specialize in producing what it did best (see Map 6.6).

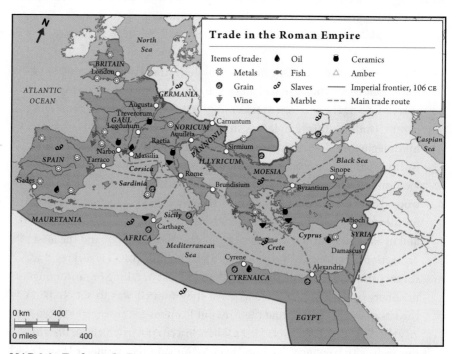

MAP 6.6   Trades in the Roman Empire   Bustling trade routes helped to consolidate Roman rule over the far-flung empire.

Two significant economic weaknesses remained, however. First was reliance on slave labor. Slaves comprised as much as 20 percent of the empire's population, so labor-intensive activities—agriculture and mining in particular—were vulnerable to labor shortages. In the ancient world, the mortality rates of slave populations usually exceeded their birth rates, which meant that societies dependent on slave labor continually needed to add new slaves to the mix just to stay even. As long as the empire kept conquering new territories—and thus acquiring new slaves—the problem was held at bay, but only temporarily. The second weakness was the fondness of the wealthiest Romans for Asian luxury goods like silk and spices, which they purchased in large quantities. This passion drained gold and silver reserves from

Roman Women   Wall painting from Herculaneum, near Rome, 1st century CE, depicting a set of ladies being groomed by a servant hair dresser.

the Roman economy. Until about 200 CE, mines were able to keep up, but productivity declined quickly thereafter, which raised the danger of currency devaluation. But during the Pax Romana years, these were only potential weaknesses; for the time being, abundance and comfort were the hallmarks of Roman economic life.

The Romans adopted many of the great Greek intellectual and artistic achievements, but popular prejudice of the time regarded Greek culture as effete. They saw it as too inclined to luxury, idleness, and pleasure, especially when compared to the manly self-discipline and pragmatism that they liked to think was the essence of Romanness. Some of this is simply the swagger of the victor, but it would be a mistake to dismiss it outright. Roman culture valued a sense of duty—to the familia, to the household gods, to one's city, and finally to the empire. A good life was a life of virtue, of owed service duly performed. These were the values the Romans brought with them into the eastern Mediterranean, where they encountered the two dominant philosophies of the Hellenistic era, Epicureanism and Stoicism (see chapter 5).

Of the two, Stoicism appealed more to the Romans. Among philosophers the most prominent Roman Stoics were the tragedian, essayist, and statesman Seneca (4 BCE–65 CE) and the former slave turned moralist and teacher Epictetus (55–135 CE). Seneca dedicated many years of his life to serving the empire, even taking on the thankless task of tutoring the teenaged Nero. In the year 65 CE Nero accused Seneca of complicity in an attempt to murder him and ordered his former teacher to commit suicide. Seneca complied by slitting his wrists, but his blood flowed

Roman Stoicism

so slowly that he never lost consciousness. He drank poison next, but it too failed to kill him. Finally Seneca immersed his slashed arms in a hot bath. The warmth opened his veins, the blood ran out, and at last he died. His protracted death brings to mind such Senecan statements as "Act toward men as though God were always watching; speak to God as though men were always listening" and "You can tell a man's character by how he receives praise" (*Epistles* 2.2 and 52.12, respectively).

In contrast to the aristocratic Seneca, Epictetus led a life of poverty and austerity. Born lame and into slavery, he nevertheless learned some philosophy from a local teacher after his owner moved to Rome and granted Epictetus his freedom. He went on to teach philosophy himself. In 93 CE he moved back to Greece and set up a school. His most memorable passage comes from his *Enchiridion* (*Handbook*):

> In life, you ought always to behave as you would at a formal banquet. A dish is being passed around and it comes to you—so reach out your hand politely and take a modest helping, and then pass the dish along without delay. If a dish does not come your way, don't act out your longing for it by stretching out your hand for it. Just wait until it comes to you. This is how you should act regarding everything in life—including children, wife, career, and wealth. (ch. 15)

Stoic ethics conformed to Roman morals in the broadest sense—with their emphasis on duty, forbearance, self-discipline, and concern for others. Above all, one ought to serve Rome, praise Rome, live for Rome—because only in the empire and its vision of the unification of all societies in a single working whole can the harmony of the world be attained. Here is how the Roman poet Virgil (70 BCE–19 CE) described the empire's destined mission:

> Others shall cast their bronze to breathe
> with softer features, I well know, and draw
> living lines from the marble, and plead
> better causes, and with pen shall better trace the paths
> of the heavens and proclaim the stars in their rising;
> but it shall be your charge, O Roman, to rule
> the nations in your empire. This shall be your art:
> to lay down the laws of peace, to show mercy
> to the conquered, and to beat the haughty down.
> (*Aeneid* 6.1012–1028)

For at least 150 years after Augustus, Romans did this rather well. Dividing society between *honestiores* ("the better people") and *humiliores* ("the

Imperial Administration

lesser people"), they provided a reliable infrastructure for urban life and a consistent form of justice for each. The honestiores consisted of the senatorial and equestrian classes, municipal officials, and army veterans, and their status entitled them to immunity from torture, lesser criminal fines, and, in capital crimes, exemption from crucifixion. (Like Seneca, honestiores condemned to death were allowed to commit an honorable suicide rather than face the intentionally humiliating and agonizing death by crucifixion.) The humiliores consisted of everyone else in the empire apart from the slaves—who, in terms of the law, were counted as property rather than people. People were expected to obey the law, pay their taxes, participate in public religious rites, and hold to the ethical duties of family care and public service; if they did so, the empire largely left them alone. Even in the prosecution of crime, Roman tradition was to allow matters to be resolved with as little state involvement as possible.

Most civil cases were tried without any public officials whatsoever. A plaintiff filed a complaint with a local magistrate called an *aedile* who maintained a list of individuals in the vicinity who held Roman citizenship. Any citizen accepted by the plaintiff and defendant could serve as judge. The aedile's role was limited to making sure the temporary judge understood the basics of the law as it pertained to the type of case he was judging. The judge's decision was then entered in the municipal records, and the matter was closed.

Taxes were collected by a tax-farming system. The imperial court determined its budgetary needs for the year and then apportioned the revenues owed by each province, district, and city to meet that need. Local officials, who presumably understood the economic realities of their own territories better than administrators back in Rome did, then collected taxes accordingly as they thought most fair and effective given local conditions. If they gathered more than they were required to send to Rome, they kept the surplus (public officials did not receive salaries); if they failed to meet their tax obligation, they were expected to make up the deficit out of their personal funds. Officials also paid for local public works out of their personal funds—roads and aqueducts, maintaining harbors and sewers, and so on. Personal profit from public taxation, therefore, was not frowned upon. In fact, some profit was necessary if the officials were to be held liable for years of deficit. What sounds like an invitation to abuse actually worked fairly well. If an official collected so much tax that the people began to grumble, Rome would hear of it quickly enough and deal with the overaggressive governor.

The system was sufficiently effective to survive even disastrous reigns like those of Caligula and Nero, whose well-known personal licentiousness went down poorly with most Romans precisely because such indecency was so very un-Roman. Domitian (r. 81–96 CE), an obsessively controlling personality, left most of the Senate disaffected by his failure to maintain the Augustan fiction of

Republican rule, but he did leave the treasury with a surplus despite an ambitious building campaign and several expensive military ventures.

HEIGHT OF THE PAX ROMANA: THE "FIVE GOOD EMPERORS"

The high point of the Pax Romana came during the reigns of the so-called Five Good Emperors: Nerva (r. 96–98 CE), Trajan (r. 98–117 CE), Hadrian (r. 117–138 CE), Antoninus Pius (r. 138–161 CE), and Marcus Aurelius (r. 161–180 CE). This was the time of the empire's greatest physical expanse and its greatest prosperity, but what really made these emperors so "good" was that they returned to the Republican fiction, giving the Senate its due respect while exercising autocratic control. Moreover, each of the five had the decency not to have a surviving heir, which allowed the Senate to appear to be the deliberative body for the selection of the next emperor. In reality, each of the five adopted his most capable general, who then became his successor after carefully going through the motions of a supposed senatorial election.

Thamagudi, Modern Timgad, Algeria   Founded by the emperor Trajan in 100 CE, Thamagudi boasted a theater, a forum, and streets paved in a checkerboard pattern.

The rulers appointed the provincial governors, district officials, and municipal chiefs who then administered the empire locally. Most came from the class of urban elites known as the **curiales**. Their chief duties were to provide justice, collect taxes, maintain roads and waterways, and keep the cities and harbors in good repair. Given the Roman means of tax gathering, these civil servants could acquire great wealth, but their sense of civic-mindedness obliged them to make up for public deficits personally. They were expected to use their own funds to provide public entertainments, food distributions, and religious ceremonies in honor of the emperors. That so many curiales did so provides an index of the strength of Roman public spirit.

◆

During the Pax Romana, in sum, the Stoic and dutiful ethos cultivated by the Romans helped them to create a remarkably stable and proud society. They saw themselves as the heirs to the Greek and eastern worlds, and they eagerly absorbed whatever in those traditions had practical value. Yet they also regarded themselves as morally superior, less inclined to luxury and ease, and dedicated to strong virtues and a hardheaded sense of pragmatic living. Those given to other values were the objects of scorn. For example, the Jews, who refused to Romanize or to serve in the army, were reviled although the Romans respected the antiquity of their traditions. Marcus Aurelius, author of the popular work known as the *Meditations*, described the secret of the Stoical Roman soul and its superiority to a new spirit that had appeared on the scene:

> A beautiful soul is one that is equally ready at any given moment to relinquish the body and give itself over to extinction and annihilation, or to continue living. Such preparedness must be the result of conscious judgment reached through reason and with dignity if it is to persuade anyone else; it must never result from obstinacy or with soul-killing display—as it does with the people called Christians. (*Meditations* 11.3)

WHO, WHAT, WHERE

Augustus	Julius Caesar	plebeians
censor	latifundia	Princeps Augustus
consul	Latins	Punic Wars
curiales	legate	res publica
equestrians	pater familias	Senate
Etruscans	patricians	Twelve Tables
imperator	Pax Romana	

SUGGESTED READINGS

Primary Sources

Epictetus. *Handbook.*

Julius Caesar. *The Civil War.*

Julius Caesar. *The Gallic War.*

Livy. *History of Rome.*

Marcus Aurelius. *Meditations.*

Plutarch. *Parallel Lives.*

Polybius. *The Histories.*

Seneca. *Epistles.*

Suetonius. *The Twelve Caesars.*

Tacitus. *Annals.*

Tacitus. *The Histories.*

Virgil. *The Aeneid.*

Source Anthologies

Beard, Mary, John North, and Simon Price. *Religions of Rome* (2005).

Cherry, David, ed. *The Roman World: A Sourcebook* (2001).

Kraemer, Ross Shepard, ed. *Women's Religions in the Greco-Roman World: A Sourcebook* (2004).

Lefkowitz, Mary R., and Maureen B. Fant, comps. *Women's Life in Greece and Rome: A Source Book in Translation* (2005).

Mellor, Ronald, ed. *The Historians of Ancient Rome: An Anthology of the Major Writings* (2004).

Shaw, Brent D. *Spartacus and the Slave Wars: A Brief History with Documents* (2001).

Warrior, Valerie M. *Roman Religion: A Sourcebook* (2001).

Studies

Aldrete, Gregory S. *Daily Life in the Roman City: Rome, Pompeii, and Ostia* (2009).

Beard, Mary. *The Roman Triumph* (2009).

Beard, Mary, John North, and Simon Price. *Religions of Rome* (2005).

Boatwright, Mary T. *Hadrian and the Cities of the Roman Empire* (2002).

Carcopino, Jérôme. *Daily Life in Ancient Rome: The People and the City at the Height of the Empire* (2008).

Eck, Werner. *The Age of Augustus* (2007).

Everitt, Anthony. *Augustus: The Life of Rome's First Emperor* (2007).

Fraschetti, Augusto. *The Foundation of Rome* (2005).

Goldsworthy, Adrian. *Caesar: Life of a Colossus* (2008).

Goldsworthy, Adrian. *The Complete Roman Army* (2011).

Goldsworthy, Adrian. *The Punic Wars* (2000).

Grubbs, Judith Evans. *Women and the Law in the Roman Empire: A Sourcebook on Marriage, Divorce, and Widowhood* (2002).

Haynes, Sybille. *Etruscan Civilization: A Cultural History* (2000).

Holland, Tom. *Rubicon: The Last Years of the Roman Republic* (2005).

Horden, Peregrine, and Nicholas Purcell. *The Corrupting Sea: A Study of Mediterranean History* (2000).

Lendon, J. E. *Empire of Honour: The Art of Government in the Roman World* (2001).

Meijer, Fik. *The Gladiators: History's Most Deadly Sport* (2007).

Milnor, Kristina. *Gender, Domesticity, and the Age of Augustus: Inventing Private Life* (2005).

Mouritsen, Henrik. *Plebs and Politics in the Late Roman Republic* (2001).

Reydams-Schils, Gretchen. *The Roman Stoics: Self, Responsibility, and Affection* (2005).

Rives, James B. *Religion in the Roman Empire* (2007).

Schultz, Celia E. *Women's Religious Activity in the Roman Republic* (2006).

Seager, Robin. *Pompey the Great: A Political Biography* (2002).

Seager, Robin. *Tiberius* (2005).

Southern, Pat. *The Roman Army: A Social and Institutional History* (2007).

Speller, Elizabeth. *Following Hadrian: A Second-Century Journey through the Roman Empire* (2004).

Strauss, Barry. *The Spartacus War* (2010).

Williamson, Callie. *The Laws of the Roman People: Public Law in the Expansion and Decline of the Roman Republic* (2005).

For additional resources, including maps, primary sources, visuals, web links, and quizzes, please go to **www.oup.com/us/backman.**

CHAPTER 7

The Rise of Christianity in a Roman World

40 BCE–300 CE

THE EARLY CHRISTIAN WORLD

The story fascinates, thrills, comforts, angers, and embarrasses at every turn, often all at once. It has touched everything from Western political ideas to sexual mores. Christianity began as an obscure reformist sect within Palestinian Judaism, at one time numbering no more than fifty or so believers. It went on, after three centuries of persecution by the Roman Empire, to become the world's most dominant faith.

The history of Christianity in the Greater West is complex, as is its legacy. One would be hard put to identify another idea, invention, school of thought, technology, or value system that has penetrated so far into the DNA of Western culture—and shaped so much of what is both good and bad in it. In this chapter we will see how Christianity arose, how it became a Roman religion, and how it absorbed such intellectual currents of the classical world as Stoic and Platonic philosophy. First, however, we must understand the

The Good Shepherd This wall painting, ca. 100–200 CE, depicts Jesus as the Good Shepherd. Note the heavily Romanized style: Jesus is beardless and wears a Roman tunic. The fresco is in the Catacombs of Saint Priscilla, under the city of Rome. Early Christians used catacombs (tunnels with underground rooms) as burial sites and meeting places for worship. It was much more common among the early Christian generations to portray Jesus as the Good Shepherd than to depict a crucifixion scene.

outlines of the Roman religion that provided the social and moral framework within which Christianity grew.

THE VITALITY OF ROMAN RELIGION

The fact of Christianity's triumph can blind us to the residual strength of traditional Roman religion. Roman cults continued to thrive for centuries, attracting new adherents and shaping both civic and personal lives by the millions. If anything, the empire's portfolio of *religiones licitae* ("legally approved religions") grew faster and stirred hearts deeper than Christianity could even hope to do. Moreover, Roman religion did not remain static but continued to develop new ritual traditions, emotional resonances, and intellectual sophistication. Rome embraced new deities by the score (including, of course, the deified emperors themselves) and built thousands of new temples across the empire. Traditional polytheistic Roman religion must be seen, in other words, as a vital, thriving, expansive, and energetic network of cults, not as a dusty relic patiently awaiting Christian conversion and enlightenment.

Growth of Emperor Worship   The expanding cult of the emperors is the most visible development in religious life. From the moment that Augustus dedicated the first temple to the deified Julius Caesar in 29 BCE, the veneration of Rome's leaders became one of the most important public rituals. The practice was intended to unite the people in

CHAPTER TIMELINE

100 BCE	50 BCE	0	50 CE	100 CE

- 40 BCE Beginning of Herodian dynasty in Judea
- ca. 5 BCE Birth of Jesus
- ca. 25 CE Jesus begins his ministry
- ca. 27 CE Jesus crucified in Jerusalem
- ca. 42–67 CE Missionary journeys of Paul
- 64 CE Great Fire of Rome: Nero blames Christians
- 64–305 CE Intermittent brutal Roman persecutions of Christians
- 66–70 CE Great Jewish Revolt
- ca. 126 CE Pantheon built in Rome

an act of thanksgiving for the blessings of the Pax Romana. The political motive behind emperor worship is obvious, but that does not mean emperor worship was insincere. In most ancient religions, divine forces permeated the physical world and caused or affected most natural phenomena, and the gods themselves wandered through our world at will and spoke to people through signs and oracles. Classical folklore and literature are full of tales of humans venturing into the afterworld, too: Odysseus and Aeneas are primary examples. So the idea that a living human ruler could be imbued with divine qualities was not out of the question, no matter how self-serving such a notion might be.

In the first three centuries CE, nearly half of all the state temples erected were dedicated to deified emperors living or dead. Statues of them were frequently added throughout the empire to temples that were already dedicated to another god or goddess. Emperors also imported into the capital city gods from regions around the empire that were associated in some way with the personal history of the ruler. Septimius Severus (r. 193–211 CE), for example, built a massive new 140,000-square-foot temple in the heart of Rome in honor of Bacchus and Hercules, the Roman variants of the Greek god and Greek hero, Dionysus and Herakles. Both figures were familiar, but their unique pairing was the cultic practice of Septimius's hometown in North Africa. It highlighted the emperor as the living embodiment of cultic and civic unity—the linchpin holding together the whole fabric of the Pax Romana.

| 150 CE | 200 CE | 250 CE | 300 CE | 350 CE |

■ ca. 140 CE **Last books of the New Testament composed**

■ 161–180 CE **Reign of Roman emperor Marcus Aurelius**

The Pantheon Construction of the Roman Pantheon was finished around 126 CE. The temple's dome, which weighs around five thousand tons, is the largest unreinforced concrete dome ever constructed. A circular opening at its top lets in a dazzling beam of light that moves around the walls, illuminating the shrines of the various Olympian deities.

The **Pantheon**, built by the emperor Hadrian (r. 117–138 CE), was an all-purpose temple dedicated, as its name suggests, to the whole roster of major deities within the empire. Consisting of a portico (or porch) with a colonnade of three ranks of granite columns, behind which rose a vast rotunda covered with a splendid concrete dome, it was—and remains—a stunning site. The Pantheon was consecrated as a Catholic church in the 7th century, named in honor of Santa Maria dei Martiri.

The imperial cult took great pains to absorb and authorize new cults in the provinces, so that religious life not only took on a unifying structure but also grew more varied while doing so. New cults arrived with every generation and every territorial expansion of the empire. The

Mystery Religions

best known were the cults of Cybele (or Magna Mater—the "Great Mother"), Isis, Mithras, and Sol Invictus (the "Unconquered Sun"), but there were countless others. These cults had diverse and often obscure origins. The Mithras cult, for example, originated in Asia Minor but claimed descent from the ancient Persian religious figure of Zoroaster, whereas the cult of Isis—which had certainly begun in early Egyptian times—took on the shape that Rome absorbed in Hellenistic Greece. Diverse origins aside, these new cults had much in common; hence historians often refer to them as **mystery religions,** or religions of salvation. All of them promised answers to the ultimate questions of human existence and a framework for worship and belief in this world while waiting for the world to come.

Were these new mystery religions a reaction against the centralizing efforts of the emperors? If so, they failed. The embrace of the new practices by Rome revitalized imperial religion in the first three centuries CE. It encouraged believers to participate in civic rituals and filled their hearts and minds with hope and comfort. In 110 CE Pliny the Younger, then governor of Bithynia, on the southern coast of the Black Sea, wrote admiringly to the emperor Trajan (r. 98–117 CE) about the resurgence in traditional religion:

It is now indisputable that temples long abandoned are being used frequently and that sacred rituals long forgotten are being observed again. The meat of sacrificial animals can be purchased anywhere one goes, too, whereas so long ago buyers of it could hardly be found. Judge from this how many peoples' lives can be reformed; all they need is a chance at repentance. (*Letters* 10.96–97)

Pliny's closing line suggests a new development in religious thought—the belief in, and the desire for, forgiveness of sins. Traditional religion stressed community with others in the present world more than the attainment of another, better life in a world yet to come. It privileged the ideas of civic virtue and ritual exactitude over ethical improvement, and it emphasized *doing* good instead of *being* good. In other words, instead of earning forgiveness of one's sins and whatever reward such forgiveness would entail, it stressed acting to unite the community.

Most of the provincial cults, like those of Isis and Mithras, did posit an after-life to which repentant believers went. (The afterlives of the unrepentant or the nonbelievers were less clear.) Those who died in the cults' good graces could look forward to an eternal reward of some sort. A 3rd-century CE epitaph erected on the tomb of Aurelia Prosodos, an Isis worshipper, by her husband, Dioskourides, reads, "To the gods of the underworld, Dioskourides, husband of Aurelia Prosodos, the best and sweetest of companions, erects this memorial. Farewell my lady! May Osiris grant you a draught of cool water." In the Isis cult, the goddess' husband Osiris revived the worthy deceased with a drink from an underworld spring, which began their enjoyment of eternal peace and pleasure.

In another innovation, several of the new cults were text oriented. With the exception of the Hebrew scriptures, previous religious writings were by and large mere collections of set prayers and ritual formulas. Influenced by the Hellenistic spread of philosophical and literary inquiry and the textual frenzy of Second Temple Judaism, however, the new religions of the first centuries CE produced a new type of religious literature. These speculative, interpretive texts explored ideas about the relationship between the mundane and divine worlds, the nature of human life, and the purpose of human suffering. The gods of the provincial cults were not simply divine potentates demanding rote prayers and well-practiced ritu-als. Instead, they were benevolent beings who understood human difficulties and desired that people live upright and ethical lives—in most cases (Isis, Mithras) to attain an otherworldly salvation, but in others (some strains of Judaism, for in-stance) simply to pursue justice and morality for their own sakes. The new texts were not scriptures—that is, they did not have the canonical status of the Jewish and later Christian writings, nor did they fill the same sort of liturgical function. Instead, they explored the intellectual ramifications of their central conceits.

Mithras and Isis   Two of the most popular religious cults in ancient Rome were those of Mithras and Isis. The Romans believed worship of the god Mithras originated somewhere in Persia, but this cannot be confirmed. The crucial episode in Mithras's story was his slaying of a sacred bull, the scene depicted here. The cult of Mithras was open only to men and was most popular among the ranks of the army. The cult of Isis, by contrast, was the domain of women. She was the goddess of marriage, health, and wisdom (especially in the realm of dream interpretation).

In so doing, these texts dissociated philosophy from religion, a development that enriched both traditions. Philosophy received a new stimulus by focusing less on the nature of the universe and more on the human lives within it. In turn, religion became increasingly a thing to think about and not simply to perform. As the ancient Greek thinker Epicurus (341–270 BCE) had famously put it, "Any philosopher's words that do not aim to relieve human suffering are pointless." The new provincial cults increasingly sought more than universal order and the submission to fate or divine desire. Instead, their followers desired solace, forgiveness, and the promise of a personal contentment. The Greater Western world entered the Common Era with a new attitude of spiritual and intellectual questing—an attitude that would shape the civilization of the next thousand years.

THE JESUS MYSTERY

Approximately 2 billion people today identify themselves as Christian; given a current world population of roughly 6 billion, Christians therefore comprise about 33 percent of the total. Islam comes in second place, with roughly 1.2 billion faithful (20 percent). Hinduism, with nearly 800 million adherents, ranks third

- ■ Christian, 1,965,993,000
- ■ Muslim, 1,179,326,000
- ■ Hindu, 767,424,000
-   Nonreligious, 766,672,000
- ■ Buddhist, 356,875,000
- ■ Tribal religion, 244,164,000
- ■ Atheist, 146,406,000
- ■ New religions, 99,191,000
- ■ Sikh, 22,874,000
-   Daoist, 20,050,000
- ■ Jewish, 15,050,000
- ■ Baha'l, 6,251,000
- ■ Confucian, 5,067,000
- ■ Jain, 4,152,000
- ■ Shinto, 3,571,000
-   Parsi (Zoroastrian), 479,000

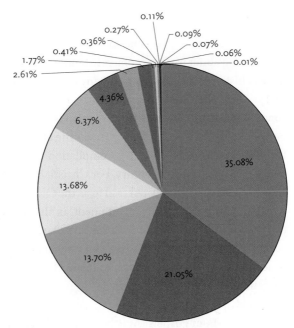

FIGURE 7.1   The World's Religions Today

(12 percent). Judaism, by contrast, makes up only about 0.20 percent of the world population, numbering a mere 15 million adherents. Jews, indeed, are almost statistically insignificant—an irony, given their remarkable place in the history of the Greater West (see Figure 7.1).

That development was neither rapid nor assured, however. Instead, Christianity spread with almost painful slowness and suffered repeated setbacks along the way. As late as 300 CE, if one could have surveyed the whole of the Roman Empire and then placed a bet on which religion in it was most likely to become the dominant religious force in the Western world, Christianity would not have been the pick. By that date, even after three hundred years of ardent evangelizing, teaching, bearing witness, and, as Christian tradition asserts, the performing of countless miracles by missionaries, Christians made up no more than 2–3 percent of the empire's population and possibly as little as 1 percent.

Moreover, biology, not conversion, accounts for the lion's share of whatever growth did occur in those years. Christians married other Christians and raised their children in the faith. Conversions did take place, however, and those who brought the gospel of Jesus to the "pagans" did so at the risk of their lives, a fact later Christians pointed to with pride. Christians had a significantly higher profile in the cities of the eastern Mediterranean than in other parts of the Roman world by 300 CE. Still, through vast stretches of the empire the very name of Jesus had yet to be heard, much less adored.

The New Testament and History

How a tiny sect thus grew to dominate Western culture is not easy to explain. Even after more than two thousand years, scholars are still trying to figure it out and still arguing about it. Two problems stand in the way. First, no one approaches the issue of historical Christianity—or any issue, for that matter—with absolute objectivity. Try as they might to remain detached, scholars are influenced by their personal convictions—even if the conviction is an ardent denial of belief. Second, our principle source for the history of Jesus's life and the careers of his early followers is the **New Testament**, which is a compilation of notoriously difficult texts written over a period of nearly a century. For Christians, the New Testament supplements the Hebrew Bible (usually referred to as the Old Testament) as holy scripture.

The canon of the New Testament as the modern world knows it did not become settled until the late 4th century. And its specific wording—reconciling variant readings and filling gaps—was not set until the early 5th century, a long time after the events it purports to relate. Twenty-seven texts comprise the New Testament (see Table 7.1):

- Four gospels (Matthew, Mark, Luke, and John), accounts of Jesus's life and teachings;
- A narrative of the actions of the original twelve apostles—the disciples hand-picked by Jesus to spread his teachings—immediately after Jesus's death;
- Seven authentic epistles (letters) by the later apostle Paul;
- Seven more epistles that tradition attributes to Paul but that he almost certainly did not write;
- Seven more epistles falsely accredited to four of the original twelve apostles; and
- The book of Revelation, a densely symbolic dream vision of the end of the world.

Not one of these twenty-seven works was written in Jesus's lifetime. Jesus himself wrote nothing and is never reported to have ordered his followers to write his teachings down. The earliest texts in the New Testament are the letters of Paul, who acknowledges that he never laid eyes on Jesus or heard him speak during his lifetime. The four gospels themselves, which provide the most detailed and precise information about Jesus, were not written until at least sixty years after his death. Nor were they necessarily written by the apostles whose name they carry. John's gospel, for example, was most likely written by a disciple of John—that is, by someone who learned about Jesus from John. Thus it likely represents John's understanding of who Jesus was and what he said and did, but few scholars believe that John himself wrote the gospel that bears his name. Hence the lateness of our

TABLE 7.1   **Books of the New Testament in the Order of Their Composition**

Year (CE)	Text	Author
50	1 Thessalonians	Paul
54–55	Galatians	Paul
55	Philemon	Paul
56	Philippians	Paul
56	1 Corinthians	Paul
57	2 Corinthians	Paul
57–58	Romans	Paul
(66–70: Jewish Revolt and Rome's subsequent destruction of the Second Temple)		
68–73	Gospel of Mark	? (attributed to Mark)
70–90	1 Peter	? (attributed to Peter)
80–85	Gospel of Luke	? (attributed to Luke)
80–85	Acts of the Apostles	? (attributed to Luke)
80–90	Colossians	? (attributed to Paul)
80–100	James	? (attributed to James, brother of Jesus)
85–90	Gospel of Matthew	? (attributed to Matthew)
85–90	Hebrews	? (attributed to Paul)
90–95	Gospel of John	? (attributed to the Beloved Disciple)
90–100	Ephesians	? (attributed to Paul)
90–100	2 Thessalonians	? (attributed to Paul)
90–100	1–2 Timothy, Titus	? (attributed to Paul)
90–100	Jude	? (attributed to Jude, brother of Jesus)
92–96	Revelation	? (attributed to John)
95–100	1–2 John	? (attributed to John)
120–130	3 John	? (attributed to John)
130–140	2 Peter	? (attributed to Peter)

closest written evidence of Jesus and his ministry. This lateness, combined with the many contradictions in the texts, leaves any effort to understand the rise of Christianity facing enormous challenges.

What are some of those contradictions? Many are simple discrepancies in chronology. The gospels of Matthew, Mark, and Luke, for example, all state that the Last Supper (Jesus's final meal with the full company of his twelve apostles, before his arrest by the Romans) took place during Passover, the Jewish holiday commemorating the exodus of the Hebrews from Egypt, whereas the gospel of John records that it occurred sometime before it. Others are flat-out contradictions of the historical record, such as Luke's famous setting of the scene of the birth of Christ:

> In those days a decree went out from Emperor Augustus that all the world should be registered. This was the first registration and was taken while Quirinius was governor of Syria. All went to their own towns to be registered. (2.1–2)

There is no evidence of a census of the entire empire under Augustus, however, only a handful of provincial censuses. Moreover, the only census of Judea that was performed when Quirinius was the governor of Syria took place in either 6 or 7 CE, which is at least a decade too late for Jesus's birth. Jesus was actually born between the years 7 and 3 BCE. The modern calendar, based on the number of years since the birth of Jesus, was invented in the 6th century by a Syriac monk who calculated backward from his own time, based on the reigns of Roman emperors, but in the process he made an arithmetical mistake—something easily done when working with Roman numerals—which explains how Jesus was actually born several years "before Christ."

Another set of contradictions in the New Testament are occasional tensions between the portrayals of Jesus's character in the gospels. Luke's Jesus, for example, shows a particular sensitivity toward women, whereas Matthew depicts a Jesus who shows hardly any interest in them at all—not even in his own mother. Mark's Jesus is a terse miracle worker who, apart from calling people to repent their sins, speaks mostly in oblique parables (short allegorical stories that indirectly convey moral lessons); John's Jesus, by contrast, is loquacious to an extreme and capable of both precise common-sense speech and sophisticated philosophical language.

A CRISIS IN TRADITION

Thus, although the basic outlines of Christian growth are fairly well known, the precise knowledge of how, when, and where the faith spread remain unclear and hotly debated. One rare point of agreement among scholars today is that the history of **Jesus of Nazareth** and the movement he founded must be understood in the context of Jewish tradition. Jesus was a Jew, as were all of his original followers, none of whom regarded their commitment to Jesus and his teachings as a denial of their Jewish identities. Indeed, they saw Jesus as the fulfillment of Jewish prophecy. In Jesus's own words, as recorded by Matthew,

> Do not think that I have come to abolish the law or the prophets. I have come not to abolish but to fulfill. For truly I tell you, until heaven and earth pass away, not one letter, not one stroke of a letter, will pass from the law until all is accomplished. Therefore, whoever breaks one of the least of these commandments, and teaches others to do the same, will be called least in the kingdom of heaven; but whoever does them and teaches them will be called great in the kingdom of heaven. (5.17–19)

These assurances might have quieted more Jewish concerns, however, if Jesus himself had been more strictly observant of Torah. Instead, he provoked widespread ire by performing work on the Sabbath, allowing his followers to call him the **messiah** ("anointed one," "Christ" in Greek), speaking scornfully of the Temple, and, most boldly of all, referring to himself as the Son of God. By Jesus's lifetime several Jewish traditions coexisted in uneasy dialogue with one another, but none of them was quite prepared for this.

The Hellenistic era had witnessed the rise of Jewish factions, divided primarily by two factors: commitment to Temple observance and the authority of the priests, *Jewish* on the one hand, and the new focus on rabbinical leadership and the "oral Torah" *Factions* (rabbinical law and its commentaries, later codified in the Talmud), on the other. Added to this mix was a potent new element: the belief in a coming *apocalypse,* or the world's imminent destruction with only the righteous saved. This apocalyptic faith resulted from the rising trend of exogamous marriage (or marriage outside of Judaism) and the exiled Jews' close contact with Zoroastrianism and its division of the world into two opposing forces, good and evil. The political scene contributed a number of factors as well. After the Maccabean revolt against the Seleucids, Judea was ruled by the Hasmonean and Herodian dynasties for a century, the last independent Jewish state until the 20th century (see Map 7.1). Although the era had helped foster a communal Jewish spirit, however, the Jews were sharply divided toward their dynasts. By long tradition Jewish kingship belonged solely to the lineage of the ancient ruler David, which made the Hasmoneans usurpers in the eyes of many. Struggles within later generations of the dynasty only confirmed their critics' opinion of them as imposters. Thoroughly Hellenized, the Hasmonean kings even bore Greek names rather than Hebrew ones. The line of Herod that replaced the Hasmoneans in 40 BCE was widely detested by the Jews, who regarded them (correctly) as puppets of the Roman state.

The kings tried to gain legitimacy by associating themselves closely with the Temple priests and their most important political allies, a party known as the

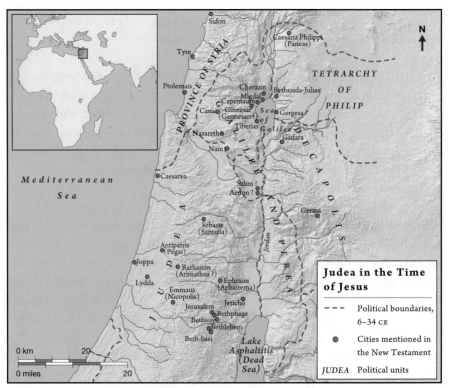

MAP 7.1   Judea in the Time of Jesus   Jesus did not travel far in his lifetime. The distance from his hometown of Nazareth to Jerusalem is roughly 65 miles. Except for his visits to the Temple in Jerusalem, he was seldom more than 20 miles from home.

Sadducees. These were one of three "philosophical sects" (*hairesis*) into which Judea was divided, according to the Jewish historian Josephus (37–100 CE); the other two were called the **Pharisees** and the **Essenes**. The Sadducees were an aristocratic party, the ideological descendants of the "Children of the Exile." They were reputedly strict upholders of Temple ritual, dedicated to the literal reading of scripture and the rejection of the oral Torah—"reputedly" because much of what is known of the Sadducees' thought comes from the testimony of writers hostile to them, including the authors of the four Christian gospels, as well as Josephus.

Opposing them were the Pharisees, the party more closely associated with the "People of the Land" and the rabbinical tradition. The most renowned figure believed to have been a Pharisee was the Babylonian scholar Hillel (110 BCE–10 CE, according to tradition), who is considered the central figure in establishing the core of the rabbinical law and its commentaries. The Pharisees generally were commoners (although, being urbanites, they regarded themselves as superior to the outlying rustics) and resisted Hellenization. They also held a number of religious beliefs that set them apart from other Jews—most notably, a belief in the immortality of the soul and the resurrection of the dead. They took the lead in advocating the arrival of a messiah, a savior of the Jewish people who would return them to freedom and safety. The Essenes, the third Palestinian sect mentioned by Josephus, are more difficult to identify. It is even possible that the name is a catchall term used by writers like Josephus to describe a host of minor Jewish sects that shared certain views. An ascetic community, they lived in isolated congregations and dedicated themselves to repentance and prayer in the hope of achieving mystical union with YHWH. The Essenes were the most eschatological sect within Judaism, meaning they were characterized by expectations of an imminent apocalyptic end of the world, although it is difficult to generalize how widely believed such ideas were.[1]

Jesus of Nazareth thus entered a Jewish world in high-voltage turmoil. When the Romans, led by Pompey the Great, conquered Judea in 63 BCE, they dismissed *Roman* and jailed the Hasmonean king and ruled in his name for twenty-five years, while *Rule* Pompey and then Marcus Crassus plundered the province mercilessly. In 40 BCE they installed the new dynasty, the Herodians. The Jews had mostly disdained the Hasmoneans, but they ardently hated the Herodians, and for good reason. Herod, named "king of Judea" (r. 37–4 BCE), was a brute who murdered anyone who stood in his way—which included two high priests, his brother-in-law, his mother-in-law, and even his wife. A lover of massive architecture, Herod built and rebuilt palaces, Roman temples, gardens, amphitheaters, hippodromes, baths, and fountains across Judea—including an ambitious restoration of the Jerusalem Temple itself. And he paid for it all with heavy taxation. Perversely, he ordered a golden imperial eagle to be installed over the gate leading into the restored Temple. When two rabbis complained of the blasphemy, Herod had them burned alive. Following Herod's death in 4 BCE, the emperor Augustus divided Judea into three provinces, one of which was administered by a Roman procurator; the other two went to Herod's sons, Herod Antipas and Philip. By the time Jesus began his ministry, sometime around 27 CE, Judea was crackling with religious rivalries and social–political tensions.

MINISTRY AND MOVEMENT

The gospels of Matthew and Luke relate a handful of episodes from Jesus's childhood and youth, but only become detailed when Jesus begins his ministry, around *Jesus and* the age of thirty. An early follower of **John the Baptist**, a Jewish revivalist *John the* preacher who prophesied the arrival of the messiah and urged his listeners to *Baptist*

---

[1]   The Essenes were probably the group whose collected writings, the Dead Sea Scrolls, were discovered at the Qumran caves near the Dead Sea in 1946.

King Herod and Jerusalem   The southern wall of the Temple Mount is shown here. It is the entrance to King Herod's expansion of the Second Temple.

penance and passionate commitment to God, Jesus took up John's cause after his own baptism by John, most scholars believe. (The word *baptize* comes from the Greek *baptizein*, a verb meaning "to dunk" or "to plunge." Jewish tradition had long involved people giving themselves ritual baths of purification; John's innovation was to actively plunge the faithful into the water.) The gospels then relate how Jesus traveled throughout Judea, performing miraculous healings, driving out demon spirits, calling people to a revivified faith and universal love, and especially teaching them about the approach of "the kingdom of God." What he meant by this last point is by no means clear. Some of his followers (and his critics) understood him to be talking about Heaven itself, God's own dwelling place; others regarded the "kingdom" as a state of spiritual grace, a soulful enlightenment. To still others the kingdom was this world, the world we inhabit, but made just and perfect by a heavenly appointed ruler, a new King David—earthly life as it should be, in other words.

The differences matter. If the kingdom Jesus spoke of was indeed a paradise and an afterlife, then he was speaking the language of the Pharisees. If he meant a spiritual state, then he was appealing to the Essenes. If he intended an earthly kingdom marked by justice and order, then the Sadducees might have been the intended audience. And still other possibilities exist. As it happened, Jesus's oblique language could have been intended to appeal to everyone, which meant that it displeased and offended far more people than it attracted. In the life-and-death struggle of 1st-century Palestine, Jewish scholars on all sides were still fighting over the exact lettering of sacred texts, their meaning, and the purposes to which they were put. For them, Jesus's words often sounded so confusing as to be provocative:

> Then the disciples came and asked him, "Why do you speak to [the crowds] in parables?"
>
> He answered, "To you it has been given to know the secrets of the kingdom of heaven, but to them it has not been given. For to those who have, more will be given, and they will have an abundance; but from those who have nothing, even what they have will be taken away. The reason I speak to them in parables is that 'seeing they do not perceive, and hearing they do not listen, nor do they understand.'" (Matthew 13.10–13)

Jesus himself did not begin to preach and to baptize until after he learned that the detested Roman-installed governor of Galilee, Herod Antipas, had arrested *Jesus and* and executed John the Baptist.[2] Jesus thus assumed leadership of a preexisting *the Twelve* popular movement, but he quickly put his own stamp on it by summoning a corps *Apostles* of personal disciples, the **twelve apostles**, who spread the idea that Jesus himself was the long-promised messiah.[3] John's more general revivalist movement thus became specifically a Jesus movement, a sect dedicated to his unique ministry. Jesus traveled throughout Galilee, Samaria, and Judea proper—an area roughly 40 miles from east to west and roughly 80 miles from north to south—and preached the primacy of a passionate love of God over a formal observance of rituals. The desire and intent behind our actions, he seemed to say, matter more than the actions themselves.

Jesus's message was forceful: If we harden our hearts against one another, we distance ourselves from "the kingdom of God"—by which he meant not only a heavenly hereafter but also a just and peaceful life on earth in spiritual

---

[2]   According to the Jewish historian Josephus, Herod Antipas killed John ("a good man who urged the Jews to be virtuous, to treat one another justly, and to worship the Lord") out of concern that he might raise a rebellion. In the gospel of Matthew (ch. 14) and the gospel of Mark (ch. 6), a different tale is told, with variants. John the Baptist had condemned Herod Antipas's marriage to Herodias, since she had previously been married to Herod Antipas's half-brother (confusingly also named Herod). At a banquet, the beautiful daughter of Herodias by her first marriage, named Salomé, performed a dance that so enchanted Herod Antipas that he offered her anything she wished—to which she replied that she wanted John the Baptist's head on a platter. Mark insists that Herodias told Salomé what to wish for; Matthew states that Salomé made the gruesome choice on her own. The gospel versions seem less likely than Josephus's bare-bones account. Presumably Mark and Matthew wanted to present a moral tale about the danger of female seductiveness.

[3]   Being twelve in number, the apostles provide a symbolic association with the Twelve Tribes of Israel. Of the gospel writers only Luke—who wrote the most fluent Greek—calls them *apostles*; Matthew, Mark, and John use the word *disciples*.

communion with one another. Our weakness is our vulnerability to sin, which makes us selfish, lustful, angry, and covetous. "Love your enemies," he urged, "[and] do good to those who hate you. Bless those who curse you, and pray for those who mistreat you." Love and forgiveness of others, he insisted, both express and inspire our love of God and guide us to the "kingdom of God."

When criticized for his inexact observance of Torah, Jesus replied that YHWH cares more for the sincerity in our hearts than for the mechanical precision of our rites. In this passage from Matthew, Jesus quotes two Torah verses:

> When the Pharisees heard that [Jesus] had silenced the Sadducees, they gathered together, and one of them, a lawyer, asked him a question to test him.
> "Teacher, which commandment in the Law is the greatest?"
> [Jesus] said to him, "'You shall love the Lord your God with all your heart, and with all your soul, and with all your mind.' This is the greatest and first commandment. And a second is like it: 'You shall love your neighbor as yourself.' On these two commandments hang all the Law and the Prophets." (22.34–40)

Jesus's own criticisms of the Pharisees and Sadducees display flashes of temper and a sharp tongue. It is small wonder that the leaders of the two groups grew irritated with him, locked as they were in a bitter struggle to lead the Jewish people and indeed to define the faith itself.

WHAT HAPPENED TO HIS DISCIPLES?

Jesus's popularity with the Jewish crowds is uncertain. Large numbers of people, perhaps even thousands at a time, regularly turned out to see him and listen to his teaching. However, many of those were mere curiosity seekers, wanting to observe one of his famous miracles, rather than true followers of his movement. To many Jews, and perhaps to most of them, he was an item in the short-term news cycle, the subject of gossip and debate, and nothing more; the evidence clearly suggests that he received only the passing attention of most Jews. Once started on his public ministry, Jesus gathered around him the twelve apostles, whom he charged with the missions of preaching, treating the ill, and exerting "power and authority over all demons" (Luke 9.1). But so long as Jesus himself lived and performed those duties, the apostles seem to have been companions more than anything else. After Jesus's death, they found their calling as the leaders and chief evangelists of the Christian communities—the story told in the book of Acts of the Apostles, which immediately follows the four gospels in the New Testament.

But it is worth noting that even Peter, the leader of the group, had moments of confusion about his mission.

What tipped the scales against Jesus in the Jewish community, ultimately, was the zeal of his disciples to have him recognized as the long-prophesied messiah. *Jewish* This, indeed, is the principal function of Matthew's gospel. Alone of the four *Rejection* gospel writers, Matthew aims specifically at a Jewish audience and focuses on de- *of Jesus* scribing those ideas and actions of Jesus that proved he was the long-promised savior. Echoes of the prophets can be heard everywhere. But there was a problem. Jewish tradition anticipated the arrival of an earthly savior, one who would create a safe, unified state for the Jews—in which justice would flourish and YHWH would be praised. Even as he embraced this designation as messiah, Jesus appeared otherwise; he was a savior of eternal souls, not the leader of a political revival. He did things no messiah was ever expected to do (such as to violate the Sabbath and speak disrespectfully of the Temple) and did *not* do the things that *were* expected of the savior. This combination made it all but impossible for most Jews to accept him in that role.

It is unclear whether Jesus's claim to be the messiah sufficed to warrant an accusation of blasphemy—the official complaint levied at Jesus by the Jewish head *Roman* council. In any event, Jesus's adoption of the title of "Son of God" set the seal on *Repression* Jewish rejection of him. Complaints about Jesus as a blasphemer mattered little to *and* the Romans, however, who regarded Jewish religious disputes with disdain. More *Crucifixion* important to the Roman prefect, Pontius Pilate, was the popular talk among Jesus's supporters that he was the "King of the Jews." This smacked of treason against the Roman state because only the emperor had the right to designate a client-king within the confines of the empire. Pilate was notorious for his high-handed brutishness even before the issue of Jesus confronted him and more than once was rebuked for his harsh methods. When Pilate ordered Jesus to be crucified (likely in or around the year 27 CE), a sign bearing the words "Jesus of Nazareth, King of the Jews" was placed on the cross above his head.[4] It was Roman practice, when crucifying criminals, to identify their crime in this way. (The six thousand supporters of Spartacus who were executed along the Appian Way by Marcus Crassus in 71 BCE, for example, had the designation of "traitor" hung over their heads.)

Pontius Pilate's career as a Roman official with a taste for rough politics is well known. The Jewish philosopher Philo of Alexandria (20 BCE–50 CE) described him as a "rigid, stubborn, and cruel [administrator] who was known to execute lawbreakers even without a trial" (*Embassy of Gaius* 38.299). Josephus describes an incident when Pilate confiscated funds from the Temple and used them to

---

4   In Latin, the sign reads *Iesus Nazarenus Rex Iudaeorum*—hence the acronym INRI that appears frequently in images of the crucifixion.

Jesus and Pontius Pilate   In this 6th-century mosaic from the church of St. Apollinaire in Ravenna, Christ is brought before the Roman prefect, Pilate, who is shown washing his hands. Jesus wears—inaccurately—a purple robe, symbolic of his kingship over all creation.

fund the construction of an aqueduct; when the Jews predictably gathered outside his court to complain, Pilate had secretly scattered dozens of armed soldiers, dressed as Jews, among the crowd. At his signal, the soldiers drew their swords and began attacking the Jews indiscriminately, killing several dozen protestors (*Antiquities* 18.3.2). Of Jesus's life and teachings, Pontius Pilate knew little and cared even less. All that concerned him was the maintenance of peace and order.[5]

After Jesus's death, the small cohort of people still faithful to him ran immediately into hiding, since the Romans were determined to stamp the sect out. Soldiers searched for them from street to street. Then, according to the New Testament, something extraordinary happened. Three days after Jesus was buried, groups of believers began to appear in the streets of Jerusalem proclaiming joyously that they had seen Jesus resurrected from the dead. In three days they had transformed, apparently as a group, from terrified fugitives hoping to escape capture into a company of bold, confident witnesses. They not only acknowledged their belief in Jesus but also broadcast it at every turn, even at the risk of death.

---

[5]   One inscription survives that attests to the existence of Pontius Pilate; it was discovered in 1962 in the ruins of a Roman theater at Caesarea Maritima and is now on view in the Israel Museum in Jerusalem. It is a dedicatory inscription written in Latin, with the English translation, "Pontius Pilate, the prefect of Judea, had the Temple to Tiberius built and dedicated it to the august gods."

For the next few decades, until they themselves began to die in the 50s, 60s, and possibly 70s CE, those early disciples traversed the eastern half of the empire telling anyone who would listen about the transformative saving power of Jesus "the Christ" (the Anointed One, literally). Threats of popular violence or state persecution posed no barrier to them. They faced execution with stoic calm, according to both Christian and Roman reports, happy to embrace the **martyrdom** that would reunite them with their savior. Faithful Christians then and now have no doubt what caused the extraordinary transformation of that small group of disciples during those three days of hiding in Jerusalem; nonbelievers can only wonder. But one thing is clear: something dramatic happened to those people.

Something dramatic also happened to someone who was not there, in hiding, and was in fact helping the authorities to track down Jesus's followers: **Saul (Paul) of Tarsus** (ca. 5–67 CE). Saul was a passionately observant and argumentative Pharisee from south-central Anatolia, a Greek speaker (*Paul* being the version of his Hebrew name in the broader society), and a Roman citizen. He studied Torah at Jerusalem in his youth with R. Gamaliel (d. ca. 50 CE)—revered as one of the greatest scholars of Jewish law in history—and acquired a solid background in Stoic philosophy. By his own admission, Paul never saw or heard Jesus but dedicated himself to persecuting his followers; he was present at, and likely participated in, the death by stoning of Stephen, the first Christian martyr, around 33 or 34 CE. Soon thereafter Paul set out from Jerusalem on the main road to Damascus, when he experienced a dramatic conversion after seeing a vision of the resurrected Christ. Paul mentions but does not describe this experience in any of his letters, but the book of Acts (written, according to tradition, by Luke) tells of it memorably:

Paul of Tarsus

> Now Saul, still breathing murderous threats against the disciples of the Lord, went to the high priest and asked him for letters to the synagogues in Damascus, that, if he should find any men or women who belonged to the Way, he might bring them back to Jerusalem in chains. On his journey, as he was nearing Damascus, a light from the sky suddenly flashed around him. He fell to the ground and heard a voice saying to him, "Saul, Saul, why are you persecuting me?" [Saul] said, "Who are you, sir?" The reply came, "I am Jesus whom you are persecuting. Now get up and go into the city and you will be told what you must do." The men who were with him stood speechless, for they heard the voice but could see no one. Saul got up from the ground, but when he opened his eyes he could see nothing; so they led him by the hand and brought him to Damascus.

After receiving baptism, Paul regained his sight and spent three years in the desert around Damascus, trying to understand the life-altering experience that had occurred to him.

Paul eventually dedicated himself to preaching Christian salvation to non-Jews, a mission that set him at odds with the apostles, most of whom regarded the message of Jesus as a mission meant solely for the Jews. The fact that Paul assumed the title of *apostle* for himself also rankled. He spent the remaining twenty to twenty-five years of his life traveling, preaching, and writing, until he was arrested by the authorities in Rome and executed in 67 CE. Paul's letters are the earliest of the New Testament texts, and they proclaim a powerful message of the hope that faith in the risen Christ offers to suffering humanity. Assuming that his letters are representative of the sum of his thinking, Paul shows no interest in anything that Jesus said or did during his lifetime. All that matters to Paul is the fact that Jesus was God incarnate and that he rose from the dead; Jesus's resurrection has defeated death, and our faith in this fact assures our own salvation. As he wrote,

> Now I am reminding you, brothers, of the gospel I preached to you, which you indeed received and in which you also stand. Through it you are also being saved, if you hold fast to the word I preached to you, unless you believed in vain. For I handed on to you as of first importance what I also received: that Christ died for our sins in accordance with the scriptures; that he was buried; that he was raised on the third day in accordance with the scriptures. (1 Corinthians 15.1–5)

It thus seems likely that the other New Testament texts were composed in part as a response to Paul's understanding of the Christian message, out of a conviction that Jesus's life mattered as much as his death. Paul's Jesus, in other words, should not become the default position. Other understandings of Jesus were just as important. Both literally and figuratively, those other understandings, it turned out, were all over the place.

CHRISTIANITIES EVERYWHERE

Whatever happened in Jerusalem to those first disciples, afterward they went out into the eastern Mediterranean determined to spread the message of Jesus. The problem, of course, was in agreeing on what that message actually was—and for whom it was intended. Was the Christian message intended for the Jews? For the Jews alone? For all people everywhere? There were factions in the early Christian movement supporting each of those views, plus others. Since Jesus and his initial disciples were all Jews, could non-Jews become his followers? And if they did, did they have to observe Jewish teaching and tradition, as the apostles themselves continued to do? If a non-Jew wanted to become a Christian, in other words, did he or she have to convert to Judaism first?

Questions like these abounded, causing many rifts to break out in the Christian movement, and the problems were exacerbated by the fact that no one had the universally recognized authority to settle such disputes as they arose. Peter was the leader of the original twelve apostles, but who should lead the movement after Peter's death in Rome in 64 CE? Peter's line of successors as **bishop** ("overseer") of the Christian community in Rome insisted that they were the heirs of Peter's own spiritual authority and hence were to be accepted as the supreme leaders of all Christians everywhere. But hardly anyone agreed with them. Why shouldn't the bishop of Jerusalem, the site of Jesus's Last Supper, crucifixion, and resurrection, take precedence? Others argued for the primacy of Antioch, the home of the first major Christian community outside of Jerusalem (see Map 7.2). Some insisted that Jesus's brother James (one of Jesus's four siblings—three brothers and a sister—mentioned in the gospels) had a hereditary right to lead the community. Still others argued that there should be no single leader at all and that guidance of the church should be left to a council of all the bishops together.

Until such matters could be resolved, the early Christians had no way to reconcile the differences in their beliefs. The apostles and early missionaries preached their messages in synagogues and market squares throughout the eastern Mediterranean, hoping to win as many converts as possible as quickly as possible, but these were the centers of ancient cultures that reached back two thousand years and more. Literacy was high because most of the people who heard Christian testimonies were versed in Hellenistic traditions. The missionaries, predictably, faced flurries of questions. Even those whose hearts were inclined to accept the new faith required some intellectual satisfaction before they were willing to commit:

- How can God be three separate beings—God, Jesus, and the Holy Spirit—and one indivisible being at the same time?
- If Jesus is "coeternal" with God, why is there no mention of him in the two-thousand-year tradition of Hebrew writings?
- If Jesus is the divine Son of God, how could he experience such human emotions as temptation, fear, and loneliness?

To crowds familiar with Hellenistic philosophy and the Hebrew scriptures, such questions were not easily ignored.

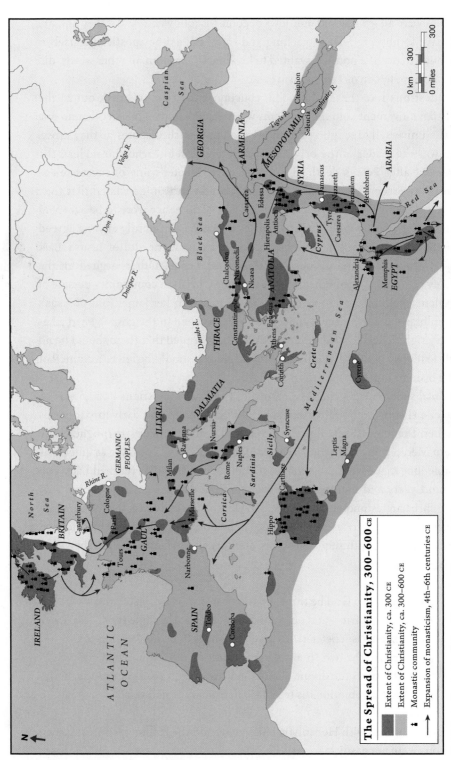

MAP 7.2   Early Christian Communities, ca. 350 CE   Christians were still a minority in the Roman Empire three hundred years after Jesus's death, but Christian communities had taken root in the eastern Mediterranean cities and started to expand into the countryside.

The Spread of Christianity, 300–600 CE

- Extent of Christianity, ca. 300 CE
- Extent of Christianity, ca. 300–600 CE
- ✝ Monastic community
- → Expansion of monasticism, 4th–6th centuries CE

Because the apostles and other missionaries often disagreed on the answers to such questions, the communities of converts they established frequently believed different things. For the first three centuries after Jesus's death, in fact, it is inaccurate to speak of Christianity (with an uppercase "C"). What existed instead were many dozens of christianities (with a lowercase "c"), each with its own beliefs, liturgical traditions, and customs. There were communities of Christians who denied Jesus's divinity and believed good works were necessary for the salvation of some Christians but not for all. Others believed that Jesus had never in fact died but instead had gone into hiding. Some maintained that Jesus had passed along some body of secret knowledge, given only to a few initiates, that gave them the key to understanding that reconciled Christian revelation with Greek philosophy. Some insisted that Jesus had never actually existed in the flesh, and that what his disciples had seen and heard was a kind of hologram. Still others insisted that baptism was all that was needed to achieve salvation. The variant versions were, in all senses of the word, difficult to reckon.

ROMANS IN PURSUIT

Whatever their theological differences, most early Christians practiced their faith in secret, gathering in homes, in remote spots outside the city, in caves, or in warehouses—wherever they might escape notice. They needed to do so because Roman authorities were still in active pursuit of them, for two good reasons. First, to the Romans religion was a public affair, a means of uniting society in the observance of shared rituals. In contrast, Christians largely withdrew from society and taught, as far as the Romans understood it, that the affairs of this world are meaningless, the only meaningful reality being one's eternal existence in the heavenly kingdom yet to come. Christians seldom served in the army and refused to perform sacrifices to the emperor, which called into question their political loyalty. To the Stoic Roman mind, engagement in the affairs of the world was a duty and a sign of virtue; to devalue the affairs of the world seemed not ascetic but immoral. Moreover, Christians still spoke of their departed Jesus as a king, and as far as the Romans saw it, loyalty to a dead traitor was as bad as loyalty to a live one. Worse still, the Christians were said to practice ritual cannibalism by taking the Eucharist, or Holy Communion, in accordance with Jesus's instructions to his disciples at the Last Supper. Indeed, the central purpose of their gathering together was to eat the physical remains of their god Jesus. Even if the Christians ate the body and drank the blood of Jesus only symbolically, in bread and wine, the idea was repulsive to Roman sensibilities.

The second thing that condemned Christians in Roman eyes was their rela- *Crushing* tionship with Judaism. The Romans had no love for the Jews, who were arguably *the Jews*

Masada   Ruins of the Jewish fortress at Masada, where rebel Jews pursued by the Roman army made their last stand in the Jewish Revolt of 66–70 CE. The Dead Sea can be glimpsed in the background. Masada is today the site where Israeli recruits take their oaths of military service.

the most volatile and troublesome people in the empire, but grudgingly respected the antiquity of their religion. When the Great Jewish Revolt of 66–70 CE erupted, Rome responded with heavy force, crushed the rebels, destroyed the Second Temple, killed untold thousands of Jews, and dispersed the rest once and for all. The slaughter was memorably fierce and was meant to be. In only a few years the Jews had passed from being, to Roman eyes, the residents of a hard-to-handle province to a despised race of stiff-necked ingrates and traitors. As the troops marched through Palestine in search of more Jews to kill or exile, they inevitably encountered groups of Christians who were eager to disassociate themselves from the Jewish majority. It is not a coincidence that the Christian gospels began to be written at this time, with their large servings of anti-Jewish language.

By the 70s and 80s CE the number of Christians who were not ethnically Jewish finally overtook the number who were. That itself required some redefinition of the relationship between the two faiths, but when the Jews became the leading active enemy of the Pax Romana, there was additional reason for the Christians to emphasize that they were not Jewish. The gospels make the case with unnerving thoroughness:

But when [John the Baptist] saw many Pharisees and Sadducees coming for baptism, he said to them, "You brood of vipers! Who warned you to flee from the wrath to come? Bear fruit worthy of repentance. Do not presume to say to yourselves, 'We have Abraham as our ancestor'; for I tell you, God is able from these stones to raise up children to Abraham." (Matthew 3.7–9)

After this Jesus went about in Galilee. He did not wish to go about in Judea because the Jews were looking for an opportunity to kill him. Now the Jewish Festival of Booths was near. . . . The Jews were looking for him at the festival and saying, "Where is he?" And there was considerable complaining about him among the crowds. While some were saying, "He is a good man," others were saying, "No, he is deceiving the crowd." Yet no one would speak openly about him for fear of the Jews. (John 7.1–2, 10–13)

Jesus said to [the Jewish leaders], "If God were your Father, you would love me, for I came from God and now I am here. I did not come on my own, but he sent me. Why do you not understand what I say? It is because you cannot accept my word. You are from your father the devil, and you choose to do your father's desires. He was a murderer from the beginning and does not stand in the truth, because there is no truth in him." (John 8.42–44)

Of course, to argue that one is not Jewish is not the same thing as to be anti-Semitic (anti-Jewish), but such an emphasis, repeatedly made over a sufficiently long time span, certainly opened the door to the evolution of a type of Jew-hatred. And as the christianities slowly spread around the Mediterranean, they continually had to repeat and refine their non-Jewishness: the diaspora of the Jews meant the side-by-side establishment of new Jewish communities in the cities as well. Wherever Christian communities took root, in other words, so too did new Jewish ones, and the efforts to explain themselves to the Romans began over and over again.

Persecution by the Romans was intermittent but brutal. Overall, many tens of thousands of Christians were arrested and killed during the first three centuries CE. The lucky ones were quickly executed; the others faced torture and humiliation before vast crowds in Roman forums. Popular resistance to Christians was ubiquitous and took many forms, from angry words to social ostracism to rough street violence, but persecution itself began in Rome as a deliberate policy before spreading, in the 2nd and 3rd centuries CE, into the provinces.

Persecuting the Christians

Catacombs of Saint Callisto, in Rome
The early Christians used underground
crypts and rock chambers to bury their
dead. The bodies were placed in niches like
the ones shown here and then sealed. The
catacombs became places of pilgrimage,
and in this way the dead continued to be
united with the living.

The first persecution occurred under Nero, during whose reign the first Christian communities were established in Rome under Peter and Paul. When the city experienced a catastrophic fire in 64 CE, Nero found the newcomer Christians to be a convenient scapegoat and contrived for them gruesome means of execution. He ordered hundreds of Christians to be covered in bloody animal skins, which made them the prey of packs of wild dogs; others were crucified; still others he had coated in paraffin and set alight as human torches. When the provincial governors took up the cause, they attempted to balance viciousness with some sense of fairness: Christians who converted back to Roman religion were forgiven, whereas those who remained Christian but held Roman citizenship were remanded to imprisonment in the capital. Only noncitizens who refused to renounce their Christian faith received the death sentence.

PHILOSOPHICAL FOUNDATIONS: STOICISM AND NEOPLATONISM

The Enduring Influence of Stoicism

Two philosophical schools offered alternatives to all the Roman and Christian faiths, even while contributing to their intellectual development: Stoicism and Neoplatonism. As we have seen, Stoicism dated back to Hellenistic times, well into the 3rd century BCE, but it received new life from Roman writers like Cicero and Seneca, who found in it the perfect expression of Roman values such as self-discipline, service to the community, and calm acceptance of divine law. Another burst of Stoic philosophy—a widespread and influential one, considering its source—came from Marcus Aurelius (r. 161–180 CE), the last of the "Five Good Emperors" discussed in chapter 6. His aphorisms, compiled in a book that he called "Notes to Myself" but is now known as the *Meditations*, appealed to many Romans and early Christians of the Pax Romana. (It helped that Aurelius wrote his book in koiné Greek, the same dialect used by the New Testament authors, which made his teachings more readily accessible to early Christians.) In line with earlier Stoic tradition, he believed the world is governed by an overarching sense of order and purpose, in service to which human lives play out. The only true happiness results from accepting one's limitations, keeping one's disappointments and frustrations in perspective, and performing one's duties to family, society, and the gods.

Aurelius's term for "order and purpose" is the Greek **Logos**, which resonated with anyone familiar with the gospel of John, where the word has much the same meaning.[6] The Logos, in the Stoic sense, gives not only a sense of the cosmos's purposefulness but also a measure of solace. It addresses the individual seeking both a place in the transient world and a permanent one in the divine world to come:

> The handiwork of the gods is replete with Providence, and the hand of Fate is not detached from nature. Rather, Fate spins and weaves the threads that Providence ordains. Everything flows from the home of the gods; more than that, a sense of needful purpose and well-being pervades the whole creation of which you are a part. Every part of the natural world contains and preserves an element of goodness that is given to it by the very nature of the world as a whole. . . . Take comfort in this thought, and live always by these doctrines. If you wish to face death with something other than mumbling confusion, give up your fascination with study, and let your heart be at rest and express simple gratitude to the gods for what they have done. (*Meditations* 2.3)

Marcus Aurelius This bronze equestrian statue of the great emperor and Stoic philosopher is on display in Rome. Marcus Aurelius's reign, which ended in 180 CE, marked the high-point of the Pax Romana.

Stoicism offered more than a set of rules to follow or a group of ideas to adhere to. Some examples include: "No action is good if performing it causes you to violate a trust or behave shamelessly" (3.7). "Do not act as though you will live ten thousand years, for death is the fate that awaits you. Therefore, while you're alive and able, seek the Good" (4.17). "Do not hold life itself to be the only thing of value. Consider the infinite measures of time and space that lie behind you and before you; in the face of these eternities, what difference does it make whether you live for three days or three generations?" (4.50). "If a cucumber is bitter, throw it away; and if your path is full of briars, change direction. That is all you need to do. It is not for you to ask, 'Why do such things exist?'" (8.50). Stoicism cultivated the soul and urged people to perform spiritual exercises through daily reflection, prayer, and contemplation of the fact of mortality. The Stoics called these practices the

---

6   Meaning "word," literally, *logos* can also be seen in the suffix "-ology" that denotes so many English terms for science—like biology, geology, and meteorology.

discipline of *askesis*—meaning "peace of mind"—from which term the English word *asceticism* derives. Many early Christian leaders saw the compatibility between their religious beliefs and Stoic ethics and used the Roman notions to explain their faith.

The Platonic tradition also kept its appeal with polytheists and, increasingly, Christians, in an amalgam known as **Neoplatonism**. A series of Plato's disciples continued teaching at the Academy long after his death in 347 BCE, most of them *The Emergence* engaged in collecting, editing, codifying, and commenting on Plato's vast *of Neoplatonism* writings. A loose network of Platonist schools also spread across the Hellenistic lands, which ensured that Plato's philosophy and his way of doing philosophy would have the most wide-reaching influence in the centuries following his death. Plato's teaching of an Ideal Universe, from which our muddled and benighted cosmos derives, harmonized with many of the new provincial mystery cults and provided them with intellectual support. Many of the Neoplatonists were equally passionate in observing their traditional polytheistic convictions. In Plato they thus found an intellectualized version of their cults.

Plutarch (46–120 CE), a wealthy Greek who was an enthusiastic supporter of the empire, dedicated his life as a priest of the oracle of Apollo at Delphi. He also composed a shelf of stylized biographies, moral essays, literary criticism, and Platonic commentaries. His best-known and best-loved work is the series of *Parallel Lives*, in which he pairs eminent statesmen from Greek and Roman history. In these lively, intimate portraits of their respective virtues (or lack thereof), his concern is not with the details of political history but with the moral character of his subjects.

As he himself put it, he was interested in "the offhand occasion, word, or anecdote . . . that brings to light men's true tempers more than the story of any of their great battles, even those in which ten thousand men may have died." Nevertheless, Plutarch knew how to tell a good story. His narratives of the disastrous Athenian campaign to Syracuse and of Pompey's defeat at Pharsalus and subsequent death, for example, are gripping set-pieces. The *Parallel Lives* have been popular ever since Plutarch's own time. Roman society read them avidly, as did most Christian scholars at least until the 4th century. In the Renaissance, Sir Thomas North (1535–1604) produced the first version in English in 1597— although he cribbed it from a French translation since he knew no Greek.[7]

Plutarch's essays, by contrast, which medieval commentators grouped under the catchall title of *Moralia* ("Ethical Matters"), have never been as popular but give an indication of the breadth of his interests. They move from "Consolation to My Wife," written after the death of their infant daughter—"Sweet wife, let

---

[7]   William Shakespeare used North's Plutarch when composing his history plays *Julius Caesar, Antony and Cleopatra*, and *Coriolanus*.

us bear this pain with patient hearts. . . . Born after four sons, she was especially dear to you; and so dearly did you long for a girl that, when she finally came, I gave her your own name. . . . She had such a gentle spirit, marvelously kind"—to "On the Delay of Divine Justice," a dialogue that tackles the problem of why evil-doers prosper. The dialogue ends with Plutarch telling a chilling parable about a scoundrel named Thespesius who lives only for pleasure and lies, cheats, and steals from everyone. He falls into a type of coma, and his admirers, thinking him dead, prepare to bury him. He wakes just in time and amends his behavior—having seen in his comalike state a vision of the punishments that await evil-doers. Plutarch's message is that divine justice exists outside of time but is certain. Yet another essay, the speculative "On the Face of the Man in the Moon," attempts a cosmology—a system for explaining the origins and structure of the entire universe. In all, the *Moralia* unite a committed Neoplatonic philosophy with a common-sense search for the alleviation of suffering. Roman religion received a jolt of intellectual rigor in the works of writers like Plutarch, which helps to account for its continued vitality.

Many early Christians felt the attraction of that rigor as well. The Alexandrian theologian Origen (185–254 CE) used the Neoplatonic notion of *emanation*—the idea that the created world results from the outward-flowing essence of life from the eternal center of the Logos. In this way he explained the migration of souls from the Heavenly Divine and out into the created world. Origen supplemented this notion with the idea of spiritual return, a kind of undertow of purified souls flowing back toward the creating center. This idea did not originate with him; his younger contemporary Neoplatonic philosopher Plotinus (204–270 CE; a poly-theist) had been elaborating the concepts of spiritual resurrection and return, as handed on to him by his own teachers, for years. But Origen was the first Christian thinker of note to explicate salvation in intellectual terms derived from a philosophical tradition.

Also Neoplatonic, but ultimately unorthodox from the Christian perspective, was Origen's denial of bodily resurrection. Origen is a unique figure in Christian history: he is regarded as one of the great Church Fathers, the first Christian phi-losopher of any note, yet most of his published ideas proved controversial and were formally condemned by later councils. He left behind an enormous body of writing; Jerome (ca. 347–430 CE), the later theologian who produced the defini-tive Latin version of the Bible (the Vulgate), credited him with nearly two thou-sand separate works. That is clearly an exaggeration. But even accounting for the texts later condemned and destroyed by church leaders, his surviving works are still voluminous.

Like the Roman cults, early Christianity received high-octane intellectual fuel injections from Stoicism and Neoplatonism. Both philosophies enriched it enormously by adding to Christianity's intrinsic emotional appeal a degree of sophistication that it had previously lacked. For the next fifteen hundred years Christian philosophers, scientists, mathematicians, and logicians were among the leading scholars in Western civilization and usually made up the majority of them. This was not necessarily because of the cultural hegemony of the Latin and Greek churches, but simply because the Christian faith itself invited, prompted, and demanded intense intellectual effort. It inspired a fascination with what is difficult and required its followers to acknowledge complex ideas about the nature of the world, human freedom, the meaning of suffering, and the purpose of existence.

Most notably, these early centuries of the Common Era introduced an emphasis on self-awareness, self-examination, and self-criticism. They urged the development of personal conscience and the constant striving for meaning and improvement, ideas that would mark Western culture indelibly. Such concerns had existed before, of course, but never with the same degree of emotional urgency and intellectual resolve. Western culture became marked by a kind of intellectual and spiritual restlessness, convinced that life has genuine meaning and purpose but never quite certain that it had discovered them. All the same, it was confident that the effort to find them was necessary and ennobling.

WHO, WHAT, WHERE

bishop	martyrdom	Pantheon
Essenes	messiah	Pharisees
Jesus of Nazareth	mystery religions	Sadducees
John the Baptist	Neoplatonism	Saul (Paul) of Tarsus
Logos	New Testament	twelve apostles

SUGGESTED READINGS

Primary Sources

Eusebius of Caesarea. *The History of the Church.*
The Gnostic Gospels.
Josephus. *The Antiquities of the Jews.*
Josephus. *The Jewish War.*
Marcus Aurelius. *Meditations.*

The Nag Hammadi Library.
The New Jerusalem Bible.
Philo of Alexandria.
Pliny the Younger. *Letters.*
Plutarch. *Parallel Lives.*

Anthologies

Ehrman, Bart D. *The New Testament and Other Early Christian Writings: A Reader* (2003).

Elliott, Neil, and Mark Reasoner, eds. *Documents and Images for the Study of Paul* (2010).

Warrior, Valerie M. *Roman Religion: A Sourcebook* (2001).

Studies

Boatwright, Mary T., Daniel J. Gargola, Noel Lenski, and Richard J. A. Talbert. *The Romans: From Village to Empire—A History of Rome from Earliest Times to the End of the Western Empire* (2011).

Brakke, David. *The Gnostics: Myth, Ritual, and Diversity in Early Christianity* (2011).

Brennan, Tad. *The Stoic Life: Emotions, Duties, and Fate* (2005).

Brown, Peter. *The Body and Society: Men, Women, and Sexual Renunciation in Early Christianity* (2008, orig. 1998).

Brown, Peter. *The Rise of Western Christendom: Triumph and Diversity, AD 200–1000* (2003).

Ehrman, Bart D. *Lost Christianities: The Battles for Scripture and the Faiths We Never Knew* (2005).

Engberg-Pedersen, Troels. *Cosmology and the Self in the Apostle Paul: The Material Self* (2011).

Ferguson, Everett. *Backgrounds of Early Christianity* (2003).

Fredriksen, Paula. *Augustine and the Jews: A Christian Defense of Jews and Judaism* (2008).

Fredriksen, Paula. *From Jesus to Christ: The Origins of the New Testament Images of Jesus* (2000).

Fredriksen, Paula. *Jesus of Nazareth, King of the Jews: A Jewish Life and the Emergence of Christianity* (2000).

González, Justo L. *The Story of Christianity*. Vol. 1, *The Early Church to the Dawn of the Reformation* (2010).

Jacobs, Irving. *The Midrashic Process: Tradition and Interpretation in Rabbinic Judaism* (2008).

Johnson, Luke Timothy. *Among the Gentiles: Greco-Roman Religion and Christianity* (2010).

Johnson, Luke Timothy. *The Writings of the New Testament: An Interpretation* (2010).

Lampe, Peter. *From Paul to Valentinus: Christians at Rome in the First Two Centuries* (2003).

Lieu, Judith M. *Christian Identity in the Jewish and Graeco-Roman World* (2004).

Luijendijk, AnneMarie. *Greetings in the Lord: Early Christians and the Oxyrhynchus Papyri* (2009).

MacMullen, Ramsay. *Romanization in the Time of Augustus* (2008).

Meier, John P. *A Marginal Jew: Rethinking the Historical Jesus*, 4 vols. (1991–2009).

Meier, John P. *The Vision of Matthew: Christ, Church, and Morality in the First Gospel* (2004).

Rasimus, Tuomas, Troels Engberg-Pedersen, and Ismo Dunderberg, eds. *Stoicism in Early Christianity* (2010).

Stark, Rodney. *Cities of God: The Real Story of How Christianity Became an Urban Movement and Conquered Rome* (2007).

White, L. Michael. *Scripting Jesus: The Gospels in Re-Write* (2011).

Wilken, Robert Louis. *The Christians as the Romans Saw Them* (2003).

Wilken, Robert Louis. *The Spirit of Early Christian Thought: Seeking the Face of God* (2005).

For additional resources, including maps, primary sources, visuals, web links, and quizzes, please go to **www.oup.com/us/backman**.

CHAPTER 8

The Early Middle Ages

300–750

T he Greater West underwent a series of shocks from the 4th to the 8th centuries that gave a radically new direction to its development. Roman might had peaked in the late 2nd century, after which imperial control entered a holding pattern while internal squabbles dominated the political scene. Those squabbles centered on a constitutional problem: the empire had never established an orderly process for succession to the throne, which meant that the death of each emperor triggered some sort of contest for power. Compounding the internal strife, the western half

THE EARLY MIDDLE AGES

of the empire fell victim to successive waves of Germanic settlers driven westward by population pressure and the advancing armies of Attila the Hun (r. 434–453) from central Asia. The Germanic peoples were immigrants and refugees more than invaders, but they were quick to draw swords when the Romans tried to check them at the Rhine and Danube rivers. The combination of internal confu-

sion and external invasion led to Roman decline in the western empire, but also to the rise of a "new Rome" in the east—Byzantium. The Byzantine Empire, with its capital at Constantinople, developed as a strongly centralized and militarized state, in which the government's close relations with the Orthodox Church proved vital to each institution's success. In the Arab and Persian Middle East

Crown of King Recesvinth
The Visigoths, a Germanic people who in 410 stunned the Greater West by sacking Rome, were justly famous for their metalwork, and this crown (worn only in formal ceremonies) is one of their best-known pieces. It is made of gold encrusted with rock crystals, pearls, and sapphires.

new networks of tribal alliances and rivalries arose that challenged control of trade and pilgrimage routes, with violent results. As we will see in the next chapter, the interplay of these developments laid the groundwork for the rise of the Greater West's third great monotheism—Islam.

These four centuries are popularly known as the **Dark Ages** in western Europe, but most scholars refer to them as **Late Antiquity**.[1] Both labels are understandable. For much of the period from 300 to 700, western Europe was a dark place indeed, filled with poverty, famine and disease, nearly constant warfare, almost universal illiteracy, and a material standard of living that is horrifying to consider. Yet many of the institutional practices and cultural values of antiquity were still alive, if in beleaguered and benighted form. Further, for the Greek-speaking lands of the eastern Mediterranean, this was a heroic age when the achievements of the ancient world were fortified by the rapid development of Christianity. From their magnificent new capital city of Constantinople (modern Istanbul) on the Bosporus—the strait separating the Black Sea and the Mediterranean—the people of the Byzantine Empire achieved a level of wealth, power, and cultural glory that were never seen again in the Greater West.

---

[1]   The term **Middle Ages** denotes the thousand-year period between the founding of the Byzantine capital city of Constantinople (ca. 330) and the start of the Italian Renaissance around 1350. Many historians object to the use of "Dark Ages" for the early medieval centuries on the basis that the name is demeaning.

CHAPTER TIMELINE

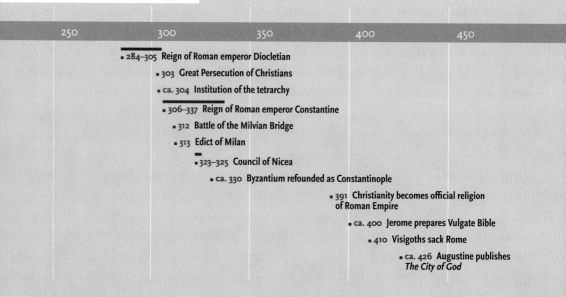

250	300	350	400	450

- 284–305 Reign of Roman emperor Diocletian
- 303 Great Persecution of Christians
- ca. 304 Institution of the tetrarchy
- 306–337 Reign of Roman emperor Constantine
- 312 Battle of the Milvian Bridge
- 313 Edict of Milan
- 323–325 Council of Nicea
- ca. 330 Byzantium refounded as Constantinople
- 391 Christianity becomes official religion of Roman Empire
- ca. 400 Jerome prepares Vulgate Bible
- 410 Visigoths sack Rome
- ca. 426 Augustine publishes *The City of God*

THE IMPERIAL CRISIS

There is no mystery to the decline and fall of the western Roman Empire: a host of internal problems coincided with a wave of foreign invasions. Historians debate the severity of specific causes, or the relative rankings of various factors, but few serious scholars dispute that the combination of internal weaknesses and external pressures did the job. The real mystery is how the empire, despite such a host of problems, managed to survive into the 5th century.

Trouble first emerged in a major way with the death of Marcus Aurelius in 180. Aurelius had designated his son Commodus (r. 180–192) to succeed him, but Commodus was a poor ruler, a snarky, ill-mannered lout who threw tantrums when he did not get his way. He thought himself a great athlete, dressed in lion skins, carried a club, and demanded that people call him Hercules (the Roman name for the Greek hero Herakles). More than once he ordered the execution of senators and officials who opposed his wishes. The political atmosphere in Rome grew toxic in a way it had not been since the infamous reign of Nero. Commodus's death set off a civil war between a host of civil and

Commodus as Hercules The emperor Commodus (r. 180–192) loved to portray himself as a manly man, rather like Russia's Vladimir Putin today, and he regularly staged rigged athletic contests in which he emerged victorious. Here he has had himself sculpted as Hercules.

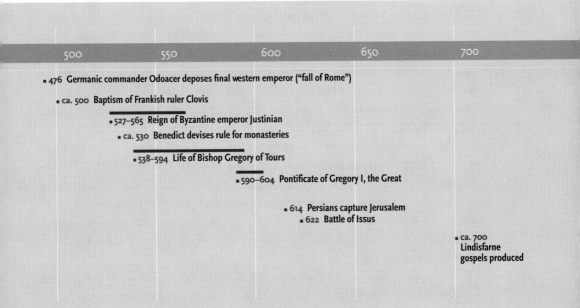

500   550   600   650   700

- 476 Germanic commander Odoacer deposes final western emperor ("fall of Rome")

- ca. 500 Baptism of Frankish ruler Clovis

- 527–565 Reign of Byzantine emperor Justinian
- ca. 530 Benedict devises rule for monasteries

- 538–594 Life of Bishop Gregory of Tours

- 590–604 Pontificate of Gregory I, the Great

- 614 Persians capture Jerusalem
- 622 Battle of Issus

- ca. 700
  Lindisfarne
  gospels produced

Internal Weaknesses military officials, and this became the unfortunate pattern for nearly every imperial succession throughout the 3rd century. The army accordingly grew in prominence as the sole bulwark against social unrest, which meant that power passed almost exclusively to a series of generals, but since each successive general's claim to legitimacy came only from having seized power by brute force, ambitious rivals in the military in turn killed each one. In the sixty-seven years from 218 to 285, there were as many as eighty-three claimants to the throne—only a handful of whom died of natural causes.

Nonstop war undermined the economy by disrupting farming and commerce, and the warmongering generals made matters worse by intermittently devaluing the currency so they would have more coinage on hand with which to pay their troops. But this triggered runaway inflation and drove hordes of laborers into the cities in search of employment or alms, causing the urban centers to become choked with homeless and desperately poor people. The smallpox virus then did the rest. By 300 the empire was reeling from disaster to disaster; the army was divided, decimated, and demoralized; and the economy sputtered and wheezed like a dying engine.

IMPERIAL DECLINE: ROME'S OVERREACH

External Pressures By cruel coincidence, this was when the imperial borders suddenly faced their most severe challenge with the inrush of the Germanic peoples along the Rhine–Danube frontier and the renewed attack of the Persian Empire, which was then under the aggressive Sassanid dynasty (224–651), in the east. The earliest Germans to arrive in large numbers, the Ostrogoths and Visigoths, advanced toward Constantinople but were bribed with money and promises of assistance if they redirected their march into western Europe. They thereby spared the cities of the eastern Mediterranean and moved instead into the underpopulated rural west, as did most of the other Germanic groups that followed, but the Persians could not be so easily disposed of. The lure of controlling the Holy Land and the Hellespont—the linchpins between the European and Asian economies—proved too great, causing the Persians to set their sights on outright conquest.

The Romans fought back valiantly but with little luck. The low point for them came in 260, when the Persians captured the emperor Valerian (r. 253–260) in battle. They held him as a slave, forcing him to kneel on all fours as a stepping stool for the Sassanid ruler when he mounted his horse. The rapid succession of emperors continued unchecked, the western provinces of the empire became overrun with invading Germanic groups, and effective government from the center all but disappeared.

Diocletian's Reforms A respite appeared with the long reign of a stern, no-nonsense emperor named **Diocletian** (r. 284–305). He came from a long line of peasant farmers in the

MAP 8.1 Persian Ascendancy   This is the most famous of the Sassanid rock reliefs, not only because of its workmanship but because of the scene it portrays: the great victory of Shapur I (r. 241–272) over the Roman emperor Valerian (r. 253–260). Valerian was captured and executed, then skinned, stuffed, and mounted on the wall at Shapur's palace.

Roman province of Dalmatia (modern Croatia), had received only an elementary education but was raised with a deep belief in the rightness of the empire, and had sought a career in the army. A talented soldier, Diocletian rose quickly through the ranks and was popular with the soldiers he commanded. When the briefly serving emperors Carus (r. 282–283) and Numerianus (r. 283–284) died—according to several ancient sources, Carus being struck by lightning and Numerianus of a mysterious eye inflammation—the army overwhelmingly threw its support behind Diocletian. He faced enormous problems: a wrecked economy, a restive army, Germanic and Persian invasions, and a bloated, inefficient administration. His solutions were as blunt and direct as his personality.

The worthless currency that had triggered the inflation could hardly be helped. Europe's known gold and silver mines were largely tapped out by Diocletian's time, and without an influx of precious metals the fiscal crisis would continue. Diocletian addressed the problem by essentially withdrawing Rome's currency from circulation and returning the empire to a barter economy. Taxes were collected in kind (clothing, food, tools, manufactured goods, or whatever),

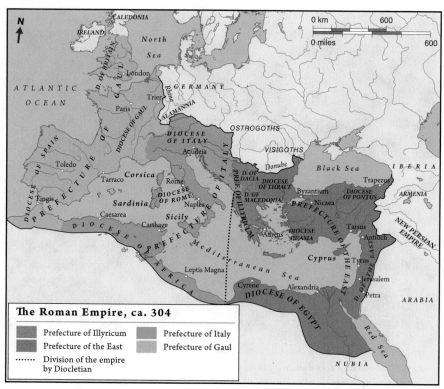

MAP 8.1   Diocletian's Division of the Empire, ca. 304   Diocletian divided the empire into two halves, each governed by an emperor (*augustus*) who was aided by an assistant ruler and designated successor (*caesar*).

and imperial soldiers were paid in the same. The debased coinage—once recaptured, melted, purified, and recast—eventually regained some of its value in Mediterranean trade, but a true money economy would not return to continental Europe until the 10th century.

Turning to the imperial army, Diocletian reformed it into separate civil and military divisions, with one force of "border troops" manning the Rhine–Danube frontier. This long line of fortified stations, together with a separate force of "palace troops," served as a roving field army that was under direct imperial command. Diocletian's border troops were essentially a form of civil militia made up of deputized residents, both Roman and German, of the frontier areas. The palace troops, the more professional fighting force, who were paid with real cash, were thus freed to concentrate on the struggle against the Persians to the east, with good results.

Last, Diocletian chose not to streamline the administration but to cut it into separate units, instituting a **tetrarchy** ("rule of four")—a new system whereby the empire was formally divided into two halves, east and west, with a separate emperor (*augustus* in Latin) for each (see Map 8.1). Diocletian appointed a fellow officer, Maximian, as augustus of the western half of the empire, retaining the wealthier eastern half for himself. Each augustus was assisted by a *caesar*, or junior emperor, who succeeded to the position of his augustus on that person's death or retirement and who then appointed a new caesar to assist him. At a stroke, Diocletian eased the bureaucratic burden on the central administration and provided a regular means for the selection of new augusti.

MARTYRDOM AND EMPIRE

Diocletian is chiefly remembered, however, for instituting in 303 the so-called **Great Persecution**, the longest and most vicious of the state attacks on Christians.

The Great Persecution

> In the nineteenth year of Diocletian's reign . . . in the month of April . . . near the time when Christians celebrate the Passion of the Savior . . . [imperial decrees] were promulgated that demanded the flattening of all Christian churches, the burning of all Christian books, the humiliation of all Christian leaders, and the imprisonment of all servants of Christ who refused to denounce their faith.

So wrote Eusebius of Caesarea (263–339), the most reliable chronicler of the Great Persecution, at the outset of his *History of the Church*. He then went on to describe, chapter by bloody chapter, the beating, flaying, decapitation, drowning, burning, rape, and mauling by animals of thousands of Christian martyrs.

Diocletian was less interested in annihilating the Christians than he was in persuading them to participate in civic celebrations of the imperial cult, however. After all, his own wife and daughter were reported to have been Christians. What mattered instead was the unraveling of social cohesion across the empire. For centuries Rome had been held together by a carefully cultivated public spirit, a sense of Romanness and the commitment to an ideal greater than parochial ethnic or religious concerns. Diocletian promoted the cult of emperor worship as a unifying force, a living symbol of everyone's participation in a world larger than themselves. The Christians' refusal to endorse the official cult, or even to give it empty lip service, seemed to strike at the very heart of the empire, and he therefore concluded that they had to be crushed into submission.

But that is not what happened, at least not with the majority of them. Many of the thousands whom Diocletian sent to their death accepted their fate with quiet resolve and even, if we can trust our sources, with some measure of happiness. Martyrdom, they felt, was a prize to be embraced. Reunion after death with the Christ whom they had served in life seemed too great a blessing to merit dreading the temporary unpleasantness that preceded it. Crowds eager for blood and tears

Medallion of Saint Mamai   Saint Mamai, an early martyr popular with the Georgian people in the Caucasus, was thrown to the lions by the Romans in 275 CE. This 11th-century medallion depicts Mamai fearlessly astride a lion while brandishing a cross, symbolizing the victory over death won by Mamai and by all believers in Christ.

certainly saw all the blood they could want but, instead of tears, too often had to put up with hymns, prayers, and laughter.

Martyrologies—the narrative records of martyrs' sufferings—can seldom be taken literally. Their whole purpose is to glorify God by testifying to both the unimaginable sufferings endured by martyrs and the stoic, calm, and joyful spirit expressed by them even when caught in the lion's maw or pierced by the executioner's blade. The more gore, the better, and the more superhuman the acceptance of brutal death, the better still. Hence, when a Christian writer like Lactantius (ca. 240–320) penned his vivid chronicle *On the Deaths of Those Persecuted for Christ*, he found it easy to identify plenty of victims of Roman cruelty; the challenge lay in maintaining the fever pitch of his descriptions of the horrors they suffered. As with the history of Eusebius of Caesarea, after thirty pages of Lactantius's nonstop beheadings, eviscerations, poisonings, burnings, and beatings, one can sense the writer's rhetorical exhaustion—and there are still three hundred pages to go.

Nevertheless, even allowing for exaggeration in the sources, enough Christians accepted their martyrdom with such grace that the Romans who witnessed it were astonished. What was it about this religion that could enable someone to accept death happily, even eagerly? Was this something to envy, or was it simply insane? It is unclear how many Romans, if any, were sufficiently moved by the martyrs' behavior to convert to the faith. Yet it is certain that the Great Persecution got more people thinking about Christianity, and perhaps talking about it, than there had been before.

A CHRISTIAN EMPEROR AND A CHRISTIAN CHURCH

In 305, having done all that he could to save the empire, an exhausted Diocletian resigned from the imperial office (the only person to do so in Roman history) and returned to his homeland farm, dedicating his last years to his private passion: growing cabbages.[2] His mechanism for the orderly transfer of power failed in its

---

2   Diocletian's passion for gardening is described by Lactantius, who became a close advisor of Diocletian's successor, Constantine the Great.

first attempt, however, and another civil war quickly engulfed the empire. When the smoke finally cleared a new emperor sat on the throne: **Constantine the Great** (r. 306–337), whose eventful reign changed everything—because he was the first Roman emperor to be a Christian.

According to the sources closest to the event, Constantine's conversion had occurred on the eve of the battle that would decide the civil war. A rival named Maxentius had also claimed the imperial title in 306; attempts to negotiate a power-sharing arrangement continually failed, and in 312 the two sides broke into open warfare. The conclusive battle took place a few miles north of Rome, at the Milvian Bridge. Reportedly, a heavenly voice spoke to Constantine in a dream and told him to embrace Christianity and to paint the cross on his soldiers' shields before the next day's battle. He did so, won the battle, became sole emperor, and committed himself to Christianity on the spot. The story seems too contrived to be true. It suggests, none too subtly, that the religion itself caused the military victory, although the soldiers can hardly have been believers. From this point on, it implies, imperial success could only come so long as the empire served the Christian God.

Constantine's Conversion

However the conversion occurred, it did in fact occur. Constantine's conversion must have been sincere, since there was no conceivable political advantage to gain from it. Christians, by the year 312, made up no more than 2 or 3 percent of the Roman population and may have constituted as little as 1 percent. Even if one considers only the urban population of the eastern half of the empire—that is, the geographic area and demographic group with the highest proportion of Christians—the new faith made up no more than 10 percent of the populace.

The impact of his conversion was immediate and dramatic. In 313 he issued the **Edict of Milan**, which legalized Christianity and guaranteed religious freedom for all faiths within the empire[3]:

Edict of Milan

> It pleases us to remove altogether the legal restraints issued heretofore regarding the Christians, any one of whom may henceforth practice the Christian faith, if he wishes, freely, openly, without molestation . . . and in free and unrestricted liberty of religious worship. . . . And moreover, in order to promote peace in our time, we grant to all religions [within the empire] the right of free and open observance of their faith.

---

[3]   Too many historians confuse Constantine's Edict of Toleration (311) with the Edict of Milan (313). The earlier decree had simply ordered an end to the Great Persecution inaugurated by Diocletian. Christians had to wait two more years for their faith to be legalized.

Christ the Almighty   This mosaic from the church of Santa Prassede in Rome shows Christ on his heavenly throne, surrounded by his apostles and two martyrs, Prudence and Praxedis. From the 4th century on, the Good Shepherd iconography of Christ (see the illustration that opens chapter 7) gave way to images of Jesus as the mighty king of Heaven or the stern judge of the Last Day. The kinder, gentler Jesus did not become the norm again until the 12th century.

Constantine did more than legalize Christianity, however; he opened the imperial coffers in support of it. He ordered that public funds be made available to compensate individuals whose property and cash deposits had been confiscated for religious reasons. He poured money into building churches, training priests, promoting evangelical missions, copying sacred writings, and setting up Christian charitable houses. He granted Christians special tax privileges and showed personal preference for selecting Christians to serve in government offices. Not surprisingly, Christianity began to spread among the people of the east at a rate never before experienced.

Traditional Roman religion remained legal for several more decades, but the momentum was now decidedly in Christianity's direction. The years of struggle and persecution were over. By the end of the 4th century the majority of the eastern Roman population had embraced the new faith, and it became the official religion of the Roman Empire in 391, thanks to the emperor Theodosius I (r. 379–395).

Permitted at last by the Edict of Milan to practice their faith openly, Christians poured into the town squares to preach—and this is when the long-simmering problems of the "christianities" came into focus. To his dismay, Constantine found

Council of Nicea

that no two Christian groups worshipped in the same way, read the same canon, or recognized the same authority. Most accepted Jesus of Nazareth as the biblical messiah and Son of God, but many did not. Most believed that he had died on the cross and rose from the dead, but many did not. Most believed that he was physically present in the consecrated bread and wine of the Eucharist, but many did not. Constantine recognized that the christianities risked continued fracturing and internal fighting unless something was done. Accordingly, he summoned an ecumenical council—that is, a gathering to establish unity of faith—to meet at the eastern city of Nicea, ordering the leaders of every Christian community in the empire to attend. With one notable exception, the bishops all came. The council lasted for two years (323–325), passed dozens of resolutions, and symbolically capped its activity by issuing the **Nicene Creed**, which has stood ever since as the universal standard, the statement *par excellence* of Christian belief. The exact wording of the Creed has been revised numerous times over the centuries. Its opening text proclaims:

> We believe in one God,
> the Father, the Almighty,
> Maker of all that is, seen and unseen.
> We believe in one Lord, Jesus Christ,
> the only Son of God,
> eternally begotten of the Father,
> God from God, Light from Light,
> true God from true God,
> begotten, not made, consubstantial
> of one Being with the Father.
> Through him all things were made.
> For us and for our salvation
> he came down from heaven:
> and by the Holy Spirit was incarnate
> he became incarnate from the Virgin Mary,
> and was made man.
> For our sake he was crucified under Pontius Pilate;
> he suffered death and was buried.
> On the third day he rose again
> in accordance with the Scriptures;
> he ascended into heaven
> and is seated at the right hand of the Father.
> He will come again in glory to judge the living and the dead,
> and his kingdom will have no end.

Constantine regarded the newly standardized Christian Church as his own dominion. He had tradition behind him: in Rome the emperor had held the title of *pontifex maximus* ("chief priest"), which made him the leader of the entire pagan cult. The empire did not distinguish between political authority and religious authority, and Constantine saw no reason to alter the arrangement simply because the religion itself had changed. Taking the formal title of "thirteenth apostle," Constantine insisted that the emperor, so long as he himself was a Christian, was by that fact alone the supreme authority over the Christian Church.

Papal Claims to Power

This brought him into conflict with the bishop of Rome, Sylvester I (r. 314–335)—the one and only bishop who had refused to attend the Council of Nicea, since doing so would have implied a recognition of the emperor's authority over the church. (Sylvester did send a representative, however, to keep an eye on things.) Sylvester claimed for himself a title previously applied to many bishops: **pope** (from *pappas*, "papa"). His argument for supreme papal authority rested on Peter, the leader of the original group of apostles who had ended his days as the bishop of the Christian community of Rome; therefore, his successors as bishop of Rome should inherit the leadership of the church. The problem for those successors was that few Christians outside of Rome accepted their logic. Peter's original authority was beyond question, but after Peter's death (in 64 CE) the leadership of the community of bishops was an open question. Why should the bishop of Jerusalem not take precedence? Or the bishop of Antioch (the first city outside of Jerusalem to have a formally organized community)? Why should leadership not be left to a free election among all bishops? As it happened, most of the popes for the first thousand years of Christian history had little authority outside of their own city of Rome. Many were respected and even granted special honors, but few were obeyed. Starting with Constantine, the holders of the imperial title assumed their own supremacy over the church and exercised it.[4]

THE RISE OF "NEW ROME": THE BYZANTINE EMPIRE

Constantine made one additional epoch-making decision: in 324, in the midst of the Council of Nicea, he decided to abandon Italy and build a new capital city in the east. He chose the site known to the ancient Greeks as *Byzantion* (in Latin, *Byzantium*), on the promontory between the Sea of Marmara and the Black Sea. This was where Europe and Asia met, the nexus of east–west trade, and the strategic node for overseeing the administration of the eastern empire. By the 4th century it seemed clear that the western half of the Roman Empire was in severe

---

[4]   Pope Sylvester did the best he could, under the circumstances. He approved the legislation of the Council of Nicea, including the Creed, and simply reissued it under his own name.

decline. And although most people hoped for its survival, Constantine and his successors recognized that the eastern half of the empire was the more important half, being the virtual cradle of Western civilization. It was an urban, commercial, literate, and sophisticated world, newly given an additional sense of unity and purpose by its now-rapid assumption of a Christian character. The western half of the empire, in contrast, was weaker, poorer, ruder, agrarian, and ultimately expendable.

From the new capital built on the site of Byzantium, now renamed **Constantinople**, the rulers of the Byzantine Empire kept their eyes trained eastward, vaguely acknowledging their links to the backward west but putting little effort into propping up the crumbling administration there. The Byzantines regarded their eastern empire as a "new Rome" purged of its pagan past and explicitly dedicated to creating a Christian realm. The new capital was formally dedicated on May 11, 330.

Growing East–West Divide

The Byzantine Empire of the 4th and 5th centuries wrapped around the eastern edges of the Mediterranean like a giant reversed letter C. It included all of today's countries of Libya, Egypt, Israel, Jordan, Lebanon, Syria, Turkey, and most of the Balkan states (see Map 8.2). Hundreds of ethnic groups resided within this zone, chiefly in the cities or within a day's journey of them. Since travel and communication were relatively easy, thanks to long-familiar sea-lanes and coastal roads, the government in Constantinople was able to retain centralized rule. The heart of the empire was the great Anatolian landmass, the center of

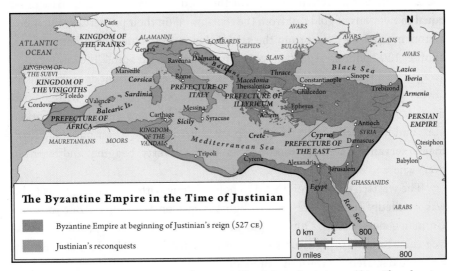

MAP 8.2   The Byzantine Empire in the Time of Justinian   Justinian and his wife and partner in rule Theodora waged war against the Germanic kingdoms in the west, aiming to reunite the empire and restore the imperial glory of the Augustan period.

grain production. Within a few generations, Byzantine society sloughed off its use of Latin and reverted to the Greek that had been the norm there until the arrival of the Romans.

The territory of Greece itself held a sentimental place in Byzantine hearts but was a relatively minor province in terms of economic and cultural life. The real nodes of energy apart from Constantinople itself were the coastal cities—Thessalonika, Ephesus, Antioch, Tripoli, and Alexandria—and a handful of inland cities like Jerusalem, Damascus, and Chalcedon. Manufacturing, trade, shipping, and finance were their lifeblood, but they also maintained hundreds of schools, academies, libraries, salons, and theaters that kept alive the classical traditions of literature, philosophy, and, to a lesser degree, science. In addition, the 4th and 5th centuries saw a frenzy of church building as Christianity at last sank its roots deeply into the culture.

The Byzantines' readoption of the Greek language represented a symbolic but also a practical turning away from the Latin-speaking west. Trade between east and west declined precipitously, since the west produced little that the east needed, apart from slaves. Beyond the disruptions and devastations caused by foreign invaders, the fundamental problem in the west was a dangerous imbalance in the distribution of wealth. Privileged families of senatorial and equestrian rank were often fabulously wealthy, but the laboring classes faced almost nonstop want and suffered repeated famines throughout the 4th and 5th centuries. Slaves, who represented as much as one-fourth of the western population by this time, fared even worse. "Many of the leading Roman families," wrote one chronicler in the early 5th century (Olympiodorus of Thebes, d. ca. 425), "have annual incomes equal to two tons of gold just from the rents owed on their properties, and if one factors in what they earn from the sale of their grain, wine, and other produce, another 1200 pounds of gold per year can be added to the sum." The lower orders scraped by on meager incomes, poor diets, and the ever-present dangers of debt. "Everywhere one turns one finds a carpetbagger," observed another writer (Libanius, d. 393), "in every territory, on every island, in every village, city, market, port, and backstreet. Everything is up for sale, including foster parents, nursemaids, servants—even the tombs of ancestors. Poverty, begging, and tears are everywhere to be found."

The "Fall of Rome"   The western empire continued to hobble along with its own augustus (who was decidedly subordinate to the augustus in Constantinople). But in 476 a German general named Odoacer put an end to the sham. He deposed the weakling ruler Romulus Augustulus (his name translates as "Little Emperor Romulus") and declared the western empire dead.

The Byzantine emperors occasionally showed some interest in influencing western matters by forming ties with several of the Germanic warlords who thenceforth dominated Europe. **Justinian I** (r. 527–565) became the most *Reign of* famous eastern emperor by reconquering much of southern Italy and the central *Justinian* part of the North African coast in an ambitious effort to reconstitute the old empire (see Map 8.2). His efforts failed in the end, however, since the economic gains from the conquests never came close to offsetting the expense of the military effort. He scored more lasting achievements with his vast construction projects within the city of Constantinople, including his completion of the magnificent church of Hagia Sophia ("Church of the Holy Wisdom") and his compilation of the *Corpus Juris Civilis* ("Corpus of Civil Law").

A dozen years went into the making of the Corpus, which brought together, organized by topic, and provided commentary on centuries of legislation concerning every aspect of civic life from taxation to criminal law. It created, in essence, a ready-to-use handbook for governing an entire society—which is precisely the use to which it was put for centuries. The Corpus formed the basis of all jurisprudence in Byzantium until the 15th century and provided a model for the development of the canon law of the Catholic Church. As the foundation of all subsequent legal study in the Greater West until the modern era, the Corpus did as much as anything else to form the legalistic bent of our modern culture.

Unfortunately, Justinian's own place in modern culture is overshadowed by a famously pornographic piece of propaganda written by Procopius of Caesaria (ca. 500–560), who served dutifully as Justinian's official biographer but also wrote, and published anonymously, a *Secret History*—now, ironically, the only work of his that anyone reads. The *Secret History* is wildly entertaining, to be sure, but it says more about Procopius's own unstable personality than about the emperor whose life it purports to tell. For example, he writes that Justinian

> was a fraud and a cheat. Hypocritical, cruelly two-faced, secretive; a practiced con artist who never showed any genuine emotion but could shed tears either of joy or sorrow, depending on the situation, whenever he perceived the need. A liar in every word—and not just in a haphazard way, but with real determination, affirming his schemes in writing and with the most solemn oaths, even in dealings with the public. But he regularly broke every agreement and pledge he ever made, like a contemptible slave who stands by his lies until only the threat of torture can drive him to confess the truth. A faithless friend and a treacherous enemy, with a crazed lust for murder and plunder; quarrelsome, extremely unruly, easily led to anything evil but stubbornly refusing any suggestion to do good. Quick to plot mischief and carry it out, but averse even to hearing a word of any noble action.

Hagia Sophia Universally acknowledged as one of the world's greatest buildings, the Hagia Sophia in Constantinople (modern Istanbul), constructed during the reign of Justinian (r. 527–565), is famous in particular for its enormous dome, supported by four giant pillars in the corners. The minarets were added under the Muslim Ottomans, who in the 15th century converted the church into a mosque. The internal view gives a sense of the massive interior and its brilliant play with sunlight.

But Procopius surpasses himself with his savage portrayal of Justinian's queen, Theodora, whom he describes as sexually insatiable, lewd, grasping, and venal. (One famous pornographic episode involves Theodora, a dozen soldiers from the imperial guard, lots of bondage, a loaf of bread, and a wild goose.) By other accounts it seems clear that Theodora was a difficult and divisive person, but Procopius's character assassination reads like the lurid ravings of an unbalanced man.

The stalling out of Justinian's military efforts turned into actual losses of territory by his immediate successors. Under emperors Maurice (r. 582–602) and Phocas (r. 602–610), Byzantium lost Egypt, Palestine, Syria, and parts of Anatolia itself to the Persians, who made another of their periodic efforts to control the western reaches of the Fertile Crescent. These were hard-fought campaigns that nearly brought Byzantium to its knees. Heraclius (r. 610–641) spent his entire reign in a life-or-death struggle to put the empire back on solid footing. But so much territory had been lost that he lacked the funds to pay his soldiers, a weakness that allowed groups of Avars, Bulgars, and Slavs to encroach on imperial lands in the Balkan region.

To combat the situation, Heraclius reorganized the army into a new system of **themes** (Greek *thema*, meaning "regiment" or "division"), which apportioned the *Heraclius's* lands of the empire to the military officers and gave them civil and economic juris- *Reforms* diction over the territories. The commanders then subdivided their zones into individual landholdings for each soldier serving under them. In this way, Heraclius stripped away the bloated, centralized imperial administration and replaced it with the army itself—which now, instead of receiving salaries from Constantinople, derived its own revenue from its landholdings and the fees it collected in return for its civic functions. It was a radical move, but one that dramatically improved military morale and effectiveness, since the soldiers henceforth had reliable sources of income and a personal stake in defending the empire from further attack.

Thus restructured, the Byzantine world achieved high degrees of prosperity and stability. Constantinople acted as the economic hub of the empire: *The Splendor of* all commerce passed through it. The city fiercely guarded its monopolies *Constantinople* on coinage, interest rates, weights and measures, and manufacturing standards, through which it exercised direct control of trade. In Justinian's time the Byzantines had learned how to cultivate silkworms and to spin the silk they produced, which allowed them to begin their own manufacturing of high-value silk cloth. The loss of market share felt by the silk traders from the Near East helped trigger a wave of wars against the Byzantines throughout the 7th and 8th centuries.

The splendor of the city was extraordinary, with hundreds of churches, fine palaces, theaters, baths, and bazaars (see Map 8.3). Most of the empire's cities suffered from Constantinople's dominance, since the capital drained commercial life from the provinces. Provincial cities continued, of course, but they became

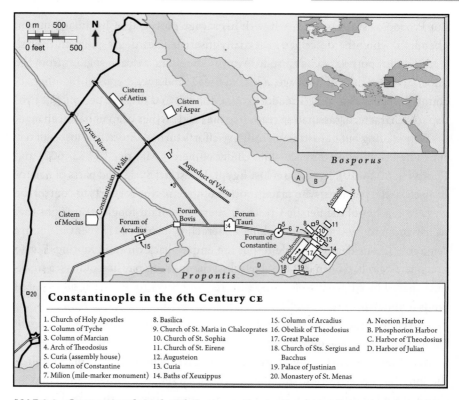

MAP 8.3   Constantinople in the 6th Century   Constantinople was the greatest city of the entire Middle Ages. Its only rivals in size, wealth, cosmopolitan culture, and architectural beauty were Cordoba (in Muslim Spain), Venice, and Baghdad.

The following legend appears within the map:

Constantinople in the 6th Century CE

1. Church of Holy Apostles
2. Column of Tyche
3. Column of Marcian
4. Arch of Theodosius
5. Curia (assembly house)
6. Column of Constantine
7. Milion (mile-marker monument)
8. Basilica
9. Church of St. Maria in Chalcoprates
10. Church of St. Sophia
11. Church of St. Eirene
12. Augusteion
13. Curia
14. Baths of Xeuxippus
15. Column of Arcadius
16. Obelisk of Theodosius
17. Great Palace
18. Church of Sts. Sergius and Bacchus
19. Palace of Justinian
20. Monastery of St. Menas

A. Neorion Harbor
B. Phosphorion Harbor
C. Harbor of Theodosius
D. Harbor of Julian

more political and religious administrative centers than sites of industry and trade. This change had important social and cultural consequences for the old class of urban elites. The descendants of the Roman curiales, they had previously formed the backbone of intellectual and cultural life, but they gradually disappeared from the 7th century on. Those curiales had been chiefly responsible for cultivating and preserving classical learning, everything from Homeric epics to Athenian stage tragedies and the works of the great philosophers. But the narrowing provincial character of the cities resulted in a narrowing of urban education as well. Primary schooling remained available in most cities, but beyond this level the only education consistently available was religious—devotional writings, hagiographies (or lives of the saints), ecclesiastical chronicles, and the like. In other words, what the provinces gained in piety they lost in general intellectual sophistication. High culture throve only in the capital.

The Renewed Persian Threat

The Persians unleashed a new campaign into the Holy Land in 612 and two years later took Jerusalem. A rebellion against the Persians by the city's Christian inhabitants led to a brutal crackdown. For three days Persian soldiers smashed

Christian shops, homes, and churches until hardly a single Christian building was left standing by 614. A late Byzantine chronicler named Theophanes described it:

> In this year, the Persians conquered all of Jordan and Palestine, including the Holy City, and with the help of the Jews they killed a multitude of Christians—some say as many as ninety thousand of them. The Jews [from the countryside], for their part, purchased many of the surviving Christians, whom the Persians were leading away as slaves, and put them to death too. The Persians moreover captured and led away not only the Patriarch of Jerusalem, Zechariah, and many prisoners, but also the most precious and life-giving Cross.

Theophanes's account is not entirely reliable in its specifics, but it seems clear that a bloodbath occurred, and it was a harbinger of things to come. From the 7th century onward, a new tone of open hostility toward non-Christians entered much Christian writing, and military conflicts in the east took on qualities of religious revenge seeking. Up to this time, Christians generally had shown much more hostility to other Christians—the old problem of the many christianities—than they had shown to non-Christians. The 7th century marks a dark turning point in Christian relations with the world. The Byzantines, reformed and reenergized, launched a counteroffensive in 622. Heraclius chose a symbolic spot for his attack: he and the army set sail from Constantinople, sailed around Asia Minor, and landed at the Bay of Issus—the exact location from which Alexander the Great had launched his conquest of the ancient Persian Empire. From there, like Alexander, Heraclius scored victory after victory until he had regained virtually all of Syria, Jordan, and Palestine.

BARBARIAN KINGS AND WARLORDS

After Odoacer deposed the final Roman augustus in 476, the western Roman Empire was replaced by a parade of semistates ruled by thuggish clan leaders. Some of these warlords offered a modicum of administration and security. Most, however, dedicated themselves to pillaging whatever food and material wealth they could find—or to attacking rivals who had already stolen what they themselves had been plotting to seize.

A 6th-century monk in Celtic England named Gildas described village life in the aftermath of Saxon raids this way:

> Sadly, the streets of our villages are filled with the ruins of once-high towers that have been pulled to the ground, with stones pried from fences

or left over from the smashing of sacred altars, with dismembered pieces of human bodies that are so covered with lurid clots of blood that they look as though the people had been run through a press, and whose only chance for any kind of burial is to rot in the ruins of collapsed homes; all the rest will simply fill the stomachs of ravenous beasts and birds. . . . To this very day not one of our villages is what it used to be. Instead, all lie desolate, routed, and ruined. (*On the Destruction of England*, ch. 24, 26)

Most of the people of western Europe, at least 90 percent of them, were reduced to subsistence farming. Probably one-half of all children born died before reaching the age of five, and one-half of all females who made it to marriageable age died before reaching the age of twenty-five, usually in childbirth. Tens of thousands of homeless refugees, and perhaps even more, roamed through the countryside at any given time, either having been driven from their homes by new waves of settlers, in flight from marauders, or in search of new territories where they could start afresh without rivals for the land. Meanwhile, the Mediterranean cities contracted into tiny hamlets—with sometimes a mere 10 percent of their former populations—and into corners of the settled urban area, leaving the emptied quarters to decay into ghost towns. Manufacture and trade beyond the immediate region became all but extinct (see Map 8.4). The sole exception was the commerce in slaves. (Slavery was ubiquitous in the ancient world and remained so in the early medieval centuries. By the 10th century, the church had developed to a point that it took action against the practice.)

Despite the miseries of the time, important aspects of Roman antiquity survived. Roman law remained in effect—inconsistently, to be sure, but not altogether forgotten. The Latin language continued as the dominant tongue in the west, and the barbarian kings did what they could to retain and emulate those elements of Roman tradition that they found useful. Intellectual life in the west was limited to the Christian monasteries that dotted the landscape from the 4th century on, but displayed real zest and ingenuity. Thus, although it was an age of poverty and chaos, it was a creative chaos. Ultimately it saw the amalgamation of the Roman, Germanic, and Christian cultures into the fascinating hybrid of medieval society.

One of the early chroniclers of the medieval era, Bishop Gregory of Tours (ca. 538–594), described the atmosphere memorably in the opening prologue to his *History of the Franks:*

A great number of things keep happening—some good, some bad. The people of the various petty princedoms keep quarreling with each other in the fiercest way imaginable, while our rulers' tempers keep

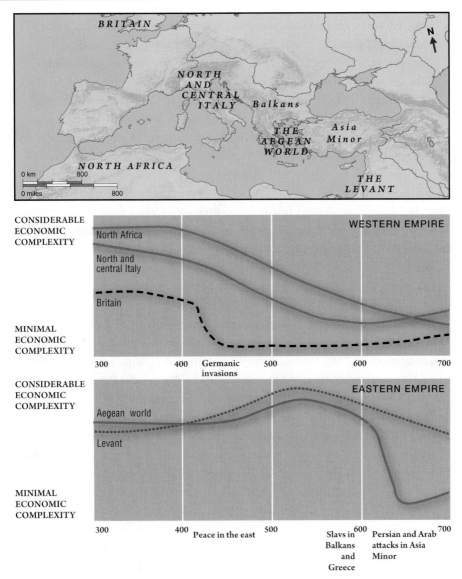

MAP 8.4 **The Economy of Europe in the Early Middle Ages** After waves of invasions and attacks, by 700 most of the people of western Europe were reduced to subsistence farming.
Adapted from Ward-Perkins, Bryan, *The Fall of Rome* (2006).

bursting into violence. Our churches are assailed by heretics, then re-taken in force by our Catholics; and whereas Christian faith burns hot in the hearts of many, it is no more than lukewarm in those of others. Church buildings are pillaged by faithless pagans as soon as they are gifted by faithful Christians. But no one has yet emerged who is a sufficiently

> skilled writer that he can record these events in a straightforward way, whether in prose or in verse. In fact, throughout the towns of Gaul [the ancient region corresponding roughly to modern France and Belgium] the knowledge of writing has declined to such an extent that it has virtually disappeared. . . . [And so] I have undertaken this present work in an effort to preserve the memory of the dead and bring them to the attention of those yet to come; but my style lacks all polish, and I have had to devote too much of my attention to the clashes between the good and the wicked.

This period from the 4th to 8th centuries was one of the longest and most dire and challenging eras in Western history. Our sources for it are few—because books seldom get written in active war zones—but enough evidence survives to provide a basic outline of what occurred. The picture is not pretty.

DIVIDED ESTATES AND KINGDOMS

The Germanic peoples who streamed into western Europe confronted innumerable challenges, not the least of which was the terrain. Most of the European continent north of the Mediterranean coastline consisted of dense forest. Newcomers faced bitter resistance from the people who had already settled open areas and so were forced to keep moving or to clear their own lands and begin farming from nothing. Moreover, various cultural traditions that had served the Germans well in the east served them ill in the more sedentary west.

Consequences of Settlement One example is the early nomadic custom of dividing a man's estate equally between his surviving sons. This practice had provided for each new generation, because herds of animals could replenish their own numbers—but a western farm could not survive such division quite so easily. By the end of the second generation, if not earlier, the distributed lands were not sufficient to support a family. The most promising options, in such a case, were either to expand one's holding by clearing more forest at the perimeter (which worked in some cases, but in others seemed only to defer the problem) or to abandon the land altogether in search of new territory elsewhere. That move, however, exposed them to more hostilities, whether from previously settled peoples, other migrating bands, or warrior thugs. And once they found new places to settle, they faced the difficulty of clearing forests, digging wells, building homes, and beginning to farm, with only the wooden tools they had managed to bring with them. (Few common farmers had metal tools at this time.) Under such conditions, most of continental Europe remained stubbornly mired in poverty until the 9th century.

The transition to agricultural life had important consequences for Germanic women. In pastoral societies, the tending of flocks is the essential labor that supports the family; thus women can contribute equally as much as men. Primitive farm work, however, requires a degree of brute physical strength that usually only men can provide. Agrarian societies therefore often value men over women and boys over girls—an important marker in the evolution of gender hierarchies. In a farming world, the most important labor a female can offer to the benefit of society is to produce more sons. This is not to suggest that nomadic, pastoral societies are egalitarian in their gender roles, but the sparse evidence that survives of the Germanic peoples suggests that rigid, sizable, and permanent differences in the relative status of men and women emerged at the time of their transition to agrarian life. The Roman historian Tacitus (d. ca. 117) wrote that in ancient times Germanic women fought alongside the men in battle, regularly voiced their opinion in clan councils, and shared in inheritance rights. Moreover, at marriage the husband owed a dowry to the bride.

By the 5th and 6th centuries, all that had changed; most Germanic women and girls were largely housebound, preparing food and rearing children, with little voice in public matters and meager inheritance rights. Exceptions existed, of course. Visigothic law, for example, declared, "Let sisters succeed equally with brothers to the inheritance of their parents; and if a father or mother dies intestate, still let sisters and brothers both succeed to the inheritance of each parent in equal measure." But women's true value in Germanic society can be seen in the law of the Salian Franks, which decreed that anyone convicted of killing a female who was in her childbearing years owed a fine of 600 shillings, whereas anyone who killed a female past her fertile years owed only one-third that amount.

The problem of divided estates hobbled as well any sort of political development after 476: a warrior might turn himself into a king by forcing his will on terrorized farmers, but he usually ended his life by dividing his kingdom among his heirs. One key example will suffice. A brutal warlord named Clovis, a member *Clovis's Frankish Kingdom* of the Germanic group known as the Salian Franks, carved out a sizable kingdom for himself in what is today mostly France around the year 500 and made himself, briefly, the most powerful ruler in western Europe (see Map 8.5). When he died in 511 his realm was parceled out to each of his four sons: Theuderic, Chlodomer, Childebert, and Lothar. Theuderic, however, went on to have two sons of his own; Chlodomer had three. And although Childebert had only daughters (who could not inherit, according to Frankish custom), his younger brother Lothar made up for him by producing seven boys. In only two generations, therefore, a single kingdom had split into twelve autonomous principalities, each with its own officials, tax system, laws, courts, weights, and measures. Any chance of stable governance usually died out quickly in such circumstances, but there is little evidence that many of the warlords were interested in even trying to provide it.

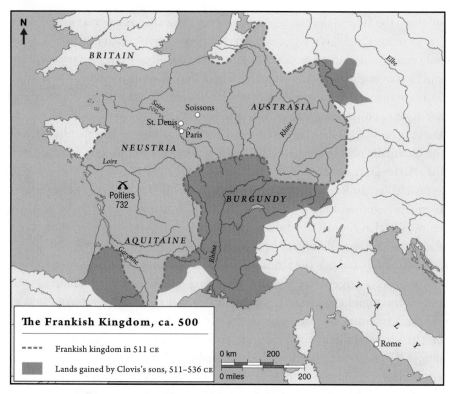

MAP 8.5   The Frankish Kingdom, ca. 500   Around 500 the Frankish warlord Clovis established western Europe's largest new kingdom in what is today mostly France.

Clovis's realm proved an exception, for two reasons. First, his adoption of Christianity around 500 CE led to him being recognized as a defender of the church. An aura of ecclesiastical blessing hence clung to his line for generations to come. Second, the family he belonged to—the Merovingians—allied itself in the late 7th century with another warlord family, the Carolingians, who succeeded them and for a time, as we will see in chapter 10, united almost all of continental Europe. But even with the exception of the Franks, the political narrative of the early medieval era is grim.

Gregory of Tours fills the four hundred pages of his *History of the Franks* with tale after tale of savagery:

> This Rauching [another Frankish warlord] was extraordinarily vain—a man filled to bursting with pride, arrogance, and impertinence. He treated his servants as though he denied they were human beings at all. . . . For example, whenever a servant stood before him, as was usual, with a lighted candle while Rauching ate his meals, he would force the poor fellow to bare his legs and hold the lit candle between his knees until it burned

down to a stub. He would then demand that a new candle be lit, again and again, until the servant's legs were entirely scorched. If the servant cried out or tried to run, a drawn sword quickly stopped him, and Rauching himself would convulse with laughter as he watched the man weep. (5.3)

Gregory relates another tale about Rauching. Two of his servants fell in love and, knowing that he would forbid their union, ran to a local priest for protection. The priest negotiated on their behalf and extracted a promise from the warlord that "he would allow the couple to stay united forever." Once the pair were back at his stronghold, Rauching ordered a massive tree to be felled and its trunk split in two lengthwise, with each half hollowed out, as one would do in making a pair of canoes. Rauching then bound the servants together, encased them in the rejoined hollow tree trunk, and buried them alive in a deep trench, saying with a roaring laugh, "See? I haven't broken my promise. I haven't 'split them up'!" (5.3).

An 8th-century writer, Paul the Deacon, in his *History of the Lombards*, vividly described a different kind of horror—the prevalence of rape, and the efforts some women made to avoid it:

> [Lombard women] used to put the flesh of raw chickens under the band that held up their breasts; and this, once the summer heat had spoiled and putrefied it, gave off a horribly foul odor. Thus when the Avars [another invading tribe] tried to rape them they found that they could not bear the stench—and thinking that the smell was natural to these women, they ran away, cursing loudly that all Lombard women stink.

Neither Gregory of Tours nor Paul the Deacon was without bias, and their specific tales of horrors must be read with a critical eye, but the general picture they draw of a Europe in constant danger of falling apart is persuasive. Until a means was found to pass on undivided realms, little significant advance in government was possible. Most early Germanic kings and princes were itinerant; they traveled constantly, bringing whatever instruments of governance they had (records, copies of laws, accounts) with them. As often as not, individuals petitioning a ruler for justice had first to overcome a basic logistical problem: finding out where the king was and then going to him.

THE BODY AS MONEY AND WOMEN AS PROPERTY

Given these difficulties, little lasting political development took place. Rule was personal, not institutional. Customs varied enormously from "kingdom" to "kingdom," from tribe to tribe, and even from clan to clan. As the Germans gradually settled the land and interacted with the old Roman populace, however, a degree of cultural assimilation occurred. Although easily 90 percent of the population remained illiterate, the old tribal customs that had been passed down orally for generations began to be written down in the 5th, 6th, and 7th centuries. These records provide our first nonliterary glimpses of Germanic values and practices.

Germanic Law Codes   Germanic law, overall, was constructed from the ground up, much like our modern system of torts, or claims of damages that result in legal rulings. Individual conflicts were dealt with as they arose and were judged by some sort of group consensus, and each case, once settled, provided a precedent for similar cases in the future. This ad hoc construction explains the somewhat random nature of the earliest written codes; they were the result of compiled specifics, not of ideological blueprints put into action. Nevertheless, some sense of consistent values emerges from the codes. In most of them, the issues of property, inheritance, marriage, and taxation are preeminent.

The most striking feature of Germanic criminal law was the apportioning of compensatory payments for the physical injury of another, a system called **wergeld**. In these brutal times, to harm or kill another man was quite literally to threaten the existence of his entire family, which depended on his labor for food production and on his strength for physical protection. Murder or assault thus threatened the family, which all too often responded to this sort of crime by declaring a blood feud. Wergeld provided an alternative to endless vendettas. The system varied in its details from tribe to tribe, but the central idea remained the same: to compensate a victim, or his or her clan, by paying for the loss of a life or for an injury to a vital or nonvital body part. Every part of the body was assigned a monetary value—so much for an arm, an eye, a foot, and so on, right down to the fifth toe on either foot.[5]

Germanic law regarded women not as property but as legal minors regardless of their age, under the more or less permanent guardianship of their fathers and husbands. Among the Salian Franks, for example, a woman who married against her father's will forfeited her rights to any family property and could be put to death by any family member. Among the Burgundians, who settled in eastern France at about the same time, a man could divorce his wife at any time and for any reason, so long as he returned her dowry and paid an additional sum as interest. Any woman who tried to leave her husband was to be drowned in a swamp. One exception to this Germanic rule was the Visigoths, who settled in Spain in the 6th century. Visigothic custom allowed an unmarried woman over the age of twenty to be a free adult, legally responsible for herself.

---

[5]   Our own personal-injury insurance policies today follow the same general idea.

Early Medieval Germanic Culture   Dating from around 600 CE, this ring, found near Bergamo, Italy, evidently belonged to a noblewoman named Gumedruta, according to the inscription. The ring was used to affix wax seals to letters and official documents.

A girl was considered marriageable when she began to menstruate and was physically capable of bearing children; this usually happened around the age of fifteen. Within marriage, strict division of labor between the sexes was the norm. Although men did the plowing—an arduous task that generally required a man's physical strength—women performed most of the daily agricultural work from that point on: planting, weeding, fertilizing, and so on. Men focused on hunting, building, blacksmithing, felling trees, and clearing swamps. Men and women worked together to bring in the harvest, however.

A generation or two after settling in their respective parts of western Europe, most of the Germanic groups experienced a severe shortage of women. This happened for two reasons. First, relentless famine had forced the settlers to practice infanticide. In times of failed crops, which were many, this was an easy, if horrific, means of preserving the food supply. And since boys did the heavy labor, infant girls were the most frequent victims of infanticide. Second, many of those girls who survived childhood subsequently died in childbirth because the strains of pregnancy and delivery on malnourished teenagers commonly resulted in their death.

The shortage of women ironically caused an increase in their relative social value, according to a crude formula of supply and demand, which the law codes came to reflect. By the 8th century, Germanic women had many more legal protections and freedoms than before. In marriage, men began to owe dowries to their brides, not the other way around, to secure a mate; this dowry became in many cases the bride's own property that she controlled directly and in her own name. The custom also arose whereby a husband owed his bride a *Morgengab*, or "morning gift," after their wedding night, to compensate her for her lost virginity. These developments hardly made early medieval life significantly brighter, but they do illustrate some of the ways that Germanic culture adapted to its new circumstances.

CHRISTIAN PAGANISM

The most visible of the new circumstances was the Germans' gradual acceptance of Christianity. The traditional religion they had brought with them into the west was polytheistic and animistic: by offering prayers and gifts to the deities, they hoped to influence the workings of nature. Wotan and Thor were two of the most significant pagan gods, and they figured large in the tales of Germanic mythology. Wotan represented the forces of the Sun; Thor of Thunder and Lightning. Many of the German tribes encountered Christianity as early as the 4th century, as missionaries rushed westward to evangelize them. But the conditions of western Europe required missionaries to follow a different strategy than they had used in the cities of the eastern and central Mediterranean. Since continental Europe had no cities where the missionaries could address the hearts and minds of the multitude, they focused instead on the smallish number of Germanic rulers, princelings, and tribal warlords.

The Jelling Stone   This 10th-century Danish runestone ("rune" refers to ancient Germanic scripts) is one of a series erected by King Harald Bluetooth (r. ca. 958–986), who is traditionally regarded as the first of his people to convert to Christianity. The stones commemorate that conversion and offer atonement for his parents' pagan hostility to the faith. "Bluetooth" wireless technology is named after Harald, for the simple reason that one of its founders was reading a novel about the king at the time that he founded his company. The company's logo consists of the runic version of the letters H and B.

Aided (the sources assure us) by stupendous miracles, the missionaries converted this upper echelon of leaders and urged them to order the conversion of their clans and tribes. Early medieval writers like Gregory of Tours and Paul the Deacon all relate fantastic tales of dramatic conversions of German rulers who then directed their victorious soldiers to receive baptism and join the cause of Christ. Of course, what usually happened in these baptisms—if anything happened at all—is that the rulers' subjects simply added Jesus to the long list of deities they continued to worship. This was sincere in its way, no doubt, but hardly reason to regard the people as Christian. Models of conversion from the top of society downward to the masses, usually either forced or enticed, can work, but they work slowly.

For many generations and possibly for centuries, medieval society was characterized by a curious, muddy amalgam of the two religions, which historians call "Christian paganism." When King Clovis ordered his followers to adopt Christianity by accepting mass baptism around the year 500, the Franks' conversion was real but incomplete. Jesus became for them a true deity but one of no more significance than the local forest god or one of their divine ancestors. Under these conditions, western Europe, in contrast to the Byzantine Empire, gradually produced a Christian religious culture that retained significant elements of pagan practice within it.

Christmas trees, for example, have nothing to do with the story of Jesus's birth. But the Germans had a tradition of honoring the tallest tree in each forest as the unique domicile of the forest's ruling deities, and so they would worship the gods by offering their tree-home various gifts, decorations, and songs of praise. This pagan ritual slowly acquired a Christian gloss until, by the 9th century, the popular incorporation of tree worship into Christian practice was complete. Another example is the popular celebration of bunnies and baskets of eggs at Easter—neither of which appears in any gospel version of the story of Jesus's resurrection. Germanic farmers owed a special tax to their tribal leaders at the onset of spring as an expression of gratitude for having helped the people to survive the perils of winter. Since theirs was a moneyless economy, they paid this tax with what they had at their disposal: baskets of eggs and springtime litters of bunnies.

CHRISTIAN MONASTICISM

The persistence of "Christian paganism" was indirectly abetted by the rise of Christian monasticism. Many religions have ascetic and contemplative elements to them, and Second Temple Judaism fairly bristled with them. For their first three hundred years, Christian missionaries were too busy in the streets and marketplaces of the eastern Mediterranean spreading the Word (usually just ahead of the Roman police) to focus on ascetic spirituality. Theirs was a call to action, not to meditation. But a Christian form of monasticism began in earnest in the 4th century. **Monasticism** rejected normal family and social life, along with the concern for wealth, status, and power. In their place, it favored a harsh life of solitude and spiritual discipline. What inspired this principled withdrawal from the world was, ironically, the gradual success of the Christian message itself.

When Constantine I announced his own conversion and issued the Edict of Milan in 313, Christianity's hour had finally arrived. And this was precisely the problem for many Christians. How could they prove to God, and to themselves, that they had the same heroic commitment to him that their ancestors had possessed, ancestors who had quite literally risked their lives every day for Christ? To be a Christian after 313 involved none of the risk, the danger, and the suffering that it had carried before. After the Edict of Milan, in fact, to be a Christian was easy, even fashionable.

For many faithful this proved intolerable, and so they intentionally sought out the loneliest, most rigorous, and most difficult way they could devise to love God—not out of spiritual masochism, but rather like athletes who push themselves to the limits of their ability in the pursuit of excellence. Men and women experiencing such desires went out into the deserts and forests, living in caves or on wind-blasted hilltops, exposed to the elements and wild beasts, scavenging for their food or begging it from passersby. Eventually, these ascetics began to live together in isolated communities where they tried to pattern their lives on those of the twelve apostles, as a sacred community united in their dedication to live by Christ's teachings.

Monasticism was extraordinarily popular in the 5th through 9th centuries, with hundreds of monastic houses established throughout the eastern and central Mediterranean, and it added a rich new element to a fast-Christianizing society. But when the movement arrived in western Europe, it had rather a different impact. There the trickle-down model of evangelization had created a religiously hybrid world in which Christianity was poorly understood and haphazardly practiced. When individuals with deep, resonant, and knowledgeable commitments to the faith entered monastic life, they helped to perpetuate Christian paganism by removing from society the very individuals most capable of correcting and deepening the Christian life of the masses.

Rule of Saint Benedict

Hundreds of monasteries and convents were established in the early medieval era, from Ireland to Hungary, from Spain to Poland, from Sicily to Sweden (see Map 8.6). Perhaps 90 percent of these houses organized their daily lives according to the **Rule of Saint Benedict**, a communal handbook written by Benedict of Nursia (ca. 480–547) to guide the monastery he had established at Monte Cassino in southern Italy. Benedict's Rule attracted so many adherents because it required relatively moderate discipline. Unlike the harsh regulations of other monastic communities, Benedict's Rule did not isolate monks and nuns from the outside world or deprive them of sleep, adequate food, or warm clothing. It also had a balanced focus on the monks' physical and intellectual, as well as their spiritual, well-being. Benedict's sister, Scholastica, is regarded as the founder of the Benedictine

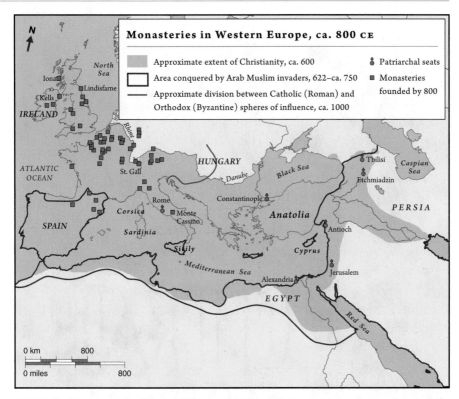

Monasteries in Western Europe, ca. 800 CE

Approximate extent of Christianity, ca. 600

Area conquered by Arab Muslim invaders, 622–ca. 750

Approximate division between Catholic (Roman) and Orthodox (Byzantine) spheres of influence, ca. 1000

🜊 Patriarchal seats

■ Monasteries founded by 800

MAP 8.6   Monasteries in Western Europe, ca. 800   Nearly every monastery and convent in western Europe was Benedictine at this time. New orders did not appear until the 10th century.

order for women.[6] Benedictine monks and nuns were required to spend several hours each day in physical labor and in study as necessary adjuncts to their central function of worship. The physical labor, which primarily involved some sort of farmwork for the monks and domestic labor for the nuns, helped to make each monastery self-sufficient. How could a community cut itself off from the world if it could not feed itself and produce its own tools, clothing, and shelter? Moreover, monasteries and convents frequently were located close together (and occasionally were administratively united), so the men and women could aid one another with specific tasks.

For the first time in Western history, physical work was seen as noble, even godly. But Benedict's insistence on study had the most immediate consequences

---

[6]   Once, after spending the day with his sister in prayer and discussion, Benedict rose to return to his monastery to sleep, in obedience to his Rule. Scholastica reportedly made a quick prayer for a thunderstorm— and God replied, forcing Benedict to stay behind, thus breaking his own Rule. Scholastica is still invoked by Catholics for protection from thunderstorms, although she should perhaps be invoked for stirring them up.

The Lindisfarne Gospels   Lindisfarne is a small island off the northeastern coast of England. In the early 7th century a monastery was founded there by an Irish missionary named Aidan (d. 651). Subjected to repeated attacks by Vikings, the monks abandoned the island in 875 and took with them all the monastery's treasures—including its famed manuscript of the four gospels, produced around 700. This is the opening page of the Gospel of Matthew.

for medieval Europe because monasteries virtually monopolized book production. Novice monks received a carefully designed education that taught them to speak, read, and write Latin, as well as the basic elements of arithmetic, geometry, astronomy, and music. This training required borrowing, copying, and commenting on the books of the western world's religious and secular learning. A constant stream of books thus flowed from monastery to monastery, creating western Europe's first libraries. We owe nearly the entire surviving corpus of classical Latin literature to the busy labor of copying and recopying by these monks. They preserved the poems of Virgil and Horace; the histories of Tacitus, Livy, and Suetonius; the speeches and letters of Cicero; and the plays of Seneca and Terence, among others. Once they had mastered the classical Latin literature, monks moved on to reading, copying, and commenting on the sacred Christian writings, preserving and extending the intellectual legacy of the faith. Until about 1100, nearly every single Christian scholar in western Europe either was a member of the Benedictines or had been educated by them.

Throughout Late Antiquity, or the early Middle Ages, monasteries were vital centers of Christian intellectual life, but they built on the foundations created by *The* a group of scholars known as the Church Fathers. Some of these figures had mo- *Church* nastic backgrounds; others were priests and bishops. Some wrote in Greek, *Fathers* others in Latin. Their work aimed at several goals: to explain Christianity to newcomers and strengthen the faith of those already in the church, to resolve the problem of the "many christianities," and to reconcile Christian faith with classical culture. Among the most important Latin Fathers were a monk, Jerome (347–420); a bishop, Augustine of Hippo (354–430); and a pope, Gregory the Great (r. 590–604); and among the Greek Fathers were Athanasius of Alexandria (ca. 298–373), Gregory of Nazianzus (ca. 329–ca. 389), and John Chrysostom (347–407)—bishops all. Jerome's greatest work was his translation of the Hebrew Bible and Greek New Testament into Latin. His version—known as the Vulgate Bible (from Latin *vulgatus*, meaning "the common tongue")—remains the official version of the scriptures in the Roman Catholic Church today. Augustine is remembered chiefly as a theologian whose masterpiece *The City of God* (ca. 426) forges a link between Christian and classical understandings of human development and history. Gregory, the first pope to have anything like the universal authority Peter's successors at Rome had always claimed, oversaw the first organized campaigns to evangelize the pagan Germans.

Of the Greek Fathers, Athanasius struggled mightily to protect the church from undue influence by the state, and he wrote a biography of the church's first monk, Antony of Egypt (d. 356). His *Life of Antony* became the model for all such hagiographies (lives of the saints), which were among the most popular literary genres of the entire Middle Ages. Gregory of Nazianzus is remembered not for a particular book (although he wrote many, chiefly exhortations to heretics to return to the church's teachings) but for his piety and dedication to putting his natural eloquence in service to God. "This is my gift to God; this is my treasure that I dedicate wholly to him. Everything else that I possessed in the world I gave up, at the command of the Holy Spirit . . . [which has been] my companion and counselor through all my life." John Chrysostom also had the gift of eloquence and is revered as one of the greatest preachers in the history of the Greek Orthodox Church.

◆

In fact, when western Europe began to emerge from the early Middle Ages, scholars and monks played a central role in the recovery. In the 8th century a new aristocratic warrior family rose to power in the northern Frankish territories. Resourceful, resilient, and ruthless, this family—the Carolingians—appointed themselves the would-be saviors of western Christendom and pursued the unification of Latin Europe with relentless focus and drive. The society they created would mark the first successful amalgam of Roman, Germanic, and Christian culture, and it laid the foundations for modern Europe.

We will pick up their story in chapter 10. For now, let us turn to the rise in the 6th century of the Greater West's third great monotheism, Islam.

WHO, WHAT, WHERE

Constantine the Great	Justinian I	Rule of Saint Benedict
Constantinople	Late Antiquity	tetrarchy
Dark Ages	Middle Ages	themes
Diocletian	monasticism	wergeld
Edict of Milan	Nicene Creed	
Great Persecution	pope	

SUGGESTED READINGS

Primary Sources

Augustine. *The City of God.*
Benedict of Nursia. *The Benedictine Rule.*
Boethius. *The Consolation of Philosophy.*
Gregory of Tours. *History of the Franks.*

Jordanes. *History of the Goths.*
Paul the Deacon. *History of the Lombards.*
Procopius. *The Secret History.*

Source Anthologies

Evans-Grubbs, Judith. *Women and the Law in the Roman Empire: A Sourcebook on Marriage, Divorce, and Widowhood* (2002).

Head, Thomas, ed. *Medieval Hagiography: An Anthology* (2001).

Maas, Michael. *Readings in Late Antiquity: A Sourcebook* (2010).

Murray, Alexander Callander. *Gregory of Tours: The Merovingians* (2005).

Smail, Daniel Lord, and Kelly Gibson, eds. *Vengeance in Medieval Europe: A Reader* (2009).

Swan, Laura. *The Forgotten Desert Mothers: Sayings, Lives and Stories of Early Christian Women* (2001).

Studies

Ando, Clifford. *The Matter of the Gods: Religion and the Roman Empire* (2008).

Banaji, Jairus. *Agrarian Change in Late Antiquity: Gold, Labour, and Aristocratic Dominance* (2007).

Bassett, Sarah. *The Urban Image of Late Antique Constantinople* (2004).

Brown, Peter. *The Rise of Western Christendom: Triumph and Diversity* (2003).

Brubaker, Leslie, and Julia M. H. Smith. *Gender in the Early Medieval World: East and West, 300–900* (2004).

Curran, John. *Pagan City and Christian Capital: Rome in the Fourth Century* (2000).

Drake, H. A. *Constantine and the Bishops: The Politics of Intolerance* (2002).

Dunn, Marilyn. *Emergence of Monasticism: From the Desert Fathers to the Early Middle Ages* (2003).

Evans, J. A. S. *The Age of Justinian: The Circumstances of Imperial Power* (2001).

Geary, Patrick. *The Myth of Nations: The Medieval Origins of Europe* (2002).

Goldenberg, David M. *The Curse of Ham: Race and Slavery in Early Judaism, Christianity, and Islam* (2005).

Halsall, Guy. *Warfare and Society in the Barbarian West, 450–900* (2003).

Harmless, William. *Desert Christians: An Introduction to the Literature of Early Monasticism* (2004).

Heather, Peter. *Empires and Barbarians: The Fall of Rome and the Birth of Europe* (2010).

Herrin, Judith. *Women in Purple: Rulers of Medieval Byzantium* (2001).

Lawrence, C. H. *Medieval Monasticism: Forms of Religious Life in Western Europe in the Middle Ages* (2001).

MacLeod, Roy. *The Library of Alexandria: Rediscovering the Cradle of Western Culture* (2000).

McCormick, Michael. *Origins of the European Economy: Communications and Commerce, AD 300–900* (2001).

Pohl, Walter, Ian Wood, and Helmut Reimitz. *The Transformation of Frontiers from Late Antiquity to the Carolingians* (2001).

Smith, Julia M. H. *Europe after Rome: A New Cultural History, 500–1000* (2005).

Wickham, Chris. *Framing the Early Middle Ages: Europe and the Mediterranean, 400–800* (2005).

Wickham, Chris. *The Inheritance of Rome: Illuminating the Dark Ages, 400–1000* (2010).

Wood, Ian. *The Missionary Life: Saints and the Evangelisation of Europe, 400–1050* (2001).

For additional resources, including maps, primary sources, visuals, web links, and quizzes, please go to **www.oup.com/us/backman.**

CHAPTER 9

The Expansive Realm of Islam

30–900

The early history and development of Islam are as difficult to determine as the origins of Christianity. As with Christianity, Islam's earliest surviving records date to several decades after the death of the charismatic figure who founded the faith—in this case, the prophet Muhammad (ca. 570–632). Literacy came to the Arabs with the Qur'an itself, authored by God and transmitted by the Prophet, but not written in definitive form until long after Muhammad's death. Moreover, the first written collections of Muhammad's non-Qur'anic teachings—the *hadith*—did not appear until more than a century after his death and hence can be regarded as less than reliable evidence, by modern critical standards. But the authority of the Qur'an and hadith are beyond questioning for many devout Muslims, just as the authority of the gospels is undoubted by many Christians, a fact that complicates efforts to determine precisely what happened, when, and why.

THE ISLAMIC WORLD, ca. 900 CE

■ Sunni Muslim states   ■ Byzantine Empire
■ Shiite Muslim states

The importance of Islam in the development of Greater Western values cannot be questioned, however. Although it built on, and in some cases conformed to, cultural norms already established among the peoples of the Arabian peninsula, the Islamic revelation helped to define attitudes toward faith and reason, women and sexuality, law and the state, and warfare and tolerance that have lasted for centuries. The phenomenally rapid spread of Islam was a matter of ethnic

The Mosque at Cordoba One of the greatest mosques of the Middle Ages was built in the Spanish city of Cordoba. The mosque was constructed atop an earlier Christian church, and many of its magnificent columns were reclaimed from nearby Roman temples.

CHAPTER OUTLINE

and military confrontation, to be sure. But it was also a complex interaction of cultural values and principles, an interaction in which the new faith adopted and absorbed as many preexisting characteristics as it suppressed, in the long march to regional dominance.

"AGE OF IGNORANCE": THE ARABIAN BACKGROUND

The Arabs had inhabited the peninsula that bears their name for many centuries.

Geography and Climate   It is a forbidding place, roughly a million square miles in area, consisting of an arid central plateau that slopes from west to east and is surrounded by several deserts (see Map 9.1). Most notable are the rocky Syrian (Nefud) Desert in the north and the Great Arabian Desert (Arabic *Rub' al-Khali*, or "Empty Quarter"), which alone makes up one-quarter of the entire peninsula.[1] Two mountain ranges exist, one running parallel to the Red Sea coast on the southwest and the other stretching along the peninsula's southeastern coast, the site of today's country of Oman. Some water is available: several stretches of marshland dot the Red Sea coastline, and large aquifers run beneath much of the peninsula, but usually at depths too great to reach. Where the levels of sand and rock are not too extreme,

---

[1]   The sands of the Great Arabian Desert reach depths, in spots, of more than 1,000 feet. Daytime temperatures, moreover, can reach 130°F (55°C) in the summer.

CHAPTER TIMELINE

0	100	200	300	400

■ ca. 27–570 **"Age of Ignorance" (al-Jahiliyya)**

some natural oases and wadis—seasonal riverbeds—occur, and it is possible to dig wells.

But the essential geographical fact of premodern Arabia is that only 1 percent of the land could support agriculture and permanent human settlement. Division of the Arab peoples is thus a natural consequence of geography. The highland plateau accommodates the grazing of sheep and goats and is the traditional home of the nomadic Bedouin tribes; the fertile southwestern coastal zone is the abode of the Yemeni Arabs. Between those extremes, pre-Islamic tradition claimed that most of the peninsula's people are descended from two legendary ancestors: Qahtan and Adnan. Qahtan, according to the tradition, was the progenitor of the "pure Arab" people (*al-Arab al-aribah*) in the southern part of the peninsula, whereas Adnan fathered the "Arabized Arabs" (*al-Arab al-musta'ribah*) of the north. By the start of Islam in the 7th century, Qahtan and Adnan were reinterpreted as the offspring of Ishmael, son of the biblical patriarch Abram/Abraham through his concubine Hagar.

Whatever their origins, many Arab tribes were united by their language, of which each group possessed its own distinct dialect. Arabic is a Semitic language, related to the tongues of the ancient Akkadians, Assyrians, Babylonians, and Hebrews, and indeed, the Arabian peninsula is thought by many to be the point of origin of all Semitic-speaking peoples. Clan and tribal identities ran deep, and everything from the dialect one spoke to the headdress one wore to the lengthy

A Tribal Culture

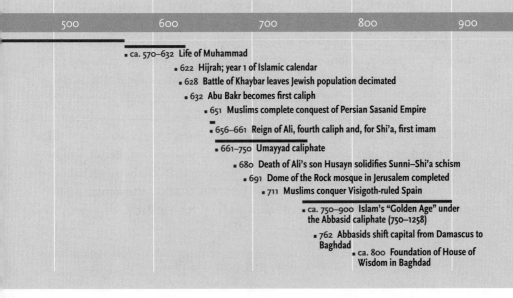

500   600   700   800   900

- ca. 570–632 Life of Muhammad
- 622 Hijrah; year 1 of Islamic calendar
- 628 Battle of Khaybar leaves Jewish population decimated
- 632 Abu Bakr becomes first caliph
- 651 Muslims complete conquest of Persian Sasanid Empire
- 656–661 Reign of Ali, fourth caliph and, for Shi'a, first imam
- 661–750 Umayyad caliphate
- 680 Death of Ali's son Husayn solidifies Sunni–Shi'a schism
- 691 Dome of the Rock mosque in Jerusalem completed
- 711 Muslims conquer Visigoth-ruled Spain
- ca. 750–900 Islam's "Golden Age" under the Abbasid caliphate (750–1258)
- 762 Abbasids shift capital from Damascus to Baghdad
- ca. 800 Foundation of House of Wisdom in Baghdad

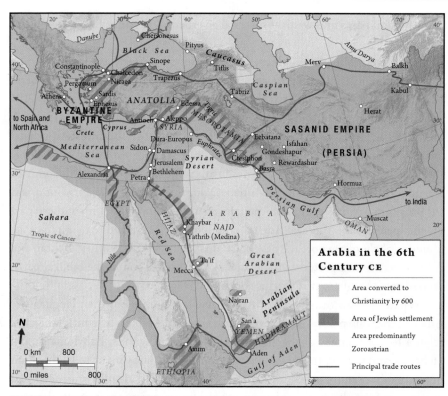

MAP 9.1   Arabia in the 6th Century CE   Most of the Arabian peninsula was, and remains, uninhabitable. Intensely isolated yet dependent on connections with the world outside, the peninsula's peoples early on developed a wary, clan- or tribal-focused sense of identity and values. The revelation of Islam fostered a sense of Arab unity that helped end decades of tribal conflict.

chain of patronyms that comprised one's name marked one as the member of a particular group, with particular social standing.[2]

Trading Networks   Such markers mattered because the peoples of Arabia lived by trade, and long-established traditions existed that gave each group specific rights and privileges. Distributors rather than growers and manufacturers, the Arabs produced few commercial goods that interested the non-Arab world, and they made their living largely by bringing luxury goods from China, India, and sub-Saharan Africa into the eastern Mediterranean. The silk route across Asia carried silks, spices, and perfumes overland from China, through India and Persia, and into Byzantium and provided opportunity for the northern Bedouin tribes, but other routes existed as well (see Map 9.1). The Yemenite tribes of the southern peninsula brought goods by ship out of India, then up the Persian Gulf, where they

---

[2]   The dialects spoken by many of the southernmost tribes have more elements in common with the Semitic languages in Ethiopia than with the Arabic dialects found elsewhere throughout the peninsula.

were handed off to the tribes of the Najd plateau. Sabaean tribes along the Red Sea coastline carried gold and gemstones from Ethiopia northward to Syria and Palestine. The Arabs, acculturated to the harshness of the terrain and mounted on their camels, made ideal long-distance carriers. Their caravans stretched across the endless miles linking east and west, north and south. The Arabs lacked a developed maritime tradition, however; foreign merchants from Persia, India, and Ethiopia brought goods to and from the peninsula by sea.

Arab historians termed the period before the advent of Islam the "Age of Ignorance" or "Age of Barbarism" (*al-Jahiliyya*). The simple absence of Islam suffices to merit the name, in Muslim eyes. Indeed, some writers used the term to embrace all of pre-

Desert Transport   Trains of camels brought Asian silks, spices, and gold to the Middle East and maintained the link between the eastern Mediterranean coast and the Arabian peninsula. Whenever possible, the caravans traveled at dawn and dusk, to avoid exertion during the blazing midday heat.

Islamic human history, but most Arabs defined **al-Jahiliyya** more precisely as the *Red Sea* period from the death of Jesus around 27 CE to the birth of Muhammad in the *Wars* year 570 CE. Many of those intervening years were in fact particularly chaotic. Clashes arose between the Roman and Persian empires, between the Byzantines and the Persians, and between Christian sects, all to the north, and in the Red Sea, between the Yemenites of Arabia and the Abyssinians of Ethiopia, to the south. These struggles caused occasional but severe disruptions of the Arab trading networks, disruptions that often boiled over into violence between tribes and clans.

A little-known and underappreciated chapter in the history of these Red Sea wars provides an important vantage point from which to view the origins of Islam. In the late 4th century the Abyssinian king of Axum, in Ethiopia, converted to Christianity, and at virtually the same time one of the Arab kings in Himyar, in southern Arabia, converted to Judaism. Both rulers and their successors energetically promoted their new faiths in their respective realms, but in 523 the then-reigning Himyari king, named Yusuf, initiated a genocidal campaign against all the Christians in his realm, whether they were Abyssinian or Arab. The plight of the victims, as the news of the bloody massacres spread, elicited a sympathetic response not only from Christian Ethiopia but also from the Byzantine Empire and its rival, the Sasanid Persian Empire, all of whom saw the massacres as a justification to seize control of Arab trade routes and centers throughout the Near East. It is within this context—of a divided Arab peninsula that felt vulnerable to outside intervention even as it was exposed to religious monotheism—that we must examine the rise of Islam.

Muhammad before Revelation

Muhammad (ca. 570–632) belonged to the Hashim clan within the Quraysh tribe, a group that had long been associated with administering the great pagan shrine in the commercial city of Mecca. This shrine, called the **Ka'ba**, was a kind of Arab pantheon, an ecumenical temple to all the pagan deities of all the Arab peoples. Pilgrims from all over the peninsula came to Mecca to pray at the shrine and present offerings to the gods. These pilgrims, together with the merchants who frequented the city, made Mecca a particularly vibrant city with more cross-cultural contact than most Arab sites. A sizable Jewish community existed too, although there is no evidence of any meaningful Christian presence before Muhammad's lifetime. With Byzantium and Persia at war in the north and Arab-Jewish and Abyssinian-Christian armies vying for power in the south, an urge to promote pan-Arab cohesion took root and fostered a militaristic streak in Arab society, conditioned to regard the entire non-Arab world as a threat to its existence. The problem was: What could unite so disparate a sprawl of tribes and clans? The answer came in the form of a divine mission and the identification of the Arabs as a new Chosen People.

THE QUR'AN AND HISTORY

Born into poverty, Muhammad began his rise in the world when he went to work for a wealthy widow named Khadija and began to handle her commercial interests. After several years, he and Khadija married. Muhammad's trading activities brought him out of Arabia and perhaps as far north as Syria, long solitary journeys that suited his meditative temperament. At some point Muhammad made contact with Judaism and Christianity, although we do not know the specifics of what he learned or how.

The Prophet Muhammad and the Faith of Islam

In the year 610, at the age of forty, Muhammad received the first of a series of dazzling visions that continued for the rest of his life. They summoned him to a unique role—as the final prophet of the One True God—and they called on the Arab people to unite and bring God's message, as delivered through Muhammad, to all the nations on earth. This message was the **Qur'an**, a divine text inscribed on a golden tablet in heaven by God himself. In his mystical transports, Muhammad heard the heavenly text being read and repeated it aloud to his followers. (In Arabic, the book's title means "recital.")[3]

---

[3]   The Qur'an itself (7.157) describes Muhammad as *ummiya*, which means "unlettered." Although some commentators insist that the word means only that Muhammad lacked a formal education, most scholars interpret it to mean that he was functionally illiterate.

The core message of the Qur'an is that all religions are false except for belief in the One True God, called *Allah* in Arabic, who created all things and has ennobled human life with a divine purpose, which is to serve and worship him through a regimen of daily prayers and adherence to his laws. The Qur'an elaborates the "five pillars of faith": (1) bearing witness to the unity of God and the prophethood of Muhammad; (2) daily prayers while facing the direction of Mecca; (3) fasting during Ramadan, the ninth month of the Islamic calendar; (4) giving alms to the poor; and (5) for those physically able and with the financial means, the obligation to make a **hajj** (pilgrimage) to Mecca. Performance of the "five pillars" gave public expression to membership in the **ummah**, the community of the faithful. To the faithful, the merciful and compassionate Allah will grant the reward of eternal bliss in a garden paradise. The remainder of sinful mankind, by Allah's stern but just judgment, will enter eternal torment in a fiery hell:

> Praise be to Allah, Who hath sent His Servant the Book, and hath allowed therein no crookedness. (He hath made it) straight (and clear) in order that He may warn (the godless) of a terrible punishment from Him, and that He may give glad tidings to the believers who work righteous deeds, that they shall have a goodly reward, wherein they shall remain for ever; further that He may warn those (also) who say, "Allah hath begotten a son": No knowledge have they of such a thing, nor had their fathers. It is a grievous thing that issues from their mouths as a saying. What they say is nothing but falsehood! (Qur'an 18.1–5)

The Qur'an identifies Christians and Jews as the "People of the Book," who deserve a measure of respect but who also have a special obligation to recognize the completion of their revelational history in Allah's Prophet. Pagan polytheisms, however, deserve little patience:

> Those who disbelieve, among the People of the Book and among the polytheists, were not going to depart (from their ways) until there should come to them clear evidence—the Messenger from Allah, rehearsing scriptures kept pure and holy: wherein are books right and straight. Nor did the People of the Book make schisms, until after there came to them clear evidence. And they have been commanded no more than this: to worship Allah, offering Him sincere devotion, being true (in faith); to establish regular prayers; and to give *zakat* [a special tax for charity, one of the five pillars of the Islamic faith]; and that is the religion right and straight. Those who disbelieve, among the People of the Book and among the polytheists, will be in hell-fire, to dwell therein (for aye [ever]). They

are the worst of creatures. Those who have faith and do righteous deeds—they are the best of creatures. Their reward is with Allah: Gardens of Eternity, beneath which rivers flow; they will dwell therein for ever; Allah well pleased with them, and they with Him: All this for such as fear their Lord and Cherisher. (Qur'an 98.1–8)

Mankind's chief responsibility is therefore submission (*islam,* in Arabic) to Allah's absolute authority—and that duty gave its name to the religion, Islam. Among the virtues that Allah commands are modesty, charity, and sobriety. Moreover, he requires tolerance of Judaism and Christianity, Islam's revelational predecessors, but directs his faithful to eradicate stiff-necked pagans who reject Islam.

Muhammad preached to the crowds in Mecca soon after his first revelation, and as the revelations continued, his message became more refined. He came to describe Islam as the final and perfect phase of the relationship established by God in his covenant with the patriarch Abram/Abraham. The Arabs themselves, he preached, are descended from Abraham's liaison with his concubine Hagar, which produced their son, Ishmael. Islam thus stands in an evolutionary relationship with Judaism and Christianity. Jesus, the Qur'an proclaims, was in the line of prophets that began with Moses. The role of the prophets was to elaborate a better

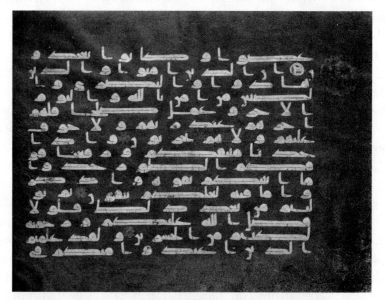

An Early Qur'an   The Qur'an is, to all Muslims, the Holy Book of God, written by him in heaven on tablets of gold. The text came to earth by means of the Prophet's revelations. God allowed Muhammad to bear witness to the holy text and recite messages aloud to his followers. These passages were saved and memorized by the community, and after the Prophet's death in 632 they were compiled and transcribed. Pictured here is a fragment from an early North African Qur'an, written in Kufic script.

understanding of God's desires, and as the Jews continued to disobey and misunderstand, God continued to send prophets—including Jesus. The Christians, however, had also failed—in failing to live up to what God expected of them and in their shocking mistake of thinking Jesus was actually God. All this had inspired Allah to make one last, full, and perfect revelation through Muhammad and the revealing of the Qur'an.

The Qur'an is a holy text like no other and presents unique challenges to critical reading. Two difficulties stand out: the text's transmission and its (real or *The* perceived) errors. First, its transmission. To devout Muslims, the Qur'an is a *Qur'an as* book written on gold tablets by Allah himself; it is the Word of God in a way that *Historical* the Hebrew or Christian Bibles are not, since there is no human agency in its *Source* creation. Muhammad's mystical revelations—hundreds of them over the course of twenty-two years—presented him with various passages of this book, which he then recited to his followers, until the entire text had been passed on. The passages were memorized by his followers as they appeared, and Muhammad, by near-universal agreement, never committed any of the passages to ink. After Muhammad's death in 632, the Prophet's companions began to collect the memorized passages on various scraps of parchment and inscribed stone, which were ultimately collected into a single manuscript that was kept first by the Prophet's successor as leader of the Muslim community, Abu Bakr (r. 632–634), and later by one of the Prophet's widows, Hafsa bint Umar (d. 665). The sole manuscript eventually went missing, but not before a later leader of the community, Uthman (r. 644–656), arranged for an authorized copy to be made, thus establishing the definitive text—an exact duplicate, without error, of Allah's handwritten original in heaven.

This leads to the second challenge posed by the Qur'an—its apparent errors. Mistakes in the Hebrew and Christian scriptures are numerous, of course, but can be explained as the results of human fallibility. Texts such as Paul's letters, after all, although divinely inspired, were written by a man sitting at a table (in Paul's case, usually in a prison cell). But how does one explain "errors" in a text that Allah did not inspire but actually wrote himself? The Qur'an, it turns out, is filled with anomalies. To begin with, how can we be certain that the authorized version prepared for Caliph Uthman correctly replicated the earlier, lost manuscript? Uthman's text introduced vowels to a text that had previously lacked them. Early Arabic writing, in common with other early ancient Near Eastern scripts, consisted only of the consonants within each word, leaving the reader to supply the vowels and punctuation out of context.[4] And if the text is indeed somehow

---

4   Try a simple example: *Rdng ths wrds s qt hrd.* Does this say "Reading these words is quite hard" or "Raiding those weirdos is [a] quiet herd"?

perfect, how does one explain the grammatical errors, skewed syntax, and fragmented sentences that abound in it? To this day, no standard critical edition of the Qur'an comparable to those made of the Hebrew and Christian Bibles has ever been published. Indeed, to many of the devout the very idea of such an edition is un-Islamic and possibly anti-Islamic, since it would be based on the assumption either that Allah is not the text's sole author or that Allah is capable of error. In either case, one is guilty of blasphemy.

Following the Qur'an, the most authoritative texts for Muslims are the collected non-Qur'anic teachings of the Prophet, known as the **hadith**. But several collections of these traditions exist, all compiled long after Muhammad's death, which further complicates their use as historical sources. The earliest surviving biography of the Prophet dates to well over a century after his death, too. So strictly speaking, there is no surviving contemporary Islamic evidence for Muhammad's life. By judicious use of the surviving much-later evidence—Qur'an, *hadith*, and biographies of the Prophet—we know much more about Muhammad, however, than we do about Moses or Jesus.

FROM PREACHER TO CONQUEROR

Muhammad preached that Allah had chosen the Arab people to bring Allah's message to the world and that this mission was therefore intended to bring an end to tribal strife. The people of Mecca, and especially the Quraysh leaders who owed their status to their role in traditional Arab religion, did not take kindly to

Muhammad's call to end the pagan cults. In 622, after twelve years of tense conflict, the Meccans drove him and his small company of believers from the city.[5] Muhammad then journeyed northward to Medina. This journey—the **Hijrah**—is commemorated by Muslims as the beginning of Islam's expansion and marks year 1 of the Islamic calendar. Medina, a commercial and cultic rival of Mecca, proved more receptive to Muhammad's teaching, and within two years Muhammad was in fact in command of the city.

Muhammad's Conquests

Success in Medina inaugurated a discernible tonal shift in the spreading of the Islamic message, since from 624 on the Prophet was in possession of an army. The Qur'anic passages revealed in Medina have a more activist and determined tone than the earlier Meccan revelations, and later Islamic texts depict the Prophet from this point on as a conqueror as much as a preacher. Ibn Ishaq (ca. 704–768), Muhammad's first biographer, proudly relates how the

---

[5]   The ninth *surah* (chapter) of the Qur'an expresses Allah's anger at the pagan leaders in Mecca who, after befriending the Prophet, had turned against him, as the local power struggle worked itself out.

Prophet defeated the Jewish community at Medina, which had allegedly plotted against him:

> Muhammad issued an order that no one was to perform the after-noon prayer until after he had reached Banu Qurayza, and he sent Ali ahead of him, bearing the Apostle's banner. The soldiers rallied when they saw it, and Ali advanced as far as the town's fortifications. While camped outside the town, Ali heard some Jews say insulting things about Muhammad, which prompted him to turn quickly and rush to meet the Apostle on the road. He told him that he did not need to come any closer or deal with the miserable Jews.
>
> "Why not?" Muhammad asked. "Did you hear them slandering me?" And after Ali replied that he had done exactly that, the Prophet went on, "Once they see me they will stop."
>
> Then the Apostle approached the Jews' fortifications and cried out, "Listen, you animals! God has rejected you and brings His vengeance upon you!"
>
> The Jews surrendered. After confining them in Medina, Muham-mad beheaded between six hundred and seven hundred of them, al-though some sources claim a number as high as eight hundred or even nine hundred.

Muhammad then began a series of rapid military ventures to defeat the Mec-cans and seize control of the entire peninsula—the first instances of a *jihad* ("strug-gle") of the sword, a holy war fought against those who persecute the Islamic believers. In 629, after five years of fighting, Muhammad was victorious. Once both Mecca and Medina were in his hands, Muhammad was able to bring most of the Arabian peninsula under his command before his death in 632. Given the sparse settlement of Arabia, the strategic key was to gain control of the handful of trade routes connecting the peninsula with the outer world. Muhammad understood this from his commercial travels. Once his Muslim forces were in a position to cut off the supply routes, the rest of the Arab tribes had no alternative but to surrender.

Before he died, Muhammad purified the Ka'ba in Mecca of its pagan trap-pings and rededicated it to Allah with a newly revealed truth: the large stone en-cased within the shrine had been sent to earth from heaven to show Adam and Eve where to build their first altar. Displaced by the Great Flood described in the Hebrew Bible, the long-forgotten stone was found by Abraham and his son Ishmael, who identified it and built a temple to house it, the first temple to Allah. The Ka'ba is that temple—and although what stands there now is a later, rebuilt temple, it still occupies the original site established by Abraham. It is thus the

Khaybar   The Khaybar oasis north of Medina was home to the largest Jewish community in Arabia, apart from the Himyari kingdom. After Muhammad led his community on the Hijrah from Mecca to Medina, in 622, he attempted to convert the Jews there, many of whom were members of a tribe known as the Banu Nadir. Jewish resistance to conversion led to tense relations with the Muslims, who were in possession of an army once Muhammad became the governor of the city. In 625 the Banu Nadir were expelled from Medina and made their way north to Khaybar. In 628 Muhammad attacked Khaybar and killed most of the Jewish population. The episode lives on in both Jewish and Islamic life. Palestinians today often shout "Khaybar! Khaybar!" when demonstrating against the Israelis. A rocket popular with the Islamist militant group Hezbollah has been popularly dubbed the "Khaybar II."

holiest site on earth to Muslims, who pray five times daily while kneeling in the direction of it. Muslims who make the required ritual pilgrimage (*hajj*) to Mecca walk in procession seven times around the Ka'ba. Those lucky enough to get next to the "House of Allah" (*Bayt Allah*, as it is known) will kiss the stone, which has the wondrous ability to absorb the believer's sins and render him pure.[6] The mosques built for communal worship by Muslims contain an inset wall notch (*qibla*) that points in the direction of the Ka'ba and provides the visual focal point for group prayers.

From the Prophet's sudden death in 632, Muslim leaders also kept an eye on the international scene, to prepare for the military expansion of Islam; Muhammad

---

[6]   According to Qur'anic tradition, the stone was originally a brilliant white in color but has absorbed so many sins over the centuries that it has turned black.

Completing the Hajj Pilgrimage (*hajj*) to Mecca is an obligation of every able-bodied Muslim. The endpoint of the pilgrimage is the sacred Ka'ba, the holiest site in Islam. Pilgrims perform a circular march (*tawaf* in Arabic) around the temple.

himself had clearly intended to advance northward into Palestine and Syria and was making plans to do so when he caught a fever and died. The long wars between Byzantium and Persia had exhausted both empires, and the time was right for the Arab advance. Muhammad had died without naming a successor, however. Most of the leading figures, known as the "Companions of the Prophet," threw their support behind Muhammad's father-in-law Abu Bakr, who took the title of **caliph** (*khalifah al-rasul Allah*, meaning "deputy of the Prophet of God").

Abu Bakr (r. 632–634) spent two years completing the conquest of Arabia and subduing Muslim groups who had rejected his succession (see Map 9.2). Upon his death, the Companions chose Umar (r. 634–644), an early convert, to succeed Abu Bakr. Umar directed his army northward, and within two years the Arabs had conquered Jerusalem, Antioch, and Damascus. Only one year later, in 637, Muslim forces took the Persian capital of Ctesiphon. According to Persian sources, the Arab soldiers were dazzled by the opulence of the capital and went on a looting spree. Taking care to send the required one-fifth of the booty to Caliph Umar, back in Medina, the army still netted enough for each soldier (reputedly eighteen thousand of them) to receive twelve thousand gold coins. Moreover, forty thousand Persian nobles were brought back to Medina as slaves.

Expansion under Muhammad's Successors

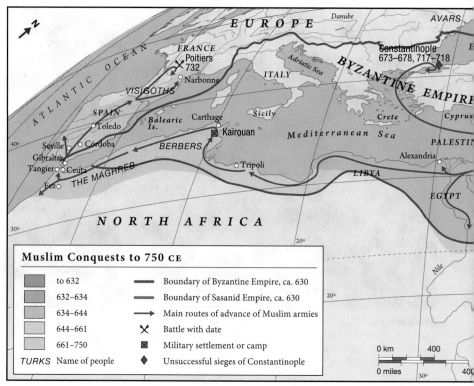

MAP 9.2   Muslim Conquests to 750   The Islamic Empire stretched from Spain to India, and until about 750 ethnic Arabs monopolized all positions of authority.

The rest of the Persian Empire surrendered to the Muslims by 651. Egypt had already fallen to the Arabs in 646—a crucial development that deprived Byzantium of a most important food source. It also triggered a quantum leap for the Muslims' development as a naval power: when the Muslims took Alexandria, Egypt's major port, two-thirds of the Byzantine imperial fleet happened to be tied up in the harbor. For a desert-dwelling people, the Arabs took to the sea quickly; this is why.

By 677 Muslim forces had reached the walls of Constantinople itself. The Byzantines drove the invaders off using a weapon called Greek fire—a naphtha-based compound that burst into flame when it came in contact with water. Undeterred, by 711 the Arabs had extended their conquests all along the coast of North Africa, had taken Sicily and the Balearic Islands, and had crossed the Strait of Gibraltar and seized Visigothic Spain. The Western world had never seen a military juggernaut like this: in 622 Muhammad and his small group of followers had been forced from their home in Mecca, yet within a hundred years those followers had conquered an empire that stretched from Spain to India, an area twice the size of that conquered by Alexander the Great (see Map 9.2).

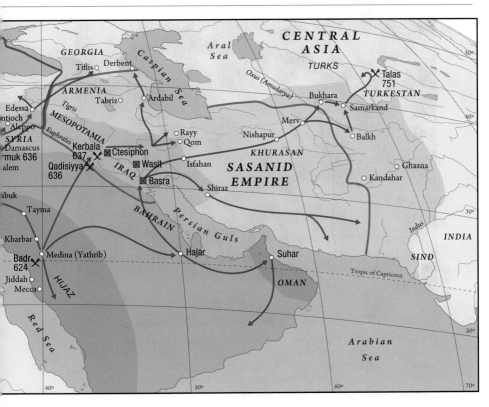

CONVERSION OR COMPULSION?

With their stunning victory over a much-weakened Persia and with their contain-
ment of a much-weakened Byzantium, there was no power on the scene capable of
halting or even slowing the Arab advance. Moreover, many people welcomed the
Muslims for the relief they brought from the ever-increasing taxes levied on them
by the Greeks and Persians to finance their wars with one another. Muslim attitudes to their new subjects took some time to work out, however.

The fraternal relationship among Judaism, Christianity, and Islam prevented
the Muslims from persecuting Jews and Christians. The Qur'an itself insists that *Attitudes*
"there is no compulsion in religion"—meaning that Jews and Christians cannot be *toward*
forced to accept Islam—since Allah's desire is for genuine conversion, not a terrified *People of*
acceptance of new faith to avoid execution. Caliph Umar (r. 634–644), in return for *the Book*
the surrender of the inhabitants of Jerusalem, had guaranteed the religious freedom
of the Jews and Christians residing there and had laid out the terms by which the
communities would live. This text, known widely as the Pact of Umar, formed the
model for the Muslim legal doctrine of the **dhimmi**, the "protected minorities"

Dome of the Rock   Completed in 691, the Dome of the Rock mosque in
Jerusalem is built upon the site, according to tradition, from which the Prophet
pushed off from earth during his mystical Night Journey through the heavens.
Apart from this tradition—which for Muslim faithful has Qur'anic authority
behind it—there is no evidence that Muhammad ever visited Jerusalem.

living under Islamic authority. The Jews and Christians, as People of the Book, deserved such treatment, in the hope that respectful handling by their Muslim rulers
would help them to see the superiority of Islam and thereby win their conversion.

*Attitudes
to the
Persians*   The Persians fared less well. Although regarded by some early Muslim leaders as another People of the Book and therefore deserving of legal protection, the
Zoroastrian Persians were widely regarded as mere pagans. And most of the Arab
soldiers and clerics, citing Qur'anic authority, claimed the right to compel the
conversion of pagans, to destroy their temples and idolatrous art, and to set fire to
their sacred writings after a four-month grace period:

> But when the forbidden months are past, then fight and slay the
> pagans wherever ye find them, and seize them, beleaguer them, and lie in
> wait for them in every stratagem (of war): but if they repent and establish
> regular prayers and pay *zakat*, then open the way for them, for Allah is
> Oft-Forgiving, Most Merciful. (Qur'an 9.5)

Arab chronicles assert that the victorious Muslims never faltered in observing the dhimmi status of law-abiding Persians; Persian sources, on the other

hand, document widespread atrocities at the local level. Surviving legal records contain no reference to a single Muslim being prosecuted for violating the rights of a Zoroastrian. That may mean that no such violations took place, but it is more likely that such violations were never prosecuted.

By the early 8th century the Islamic Empire was an unqualified military success, but it consisted of a small group of ethnically Arab Muslims governing an enormous and overwhelmingly non-Arab and non-Muslim population. From the Atlantic coasts of Spain and Morocco to the Indus River valley in India, the Arabs ruled a polyglot mix of Romano-Hibernians, Visigoths, Berbers, Egyptians, Syrians, Jews, and Persians (to name only the most prominent groups). In much of the empire the Arabs made up less than 1 percent of the population. Subjects were encouraged to convert to Islam through positive appeals and by imposing restrictions on non-Muslim activities. The most important restriction, rigorously monitored, was a complete ban on any public expression of a non-Islamic faith or of any criticism of Islam.

Conversion brought with it membership in the ummah, immunity from non-*zakat* taxes, military and political preferment, and economic privileges, in addition to the innate spiritual blessings of the faith. Non-Muslims possessing dhimmi status had to pay a heavy poll tax (*jizya*). Beyond the ban to practice their faith or discuss it in public, they could not testify against a Muslim in a court of law and had to wear special items of clothing that identified their inferior status—usually a wide belt called a *zunnar*. Although Muslims could take dhimmi-status wives, their offspring were automatically regarded as Muslim. Islamic law forbade dhimmis to construct new houses of worship for themselves, and strict jurists denied them the right to fix older houses falling into disrepair, since such construction work would effectively constitute a public expression of their faith. As a result churches, synagogues, and Zoroastrian temples everywhere decayed until they were no longer safe for use, and the communities that had used them gradually ceased to worship as communities.

Given this combination of positive enticements to convert and restrictive discouragements to continue in their own faith, the subjects of the Arab empire gradually began to embrace Islam. Most Persians remained loyal to the Zoroastrian tradition, especially those who lived in the countryside. By 750, one hundred years after their defeat by the Arabs, perhaps 90 percent of Persians still practiced Zoroastrianism. To accelerate conversion, the Arab rulers offered cash payments to Persians who would attend Friday prayers and awarded new deeds to landowners who would convert and agree to pressure their tenant-farmers to adopt the new faith. Slaves were given their freedom in return for converting. The Persian chronicler al-Tabari (d. 923) famously described early Arab policy toward the Persians as "to milk them until they are dry, and then to suck out their blood." Nevertheless, the process was slow, and it was not until the 10th century that Islam became the majority religion throughout the empire.

THE ISLAMIC EMPIRE

From Muhammad's death in 632 until 750, the Islamic Empire was a military state focused on expansion of borders and the monopolization of military, economic, and political power by the Arabs who had received Allah's revelation. But as larger numbers of people embraced the new religion, voices arose that promoted a new understanding of the caliphate as a Muslim state rather than a specifically Arab one—that is, as a community based on religious rather than ethnic identification. As the early Christians had done in the 4th and 5th centuries, the Muslims of the 7th and 8th centuries reinvented their faith as a multicultural hybrid.

The Abbasid Caliphate

This process became formalized with the rise of a new dynasty, which seized control of the caliphate in 750: the **Abbasids**, who boldly abandoned the Umayyad capital of Damascus and built a new one far to the east—**Baghdad**, which remains the capital of modern Iraq. The move was as important, both symbolically and geopolitically, as Constantine's move from Rome to Constantinople.

The first 150 years, from 750 to about 900, of the Abbasid era (750–1258) is generally regarded as Islam's Golden Age. From their magnificent new capital at Baghdad the caliphs transformed Islam's original Arab culture. At the heart of Abbasid policy was the earnest, although cautious, welcoming of the involvement and traditions of the *mawali* ("clients," literally), the non-Arab Muslims. This new, open attitude was driven in part by simple pragmatism: by 750, ethnic Arabs were no longer the numerical majority of Muslims. Taken together, Berbers, Egyptians, Kurds, Persians, and Syrians greatly outnumbered the relatively small group of Arabs who still monopolized all positions of political, military, and religious authority.

Among the *mawali*, the largest single group by far were the Persians. The first wave of transformation under the Abbasids, therefore, was the intentional spread and promotion of Persian culture—the so-called Persianization of Islam. Administrative integration came first. Persia, of course, had long experience with administering a vast empire, going back to Cyrus the Great. Their tactic then had been a carefully controlled system of provincial governors called *satraps*; this same idea reemerged under the Abbasids as a network of new officials called *viziers*. A **vizier** (from Arabic *wazir*, meaning "helper" or "assistant") was the governor of a district and the personal representative of the caliph, a combination of administrator and ambassador.

To offset the danger of decentralizing imperial power, the Abbasids increased the number and extent of the state-owned estates (*sawafi*) within each province; overseeing these estates was one of the duties of the viziers. The Abbasids also increased the fiscal contributions owed by each province to Baghdad. With the new income, the Abbasids developed the city of Baghdad itself, improved the pay of the army, and continued developing the infrastructure that held the Islamic world together. Moreover, they withdrew from the viziers the authority to appoint local religious judges, or *qadis*, and monopolized control of all judicial appointments. Still, loss of authority proved inevitable. The viziers in Syria and Anatolia bore the brunt of continuing the offensive against Byzantium throughout the 9th and 10th centuries, a war they largely financed by themselves, which resulted in their increased autonomy from Baghdad and, ultimately, as we will see in chapter 10, the breakup of the Abbasid Empire into competing caliphates. Nonetheless, the Abbasids remained in nominal power until another conquering people, the Mongols, captured Baghdad in 1258.

SUNNIS AND SHI'A

The early Abbasid centuries may have been Islam's Golden Age, but they also witnessed a fundamental break in the Muslim world—the split between the Sunnis and the Shi'a. Caliph Umar died in 644, stabbed by a Persian slave who resented the Arab takeover. When the Muslim leaders met to select the next caliph, two main contenders vied for the position: Uthman ibn Affar, an early convert from the Umayyad clan among the Quraysh tribe, and Ali ibn Abi Talib, the Prophet Muhammad's nephew and husband of Muhammad's only surviving child, Fatima. Most of the community preferred Uthman, who subsequently became the third caliph (r. 644–656), the ruler who oversaw the production of the authorized text of the Qur'an. The disgruntled Ali did not have to wait long for his turn, however, since Uthman was murdered by a party of Egyptian rebels who saw no reason why Egypt's acceptance of the Islamic faith had to entail the country's political subjection to the culturally inferior Arabs.

Ali was elected to succeed Uthman, becoming the fourth caliph (r. 656–661), and he quickly established his capital at the fortified eastern city of Kufa, on the banks of the Euphrates River about 100 miles south of Baghdad. The move from Medina disappointed many Arab leaders, who felt it as an insult to their homeland and therefore transferred their allegiance to a kinsman of the slain Uthman, a figure named Mu'awiya who had served as the provincial governor of Syria and resided in Damascus, a heavily Arabized city. Tensions between Mu'awiya and Ali rose with each passing year and could well have broken out into full-scale civil war, except that Ali was murdered in Kufa in the year 661 by a local rebel. It is a complicated narrative filled with names that are unfamiliar to most readers, but one whose consequences were important.

In the short term, the caliphate would remain in Umayyad hands until 750. In the long term, however, this series of elections, rebellions, and murders triggered the schism between the Sunnis and Shi'a. (In Arabic *Shi'a* is the plural noun, *Shi'i* is the plural adjective.) The rift is both political and religious. **Sunni** Muslims regarded selection by the community as the sole legitimate means to

The Sunni–Shi'a Schism

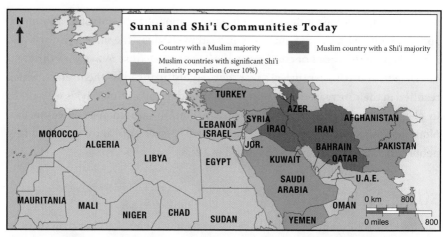

MAP 9.3   Sunni and Shi'i Communities Today   While communities of Shi'a can be found everywhere in the Muslim world, they have tended to concentrate in particular areas—most heavily in the Persian east (today's Iran and the southern regions of Iraq).

leadership of the Islamic world. The **Shi'a**, on the other hand, insisted that political and religious legitimacy could pass only to members of the Prophet's hereditary line. For them, Ali and his descendants via Fatima were thus forever the true successors to Muhammad. The Sunnis take their name from the *sunan* ("principles" in Arabic), the written and oral legacy of the Prophet's teachings and personal actions. The Shi'a (whose name derives from *shi'at Ali*, "the party of Ali") stress the divine appointment of the **imams**, the heavenly appointed heirs of Muhammad, whose words and judgments they regard as infallible. The Shi'a regard Ali as the first imam and the first true caliph, and consequently they reject most of the religious customs established under the first caliphs—Abu Bakr, Umar, and Uthman—and their Umayyad successors.[7]

The antagonism between Sunnis and Shi'a grew sharper as their traditions developed. By 800 the Shi'a comprised roughly a tenth of the Islamic world, and although Shi'i dynasties later rose to power in Egypt and parts of North Africa, the area of Persia that is now Iran quickly became and remained the heartland of Shi'ism (see Map 9.3).

The rift between Sunni and Shi'i Muslims widened and grew increasingly bitter with every generation. The dispute involved more than competing claims to inherit the Prophet's mantle as leader of the Islamic community. Rather, an explicitly religious element entered the tradition. The death in battle of the beloved Shi'i leader Husayn ibn Ali al-Shahid, Ali's son, in 680 had inspired the creation of a

---

[7]   Several denominations of Shi'ism developed in the early centuries, differing from one another primarily in the individuals each recognized as a true imam.

messianic narrative. Popular belief expected Husayn's return as the *Mahdi*—the "Guided One" who will emerge at the end of time and secure Islam's ultimate victory on earth. This belief now evolved into the Shi'i doctrine of the "hidden imam."

What differentiated the various sects of Shi'ism that emerged in Abbasid times was the number of true imams each group recognized, before the final imam went into hiding to await the moment of messianic return. The Shi'a, bound by their allegiance to Ali's descendants, thus incorporated the religious teachings and legal judgments rendered by those imams. In this way, their varying political programs transmuted into a web of traditions very much at odds with those of the Sunni majority.

The Abbasids were in a bind. To retain the support of the Islamic majority they had to champion Sunni orthodoxy, yet they owed their dynastic success to the backing they had received from the Shi'a. Moreover, the open bias they *The* showed for promoting Persians at court led to demands by other *mawali* groups *Abbasid* for similar treatment. The rulers embraced as many aspects of the various *mawali* *Response* cultural traditions as could be harmonized with Islamic teaching, whether Sunni or Shi'i. The Persians, for example, had an ancient custom of veiling of their women whenever they appeared in public. This was done not to denigrate women but to express ethnic pride: inferior non-Persian men had no right to look upon a Persian woman. The veil was a badge of honor, an expression of superiority. This Persian practice harmonized well with the Qur'anic demand for sexual modesty, and thus it became generally Islamized.

ISLAM AND THE CLASSICAL TRADITIONS

The Arabs' conquests exposed them to the Greater West's centuries-long intellectual, scientific, and artistic traditions, but they disdained any aspect of *Preservation* Zoroastrian learning and resented the Persians' embrace of Shi'ism. This *of the Latin* made the Arabs much more open to the Greco-Roman and Judeo-Christian *West's* intellectual legacy. The Arabs were new to literacy, however, and could not *Cultural* access the texts available to them in the countless libraries of the Near East *Legacy* and North Africa. Starting in the 8th century, groups of Syrian Christians— mostly scholar-monks—began to translate the writings of the ancient Greeks and Romans into Arabic for the benefit of their new rulers. Soon, scholars in North Africa, Sicily, and Spain became involved. Their activity was prodigious: within two or three generations the whole corpus of Western thought lay available for Muslim scholars to read. It included the mathematical and geometrical works of Euclid and Archimedes, the medical knowledge of Hippocrates and Galen, the historical texts of Herodotus and Thucydides, the books of the Hebrew Bible and the New Testament, and works of geography, astronomy, poetry, and

Veiled Women   This 17th-century fresco from Safavid Iran is a late rendering of an early episode in Islamic history. It shows a group of women mourning the dead during one of the expansionist wars of the first Islamic century (650–750 CE). The veiling of women, practiced by most Near Eastern peoples to some degree, was particularly associated with Persian culture, and it came to be the enforced norm within Islam after the Abbasid dynasty relinquished Arab Damascus and moved the capital east to Baghdad. The so-called Persianization of Islam then commenced. The Abbasids remained in power until the Mongols destroyed Baghdad in 1258.

law. Roman histories, legal texts, Stoic meditations, and technical treatises were available too. The leading Muslim scholars absorbed most of this knowledge eagerly, finding in it much that was of immediate practical value. Indeed, with the support of the caliph's court, scholars established a large library and institute for the study of classical texts called the "House of Wisdom" (*bayt al-hikma*).

As a rule, any text or genre of inquiry that could be reconciled with Islamic doctrine received a warm welcome. But the Greco-Roman philosophical tradition, specifically, was another matter altogether. Why would anyone look to pagans like Plato and Aristotle for answers to questions about the purpose of human life, the nature of truth, the definition of justice, or the understanding of morality? After all, all those answers were available in the Qur'an and the *hadith* and the body of Islamic law that grew out of them, the **shari'a**.

Numerous Islamic scholars did read Greek philosophy, however—especially the works of Aristotle. Al-Kindi (d. ca. 870), al-Farabi (d. ca. 951), Ibn Sina (d. 1037), al-Ghazali (d. 1111), and Ibn Rushd (d. 1198) all wrote brilliant commentaries on it. Al-Kindi was one of the first to argue that philosophy posed no difficulty for pious Muslims:

> Aristotle, the greatest of the Greek philosophers, wrote that "we should be grateful to the fathers of those who have contributed anything of truth, since they were the cause of the philosophers' existence." . . . How beautiful is his statement. We need feel no shame in appreciating the truth or in acquiring it from wherever it comes from—even if the truth comes from peoples and races far distant from us and far different from us. To the man who seeks truth, nothing is more important than the truth. Truth cannot be disparaged, and neither should be the one who speaks it or conveys it. Truth, indeed, diminishes no one and exalts all.

To the great bulk of Islamic society, however, philosophy was irrelevant, a brain-churning waste of time when one could be pondering the Qur'an and the judgments of Islamic legal scholars. Greek tragedy also fell on deaf ears among the Muslims because the idea of an inexorable fate other than the determination of the all-knowing Allah was anathema to them. Consequently, the great plays were neglected absolutely—never performed, never recopied, never commented on. The epic poetry of the Greeks and Romans also held no interest for Muslim readers, who preferred the stories of their own heroes, whose exploits they related in prose and verse—such as the great collection of tales called the *Shahnameh* ("The Book of Kings") by the Persian poet Ferdowsi (d. 1020)—and in histories. The Arabs especially excelled in historical writing, with figures like Ibn Ishaq (Muhammad's first biographer, d. 768), al-Waqidi (d. ca. 822), and al-Masudi (d. 956). It remains unclear, however, how much attention Muslim historians paid to classical writers like Herodotus, Thucydides, or Tacitus. Intrigued by what they read or heard about, the caliphs maintained two principal centers for this translation in the late 8th and throughout the 9th century, both located in Baghdad. One was led by the Arab scholar al-Kindi (d. ca. 870) and the other by the Syrian Christian physician Hunayn ibn Ishaq (d. ca. 873). Hunayn ibn Ishaq also made the first translation of the Septuagint version of the Bible into Arabic.[8]

Muslim writers excelled in two genres especially—histories and travelogues. Like the Romans before them, the Muslims explored the history and geography of their newly acquired territories both as a pragmatic measure (the better to govern them) and as propaganda (to illustrate the advantages brought by the arrival of

---

[8]   By the time of the Abbasid takeover in 750, fully 50 percent of all Christians worldwide lived under Islamic rule. As they became Arabized, it became necessary to translate the scriptures into Arabic. Hunayn ibn Ishaq, incidentally, is not the same Ibn Ishaq who wrote the biography of Muhammad.

Islam). Many of the histories focused on a particular tribe, city, or region, but ambitious writers like al-Baladhuri (d. 892) and al-Tabari (d. 923) composed massive chronicles of the entire empire. Among the most famous of Muslim travel writers was Ibn Fadlan (d. ca 950), who journeyed north into what is today Ukraine and western Russia; to him we owe the classic description of Viking burial customs. A genuine spirit of curiosity about other cultures informs his (and other writers') descriptions, but so too does a judgmental sense of Arab superiority:

> The Rus are the dirtiest creatures God ever made. They defecate and urinate anywhere, without shame. Like beasts, they do not wash their privates after sex and do not wash their hands after eating. After their travels they drop anchor (or, as with the ones I saw, tie up their ships along the shore of a river like the great Volga) and build large wooden huts for themselves on the shore. Each hut can hold between ten and twenty people. Inside, each man rests on a couch. They have lovely slave girls with them, whom they will sell to slave-merchants eventually, and each man has sexual intercourse with a slave girl whenever he wishes, even in front of his companions. Sometimes the whole company gets involved, each with his own girl, all in each other's presence. If a merchant happens along who wants to buy a girl, he simply looks on and waits for the man to be finished.

The al-Kindi school focused on philosophical, literary, and logical texts, whereas the ibn Ishaq school tended to emphasize the Greek scientific and medical writings. Muslim scholars showed little interest in the Romans, whose intellectual works they regarded as derivative of the Greeks, although they did admire the Romans' adeptness with technology. But for every eager scholar wanting to pursue Greek knowledge, dozens of suspicious clergy cautioned against the ideas of unbelievers. The early Christian communities had exhibited a similar hesitation toward pagan Greek learning, until figures like Augustine of Hippo showed that classical learning posed no intrinsic threat to Christian orthodoxy and could in fact help to clarify Christian ideas and beliefs. Resistance to the Greek tradition was as tenacious and passionate as the support expressed for it by scholars like al-Kindi.

The Challenge of Classical Greek Culture

Few of the great Muslim philosophers could read Greek; most depended on the translations made for the caliphal court. And like academics everywhere, some of them claimed more expertise than they actually had. Here is al-Kindi's thumbnail synopsis of Aristotle's *Metaphysics*:

> In the work called *Metaphysics* Aristotle sought to explain those things that exist yet do not possess matter; and how these things may co-exist with things that do have matter—and yet remain unconnected to

matter and separate from it. He sought also to affirm the Oneness of God (the Great and Almighty), to explain God's many beautiful names, and to explicate how God is the causal agent of everything in the universe, making everything perfect—for God is the God of the universe, governing everything in His complete and perfect wisdom.

But Aristotle never said anything remotely like this. Was al-Kindi a charlatan? Certainly not. Rather, he wished to deflate clerical concerns about the dangers in seeking knowledge from non-Islamic traditions. He therefore tried to deflect criticism by making Aristotle sound like someone who would surely have been a Muslim if only he had been lucky enough to live in Islamic times.

At other times al-Kindi felt free to express Aristotle's views clearly:

> There is nothing shameful in admiring, and even in acquiring, the Truth, no matter where It comes from. To the student of Truth there is nothing that matters except Truth, and Truth is never cheapened or lessened by the person who states it, not even if he comes from a distant land and belongs to a backward nation. Indeed, Truth belittles no one and ennobles all.

Those interested in Greek philosophy thus faced a twofold problem: to show how a pagan discipline could explain Islamic truth while preserving the authority of revelation. Does revealed truth need logical explication? Does logical explication undermine the authority of the revelation?

Islamic thinkers had started to wrestle with these questions even before their discovery of the Greek tradition. From Muhammad's death in 632, Muslims and would-be Muslims had tried to answer a number of fundamental questions about the faith—the kinds of questions that anyone intrigued by the faith might raise. Was the Holy Qur'an created, or had it existed in heaven from all eternity? If it was present from the Creation, then why did Allah bother with the partial and imperfect Jewish and Christian revelations? And why does the Qur'an's message appear to change? How can it call first for Arabs to embrace Islam for repentance of their sins and to foster pan-Arab unity when later it calls Arabs to bring the message of Allah to the entire world? Another group of questions centered on Allah's attributes. In stating that Allah sees everything, hears our prayers, speaks, has knowledge, exerts will, and wields power, does the Qur'an imply that Allah is anthropomorphic—a kind of eternal man? And a third set of questions asked whether Allah's omniscience implies that every human's destiny is predetermined. Do we have free will, or has Allah, in knowing our ultimate fates, effectively set our ultimate fates?

The practical and immediate need to confront these matters resulted in a body of ideas and disciplines known as **kalam** (literally "speech" or "word," but usually translated as "theology"). *Kalam* was not philosophy and did not aspire to be. Instead, it was a method of inquiry into a limited number of specific issues that needed resolution, and its goal was to ease Islam's acceptance by cultures with long-established traditions that privileged rational thought. Reason, of course, is a universal trait. But the value placed on reason, in preference to other ways of knowing, is a cultural one. As Islam developed and as questions about the fundamental nature of Allah, the Qur'an, and human free will were articulated, Sunni leaders resolved them by seeking a consensus among the community of scholars. This was the tradition known as *ijma'* ("consensus"), a principle that embraced the use of reason to resolve a religious question. But *ijma'* was not open-ended. Once the community's answer on any given question had been authoritatively expressed, the question was considered closed for all time. Tradition trumped any rethinking of any issue.

But the Christian-initiated translations of the Greeks posed another problem: as a result of the monks' work, Muslim scholars encountered real philosophy (*falsafah* in Arabic), or open-ended rational inquiry. In philosophy, the answer given to any question does not close the matter; rather, it invites continual reappraisal. Philosophy is therefore as much an attitude of mind as it is any particular body of ideas, and it does not attempt to produce a desired goal. The liberal

Truth Attainable by Rational Argument   In this scientific manuscript from 13th-century Persia, two great rationalists, Aristotle and his pupil Alexander the Great, lead a discussion of the medicinal properties of certain animal organs and secretions. The eighteenth chapter (*sura*) of the Qur'an discusses a wise ancient ruler who held dominion "from the rising of the sun to the setting of the sun"; commentators have associated this figure with Alexander since the 8th century.

atmosphere of the early Abbasid years allowed philosophy to bloom, as the caliphs al-Rashid (r. 786–809), al-Ma'mun (r. 813–833), al-Mu'tasim (r. 833–842), and al-Wathik (r. 842–847) encouraged new translations of and commentaries on the Western philosophical canon. They promoted as well the study of the philosophical and scientific traditions of Zoroastrian Persia and Buddhist India. In addition to the House of Wisdom at Baghdad, these caliphs also opened a second center for liberal studies at Basra, in Iraq.

Opinions varied on the acceptability of the new cultural injections, but for the moment the inclusionists won. Prominent among these was a group of scholars known as the Mu'tazilites ("the Dissenters"). The Mu'tazilites held widely varying views, but they shared a belief that whenever tradition and reason were in conflict, the scale tipped in reason's favor. Another way to describe the Mu'tazilites is as the party inclined to prevent *ijma'* from sealing off intellectual inquiry. For this reason alone, they were generally disliked and distrusted by most Sunnis, but what earned the Sunnis' real ire was the Mu'tazilite position on the "createdness" of the Qur'an. The caliph al-Ma'mun (r. 813–833), a strong Mu'tazilite sympathizer, even proclaimed this position the official doctrine of the state and required appointees to public office to swear allegiance to it. He triggered a violent revolt and died soon thereafter under suspicious circumstances.[9]

Islam's effort to absorb classical Greco-Roman culture was therefore a highly fraught business. Sunnis and Shi'a judged the issue from different vantage points and by different methods, and disagreements were many and wide within each group. For every inclusionist like al-Kindi and the Mu'tazilites, there were dozens of exclusionists who regarded the effort to harmonize their faith with classical Greco-Roman or Zoroastrian culture as pointless at best and dangerous at worst. In this way Islam extended the general tendency in the Greater West to pursue reform movements, whenever they were thought necessary, as efforts to restore a lost preexisting purity.

The dangers of cultural borrowing and intellectual innovation played a role in the development of the singular Muslim custom of spiritual concealment, *takiyya*. Interpreting the Qur'anic verse "Whether ye hide what is in your hearts or reveal it, Allah knows all" (3.29) in a somewhat generous way, Islamic jurists in both the Sunni and the Shi'i camps provided a justification for the intentional hiding of what one believes. Thus a Shi'i Muslim could pretend to be a Sunni, or vice versa, to protect oneself without incurring divine displeasure. For Shi'i Muslims *takiyya* grew in importance from a bitter necessity during times of Sunni persecution to a fundamental and obligatory duty, the denial of one's faith as an expression of it.

---

9   One tradition asserts that al-Ma'mun was resting by a river and asked some courtiers what he should eat. They just happened to have some dates at hand. He died on the spot, presumably poisoned.

WOMEN AND ISLAM

The expansion of Islam, like the spread of all world religions, profoundly affected the status and treatment of women. As with Christianity, Islamic teaching on women's roles and rights in society developed as a dialogue between the revealed truth of the faith and the traditional norms and values of each society into which the faith was introduced. The picture that emerges is complex. Women in the early Muslim world did not enjoy anything approaching equal rights with men—but neither did they in the Christian or Jewish worlds. Women's experiences varied depending on ethnicity, social class, economic status, educational level, and geographical location, all of which make accurate generalizations about Islam and women difficult to assert with any degree of fairness.

The Qur'an makes plain that women share equally in the primary responsibility of all Muslims to remain obedient to Allah's commands. In recounting the Creation story of Adam and Eve in the Garden of Eden, the Qur'an rejects the biblical tradition of identifying Eve as the temptress who seduces Adam into sin; rather, both share responsibility for their sin and an equal portion of the punishment. Nevertheless, the Qur'an emphasizes the comparative physical weakness of women and their concomitantly increased vulnerability in a harsh world. The entire fourth chapter (*sura*) of the Qur'an is dedicated to the topic of women. This *sura* was revealed to Muhammad, according to tradition, after the battle of Uhud in 625, the first military defeat suffered by the Muslims, one in which many Muslim soldiers died, leaving behind a large number of widows and orphans. Islamic law requires that widowed women receive a guaranteed portion of their husbands' estates and that divorced wives are entitled to having their dowries returned to them. In pre-Islamic times, neither provision was the norm. The Qur'an also asserts the right of women to give testimony in legal cases, although a woman's testimony is considered only half as worthy as that of a man, and to bring suit for damages in civil cases. These too were innovations in Arab tradition. This *sura* also permits a man to have as many as four wives, but it obliges him to treat each wife with equal respect. Polygamy was an ancient custom among the Arab tribes, and a man was previously allowed to take as many wives as he wanted, without any social requirements on how he treated them. The Qur'anic tradition therefore represented a reining in of the practice.[10]

On the Sunni side, some Yemeni and Bedouin tribes had long practiced a legalized form of concubinage. In *mut'a* (literally "pleasure" or "enjoyment"), a man married a woman for a prearranged period of time—a year, a month, a week, or

---

[10]   Muhammad himself had a total of eleven wives (thirteen, according to some sources), but seldom more than four at any given time. His serial marriages may have aimed at ensuring the unification of the Arab tribes by forging alliances across Arab society.

even a single day—and paid her a prorated dowry in return for his "enjoyment" of her.[11] It is unclear how widespread the practice was in pre-Islamic times, but some evidence dates it to as early as the 4th century CE among the Bedouin and possibly even earlier among groups of Egyptian traders. Several later writers claimed that Muhammad himself had practiced it (al-Tabari, *Chronicle* 1.1775–1776). Many Sunni jurists rejected *mut'a* and the assertion that the Prophet had ever been involved in it. But from the time of the legal scholar al-Shafi'i (d. ca. 819), a compromise allowed it, provided that the term of the marriage did not appear in the written marriage contract. The Shi'a, in contrast, championed *mut'a* from the start (and still practice it widely today).

Above all, Islam demanded of women obedience and modesty—obedience to religious tradition and social norms of gender roles and modesty of dress, demeanor, and speech. To lesser extents, it demanded the same of men. As the very name of the faith makes plain, the most important value for men and women to aspire to is submission. Misogyny certainly existed, even throve, in medieval Muslim society, but it is not an intrinsic part of the Qur'anic call itself. Ethnic, tribal, and class-based prejudices both spawned and encouraged misogynistic practices and attitudes. Islam softened many such customs. Among the pre-Islamic Arabs, for example, no restrictions were placed on a father's right to control and discipline his wives or children. In its way, such a tradition resembled the Roman custom of patria potestas or the classical Athenian strictures regarding women. Restrictions on women's movement in public—whether veiled or not, whether accompanied by an adult male family member or not—predated Islam and probably originated in the exceptionally dangerous nature of movement through the peninsula. The Qur'an itself says nothing about the subject.

◆

Arab culture, and to a lesser extent Persian culture, was undoubtedly patriarchal and paternalistic. Islam tempered and softened the harshest elements within both worlds, but in its desire to adopt and adapt to the many cultures that it encompassed, the faith allowed as many of preexisting life practices to endure as possible. Whether one looks at early Islam's political, intellectual, or cultural development, one is left with the impression not of a new and ideologically zealous culture forcing itself upon preexisting societies, but of an intricate interplay between a developing corpus of religious principles and a complicated, heterogeneous world over which Islam—seemingly in the blink of an eye—suddenly held sway.

---

[11] For a marriage of only one day, the marriage price could be as low as a handful of grain or dates.

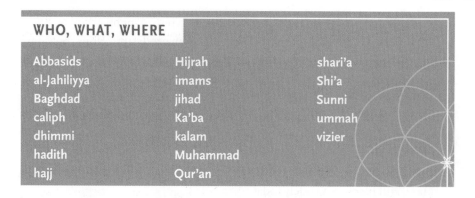

WHO, WHAT, WHERE

Abbasids	Hijrah	shari'a
al-Jahiliyya	imams	Shi'a
Baghdad	jihad	Sunni
caliph	Ka'ba	ummah
dhimmi	kalam	vizier
hadith	Muhammad	
hajj	Qur'an	

SUGGESTED READINGS

Primary Sources

Al-Bukhari. *The Hadith.*

Al-Kindi. *On First Philosophy.*

Ferdowsi. *Shahnameh (The Book of Kings).*

Ibn Fadlan. *Risala (Travels).*

Ibn Ishaq. *Life of the Prophet.*

The Qur'an.

Anthologies

Constable, Olivia Remie, ed. *Medieval Iberia: Readings from Muslim, Christian, and Jewish Sources* (2011).

Lopez, Robert S., and Irving W. Raymond, trans. *Medieval Trade in the Mediterranean World: Illustrative Documents* (2001).

McGinness, Jon, and David C. Reisman. *Classical Arabic Philosophy: An Anthology of Sources* (2007).

Renard, John. *Islamic Theological Themes: A Primary Source Reader* (2014).

Shinners, John, ed. *Medieval Popular Religion, 1000–1500: A Reader* (2006).

Studies

al-Khalili, Jim. *The House of Wisdom: How Arab Science Saved Ancient Knowledge and Gave Us the Renaissance* (2012).

Bennison, Amira K. *The Great Caliphs: The Golden Age of the Abbasid Empire* (2010).

Bowersock, G. W. *The Throne of Adulis: Red Sea Wars on the Eve of Islam* (2013).

Caswell, F. Matthew. *The Slave-Girls of Baghdad: The Qiyan in the Early Abbasid Era* (2011).

Cook, Michael. *Commanding Right and Forbidding Wrong in Islamic Thought* (2001).

Cotton, Hannah M., Robert G. Hayland, Jonathan J. Price, and David J. Wasserstein. *From Hellenism to Islam: Cultural and Linguistic Change in the Roman Near East* (2012).

Crone, Patricia. *God's Rule: Government and Islam—Six Centuries of Medieval Islamic Political Thought* (2005).

Crone, Patricia. *Meccan Trade and the Rise of Islam* (2004).

Crone, Patricia, and Martin Hinds. *God's Caliph: Religious Authority in the First Centuries of Islam* (2003).

Donner, Fred McGraw. *Muhammad and the Believers: At the Origins of Islam* (2010).

El Shamsy, Ahmed. *The Canonization of Islamic Law: A Social and Intellectual History* (2013).

Friedmann, Yohann. *Tolerance and Coercion in Islam: Interfaith Relations in the Muslim Tradition* (2003).

Goldenberg, David M. *The Curse of Ham: Race and Slavery in Early Judaism, Christianity, and Islam* (2005).

Griffith, Sidney H. *The Church in the Shadow of the Mosque: Christians and Muslims in the World of Islam* (2008).

Haider, Najam. *Shi'i Islam: An Introduction* (2014).

Hawting, G. R. *The First Dynasty of Islam: The Umayyad Caliphate, AD 661–750* (2000).

Hoyland, Robert G. *In God's Path: The Arab Conquests and the Creation of an Islamic Empire* (2014).

Kennedy, Hugh. *The Prophet and the Age of the Caliphates: The Islamic Near East from the Sixth to the Eleventh Century* (2004).

Khalek, Nancy. *Damascus after the Muslim Conquest: Text and Image in Early Islam* (2011).

Levy-Rubin, Milka. *Non-Muslims in the Early Islamic Empire: From Surrender to Coexistence* (2011).

Marsham, Andrew. *Rituals of Islamic Monarchy: Accession and Succession in the First Muslim Empire* (2009).

Mottahadeh, Roy P. *Loyalty and Leadership in an Early Islamic Society* (2001).

Turner, John P. *Inquisition in Early Islam: The Competition for Political and Religious Authority in the Abbasid Empire* (2013).

Young, M. J. L., J. D. Latham, and R. B. Serjeant. *Religion, Learning, and Science in the Abbasid Period* (2006).

Zadeh, Travis. *Mapping Frontiers across Medieval Islam: Geography, Translation, and the Abbasid Empire* (2011).

For additional resources, including maps, primary sources, visuals, web links, and quizzes, please go to **www.oup.com/us/backman**.

CHAPTER 10

Reform and Renewal in the Greater West

750–1258

In the middle of the 8th century, separated only by a year, two palace coups took place 2,000 miles from each other. Such events were commonplace in both realms and often involved blindings, beheadings, and poisonings—with at least one monarch ripped apart by having her limbs tied to four horses driven in four directions.[1] At first, perhaps, these two seizures of power did not seem remarkable. But each set its society on a new course of development and brought their worlds into direct and lasting conflict. One brought on the Carolingian dynasty that culminated in the reign of Charlemagne in western Europe; the other introduced the Abbasid caliphate based in Baghdad. Both would fundamentally shape the history of the Greater West.

THE GREATER WEST, ca. 1200

The centuries that followed witnessed much of the best and the worst of their societies' medieval era. They included unimagined prosperity, intellectual advance, artistic

Astrolabe A 12th-century astrolabe from Muslim Spain. The increase in maritime trade across the Mediterranean by 1000 owed a lot to technical innovations introduced by Muslim and Jewish scientists, many of whom worked in Spain.

---

1 This unlucky individual was Brunhilde, a Visigothic noblewoman who married Sigebert, the king of Austrasia (a territory in the eastern reaches of today's France).

- Two Palace Coups
- The Carolingian Ascent
- Charlemagne
- Imperial Coronation
- Carolingian Collapse
- The Splintering of the Caliphate
- The Reinvention of Western Europe

- Mediterranean Cities
- The Reinvention of the Church
- The Reinvention of the Islamic World
- The Call for Crusades
- The Crusades
- Turkish Power and Byzantine Decline
- Judaism Reformed, Renewed, and Reviled

CHAPTER OUTLINE

flourishing, religious revival, and political development—but also fiery hatred, social oppression, academic censorship, and xenophobia. They defined the broad division in Islam between Sunnis and Shi'a, still evident today, and the reinvention of Europe with feudal society and medieval cities. Perhaps most notoriously they included the Crusades in the Holy Land and also a new chapter in Jewish history.

TWO PALACE COUPS

The Abbasid Takeover

The first coup took place in Damascus in 750, when the Sunni family known as the Abbasids, members of the Banu Hashim clan, which traced its ancestry back to the great-grandfather of Muhammad, rebelled against the Umayyad rulers of the Islamic Empire. The Umayyad dynasty had never been popular. Despite building the shrine of the Dome of the Rock in Jerusalem and the Great Mosque in Damascus, they were seen (probably correctly) as more interested in power than in the faith. They only made things worse by reserving all positions of leadership in the empire for ethnic Arabs. Their prejudice led to severe economic and social trouble, as large numbers of Egyptians and Persians converted to Islam, abandoned their farms, and migrated to the cities, where they expected to receive preferment. The subsequent decline in agricultural production caused food prices to spike and imperial revenues to fall. The empire's cities swelled with disaffected

CHAPTER TIMELINE

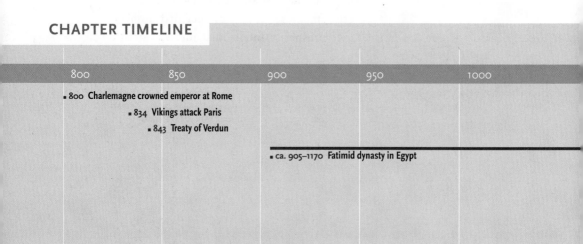

800	850	900	950	1000

- 800 **Charlemagne crowned emperor at Rome**
- 834 **Vikings attack Paris**
- 843 **Treaty of Verdun**

- ca. 905–1170 **Fatimid dynasty in Egypt**

populations, who found out the hard reality that membership in the *ummah*, the Islamic community, depended very much on the color of one's skin.

As unrest gained pace in the 8th century, the Abbasids, based in Khurasan, in northeastern Iran, began laying the groundwork for regime change. Although themselves Arab, the Abbasids championed a multiethnic vision of Islam. They cagily sought support among the Shi'a who had taken refuge in Iran with false promises of elevating their choice to the caliphal throne after the coup. Finally, in 750, they struck. Led by family patriarch al-Saffah ("the Slaughterer"), they routed the Umayyads on the battlefield, took control of the state, and promptly moved the capital eastward to their newly established city of Baghdad.[2] The Abbasids presided over the opening of the Islamic world to non-Arabs. Persians especially rose to prominence under the new regime, winning positions at court, in the provincial government, and in the Islamic schools. This began a sweeping process of cultural change, sometimes known as the "Persianization" of Islamic culture.

The second coup was much less bloody but no less epoch-making. The Frankish warlord-kings who had held sway over northern Gaul since Clovis's acceptance of Christianity around 500 were on the whole a sorry lot. These were the Merovingians, who fought incessantly, plotted even more, and showed no

The Carolingian Takeover

---

[2]   Al-Saffah invited the remaining Umayyads to a reconciliation dinner. Just as the first course was being served, his agents sprang from their hiding places, knives flashing. Only one Umayyad family member escaped.

1050	1100	1150	1200	1250

- ca. 1050 Medieval agricultural revolution at its height
- 1054 Great Schism between Latin and Orthodox churches
- 1066 Norman conquest of England under William I
- 1071 Byzantines defeated by Seljuk Turks at Manzikert
- 1077 Holy Roman Emperor Henry IV does penance before Pope Gregory VII
- 1095 Pope Urban II calls First Crusade
- 1096–1099 First Crusade
- 1100 Banking industry emerges in Italy
- 1122 Concordat of Worms ends investiture conflict
- 1135–1204 Life of Maimonides, Jewish philosopher
- ca. 1150–1212 Reconquista of Muslim Spain
- 1187 Muslim reconquest of Jerusalem
- 1204 Crusaders of Fourth Crusade sack Constantinople

persuasive interest in doing more with rulership than acquiring wealth and root-ing out real or suspected rivals. From the mid-7th century on, they are known as the "do-nothing kings," whose ineffectiveness enabled local warlords and officials to usurp power for themselves.

The most successful of the usurpers was a family from northeastern Gaul known as the Carolingians. By the early 700s Pepin of Heristal was serving as a regional Merovingian official but was in reality an all-but-autonomous ruler. He passed his position on to his only, although illegitimate, son, **Charles Martel** ("the Hammer," d. 741), who added much of northwestern Gaul to the family domain and gave the name Carolingian (from *Carolus*, Latin for "Charles") to the dynasty. The secret to the Carolingians' effectiveness was a combination of vision, ruthlessness, and luck. The family early on developed a view of themselves as the self-appointed saviors of Christian Gaul and eventually of western Europe, des-tined like the biblical David to replace the rejected king Saul (that is, the Merovin-gian house) and establish a righteous and lasting realm.

For four or five generations the family advanced their dedication to unit-ing and strengthening western Christendom. One of the most dramatic events in this pursuit was Charles Martel's victory in 732 over Spanish Muslim forces that effectively stopped the Islamic advance into Europe. In 751 Charles Martel's son Pepin the Short completed the takeover of the Merovingian throne by persuading the papacy to recognize him as the true legitimate king of the Franks. The last Merovingian was deposed and the first Carolingian king enthroned.

THE CAROLINGIAN ASCENT

Pepin the Short (r. 751–768) became the king of the Franks by the acclaim of his people and the recognition of his title by Pope Stephen II (r. 752–757). He and his son and successor, Charlemagne (r. 768–814), stressed practical needs of stabilizing their realm and building an independent empire. The pope, for his support, gained in the Carolingian monarchy a military ally against the newest Germanic group to rip through Italy—the Lombards—and a tacit rec-ognition that the Holy See was the arbiter of political legitimacy in Europe. Pepin and Charlemagne confirmed the pontiff's position as the secular ruler of the so-called Papal State, a wide swath of land across the middle of the Italian peninsula. With a strong ally and steady source of income, the papacy was able at last to exercise some genuine authority in the Christian world, although the precise nature and extent of that authority remained uncertain for many years.

There is something of an irony in the Carolingians' success. Genuinely pious and dedicated to the evangelization of barbarian Europe, they nonetheless owed *The Means:* their rise to power to their oppression of local churches. As early as the 720s, the *Ransacking* Carolingians had ransacked the monasteries in their domains to raise the reve- *the* nues they needed to pay their soldiers. Monasteries, after all, were the wealthiest *Monasteries* institutions in western Europe, possessors of large estates well run with collective labor forces. Their sacristies were often filled with valuable items bequeathed by pious neighbors. Some of them also held deposits of cash or valuables from nervous owners who feared leaving them in their own homes. Carolingian forces presented the monasteries with a simple choice: these are barbarous times, and you can either give us your valuables to pay for our soldiers or you can be left alone to face certain annihilation by Germanic invaders or, even worse, the advancing Muslims. With their purses thus filled, the Carolingians' army swelled in size, enabling them to bring more and more of France under their authority. Charles Martel's great victory over the Muslims in 732, on the plain between Tours and Poitiers in midwestern Gaul, solidified the family's heroic status and justified (in their own minds, at least) their manhandling of the monks. As a source known as the *Chronicle of Saint-Denis* put it,

> The Muslims were marching to the city of Tours in order to destroy it, the Church of Saint Martin, and all the surrounding countryside, when Charles—that illustrious prince—opposed them at the head of his whole army. He set his soldiers in formation and fell upon the enemy as ferociously as a hungry wolf falls upon a stag, until, by the grace of Our Lord, he had slaughtered on the field 300,000 of the enemies of Christianity, including their king Abd ar-Rahman. This was how he came to be called Martel ["hammer"], for he struck down his foes on the field as though he were a hammer made of iron, or steel, or some other type of metal. And the most amazing thing of all was the fact that he lost only fifteen hundred of his own men that day.

Victory followed victory, and by the end of Pepin the Short's reign in 768, almost all of modern France lay under Carolingian control.

What distinguished the Carolingians from other warlord families was their genuine dedication to transforming the societies they ruled. Charles Martel and *The Goal:* Pepin the Short built nearly as many monasteries as they ransacked, and they es- *Christian* tablished scores of new churches and schools. Charlemagne is credited with hun- *Rule* dreds more. They supported missionary work among the Germanic peoples and at least attempted to develop an infrastructure of roads and bridges that would

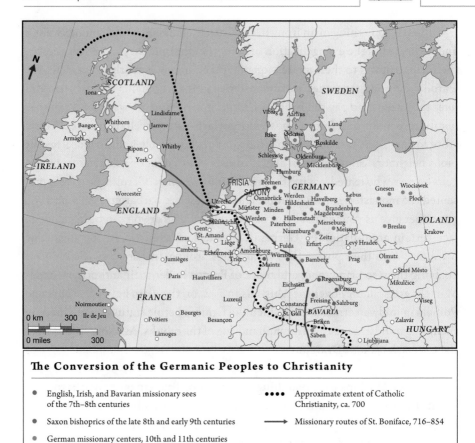

The Conversion of the Germanic Peoples to Christianity

- English, Irish, and Bavarian missionary sees of the 7th–8th centuries
- Saxon bishoprics of the late 8th and early 9th centuries
- German missionary centers, 10th and 11th centuries
- •••• Approximate extent of Catholic Christianity, ca. 700
- ⟶ Missionary routes of St. Boniface, 716–854

MAP 10.1   The Conversion of the Germanic Peoples to Christianity   The conversion of the Germanic peoples occurred over centuries. It was led by individual missionaries whose activities were approved, but not directed, by religious and political authorities.

connect villages and towns. The Carolingians were also distinguished by their stable succession pattern: for several generations in a row they produced a single heir who inherited the entire family domain, without the pressure to divide it among siblings.[3]

The greatest missionary of the age was **Boniface** (680–754), an Anglo-Saxon monk who spent forty years preaching to the Germanic peoples of the north, founding monasteries, churches, and schools with undiminished zeal (see Map 10.1). He had the ardent backing of the Carolingian court, "without which,"

---

[3]   The Carolingians did not rely on luck alone. They kept scores of mistresses and limited intimacy with their wives to the minimum needed to produce a male heir. Their method was not foolproof; in fact, several of the Carolingians did produce multiple legitimate heirs. Disease and warfare carried off most of them before political division occurred. In a few cases, a sudden assassination or imprisonment sufficed.

Boniface wrote in a letter to a friend, "I could neither administer my churches and defend my clergy nor continue the fight against idolatry." Charles Martel, in fact, created four dioceses in southern Germany in his honor (at Salzburg, Regensburg, Freising, and Passau) and appointed him metropolitan, or supreme administrative officer among a group of bishops, over all German lands east of the Rhine River. In return for this support, Boniface made sure that all the bishops he appointed, from the Low Countries to Saxony, declared loyalty jointly to the papacy and to the Carolingian ruler. The relationship between Rome and the Carolingians can be thought of as a partnership, although one in which the Carolingians had the dominant role.

CHARLEMAGNE

Following Pepin the Short's death, **Charlemagne** ("Charles the Great") spent forty years campaigning across Europe, expanding his realm into northeastern Spain, eastern Germany, Italy, Bohemia (part of today's Czech Republic), the Hungarian plain, and the northern reaches of the Balkans (today's Slovenia, Croatia, and Bosnia and Herzegovina). His great goal was to unite Latin Europe under a single government with a comprehensive legal system, a network of churches and schools, a reliable basic infrastructure, and a regularized system of weights and measures (see Map 10.2).

Charlemagne's energy was prodigious. According to Einhard's *Life of Charlemagne*, a biography written to order during the reign of Charlemagne's heir, Louis the Pious (r. 814–840), he also suffered from lifelong insomnia, which he inflicted on his courtiers:

> He habitually awoke and rose from his bed four or five times a night. He would hold audience with his retinue even while getting dressed or putting on his boots; if the palace chancellor told him of any legal matter for which his judgment was needed, he had the parties brought before him then and there. He would hear the case and render his decision just as though he was sitting on the bench of justice. And this was not the only type of business he would carry on at these hours, for he regularly performed any one of his daily duties, whether it was a matter for his personal attention or something that he could allocate to his officials. (ch. 24)

A pragmatic streak led the Carolingians to pursue a limited form of meritocracy; perhaps they had no real alternative. After all, the relentless traveling of the royal court exposed them to a parade of ineptitude. Everything from illiterate priests to judges with no knowledge of the law made the need for reform clear. Thus anyone

MAP 10.2 Charlemagne's Empire   The Carolingian realm at its height reunited most of the European part of the western Roman Empire.

with a useful skill could find service somewhere in the regime. Stable government required a central base of operations, and so Charlemagne built the first permanent capital of any Germanic ruler. To this capital at Aachen (Aix-la-Chapelle, on today's French–German borderlands), the court brought poets and theologians from Spain, historians and legal scholars from Italy, grammarians from Ireland, and biblical scholars from England. But they also scouted out skilled stonemasons, carpenters, metalsmiths, scribes, weavers, tanners, musicians, coopers, and herbalists. Social background usually took a backseat to the more important issue of ability.

Putting these scholars, artists, and craftsmen to work, Charlemagne's court inaugurated a cultural revival known as the **Carolingian Renaissance** (named *The* after the remarkable Italian Renaissance discussed in chapter 12). Under the di- *Carolingian* rection of an earnest Englishman named Alcuin (730–804), hundreds of monas- *Renaissance* tic scribes created whole libraries by producing copy after copy of the classical and Christian authors, grammarians explained the workings of Latin composition, and poets sang the glories of Carolingian rule in classical meters. Most of the Carolingian Renaissance consisted of a kind of cultural salvage operation—preserving, cataloging, copying, and distributing works of the classical and Christian past. But in that work they introduced a number of innovations, one of the most important of which was a new technique of writing.

INROMANTIMESTEXTSWEREWRITTENLIKETHISALLI-NCAPITALSANDWITHOUTPUNCTUATIONORSPACESBE-TWEENTHEWORDS

The Romans' practice had two aims: to save space on expensive writing surfaces and to support their practice of oral reading. (Most people will find the collapsed sentence above is easier to read aloud than silently.) Alcuin soon found that his army of scribes found Roman script too confusing (medieval monks, after all, were supposed to maintain silence unless addressed by a superior), which led to endless copying errors. Hence he broke with tradition and created a new way of writing—a script called Carolingian (or Caroline) minuscule, which used upper- and lowercase letters and introduced spaces between words. Alcuin's inventions not only made it easier for scribes to produce reliable texts, but also resulted in a new way of reading that made it a private, silent pleasure rather than an oral, communal one.

The Carolingian Renaissance was a court-directed enterprise and as such it reflected and expressed the court's interests. Simply put, most of the works produced aimed specifically to strengthen either the Roman Catholic Church or the Carolingian dynasty. What they did not aim

Carolingian Minuscule Script   In order to minimize scribal errors and ease comprehension, the Carolingian court introduced lowercase letters and word spacing. This 8th-century page is a table of contents for a manuscript of the Salic Laws.

to do was to distinguish between the authorities held by each—since such a distinction did not exist. In Carolingian eyes, all power belonged to the king.

Charlemagne's Rule

Charlemagne viewed power and status as commodities that he alone possessed and could parcel out at will. He governed his vast realm by delegating local, provincial authority to a caste of counts (*comites* in Latin) who represented the king and exerted power in his name, but these were not hereditary positions. The title of count was a job description, not a designation of social class. Charlemagne could appoint the lowest-born peasant as count, if he wished, and that count's position of honor would be equal to that of any count who claimed an aristocratic background. Ability and loyalty to the throne were what mattered most. The court held several assemblies each year, to which various counts and other officials were summoned. A typical summons read like this:

> In the name of the Father, and of the Son, and of the Holy Spirit. Charles, the most serene, august, heavenly crowned, magnificent, and peaceful emperor, and also, by God's mercy, the King of the Franks and of the Lombards, to Abbot Fulrad.
>
> You are hereby informed that I have decided to convene my General Assembly this year in eastern Saxony at the place called Stassfurt, on the Bode River. I therefore command you to come to this place on the fifteenth day before the calends of July—that is, seven days before the Feast of Saint John the Baptist—with all your men suitably armed and at the ready, so that you will be prepared to head out from that place in any direction I choose. In other words, come with arms, gear, and all the food and clothing you will need for war. Let every horseman bring a shield, lance, sword, knife, bow, and supply of arrows. Let your carriage train bring tools of every kind: axes, planes, augurs, lumber, shovels, spades, and anything else an army might need. Bring also enough food to last three months beyond the date of the assembly, and arms and clothing to last six.
>
> I command, more generally, that you should see to it that you travel peacefully to the aforesaid place, and that as your journey takes you through any of the lands of my realm you should presume to take nothing but fodder for your animals, wood, and water. Let the servants belonging to each of your loyal men march alongside the carts and horsemen, and let their masters be always with them until they reach the aforesaid place, lest a lord's absence be the cause of his servants' evildoing.
>
> Send your tribute—which you are to present to me at the assembly by the middle of May—to the appointed place, where I shall already be. If it

should happen that your travels go so well that you can present your tribute to me in person, I shall be greatly pleased. Do not disappoint me now or in the future, if you hope to remain in my favor.

The counts owed their status entirely to the king's favor, not to any birthright of their own. Moreover, the king trained and sent out teams of *missi dominici* (literally, "dispatched royal agents" or "traveling lords"), who moved in regular circuits throughout the realm, reviewing comital records, holding open courts, and inviting the local populace to come forth with complaints about the job performance of the counts.

It was a system of government that was meant to evoke the ruling style of the

Charlemagne's Chapel at Aachen   Charlemagne had his palace chapel modeled after the church of St. Ambrose in Ravenna, Italy. Ravenna had been the de facto capital of the Roman Empire since the 3rd century, and of the western Roman Empire after the transfer to Constantinople in the 4th. His throne was placed at one end, the altar and a shrine to the Virgin Mary at the other.

ancient Roman emperors, seeking a balance of centralized aims and local needs. The Carolingians admired the Roman idea of getting their subjects to see themselves as part of a larger civilization, although in the Carolingians' case the larger civilization was Latin Christianity, not Roman polytheism. When building his palace complex at Aachen, Charlemagne ordered its chapel to be modeled on the Byzantine church of San Vitale that Justinian had built in Ravenna. And he had nearly identical marble pillars, stone columns, and glittering wall mosaics (and the appropriately skilled workmen) hauled north from Italy to do it.

IMPERIAL CORONATION

Charlemagne sought to elevate himself and his empire to the imperial dignity enjoyed by Byzantium. He made protection of the pope and Roman orthodoxy an essential component of his mandate. The culmination of his efforts took place on Christmas Day in the year 800, in Rome, when Pope Leo III (r. 795–816) placed a crown on Charlemagne's head and proclaimed him Augustus, the title of the first Roman emperor. The significance of the coronation was symbolic and also more than symbolic. The symbolic significance had to do with the date. The traditional Anno Domini system of dating (today designated instead as the Common Era)—that is, reckoning the years from the purported time of Jesus's birth—was then still a novelty. It had been created by a Syrian monk in the 6th century but had only become used in the west after the English scholar-monk Bede (d. 735) had promoted its use. By the time of Charlemagne's coronation, most literate people in Europe used the new system. Still, the bulk of the population probably still thought in terms of the old system (called annus mundi II) they had inherited from earlier times, and according to this system the year 800 was actually the year 6000.

Einhard reports that Charlemagne was surprised and incensed by the coronation. He would not have attended Mass even on Christmas if he had known what Leo was planning to do. But Charlemagne had been in Rome since early November, and the man who never slept would never have been caught in an unplanned coronation. More likely, some mishandled detail in the crowning ceremony caused his angry outburst. Regardless, Charlemagne probably took advantage of the calendrical quirk of the year 800/6000 to make his coronation signal the start of a bright new age in history.[4]

Message to Byzantium However, the significance of his coronation was far more than symbolic: it sent a political message to Byzantium. Seeking support for their claims to political legitimacy, early medieval rulers like Clovis had frequently turned to the Greeks. The Byzantines, for their part, regarded the Latin westerners as ill-mannered and backward poor cousins, nominally members of the Christian family but hardly the sort of relatives one boasts about. Most Byzantines, in fact, regarded the loss of western Europe as a blessing in disguise. Charlemagne's coronation, however, changed everything. By assuming the imperial title, he effectively declared the Carolingian court independent of and equal to the Greek east. Moreover, by receiving the crown from the pope, the Carolingians established a way to pass on the imperial title in which the Byzantines had no role.

Constantinople was not pleased with this declaration of independence but was powerless to do anything about it. Compounding matters, the throne in Constantinople was occupied at the time by an unpopular ruler, Irene (r. 797–802), who had seized power by organizing a coup against her ineffectual son Constantine VI (r. 776–797). Charlemagne sent Irene an embassy and proposed marriage. If the marriage happened, his ambassadors urged, the eastern and western empires would unite, the growing rift between the Latin and Greek churches would heal, and the Christian world could mount a powerful joint offensive against Islam. Irene was inclined to accept, but she fell from power before she could give her answer. Her interest in marrying Charlemagne was the last straw

---

4   Think of Charlemagne at his coronation as almost like a modern politician who coordinates speeches and ribbon-cutting ceremonies to coincide with significant anniversaries.

for several Byzantine high officials, who seized Irene, cut off her hair, and forced her into a convent, never to emerge. Once in the convent, she seems to have accepted her fate with grace, seeing her life as a nun as a penance for her cruelty to her son. She died in 805. Charlemagne was so furious at this spoiling of his grand plan that he even formed a brief alliance with the Abbasid caliph in Baghdad, Harun al-Rashid (r. 786–809), to mount a two-pronged invasion of Byzantium. Nothing came of it—except that Charlemagne received, among other fine gifts from the caliph, the first elephant he had ever seen.

CAROLINGIAN COLLAPSE

Carolingian luck ran out after Charlemagne's death in 814. At his death, Charlemagne's crown passed to his sole surviving heir, Louis the Pious (r. 814–840), but Louis had few of his father's gifts. Studious and well-meaning, he nevertheless lacked charisma and quick wit. He was also intensely straitlaced and moralistic—hence his nickname—and banished from court all the dancing girls and mistresses who had made his father's sleepless nights less lonely. Even worse from the dynastic perspective, Louis was determined to make up for his father's sexual libertinism by remaining staunchly faithful to his wife. As a result Louis was survived by three sons.

In 843, shortly after Louis's death, these sons agreed to the **Treaty of Verdun**, which divided the empire into three parts: Charles the Bald received the western *Treaty of* part, Lothar the middle, and Louis the eastern part (see Map 10.3). Although of *Verdun* course no one knew it at the time, this treaty roughly defined the political contours of western Europe that exist today. Other than brief periods under Napoleon and Hitler, Europe would never again see as large a unified state as it had under Charlemagne.

After the Treaty of Verdun, the delicate sense of cultural unity across Latin Europe fostered by Charlemagne dissolved almost immediately into factionalism. The large-scale division of the empire was accompanied by decentralization of power at the local level. Nobles increased their authority in their own territories and built up groups of military followers who were primarily loyal to them, not to some distant king or emperor. Civil war became incessant, and Europe in the 9th and 10th centuries seemed likely to slip into another Dark Age.

Exacerbating the internal rot, new waves of invaders attacked Europe. Another nomadic group emerged from the central Asian steppe and marched into the *The* plains of eastern Europe below the Danube River. These were the Magyars, the *Magyars* ancestors of today's Hungarian nation. They were a localized threat, however, encroaching only on the easternmost former members of the Carolingian state, although the people of northern Italy also had some reason to fear them.

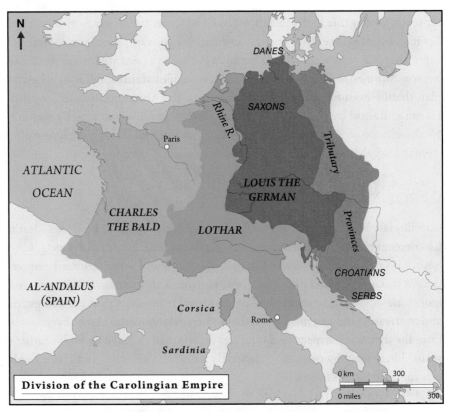

MAP 10.3   Division of the Carolingian Empire, 843   Charlemagne's three grandsons divided the empire among themselves with the Treaty of Verdun. The treaty helped to confirm a lasting political and cultural distinction between France and Germany.

The
Vikings

A much greater threat came from the north—the Vikings ("sea raiders"). Their hordes had begun to beset Latin Europe as early as Charlemagne's time; as the Carolingian state fractured, the invasions gained pace.

What made the Viking threat so severe was the unpredictable nature of their attacks. Unlike the Magyars—a large, slow-moving land force—the Vikings raided in smallish groups of perhaps two dozen fighters per warship. Those ships, moreover, were designed to sail in as little as 3 or 4 feet of water, which meant that the Vikings could move upriver. Most of Europe's rivers flow northward and westward—opening directly on the Atlantic, the North Sea, and the Baltic Sea— in other words, directly in front of the Vikings' approach. The attackers were thus able to move with terrific speed and attack far inland. Viking warships attacked Paris in 834, during the reign of Louis the Pious, and even sacked Seville, the capital of Muslim Spain, about a decade later. There was no advance warning for these raids. The Vikings simply appeared all of a sudden, attacked and pillaged, and disappeared before any kind of defense could be mounted. And of course the incessant civil war that followed the Treaty of Verdun only made the problem worse. Here is how a church council lamented the suffering of the time:

> Our cities are depopulated, our monasteries wrecked and put to the torch, our countryside left uninhabited. . . . Indeed, just as the first humans lived without law or the fear of God and according only to their dumb instincts, so too now does everyone do whatever seems good in his eyes only, despising all human and divine laws and ignoring even the commands of the Church. The strong oppress the weak, and the world is wracked with violence against the poor and the plunder of ecclesiastical lands. . . . Men everywhere devour each other like the fishes of the sea.

In the words of the Old Norse poet Snori Sturluson (1179–1241), the Vikings "were like mad dogs or wolves, biting the edges of their shields, / and were as strong as bears or bulls. They killed men everywhere / and nothing could stop them—not fire, not steel." No wonder that scattered figures across Europe, gathering crowds of frightened followers around them, began to proclaim the end of the world.

And then the Muslims came again.

THE SPLINTERING OF THE CALIPHATE

The multicultural vision and policy of the Abbasids outraged many and inspired a predictable backlash. "O Lord," cried one offended Arab elitist, "the sons of whores have multiplied so much—please guide me to another land where I need not deal with bastards!" And as it happened, many were guided away from the cosmopolitan empire. The last Umayyads had fled as far as Spain, where they officially seceded from the caliphate and declared an independent kingdom of their own in 756. Other regions soon followed suit: Algeria broke away in 779; Morocco in 789; Tunisia in 800; Khurasan (northeastern Iran and part of Afghanistan) in 819; Sind (roughly the territory of today's Pakistan) in 867; and Egypt, too, in 868, only to have its rebels overthrown and succeeded by a new dynasty called the Fatimids in 905. So too did numerous smaller princedoms. Thus the cultural glories of the Abbasid Golden Age came at the cost of the political shattering of the empire (see Map 10.4).

Many issues beyond concern about heretical ideas played into the disintegration. Other issues were ethnic pride and racial bias, a sense of unfair commercial and tax policies, and frustration over the perceived stalling out of strong jihad in favor of soft intellectualism. It is no coincidence that the splinter states became seedbeds for strict conservative reform movements, such as the Almoravids and the Almohads in North Africa and Spain. These sects, and others like them, called for halting what

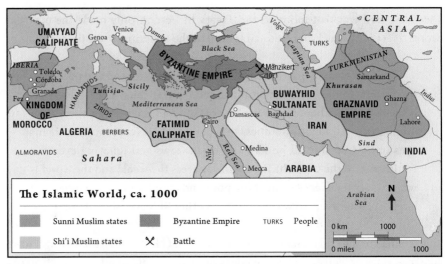

MAP 10.4 The Islamic World, ca. 1000   By the start of the 11th century, the political unity
of the Abbasid caliphate was shattered.

they regarded as the cosmopolitan rot that had beset Islam. They demanded a return
to the militarism, discipline, and order of the great conquering age of the Prophet
and his Companions. Only by restoring the active spirit of jihad, the reformists asserted, could the great cause of bringing Islam to the world be fulfilled.

Increasing Muslim Hostility toward Jews and Christians

Two important developments coincided with the breakup of the Islamic
Empire. First, internally, Muslims had become the majority in two or three generations. Conversion, coercion, and emigration had caused the Jewish and
Christian populations to shrink. Most Muslims states still recognized the legal
rights of their non-Muslim subjects as dhimmis. But it is one thing to live in tolerance with foreign communities that vastly outnumber one's own and quite another when one's own community has become the majority and the other groups
suddenly appear as out-of-place foreigners. Acts of anti-Jewish and anti-Christian
hostility grew increasingly common through the 9th and 10th centuries, especially in areas experiencing temporary economic troubles. They became common
features, too, of the reformist movements of the age. This was popular violence
rather than state-run persecution in most cases, although the victims may not
have appreciated the difference.

Islamic State Efforts to Expand Commerce

Second, this fracturing of the caliphate coincided with the breakup of the
Carolingian Empire. With western Europe entering another dark period, many of
the splinter Islamic states saw an opportunity to expand commerce. After all,
whether for dynastic, ethnic, or religious reasons, they tended to dislike one another intensely and preferred to trade with Christian Europe rather than with
their Islamic neighbors, and hence the new wave of Islamic attacks on Europe in

the 9th and 10th centuries, coinciding roughly with the Magyar and Viking invasions. By 850 Muslim forces had conquered Sicily, parts of southern Italy, and the Balearic Islands, and they had made successful raids on Sardinia, Corsica, and the cities of Marseilles and Rome. But the Islamic attacks were not campaigns of conquest. Rather, they were attempts to carve out zones of interest, economic trading posts, and certain resources. And, as often as not, they were competing with one another to create these zones. For example, the Aghlabids of Tunisia seized Sicily in part to make sure that the Rustamids of Algeria did not get it.

All these developments transformed European and Muslim relations, which had been characterized by violence, distrust, and suffering. When the smoke cleared, Latin Europe and the Islamic world were each profoundly different places than they had been before. In the following sections we will examine how the Christian and Muslim worlds reinvented themselves between the 10th and 13th centuries.

THE REINVENTION OF WESTERN EUROPE

European reinvention followed two main lines of development—in the north via a new network of lords and vassals, bound by feudal bonds, and in the south by the growth of cities, powered by trade. The church, beset by corruption of astonishing proportions, responded with a reform movement of its own that remade the institution and put Christian life on a wholly new trajectory. The combination of these reinventions—social, civic, and spiritual—led directly to some of the greatest achievements of the medieval era. They also paved the way for the Crusades.

Across continental western Europe the decay of the state and the pressure of foreign invasion drove farmers and their families to abandon their scattered *The* homesteads and to take shelter in groups, under the protection of whatever strong- *Manorial* man might exist in the district. Having little or nothing else to give in return for *Order* protection, they offered their labor. By this simple demographic shift, a society of individual farmers evolved into a new society based on **manors**—collective farms under the authority of lords. The lords owned the land and the major share of its annual yield, although the work was done by dependent farmers called **serfs**. Serfs were not slaves, although their daily lives differed little from slavery; lords could not buy and sell serfs as though they were mere property. Rather, serfs and lords were tied together by complex networks of mutual duties and rights. Serfs could not leave the manor, for example, or marry their offspring to someone from another manor, without their lord's permission. Lords were required to resolve disputes between serfs. The services owed back and forth made medieval manors like miniature communities, like agrarian states unto themselves (see Figure 10.1).

The peasants brought varied backgrounds to their collective work, including knowledge of techniques like crop rotation (planting fields with a different crop

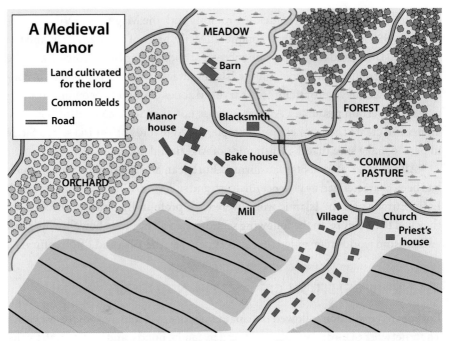

A Medieval Manor   This schematic rendering of a manor illustrates its self-sufficiency as an economic entity.

in each season, so as not to deplete the soil), the use of wheeled plows, and the invention of horseshoes (which allowed quicker and more agile horses to replace lumbering teams of oxen as draught animals). Crop yields nearly doubled as a result. By living and working collectively, sharing labor, skills, and resources, farming on manors became much more productive. Crop surpluses became the norm, and by about 950, the height of what some historians call an "agricultural revolution," western Europe became a food exporter for the first time in its history. It was largely to secure access to this food supply that the rump states of the broken Abbasid Empire began to compete for trading zones along the Mediterranean coast. And this trade allowed the new class of manorial lords to become rich—rich enough eventually to give up wooden manorial houses for stone castles.

But the manorial lords lacked any real political legitimacy. They were, in many cases, of questionable ancestry and social status, men to whom war refugees had fled in desperation. These warlords (the Latin term is *milites*) used a variety of strategies to legitimate themselves. One popular option was simply to invent aristocratic genealogies for themselves, claiming descent from the Carolingians. Another method was to form ties with other *milites*—a medieval equivalent of the modern practice of governments recognizing one another.

The Ties that Bound   In this scene from the Bayeux Tapestry (1067), the earl of Wessex, Harold Godwinson, swears his fealty to Duke William of Normandy.

By securing the support of other *milites* in the region, a warlord acquired at least a veneer of political authenticity.

These relationships between warlords had substance: some forms of military service, counsel, and economic assistance were invariably involved. Since each warlord differed in the amount of land or social recognition he commanded, these relationships slowly took on a hierarchical form, with a senior partner and a subordinate one—hence the terms **lord** and **vassal**, respectively. In forming a tie, a lord bestowed on the vassal dominion over a fief—that is, an allotted manor or manors—and the vassal in turn pledged in a public ceremony to serve the lord loyally. These public rites varied widely across Europe, but evidence suggests that often the lord handed over a clod of earth to symbolize the fief being bestowed. Since the Latin word for "fief" is *feudum*, these relationships came to be generally known as **feudal bonds**.

By about 1000, these connections had spread across much of northern Europe; by 1100 they dominated it. Manors and feudal relations helped create a new society based on land tenure and ties of personal loyalty. Serfs worked for a landlord in return for the security and primitive justice he provided, whereas *milites* were bound to one another as lords and vassals. Again, the system varied from territory to territory. The feudal networks in France, for example, were significantly more elaborate, hierarchical, and complicated than those in Anglo-Saxon England, which had never been part of the Carolingian Empire. When William, duke of Normandy, known to posterity as William the Conqueror (r. 1066–1089), seized the island in 1066 and parceled out the lands to his leading noblemen-vassals, he made it all but impossible for them to redistribute the land to vassals of their own. Germany added its own twist, as great lords created feudal relations with high-ranking churchmen—abbots and bishops. Since these men would presumably not be producing heirs, there was little danger of the feudal lands becoming hereditary holdings. German towns along the Baltic coast also developed a trading network that reached from Denmark to Sweden and northern Russia, a network that developed into a commercial cartel known as the Hanseatic League.

MEDITERRANEAN CITIES

Mediterranean Europe followed a different trajectory. By long-standing custom, social position there had depended less on controlling land than on participating in the public life of the community: merchants, financiers, civic officials, and professionals formed the backbone of southern European life. Urban life had declined during the long centuries of the Dark Ages—some cities had collapsed to the point where they had only one-tenth of the ancient population levels—but revived under the short-lived stability of the Carolingians. Food surpluses from the new manors gradually made their way into urban markets. The Muslim attacks of the 9th and 10th centuries forcibly (and probably unnecessarily) opened those markets to trade with North Africa; cities like Barcelona, Montpellier, Marseilles, Genoa, Pisa, and Venice were the first to establish permanent commercial relations with the Muslim countries, and as a result they witnessed a dramatic rise in their wealth and power (see Map 10.5).

Economic Powerhouses of Europe

The Mediterranean accordingly roared back to life, and from about 1000 to 1400 these cities were the economic powerhouses of Europe.[5] At the same time, the Byzantines' territorial losses to the Abbasids forced them to reorient their military and commercial attention northward into the Slavic Balkan lands and the territories around the Black Sea. As the Greeks gradually relinquished their control of the sea-lanes in the eastern Mediterranean, the Latin cities moved in aggressively. More cities joined in—Amalfi, Naples, Venice—and soon Latin Europe's commercial network, having expanded throughout the Mediterranean, spread around Spain, through the Gulf of Biscay, and into the North Sea. They brought lumber, minerals, wool, and metal ores to the manufacturing

---

[5]   In 1150, the annual commercial tax revenue from the city of Palermo alone was four times that from the entire kingdom of England.

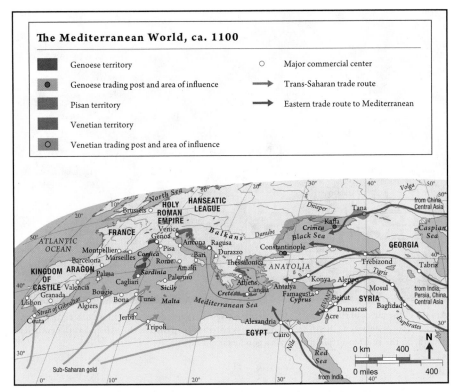

MAP 10.5   The Mediterranean World, ca. 1100   Control of trade routes and access to commercial centers played as great a role as religious rivalries in Mediterranean life.

centers along the coast, transporting eastern silks, spices, metalwork, and dyed cloth back to the west. Developments in ship design led to larger and swifter commercial vessels, capable of delivering larger cargoes at less cost. Meanwhile, the growing use of financial instruments like letters of credit, also known as bills of exchange, reduced the danger of carrying large amounts of cash. By the late 11th century, an embryonic banking industry had already emerged in Italy.

Mediterranean cities quickly became multiethnic emporia, much as they had been during the Pax Romana. A visitor to 12th-century Barcelona or Pisa, for example, would find the streets and markets crowded with merchants from Alexandria, Athens, Brussels, Lisbon, Palermo, and Tunis, as well as a dozen other places—with more than a sprinkling of Jews from all around the Mediterranean. The interaction among groups was regulated by complex systems of municipal and religious laws, ethnic customs, class privileges, and commercial traditions. Merchants of different ethnicities, cities, or social strata each had specific rights and privileges, negotiated with municipal governments. To keep straight who was who, Mediterranean cities began to use dress codes known as sumptuary codes to identify people. These sumptuary codes elaborately

Amalfi The cities of the western Mediterranean saw a tremendous surge in wealth and vitality, as trade routes between Christian and Muslim territories reopened in the 9th and 10th centuries. Amalfi, on the southern Italian coast, is a good example.

regulated styles of dress, types of fabrics, headgear, footwear, numbers of buttons, and the sorts of decorative badges, pins, and scarves each person could wear. The idea was not to shame groups but to establish the rules of their engagement.

The communicative calculus could be elaborate: a Muslim cloth merchant from Famagusta (in Cyprus), for example, conducting business in Montpellier with a Christian member of the jewelers' guild from Marseilles was entitled to a specific set of legal rights. One had to know whom one was dealing with, or there was no deal. Moreover, since different groups often had different housing and dietary requirements, the custom quickly arose of segregating the cities: merchants from cities that did a lot of business with one another were awarded buildings, streets, or even whole neighborhoods to themselves. There they had special houses, butcher shops, alehouses, and worship sites so that each could live according to their own customs.

Most cities were governed by municipal councils and various administrative executives, usually drawn from the urban elites. This group consisted of local rural aristocrats, well-to-do merchants, the professional classes (bankers and lawyers, chiefly), and representatives of the leading artisanal and commercial guilds (professional associations, similar to modern cartels, that set prices and manufacturing standards within a given town).

THE REINVENTION OF THE CHURCH

The Catholic Church also reinvented itself in the post-Carolingian centuries. It needed reform badly, because many forms of corruption had taken hold by the 9th and 10th centuries, owing to the *milites*, the secular warlords in Latin Europe. Simply put, the warlords, to raise funds for their armies, revived the old Carolingian practice of ransacking their own churches and monasteries. Many simply plundered and ran off with the spoils, but others conceived of a longer-term strategy for tapping into ecclesiastical wealth: they expelled the clerical leaders (often by killing them) and sold the positions to their military and political underlings and supporters. By placing their clients in ecclesiastical positions, the warlords secured a set percentage of the churches' annual revenues. In turn, they rewarded their followers with fancy titles, accoutrements, salaries, and prestige. This abuse, known as **simony**, was rampant, from village churches and small monasteries to large episcopacies and even the papacy. Few religious houses avoided the onslaught.

The chronicles of the 10th and 11th centuries abound with abominable behavior by warlord lackeys in church positions. The nadir was reached in Rome. During a period remembered as the "Pornocracy" (904–984), the papacy was bought and sold numerous times among the leading families in Roman politics. Pope John XII (r. 956–963), who did not himself purchase the papacy but received it from his father, who arranged his election to the office as an eighteenth birthday present, was reported to have sold the bishopric of one town to a ten-year-old boy, as a birthday present from the boy's father.[6] The tradition of state control of the church dated back to the emperor Constantine and the Council of Nicea (discussed in chapter 8). The more recent tyranny of the Carolingians had been stark, but they never abused the church in the same way that the warlords now did. The fundamental reform required was to insist on the churches' freedom from secular control. *Libertas ecclesie!* ("Freedom for the church!") became the demand of the reformers.

The reform movement began at the grassroots level, on the new manors, where the problem of simony was felt most acutely. To the peasants, simony not only looked bad but also created a profound spiritual crisis. The Carolingians,

---

[6]   John's favorite mistress, it was said, wore a papal crown, sat on a throne, and turned one wing of the papal palace into a whorehouse. He died in bed with a married woman.

after all, had struggled mightily to promote Christian education and to improve the quality of parish church life. As a result, by the mid- to late 10th century probably a clear majority of western peasants were meaningfully, knowledgeably Christian. And the one teaching they all knew was that they needed the sacraments to achieve salvation, especially baptism.

But does a "priest" who is a simoniac—who got his job only by buying the title from a warlord—actually have sacramental authority? Even if the "priest" does perform a Eucharist, are the bread and wine of that ceremony truly turned into the body and blood of Christ? And if not, is the ceremony of any value at all? If a peasant couple has a sickly infant whom they want to have baptized, is the baby truly baptized if the priest is a simoniac? The question was not theoretical: probably one-half of all children born in Europe at this time died before the age of five. Since Catholic doctrine maintained that only baptized Christians can be saved, the couple's baby would presumably suffer eternal damnation because of the illegitimacy of the priest's action. It gets more complicated, too: What if the priest in question had been properly trained for his vocation, but his ordination to the priesthood had been performed by a simoniac bishop? Or if that bishop's elevation to the episcopacy had been performed by a simoniac archbishop—perhaps by that ten-year-old boy appointed by John XII?

Outraged peasants understood one thing quite well: this problem existed because the *milites* had taken over the churches. Warlords no longer merely controlled the peasants' lives on the manors; their greed for church revenue now placed even the peasants' eternal souls in jeopardy. Demands for freeing the churches from the warlords' clutches therefore began on the manors, where the population could express collective complaint. These rallies for reform, called "Peace of God" assemblies, began as individual demonstrations. However, they multiplied in number, since peasants everywhere had essentially the same complaint and the same sole method of protest available to them. They thus took on the appearance of a movement—indeed, the first mass movement in Western history.

Movements need leadership. That leadership came from Latin Europe's bishops. The reawakening of Europe's cities had revived the episcopacies as well. Although defined as the spiritual descendants of the original twelve apostles, bishops had always been second-tier figures in the Latin Church. When more than 90 percent of the population lived in the countryside, churchmen in cities lacked prestige—especially since hardly any cities in continental Europe were of any real size.[7]

---

[7]   In Charlemagne's time, for example, the city of Paris was only 7.5 acres in area. In comparison, the university campus at which I teach, Boston University, is 75 acres in area.

Monasteries had always been the real centers of power in Latin Christianity, going back to the Benedictine order established in the 6th century. Most of the scholars drawn into the Carolingian court had been monks and abbots, and monastic wealth (when it was not plundered) was the largest accumulated treasure in most districts. As cities grew in size and number, the relative importance of bishops did too. And they seized on the Peace of God assemblies as a means to place themselves at the forefront of church reform. Bishops began to convene regional councils, schedule and organize assemblies, arrange for large-scale public masses, commission speakers, issue calls for specific *milites* to relinquish their strangleholds over their churches, and above all promote themselves as the leaders of church reform. The more success they had in winning their own churches' freedom, the faster they rose in popular estimation.

By the time the reform reached the papacy—the last part of the church to be reformed—the bishops were clearly the dominant power brokers. But as the bishops took center stage, so too did the pope—who was, after all, the bishop of Rome.[8] The second half of the 11th century was filled with diplomatic, rhetorical, and military wrangling between Rome and its rivals. Two issues stood out, among many: lay investiture and papal supremacy. Most political rulers by this time acknowledged (grudgingly, perhaps) that the church should appoint its own priests and bishops, but they wanted to retain their own role in the process by insisting that they, as the leaders of secular society, should invest (that is, formally bestow upon) all clergy with the lands and revenues that came with their offices. Even more important were the differences of opinion regarding the specific authorities and privileges assumed by the new, reformed papacy. What powers did the pope have, need to have, and ought to have? What limits should there be on papal power? This issue was especially important to the Eastern Orthodox churches, most of whose bishops were willing to recognize the pope as a "first among equals" but adamantly refused the notion of a papacy that ruled over all bishops (and by extension over the entire church). Rome's claim to supreme authority over all Christians rankled both the Byzantine emperor and the patriarch at Constantinople.

Half-hearted efforts at reconciliation came to an end in 1054, when the pope, Leo IX (r. 1049–1054), and the patriarch, Michael Cerularius (r. 1043–1059), angrily expelled each other from the church. This mutual excommunication initiated a formal break between the Latin and Orthodox churches that came to be known as the **Great Schism**. As the split between the Christian leadership

The Great Schism

---

[8]   At first, the overwhelming majority of popes came from monastic backgrounds. In the second thousand years of Christianity, more than 90 percent of popes were bishops before rising to the Holy See.

widened, Rome and Constantinople openly competed for the allegiance of new converts in eastern Europe and Russia. Leo spent much of his time as pope on the road, bringing the majesty of the office to the eyes of Europe's commoners for the first time, and his successor, Nicholas II (r. 1059–1061), created the College of Cardinals (cardinals being officially appointed advisors to the Holy See)—which subsequently acquired sole power to elect the next successor to Peter. The pontificates of Leo and Nicholas were, each in its own way, declarations of papal power.

The Gregorian Reform

Pope Gregory VII (r. 1073–1085), however, was the staunchest advocate of the primacy of the pope as the leader of all Christian peoples, so much so that the entire reform movement is commonly referred to as the **Gregorian Reform**. Within the church, Gregory campaigned to improve the moral and educational caliber of the clergy by holding the priesthood to high standards of competence and also—especially in matters of sexual behavior—to stringent standards of conduct. He also demanded strict conformity to the standard religious services authorized by the church hierarchy and the use of Latin as the universal language of Christianity. Thus, under Gregory VII, the movements for clerical reform and centralization of authority within the church merged.

Gregory demanded an end to **lay investiture**—the selection and appointment of church officials by secular authority—and secular control over church lands. In a deliberately public disagreement with the German emperor Henry IV (r. 1056–1106), Gregory challenged the emperor's authority to appoint bishops within his domains. The struggle for control of the church pitted the most powerful secular and sacred rulers of Christendom against each other. Gregory invalidated Henry's right to rule over his territories and encouraged the emperor's enemies among the German princes to rise against him. As rebel forces gathered, Henry was forced to prostrate himself before the pope and beg forgiveness.

The Investiture Conflict   Holy Roman Emperor Henry IV, facing rebellion from his nobles, pleads with Countess Matilda of Tuscany to help persuade Pope Gregory VII to end the conflict. Matilda dominated northern Italy at this time, and so long as she supported Gregory (which she did), Henry's troops could not advance to put pressure on the pope to relent. This image appears in an 11th-century manuscript of *The Life of Matilda, Countess of Tuscany.*

This was the tipping point in what has come to be known as the investiture conflict, and all sides recognized a need to find a compromise. In 1122 it was reached: the **Concordat of Worms**, signed in that year, reconfirmed the church's right to appoint its own clergy, but the secular rulers retained the right to bestow all the lands and revenues associated with those appointments. The great reform, everyone hoped, was finished.

THE REINVENTION OF THE ISLAMIC WORLD

From the 9th century onward, the political history of the Islamic world was exceptionally turbulent and complicated. The western rump states went through numerous shifts in dynastic rule (usually violently), oscillated between conservative and liberal efforts to reform their societies, and constantly redefined their relations with Latin Europe. In the central zone of the Near East, the arrival of yet another Asiatic group—the Seljuk Turks—in the early 11th century set off a chain reaction of wars, rebellions, and coups that destabilized the region just at the time when trade relations with Christian Europe were reopening. Farther to the east, a powerful resurgence of Turkic and Persian cultures brought enormous and lasting changes to the caliphate.

The westernmost Islamic states, from Spain to Libya, were centers of manufacture. Ceramics, textiles, glassware, and metalwork were the dominant industries, after agriculture. The ethnic Arabs who monopolized the political and military commands disdained agriculture; slaves performed much of the labor, along with most of the menial tasks in urban life. Sub-Saharan black Africans, acquired by Moroccan traders working down the coast, made up much of the slave population. Tax records from the city of Cordoba attest to eight thousand black slaves in that city alone in the early 11th century. Apart from the great cosmopolitan city of Cordoba—the home of the Great Mosque and a palace library filled with more than 400,000 volumes—the western states of Spain and across North Africa were not renowned as centers of intellectual life.[9] In the 9th and 10th centuries the rulers remained focused on spreading the faith among their subjects. Islam became the majority religion across North Africa by the early 11th century, which coincided with the rise of new dynasties made up of ethnic Berbers, who regarded the long Arab monopoly as a failed enterprise. These new dynasties—in Morocco, Algeria, Tunisia, and Libya (then called Tripolitania and

Western States

---

[9] One notable exception was the brilliant Andalusian philosopher Ibn Rushd (1126–1198, better known in the West as Averroës). In his lifetime, however, Ibn Rushd was widely regarded with suspicion for his eager embrace of Aristotelian rationalism. He was constantly driven from court to court, city to city, by those opposed to his openness to non-Islamic tradition.

Cyrenaica)—were frequently characterized by martial jihadist campaigns to "purify" society of elements not sufficiently Islamic. Popular attitudes to resident Christians and Jews hardened noticeably.

Islamic Heartland

In the Near Eastern heartland the contest between established Arab leaders and the newly converted Turks provided the chief political narrative (see again Map 10.4). This was by far the most ethnically, linguistically, and religiously diverse region in the Islamic world: Arabs, Syrians, Persians, Turks, Kurds, Berbers, Copts, Jews, Armenians, and a dozen others were all on the scene, representing every Islamic, Christian, and Jewish sect. Although technically part of the Abbasid caliphate, most of the Holy Land region in the 10th and 11th centuries consisted of a sprawl of independent principalities. Clashes across ethnic and religious lines were common, but the region retained its commercial vitality as the linchpin between the Mediterranean and the Silk Road economies, with Jerusalem and Damascus the most important cities. Industry, commerce, and finance—all urban phenomena—were the most important elements in the economy, and each group in each community carefully guarded its traditional rights and privileges. Schools and libraries were numerous but chiefly sectarian. Most of the population managed a stable way of life, although trouble usually arose when local dynasties changed, which provided opportunities for extremist groups in all sects to flex their muscles and carve out areas of dominion for themselves.

The eastern realm of Islam centered on the capital of Baghdad but reached all the way to India. So vast an area was difficult to administer, and so challenges to Abbasid rule were constant—which led the Abbasids to turn to the Asiatic Turks as military allies just as they had earlier turned to the Persians. The Abbasids carefully promoted and paid honor to the cultural traditions of their allies. They embraced the spread of the Persian and Turkish languages; they employed Persian and Turkish elements in their architecture and pictorial arts; and they encouraged Persian and Turkish literary and scientific traditions. Perhaps most significantly, they aided the spread of the spiritual tradition of **Sufism**, a mystical form of Islam that emphasizes personal experience of the divine over obedience to the Qur'an and Islamic law. This was the most culturally "open" territory in the Islamic world, but it is worth noting that this openness resulted as much from political pragmatism as from a generosity of spirit. The flowering of intellectual life and artistic culture centered on Baghdad was the glory of the age, until it came to a fiery end when the Mongols demolished the city in 1258, slaughtering more than 300,000 people in twelve days and burning hundreds of libraries, temples, hospitals, palaces, and art collections in the process.

THE CALL FOR CRUSADES

Between 1096 and 1291 Latin Europe undertook a series of large-scale military campaigns to win back the Holy Land, which had been under Muslim control since 639. Numerous small-scale efforts continued after that but amounted to little. Nonetheless, the Crusades changed societies and regimes throughout the Mediterranean.

The Crusades are unique in European history because they are the only wars that were formally sanctioned and blessed by the church. To take part in them was considered not only morally justifiable but also a positive spiritual action. These wars, the church proclaimed, pleased God and made one a better Christian—to the point that if a soldier died on a crusade, he was assured forgiveness of all his sins and eternal salvation (assuming that he had had a penitent heart and pure motives). The church called for crusades, preached them from the pulpit, formally inducted their leading fighters, and arranged their financing. As enthusiasm for crusades to the Holy Land waned in the 13th century, the Crusades' mechanisms of preaching and finance were brought to bear on conflicts elsewhere in Europe.

Although a new phenomenon, the Crusades were nevertheless a product of the centuries that had preceded them. If one disregards the religious motive that lay behind them, the Crusades appear as simply another chapter in the centuries-old struggle for control of the eastern Mediterranean shorelands. These lands offered access to both the European economy, centered on the sea, and the overland Asian economy composed of the great silk and spice routes. Its geographical location made the Holy Land valuable long before it became holy. The Phoenicians and the Hittites had fought over it. So had the Egyptians and the so-called Sea Peoples, the Hebrews and the Canaanites, and the Persians and the Greeks. The Romans came next, then the Persians again, the Byzantines after that, and then finally the Arabs under Muhammad. And the litany of conflicts continued after the Crusades ended. In short, the Crusades had a larger context of Greater Western struggles that involved many more factors than religion alone. Yet the religious factor is what makes the Crusades unique. To find ways to justify warfare is one thing, but how did the Latin West ever develop the idea that Jesus wanted his followers to kill Muslims?

Part of the answer lies in the great Gregorian Reform effort, in which intellectual reform was as important as institutional renewal. At the many councils convened during the 10th and 11th centuries, the church debated, among many other things, the theology of warfare. Under what conditions, if any, may a Christian legitimately use physical violence? Jesus had preached "Blessed are the peacemakers" and had accepted his own torture and death, but did that necessarily imply that Christians must never use any kind of force? Did the bravery of the

The Christian Explanation

martyrs of the first Christian centuries require all Christians to forego self-defense when attacked? If one sees a criminal brutally assaulting a woman, is one committing an un-Christian act by beating him into submission?

Such questions were not hypothetical. Latin Europe was overwhelmingly Christian by the late 11th century, but it was also a society organized for warfare—a secular hierarchy of warlords in the north and an aggregation of maritime cities, each with its own militia, in the south. The reformed church needed to find ways to manage and restrain conflicts. One method it employed was the Truce of God, a solemn ban on warfare on holy days and on assaulting pilgrims. Those who violated the Truce were excommunicated. Christian warfare was acceptable, the church decreed, only if it met three criteria: it must have a just cause, it must be fought in a just way, and it must be declared by a just authority.

By 1096, many Europeans believed that warfare against Islam was indeed a just cause. After enduring centuries of persecution under the Romans, Christians in the Holy Land, across North Africa, and throughout the Mediterranean faced conquest by the followers of Muhammad. In creating the great Islamic Empire, after all, Muslim armies had killed hundreds of thousands of Christians and Jews. Under the early caliphs there had been a concerted effort to protect the empire's dhimmis, but as the years went by and Muslims gradually became the majority group within the overall population, hostilities toward Christians and Jews increased. As Islamic unity then shattered into a maze of ethnic, sectarian, and dynastic rivalries, popular willingness to tolerate the non-Muslims in their midst only declined. The 10th and 11th centuries saw repeated popular attacks on Christians and Jews and sporadic state-run persecutions.

The popularity of pilgrimage as a Christian devotion complicated matters further. For centuries waves of pilgrims had ventured from Europe to the Holy Land—with Muslim blessing—to worship at the sites associated with Christ. Pilgrimage, however, is by its very nature a public display of faith and therefore at odds with dhimmi law. Muslim ire focused on the European pilgrims traveling through their lands, less so on their own Christian subjects, and those pilgrims began to experience bitter street-level harassment and violence. Soon enough, however, intolerance of the dhimmis themselves took root in many places. Islamic reform groups like the Almohads and Almoravids in Spain and North Africa made no secret of their determination to crush the Christians and Jews living among them. In 1009 the Egyptian ruler al-Hakim (r. 996–1021) demolished the Church of the Holy Sepulcher in Jerusalem (the church built over what is believed to have been Jesus's actual tomb) and ordered every church and synagogue in his realm similarly destroyed. Christians across Europe were horrified but not altogether surprised. To take up arms against such attacks therefore seemed to satisfy the requirement of a just cause.

Church of the Holy Sepulcher What the crusaders were after: the tomb of Christ at the Church of the Holy Sepulcher in Jerusalem. The present chapel structure was built in the 13th century. Earlier buildings were damaged or destroyed by various attackers, the most notable being the Egyptian caliph al-Hakim in the early 11th century.

But it was the Seljuk Turks whose arrival near the holy sites in the 1060s and 1070s did the most to interrupt the passage of pilgrims. The Abbasids had long courted the Turks, whose military might was considerable, and hoped to use them against Shi'i princes in Syria, Palestine, and Egypt who refused to obey Baghdad. The Turks were new to Islam and burned with the zeal often found among recent converts. With the caliphs' blessing they marched westward, defeated the Byzantine army at Manzikert in 1071, and spread throughout Anatolia, setting up an independent state. But many of the nomadic warriors refused to settle down and raided the Arab-led states to their south. The threat to the splinter states inspired them to crack down on their dhimmis in a show of force. The age demanded an expression of rigorous jihad, and it got it.

THE CRUSADES

There were eight major crusades, and all except the First Crusade ended in failure. The soldiers of the first campaign conquered the Holy Land in 1099 and carved four separate states out of it (see Map 10.6). These became nominally Christian

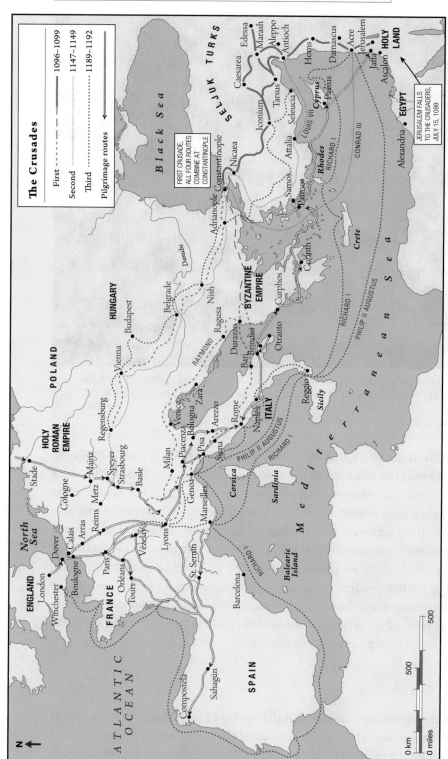

MAP 10.6   The Crusades   The First and Second Crusades took the land route from western Europe to the Holy Land, since the difficult pilgrimage was intrinsic to the religious zeal that drove the campaigns. The Third Crusade used a combined land and sea approach. All crusades to the Holy Land thereafter were exclusively maritime affairs.

states, although the overwhelming bulk of their populations were Muslims, Jews, and non-Latin Christians.

Despite their violent creation, however, the states quickly developed internal policies that granted as much autonomy as possible to the native groups. The crusaders turned into surprisingly lenient rulers, as evidenced by the contemporary chronicler Ibn al-Athir's (1160–1233) claim that thousands of Muslims and Jews migrated to the crusader states because they found life under the crusaders' rule preferable to life under the warring Arab and Turkish warlords. (It was for this claim, presumably, that the terrorist group ISIS desecrated al-Athir's tomb in Mosul, Syria, in June 2014.) Christian trade with Muslims continued in the Mediterranean cities throughout the Crusades—and in fact increased steadily. Muslim sources of the age never present the struggles for the Holy Land in religious terms, and the Christian conquest of Jerusalem in 1099 triggered no groundswell of outrage outside of Palestine itself. For two centuries, outraged resistance to the crusaders' control of the Holy Land was found only in the immediate area; contemporary evidence suggests that the Islamic world as a whole was more concerned with the arrival of the Turks (11th–12th centuries) and the approach of the Mongols (12th–13th centuries).

No kings were involved in the First Crusade (1096–1099), which may be one reason why it alone was an unqualified success. Led by a handful of French and Flemish noblemen, the crusaders marched to Constantinople, where the wary Byzantines gave them fresh supplies and urged them to head as quickly as possible to Anatolia. Turkish cavalry harassed them repeatedly for months, picking off thousands of soldiers while avoiding pitched battle, until the crusaders made it to Antioch, where they regrouped before their further push southward. Finally in 1099, after they had been on the way for three years, they reached Jerusalem, which they took after a month-long siege. *The Course of the Crusades*

The Second Crusade (1147–1149) came two generations later, when King Louis VII of France, determined to stop local incursions against the crusader-held territories, led a disastrous campaign that ended with his failed siege of Damascus, after which he led his troops home in shame. The Third Crusade (1189–1193) was perhaps the most dramatic. It was led by King Richard the Lionheart of England (r. 1189–1199), King Philip Augustus of France (r. 1180–1223), and Emperor Frederick Barbarossa of Germany (r. 1155–1190). Their opponent was Salah ad-Din (better known in the west as Saladin), the ethnically Kurdish sultan of Egypt and Syria (r. 1174–1193) and founder of the Islamic Ayyubid dynasty. The bulk of the fighting consisted of grueling face-to-face battles. Finally the two sides struck a deal that gave the Muslims control of Jerusalem but guaranteed Christians and Jews the right to visit the city.

That truce unfortunately vanished only a few months after the crusade's end, when Saladin unexpectedly died. Only one of the subsequent crusades ever made it to the Holy Land. The Fourth Crusade (1202–1204) got diverted to

The Siege of Antioch   William of Tyre's *Histoire d'Outremer* ("History of Events across the Sea") is one of our best sources for the first two crusades and the internal life of the crusader states between wars. Here the 1098 siege of Antioch—the most strategically important battle of the First Crusade—is depicted. After taking Antioch, the crusaders had a regional base that could be resupplied by sea.

Constantinople (which the crusaders seized and held for the next seventy years). The Fifth (1217–1221), Seventh (1248–1254), and Eighth (1270) crusades all focused on Egypt and North Africa. Only the Sixth Crusade (1228–1229), led by the joint Sicilian king and German emperor Frederick II (r. 1220–1250), produced a qualified success when Frederick managed to negotiate the surrender of Ayyubid control over the Holy Land.

A separate and special case of the crusades was the Spanish Reconquista (711–1492). The Muslim armies that seized Spain in 711 retained control of about 80 percent of the peninsula. The northernmost tier remained in Christian hands, although this territory were divided among a half-dozen different royal families. Muslims' treatment of their Christian subjects initially was harsh but generally followed the strictures established for dhimmi communities. By the late 10th century, however, as the majority of the population became Muslim, patience with the Christian minority ran out and open persecution, though still intermittent, became increasingly common, which led the northern territories to begin attempts to regain control of the peninsula—which they finally accomplished in 1492. The Reconquest was not a continuous victory march southward, however. The border between Christian Spain and Muslim Spain fluctuated considerably, and individual territories were conquered, lost, reconquered, and lost yet again numerous times. Only some of the campaigns were technically crusades, recognized and supported by the church; most were undertaken, and regarded, as local efforts to extend royal prerogatives.

The Impact of the Crusades   Although a largely failed enterprise, the Crusades had a lasting impact on the Greater Western societies. Europe's kings henceforth showed renewed interest in controlling the churches within their realms; the Mediterranean states, having benefited from transporting and supplying the crusading armies and Christian outposts in the Holy Land, now commanded the sea-lanes throughout the entire basin. Medieval literature explored new settings and techniques after exposure to Islamic traditions. The "framed-narrative" technique in the wildly popular *Tales of the Arabian Nights* (in which a series of individual stories are linked by an over-arching single story) provided the model for European works like *The Decameron* of Giovanni Boccaccio and *The Canterbury Tales* of Geoffrey Chaucer. And the complexity of financing the Crusades inspired advances in banking techniques across Europe.

Caught between crusaders from the west and Turks from the east, the Byzantines survived by playing one side off the other. They no longer had the military might to assert themselves and became adept at diplomatic manipulation, acquiring for themselves a reputation for trickery and unreliability. The crusaders came to despise the Byzantines as much as the Muslims, which explains the wild violence unleashed when the soldiers of the Fourth Crusade (1202–1204) sacked Constantinople.

TURKISH POWER AND BYZANTINE DECLINE

The crusader era witnessed dramatic change in the Middle East. First, the arrival of the Turks upset and ultimately overthrew the Arab rulers of the Middle East. In their place, the Turks created an independent state in Anatolia, called the Sultanate of Rum, and a second Turkish-dominated state in a reunited Egypt and Syria, called the Mamluk Empire (see Map 10.7). The Mamluks (Arabic for "slave") originated as an elite bodyguard unit for the Abbasid caliphs. Their name derives from the Turkish practice of kidnapping and enslaving Christian children throughout the Middle East, forcibly converting them to Islam, and putting them through an extraordinary military discipline and training. These slave-soldiers were thus culturally Turkish (by forced adoption) and were independent of the tribal loyalties of the regular Muslim armies.

Nominally subject to the caliphs in Baghdad, the Mamluk Empire and the Sultanate of Rum comprised the center of Islamic power. In 1258 Abbasid power disappeared entirely when the Mongols destroyed Baghdad; the Mongols' own self-proclaimed drive for world domination ended when they were decisively defeated themselves by the Mamluks only two years later. Turkish hegemony over the Islamic world would last in one form or another until the early 20th century.

In the second major shift that the Middle East experienced during the crusader era, the Byzantine Empire effectively ceased to exist as a world power. After the crusaders wrecked Constantinople in 1204, they held on to the empire for more than seventy years, parceling it out to themselves as fiefdoms. For three generations the usurpers plundered Byzantium and all its holdings, determined to crush the Orthodox Church and replace it with Roman Catholicism. By the time they were driven out, in 1278, the empire was in tatters and lived on only as a weak confederation of four minor states. Through diplomatic maneuvers, it managed to

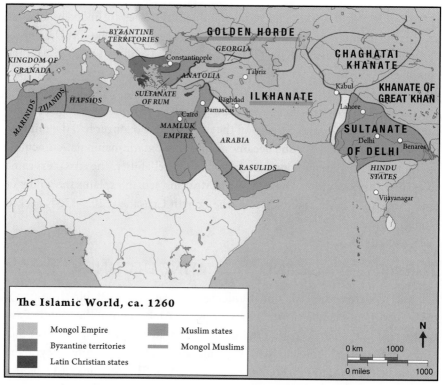

MAP 10.7   The Islamic World, ca. 1260   The Mongol conquest of Baghdad in 1258 was the greatest single military disaster ever visited on the Islamic world. More Muslims were killed in the Mongol advance than were killed in all of the Crusades combined.

survive until its final defeat by the Ottoman Turks in 1453, but for much of its last two centuries the Byzantine Empire consisted of little more than the city of Constantinople itself.

JUDAISM REFORMED, RENEWED, AND REVILED

Scattered by the Romans in 70 CE, the Jews of the Diaspora were left stateless, exiled from their homeland, hounded by Christian evangelists, and still subject to persecution by the Romans. Yet the Jews survived—by adapting imaginatively to the societies where they lived while holding to the core of their traditions. As a Mediterranean people, they had dispersed, predictably enough, around the sea basin (see Map 10.8). In most places local laws forbade them to own farmland, and hence the Jews of the Diaspora became even more heavily urbanized than they had been before. Life in cities, moreover, offered them a measure of safety, since they tended to live as discrete communities.

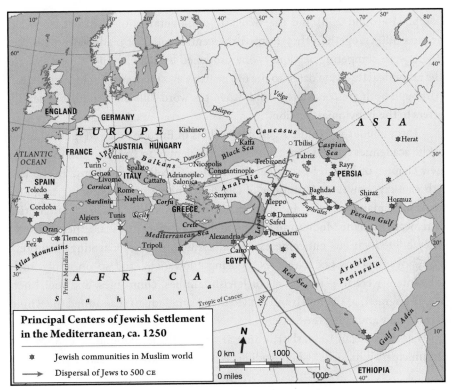

MAP 10.8 Principal Centers of Jewish Settlement in the Mediterranean, ca. 1250 By the 13th century Jewish life was more urbanized than ever before.

In their own designated neighborhoods, they could have at least limited security and autonomy.

The class and sectarian rifts that had characterized life in Judea in Christ's time ceased to have meaning. They were all exiles now, and the Temple was no more. The rabbinical strain of Judaism that traced its roots to the Babylonian Captivity hence became the norm for Jewish life. In city after city, Jews established their synagogues and schools, their butcher shops and eateries, and settled into lives as merchants and professionals.

As during their first exile in Babylon, the Jews quickly found that life as a religious minority presented challenges not addressed in the Torah. How does one live a Jewish life in a non-Jewish world? The rabbis set to work gathering, sifting, organizing, and commenting on the decisions handed down by earlier religious judges. At the same time, new judgments were being rendered from one end of the Mediterranean to the other. These judgments and the precedents on which they rested were studied at the great rabbinical academies and eventually codified in the **Talmud**. It had two parts—the *Mishnah* (the collected rabbinical laws, compiled around 200) and the *Gemara* (commentaries on the laws compiled around 500). Together, they formed the central pillar of medieval Jewish life. There were competing versions—one produced by scholars in Babylon (where the rabbinical tradition dated to the 6th century BCE) and another in Jerusalem.[10] Although both are considered valid, when the word *Talmud* is used, it generally refers to the Babylonian version.

Throughout the Middle Ages, most rabbis in Europe received their training at the academies in the Levant, either in Jerusalem or in Baghdad. An important new chapter of Jewish history began with the Carolingian collapse in the late 9th century, however. A number of late Carolingian princes, hoping to ignite some local manufacturing and commercial activity, invited Jewish communities to relocate from the Mediterranean and to settle permanently in northern Europe. They offered various enticements—legal autonomy under Carolingian protection, advantageous tax schedules, housing allowances, and so on. Once such guarantees were in place, scores of Jewish families, companies, and social networks migrated to the north and settled in the small towns that dotted the Rhine River valley and along the Seine.

For example, in 1084, shortly after arranging the legal founding of Speyer as a municipality, its lord, Bishop Rudiger, issued the following charter:

> In the name of the Holy and Indivisible Trinity, I, Rudiger, by the grace of God bishop of Speyer, having completed the task of establishing Speyer as a legally recognized city, determined to increase the city's honor a thousand-fold by bringing a community of Jews to live permanently within it; and so I invited in Jews from abroad and from Jewish communities in other towns. Moreover, I enclosed them within a fortified wall, lest they be too easily harmed by the rioting common people.... I gave them license and privilege to work at money changing according to their desire . . . and I bestowed upon them, from the Church's holdings, a burial ground for their own possession and use. . . . As much as I am the ruler of Speyer's [Christian] residents, so is the archisynagogos [rabbi] for the Jews [therein]: he has power to judge all disputes and petitions brought before him. . . . In general, I have granted to the Jews of Speyer—as a crowning grace to my benevolence—statutes of such benefit to them as to be unequalled anywhere in Germany.

As decades passed, these small communities prospered and grew.

---

[10]   Although called the Jerusalem Talmud, it was actually compiled by scholars in and around the city of Tiberias, along the western shore of the Sea of Galilee.

Jewish Synagogue and Christian Church   During the centuries-long Christian reconquest of Spain from Muslim control, many towns and villages changed hands numerous times. Mosques were turned into churches, then back into mosques, then again into churches, over and over. Synagogues were also built, taken over, handed back, and reclaimed for another repeatedly. This 13th-century building in Toledo, in central Spain, was a mosque that was eventually converted into the church of Santa Maria la Blanca. Skilled craftsmen of all faiths found work in the near-constant renovation. In a handful of Christian churches in Spain, the vine-tracery patterns carved on arches by Muslim stonemasons turn into Arabic lettering and spell out the creed: "There is no God but Allah, and Muhammad is his Prophet."

Although they remained in contact with the Mediterranean communities, northern Jews soon began to follow a different path of development from *Different* southern Jews. These different paths ultimately resulted in the formation of *Paths of* two distinct Jewish cultural traditions—that of the Ashkenazim in the north *Development* and the Sephardim in the south. The Ashkenazim were the most geographically remote from their homeland, surrounded by hostile Christians who rejected the late Carolingians' courting of Jews. They therefore turned inward, developing a brilliant conservative culture that focused on preserving Talmudic tradition at all cost. The Sephardim, comfortably Mediterranean, were in constant contact with Arab, Greek, and Latin cultural developments, and they participated more directly in intellectual exchange and changes in cultural norms. The stark contrast between Ashkenazic and Sephardic Judaism became apparent when groups from both traditions migrated back to the Holy Land when it was under crusader control. They wore different styles of clothing, followed different liturgies and rituals, and spoke different vernaculars.[11] Providing separate synagogues, butcher shops, markets, and housing for both communities challenged the ingenuity of the crusader-state regimes and led to near-constant low-grade social friction.

North or south, east or west, medieval Jews lived in their separate districts in the cities. And these districts were frequently encircled by protective walls both to mark the territory of Jewish autonomy and to protect the Jews from angry Christian mobs. (The local rabbi possessed the key to the gate.) The church insisted that the only proper Christian response to the Jews was tolerance and coexistence—and that it was the church's special responsibility to protect the Jews. As Pope Innocent III (r. 1198–1216) put it in 1199,

> No Christian may use violence in order to force a Jew to receive baptism . . . for no one who has not willingly sought baptism can be a true Christian. Therefore let no Christian do a Jew any personal injury—except in the case of carrying out the just sentence of a judge—or deprive him of his property, or transgress the rights and privileges traditionally awarded to them. Let no one disturb the celebration of their festivals by beating them with clubs and hurling stones at them; let no one force from them any services which they are not traditionally bound to render; and we expressly forbid anyone . . . to deface or violate their cemeteries or to extort money from them by threatening to do so.

But a declaration like this is usually a tacit recognition that such crimes did occur—which they did, frequently. Popular violence against Jews was a constant element of medieval life. Almost without exception, a papal call for a crusade to the Holy Land triggered a popular uprising against the Jews. Most infamously, in 1096 rabid crowds murdered hundreds of Jews in the German cities of Cologne, Mainz, and Worms. In the aftermath of these slaughters, the church took measures to prevent anti-Jewish violence whenever it summoned a crusade, but those measures usually failed. Official forms of persecution existed too. In the French city of Toulouse, for example, a representative of the Jewish community was required to stand on the steps of the Christian cathedral every year on Good Friday and be publicly slapped in the face by the bishop.

Despite the harsh circumstances confronting them, the Jews of the 9th to 13th centuries flourished. Their communities benefited from the economic

---

[11]   The southerners spoke early forms of Ladino, related to Old Spanish. The northerners spoke early forms of Yiddish.

growth of the era, which they had helped to produce. Their synagogues and schools brimmed with life, and many Jews played important roles in Christian society as advisors, teachers, translators, and intermediaries. Two of the greatest Jewish thinkers of all time emerged at this time too: Rashi (1040–1105) and Maimonides (1135–1204). Rashi, an Ashkenazic Jew, lived in northern France and is regarded as the supreme commentator on the Torah. To the present day, printed editions of the Talmud include Rashi's line-by-line commentary on each page. Rashi's commentaries on the Hebrew Bible were important not only to Jewish scholars but also to certain Christian ones, since his mastery of biblical Hebrew clarified hundreds of passages that had frustrated textual scholars for centuries. Later Franciscan commentators like Nicholas of Myra had a special affinity for his writings. Maimonides, by contrast, was Sephardic, having grown up in Seville. The arrival in Spain of the Almohads, one of the brutal Sunni reformist sects, made life there untenable, so Maimonides traveled throughout the Mediterranean. He settled at last in Cairo, where he worked as a physician during the day and spent his nights writing legal texts, medical treatises, biblical commentaries, and philosophy. His two major works were the *Mishneh Torah*—an enormous compilation of Jewish law, with commentary— and the *Guide for the Perplexed*, a brilliant but difficult analysis of the relationship between reason and faith.

◆

These centuries witnessed the cultural maturation of Christian Europe and the Islamic Near East as the two faiths developed most of the institutions, traditions, and value systems that would characterize them into the modern age. In each case, that maturation emerged from the complex interplay of religion, ethnic and social customs, and the intellectual legacies of the ancient world. Jewish ideas and values developed as well, coalescing into the dominant strains that carried Jewish life into the early modern era.

WHO, WHAT, WHERE

Boniface	feudal bonds	serfs
Carolingian	Great Schism	simony
Renaissance	Gregorian Reform	Sufism
Charlemagne	lay investiture	Talmud
Charles Martel	lord	Treaty of Verdun
Concordat of Worms	manors	vassal

SUGGESTED READINGS

Primary Sources

al-Baladhuri. *The Origins of the Islamic State.*

Benjamin of Tudela. *Itinerary.*

Einhard. *The Life of Charlemagne.*

Ibn al-Athir. *The Universal History.*

Ibn al-Haytham. *The Advent of the Fatimids.*

Maimonides. *The Guide for the Perplexed.*

Rashi. *Commentary on the Torah.*

al-Tabari. *The History of al-Tabari.*

Theophanes. *The Chronicle of Theophanes the Confessor.*

Anthologies

Allen, S. J., and Emilie Amt, eds. *The Crusades: A Reader* (2003).

Constable, Olivia Remie, ed. *Medieval Iberia: Readings from Muslim, Christian, and Jewish Sources* (2011).

Dutton, Paul Edward, ed. *Carolingian Civilization: A Reader* (2004).

Lopez, Robert S., and Irving W. Raymond, trans. *Medieval Trade in the Mediterranean World: Illustrative Documents* (2001).

Shinners, John, ed. *Medieval Popular Religion, 1000–1500: A Reader* (2006).

Studies

Bachrach, Bernard S. *Early Carolingian Warfare: Prelude to Empire* (2000).

Beckwith, Christopher I. *Empires of the Silk Road: A History of Central Eurasia from the Bronze Age to the Present* (2009).

Chazan, Robert. *God, Humanity, and History: The Hebrew First Crusade Narratives* (2000).

Chazan, Robert. *The Jews of Medieval Western Christendom: 1000–1500* (2007).

Christie, Niall. *Muslims and Crusaders: Christianity's War in the Middle East, 1096–1382, from the Islamic Sources* (2014).

Constable, Olivia Remie. *Housing the Stranger in the Mediterranean World: Lodging, Trade, and Travel in Late Antiquity and the Middle Ages* (2003).

Cook, Michael. *Commanding Right and Forbidding Wrong in Islamic Thought* (2007).

Crone, Patricia. *Meccan Trade and the Rise of Islam* (2004).

Crone, Patricia, and Martin Hinds. *God's Caliph: Religious Authority in the First Centuries of Islam* (2003).

Davidson, Herbert A. *Moses Maimonides: The Man and His Works* (2004).

Friedmann, Yohanan. *Tolerance and Coercion in Islam: Interfaith Relations in the Muslim Tradition* (2003).

Griffith, Sidney H. *The Church in the Shadow of the Mosque: Christians and Muslims in the World of Islam* (2008).

Heather, Peter. *Empires and Barbarians: Migration, Development, and the Birth of Europe* (2009).

Hillenbrand, Carole. *The Crusades: Islamic Perspectives* (2008).

Jotischky, Andrew. *Crusading and the Crusader States* (2004).

Kennedy, Hugh. *The Prophet and the Age of the Caliphates: The Islamic Near East from the Sixth to the Eleventh Century* (2004).

Khamis, Ulrike al-. *Early Capitals of Islamic Culture: The Art and Culture of Umayyad Damascus and Abbasid Baghdad, 650–950* (2014).

McCormick, Michael. *Origins of the European Economy: Communications and Commerce, AD 300–900* (2002).

Moore, R. I. *The First European Revolution, c. 970–1215* (2000).

Peri, 'Oded. *Christianity under Islam in Jerusa-lem: The Question of the Holy Sites in Early Ottoman Times* (2001).

Ray, Jonathan. *The Sephardic Frontier: The Re-conquista and the Jewish Community in Me-dieval Iberia* (2008).

Tolan, John V. *Saracens: Islam in the Medieval European Imagination* (2002).

Tyerman, Christopher. *God's War: A New His-tory of the Crusades* (2009).

Wickham, Chris. *Framing the Early Middle Ages: Europe and the Mediterranean, 400–800* (2007).

Wickham, Chris. *The Inheritance of Rome: Il-luminating the Dark Ages, 400–1000* (2009).

For additional resources, including maps, primary sources, visuals, web links, and quizzes, please go to **www.oup.com/us/backman.**

CHAPTER 11

Worlds Brought Down

1258–1453

The 13th and 14th centuries were an age of unparalleled achievement and trauma. The earliest signs of a recognizably modern European world appeared—parliamentary government, an embryonic form of capitalism, universities, the emerging primacy of science, and the spread of literacy and vernacular culture. Modern technologies like mechanical clocks, eyeglasses, magnetic compasses, and paper mills came into use. So too, however, did violent practices like the inquisition against heretics and the persecution of Jews. The Catholic Church assumed the basic institutional form it has today, but it also witnessed an extraordinary wave of popular mysticism and lay evangelism. Some even feared that lay revelation would displace the Church as the mediator between God and man. Interest in science surged, in the confident belief that the cosmos was a rational structure whose deepest secrets could be discovered. At the same time, the greatest scientific mind of the age, English friar and scholar Roger Bacon, warned that the Antichrist, fast approaching, would appear

THE GREATER WEST, 1453

A World Turned Upside Down Pictured here is the battle of Crécy (1346), the first great battle in the Hundred Years' War. The English are on the left, with infantry longbowmen shown—inaccurately—in the front lines. Confronting them are the mounted knights of France. Much bloodshed ensued, ending in a surprise English victory. Similar slaughter occurred at Poitiers (1356) and Agincourt (1415), although the war ended, in 1453, with the French victorious.

in the guise of a scientist. Economically, Europe finally overtook the Islamic world in wealth and ingenuity, yet its very success carried within it the seeds of catastrophe. It also contributed to a growing willingness of society to ignore the teachings of the Church.

The Islamic world similarly shone, even as it split permanently into distinct civilizations. The Mongols brought the caliphate to a sudden and savage end, but their equally swift withdrawal from the scene opened the door to new Muslim conquests, eastward into India and across the Red Sea into sub-Saharan Africa. Two new powerful Islamic states emerged—the Mamluks in Egypt and Palestine and the Ottoman Turks in Anatolia and Syria. Sectarian differences continued, but the urgency of the conflicts between them abated. However, the Sufi movement, which the advance of the Turks westward had accelerated, remained a challenge for Islamic society. The Ottomans' sack of Constantinople in 1453 put an end to the long-exhausted Byzantine Empire, and their subsequent advance into southeastern Europe brought the entire Greater West into a new alignment, with the Turkish superstate now serving as a bridge between Christian Europe and the Middle East.

It is important to consider these two centuries together because the ways in which societies responded to the shared horrors of the 14th century—a perfect trifecta of famine, war, and plague—were largely shaped by what had happened in the 13th.

CHAPTER TIMELINE

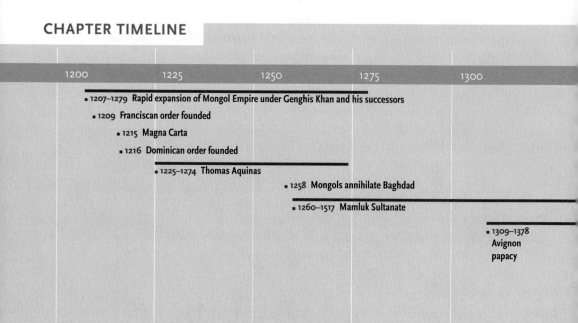

1200	1225	1250	1275	1300

- 1207–1279 Rapid expansion of Mongol Empire under Genghis Khan and his successors
- 1209 Franciscan order founded
- 1215 Magna Carta
- 1216 Dominican order founded
- 1225–1274 Thomas Aquinas
- 1258 Mongols annihilate Baghdad
- 1260–1517 Mamluk Sultanate
- 1309–1378 Avignon papacy

LATE MEDIEVAL EUROPE

Latin Europe's history had been shaped by two opposing waves of development. The dual economic and cultural engine of the Mediterranean region spread its influence northward, bringing elements of cosmopolitan urban life, intellectual innovation, and cultural vibrancy into the European heartlands. Political leadership, however, came from the north, as the monarchies of England and France and the Holy Roman Empire pushed their boundaries southward, drawn by Mediterranean commerce and the gravitational pull of the papal court. The cross-fertilization of north and south benefited each and fostered Europe's ability to reform and revitalize itself. In the Muslim world, by contrast, innovation came largely from outside, in the dominance of Islamicized foreign rulers—the Ottoman Turks and their ethnic cousins, the Mongols and Tartars.

Feudal England, France, and the Holy Roman Empire were the leading powers of the age. Their kings and princes dominated the political scene, and *Political* their soldiers provided the overwhelming bulk of the crusaders. From the 11th to *Power* 13th centuries, they continually extended their power southward to reach the Mediterranean. The Holy Roman emperors had claimed sovereignty over northern Italy since the 10th century. The apex of German might in Italy was reached around 1200, when the new Hohenstaufen dynasty acquired by marriage the throne of the kingdom of Sicily and Naples. France's Capetian dynasty, which came to power in 987 with little more than the city of Paris to its credit, engaged

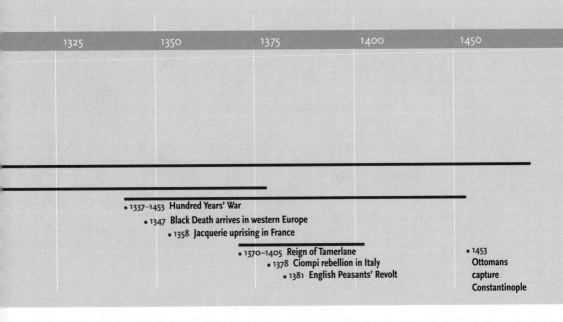

1325   1350   1375   1400   1450

- 1337–1453 **Hundred Years' War**
- 1347 **Black Death arrives in western Europe**
- 1358 **Jacquerie uprising in France**
- 1370–1405 **Reign of Tamerlane**
- 1378 **Ciompi rebellion in Italy**
- 1381 **English Peasants' Revolt**
- 1453 **Ottomans capture Constantinople**

in five generations of aggressive diplomacy: through marriage, it brought more and more of central and southern France into the family domain. By the reign of Louis VII (r. 1137–1180), its control reached as far south as the Pyrenees, although it still lacked a Mediterranean outlet—which finally came with the Albigensian Crusade waged by Philip IV (r. 1180–1223) against the Cathar heretics in southern France and the marriage of Louis IX (r. 1226–1270) to Margaret of Provence. England's monarchs had pursued similar aims. At its zenith, in the reign of Henry II (r. 1154–1189), the royal domain included England, Normandy, Brittany, Maine, Anjou, Gascony, and Aquitaine. As Henry's successors—Richard the Lionheart (r. 1189–1199), John (r. 1199–1215), and Henry III (r. 1215–1272)—gradually lost control of the French territories, they compensated by opening a strategic offensive in the Mediterranean marriage market.

The countervailing wave was the northward spread of Mediterranean urban institutions and commercial techniques. Cities proliferated in the 12th and 13th centuries across feudal Europe and brought with them Roman law, notions of municipal citizenship, representative government, commercial and artisanal guilds,

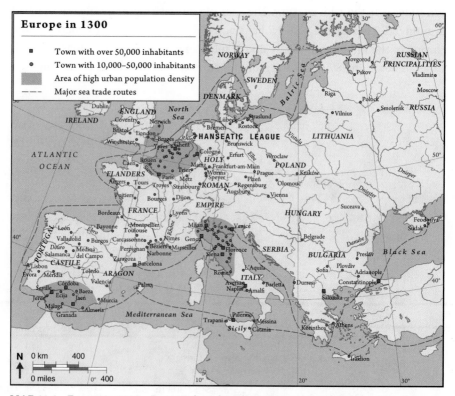

MAP 11.1 Europe in 1300   By 1300 the politically dominant kingdoms of northern Europe had extended their borders to the economically dominant Mediterranean region. Venice retained control over most of the eastern sea, while Barcelona and Genoa held sway over most of the western sea.

schools and universities, and even Mediterranean dress codes. These eased the interactions of the increasingly polyglot and ethnically varied cities (see Map 11.1).

The church, too, reached the zenith of its worldly power. The Gregorian Reform discussed in the preceding chapter (named after Gregory VII, r. 1073–1085) had *Papal* resulted in a sturdy, hierarchical organization—of priests, bishops, archbish- *Authority* ops, and, at the summit, the Holy Pontiff, the pope. Popes like Innocent III (r. 1198–1216) and Gregory IX (r. 1227–1241) exercised a degree of worldly power that no earlier popes had ever had. The new papacy based its authority on a principle called *plenitudo potestatis*—literally "fullness of power" but better translated as "ultimate jurisdiction"—which stressed the church's responsibility toward the world. On the Day of Judgment, it argued, every person must stand before God and be held responsible for his or her sins, but the church must also be held accountable for God's judgment. Did your priest teach you the proper doctrines and morals? Did he help guide you through life's challenges and temptations? Did he nourish you with the sacraments? Since the clergy bear some responsibility for every person's ultimate fate, the church must have a right to pronounce on the doings of our lives, particularly those with a moral component. *Plenitudo potestatis* did not assert the church's right to control individual lives, only its right to be heard.

SCHOLASTICISM

Through its bishops, the church oversaw the universities of Europe (see Map 11.2). This was the great age of **scholasticism**—really a curriculum rather than a philosophy. Scholastic learning was based on the conviction that the whole of the cosmos was rationally ordered: God, having created man as a rational creature, has given him the ability, but also the responsibility, to determine the universe's operation. Not surprisingly, the rediscovered works of Aristotle took center stage, since his inductive method proved most amenable to the study of nature. Scholastic writers specialized in a type of encyclopedia called a *summa*, which attempted to summarize all existing knowledge on a given topic. Many of the scholastics were members of the Dominican or Franciscan orders (discussed later in this chapter) and taught in universities. On the whole, they believed in the human capacity to discover truth in all areas of human experience. Apparent inconsistencies in human knowledge are merely imperfections in our own understanding, not flaws in nature.

No one will ever award Albertus Magnus (1193–1280)—or his brilliant pupil Thomas Aquinas (1225–1274)—prizes for prose style. They wrote in an *Thomas* annotated outline form: lists of questions followed by lists of answers, with *Aquinas* subsections, objections, and counterassertions inserted wherever deemed

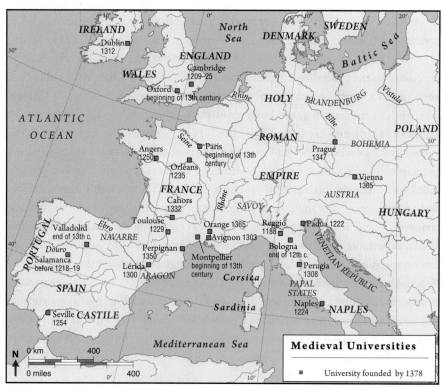

MAP 11.2   Medieval Universities   By the 12th century, universities eclipsed monasteries and cathedral schools as the most prestigious centers of learning in Latin Christendom. They attracted students—all male—from many lands and helped to forge a common elite culture across most of Europe.

appropriate. One might be reading lines of code for a computer program. For them, elegance lay in the thought behind the words, not in the words themselves. Indeed, any stylistic flourishes that drew attention away from the ideas undermined the force of the argument. True beauty lay in the perfectly rational ordering of God's creation and in the perfectly rational representation of it in words. Here, for example, Aquinas argues that the soul does not die when the body does:

> If the destruction of the body means the destruction of the soul, then it must follow that any weakening of the body entails a weakening of the soul. But in reality, if the soul is weakened in any way by a weakening of the body, that is only coincidental . . . and if our understanding flags or falters because of fatigue, injury, or weakness in the body—this is not necessarily fatigue, injury, or weakness in the understanding itself but only in those bodily faculties that the understanding utilizes. (*Summa contra Gentiles* 2.79)

The prose is bloodless (even more so in the original Latin). The point of it is to strip away rhetorical effect so that the beauty of God's Truth—in this case, the eternality of the human soul—can shine through, like sunlight through a windowpane.

Scholasticism represents a powerful moment in the history of Western culture, when it seemed possible to understand everything. The cosmos appeared to work with a formal perfection, and the limits of the human intellect seemed boundless. But unlike the distant and indifferent Creator of the deists of a later time, the God of the scholastics was present, active, brilliant, and benign—an artist and scientist. The rational mind, Aquinas and others insisted, is not a tool but a beautiful gift through which we can perceive all the divine and hidden harmonies of life. This confidence overflowed into other areas of medieval life, like the creation of literary masterpieces like Dante's *Divine Comedy* (written between 1313 and 1321), in which the poet crafts his own salvation via a journey through an afterlife (Hell, Purgatory, Paradise) of his own design, and the construction of soaring Gothic cathedrals. Marked by pointed arches, ribbed vaulting, flying buttresses, and stained-glass windows, Gothic churches appealed to the senses in the way that Thomas Aquinas's *Summa* appealed to human logic and reason: both were designed to lead people to knowledge that touched the divine. It would be a long time before the European world was again so self-confident.

In science the most brilliant and divisive figure was Roger Bacon (1214–1292), a sharp-tongued English Franciscan who delighted in disparaging the "idiot jackasses" *Roger Bacon* he found in the leading universities. Bacon was convinced that the natural world formed a perfect enactment of God's grand design, but that the beauty of the whole could only be perceived after one had mastered all of the individual sciences. He threw himself with gusto into learning Arabic, Greek, and Hebrew and the scientific and philosophical traditions within them, as well as every science from astronomy to zoology; then he set himself to write a grand synthesis—a kind of *summa scientifica* that would encompass the entire natural world as an organic whole, divinely created and rationally ordered. Because of his brashness, his Franciscan order placed Bacon under house arrest and forbade him to write, but not until he had penned a prospectus for the project, a lengthy book known as the *Opus maius* (*Major Work*).

Interior of Sainte-Chapelle, Paris   The stained-glass windows of Sainte-Chapelle (1246–1248) are a fine example of the vibrancy of Gothic art. The pointed arches and ribbed vaulting of the Gothic style can be seen clearly.

Whether in philosophy, science, medicine, law, or any other intellectual field, the central assumptions of the scholastic writers of the late Middle Ages were that the world made sense; that it was rationally ordered; and that all its various truths, once learned, were in harmony with one another. The "unity of Truth" is how they described it. And God, who gave man the gift of reason, intended for him to discover it.

MYSTICISM

In apparent contrast to the intense rationalism of the scholastics, mysticism, or the experience of direct contact with God, was also among the central aspects of the age. It was hardly a new phenomenon. The voices that had sent Abraham on his first wanderings in the Holy Land, the burning bush on Mount Sinai through which Moses heard God's commands, the warnings of the biblical prophets—all these were God's piercing of the veil between the divine world and our own. In the early Christian era, Church Fathers like Jerome and Augustine reported mystical revelations. God spoke to the masses countless times through the miracles of the saints. What was unique about the mystical experiences of the late Middle Ages was their sheer number. Many hundreds—even thousands—of people claimed to have experienced God, in the form of either visions or otherworldly voices. They included austere Carthusian and Cistercian monks and nuns (two relatively new monastic orders discussed later in this chapter) and courtly poets, but also everyday peasants and town dwellers—school teachers, lawyers, shopkeepers, midwives, government officials, children, and the elderly.

Some people had single life-altering visions; some had repeated experiences; others had literally hundreds of powerful, stirring episodes of contact with the divine. These revelations centered on Christ. People heard Christ, saw Christ, spoke with Christ, embraced Christ, and kissed Christ. Moreover, the Christ whom they encountered was not the stern, lordly King of Heaven and Judge of the Last Day (the most common images of Christ in early medieval art). Rather, he was the gentle, caring Christ who suffered and died out of his love for all mankind. One mystic, an Englishwoman named Margery Kempe (1373–1438), speaking in the third person, describes how, on a pilgrimage to Jerusalem,

> [she] wept and sobbed as plenteously as though she had seen Our Lord with her bodily eye, suffering His Passion at that time. Before her in her soul she saw Him verily by contemplation, and that caused her to have compassion. And when they came up on to Mount Calvary [the hill outside Jerusalem where Jesus was crucified], she fell down because she could not stand or kneel, and rolled and wrestled with her body,

spreading her arms abroad, and cried with a loud voice as though her heart would burst asunder; for, in the city of her soul, she saw verily and clearly how Our Lord was crucified.

After she returned to England, the sightings continued:

> When she came home to England, [the visions] came seldom at first, as it were once a month, then once a week, and afterwards daily; and once she had fourteen [visions] in one day, and another day she had seven, and so on, as God would visit her, sometimes in church, sometimes in the street, sometimes in her chambers, sometime in the fields, whenever God would send them, and she never knew the time nor the hour when they would come.

Two aspects of the mystical exaltations stand out. First, people experiencing contact with God did not come away with new insights into theological mysteries or dramatic new interpretations of scripture. They did not know how to live better or make the world a safer and more prosperous place. Time after time, they described their experiences simply as intense waves of emotion. They felt an overwhelming sensation of God's love—as though God wanted only to remind people that He had not forgotten them. He sees their suffering and wants to reassure them that they are loved. An account from another Englishwoman, Julian of Norwich (1342–1416), reads:

The Message of God's Love

> I have begged repeatedly to understand what God meant by these visions ever since I had them. Finally, after more than fifteen years, I received the answer, for I heard in my soul the following words: "Would you like to know the Lord's message in all this? Then learn this well: Love was His message. Who showed this message to you? Love did. What did He show you? Love. Why did He show it to you? Out of Love. Hold on to this idea and you will forever grow in your knowledge and understanding of Love; otherwise you will never know or learn anything."
>
> And this is how I learned that Love was Our Lord's message. I saw with certainty that even before God created us He loved us, and that His Love has never slackened, and that His Love shall endure forever. All the works He has done have been done out of this Love; in this Love He has created all things for our good use; and in this Love our lives are everlasting. We began to exist at the moment of our creation, but the Love that made us was in God from the beginning of time. Our truest beginning is therefore in His Love, and all of this we shall see in God, without end.

Women Mystics

Second, mysticism privileged women. Vastly greater numbers of women reported experiencing this sort of contact than men did, and it seems likely that even greater numbers of women experienced the visions without reporting them. Hildegard of Bingen (1098–1179) was a noble-born German abbess who dramatically described her visions in prose, painting, and music. Hadewijch of Flanders (d. ca. 1245) composed a long sequence of poems and letters that described her own "mystical marriage" to Christ in the vocabulary of courtly love. Julian of Norwich, quoted above, was an educated commoner who at the age of thirty had sixteen separate visions. As a result, she became a recluse and devoted the rest of her life to puzzling out what had happened to her. Her *Revelations of Divine Love* is one of the most moving of all mystical books. Catherine of Siena (1347–1380) started seeing visions in early childhood. For several years she hid from the world, a recluse in her crowded family home (she was the twenty-second of twenty-four children), but at the age of twenty she dedicated herself to social reform and became a tireless advisor to princes and popes. Her visions continued throughout her life.

Although many mystics criticized contemporary problems in the church, none saw themselves as rebels against it. In fact, most took special care to champion orthodox doctrine. But the sheer number of late medieval mystics suggests a grave dissatisfaction with the church and the world.

THE GUILD SYSTEM

The mystical exaltations may have had something to do with the economic vibrancy of the late Middle Ages. The medieval economy had grown at an impressively steady rate since the late 11th century. Fueled by agricultural surplus and the reopening of commercial ties with the Islamic world, it saw advances in financing, manufacturing, and shipping. But not everyone was pleased with this embryonic form of capitalism. The church, itself among the wealthiest of institutions, had a conflicted relationship with it because capitalism functioned on the use of credit. Credit—that is, the loaning

Hildegard of Bingen   Hildegard was a beloved abbess, a renowned mystic, and perhaps the first multimedia artist. When, in her late thirties, she admitted to her brother (who was a priest) that she had started having visions as a child and in fact still had them, he urged her to write. She wrote several books in which she tried to put her experiences into words. When she decided that her writings were inadequate, she put down the pen and took up a brush, composing dozens of ecstatic, expressive paintings. When that too proved insufficient to her, she composed music in the hopes that here at last she could describe what it feels like to be in God's intimate presence. Much of her music survives and is available on recordings. In the image presented here, she begins to write. The manuscript from which this image was photographed was destroyed in World War II.

of money at interest—was morally suspect to many churchmen, since it entailed profiting from someone else's need. The very success of the economy raised the potential danger of materialism. The more money, possessions, property, and investments people had, the church feared, the more time they would devote to their management. God does not care about the value of our possessions, the church counseled, but about the value of our lives. Wealth is indeed better than poverty, but it is not intrinsically good.

That did not stop people from pursuing wealth by an impressive array of new techniques. Among the most important innovations was the guild system. A medieval **guild** somewhat resembled a modern trade association or cartel: it set prices, quality standards, methods and volume of production, and wages paid to workers. It also assigned market shares to individual artisans or merchants. Each city had its own guilds, usually one for each artisanal industry (such as brewing, weaving and dyeing, or metalwork) and another set for the commercial companies (finance, trading, shipping) that brought the goods to market. Guilds played important roles in urban life, funding charities, schools, and hospitals. Among the bylaws of the wine and beer merchants' guild at Southampton, England, in the 13th century, for example, was this provision:

> Whenever the guild is in session the lepers at [the hospital of] La Madeleine shall receive in alms from the guild eight gallons of ale, as shall the sick in [the hospitals of] God's House and Saint Julian's. The Franciscans shall receive eight gallons of ale and four gallons of wine; and sixteen gallons of ale shall be distributed to the poor from whatever spot the guild meets at. . . . If any guild member should fall into poverty and cannot pay his debts, and if he is unable to work and provide for himself, then he shall receive from the guild one mark [of silver] every time the guild meets in session, in order to relieve his suffering.

Guilds not only complemented but also at times nearly replaced the charitable functions of the church. The reach of the church in the late Middle Ages was extensive. It orchestrated crusades, ran and policed the universities and cathedral schools, oversaw the workings of the marketplace, judged the activities of Europe's bedrooms, excommunicated kings and princes, warred with them on

Two Master Craftsmen   The Italian sculptor Nanni di Banco (1383–1430) carved this relief of a stonemason and a woodcarver in honor of the Florentine builders' guild.

occasion, and staged councils to determine ever-finer details of canon law. Many feared it had lost sight of its central mission of ministering to the people. This was the impetus behind the founding of the mendicant orders, groups dedicated to assisting the clergy in the performance of their evangelical mission. These orders grew rapidly in number, size, and popularity, and their astonishing success can be attributed to two principle factors—their unique dedication to serving the common people and the fact that they, unlike the clergy they assisted, opened their membership to women.

THE MENDICANT ORDERS

Franciscans and Dominicans

The two leading **mendicant orders** were the Franciscans and the Dominicans. The Franciscans, established in 1209 by St. Francis of Assisi (1181–1226) and approved by Pope Innocent III, dedicated themselves to preaching and service to the urban poor. They begged for alms and food and donated whatever they collected to the destitute. They preached Francis's simple message of love, forgiveness, and charity.[1] People flocked to them wherever they went. The Dominicans, on the other hand, aided the church's teaching mission. From the church's perspective, too many faithful, especially in the countryside, still lacked proper religious instruction and so drifted into heresy. Heresies, in fact, enjoyed something of a golden age in the 13th and 14th centuries. Dominic de Guzmán (1170–1221), an earnest Spanish cleric, established the order named after him (officially known as the Order of Preachers) in 1216 in the hopes of bringing the heretical back into the Catholic fold. He viewed heresy as the product not of human evil or of Satanic mischief but of the church's failure to provide appropriate religious education. In response, the Dominicans established schools across Europe, debated heretical ideas, and preached tirelessly.

Catharism and Lollardy

The two most prominent heresies were Catharism and Lollardy, and both were profoundly critical of the church (see Map 11.3). The Cathars posited two separate and equal gods, one absolutely good and the other absolutely evil. Trapped in the cosmic war between them, humans were condemned to a miserable cycle of reincarnation. To the Cathars the physical universe was the creation of the evil deity; our souls, by contrast, were created by the good god. We therefore participate in the cosmic struggle by overcoming our own physicality, the demands of the flesh, and the human concern for material wealth. Once we have achieved the appropriate spiritual state, we break the cycle of reincarnation and our souls are released

---

[1]   Francis of Assisi, whose name Cardinal Jorge Bergoglio took when he was elected pope in 2013, was revered not for the brilliance of his thought but rather for the dedication with which he endeavored to live simply in imitation of Jesus's earthly life.

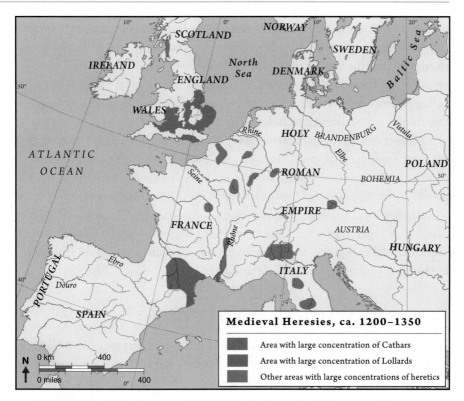

MAP 11.3 Medieval Heresies, ca. 1200–1350 Heretical ideas could be found almost anywhere, but individual groups of heretics tended to conglomerate in particular areas. The Lollards resided chiefly in England, while the Cathars predominated in southern France and parts of northeastern Spain.

from our bodies in a spiritual exaltation that tips the cosmic scale in favor of the universal good. The Lollards were almost dull in comparision.

Lollards condemned church corruption and worldliness. They believed in the right of nonpriests to preach, and they taught that to live according to the spirit of Christ is more important than to follow the many letters of the church's laws. The Lollards had no common body of doctrines; they shared instead a general anticlericalism toward Rome, whose obvious wealth and involvement with earthly matters corrupted its spiritual authority in their eyes.

The Dominicans confronted these and other groups with relentless preach- *Inquisition* ing and arguing. Dominicans were confident that the errant had only to hear Christian truth properly presented and they would return to the church's embrace confidently and with gratitude. Of course, it did not always work out that way, which led to the development of a sterner educational tool—the inquisition. The **inquisition** began as a pedagogical program to counter heresy: determine what an individual or group actually believed and then demonstrate its errors.

Its origin lay in a principle of ancient Roman law similar to our modern "probable cause" hearings. According to this principle, certain crimes are so detrimental to society that the state has a right, indeed a responsibility, to investigate pre-emptively if there is a reasonable likelihood that the crime might be in the offing. Heresy fell into this category because it imperiled the soul not only of the heretic; any innocent bystander might succumb.

Like other interrogation methods used in medieval times, inquisition did not shy away from using physical force. But the Inquisition (with an uppercase I) of popular legend and Hollywood films, with black-hooded sadists plying red-hot pincers in dank dungeons, largely came later, during the 15th and 16th centuries. Nevertheless, medieval inquisitions used enough coercion and manipulation to earn a dark reputation. The Dominican friars became especially associated with inquisition, although the overwhelming majority of them dedicated themselves to teaching, preaching, and peaceful ministry.

EARLY REPRESENTATIVE GOVERNMENT

Modern democracy has its immediate roots in the parliamentary tradition created by late medieval society. By 1300 nearly every state in Latin Europe, large or small, had some sort of representative assembly that possessed genuine power, usually by means of controlling the king's or prince's access to tax revenue.

Noble advisory councils were nothing new. But the late medieval addition of representatives of the common people signified the real breakthrough. The governments' need for revenue drove the issue but does not explain it entirely. Since Europe's nobles and churches remained exempt from taxation, the king's only recourse for new revenues was to tax the free commoners in the cities. The urban classes responded positively, for the most part, provided that the king granted them in return a voice in the formation of government policy. By 1100 such commoners' councils held an advisory role in government, but by 1300, when the urban manufacturing and commercial sectors represented the bulk of their realms' collective economic output, the urban classes had expanded their advisory role into power to initiate legislation for the king and the authority to veto the king by controlling his purse.

The English Parliament

The transition was not always smooth. Constraints on royalty in England included the signing of the Magna Carta in 1215 and the Provisions of Oxford in 1258, and both came about after high drama and much strong-arm maneuvering. The **Magna Carta** is principally a conservative document in which the king confirmed the long-standing rights and privileges of England's nobles. But it did contain one important innovation—an explicit recognition that the king is not above the law. The Provisions of Oxford was the first formal document to enshrine the idea that royal rights were limited and that other facets of government, under the control of the lower orders, possessed constitutional authority. England's governing body came to be known as the **Parliament**, and it consisted of two bodies—the House of Lords and the House of Commons. (The nobles insisted on separate buildings, so that they would not have to mingle with the commoners.)

In France, the Capetian kings from Louis VIII (r. 1223–1226) on were hobbled not only by their feudal obligations to the nobles but also by their practice of awarding land grants (*apanages*) to the younger sons of each Capetian generation. As consolation prizes for not inheriting the crown, apanages were independent provinces that required their holder to perform no service to the throne. The Capetians therefore had even greater need to seek the financial assistance of the urban populace, which they did by developing the French parliament—the **Estates General**. *The French Estates General*

The German case was more complicated. Frederick II (r. 1212–1250) had inherited the Holy Roman Empire from his father and the Kingdom of Sicily (which included southern Italy) from his mother and frankly had little interest in his German lands at all. His southern realm was wealthier and more cosmopolitan. Frederick encouraged urban growth within Germany but also issued, in 1231, the Constitutions in Favor of the Princes of Germany, which severely curtailed the power of those cities and indeed of his own feudal claims to privilege. He gave up a strong German monarchy in return for the German princes' leaving him alone to pursue his own goals in the Mediterranean. Nevertheless, his actions helped solidify the gains made in establishing the German parliament—known as the **Diet**. *The German Diet*

By 1250 or thereabouts, the balance between the authority and status of the commoners and that of the nobles was changing dramatically. The warlords (*milites*) had easily justified their emergence in the 11th century, with their monopoly on political power and privileged status. Three struts bolstered their authority: economic wealth, literacy, and military service. They generated through their manors the largest portion of economic production in the realm. They alone could perform government service, since they had a virtual monopoly, among the laity, on literacy, and they provided the dominant and most effective military service. But the rise of the urban economy had shifted economic dominance within Europe to manufacturing and commerce instead of agriculture, and the spread of literacy among city dwellers had opened up civil service to commoners. Government became professionalized, in other words, and men of noble birth began to shun the lesser offices of civil administration. That left room for commoners to enter and replace them. As the struts that legitimated noble authority gradually disappeared, voices began to murmur darkly about unjustified privilege. *Threats to Noble Authority*

THE WEAKENING OF THE PAPACY

Confrontation at Anagni

Pope Boniface VIII (r. 1294–1303) had begun his pontificate with a splendid jubilee that brought as many as a million pilgrims into Rome, but papal stature had declined precipitously since then. Boniface, a rock-ribbed papal triumphalist, had provoked widespread ire by his insistence that "it is absolutely necessary to every single human being's salvation that he be subject to the Roman pontiff"—a declaration that he meant most literally. The claim was not new, but Christians everywhere chafed at the tone. Philip IV of France (r. ca. 1285–1314), who understood Boniface's claim as undermining his own desire to tax the French clergy, responded by issuing an arrest warrant for the pope, accusing him of everything from murder and bribery to devil worship and sodomy. When Philip's soldiers hunted down Boniface at his vacation residence in the central Italian town of Anagni, they slapped and beat the old man mercilessly (Boniface was then nearly seventy). Boniface's humiliation demonstrated the limits of papal control, and he died within days.

The Avignon Papacy

More troubles followed in quick succession. In 1305 the College of Cardinals met in Rome, after the death of the briefly reigning Pope Benedict XI (r. 1303–1304), and elected a Frenchman to the Holy See, who took the name Clement V (r. 1305–1314). Clement proved so unpopular with the crowds in Rome, however, that he had to flee the city in fear of his life; he and all the cardinals who had voted

The Papal Palace at Avignon   Political conflicts in Rome forced the papal court to flee the city and take refuge in Avignon in southern France from 1305 to 1378. The palace they constructed is more forbidding than welcoming, a symbol of a church under siege.

for him took refuge in southern France, where they built themselves an immense palace whose imposing walls and thick gates reflected the defensive posture of the papacy.

From 1305 until 1378 the papal court stayed behind those walls. This era is thus known as the **Avignon Papacy**. All five popes of those years were Frenchmen, and none of them is remembered with much admiration. For decades their chief concerns seems to have been manipulating international politics so that they could be restored to Rome and insisting on papal rights to complete obedience by the faithful. Decrees and demands flowed endlessly from the palace gates, but the popes themselves were all but absent from Christian life.

NOBLE PRIVILEGE AND POPULAR REBELLION

The word *chivalry* derives from the French word for horsemanship (*chevalerie*) and originally denoted skill at mounted shock combat: heavily armored knights *The Code* astride thundering warhorses, bearing swords, lances, maces, and flails. Knights *of Chivalry* proved their worth at tournaments, fighting other knights in all-too-real contests in which many were killed. They sought not merely renown but also position as a vassal to higher lords in search of loyal underlings. *The Song of Roland*, a popular epic poem written down around 1100, depicted its hero as the very summit of knightly perfection—an unsurpassed warrior loyal to his lord but to little else. The fictional Roland exhibits no qualities other than his usefulness on a battlefield. By 1200, however, a significant change had occurred, and the ideal knight portrayed in literature was more a figure like Sir Lancelot, Sir Galahad, or Saint Perceval of the Arthurian legends. All were still champion fighters, but they were also models of **chivalry** in a new sense—comportment, noble demeanor, learning, and piety. They were sensitive to music and art and, above all, were chivalric lovers of virtuous noblewomen.[2]

An Italian-born French writer named Christine de Pizan (ca. 1364–1430) is one of our best sources regarding chivalry. She was Europe's first female professional writer, having turned to her pen as her only means of support after the death of her nobleman husband in 1390. Over the next forty years she produced hundreds of poems and many volumes of allegorical tales, biographies, translations, literary criticism, and commentaries on politics, religion, and society. Throughout it all her central theme was the failure of society to value women appropriately. The cult of chivalry, as she saw it, helped to smooth the rough edges of aristocratic behavior toward women, but this gain came at the cost of turning

---

2   Lancelot's mistake was not in loving Arthur's queen, Guinevere, but in loving her with the wrong kind of love, adultery.

women into adored figurines—angels on pedestals. Worse still, Christine suspects that for all their showy declarations of courtly love, most men are still motivated by mere lust. At the end of her most famous book, an allegory called *The City of Ladies*, she urges her readers to "chase away all lying flatterers who use every trick and stratagem they can think of to get that which you should preserve above all—your honor and reputation. Oh ladies! Run away from their foolish declarations of love! Run, for Heaven's sake! Run! Nothing good can come of their tricks."

Over the course of the 13th and 14th centuries, as aristocrats sought to maintain leadership of society, chivalry took on newer and more symbolic roles. Coats of arms, for instance, which had originally served the practical purpose of identifying battlefield participants, began to adorn everything a nobleman owned, from tableware and fireplace masonry to goblets, gloves, and stationery. Aristocrats not only patronized musicians and poets but also now endowed colleges, scholarships, chapels, and hospitals and emblazoned them all with their names and heraldic signs. Genealogy became a passion of the elite, and its results (often fanciful) were published in books and embroidered on tapestries. Songs, tales, and histories enumerated their elevated sensibilities. Commerce and trade were denigrated as beneath the dignity of a lord. The noble class felt the need to emphasize at every turn the chasm that separated it from commoners: the nobles were not different because they were privileged, they seemed to say, but were privileged because they were different. And the difference was essential, not functional.

A Noble Warrior?   Mounted shock combat—that is, armored knights atop armored warhorses—was the premier technique of warfare in the Middle Ages. The *Manesse Codex*, from which this image is taken, is a famous compilation of German chivalric poetry dating to about 1300. The knight shown here is not drawn to life (where are his weapons?) and should be regarded only as representative of the noble grandeur of chivalrous knighthood.

But the military role of the knightly class remained and sufficed to maintain the hierarchy. So long as mounted shock cavalry remained the premier fighting force, commoners might complain about abuses of privilege, but not about the very idea of privilege. In contrast, popular rebellions of the late Middle Ages— the three best known are the Jacquerie uprising in France (1358), the Ciompi Rebellion in Italy (1378), and the Peasants' Revolt in England (1381)—shared a common element: they questioned the very order of medieval society, not merely the abusive actions of a few elites within it. None was ultimately successful, but they gave powerful expression to the resentment of the commoners against continuing noble privilege.

An anonymous poet of the time asked,

> When Adam delved and Eve span,
> Who was then the gentleman?

Although simply phrased, it was a radical question: When God created the world in all its original perfection, were there any "gentlemen"? Any privileged few who lived off the labor of the many? If not, then the existence of them now must be a distortion of God's original intent, which could be no other than the equality of all mankind.

The couplet was referred to in a sermon delivered by one of the leaders of the **English Peasants' Revolt**, a Lollard priest named John Ball (1338–1381). The story is retold in the *Historia Anglicana* of Thomas Walsingham (d. 1422):

The English Peasants' Revolt

> *When Adam dalf, and Eve span, who was thanne a gentilman?:* From the beginning all men were created equal by nature, and that servitude had been introduced by the unjust and evil oppression of men, against the will of God, who, if it had pleased Him to create serfs, surely in the beginning of the world would have appointed who should be a serf and who a lord.

Ball ended by recommending

> uprooting the tares [weeds] that are accustomed to destroy the grain; first killing the great lords of the realm, then slaying the lawyers, justices, and jurors, and finally rooting out everyone whom they knew to be harmful to the community in future.

In the 14th century several simple, inexpensive technologies developed in weaponry, which knocked the third and final strut—military protection—out from under aristocratic claims to justified privilege. The two most significant weapons were the longbow and the crossbow, which appeared first in Wales and

Innovations in Weaponry

Scotland, where they were used to repulse the English armies of King Edward I (r. 1272–1307), and possibly even before that. Prior to this time, bows were largely used by noble cavalry. The physical challenge of sitting astride a broad warhorse while fully armored, however, meant that knights' bows were relatively short in length and hence of limited power and range. The Welsh and the Scots, however, hit upon the idea of turning bows into infantry weapons instead, which allowed them to increase the length of the bow significantly. Longbows—familiar today as "bows and arrows"—were often a full 6 feet long, and their arrows could pierce a suit of armor at a distance of 200 yards.

The crossbow was the medieval equivalent of a sawed-off shotgun, and it shot thick metal darts called *quarrels*. A ratcheted steel gear, turned by a steel crank, drew the bowstring; once released, the quarrel likewise could pierce plate armor and even shatter the bones it protected.[3] Crossbows date back to Alexander the Great. The late medieval weapon, however, used a steel, not wooden, bow piece, which gave it tremendous force and required the crank to arm it. The crossbow was designed for close-range killing and holds the distinction of being the first weapon ever banned by the Catholic Church—not for its deadly force per se but because it allowed the unthinkable: with it, commoners could kill noblemen almost at will. This was more than social inversion, the church declared; it was an intrinsically immoral attack on God's ordering of society.

THE HUNDRED YEARS' WAR

The **Hundred Years' War** (1337–1453) was the longest (although not continuous) war in Western history—and almost the longest in preparation. England and France had experienced fierce tensions and rivalries since 1066, when, as we saw in chapter 10, William the Conqueror crossed the English Channel with his army and conquered England. From this time on, the English kings, as kings, were autonomous sovereigns but, as dukes of Normandy, also vassals of the throne in Paris. French kings were thwarted whenever they tried to curb the ambitions of their Norman vassals, however. And when the Norman kings managed to acquire even more French territories through strategic marriages—such as the marriage of Henry II (r. 1154–1189) to Eleanor of Aquitaine—the vassals stood more powerful and respected than the lords.

Origins and Course of the War   Matters came to a head when England's king Edward III (r. 1327–1377) claimed the French throne for himself in 1337. Legally, his claim was correct, because he was married to the last remaining Capetian heir of France's king

---

3   In Spain, the crossbow may have been used as a surgical tool. A quarrel embedded in a soldier's bone could be removed by tying it to a quarrel shot by a crossbow in the opposite direction.

Philip IV (r. 1285–1314). However, the French court, which recognized Philip VI (r. 1328–1350) of Valois as king (the Valois took over when the Capetians had no male heir), would have none of it, and the war began. On again, off again, the Hundred Years' War left the French countryside ravaged and its people dispirited (see Map 11.4). The English, who were vastly outnumbered, avoided pitched battles and instead sent innumerable small raiding forces, armed with longbows and crossbows, which could pierce the French suits of armor and render mounted knights ineffective. Their mission was to vandalize as much French territory as possible, terrorize the people, and then return to England before the French could muster their enormous feudal army.

At stake was not simply dynastic territorial rights but an entire way of life. As one chronicler described an early English victory, at the battle of Crécy in 1346,

> The English [longbow] archers stepped forward and shot their arrows with great might—and so rapidly that it seemed a snow-blizzard of arrows. When these arrows fell on the Genoese [one of France's allies at the time]

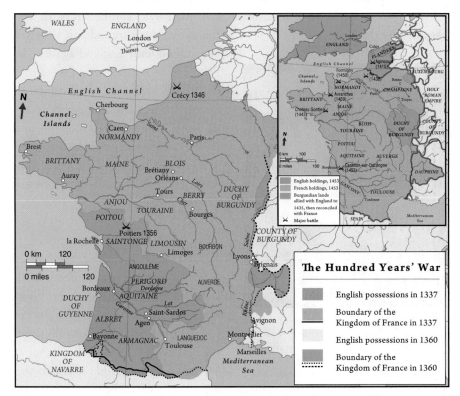

MAP 11.4   The Hundred Years' War   During the Hundred Years' War, English kings contested the French monarchy for the domination of France. For many decades the English seemed to be winning, but the French monarchy prevailed in the end.

and pierced their armor, they cut the strings of their own weapons, threw them to the ground, and ran. When the king of the French, who had arrayed a large company of mounted knights to support the Genoese, saw them in flight he cried out, "Kill those blackguards! They're blocking our advance!" But the English kept on firing, landing their arrows among the French horsemen. This drove the charging French into the Genoese, until the scene was so confused that they could never regroup again. . . . [When the slaughter ended,] it became clear that the French dead numbered eighty banners [flag-bearers], eleven princes of the realm, twelve hundred knights, and thirty thousand commoners.

Joan of Arc and France's Victory

The war ended with an improbable French victory, led by a charismatic peasant girl named **Joan of Arc** (ca. 1412–1431), who claimed to have received messages from Heaven telling her to drive the English from France. Unlike most mystics of her time, however, Joan received concrete messages outlining what was expected of her: to take control of the French army, inspire the French soldiers, and drive the English from the land. The French army briefly rallied under her leadership and scored several victories, until Joan was captured in battle and executed by the English in 1431. Shortly thereafter, the Burgundians, who had been allied with England against the French, reversed course and sided with the French. With their newly combined forces, the French and Burgundians drove the English from the land, and in 1453 a permanent peace was settled. The first death knell of the feudal aristocracy had been sounded, however, despite the victory.

Joan of Arc   This early image of Joan of Arc shows her in armor but without her hair cropped. Joan cut her hair short in a conscious effort to appear manly; after her capture, this gender-bending display was used as evidence of her supposed witchcraft and heresy. In reality, Joan's ease at cutting across social boundaries—a commoner, leading an aristocratic army—unnerved people as much as her violation of gender norms did. She was only nineteen when she was put to death.

THE PLAGUE

Another even more dire death knell sounded for the whole Greater Western world in late 1347, when a fleet of Genoese merchant ships returning from the Black Sea arrived in the harbor at Messina, Sicily. Aboard the vessels was a pack of rats carrying the bubonic plague. This disease originated in eastern Asia and had worked its way westward along the trade routes; the violent advance of the Mongol army under Genghis Khan (ca. 1167–1227) and his successors probably sped matters up considerably. Since the disease had never existed before in the west, the people had no biological means of fighting it off, and it took several centuries for the necessary antibodies to develop among the populations at large. Waves of the plague—known popularly as the **Black Death**—therefore returned to the Near East and Europe until well into the 18th century.

This was the single worst natural disaster in Greater Western history, killing as many as 50 million people in less than three years—roughly one-third of the European and Muslim populations (see Map 11.5). A Sicilian eyewitness, Michael of Piazza, recorded the following:

Reactions to the Black Death

> At the start of November [in 1347] twelve Genoese galleys . . . entered the port at Messina. They carried with them a disease so deadly that any person who happened merely to speak with any one of the ships' members was seized by a mortal illness; death was inevitable. It spread to

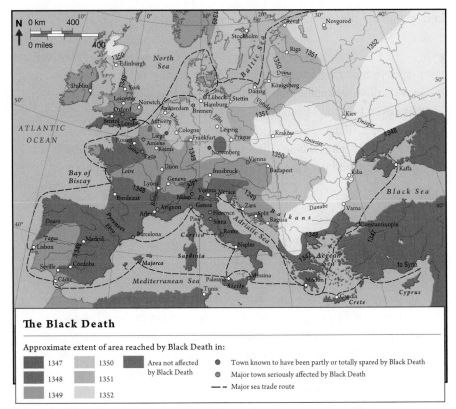

The Black Death

Approximate extent of area reached by Black Death in:

1347	1350
1348	1351
1349	1352

Area not affected by Black Death

● Town known to have been partly or totally spared by Black Death
● Major town seriously affected by Black Death
--- Major sea trade route

MAP 11.5   The Black Death   From Sicily, the plague spread outward in concentric circles. Its waves of death needed only two years to kill more than 20 million people in Europe alone.

everyone who had any interaction with the infected. Those who contracted the disease felt their whole bodies pierced through with pain, and they quickly developed boils about the size of lentils on their thighs and upper arms. These boils then spread the disease throughout the rest of the body and made its victims vomit blood. The vomiting of blood normally continued for three days until the person died, since there was no way to stop it. Not only did everyone who had contact with the sick become sick themselves, but also those who had contact only with their possessions. . . . People soon began to hate one another so much that parents would not even tend to their own sick children. . . . As the deaths mounted, crowds of people sought to confess their sins to priests and to draft their wills . . . but clergy, lawyers, and notaries refused to enter the homes of the ill. . . . Franciscans, Dominicans, and other mendicants who went to hear the confessions of the dying fell to the disease—many of them not even making it alive out of the ill persons' homes. (*History of Sicily*)

In England, the canon Henry Knighton wrote,

At the same time sheep began to die everywhere throughout the realm. In a single pasture one could find as many as five thousand carcasses, all so putrefied that no animal or bird would go near them. . . . Moreover, buildings both large and small began to collapse in all cities, towns, and villages, for want of anyone to inhabit them and maintain them. In fact, many whole villages became deserted; everyone who lived in them died and not a single house was left standing. (*Chronicle*)

In Paris, French writer Jean de Venette described a popular reaction to the crisis:

Some said that the pestilence was the result of infected air and water, . . . and as a result of this idea many people began suddenly and passionately to accuse the Jews of infecting the wells, fouling the air, and generally being the source of the plague. Everyone rose up against them most cruelly. In Germany and elsewhere—wherever Jews lived—they were massacred and slaughtered by Christian crowds, and many thousands were burned indiscriminately. The steadfast, though foolish, bravery of the Jewish men and women was remarkable. Many mothers hurled their own children into the flames and then leapt in after them, along with their husbands, in order that they might avoid being forcibly baptized. (*Chronicle*)

The Spanish Muslim writer Ibn Khaldun (1332–1406) summarized the ruin this way:

> It was as though humanity's own living voice had called out for oblivion and desolation—and the world responded to the call. Truly Allah inherits the earth and all things upon it. (*Muqaddimah*)

People tried every medicine, folk cure, and prayer they knew, all to no effect. In several instances townsfolk, who knew that the disease had something to do with rats, intentionally burned their entire towns to the ground to drive the rats away, but this of course only accelerated the spread of the contagion. By the time the plague had spread its way through nearly every corner of Europe, North Africa, and the Near East, it had left behind piles of corpses so massive that people hardly knew what to do with them. Scores of "death ships" bobbed directionless on the seas, every person on board dead, with the victorious rats silently gnawing on their remains.

The consequences of the catastrophe were innumerable. The fatalities, cou- *Consequences* pled with the fear of interpersonal contact, halted agricultural and industrial *of the Crisis* production and severed all commercial ties. The death of so many farm ani- mals had equally long-term effects: wool and dairy production all but ceased, and the loss of oxen and horses as draught animals meant that farming would be slow to restart. Once the immediate crisis passed, twin spirals of inflation and reces- sion followed. Urban workers who had survived could demand higher wages for

Burying Plague Victims   This page from the *Annals* of Gilles de Muisit, late 14th century, shows crowds in Tournai (Belgium's oldest city) struggling to bury all the dead left in the Black Death's wake.

their labor, and this, combined with the general scarcity of goods, triggered rapid increases in prices. Rural workers faced a different problem. So many people had died that even decreased food production met local needs—and hence food prices dropped precipitously. When rural workers demanded lower rents for their work on the land, the landlords could hardly refuse. But the collapse in crop prices hurt the farmers more than the decreased rents helped them. So in general terms, urban workers who survived the Black Death profited from the decimation, whereas rural workers were driven even deeper into poverty.

Each return of the Black Death over the centuries left new iterations of the same miseries in its wake. No epidemic ever reached the hopeless severity of the first wave, but fear of the plague haunted the Greater West for many generations.

THE MONGOL TAKEOVER

The 13th and 14th centuries witnessed the near-complete takeover of the Islamic world by a new wave of foreign conquerors, who dominated Muslim life for the next three hundred years, reconfiguring its map and introducing new cultural and social elements into Islamic identity. Leadership of Islam had long been monopolized by two groups, the Arabs and the Persians. Although often in tension with each other, they had nevertheless worked out some sort of creative cultural compromise. The arrival of two groups of newcomers, however, renewed cutthroat competition between the Muslim states. Neither group was monolithic. Instead, each was a compound assemblage made up of numerous tribes and clans linked by language: the Mongols and the Turks.

Rise of the Mongols

The most destructive of the invaders were the **Mongols**, who began moving westward in the 12th century. No one knows the precise origin of the Mongols. Ancient Chinese records trace them back to a group they called the Donghu (3rd century BCE), which was actually a confederation of various peoples speaking related dialects of an early version of the Mongolian language. But some scholars claim to see elements of early Turkish dialects in the Donghu as well. Certainly the Mongols, as they spread across Asia, maintained continuous contact with Turkish-speaking groups and absorbed elements of Turkish culture. As the two groups gradually merged, they became known in the west as the *Tartars* (a word that derives from the Latin *Tartarus*, "hell").

Nomadic peoples of the steppes found it natural to form occasional alliances and confederations—and to disband them just as casually. When gathered, these armies were often of considerable size. Fighting on horseback, they moved quickly and specialized in lightning strikes on other nomadic groups and small population centers. Siege machinery was largely unknown to them, which allowed fortified cities to withstand their assaults. The Mongols were a diverse group of tribes along the northern and northwestern borders of China, and the Chinese themselves had been traditionally among the Mongols' favorite targets for raiding. Centuries of such attacks had prompted the Chinese to build the Great Wall, a series of fortifications made of stone, brick, pressed earth, wood, and other materials. Although not impregnable, the wall repulsed attackers and migrants alike with sufficient success that it was a major reason for the seemingly endless waves of invaders and nomads who moved westward across Asia and into the Western world.

Under their brilliant but brutal commander Temüjin (ca. 1167–1227), the Mongols forged another of their periodic confederations. Better known by his title of **Genghis (Chinggis) Khan**, or "Universal Ruler," he broke through the wall in 1207 and subdued the northern half of China. The Chin emperor surrendered in 1214 and awarded Genghis Khan an enormous tribute payment of gold and silver coins, which sources say required three thousand horses to carry. At this point Genghis might have stopped his conquests, because in diplomatic records he referred to himself as the "supreme emperor of the east" and wrote to the Abbasid ruler in Khwarezmi (in modern-day Iran) as the "supreme emperor of the west." The arrogant al-Nasir (r. 1180–1225) rejected Genghis's peace offering, however, and slaughtered all 450 members of the diplomatic embassy he had sent. This called for revenge, and in 1219 Genghis Khan moved westward and quickly crushed what was left of the Abbasid state.

Conquests under Genghis Khan

Genghis left local rulers in place, so long as they swore unquestioning obedience to him, and he installed Mongol tax collectors in each region to ensure a flow of revenue into his coffers. Some towns rebelled and slew these Mongol officials as soon as Genghis had moved on, which prompted the great khan to return in wrath and annihilate entire populations. Once he was even reported to have ordered the killing of every living creature in a city, including its domesticated animals. Ali ibn al-Athir (1160–1233), the great Kurdish historian, described the Mongols memorably in his *Universal History*:

> Even Antichrist, though He strike down all those who oppose him, will spare those who follow Him—but these Mongols spared no one, not even men, children, or women; they even ripped open the stomachs of women who were pregnant and killed their unborn children. . . . These people came out of the lands of China and attacked cities . . . in Turkestan . . . and advanced on Samarkand, Bukhara, and other sites in Transoxiana. One of their armies made it as far as Khurasan and continued their campaign of conquering, pillaging, and ruining until they reached . . . the borders of Persia, Azerbaijan, and Iraq, . . . all of which they destroyed and wholly depopulated, except for a small remnant, in less than a year's time.

Coming as it does near the end of the *Universal History*, ibn al-Athir's passage denotes the apocalyptic role he saw the Mongols to be playing. Surely the end of the world was nigh if such malevolent power as the Mongols possessed could roll over the world at will. Had he lived another quarter century, ibn al-Athir would have seen his worst imaginings realized.

Expansion under Genghis's Successors

The Mongol conquests were far greater than those achieved by any earlier people, or by any people since Genghis Khan died in 1227, and after a bitter fight among brothers he was succeeded by his third son, Ögedai (r. 1227–1241), who continued to push the borders of the Mongol-dominated realm farther west until they reached Anatolia. Another branch of his army, moving north of the Black Sea, threatened Hungary and even reached northward to the Baltic Sea and southward to the Balkans. Under Hulagu (r. 1256–1265), a general under the command of his ruling brother Möngke Khan (r. 1251–1259), the Mongols annihilated Baghdad in 1258. According to Muslim sources, as many as 300,000 people were killed in a two-week-long orgy of slaughter. The Mongols destroyed the royal library (one chronicle reports that the Tigris River ran black from the ink of all the books hurled into it) and burned dozens of mosques, schools, and hospitals. At the end, Hulagu had the Abbasid caliph,

The Siege of Baghdad The Mongol conquest of Baghdad in 1258 ended the caliphate, the main political institution of the Islamic world since the death of Muhammad. This illustration of the siege of Baghdad from a 15th-century Persian manuscript shows the last Abbasid caliph, al-Musta'sim (r. 1242–1258), submitting to the Mongol khan Hulagu (r. 1256–1265).

al-Musta'sim (r. 1242–1258), rolled up in a Persian carpet and then trampled by Mongol horsemen.

A contingent of Mongol soldiers then pressed farther westward as far as Damascus but were finally repulsed in 1260 at 'Ayn Jalut, near Nazareth, by a Mamluk army coming out of Egypt. The Mongol realm reached its greatest extent in 1279, when Kublai Khan, one of Genghis's numerous grandsons, conquered southern China. By then the Mongol Empire covered some 12 million square miles of land, nearly one-quarter of the Earth's land surface (see Map 11.6).

At the height of their power the Mongols controlled an almost unimaginably vast empire, from Beijing to the Euphrates River and from Moscow to the Arabian Sea. In their wake, they left behind vast numbers of dead. In China alone, census records show that the population in 1200, before Genghis Khan's invasion, stood around 120 million people; in 1300 it figured only 60 million. Ibn Battuta (d. 1378), the famous Spanish Muslim traveler, reported that Persia's population fell from 2.5 million in 1220 to a mere 250,000 in 1260. Some estimate that fully half of Russia's population died as a result of the Mongol conquests. Fra Giovanni

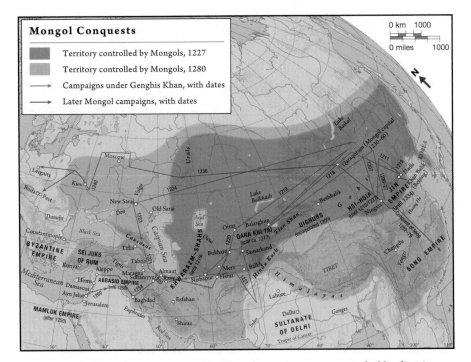

MAP 11.6 The Mongol Conquests The Mongol conquests were among the bloodiest in human history. Within China alone, the Mongols under Genghis Khan killed 20 million people. His successors did their best to equal those numbers as they tore through central Asia, Russia, Persia, and the Middle East.

di Pian Carpini, an eyewitness to the destruction of the Russian capital city of Kiev, described it this way:

> When the Mongols launched their next attack, upon Russia, they caused enormous destruction, leveling many cities and fortresses and butchering countless men. They besieged Kiev, the capital, for a long time—and when they finally took it they put to death nearly everyone living in it. When my companions and I traveled through that area, we saw the skulls and bones of innumerable corpses lying everywhere on the ground. Kiev at one time had been a large and densely populated city, but now it hardly exists at all—a mere two hundred homes still stand, and every one of their inhabitants has been reduced to slavery. (*History of the Mongols*)

Mongol Rule

The Mongols had little interest in actual governance; they left most of the peoples under their control free to live according to their traditional laws and customs, provided that they sent taxes and tribute whenever asked and obeyed without question any new law that the khans decreed. The Mongols understood the significance of trade, however, and were scrupulous about awarding and enforcing safe-passage guarantees to merchants (who paid handsomely for them). Beyond this, however, they showed no real concern for administration, relying instead on massive violent retribution against any group who resisted Mongol authority to keep peace and order. Time and again, they slaughtered entire towns and villages, punishing collectively any infraction committed by anyone. Merchants and travelers moving across Asia commented repeatedly on the tranquility and order they saw everywhere throughout the Mongol-controlled continent, but as Fra Giovanni recognized in the ruins of Kiev, the tranquility was really the paralysis of brutalized people.

IN THE WAKE OF THE MONGOLS

Mongol Successor States

The Mongols began to fight among themselves after the death of Genghis's grandson Kublai Khan (r. 1260–1294), and the enormous territory they held broke into a number of smaller although still considerable states. The most important of these were the Khanate of the Golden Horde, which dominated the southern Russian steppe; the Il-Khanate, which ruled over most of the previously Persian-controlled part of the Islamic Empire; the Chagatai Khanate, which controlled central Asia; and the Yuan dynasty in China, which held nominal leadership over all the Mongol realms from its capital in Beijing (see Map 11.7).

Numerous Western states and individual rulers attempted to forge some sort of peaceful relations with the Mongols. Louis IX of France famously sent an

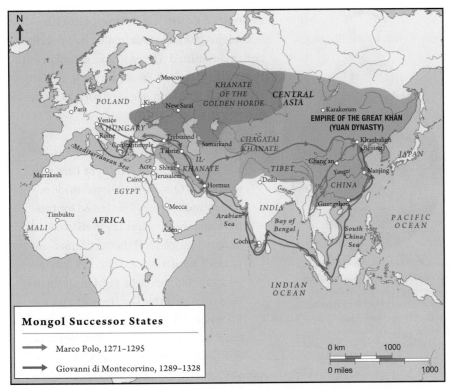

N

Mongol Successor States

→ Marco Polo, 1271–1295

→ Giovanni di Montecorvino, 1289–1328

0 km _____ 1000
0 miles _____ 1000

MAP 11.7 The Mongol Successor States   The Mongols were warriors, not statesmen, and their vast conquests quickly broke up into a patchwork of separate khanates held together by brute force—much as had occurred in the wake of Alexander the Great's conquests in the 4th century BCE (see Map 5.3).

emissary to Batu Khan (r. 1227–1255), khan of the Golden Horde, congratulating him on his conquests and offering to bestow those lands on him officially in return for Batu's conversion to Christianity, pledge to become Louis's vassal, and payment of an annual tribute. Batu responded that he would teach Louis a lesson by burning Paris down around his ears.

Nonetheless, because the Mongols were willing to deal with Westerners, one effect of their conquests was to open China to European travelers for the first time. The most famous of these travelers was Marco Polo (1254–1324), a Venetian merchant who claimed to have spent twenty years in the court of Kublai Khan—"claimed" because not all scholars agree that Marco Polo actually made it to China. Nonetheless, the account of his travels stimulated other Europeans to seek out the fabulous riches of the East. Christopher Columbus's copy of *The Travels of Marco Polo* still survives.

Among the first travelers from the West were teams of Franciscan missionaries sent by the church with the optimistic charge of converting the great khans to Christianity. One of these was Fra Giovanni di Montecorvino (1247–1328), who

The Opening of China to the West

A Mongol Passport The court of the Mongol ruler Kublai Khan (r. 1260–1294) issued this engraved safe-conduct pass, which guaranteed its bearer safety while traveling through the Mongol lands. The inscription reads: "By the strength of Eternal Heaven, an edict of the khan. He who has not re-spect [for the bearer of the passport] shall be guilty."

established a church at Beijing, built a Christian school for 150 slave children he had purchased and manumitted (freed), and translated the Psalms and the whole of the New Testament into Tartar for them. He sent back to Rome an extraordinary letter:

> I, Fra Giovanni di Montecorvino, set out from the city of Tauris, in Persia, in the year of Our Lord 1291 and made my way to India, where I remained for thirteen months . . . and baptized about a hundred people. . . . I then continued my journey until I made it all the way to [China], the realm of the Great Khan who rules over the Tartars and to whom I presented the letter of our Holy Father the Pope, inviting him to adopt the Catholic faith of Our Lord Jesus Christ. The Khan is too set in his idolatrous ways to change, although I must record that he has extended great friendship to us Christians in the years I have been living here in his realm. . . . I have built a church in [Beijing], where the Khan has his chief residence, . . . and in this church I have baptized some six

Papal Gift to the Great Khan   This is a copy of a now-lost original painting by Zhou Lang in 1342, depicting the arrival of a gift horse from Pope Benedict XII (r. 1334–1342) to the last Mongol ruler of China, Shundi (r. 1333–1370). The gift was brought to the Chinese court by a Franciscan emissary named Fra Giovanni di Marignolli (ca. 1290–1360).

thousand people, as near as I can reckon. . . . I believe it is possible that, if I had had two or three comrades to aid me, the Khan himself might have been baptized by now, and for this reason I beg that if any friars are willing to come this far and dedicate themselves to so great a task . . . then they will come. . . .

It has been twelve years since I had any news of the papal court, our Franciscan order, or the general goings-on in Europe. Two years ago a fellow from Lombardy came here—a surgeon—and spread the most vicious rumors about the papal court and other matters [Fra Giovanni refers here to Boniface's humiliation by Philip IV at Anagni], but since these blasphemies are too horrible to be true I beg to hear the truth and pray that my fellow Franciscans, to whom I address this letter, do all they can to bring my request to Our Holy Father the Pontiff. . . . As for myself, I have grown old and gray; even though I am only fifty-eight, toil and trouble have aged me. I have acquired a working knowledge of the language and script used by the Tartars, and have already translated the New Testament and the Psalter for them. . . . To the best of my knowledge there is no king or prince anywhere in the world who can compare to the Great Khan in terms of the vastness of his realm, the number of his subjects, or his wealth. But here I must now stop.

[Beijing], the eighth of January, in the year of Our Lord 1305.

Two years later, Pope Clement V (r. 1305–1317) appointed Giovanni the archbishop of Beijing and sent him the assistants he had requested.

PERSIA UNDER THE IL-KHANS

The Mongols were themselves shamanistic, meaning that they followed tribal spiritual leaders who were in contact with the spirit world and worked as miracle healers. The Tartars who succeeded them were generally tolerant of other religions and did little to hinder the development of either Christianity or Islam. There were, of course, exceptions. One early emir (prince) of Il-Khan Persia (modern-day Iraq and Iran), Nawruz (d. 1297), issued a decree:

> All [Christian] churches shall be torn down, their altars destroyed, and all celebrations of the Eucharist shall cease; moreover all hymns of praise and ringing of bells to call Christians to prayer shall be abolished. I decree too that the leaders of all Christian and Jewish congregations shall be killed.

Il-Khan Rule and Culture

But although several prominent Mongols did convert to Christianity, Islam was far more successful in spreading its message among not only the Mongols themselves but also their tributary peoples. Since the arrival of the Seljuk Turks in the 11th century, a significant number of Muslims were Turkish speaking. This gave the Muslims a considerable advantage in proselytizing, because the long history of interaction between the Turks and Mongols had fostered widespread understanding of their respective languages. Moreover, groups of Turks had traditionally been among the Mongols' chief steppe allies in the occasional confederations of tribes that formed and dissolved over the centuries. Mahmoud Ghazan (r. 1295–1304), ruler of the Il-Khan kingdom in Persia, converted to Shi'a Islam—probably as a political move. (Rumor had it that he continued to practice shamanism privately.) He then declared Islam the official religion of the state.

A few cultural and intellectual highlights stand out in the Il-Khan period. Rashid ad-Din Hamadani (1247–1318) was a physician and historian; his encyclopedic *Jami al-Tawarikh* (*Compendium of Chronicles*) is one of the greatest of medieval world histories. Hafez Shirazi (1325–1390) is perhaps the best loved of all Persian poets to the present day; his lyrical verses praise the beauty of the human form in language reminiscent of religious mysticism. Scholars in Il-Khan Persia also translated Chinese medical texts, and artists perfected blue-and-white ornamental tile work.

The Il-Khan rulers never enjoyed much popularity with the peoples of Iraq and Iran, however. Turkish gradually replaced Mongolian as the official court language, and Turks and Mongols held the supreme political and fiscal offices. Ethnic Persians, however, continued to make up the bulk of the civil administration throughout Iraq and Iran. Too much of Il-Khan policy was aimed at diverting wealth into Mongol hands for there to be any popular base to their power. After 1335 there

Tamerlane on His Throne   There is no universal Islamic prohibition against representational art; rather, there is a general, ethnically Arab aversion to it. The Persian and Turkish artistic traditions embraced representational art from the start. Here we see Tamerlane (r. 1370–1405) receiving an audience of nobles and courtiers on the occasion of his accession to the throne in Samarkand, in eastern Iran. This image comes from the *Zafarnama* ("Book of Victory"), a history of Tamerlane by Sharaf ad-Din Ali Yazdi, a 15th-century Persian writer.

were no more Mongols in charge, since the Il-Khan line died out; this triggered a long series of civil wars between petty emirs. Adding to Persia's troubles, a new dynasty in China—the Ming—came to power, conquered Mongolia, and cut off the silk routes across central Asia. Persia's economy consequently went into a tailspin.

Another Tartar warlord, around 1400, named Timur the Lame, or **Tamerlane** (r. 1370–1405), briefly terrorized Iraq and Iran while trying to reestablish Tartar supremacy. Historians often refer to him as the final Mongol emperor. Tamerlane cut a huge swath of destruction: Baghdad, Delhi, Isfahan (where he notoriously ordered forty thousand citizens beheaded and had a pyramid made of their skulls), Aleppo, Damascus, and Iznik. He burned mosques, schools, and libraries everywhere he went, ordered all Christian churches torn down, and rounded up all the most skilled artisans and deported them to his own capital at Samarkand, where they were forced to finish their lives constructing palaces and monuments in his honor. No one mourned his passing, and it would take many generations for Iraq and Iran, already smarting from earlier Mongol atrocities, to recover from the damage he had inflicted on them.

Reign of Tamerlane

The Mamluk Sultanate

A NEW CENTER FOR ISLAM

The Turkish-led Mamluk Sultanate largely escaped the catastrophic violence of the Mongols. And so it became, for 250 years, a stronghold of western Islamic civilization. Stretching from modern-day Libya and Egypt on the African coast to northern Syria, the Mamluk Sultanate centered on the great cities of Alexandria, Cairo, Jerusalem, Damascus, Antioch, and Aleppo (see Map 11.8). It lasted through two distinct periods: the Bahri (1250–1382) and the Burji (1382–1517).

The **sultan** was a military officer, a general in chief, and the position was therefore determined by the army. Most sultans in fact gained office by selection

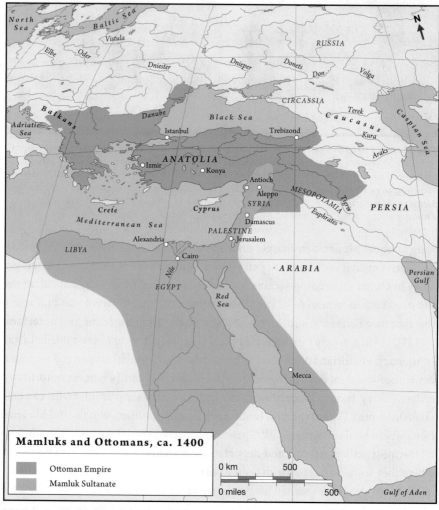

Mamluks and Ottomans, ca. 1400

- Ottoman Empire
- Mamluk Sultanate

0 km   500

0 miles   500

MAP 11.8   Mamluks and Ottomans, ca. 1400   With the Tartars entrenched farther to the east, the Mamluks and Ottomans divided the western Islamic world between them.

from the leading generals. A few sultans did attempt to pass their position on to
their sons, but usually the heirs were ousted by rival generals. The Bahri and the
Burji were both foreigners to the region. The Bahri sultans were Kipchak Turks,
an ancient people who had originated in Siberia and slowly migrated westward,
reaching the Middle East around 1050, where they found employment in the
highly disciplined ranks of the Mamluk soldiery. The Burji, by contrast, were
ethnic Circassians, an obscure group from the Caucasus Mountain region who
spoke Turkish in addition to their ancestral Adyghe language. (The name *Circassian* comes from the Turkish for "people from the Caucasus.") Both periods were
characterized by short-lived sultanates: twenty-seven reigns in the Bahri era (an
average of four years apiece) and twenty-six in the Burji (an average of a little
more than five years apiece).

Islam had been an international multiethnic religion since the late 7th century, but political, religious, and social authority had been monopolized for more
than six hundred years by just two groups, Arabs and Persians. The rise of the
Mongols and Turks not only shattered those monopolies but also drove the long-
ruling societies into secondary status in their own homelands. They would not
fully emerge from the political shadows until the 20th century. Moreover,
Mamluk rule, occasioned as it was by military force, relied on force to sustain
itself.[4] The atmosphere of violence both colored and contributed to a sense of
failed jihad. The crusaders had been driven from the Holy Land in 1291, it is true,
but Islam as a geopolitical force was in retreat. The Christian Reconquista in
Spain gained pace through the 13th and 14th centuries, and the survival of
Constantinople continued to rankle because Muslims had been trying to take
the city for nearly seven hundred years. The great capital city of Baghdad had also
been flattened. And the advance of the Mongols, some of whom had nominally
converted to Islam, did nothing to slow the spread of Orthodox Christianity among
the peoples of Russia and the Balkans, whom they dominated politically for
several centuries.

In the Mamluk state, therefore, a concerted effort to restore a strong, authoritarian Islam continued. This was ironic, since many of the Mamluks—from some
of the sultans down to the common soldiers—were Muslim in name only. Many
soldiers never even bothered to learn to speak Arabic and regarded Arabs and
Egyptians alike with disdain. In this regard, they resembled the supposedly
Muslim Il-Khan ruling class in Persia, and, being largely uncommitted to religion
in general, they thereby acquired reputations for religious tolerance that are not
quite deserved.

---

[4] More than half of the Mamluk rulers were assassinated or executed after mostly sham trials. More than
half of the remainder were forcibly deposed or resigned under threat of deposition.

The greatest of the Mamluk rulers was the first: Baibars (r. 1260–1277), who famously crushed the Seventh crusade led by Louis IX, defeated the Mongols at 'Ayn Jalut in 1260, and recaptured the city of Antioch in 1268—a victory that sealed the ultimate defeat of the remaining crusader states. He also perfected what became the distinctive Mamluk system of granting lands to officers and soldiers in return for their military service. Rather like the network of feudal relations in Latin Europe, only stripped of Europe's complex system of social and constitutional obligations, this system left common farmers at the mercy of their Mamluk overlords. By 1300 or so, fully one-half of whatever revenues each lord raised was owed to the sultan, which guaranteed him sufficient funds to keep adding new slaves to the army. Fortunately for the sultan, much of the spice trade from east Asia had been rerouted to avoid the Mongols and

Mamluk Decorative Lamps   These lamps date to the first half of the 14th century and are made of enameled glass. They were produced in the Mamluk Empire, which then was composed of Egypt, Palestine, and Syria. The inscription reads that they were created in honor of Sultan Badr ad-Din al-Hasan, who ruled the area at the time when the Black Death hit.

came instead by ship around the Arabian peninsula and up through the Red Sea, thus entering Egyptian markets directly. Therefore, the Mamluk Sultanate remained extraordinarily wealthy, although the bulk of the wealth was monopolized by the ruling elite.

With so much wealth at their disposal, the Mamluk sultans did more than expand their armies: they also patronized art in intentionally showy but often brilliant ways. Sumptuously woven textiles and carpets became a hallmark of their courts (and highly prized commodities among the European well-to-do). Their palaces were showcases for decorative glass, enameled lamps and statuary, exquisite ironwork, and libraries filled with books of fabulously ornate calligraphy and jeweled bindings. Moreover, the Mamluks built scores of new mosques and madrasas (religious schools) and bestowed lavish endowments on them. The Mamluks had a particular enthusiasm for Sufism—which, as discussed in chapter 10, the bulk of Sunnis had difficulty reconciling themselves to—and brought hundreds of Sufi masters and thousands of Sufi texts into their realm.

In a conservative reaction against Mamluk ostentation and support of Sufism, the most vigorous intellectual life under the Mamluks was found among the Arabs, Egyptians, Kurds, and Syrians who smarted under the new regime. The most influential thinker of the era was Ibn Taymiyyah (1263–1328), a prolific legal scholar whose works urged a return to the stripped-down essentials of Islam, insisted on conservative readings of the Qur'an and *hadith*, and raged against the dangerous influence of Sufism. (One of his favorite words to describe Sufism was *bid'a*—"reckless innovation" or even "newfangled nonsense.") Taymiyyah insisted on the Qur'an's absolute authority and rejected any efforts to interpret its meanings apart from the most literal and exact. Although trained in *kalam* (theology) and philosophy, he rejected speculative thought as fundamentally un-Islamic and called for all Muslims to adhere to jihad against all the enemies of the faith—among whom he included the Mongols and the Shi'a. He also called on Muslims to reject the cult of Islamic saints, which he regarded as an impious absorption of Christian practice.[5] And perhaps most significantly for later centuries, he ardently championed the restoration of ethnic Arab leadership over international Islam.

Conservatism and Reaction

The Black Death decimated the Islamic world just as it did the European world, and the Mamluk Sultanate never fully recovered from the blow. In Cairo alone, as many as forty thousand people perished. When the Burji regime replaced the Bahri in 1382, they made factionalism even worse by purging the Turkish elite and installing their Circassian fellows, through whom they ordered

---

[5]   "Many of these saints' venerators do not even know that this is a practice derived from the Christians. May Christianity and its followers be accursed!" (*Kitab Iqtada*).

even heavier taxation of the common populace. The Burji likewise earned well-deserved reputations for graft and corruption that further alienated them from their subjects in Egypt and Syria. But so long as the Mamluk military machine stood supreme, there was little anyone could do about them.

By 1500, however, two things had occurred that brought Mamluk power to an end. First, Portuguese explorers had rounded the African continent and interjected themselves into the spice and silk trade coming out of India, thus depriving the Mamluks of desperately needed revenue. Second, the Ottoman Turks, whose enthusiastic embrace of gunpowder and cannons gave them a clear tactical advantage over all rivals, challenged Mamluk control of Syria and Palestine with an assault on Aleppo. This gained, the Turks pressed farther southward, taking all of Syria in less than a year and in early 1517 capturing Cairo itself, putting an end to the Mamluk era. The establishment of Ottoman power inaugurated Islam's modern era.

THE OTTOMAN TURKS

The **Ottoman Turks** (tribal cousins of the Seljuk Turks of two centuries earlier) had arrived in force in the late 13th century, under their charismatic leader Osman (r. 1281–1324). No one would have predicted it, but the Ottoman regime gave the Islamic world its lengthiest, most stable, and most prosperous rule. To a certain extent, they had the Mongols to thank for that. The Mongols' devastation had been so vast, and their extortion of wealth afterward so extensive, that Iraq and Iran required at least a century to recover. Meanwhile, the realm of the Seljuk Turks, who had dominated most of Anatolia since their victory over the Byzantines at Manzikert in 1071, had broken up into a sprawl of warring principalities, which the Ottomans were then able to pick off one at a time. The turning point was a severe defeat inflicted on the Seljuks by the Mongols in 1243 at Köse Dağ in northeastern Anatolia.

Ottoman Expansion and Consolidation   In 1453 the Ottomans under their leader **Mehmed II** (r. 1451–1481) achieved what Muslim armies had dreamt of since the 7th century—the conquest of Constantinople, capital of Byzantium. Only the Mamluks, far to the south, rivaled the might of the Ottomans (see Map 11.8). By 1500 even the Mamluks were in retreat, leaving the Ottomans as undisputed leaders of the Islamic world, a position they held until they finally fell from power in the aftermath of World War I. Through most of its long history, the Ottoman Empire comprised most of North Africa, the Hijaz (that is, the western coastal strip of Arabia including the holy cities of Mecca and Madina), Palestine, Mesopotamia, Syria, Anatolia, the Balkans, Hungary, and the Crimea. This was an area larger than the Byzantine Empire had ever been.

They had the advantage of arriving on the scene in the late 13th century when everyone else but the Mamluks were weakening. Under the Seljuks, much of the Greek Orthodox and Armenian Christian populations had been driven off the land by the Turkish leaders' need to award land parcels to their soldiers. Unattached Turkish frontier warriors and mercenaries (called

THE OTTOMAN EMPIRE AT ITS GREATEST EXTENT

ghazis, in Turkish) made things worse, massacring and enslaving Christians in roughly equal numbers in the 12th and early 13th centuries. Famines and disease took care of much of the rest. By the time the Ottomans came to power, the Turks' scorched-earth policies had emptied most of the Anatolian countryside. Many of the displaced Christians relocated to the Balkan and Black Sea territories, where the Byzantines still exercised some control, whereas town dwellers preferred to emigrate into Latin Europe, especially Italy. Those Christians who remained faced punitive taxation and various forms of social discrimination, and occasionally some entire villages converted to gain a sounder footing under the new regime. By 1300 Anatolia was overwhelmingly Muslim, and the Ottomans responded by building hundreds of new mosques, madrasas, and hospitals—even temporary housing for new converts, as a means of instructing them in Islamic customs.

The Ottomans had an even stronger enthusiasm for Sufism than the Seljuks had, and they consequently brought in Sufi preachers in huge numbers. The Sufis bore special responsibility for converting the remaining Christians, which they did by emphasizing a kind of religious syncretism not seen since Roman times. Sufi sermons drew direct parallels between the biblical twelve apostles and the twelve Shi'i imams; others presented Allah, Muhammad, and Ali as an Islamic Trinity. The way had been prepared for these preachers by earlier figures like the great Sufi poet Jalal ad-Din Muhammad Balkhi (1207–1273), better known in the West as **Rumi**, who penned thousands of verses, a number of sermons, and a famous collection of letters. Although he was a strict Muslim, Rumi's poetry frequently aimed at an ecumenical appeal:

> In search of Allah I ventured among the Christians and looked upon the Cross,
> But I did not find Him there;
> I entered pagan temples and looked upon the idols,
> But I did not find Him there.
> I explored the mountain cave at Hira [the site of Muhammad's first Qur'anic revelation]
> And even went as far as Kandahar, but I did not find Him there.
> So I made up my mind to climb to the top of Mount Caucasus,

> But there I found only a phoenix's nest.
> Turning around, I set out for the holy Ka'ba, the refuge of young
>   and old,
> But I did not find Him even there.
> Trying philosophy next, I looked for insight in the writings of Ibn Sina,
> But I did not find Him there. . . .
> Finally, at last, I looked in my own heart, and found Him;
> He had been there all along. (Quatrain 1173)

Rumi's writings champion Islam without disparaging other faiths. His approach seemed too gentle to many of his contemporaries, especially those Sunnis who were ill at ease with Sufi emotionalism. Yet the beauty of his poetry secured him an avid readership that lasts to the present day. Another Turkish poet, Yunus Emre (1240–1321), likewise excelled at combining the language and imagery of mystical spirituality and earthly delight. The appearance of such poets, and their immediate and enduring popularity, parallel the European development of its vernacular literatures.

The unsettled nature of much Muslim life, as the Il-Khans plundered Iraq and Iran and as the Muslims in Spain confronted the Reconquista, meant a continuous flow of immigrants into the Ottoman lands. Judges, theologians, engineers, and civil bureaucrats, as well as farmers and artisans, poured into the region in large numbers. This influx of skilled labor and administrative talent enabled Ottoman society to stabilize quickly as a developed economic and political entity. And the Byzantine collapse opened Thrace, Macedonia, and the Balkans to Turkish expansion too. Under Murad I (r. 1359–1389) the Turkish army added most of Bulgaria to the Ottoman domain as well, although Murad himself died shortly thereafter in battle against the Serbs at Kosovo. In formalizing the peace accord after the fray, a prominent Serb princess married Murad's son and heir, Bayezid I; the union was reportedly an unusually happy one. Even more significantly, Serbian forces promptly joined up with Bayezid and helped him to attack Bosnia, Herzegovina, and parts of Hungary.

The stronger the Ottomans became, however, the more suspicious of them the Mongol Il-Khans in Persia and the Mamluks in Egypt grew. The popularity of Sufism among the Turks, and its sometimes troubling ecumenical traces, added to the popular hostility toward them. Bayezid I (r. 1389–1403) went so far as to name his first three sons Musa (Moses), Issa (Jesus), and Mehmed (Muhammad), which was beyond the pale in most Sunni eyes. When the Ottoman rulers, mimicking the Mamluks, formed their own personal bodyguard of slave-soldiers, called **Janissaries** (after the Turkish *yeniçeri*, meaning "new soldier"), they conscripted Greek Christian boys to supplement Turkish recruits, a practice known

The Conquest of Constantinople   This fresco on the outer wall of a Byzantine church, painted around 1537, depicts the 1453 siege of the city led by Sultan Mehmed II (r. 1451–1481). The massive cannons used by the Ottomans to break the defenses had been forged in Hungary by the ironworkers' guild, in hopes that the Turks would settle for Constantinople and leave the Hungarians alone. They were wrong.

as *devshirme*. Although these boys were raised as Muslims, the Mongols and Mamluks used the makeup of the Janissary corps as further evidence of the Ottomans' weak commitment to Islam and justification for their own attacks on the state.

Despite those attacks, the Turks entered the 15th century as the clear leaders of international Islam. Turkish replaced Arabic and Persian as the language of diplomacy, and ethnic Turks filled the upper ranks of the civil and military hierarchies. When Constantinople was finally taken in 1453, it was renamed Istanbul ("the city") and established as the new capital of the Turkish state. The choice was doubly symbolic: not only did the Islamic world itself now stand triumphant over the Byzantines, but also the Ottomans, unlike all earlier Muslim leaders, took up residence in the very city that straddled Asia and Europe. Islam would henceforth be a civilization on two fronts, facing both east and west, rooted in the faith that arose from Arabia but as much involved in Western ways as in Eastern. It was no coincidence that what enabled the great sultan Mehmed II to finally achieve the conquest of Constantinople was his use of massive cannons that had been forged for him by engineers in Hungary. It was an Eastern army with Western technology.

The New Capital of Istanbul

The dominant spirit of the age, before the catastrophes of the 14th century, was a willingness, a confident willingness, to question the values of society and state—not necessarily to challenge or undermine them but to express a conviction in progress, a belief that human experience and understanding not only change but also move forward with time. When that faith in progress confronted the devastations of the 14th century, however, the collapse of old certainties left behind it an overwhelming sense of loss and bewilderment. No one could have predicted that the crises of the 14th century would spark one of the greatest periods of cultural achievement in European history, the Renaissance.

WHO, WHAT, WHERE

Avignon Papacy	Hundred Years' War	Ottoman Turks
Black Death	inquisition	Parliament
chivalry	Janissaries	Rumi
Diet	Joan of Arc	scholasticism
English Peasants' Revolt	Magna Carta	sultan
Estates General	Mehmed II	Tamerlane
Genghis (Chinggis) Khan	mendicant orders	
guild	Mongols	

SUGGESTED READINGS

Primary Sources

Anonymous. *The Secret History of the Mongols.*

Alighieri, Dante. *The Divine Comedy.*

del Carpine, Giovanni Pian. *History of the Mongols.*

Froissart, Jean. *Chronicles.*

Ibn Battuta. *Travels.*

Ibn Khaldun. *The Muqaddimah.*

Ibn Taymiyya. *Following the Straight Path.*

Ibn Taymiyya. *The Goodly Word.*

Kempe, Margery. *The Book of Margery Kempe.*

Pizan, Christine de. *The Book of the City of Ladies.*

Rumi. *Complete Poems.*

Anthologies

Aberth, John. *The Black Death: The Great Mortality of 1348–1350; A Brief History with Documents* (2005).

Avery, Peter. *The Collected Lyrics of Hafiz of Shiraz* (2007).

Dean, Trevor, trans. *The Towns of Italy in the Later Middle Ages* (2000).

Doss-Quinby, Eglal, Joan Tasker Grimbert, Wendy Pfeffer, and Elizabeth Aubrey, eds.

and trans. *Songs of the Women Trouvères* (2001).

Massoud, Sami G. *The Chronicles and Annalistic Sources of the Early Mamluk Circassian Period* (2007).

Murray, Jacqueline, ed. *Love, Marriage, and the Family in the Middle Ages: A Reader* (2001).

Studies

Aberth, John. *From the Brink of the Apocalypse: Confronting Famine, War, Plague, and Death in the Later Middle Ages* (2001).

Allsen, Thomas T. *Culture and Conquest in Mongol Eurasia* (2001).

Amitai-Preiss, Reuven. *Mongols and Mamluks: The Mamluk–Īlkhānid War of 1260–1281* (2005).

Arnold, John. *Inquisition and Power: Catharism and the Confessing Subject in Medieval Languedoc* (2001).

Beckwith, Christopher I. *Empires of the Silk Road: A History of Central Eurasia from the Bronze Age to the Present* (2010).

Blumenfeld-Kosinski, Renate. *Poets, Saints, and Visionaries of the Great Schism, 1378–1417* (2006).

Cahen, Claude. *The Formation of Turkey: The Seljukid Sultanate of Rūm; 11th to 14th Century* (2001).

Clark, Victoria. *Why Angels Fall: A Journey through Orthodox Europe from Byzantium to Kosovo* (2000).

Cohn, Samuel K., Jr. *Lust for Liberty: The Politics of Social Revolt in Medieval Europe, 1200–1425; Italy, France, and Flanders* (2006).

Dunn, Alastair. *The Peasants' Revolt: England's Failed Revolution of 1381* (2004).

Dyer, Christopher. *Making a Living in the Middle Ages: The People of Britain, 850–1520* (2003).

El-Cheik, Nadia Maria. *Byzantium Viewed by the Arabs* (2004).

Finkel, Caroline. *Osman's Dream: The History of the Ottoman Empire* (2007).

Goffman, Daniel. *The Ottoman Empire and Early Modern Europe* (2002).

Imber, Colin. *The Ottoman Empire, 1300–1650: The Structure of Power* (2009).

Inalcik, Halil. *The Ottoman Empire: The Classical Age, 1300–1600* (2001).

Inalcik, Halil, and Donald Quataert, eds. *An Economic and Social History of the Ottoman Empire* (2005).

Komaroff, Linda, and Stefano Carboni. *The Legacy of Genghis Khan: Courtly Art and Culture in Western Asia, 1256–1353* (2002).

Leopold, Antony. *How to Recover the Holy Land: Crusading Proposals of the Late Thirteenth and Early Fourteenth Centuries* (2000).

Liu, Xinru. *The Silk Road in World History* (2010).

Pegg, Mark Gregory. *The Corruption of Angels: The Great Inquisition of 1245–1246* (2001).

Rouighi, Ramzi. *The Making of a Mediterranean Emirate: Ifrīqiyā and Its Andalusis, 1200–1400* (2011).

Rubin, Miri. *Gentile Tales: The Narrative Assault on Late Medieval Jews* (2004).

Sumption, Jonathan. *The Hundred Years War* (2000–2011).

For additional resources, including maps, primary sources, visuals, web links, and quizzes, please go to **www.oup.com/us/backman**.

TEMPLA DOMVM EXPOSITIS·VICOS·FORA·MOENIA·PONTES:
VIRGINEAM TRIVII QVOD REPARARIS·AQVAM·
PRISCA LICET·NAVTIS·STATVAS·DARE·COMMODA·PORTVS:
ET VATICANVM·CINGERE·SIXTE·IVGVM:
PLVS TAMEN VRBS·DEBET·NAM·QVAE·SQVALORE·LATEBAT:

Renaissances and Reformations

1350–1563

Pope Sixtus IV Sixtus IV (r. 1471–1484) is remembered for building the Sistine Chapel, establishing the Spanish Inquisition, and developing the Vatican Library. Record collection had long been professionalized in the papal court; in fact, references to standing administrative offices with bureaucratic support date back to the 6th century, but a formal library was another matter. Sixtus saw the need for a centralized permanent collection of the church's manuscripts. Pope Nicholas V (r. 1447–1455) was the library's actual founder, but Sixtus greatly expanded and reorganized it and also made it available to scholars. Sixtus was a Franciscan, one of the last of his order to hold the papacy, but quickly became enamored of the pomp and splendor of the Renaissance court. He appointed a half-dozen of his nephews to the College of Cardinals, including Giuliano della Rovere—the tall figure in the center—who later became Pope Julius II (r. 1503–1513), the target of Erasmus's great satire *Julius Excluded from Heaven*.

THE GREATER WEST, ca. 1550

The Renaissance, the period in Europe roughly from 1350 to 1550, is one of the few eras in Greater Western history that named itself. The cultural elite of the time believed they were living in an age of self-conscious revival. They were bringing back to life the ideas, moral values, art, and civic-mindedness that characterized, they believed, the two high points of Western culture: Periclean Athens and Republican Rome. One of the first to use the term was the Italian writer, painter, and architect Giorgio Vasari (1511–1574). After a thousand years of medieval barbarism, Vasari claimed, Italian artists and thinkers had bravely restored the lost perfection of art and philosophy as known to the ancients. An earlier Renaissance writer on education, Pier Paolo Vergerio (1370–1444), insisted that only the study of the classical liberal arts could lift society from the moral and spiritual decay of the medieval era. "Only those liberal arts," he proclaimed, "are worthy of free men; they alone can help us to attain virtue and wisdom ... [and fill in the gaps in our moral knowledge] which the ignorance of the past centuries has intentionally created."

Una rinascità was a "rebirth" of classical values that gave fresh hope and creative energy to Europe. It also led to the greatest eruption in Greater Western religion since the birth of Islam—the Protestant Reformation.

REBIRTH OR CULMINATION?

Not everyone in the Renaissance shared Vasari's and Vergerio's sense of the near-mythic magnificence of antiquity, and it took some time for the French version of the word rinascità, renaissance, to catch on. It did not acquire positive connotations until the English writer John Ruskin (1819–1900) used it in his famous study of architecture, The Stones of Venice (1851): "This rationalistic art is the art called Renaissance, marked by a return to pagan systems" (1.1.23). Most of Vergerio's and Vasari's contemporaries were simply grateful to have been born after the filthy muddle of the Middle Ages. Francesco Petrarch (1304–1374), usually regarded as the father of humanism and the first Renaissance writer, expressed this nostalgia for the deep past of Rome and Athens. In an open letter written toward the end of his life, called the Letter to Posterity, he recalls his youthful studies:

CHAPTER TIMELINE

1300	1330	1360	1390	1420

■ 1304–1374 Petrarch

■ 1434 Cosimo de' Medici assumes power in Florence

I had more of a well-rounded mind than a keen intellect, and was naturally inclined to every type of virtuous and honorable study but especially to moral philosophy and poetry. After a while, it is true, I began to neglect poetry in favor of sacred literature, in which I soon found a buried sweetness that I had previously acknowledged to be there but only in a perfunctory way; now however I found its sweetness so great that poetry became a mere afterthought for me. Out of all the subjects that intrigued me, I fixed especially upon antiquity—for the truth is that our own age repels me and has always done so. Indeed, were it not for the love of those I hold dear, I would rather have been born in any age but our own. I have spent most of my life thinking about other eras, in fact, as a way of ignoring my own, and that is why I have always loved the study of history.

However, the Renaissance—or the early part of it, anyway—shared more with its preceding age than it wanted to admit. The three elements most characteristically associated with the Renaissance—classicism, humanism, and modern statecraft—represent no essential break with medieval life at all. They may in fact be thought of as the culmination of medieval strivings.

The cult of classical learning and literature had its origins in early Christian monastic life. Novice monks had long been directed to study the Roman poets *Classicism* Virgil and Horace, the historians Suetonius and Sallust, and the playwrights Terence and Seneca. It was their means to learn Latin before being granted access to

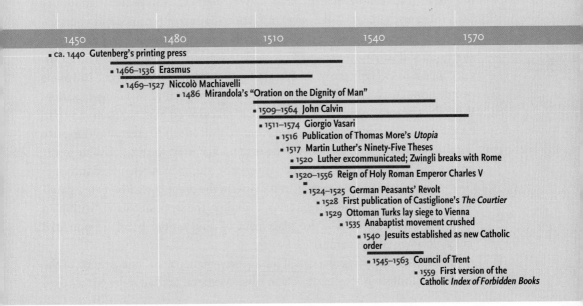

1450	1480	1510	1540	1570

- ca. 1440 **Gutenberg's printing press**
- 1466–1536 **Erasmus**
- 1469–1527 **Niccolò Machiavelli**
  - 1486 **Mirandola's "Oration on the Dignity of Man"**
- 1509–1564 **John Calvin**
- 1511–1574 **Giorgio Vasari**
  - 1516 **Publication of Thomas More's *Utopia***
  - 1517 **Martin Luther's Ninety-Five Theses**
  - 1520 **Luther excommunicated; Zwingli breaks with Rome**
- 1520–1556 **Reign of Holy Roman Emperor Charles V**
  - 1524–1525 **German Peasants' Revolt**
  - 1528 **First publication of Castiglione's *The Courtier***
  - 1529 **Ottoman Turks lay siege to Vienna**
  - 1535 **Anabaptist movement crushed**
  - 1540 **Jesuits established as new Catholic order**
- 1545–1563 **Council of Trent**
  - 1559 **First version of the Catholic *Index of Forbidden Books***

the scriptures and the patristic literature (the texts of the Church Fathers). The works of Aristotle, Ptolemy, Galen, and Euclid, moreover, had dominated university education from the start. But the great scholars of the Renaissance broadened this core canon by seeking out long-lost manuscripts; virtually anything by a classical author was of interest. Petrarch himself unearthed Cicero's *Letters to Atticus*, lying unused and unknown on a dusty library shelf in Verona for centuries, and brought out a new edition of it.

What distinguished the Renaissance approach to the classics was a passionate conviction that they contained all that humans have best thought and best expressed. It was simply impossible not merely to be educated but also to be a complete, satisfied, and accomplished human being without knowing the wisdom of the ancients. Pier Paolo Vergerio described the classical canon as "the only literature whose study helps us in the pursuit of virtue and wisdom, and brings forth in us those most sublime gifts of body and mind that ennoble men's spirit and that are properly regarded as second only to virtue itself as our most dignified attainment." Renaissance scholars traveled through scores of libraries and archives, sifted through piles of manuscripts, corrected the minutest scribal errors, and commented prolifically on the cultural context and multiple meanings of a writer's text. Moreover, these scholars put their learning to use in original works of their own, in every genre from poetry to stage drama, epistles to essays, histories to philosophical treatises.

Humanism   The concern in this period to develop human potential, to value the particular, and to assert the inherent dignity of each person is called **humanism**. The idea itself was not new, but the degree of emphasis placed on it was. The catastrophes of the 14th century had inspired many to doubt the values and assumptions of the high medieval era—the belief in a rationally ordered cosmos and a benevolent deity, the naturalness of a hierarchically structured society, the conviction that good will triumph over evil. The Black Death, after all, had shown no apparent concern to kill only the wicked, and the other calamities of the time had made people grow suspicious of accepted systems of thought and social organization. What does one do when everything a society takes for granted has been shown to be a sham? The world is a perilous place, denying all efforts to create anything like order or meaning. The best one can do is to find comfort, beauty, or value in the broken shards of the world scattered at one's feet. Humanism celebrated such specific pleasures: the precise arch of an eyebrow or the drape of a garment in a painting, the warm hue of sunlight entering a window, the sense of balance within an enclosure created by the artful placement of objects, the beautiful potential energy in a tensed coil of muscle.

A focus on the particular called for a representational art, one attuned to the hard but transitory reality of objects in time. Medieval art had more widely used

symbolic and allegorical representations. Starting with the
Florentine painter Giotto di
Bondone (1267–1337)—a generation before Petrarch—artists
strove for a more naturalistic,
three-dimensional style of depiction. By the early 1400s linear
perspective was introduced in
painting, heightening the senses
of depth, solidity, and realism the
artists evoked. The 1427 fresco of
the Holy Trinity painted for the
church of Santa Maria Novella in
Florence by Masaccio (1401–
1428) marked the maturity of
the new techniques.

Scholars in the Renaissance
still wrote in Latin, although
most of the creative literature of
the age was in the vernacular, or
local languages. This too reflected medieval practice, but
for a different reason. In the
Middle Ages, scholarship was
written in Latin because it was
the common tongue of the
learned. Physicians in Spain

The Holy Trinity (in Perspective)   The Italian artist Tommaso
Masaccio (1401–1428) painted this masterwork in the church of
Santa Maria Novella in Florence. It is among the first Renaissance
paintings to employ linear perspective, in which parallel lines are
represented as converging so as to give the illusion of depth and
distance. Above Christ's head appear the Holy Spirit, in the form of a
dove, and the head of God the Father. The man and woman shown in the
lower corners are presumably the patrons who commissioned the work.
Their clothing suggests that they were commoners rather than nobles.

could communicate with physicians in Hungary or Denmark; mathematicians in
England could be read in Portugal or Poland. In the Renaissance, however, scholars wrote in Latin (or sometimes in Greek) out of a conviction in the intrinsic superiority of the classical languages. Latin and Greek, in the "pure" forms used in
ancient times, were seen as uniquely capable of expressing complex thought.
Hence scholars sought to take the living Latin and Greek they had inherited and
purge them of what they considered barbarisms and corrupt usages. Words,
phrases, and grammatical constructions that came into use in the postclassical era
were avoided in the effort to return to the purity of ancient Latin. The results were
disastrous and effectively killed Latin as a living language. Imagine a demand
today to make Shakespearean English the only form of English worthy of public
discourse.

The most famous of Renaissance descriptions of humanism came from Giovanni Pico della Mirandola (1463–1494), a young man of great and varied learning. His "Oration on the Dignity of Man" (1486) lays out the fundamental elements of the movement:

> I read somewhere of a Muslim writer named Abdullah who, when asked to identify the most wondrous and awe-inspiring thing to appear on the world's stage, answered, "There exists nothing more wondrous than Man." . . .
>
> But when I began to consider the reasons behind these opinions, every particular of their arguments for the magnificence of human nature failed to persuade me.

The unconvincing arguments include man's existence as a rational creature or as master of the physical world. What strikes Pico della Mirandola as the essential and glorious point about humans is rather something else: to us alone has God given the freedom and ability to be whatever we want, to become whatever we desire, and to achieve whatever we wish. A flower has no choice but to bloom, wither, and die; a stone may serve as a building block, a projectile, or a hindrance in the road, but it has no destiny of its own, no yearning to become something. Humans alone, he insists, are free to be whatever we wish to be:

> You alone, being altogether without limits and in possession of your own free will, . . . have it within you to establish the limits of your own nature. . . . Alone at the dark center of his own existence, yet united with God, Who is Himself beyond all created things, Man too exists beyond every created thing—and who can help but stand in awe of this great Fate-forger? Even more: How is it possible for anyone to marvel at anything else?

To describe man as, essentially, his own creator was to flirt with heresy—and Mirandola did in fact run afoul of the church. Consequently he issued a number of corrections and retractions and announced his interest in becoming an obedient monk. He died suddenly at age thirty-one, however, poisoned by an enemy who had slipped arsenic into his wine. His fate should not distract us, however, from recognizing the fundamentally religious nature of humanism. Humanism was not a secular philosophy. It sought to define the place of humanity in God's divine plan, to parse the relationship between man and God, and so to glorify both.

The third major element of the Renaissance was statecraft. The concept of a

Statecraft   state is a relatively modern one. A state as a thing in itself, independent of the people who comprise it and following its own norms and rules, requires a degree of abstraction. Earlier notions of government had regarded the state as a network of personal relationships, but not necessarily as a distinct object. It had the king at the center, with his web of obligations and privileges to his nobles, his commoners, and the church. Exceptions to this model existed, of course, but until the 13th century they were in the minority.

Renaissance theorists and power brokers, taking their cue from late medieval writers like Brunetto Latini (1220–1294) and Marsiglio di Padova (1275–1342), thought of the state in a new way. The political state was a thing, a part of the natural world, and it functioned according to rules. Political leaders who understood this governed most effectively because they could direct the state by means of its own internal logic. Statecraft therefore involved understanding systems of law, taxation, and economy. It involved the intricacies of diplomacy and negotiation, the mechanisms of crowd control, the manipulation of public opinion, and the knowledge of when to deceive or to exert force. Idealism had no part in it, and

The Ambassadors   This powerful painting by Hans Holbein the Younger (ca. 1497–1543), *The Ambassadors*, depicts a French nobleman dispatched to London on a diplomatic errand, together with his friend, a French bishop. Together they represent the active and the contemplative modes of life, with objects representing knowledge, power, and art in the background. The diagonally oriented object in the foreground, when looked at obliquely, is a skull representing death.

politics became a hard science rather than an expression of personal desire. For that very reason, however, it offered the perfect site for educated men of the Renaissance. Conscious of their abilities and dedicated to the ancient Roman virtue of civic-mindedness, they could take their proper place within the world by mastering its rules and methods.

THE POLITICAL AND ECONOMIC MATRIX

Renaissance Roots in Urban Italy

Europe needed men of ability, Italy especially. Italy was by far the most developed urban society in Europe, followed closely by southern France and eastern Spain, yet its political scene was a mess. The northern city-states, where the Renaissance began, had long been under the leadership of the Holy Roman emperor, at least in name. Since the 10th century Holy Roman emperors had brought armies over or around the Alps, intermittently but repeatedly, to reassert their claims—and most of Italy's city-states opened their gates, bowed deeply, and paid their ritual and financial tribute. But once the armies were safely back in Germany, the Italians instantly returned to their independent republican ways.

By the start of the Renaissance many northern Italians wanted to end permanently the imperial claims over their territories. Others, however, saw some utility in the on-again, off-again imperial connection and so opposed autonomy. This scenario, in which the papacy became deeply involved, led to strife between and within each of the city-states. By the time of the 14th century's disasters, northern Italy was a mercenary's dreamscape. Wars large and small, palace coups, assassinations, plots, pillagings, enforced exiles, and institutional corruption had spread everywhere (see Map 12.1).

Political Transformation of Italian City-States

A unique feature of the Italian scene, however, helped pave the way for the Renaissance. Italian nobles tended to live within the cities, although their rural estates were distant, and hence they played an active role in urban culture that nobles in northern Europe did not. That included both established lineages and wealthy commoners whose riches had helped them purchase aristocratic titles. Moreover, the elitist bias against trade and commerce that characterized northern European aristocratic society was much less virulent in Italy. Hence, by 1400, ties (usually volatile) had developed between the urban aristocrats and the mercantile and banking families of the burgher class. This connection allowed the upper classes to usurp republican government and to institute direct, often-tyrannical control over the city-states. Most who did so, imitating the 1st-century emperor Augustus, maintained the fiction and rituals of republican government while establishing despotic rule.

Most city-states thus had actual, if barely functioning, republican governments between 1350 and 1450 (the first half, roughly, of the Renaissance) but oligarchic

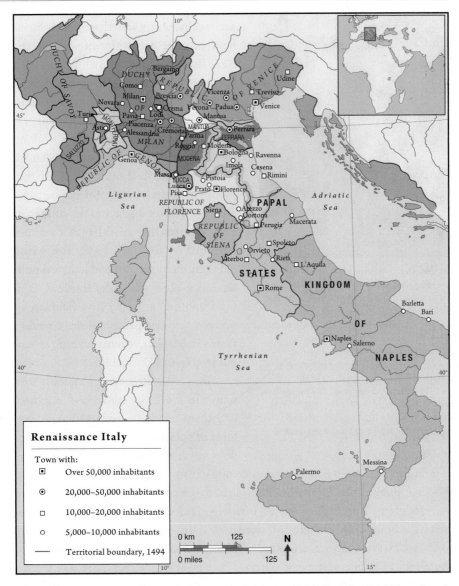

MAP 12.1   Renaissance Italy   The political map of Renaissance Italy differed little from that of medieval Italy: a large Kingdom of Naples in the south; the perennially embattled Papal States in the center, and a sprawling matrix of city-states in the north. Most humanistic activity took place in the north and in the court cities of Rome and Naples.

governments from 1450 to 1550 (the second half). In Florence, for example, the Medici family, which had risen through the ranks in banking and textiles, came to political prominence shortly after 1400. Through three generations—under Cosimo de' Medici (r. 1434–1464), Piero de' Medici (r. 1464–1469), and Lorenzo de' Medici (r. 1469–1492)—they governed a pretend republic. In 1531 the family became the hereditary dukes of Florence (later elevated to the status of an

The Medici and the Magi   Wealth has its privileges, among which has been the tradition of artists inserting portraits of their patrons into their religious paintings. Usually this was done by placing the patron somewhere within the frame of the original biblical story, but with this painting of the Three Magi coming to worship the child Jesus, the Renaissance master Benozzo Gozzoli (1420–1497) has gone one step further by portraying Cosimo de' Medici and his family members as the guides who brought the Magi to the infant Jesus. The imposition is apt, since the gifts brought by the Magi (gold, myrrh, and frankincense) were symbolic of the finance and spice trades that brought the Medici their enormous wealth.

archduchy) and placed three family members on the papal throne during the Renaissance—Leo X (r. 1513–1521), Clement VII (r. 1523–1534), and Leo XI (r. 1605). In Milan, the famous Visconti and Sforza families followed similar trajectories, with the Visconti family taking the ducal title in 1369 and holding it until the family line died out in 1447. At that point the Sforza family (of peasant origins, with several generations of mercenary soldiers thrown in) took over and governed by fiat until 1535. The d'Este family in Ferrara, who had led local politics since 1264, won a ducal title in 1452 (and another in 1471) and held on to power until 1597; likewise the Gonzaga family in Mantua, where they ruled without stop from 1328 to 1708.

The concentrations of wealth and power in these city-states, and in others like them, made possible elaborate systems of patronage, which gave a tremendous boost to intellectual and artistic life.

A Culture of   Again like Augustus, Renaissance oligarchs put their resources to work in
Consumption   the public sphere. They commissioned scores of palaces, chapels, public fountains and market squares, mausoleums, fortifications, libraries and museums, schools, and hospitals. All were done in the newest styles and were richly decorated with paintings, sculptures, frescos, and tapestries—and they provided hundreds of opportunities for scholars, artists, and architects. Art was not for art's sake alone in the Renaissance: it expressed humanist values and aesthetics while serving to elevate the civic spirit and also promoted the glory and wisdom of the patron whose support made the art possible.

The depressed economy contributed as well, since labor costs were comparatively low. The building frenzy of the 14th and 15th centuries therefore represented a jobs program: it bolstered support for the regimes by putting people to work. Manufacturing still limped along, since the shrunken population meant a decreased need for most goods; the demographic recovery was slow across Europe. The city of Toulouse, for example, had numbered thirty thousand in the early 14th century, and by the early 15th it had only eight thousand. Within Italy,

Genoa had lost more than one-third of its population; Bologna and Milan had each lost half; Florence had lost three-fourths. Many towns did not regain their 13th-century populations until the 20th century. Moreover, the ongoing struggles against the Ottomans, who pressed their frontiers to the gates of Vienna, interrupted trade with Asia. Even with such drastically reduced numbers, the drift of the rural poor into the cities ensured a constant labor surplus. Labor costs therefore were cheap, making the vast construction projects of the Renaissance possible.

The rich are with us always. Even in a depressed economy, concentrations of capital exist and often grow, so long as the possessor is lucky or clever (or corrupt) *Economic* enough to seize the opportunities. In the Renaissance, those opportunities ex- *Inequality* isted, especially in finance and armaments. With so much construction to perform and so much war to wage, those with capital were able to lend it at handsome rates of interest. Meanwhile, manufacturers found markets always in search of weaponry and construction equipment. Venice's Arsenal—its shipbuilding factory— employed three thousand laborers at the start of the 15th century. Tax records from that time show that two-thirds of the city's merchants made at least 6,000 ducats per year, and one-half of those fortunate merchants actually made well over 12,000.[1] Seven merchants actually had annual incomes of more than 140,000 ducats. Such severe inequities in the distribution of capital ensured that rents and wages worked in favor of the elite. So did the power of the guild leaders and urban nobles. In Milan, a mere 5 percent of the population controlled one-half of the city's wealth. No wonder they had the ability to commission palaces, endow museums and libraries, dress in expensive silks and furs, and commission such splendid works of art. The Renaissance, for all its cultural glories, was a miserable time to be a poor farmer or a simple workman—which is precisely what the overwhelming majority of people were.

THE RENAISSANCE ACHIEVEMENT

Art and intellectual life tend to thrive when supported. The cult of patronage— that is, the eager support of painters, sculptors, poets, and scholars as a sign of one's sophistication—and the appreciation of individual talent gave a tremendous impetus to new forms of expression and the pursuit of knowledge. The influx of scholars and artists from the east also contributed as the Ottomans closed in on the remnants of Byzantium. One Sicilian humanist, Giovanni Aurispa (1376–1459), rushed to Constantinople in the years leading up to the Turkish

---

[1]   A Venetian ducat of that time was minted of roughly 0.125 ounces (one-eighth of an ounce). An approximate contemporary estimate of the value of 6,000 ducats would be about $1.2 million.

A Renaissance Print Shop   The printing press made written materials available to the population on a vast scale, but printing was nevertheless a slow and laborious process. In this scene two workers are setting type in a frame, while in the front, to the right, another worker fixes the type in place and inks it before placing it in the press. The worker in the front, to the left, carefully peels a printed sheet from its frame. This woodcut was created by the Swiss artist Jost Amman (1539–1591).

siege and came back with more than two hundred manuscripts that might otherwise have gone up in flames. Copyists were hired by the hundreds in every city to get texts like these reproduced and circulated. By 1400 Florence had opened the first lending library in Europe; one could actually borrow books and bring them home rather than have to read them on site, as before. The invention of the printing press by Johannes Gutenberg around 1440 allowed books to pour over Europe like a tide. Aldus Manutius (1450–1515) was the most celebrated of humanist publishers; his printing house in Venice produced editions of well over a hundred Latin and Greek texts before his death.

The Triumph of Vernacular Literature   Vernacular literature also began to appear in print. This is important because most of the truly memorable literature produced in the Renaissance was in the common, not the learned, tongues. Petrarch's great sequence of sonnets and other poems to his beloved Laura—the *Canzoniere* (*Song Book*)—have proved enduringly popular, whereas his Latin epic poem about the Roman general Scipio Africanus—called *Africa*—is turgid and lifeless. Much better is Ludovico Ariosto's (1474–1533) immense, and immensely entertaining, mock-epic *Orlando Furioso* (*Crazed Roland*). It tells of the mad adventures of Charlemagne's knight Roland, who loses his mind when his beloved Angelica falls in love with a Muslim prince and moves to China. Roland promptly turns into a one-man juggernaut, rampaging through Europe, Asia, and Africa and destroying everything in sight. Giovanni Boccaccio (1313–1375) wrote the first Italian novel—called *Filocolo* (*The Love Afflicted*, 1336)—but is best remembered for his collection of thematically linked short stories called *The Decameron* (*Ten Days*, 1353), in which ten friends escape from plague-ridden Florence into the countryside and entertain themselves by each one telling a story to the rest every day for ten days.

Not many Renaissance stage plays have lasted; only two are still widely read and produced today. Pietro Aretino (1492–1556), known in his lifetime as the "Scourge of Princes" for his scathing wit and willingness to blackmail the prominent when short of funds, wrote several brilliant bawdy comedies. His best play, a comedy called *La Cortigiana* (*The Woman Courtier*), tells of an upright wealthy citizen from Siena who receives an appointment as a papal cardinal. Traveling to Rome for his installation, he sees a beautiful young woman sitting at a window and decides he must have her as a mistress. The comedy ensues when a scheming con artist tries to teach the elderly man how to flatter and entice the young beauty—all the while pursuing a plan of his own.

The other great Renaissance comedy is *La Mandragola* (*The Mandrake Root*), by Niccolò Machiavelli (1469–1527). The play, which appeared in 1518, tells of another upright elderly man, Nicia, newly married to a stunning but sexually shy beauty named Lucrezia. Unable to convince his bride to sleep with him, the foolish husband confides in a dashing young ne'er-do-well named Callimaco, who, desiring Lucrezia for himself, hatches a plot. He tells Nicia that he has learned, through careful study of ancient Greek scientific manuscripts, of a potion made from mandrake root. When given to a woman, it instantly enflames her with a lust that cannot be denied. The drug has an unfortunate side effect, however: the first man to have sex with the woman will die immediately afterward. Nicia declares that he wants Lucrezia, but not enough to die for it. Callimaco then announces— tremblingly, hesitantly—that he himself suffers from an unspecified mortal illness and has only a few days to live. So great is his admiration for Nicia and his desire to perform a useful service before he dies that he volunteers for the suicide mission.

La Mandragola surprises most people who read or watch it. They usually come to the play knowing Machiavelli from another work of his, a small political treatise called *The Prince*. In 1499 the people of Florence had overthrown the Medici oligarchy and restored republican government. Machiavelli, a Florentine, loved and served its republic with passionate dedication for thirteen years, from 1499 to 1512—as a diplomat, civil servant, and military overseer. Late in 1512, however, a counterplot restored Lorenzo de' Medici to power. Machiavelli was dismissed, arrested for conspiracy, tortured, and ultimately released. In retirement at his country estate, he then gave himself over to study and writing.

Machiavelli's The Prince

The Prince, although he never published it, was the first thing Machiavelli wrote after his release from prison. (He wrote it in a matter of weeks, then circulated it among a small circle of friends and dedicated it to Lorenzo de' Medici— probably in hopes of winning a position in the new government.) It is a notorious book, praised by some for its clear-eyed realism about how political power actually works and vilified by others as little more than a how-to manual for thugs. Society, Machiavelli argues, benefits more from stable order than from benevolent instability. Therefore, a prince's first responsibility is to secure his own power, even if the exercise of that power is unjust. Ruthlessness should not be pursued for its own sake, but a wise prince will never rule it out altogether. A prince ought always to maintain an upright public appearance, but behind the scenes he should use any means at his disposal—including lying, cheating, stealing, or killing—to maintain power. Although *The Prince* never uses the phrase, its essential message is that in politics the end justifies the means.

Once the book was published, five years after Machiavelli's death, people read it with a shudder of horror. Machiavelli's defenders point to the chaotic state of Italian politics at the time, with French, German, and Spanish invaders at every turn. *The Prince*, they suggest, is simply a plea for a no-nonsense messianic figure who would restore Italian liberty. Perhaps. Machiavelli's letters, however, show that he was a man of republican Florence, first, last, and always. He would have been delighted to see Ferrara, Mantua, Milan, Pisa, or Venice crushed by a foreign army if that were to Florence's gain. Complicating matters, he dashed off *The Prince* in a few weeks. Machiavelli then spent four years (1513–1517) composing his major work, *Discourses on Livy*, which elaborates a complex and passionate argument on the superiority of republican government to any other type of political organization. Because no one except specialist scholars ever reads the *Discourses*, it has escaped popular notice that it demolishes nearly every idea put forth in *The Prince*. "No properly run republic should ever find it necessary to overlook the crimes of any given citizen because of his supposed excellence.... Governments of the people are superior to any government by a prince" (1.24, 1.58).

Less controversial were Marsilio Ficino (1433–1499) and Baldassare Castiglione (1478–1529). Ficino was a celebrated philosopher who spent his career at the Medici court. He had mastered classical Greek as a young man and became a devout exponent of Neoplatonism. His greatest achievement, in fact, was a translation into Latin of the entire corpus of Plato's writings. Until its publication in 1484, Plato had hardly been known in Latin Europe, and Western intellectual life had been long dominated by Aristotle. Ficino's other major works include a long treatise, *On Platonic Theology*, which explicates Christian doctrine on the immortality of the soul using Platonic ideas. He argues that the unique, characteristic destiny of the human soul is to investigate its own nature, but such investigation inevitably results (at least temporarily) in confusion and misery. Hence the ultimate goal of the soul is to rise above physicality, to become disembodied, and to achieve union with the divine. As a hybrid philosophical and mystical treatise, it is a stunning exercise. Ficino was the tutor of many Neoplatonists, most famously of Giovanni Pico della Mirandola, the author of the "Oration on the Dignity of Man."

Castiglione's The Courtier

Castiglione came from an ancient noble family near Mantua and spent his entire life in the circle of social and political elites. He served as a personal aide and confidante to the marquis of Mantua and then to the duke of Urbino and spent several years in Rome as an ambassador to the papal court, then several more as papal envoy to the royal court of Spain in Madrid. He is remembered primarily for *The Courtier* (1528), which is a kind of memoir written in the form of a fictional philosophical dialogue. In it he laments the passing of the

Renaissance's golden era, when humanism was at its height. By 1500 Italy was overrun by ambitious foreigners, and courtly life as Castiglione had known it (or at least as he chose to remember it) had declined into a tawdry arena of power grabbing, money grubbing, and social climbing. He depicts fictionalized versions of the companions of his youth—elegant, charming, cultivated, effortlessly superior to everyone—who spend four evenings in an extended conversation about the qualities of an ideal courtier.

To Castiglione the courtier is above politics: he graciously advises any figure deemed worthy of attention but does not advocate any particular political philosophy. This marks a shift from the original ideal of humanism, which expected a passionate civic spirit from its adherents. Castiglione's figures expound on the need for courtiers to appreciate music and poetry; to excel at dancing, sports, and refined conversation; to understand the importance of fashion as well as affairs of state. In short, courtiers should exist beautifully, all the while exuding an air of nonchalance and unpracticed elegance. *The Courtier* was extraordinarily popular, going through more than one hundred editions between its appearance in 1528 and 1616. Its significance lay in its elegiac mood: at a time when many of Europe's nobles were being displaced from political life, Castiglione consecrated for them the qualities that lifted them forever, in their own minds, above the common rabble.

CHRISTIAN HUMANISM

As the ideas and values of the Renaissance spread outward from Italy, they took on new styles, concerns, and emphases. Ultimately, if indirectly, they led to the shattering of the religious unity that had marked Latin Europe since the advent of Christianity.

It took some time for humanism to catch on in the north. The prolonged agony of the Hundred Years' War in England and France certainly impeded the spread of the new learning. So did the resistance of the universities of Paris and Oxford—both strongholds of Aristotelianism. As for Germany, intellectual life there had long been centered in the royal and aristocratic courts. By this time Germany had fractured into hundreds of principalities (nominally under the authority of the Habsburg dynasty, but effectively autonomous), and its relatively few universities did not rush to embrace new ideas.[2] When humanism did finally begin to take root throughout Europe, around the year 1500, it developed along a variety of trajectories; especially significant among them was a kind of humanism that came to be known as **Christian humanism.**

---

[2]   Munich did not acquire a university until 1472. Even then, the university was at Ingolstadt, several miles away.

The Four Holy Men   "A panel on which I have bestowed more care than on any other painting" is how the German Renaissance master Albrecht Dürer (1471–1528) described this powerful group portrait, completed in 1526. It depicts, from left to right, St. John the Evangelist, St. Peter (holding his ever-present key to paradise), St. Mark, and St. Paul the Apostle (who carries a copy of the Bible and a sword, the latter being a reference to his martyrdom). Dürer was a passionate supporter of the Lutheran Reformation, and the bottom portion of each panel (since lost) bore passages from Luther's German translation of the scriptures.

Like early humanism, Christian humanism rejected scholastic system building and looked to the past for new models of thinking and behavior. However, Christian humanists showed a strong preference for texts and traditions that contributed specifically to religious faith. Their goal was not to become better all-round individuals, but better Christians. Consequently, they focused less on the writings of the ancient philosophers and poets and more on the early writings of the Christians—especially the New Testament itself. In the visual arts, Christian humanists showed little interest in depicting classical pagan themes; rather, painters and sculptors avidly adopted Renaissance techniques to produce striking new presentations of biblical imagery. The Christian humanists were passionate reformers, dedicated to promoting Christian education and practical piety through the preparation of newer and better texts.

The Christian humanists were not yet anti-Catholic, only anticlerical. The shortage of priests had always been more dire the farther north one traveled in Europe, with exceptions in cities like Paris, London, and Mainz, but the problem had been persistently acute since the Black Death. Clergy at the grassroots level were in painfully short supply, and those who were available were often poorly trained. Hence northerners had developed strong traditions of lay piety. They focused less on the church's sacramental life and more on the simple reading of scripture, the singing of hymns, and communal prayer. Religious fraternities and sororities abounded, offering many a life of organized piety, education, and moral rigor that deemphasized ecclesiastical dogma and ritual.

The Brethren of the Common Life   The best known of these organizations was the Brethren of the Common Life, established in Holland in the late 14th century; its reputation for pious simplicity and educational excellence spread quickly across Europe. The Brethren community preached what they called the "new devotion" (*devotio moderna*), based on the idea of replicating in one's own life the actions and attitudes of Jesus, rather than the formal doctrines and disciplines of the church. An early member of the Brethren, Thomas à Kempis (1380–1471), wrote *The Imitation of Christ,* which went on to become the most widely read and frequently translated Christian devotional book in Europe. But the most famous alumni of the Brethren were Desiderius Erasmus and Martin Luther.

ERASMUS: HUMANIST SCHOLAR AND SOCIAL CRITIC

Erasmus (1466–1536) was arguably the greatest of all humanist scholars, admired for the breadth of his classical learning, his quick wit and generous spirit, and the elegance of his writing. The illegitimate son of a Dutch priest in training and a physician's daughter, he grew up in Rotterdam and received his primary education at home. In 1483, however, both of his parents died in a new outbreak of the plague. Supported by the Brethren of the Common Life, Erasmus entered a series of monastic and lay-fraternal schools, where he was unhappy with the communities' frequently dour discipline but delighted in their extensive libraries. In 1492, brilliant but penniless, he took monastic vows, entered an Augustinian house, and was soon ordained to the priesthood. He hated monastic life, however, and thought most of his fellow monks joyless and haughty automatons. Fortunately, a bishop from Cambrai, not far away in northern France, heard of Erasmus's brilliance and took him on as a personal secretary in 1495. The bishop urged Erasmus to pursue more formal study and sent him to the University of Paris.

Once he had finished his degree, Erasmus set out for England, where he had been invited to lecture at the University of Cambridge. Freed from the bishop's service, Erasmus spent the rest of his life as an itinerant scholar, lecturing at various universities and visiting one noble court after another. Chronically short of funds, he was offered many lucrative academic posts throughout his life but declined them all, preferring his freedom. He also rejected several offers to be appointed a Catholic bishop and two nominations to the College of Cardinals. He studied and wrote constantly, even while traveling. In fact, he claimed to have written much of his most famous work, *The Praise of Folly* (1509), while on horseback during a trip to England to visit his friend and fellow humanist Thomas More. He died in Basel, Switzerland, in 1536.

Despite such an unsettled life, Erasmus produced an astonishing amount of writing. His letters alone fill eleven fat volumes in their standard edition. He wrote in three distinct voices. His most popular works were witty satires like *The Praise of Folly* that aimed to entertain people while pointing out society's flaws and foibles. A personified figure of Folly here delivers a monologue on the crucial but unappreciated role she has played in human history. Everyone from kings and princes to peasants and peddlers, she claims, owes something to her for the simple reason that humans all prefer foolishness to common sense. Every page of history proves her

Erasmus the Satirist

Erasmus of Rotterdam Given the fact that he was the most traveled, best-connected, and most highly regarded religious scholar in Europe, there are surprisingly few contemporary portraits of Erasmus, the man who made a heroic last-ditch effort to reform Catholic Christianity before Martin Luther's break with Rome. This portrait, by fellow Dutchman Quentin Metsys (1466–1530), captures the quiet determination of the man. Despite his gift for satire and enjoyment of good (and sometimes bawdy) humor, Erasmus dedicated long years of work to exposing problems within the Catholic Church and promoting a spiritual rejuvenation that would keep all Christians within the arms of the church. His failure marks an important turning point, since most of the great reforms in the church in earlier centuries had been inspired from without. From Erasmus's time to the present, Catholic reform has been largely driven from within the institutional leadership.

point. In works like this, or his popular *Colloquies* (1518), Erasmus lampoons pedantic teachers, hypocritical clerics, greedy landlords, shrewish wives, petulant youths, preening nobles, untrustworthy merchants, and others with a wit that is pointed but almost never mean-spirited.

Erasmus's most notorious satire, though, is a prickly piece called *Julius Excluded from Heaven* (1513), a lengthy sketch depicting a confrontation at the Gates of Heaven between the recently deceased Pope Julius II (r. 1503–1513) and St. Peter. Julius is drunk when he arrives and tries to unlock the gates with the key to his private money chest. Asked to account for his many sins, ranging from murder to sodomy, Julius replies that his sins were all forgiven "by the pope himself"—meaning, of course, Julius himself. When St. Peter refuses to admit Julius into heaven on account of his excessive concern for worldly power and war making, the pope throws a fit, threatens to excommunicate Peter, and announces that he will raise an army to burst through the gates and take Paradise by force.[3]

Erasmus the Educator

In his second voice, Erasmus composed a long series of moral polemics, earnest in tone yet intended for a general audience. In these books—like *Handbook of the Christian Soldier* (1503), *Education of a Christian Prince* (1516), and *The Complaint of Peace* (1517)—he condemns empty religious formalism and urges people to seek out the vital spirit of Christ as depicted in the Bible. They should live simply, honorably, peaceably, and with sincere conviction. Both these serious and his satirical works were immensely popular: it has been estimated that by Erasmus's death in 1536 some 15 percent of all the printed books purchased in Europe had come from his pen.

In his third voice, Erasmus toiled at the most detailed and exacting textual scholarship—revised and annotated editions of the writings of the Latin Fathers

---

[3] At one point the pope complains to St. Peter, "You would not believe how *seriously* some people take little things like bribery, blasphemy, sodomy, and poisoning!"

Ambrose (d. 397), Jerome (d. 420), and Augustine (d. 430). He followed these projects with his masterpiece, a new critical edition of the Greek New Testament (1515), whose fifth and final version appeared in 1535. Known as the Received Version (*Textus receptus*), it was used by most early translators of the New Testament into English and other vernaculars. These works had a much smaller readership, understandably, but he regarded them as his chief legacy to the world.

Erasmus the Scholar

MARTIN LUTHER: THE GIFT OF SALVATION

Among those who used Erasmus's New Testament as the basis for a vernacular translation was **Martin Luther** (1483–1546), the German monk whose agonized quest for salvation triggered the break with the church known as the **Protestant Reformation**. Like the humanists who sought to restore ancient morals, Luther sought to re-create what he believed to be Christian belief and practice as they had existed in the apostolic church. He saw himself as a restorer, not a revolutionary, a liberator rather than an insurrectionist. A brilliant biblical scholar, Luther had the gift of expressing his ideas in clear, forceful language that ranged easily in emotional pitch from exquisite descriptions of God's loving kindness to the coarsest verbal abuse of his foes (who consisted of anyone who disagreed with him). His charisma, energy, and passionate feeling were immense; he needed such powerful drive because his ultimate goals—once he decided that compromise with Rome was impossible—were nothing less than the complete overthrow of Catholic tradition and the resetting of the Christian clock, so to speak, fifteen hundred years back.

Luther was born—proudly—of modest, laboring stock in northern Germany. His hardworking parents instilled piety and order in him from an early age, and when it came time for his education they sent him to a school run by the Brethren of Common Life. Hoping to establish his son in a legal career, Luther's father then sent him to the University of Erfurt, but Martin was drawn instead to theology and the classical languages. In 1505, aged twenty-two, he shattered his father's hopes by taking vows as an Augustinian monk. A mere two years later he was ordained a priest.

His vocation brought him no peace, however. Belief in God tormented Luther because he could see no way to please Him. God's majesty was so immense, so vast, and so inconceivably great that Luther found it impossible to believe that anyone could merit salvation. No one deserves to be saved, he believed, for the simple reason that no one can deserve to spend eternity in God's presence. How can anyone possibly claim to merit that? And yet that was precisely what Christian tradition told him to pursue—a life of prayer, repentance, good works, and devotion that would earn him the salvation Christ had promised to everyone who did so. Luther observed his monastic discipline with fanatical determination, even to

Crisis of Faith

the point where his abbot feared for his sanity. And yet the fear that nothing he did could possibly justify his standing before God never left him. So sharp grew his agony, he later wrote, that he began to despise God for having created a game that we cannot win—and then punishing us with eternal torment for losing it:

> Even as a blameless monk I still felt certain that in God's eyes I was a miserable sinner—and one with a very troubled conscience—for I had no reason to believe that God would ever be satisfied by my actions. I could not love a righteous God who punished the unrighteous; rather, I hated Him. I was careful never to blaspheme aloud, but on the inside, in the silence of my heart, I roiled and raged at God, saying, "Is it not enough for You that we, miserable sinners all, are damned for all eternity on account of original sin [the notion that, as a result of Adam and Eve's misbehavior, all human beings come into the world with a moral stain upon them from birth]? Why do You add to our calamity by imposing the Ten Commandments on us as well? Why add sorrow upon sorrow through the Gospel teachings, and then in that same Gospel threaten us with judgment and wrath?"

Epiphany in 1513

But then came the breakthrough. Having been sent by his exhausted abbot to teach theology at the University of Wittenberg, Luther, in 1513, was preparing lecture notes on St. Paul's epistle to the Romans, a text he had read countless times before, when suddenly a new insight flashed through his mind:

> I pondered these words night and day until, at last, God had mercy on me and gave me to understand the connection between the phrases "The justice of God is revealed in the Gospel" and "The just will live through faith" [Romans 1.16–17]. I suddenly began to understand that God's justice—that is, the justice by which a just person may live forever—is a gift of God won by faith. . . . All at once I felt reborn, as though I had entered Paradise through gates thrown wide open, and immediately the whole of Scripture took on a new meaning for me.

In other words, *of course* God knows that we do not "deserve" salvation. But salvation is God's gift to us, and He simply wants us to have it anyway.

After this revelation, he tells us, the rest of the scriptures' meaning lay open to him, as though he were reading the words for the first time. To be righteous in the eyes of God, one did not have to confess one's sins to a priest, give alms to the poor, or perform ritual devotions like pilgrimages or vigils. One did not have to follow rites like reciting of the rosary or abstaining from meat on Fridays. One

Martin Luther and Katherina von Bora   The German painter Lucas Cranach the Elder (1472–1533) produced this dual portrait of the great Protestant reformer and his wife; this painting, in fact, may have been produced in honor of their betrothal. (Cranach was present at the ceremony.) Their marriage was an unusually happy one, perhaps the only thing in Luther's life that never caused him any agony.

attains righteousness simply by having faith in Christ; one must simply accept the salvation He offers as an unmerited gift. This idea became canonized in Luther's understanding of **justification by faith alone** (*sola fide* in Latin). It results not from our merit but from God's grace alone, as expressed uniquely through Christ's sacrifice on the cross. Moreover, everything that God requires of us is expressed not through the teaching authority and tradition of the church but through the words of scripture alone. Anything beyond biblical teaching is superfluous to salvation at best and an impediment to it at worst. Few of these ideas were new. In fact, many of them had been enunciated centuries earlier by Augustine (d. 430), the founder of Luther's own monastic order. But Luther carried them to a degree far beyond Augustine or any other theologian.

LUTHER'S REBELLION AGAINST THE CHURCH

Luther's theology offended the church because it made the church irrelevant. From the time of the Gregorian Reform in the 11th century, the Catholic Church had developed its theology of salvation with itself as the irreplaceable intermediary between God and humanity. The church and the believer worked together to effect salvation, through teaching and ministry, the sacraments and pious action. The relationship was not a crude contract, although many saw it that way and had been making similar complaints since at least the second half of the 14th century.

Anti-Catholic Propaganda   This anonymous woodcut of 1520 by a German satirist depicts the devil (complete with wings and clawed feet) sitting on a letter of indulgence and holding a money collection box. The devil's mouth is filled with sinners who presumably bought letters of indulgence in good faith, thinking they had been absolved from their sins. Illustrations such as this, often printed as broadsheets and sold very cheaply, clearly conveyed criticism of the church to people who could not read.

What prompted Luther's rebellion against the church was not merely his new understanding of scripture—because it was not, after all, new. Rather, it was his ire over the church's practice of selling **indulgences,** a monetary donation to the church as a means to satisfy some of the requirements for the forgiveness of sin. A quick theological aside: from the 12th century on, Catholic doctrine had understood penance for sin to have the four elements of contrition, confession, absolution, and satisfaction. One first has to repent honestly for what one has done; second, one must confess the sin fully to a priest; third, one receives absolution from that priest if the confession is sincere and genuine; and fourth, one must then make some sort of restitution for what one did. An indulgence—earned by some explicit act of charity or devotion—was a way of meet-

Indulgences for Sale   ing the fourth demand. A special donation to the church was one way of earning an indulgence. Hence, although it was not an act of "purchasing forgiveness," it certainly could look like one—especially if the process was abused. And it was, egregiously, in Luther's time.

Many people had criticized the practice, including Erasmus. The Renaissance popes, as involved as ever in Italian politics, had waged wars against various despots, had tried to resist the advancing Ottoman Turks, and had expanded the church's network of universities across Europe. As a result, they were in constant and desperate need of funds, and many turned to the offering of indulgences as a reliable means of raising cash. An enormous campaign spread throughout Germany and Italy to raise funds for the construction of the huge new St. Peter's Basilica in Rome. In 1517 Martin Luther, just recently released from his spiritual tortures, witnessed the abusive and predatory selling of indulgences in both regions and was outraged. The symbolic starting point of the Protestant Reformation was not his biblical epiphany in 1513 but his **Ninety-Five Theses** of 1517—a manifesto condemning the theology of indulgences.

The Ninety-Five Theses   The Ninety-Five Theses are simply a list of assertions that Luther declares himself prepared to argue—the arguments themselves are not part of the text. This sort of bulletin of ideas was a common practice in universities of the time.

The Basilica of St. Peter in Rome   Four Italian artists share the bulk of the credit for this late Renaissance masterpiece of architecture and art: Donato Bramante (1444–1514), Michelangelo Buonarroti (1475–1564), Carlo Maderno (1556–1629), and Gian Lorenzo Bernini (1598–1680). It is the largest church in Europe, and it took 120 years to complete its construction and decoration. By centuries-old tradition, its altar is built over the site of St. Peter's tomb.

Like the modern custom of publishing the prospectus of one's doctoral dissertation, it invited argument and discussion. He got it. Pope Leo X (r. 1513–1521) spent three years examining Luther's position and finally responded with a papal bull on June 15, 1520, called *Exsurge Domine* ("Arise, O Lord"). He condemned forty-one of the theses as heretical, and he gave Luther sixty days to withdraw the offending statements. Luther answered by publicly burning his copy of the bull on December 10, exactly sixty days after it was issued. After this, there was only one action Leo could take: On January 3, 1521, the pope excommunicated Luther and banned his writings. Enforcement of that ban, however, was a matter for civil authorities, and consequently Luther was ordered to appear before an imperial court (diet) in the German city of Worms. Luther appeared but boldly refused to recant anything he had written; he then fled the scene at night, before the diet passed sentence on him. A powerful German prince—Frederick III of Saxony (r. 1483–1525)—gave him refuge. From this point on, little effort was made to mend fences. Disaffected Christians across Germany flocked to Luther's message by the thousands and then by the tens of thousands. Within a few years the religious unity of Christian Europe was permanently sundered.

Earlier, in 1520, Luther's *Address to the Christian Nobility of the German Nation* had laid out his vision for the organization and administration of his reformed church. Since there was no supreme spiritual authority—each believer needing only his or her Bible and conscience—Protestant churches needed only secular administration and guidance. For that, Luther turned to the princes. A prince who formally broke with Rome and converted to Lutheranism was entitled, Luther wrote, to confiscate the Catholic ecclesiastical lands, properties, and wealth within his principality and to lead the administration of the new reformed churches. The temptation was great, but most princes feared that seizing the extensive holdings of the churches and monasteries would cause the Holy Roman Emperor Charles V to rush to Catholicism's defense. Hence, although most of the nobles converted to Lutheranism, they hesitated to start plundering.

"The Pope is the Antichrist, and the Catholic Church is the most unruly of all crooks' lairs, the most brazen of all brothels, and the Kingdom itself of Sin, Death, and Hell," Luther wrote in a late book titled *On the Roman Papacy: An Institution of the Devil*. Pope Leo, for his part, dismissed Luther as "a German drunkard who will mend his ways once he sobers up." With so much at stake in terms of geopolitics, it is not surprising that the rhetoric of the religious dispute became feverish. Catholics and Protestants at all levels of society hurled abuse at each other.[4] Erasmus and Luther, for a while, had maintained a civilized debate in print over theological issues like free will, the workings of divine grace, and the interpretation of scripture. (The two men never met personally.) Other than that, however, most of the religious battle was in poisonous language. When large numbers of German peasants were persuaded by radicals to rise up in arms against their landlords in 1524 and 1525 in a rebellion known as the **German Peasants' Revolt**, Luther responded savagely. Whereas the peasants had been stirred by Luther's insistence on the dignity of all believers, he called on the princes to take bold action.

Luther and the German Peasants' Revolt

If his aim was to scare the peasants into submission, *On the Thieving, Murderous Hordes of Peasants* was a brilliant success:

> Therefore every one of you [German princes] who can, should act as both judge and executioner. . . . Strike [the peasants] down, slay them, and stab them, either in secret or in the light of day . . . for you ought always to bear in mind that there is nothing more poisonous, dangerous, or devilish than one of these rebels. . . . For baptism frees men's souls

---

[4]   Although they came to be known as *Protestants* ("those who protest"), Luther and his followers called themselves *Evangelicals*.

alone; it does not liberate their bodies and properties, nor does the Gospel call for people to hold all their goods in common. . . . Fine Christians these peasants are! There can hardly be a single devil left in hell—for I do believe they have all taken possession of these peasants, whose mad ravings are beyond all measure. . . . What a wonderful time we live in now, when a prince can better merit heaven by bloodshed than by prayer!

Most of the rebels, denied Luther's expected support, laid down their weapons at once. The rest were quickly defeated in a battle at Frankenhausen in May 1525, and the revolt ended. The rebel leader, an apocalyptic firebrand named Thomas Müntzer (1488–1525), was executed. The cost of victory was high, however. As many as 100,000 people lost their lives.

After this, the "Protestantization" of Germany gained pace, as the princes now rushed to support Luther's program and seize church lands and treasur- *Protestantism* ies. Sincere religious conviction undoubtedly motivated them, but political *Spreads and* and economic factors obviously were also at play. By formally adopting the *Divides* Lutheran cause, princes acquired—with Luther's own blessing—the authority to appoint pastors to the new churches. This effectively placed the nobles in charge of the entire institution. Freed from having to meet their former fiscal obligations to Rome or to recognize the authority of ecclesiastical courts, the princes likewise ensured the obedience of the new Lutheran churches to noble demands. The policies they developed came to be summarized by the phrase, "The religion of the ruler determines the religion of the land" (*Cuius regio, eius religio*). And most of the princes promoted the new *religio* to strengthen their grip on the *regio*.

The Catholic–Protestant rift thus became an unbridgeable chasm. What began as an in-house theological dispute took on more and more political and social elements with every passing year. Two interconnected issues now took on special significance: the constitutional arrangement within Germany and the threat posed by the Turks.

For two centuries the four hundred or so German princes had enjoyed inde- pendence from imperial control, while the Habsburgs went about adding to their *Charles V* domain in eastern Europe and marrying available heiresses throughout the con- *Comes to* tinent. When Charles V (r. 1520–1556) came to the throne, he inherited, by a *Power* genealogical quirk, several lines of the Habsburg family legacies. These territo- ries, when considered in the aggregate, put him in the sudden and unexpected position of having the German princes surrounded (see Map 12.2).[5]

By constitutional tradition, Charles had no cause to take advantage of his position by imposing his rule on the princes. However, since he was, as Holy Roman emperor, the leading royal defender of Catholicism, he considered

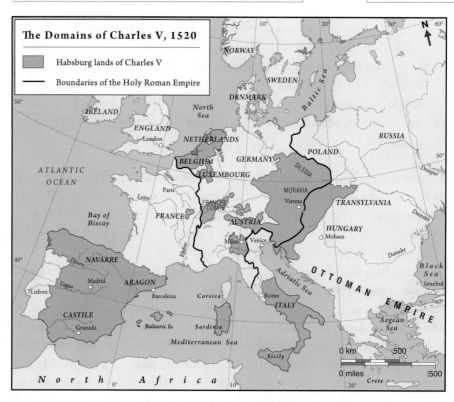

MAP 12.2   The Domains of Charles V, 1520   Charles V (r. 1520–1556) inherited several lines of Habsburg family territories, with the result that he dominated the continent.

seriously his obligation to combat the Protestant heresy. The princes, for their part, had good reason to support Luther: he had essentially given them control of the churches aligned with his movement.

The Turkish Threat

The Turkish threat was complicated. Ottoman forces had driven deep into Europe after taking Constantinople in 1453, in the hope of weakening Christendom generally and stopping Habsburg advances specifically. Charles V, naturally, spearheaded the effort to hold them at bay. But many Protestant princes hoped to form an alliance with the Ottoman sultan, Suleiman the Magnificent

---

[5]   His formal title(s), used on all his official records, ran as follows: "Charles, by grace of God the elected Holy Roman Emperor, forever August, King in Germany, King of Italy, Castile, Aragon, León, both Sicilies, Jerusalem, Navarra, Granada, Toledo, Valencia, Galicia, Majorca, Sevilla, Sardinia, Cordova, Corsica, Murcia, Jaen, the Algarves, Algeciras, Gibraltar, the Canary Islands, the Western and Eastern Indies, the Islands and Mainland of the Ocean Sea, etc. etc., Archduke of Austria, Duke of Burgundy, Brabant, Lorraine, Styria, Carinthia, Carniola, Limburg, Luxembourg, Gelderland, Athens, Neopatria, Württemberg, Landgrave of Alsace, Prince of Swabia, Asturia and Catalonia, Count of Flanders, Habsburg, Tyrol, Gorizia, Barcelona, Artois, Burgundy Palatine, Hainaut, Holland, Seeland, Ferrette, Kyburg, Namur, Roussillon, Cerdagne, Zutphen, Margrave of the Holy Roman Empire, Burgau, Oristano and Gociano, Lord of Frisia, the Wendish March, Pordenone, Biscay, Molin, Salins, Tripoli and Mechelen, etc."

(r. 1520–1566), who had come to his throne at roughly the same time as Charles V came to his. Such a pact, they hoped, would leave Charles as the surrounded party and thereby neutralize his power. Diplomatic relations between Protestant rulers and Suleiman were extensive. The Turks had large numbers of Jews and Christians living within the European part of their empire, and for the time being, at least, they treated them with the tolerance required by dhimmi law. Dhimmi law did not protect Christian and Jewish buildings, however, as Suleiman's forces advanced through southeastern Europe. When the Turks overran Buda, the capital of Hungary, they delighted in destroying churches and synagogues throughout the city. Indeed, they set aflame a collection of Renaissance art as rich as anything in Florence or Milan.[6]

Suleiman's advance compelled Charles to mobilize his forces, but since the Turks were not yet threatening Habsburg lands directly, Charles bided his time. The Lutheran princes kept negotiating with Suleiman to keep the pressure up. An alliance did not happen in the end, but Suleiman

Turkish Atrocities   Throughout the 16th and 17th centuries the Ottomans made repeated efforts to expand their control in southeastern Europe, twice getting as far as the gates of Vienna. This woodcut depicts popular fears of Turkish savagery. "Such amusements are common in all wars," warned Erasmus in 1530, when this image was published. The Turks did commit atrocities like those shown here, but no more so than what European Catholics and Protestants inflicted on one another (and what both sometimes inflicted on the Jews) throughout the religious wars of the 16th and 17th centuries.

concluded that Charles was too weak to offer any real resistance and so launched a fresh attack in 1526 and quickly took most of Hungary. After a brief pause he advanced his army as far as Vienna, to which he laid siege in 1529. At this point even the Protestants were worried. Luther published in that same year the pamphlet *On the War against the Turks*, in which he called for a united European front against the Ottomans yet rejected as un-Christian the notion of a crusade. Suleiman's siege failed, however, and the Turkish advance was temporarily stopped.

THE REFORMATION GOES INTERNATIONAL

Like other reformers before him and since, Martin Luther believed that those who joined him in rebellion would agree with his proposals for the future. But things seldom turn out that way. People, it seems, unite more easily in opposition

---

6   Buda—supposedly named after Bleda, Attila the Hun's older brother—was much later incorporated with the small nearby town of Pest to become today's Budapest.

to a present evil than they rally around a new vision of future good. With its spread beyond Germany, especially in the legacy of John Calvin, Protestantism in fact thrived on divisions.

When Luther began his revolt, many among the pope's advisors recommended immediate and dramatic action. Luther, after all, seemed intent on tearing down the entire Catholic tradition. However, just as many others counseled a quietist approach. Once Luther validated the idea that people can interpret the scriptures for themselves, they pointed out, people would soon disagree with Luther's interpretations as much as they disagreed with Rome's. The rebellion would then splinter into countless factions and soon disappear under its own dead, fractured weight.

Each group of advisors was half right. At the start, Luther saw his actions as a much-needed campaign to correct flaws in Catholic belief and practice, not as a drive to destroy the church. He was a reformer, not a revolutionary. Dramatic counteraction was indeed called for, but not in the urgent sense recommended by the alarmists. As for the second group, they saw correctly the coming splintering of the reformers into rival groups, but their assumption that division meant failure was wrong. They had severely underestimated the intensity of anticlerical feeling—and the deep resentment of the church's abuses and failings. By the time they realized their mistake, it was too late. Luther and his followers had flooded Germany with polemical pamphlets, sermons, hymnals, catechisms, and above all the Bible itself in translation.

It took a generation, more or less, for Luther's ideas to catch on outside of Germany. His basic ideas were known. How could they not be, considering the enormity of the scandal he had caused? However, Luther wrote most of his works in German—since vernacular scripture reading and vernacular worship were so central to his theology. And translators did not rush to bring his works into other tongues. Luther had taken care to produce a number of pamphlets and broadsides in Latin to encourage the spread of the revolt. His ongoing debate in print with Erasmus—the most revered scholar in the Christian world—also kept his program in the spotlight. Still, when Protestantism did start to spread, it did so on the heels of the spread of Christian humanism. Many saw that intellectual effort as preparation for the spiritual regeneration coming out of Germany.

Not all Christian humanists were, or became, Protestant. Many of the most famous, in fact, remained staunchly Catholic. What contributed to the spread of Protestantism was not humanism itself but rather the dialogue between Renaissance and Reformation. It was the spirit of questioning, of returning to ancient sources. Many heard that dialogue and clung ever-more fiercely to the Catholic tradition. Many others, however, who might otherwise never have thought it possible, heard in the debate a calling to a wholly new, and newly holy, path.

Scholars and Activists   The best of the Christian humanist scholars were all dedicated Catholics: Guillaume Budé (1467–1540), Jacques Lefèvre d'Étaples (1455–1536), Cardinal

Francisco Ximénez de Cisneros (1436–1517), and Joan Lluís Vives i March (1493–1540). Other writers—primarily Protestants like Ulrich Zwingli (1484–1531) and John Calvin (1509–1564)—remain better known and were more historically significant because of their activities in the world. But pure scholars should have their due, too.

Budé was a classical linguist, one of the finest Greek scholars of his generation. Supported by the French royal court, he produced a Greek lexicon that remained the standard for scholars for nearly two hundred years. He also founded the school that later became the Collège de France and the library that ultimately grew into the Bibliothèque Nationale, both in Paris. Lefèvre, also a royal favorite, was an industrious writer of biblical commentaries as well as editions and translations of patristic texts. In 1530 he published the first ever translation of the entire Bible into French.

Cisneros held immense power in Spain: he was the archbishop of Toledo, was twice the regent for the crown, and served as Grand Inquisitor at the high point of that institution's power in Spain. As a statesman Cisneros was blunt and direct to the point of cruelty. He ordered the forced baptism of the Muslims of southern Spain and the burning of Arabic manuscripts in the library at Granada. As a scholar, however, he was patient in the extreme: he spent fifteen years producing the *Complutensian Polyglot Bible*—an impressive work that reproduced, in parallel columns, the best texts then available of the entire Bible in Aramaic, Greek, Hebrew, and Latin.

Lluís Vives, a much more sympathetic figure, dedicated long years to social reform as well as to reform within the Catholic Church. He was an earnest champion of education for women and welfare for the poor. The fourth-generation son of a *converso* family—that is, a Spanish family that had once been Jewish—he witnessed the Inquisition's execution of his father, grandmother, and great-grandfather.[7] And

Polyglot Bible   A page from the *Complutensian Polyglot Bible* (1514–1517) published by Cardinal Francisco Cisneros, one of the great humanistic achievements of the Renaissance. The three main columns present the biblical text in Hebrew, Latin, and Greek, while underneath are printed passages in Aramaic, where they survive, and alternative readings. The Complutensian edition was used extensively by the English translators who produced the King James Bible (Authorized Version) in 1611.

---

[7]   As we saw in chapter 11, scholars use *inquisition*, with a lowercase *i*, to refer to the inquisitorial process in the Middle Ages. Uppercase *Inquisition* is reserved for the Renaissance, when what had been a legal process turned into a formal institution.

although he never wavered in his Christian commitment, he left Spain as soon as he could and never returned. After studying in Paris, he became a professor of philosophy at Oxford and spent his time between Oxford and the royal court in London, where he served as private tutor to the Tudor family.

Zwingli

Among the Protestant humanists, the most influential were Ulrich Zwingli and John Calvin. Zwingli left behind more than twenty volumes of writings—sermons, biblical exegesis, topical essays, some poetry—but little of this is read by anyone other than specialists. His impact was in the world of action rather than thought. He was born to a Swiss farming family and received a good although unremarkable education. In 1498 he enrolled at the University of Vienna but was expelled for reasons no one has ever discovered. He was ordained a priest and spent several years as a military chaplain. A crisis of conscience, however, led him to withdraw from his post and take up duties as a simple parish priest in a small village in Switzerland. This position gave him ample time for self-education, and in a few years he had mastered Greek and acquired a usable knowledge of Hebrew.

By 1516 personal study of the scriptures had inspired Zwingli to doubt the value of much Catholic doctrine and ritual, but he was too timid to admit his opinions publicly until Martin Luther published the Ninety-Five Theses. Zwingli then dedicated himself to the twin goals of supporting Luther's Reformation and securing Switzerland's independence from French, Italian, and imperial meddling. He formally broke with Rome, and by 1522 most of the German-speaking cantons of Switzerland had done the same and had placed themselves under Zwingli's leadership. He moved to Zurich, which became second only to Luther's Wittenberg as the unofficial capital of the Protestant movement.

Zwingli's brand of Christianity differed from Luther's in a number of specifics. In fact, Zwingli, who did not meet Luther personally until 1529, is one of the first examples of a Protestant who broke away from the movement's founder. He died in battle against armies from the Catholic southern portion of Switzerland, and the embryonic church he had created became subsumed by the new church created by John Calvin.

The Anabaptists

A brief but violent interlude, however, preceded Calvin on the scene. Several dozen radical members of Zwingli's church at Zurich quit Switzerland and took up residence in exile at Münster, in northwestern Germany. Disgusted by what they considered the immoral joining of Protestant religion with secular government (Luther and the German princes, Zwingli and the Swiss town councils), they established themselves as an apocalyptic sect known as the **Anabaptists**. Their name means "rebaptizers" because the group rejected infant baptism as meaningless by itself and called for a second baptism in adulthood. They also embraced a literal reading of scripture, polygamy (although the extent of this is still debated), and the imminent approach of Christ's Second Coming. The sect came under the charismatic leadership of Jan van Leiden (1509–1536), who proclaimed himself the successor to the King David of biblical times and his Münster church as the reincarnation of the Jerusalem Temple. Zwingli and Luther both denounced the group, as did all the Catholic rulers of the time. Persecutions followed as Münster was stormed by the Catholic prince (and bishop) of the city, the Anabaptists were tortured and executed, and their sympathizers across Europe were arrested.[8]

By the time John Calvin established his own Reformed Church in Geneva, the conflict between rival Christianities had moved well beyond a war of words. Most of the Scandinavian territories (Finland was the exception) had declared for Lutheranism by the end of the 1520s. Lutheranism had also sunk deep roots in northern Germany and parts of Poland, Hungary, and the Low Countries. England was, for the time being, still staunchly Catholic, although Henry VIII's (r. 1509–1547) marital woes led him in 1534 to break with Rome and establish the Church of England, as we will discuss further in chapter 14 (see Map 12.3).

CALVIN: PROTESTANTISM AS THEOLOGY

At first glance, **John Calvin** seems an unlikely revolutionary. Quiet, reserved, and intensely bookish, he studied (under pressure from his father) for a legal career at the University of Bourges, where he fell under the spell of humanist classicism. At about the same time—somewhere around 1530—he had an evangelical conversion that changed his entire life. He described the event in the introduction to his later *Commentary on the Psalms*:

> All at once, God overpowered my mind, which at that point was far more incorrigible in such matters than one might expect in one so young, and opened it [to the Truth]. Having been given this sampling of, this introduction to, true godliness, I instantly burned with such a passion to have better knowledge of it that, even though I never abandoned my other studies entirely, I pursued them with much less drive than before.

If his account is accurate, his was an intellectual rather than mystical conversion, although it was no less passionate for that. True to his bookish nature, he

---

8   Crushed by its enemies, the Anabaptist movement disappeared. The Mennonite church, founded by Menno Simons (1496–1561) of Holland, is a late offshoot that still survives.

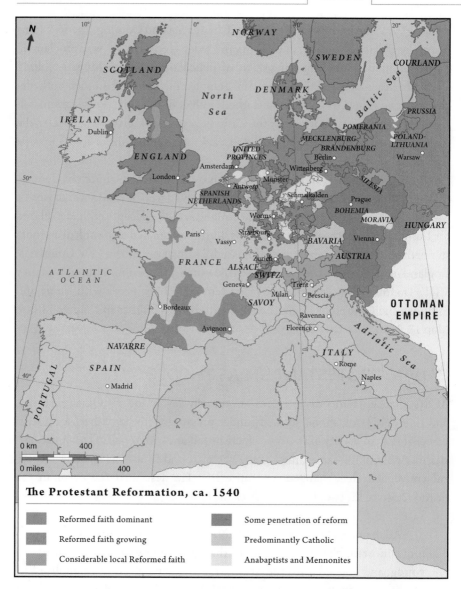

MAP 12.3   **The Protestant Reformation, ca. 1540**   By 1580, the reformation of the Church
had spread rapidly across northern and central Europe, but it was never a uniform movement.
Reform was always at a local level. Italy and Spain remained predominantly Catholic. France,
the Low Countries, southern Germany, and central Europe were hotly contested, but England,
Scotland, northern Germany, and Scandinavia were decisively Protestant by the end of the
16th century.

turned almost immediately to writing the first edition (1535) of his main
work, *Institutes of Christian Religion*, which he continued to revise until his
death. (Its final and definitive editions appeared in 1559 in Latin and in 1560
in French.)

The *Institutes* was the first work to lay out the emerging theology of Protes- *Calvin's*
tant Christianity in a systematic, logical, organized way. Here is a representative *Institutes*
passage on how the Reformed Church uses discipline: *of Christian Religion*

> It is necessary, likewise, to distinguish between different kinds of
> sins, for some are only minor infractions whereas others are enormous
> and enormously wicked crimes. In order to correct the latter, mere
> warnings and reproofs do not suffice, and one must resort to sterner
> measures—as Paul shows [1 Corinthians 5.1–5] when he does not allow
> himself to rest content after having condemned the man of Corinth who
> had committed incest, but immediately excommunicates the man after
> his conviction for the crime. Now we begin to see how the spiritual au-
> thority of the Church, which corrects sins according to God's Word, pre-
> serves our health, orders our lives, and establishes bonds of unity among
> us; for whenever the Church banishes from the community those guilty
> of adultery, fornication, theft, robbery, sedition, false witness, or any
> other crimes of that sort, or when it banishes those stubborn people who
> criticize God's Holy Judgment, even after having been admonished for
> lesser sins, it [the Church] exercises no unauthorized rational power but
> only the jurisdiction that God Himself has given it. . . . Anyone who be-
> lieves that the Church could even exist without this power to discipline
> is sorely mistaken—for how could we do without the very thing that
> God saw fit to give us? The reasons why this is necessary will be made
> clear in its action. (4.12.4)

Martin Luther, like his model St. Augustine, had been far too impulsive and emotive a writer ever to write anything like this.

Calvin shared Luther's central, defining notion of an infinitely majestic, all-
powerful, and all-knowing God whose transcendent might and will are in *The*
absolute control of the entire cosmos. But Luther softened this commanding *Concept of*
image by emphasizing the infinitely merciful, because unmerited, love that *Predestination*
God feels for us. Calvin stressed instead the unfathomable mystery of God's justice. Since He is all-knowing, argued Calvin, God has known since the moment of
Creation which human beings are to be saved and which are to be damned—and
these fates are sealed absolutely by the sheer force of God's will. There is nothing
any human being can do to alter his or her fate. All is predestined and beyond our
capacity to understand. Does this concept of **predestination** mean that many
apparently "good" people will be punished in hell while many apparently "bad"
people will be rewarded in heaven? Yes, it does, but this, to Calvin, is simply the
consequence of our complete inability to understand God's purpose, rather than

a sign of God's supposed hypocrisy. We must remain faithful to the belief that God's ways are ultimately and supremely just, even if we cannot comprehend them. In essence, what Calvin called for was an attitude of radical humility before God, an absolute submission of the soul to the Almighty's wisdom, power, and righteousness.

But this is not an attitude of passivity. It is precisely because we cannot know whether we are among the *Elect*—his term for those predestined for salvation—that Calvin demands of his followers the strictest possible adherence to moral standards. To the Elect, he writes, good ethical behavior will come naturally and

Spread of Calvinism

be the sign of their chosen status. To those who are not elected, their moral behavior will not affect their ultimate fate in the slightest—but they therefore have all the more reason to live according to a godly standard. The joy of such a life is in fact the only meaningful pleasure they will have before confronting the eternal torments of hell. Membership in good standing in the Reformed Church—Calvin's name for the branch of Christianity he established—is a likely indicator that one is among the Elect. Membership in the despised Roman Catholic Church or the Orthodox Church is as likely an indicator that one is not. But although being a Calvinist immeasurably improved one's odds of salvation, it alone determined nothing. The central concern of life therefore should not be the destiny of our individual souls but the fulfillment of God's purpose on the entire earth.

Calvinist Churches: Geneva   This church, dedicated to St. Peter, contrasts sharply with the audacious grandeur of the Vatican basilica. Sometimes referred to as the "adopted home" church of the Swiss reformer John Calvin, it is, stylistically, a hodge-podge, with structures and elements from every century since the 12th. The interior is shorn of decoration apart from the architectural elements: no mosaics, frescos, paintings, or sculptures; nothing to distract the worshipper from the Word being preached from the pulpit.

Calvin's teachings found receptive audiences all around Europe. Apart from its success in Switzerland, Calvinism became the dominant creed in Holland (where it became known as the Dutch Reformed Church), in Scotland (where it was called the Presbyterian Church), in parts of France (where Calvinists were called Huguenots), and in parts of England (where they were ultimately called Puritans). The theocratic state he established in Geneva earned a well-deserved reputation for severity, but Geneva also earned a reputation for modest, honest, and godly behavior. Calvinist communities emphasized simplicity and austerity in worship. Anything that smacked of Catholic ritual or hierarchical structure was eschewed. Instead, churches were communities of equals—joined together in prayer, scriptural reading, hymn singing, and listening to sermons. How can there be a pecking order among the Elect? Sermons indeed form the centerpiece of Calvinist worship, since they are by nature ruminations on scripture. Calvin himself was too gifted a scholar to insist on only literal readings of the Bible, although he tended to seek out symbolic or other interpretations only after considering the literal first.

Still other reformers and groups branched off to form new denominations, but these were considerably smaller in size and tinged with elements of ethnic or national rebellion. Lutheranism and Calvinism were the two with the greatest international appeal, and by 1550 they had torn the religious fabric of Europe asunder. Only in the late 20th century, in the aftermath of two World Wars and the Holocaust, would there arise serious efforts to reconcile the fissures in Christianity.

THE GODLY SOCIETY

Although they were intent on religious reform, Luther, Calvin, and the other Protestant leaders did not think of themselves as social reformers. Indeed, as we have seen, when radicals like Thomas Müntzer, leader of the German Peasants' Revolt, interpreted Luther's theology as a call to social rebellion, Luther called for the rebels' extermination. The reformers, in fact, relied on existing social and political structures for their vision of a new Christendom: from feudal princes in Germany to urban elites in Switzerland, the existing social models provided the backbone of the Protestant campaigns.

And a strong backbone was needed, according to Luther, Calvin, and others. Human nature was too depraved, too ensnared in its own sinfulness, to be trusted. *The* Figures of authority were needed to provide discipline. Protestant theology *Patriarchal* championed the notion of the "priesthood of all believers"—meaning that each *Order* individual could discern the teachings of the Bible for him- or herself. But only strong and demanding leaders could make sure that people lived according to the truths they read in scripture. Hence Luther granted power to the German princes to enforce the teaching of the new Lutheran churches within their domains. Calvin established the town councils of the Elect to supervise, judge, and punish the Reformed citizens of Geneva and elsewhere.

Both men wrote extensive commentaries on the following passage from the New Testament:

> Let every person be subject to the governing authorities, for there is no authority except from God, and those authorities that exist have been instituted by God. Therefore whoever resists authority resists what God has appointed, and those who resist will incur judgment. For rulers are not a terror to good conduct, but to bad. Do you wish to have no fear of the authority? Then do what is good, and you will receive its approval; for it is God's servant for your good. But if you do what is wrong, you should be afraid, for the authority does not bear the sword in vain! It is the servant of God to execute wrath on the wrongdoer. Therefore one must be subject, not only because of wrath but also because of conscience. (Romans 13.1–5)

The Patriarchal Family Since sinfulness is present in us from birth, disciplined authority needed to be as much a cornerstone of parenting as was love itself. Hence Protestant social ideology called for the patriarchal family as the fundamental unit of godly society. In that family, the man stood as the undoubted leader, charged with the protection and care of the whole household. The mother was subject to her husband's authority and given the special task of beginning the moral and spiritual

The Patriarchal Family   Cornelius Johnson (1593–1661) was a popular portraitist among the English aristocracy of the 17th century. This painting from 1640 shows Arthur, 1st Baron Capell (1604–1649), together with his family, posing before their formal garden. Note that of the three females in the picture (his wife in the center and his two daughters at the right), Lady Elizabeth Capell is looking respectfully at her husband, daughter Mary is gazing at her baby brother, and daughter Elizabeth is looking shyly to the right; only the males in the picture look directly at the viewer.

education of their children. Luther and Calvin here drew on Paul's epistles: "Wives, be subject to your husbands as you are to the Lord. For the husband is the head of the wife just as Christ is the head of the church, the body of which He is the Savior. Just as the church is subject to Christ, so also wives ought to be, in everything, to their husbands" (Ephesians 5.22–24).

Husbands and fathers exercised their authority in a variety of ways. Physical discipline was permitted within certain limits, but men were expected above all to lead by setting examples of rigorous and godly behavior. To help them, most Protestant denominations offered some form of personal and family counseling. They also emphasized Bible reading within all family devotions. But since the godly family was the basic unit of godly society, the society itself had an intrinsic right to step in and exert authority when a parent failed. Public shaming, social ostracism, banishment from church life, and imprisonment were widely practiced.[9]

In the godly society, sexual morality played an important role. At least in their first two or three generations, Protestant Christians placed a significantly sharper and more constant focus on sexuality than did their Catholic peers. Chastity before marriage and fidelity within it remained the moral ideal for all Christians, but Catholic Europe had long allowed a certain liberality in sexual matters, especially for men. Prostitution, although regulated, had been legal throughout Europe for centuries, for example, and no social stigma fell on the men who frequented prostitutes.[10] One way that Protestants sought to curb prostitution—apart from simply closing down the brothels—was through early marriage. With access to legitimate sexual release, they believed, men would not be tempted to resort to illegitimate means.

Sexual Morality

---

[9]   The Scottish reformer and founder of the Presbyterian tradition, John Knox (1514–1572), wrote a vitriolic treatise called *First Blast of the Trumpet against the Monstrous Regiment of Women* (1558). The tract takes aim specifically at England's Queen Mary and her heavy-handed efforts to restore Catholicism in the realm (discussed in chapter 14), but its general attitude regarding women's biblical call to subservience to men is clear. "To promote a woman to bear rule, superiority, dominion, or empire above any realm, nation, or city, is repugnant to nature; contumely [an insult] to God, a thing most contrary to His revealed will and approved ordinance; and finally, it is the subversion of good order, of all equity and justice. In the probation of this proposition, I will not be so curious as to gather whatsoever may amplify, set forth, or decor the same; but I am purposed, even as I have spoken my conscience in most plain and few words, so to stand content with a simple proof of every member, bringing in for my witness God's ordinance in nature, His plain will revealed in His word, and by the minds of such as be most ancient amongst godly writers. And first, where I affirm the empire of a woman to be a thing repugnant to nature, I mean not only that God, by the order of His creation, has spoiled [deprived] woman of authority and dominion, but also that man has seen, proved, and pronounced just causes why it should be. Man, I say, in many other cases, does in this behalf see very clearly. For the causes are so manifest, that they cannot be hid. For who can deny but it is repugnant to nature, that the blind shall be appointed to lead and conduct such as do see? That the weak, the sick, and impotent persons shall nourish and keep the whole and strong? And finally, that the foolish, mad, and frenetic shall govern the discreet, and give counsel to such as be sober of mind? And such be all women, compared unto man in bearing of authority. For their sight in civil regiment is but blindness; their strength, weakness; their counsel, foolishness; and judgment, frenzy, if it be rightly considered."

[10] Men had tended to put marriage off until they were established in a trade, which could take until their thirties.

The era also witnessed new efforts to combat homosexuality. Same-sex eroticism had been regarded as a sign of weakness since Roman times. Christianity added the notion that the activity was immoral since it denied the procreative function that was sexuality's whole intent and purpose. Until the 13th century, however, homosexuality was not a criminal offense. By 1260 in France, homosexual acts became punishable by death. Comparable measures were instituted across Europe, at both the national and the local levels, although it remains unclear how often such laws were enforced. Hostility to homosexuality increased with the need to rebuild the population after the Black Death as well. Although Renaissance classicism brought more liberal attitudes, in Florence alone more than fifteen thousand people were arrested for sodomy between 1432 and 1502 (although not all were convicted). The Spanish Inquisition arrested more than fifteen hundred people on charges of homosexual acts between 1540 and 1700.

Protestantism's emphasis on biblical truth (*sola Scriptura*) sharpened antihomosexual sentiments significantly, although formal condemnations came mostly at the local levels of government.[11] One notable exception was England's "Buggery Act," passed in 1533 under King Henry VIII, whose break from Rome we will examine in chapter 14. The act remained in force until 1861, when the death penalty it called for was replaced by a sentence of life imprisonment.

Forasmuch as there is not yet sufficient and condign [deserved] punishment appointed and limited by the due course of the Laws of this Realm for the detestable and abominable Vice of Buggery, [whether] committed with mankind or beast: May it therefore please the King's Highness, with the assent of the Lords Spiritual and the Commons of this present parliament assembled, that it may be enacted by the authority of the same, that the same offence be from henceforth adjudged a felony, and that such an order and form of process therein to be used against the offenders as in cases of felony at the Common Law; and that the offenders being hereof convicted—by verdict, confession, or outlawry— shall suffer such pains of death, and losses and penalties of their goods, chattels, debts, lands, tenements, and [inherited properties], as felons do according to the Common Laws of this Realm; and that no person offending in any such offence shall be admitted to [the king's] clergy; and that Justices of the Peace shall have power and authority within the limits of their commissions and jurisdictions to hear and determine the said offence, as they do in the cases of other felonies.

---

[11] Just six passages from the Bible explicitly condemn homosexuality, and two are simply New Testament restatements of Old Testament proscriptions. The scriptures record no direct teaching from Jesus.

What makes any type of sexual activity a crime against the state instead of a matter of personal morality? In Protestant Europe, where the state had become the administrative head of the religious community, a sin against public morals was also a crime against civil society. Hence homosexuality—along with adultery, masturbation, foul language, gambling, and drunkenness—required a civil response. Sixteenth-century Protestants read the Bible as mandating the two-parent, heterosexual, married, nuclear family. Any sexual activity outside that norm was in essence a threat to the godly state.

THE REBIRTH OF SATIRE

A literary genre that thrived outside the norms of taste was satire, which roared back to life in the 16th century. The conjunction of increasing literacy rates and the mass availability of printed texts generated a demand for literary entertainment unlike anything the Western world had experienced before. Not that the love of storytelling was itself new, but oral tradition could now give way to print on paper. Reading became a common pleasure of everyday life, no longer the reserve of scholars and monks. Printing houses across Europe poured out a steady stream of poetry, histories, stage dramas and comedies, travelogues, essays, memoirs, popular science tracts, and collections of letters and speeches.

Not everyone in Europe was reading Erasmus, Luther, and Calvin constantly—which is probably a good thing. In addition to Machiavelli and Aretino, three European writers stand out in the first half of the 16th century: Thomas More, Ulrich von Hutten, and François Rabelais. They could hardly have been more different in their personalities and life stories, but the most famous works of all three were satires.

Satire had been one of the most popular literary genres among the Romans. The English word *satire*, which appeared for the first time in 1509, in fact derives from Latin *satura* (denoting a witty poem that ridicules vice). "Satire is all ours," once bragged Quintilian (36–96 CE), Rome's greatest literary scholar. But satire had all but disappeared during the Middle Ages. Levity about the world's idiosyncrasies and human foibles did not appeal much to the monks who established the classical canon in their scriptoria. With the rise of classical humanism, however, satire returned as a favorite literary genre. There were, after all, plenty of people to ridicule: warmongering popes, fey aristocrats, affected scholars, grasping financiers, humanistic despots, self-absorbed artists.

Erasmus helped to revive prose satire with his *Praise of Folly*, and satire in prose, in fact, became the preferred style in the 16th century. His close friend Thomas More (1478–1535) penned a popular book called *Utopia*

Thomas More's Utopia

Utopia   This woodcut by Ambrosius Holbein (ca. 1494–1519)—older brother of the famous artist Hans Holbein (ca. 1497–1543)—was the frontispiece for a 1518 edition of *Utopia*. Against a backdrop of the fictional island, Raphael Hythlodaeus describes the Utopian way of life to More.

(1516).[12] It consists of two parts, the first being an imaginary discussion between More and a traveler-adventurer named Raphael Hythlodaeus on the various ills then besetting Europe. High on the list are pervasive poverty, religious intolerance, the failure of systems of justice, and the propensity to war. In the second part, Hythlodaeus describes for More his travels to a "perfect society"—a far-distant island in the Atlantic named Utopia (which is an Anglicized version of the Greek phrase "no place").

Utopia is a crescent-shaped island, 200 miles across, in which the population lives in scattered communities of about seventy-five thousand each. All goods are held in common; citizens take turns, in two-year shifts, farming the land and working at artisanal crafts; medical care and primary education are free and available to all. There are no lawyers; all wives are subservient to their husbands, to whom they must confess their sins once every month; and the penalty for pre- or extramarital sex is enslavement. There are a lot of slaves, consequently, who do most of the hard labor. Although meant as a satire, there is nothing in *Utopia* to make a modern reader laugh, because More was largely humorless. (According to a family memoir, he laughed at court jesters when they made pratfalls, but at little else.) *Utopia* remains a valuable book, however, not least for the insight it provides into its author's mind.

Hutten's Letters of Obscure Men   Far more successful as satire is the fictitious *Letters of Obscure Men* (1517) by Ulrich von Hutten (1488–1523), a swashbuckling imperial knight and occasional humanist writer. In 1515 the Duke of Württemberg killed a beloved cousin of Hutten whose wife he had designs on. Hutten responded by publishing blistering Latin poems that ruined the duke's reputation and led ultimately to his overthrow. They made Hutten famous, and in 1517 Maximilian I (r. 1493–1519) appointed him the poet laureate of the German Empire. In that same year, Hutten became a passionate supporter of Martin Luther and coauthored, with his humanist friend Johann Jäger (1480–1539, who used the pseudonym Crotus Rubeanus), the *Letters of Obscure Men*.

---

[12] More is best known as the royal chancellor who refused to recognize Henry VIII's annulment of his marriage to Catherine of Aragon and opposed the king's plan to establish a national church under royal control that would deny the supremacy of the pope (discussed in chapter 14). He paid for his opposition with his head.

Filled with clever wit and broad, coarse humor, the *Letters* purport to be addressed to a prominent nobleman by fanatical Catholic monks and friars regarding why it is necessary to burn Jewish books like the Talmud and anti-Christian polemical literature. The diatribe is in reference to a real event: the dispute, several years earlier, between the famed humanist scholar Johann Reuchlin (1455–1522) and a group of zealous Catholic Inquisitors who had argued for the same cause. (The title echoes the *Letters of Notable Men* that had passed between Reuchlin and his adversaries.) The *Letters* were written in intentionally bad Latin, making much of their humor impossible to convey in English. Reading them, it is clear that Hutten never lost his hatred of Catholic monks, who might well respond to Protestantism and satire with book burnings, and this book is a settling of old debts. He gives his monks outrageous names like Brother Goatmilker and Brother Shitshoveller, attributes every sort of lechery to them, and describes them nervously defecating under their robes during public debates. His aim is less to defend the Jews (although he was indeed an opponent of the book burnings) than to ridicule the pretensions and hypocrisy of the Catholics. The aristocrat who receives the letters—a real figure in Hutten's time—also comes in for a lambasting. The monks sordidly declare their passionate relations with his wife.

The best known of the three satirists was François Rabelais (ca. 1494–1553). Born to a wealthy country lawyer, he received a sound education before entering *Rabelais* the Franciscan order sometime around 1510 and becoming a priest about a decade later. He traveled to libraries around France and earned a reputation as a first-rate classical scholar, but in 1524 he suffered the indignity of having his Greek books confiscated by one of his superiors, who thought they might lead to heresy. Rabelais successfully petitioned Pope Clement VII (r. 1523–1534) in 1524 for release from his Franciscan order and to be allowed to join the Benedictines. Through his new order he studied medicine in Paris. However, since he disliked Benedictine life too, he broke his vows and moved to the University of Montpellier to continue his medical training. He finished in record time, quickly sired two children with a local widow, and then moved on to practice medicine in Narbonne and Lyons.

In 1532 Rabelais published a brief satirical novel, *The Horrible and Terrifying Words and Deeds of the Renowned Pantagruel, King of the Dipsodes*. When this proved unexpectedly popular, he followed it with three more volumes that continue Pantagruel's adventures while also providing, in another volume, the backstory of Pantagruel's father, Gargantua. The five books are now published together as a single work, *Gargantua and Pantagruel*. (A supposed sixth book, written by an opportunistic forger, appeared in 1564, eleven years after Rabelais's death.) Gargantua and Pantagruel are giants—enormous, misshapen, driven by inexhaustible appetites of body and mind, and delighting in broad scatological humor—and the same can be said of *Gargantua and Pantagruel* the novel, a vast, loose-jointed sequence of episodes in the protagonists' lives. The closest it comes to offering a coherent story is a lengthy rambling narrative in Books 3 and 4 about their efforts to help a friend. (Another giant, named Panurge, wishes to locate an oracle known as the Sacred Bottle for help deciding whether to marry a girl whose fidelity is uncertain.) Although lively, the novel is shapeless, repetitive, and overlong.

What was its purpose? Rabelais certainly wanted to entertain his readers and make them laugh. "Mirth is my theme, and tears are not, / For laughter is man's proper lot" is the famous ending couplet of Rabelais's verse preface. *Gargantua and Pantagruel* and *Letters of Obscure Men* are the only truly funny books written in that unfunny century. Being satire, the laughs they raise come at someone's expense; we laugh because someone is being ridiculed. Both books have numerous targets, but they share one in particular, the Catholic clergy. Whereas Hutten attacks them from the Protestant side, Rabelais offers a Catholic in-house attack.

The wounds he inflicts, however, result not from rapier wit but from a heavy two-handed broadsword. He mocks dry-as-dust scholastic theologians and pompous overfed monks by exaggerating their flaws a hundredfold. He lambasts puritanical morality by having his heroes indulge in orgies of food, sex, and drink that would make a Roman emperor blush. Bodily functions stain every page. In one early passage (1.17), Gargantua caps off a drinking binge by untying his codpiece and urinating so much he floods the entire city of Paris, "drowning 260,418 people, plus women and children."

Still, the book's verbal energy is extraordinary. Rejoicing in his freedom from church Latin, Rabelais pours words onto the page in a kind of vernacular euphoria. The novel is a hymn to the French language and a celebration of human freedom: freedom to think, to scoff, to lust, to indulge in manic excess, to coin words, to imagine outrageous scenes, to offend, to risk boredom, and to delight in whimsy. Ultimately, it is about the freedom to hope for a better world than the one we live in. As a work of art it has failings, but as the expression of an irrepressible spirit it can never cease to fascinate. And that spirit is humanism.

CATHOLIC REFORM AND THE COUNCIL OF TRENT

Whether it followed a humanist line or another, Catholic reform was certainly needed, and figures like Erasmus and More spent their lives calling for it. Even the most worldly of Renaissance popes recognized that many of the faithful were put off by the church and its cumbersome institutions. The problem was how to find reforms that would please everybody. Through much of the 14th and 15th centuries, when the Holy See was a political football of the Italian nobility, a movement arose to strengthen the role of general councils in ecclesiastical governance. The popes, many of them more concerned with their personal fates than with the office they held, opposed this "conciliarism" vehemently, but the resulting deadlock only aggravated the problems that both sides were supposedly trying to address. The success of Protestantism produced urgent calls for a general council; papal dithering only made the calls more insistent. But then, surprisingly, the Protestant juggernaut stalled. By 1540 every state in Europe that would become Protestant had done so; no new national-scale conversions were won by any of the major Protestant branches (see Map 12.3).

Beginning with Pope Paul III (r. 1534–1549), the court in Rome finally took the lead in bringing on reform. He appointed a commission of high-ranking clerics to investigate church abuses; this commission's final report, published in 1536, laid bare scores of problems in the administration of the papal court, the actions of the bishops, and the shortcomings in parish life. In 1537 Paul issued a bull condemning the enslavement of the indigenous peoples of the New World (discussed in the next chapter); in 1540 he confirmed the formation of the Society of Jesus, or the Jesuits, a teaching and missionary order; and in 1542 he authorized the creation of the Holy Office—that is, the Roman Inquisition. Last, after securing guarantees that its proceedings would be subject to papal approval, he called for a full ecumenical council to study and propose solutions to the general reform of Catholic life, which has come to be known as either the **Catholic Reformation** or the **Counter-Reformation**. This **Council of Trent**, which convened (with a few intermissions) from 1546 to 1563, was the most important assembly of its kind until the Second Vatican Council of 1963–1965.

Although the religious revolt in northern Europe was obviously its trigger, the Council of Trent was more than a response to Protestantism; efforts at reform *The* had begun long before Luther appeared on the scene. Nevertheless, the Council's *Plan for* initial actions offered no hint of compromise but rather highlighted the differ- *Renewal* ences between what it regarded as Catholic truth and Protestant lies. If anything, they asserted the Catholic position with even more force than before. The problems confronting the church, the Council believed, were not with doctrine itself but with the ways in which doctrine was taught to the people. The changes most needed were therefore in leadership and organization.

Paul III's successor, Pope Julius III (r. 1550–1555), devoted himself to personal pleasure—in particular, his infatuation with an illiterate, fourteen-year-old street beggar named Innocenzo. Julius moved Innocenzo into the Vatican palace, awarded him several wealthy benefices, appointed him the abbot of the monastery of Mont Saint-Michel, and made him a cardinal. Julius, thankfully, was around for only a few years, and the popes who succeeded him pressed the Council to reach even further in its ambition: Paul IV (r. 1555–1559) and Pius IV

Catholic Reform   Pope Paul III (r. 1534–1549), in an oil portrait by the great Venetian artist Titian (Tiziano Vecellio, 1490–1576), called for the Council of Trent (1545–1563), whose pomp and circumstance are also on display here. Initially summoned in 1537 to lay out the plan for the Catholic Reformation, the Council was delayed for financial and bureaucratic reasons; it finally met, ironically, when Martin Luther had taken to what was to become his deathbed.

(1559–1565).[13] The Council ordered a streamlining of the church bureaucracy, outlawed ecclesiastical pluralism (the practice of a single individual holding appointments to serve in multiple parishes or dioceses), and heightened the responsibility of bishops to oversee the life of their provinces. Most important of all, it charged them with improving the education of their clergy and of the flocks they served. To assist them, the church helped to build hundreds of new parish schools to train teachers. At the higher levels, the church increased the funding for universities and reorganized curricula.

THE SOCIETY OF JESUS

Several new ecclesiastical orders joined the campaign and dedicated themselves specifically to education: the Ursulines ("Company of Saint Ursula"), founded in 1535 and papally approved in 1544, created a network of schools for girls across Europe and soon in the New World. More famous still was the Society of Jesus, commonly called the **Jesuits**, found by St. Ignacio de Loyola (1491–1556) in 1540. "A Society founded for a single, central purpose—namely, to strive for the defense and propagation of the Faith, and for the progress of souls in Christian life and doctrine," the Jesuits dedicated themselves to preaching and teaching at all educational levels, although historically they have tended toward higher education. Founded as they were by a former soldier—Loyola, a Spanish noble and career military man, experienced a conversion while recuperating from severe battle wounds received in 1521—the Jesuits formed a compact and highly

---

[13] Julius is the last pope known to have been sexually active and explicitly homosexual.

centralized organization. They took vows of poverty, chastity, and absolute obedience to their superiors, especially to the pope, and became the church's most successful tool in bringing Christianity to the outside world.

Within ten years of their founding, the Jesuits had established mission schools in India and Japan, and by 1600 they had extended their reach into South and North America and into sub-Saharan Africa. And since the Council of Trent particularly emphasized the doctrinal point that for Catholics, unlike Protestants, doing "good works" was an essential requirement of Christian living, the reformed church stepped up its involvement in charitable work among the world's poorest peo-

Jesuit Missionaries   The Jesuits were pivotal in revitalizing the Catholic Church's evangelical and educational missions. In this 18th-century painting from Lima, Peru, the order's founder, St. Ignatius Loyola, appears in the center, flanked by two loyal followers, St. Francis Borja and St. Francis Xavier. At the bottom, figures representing Africa, Asia, North America, and South America bear witness to the extent of Jesuit missionary activity.

ples. The combined efforts of these new orders, especially in their conflation of schoolroom teaching and service, helped gain many converts in the New World. They even returned many Protestant believers in southern Germany, parts of Bohemia, and throughout Poland–Lithuania to Catholicism.

The Jesuit Mission: Education and Conversion

Education required books, however, and education in the Catholic faith faced a potential obstacle: non-Catholic books were easily available too. The post-Trent church confronted the problem—or thought it had done so—by producing an *Index of Forbidden Books*. The first version of the *Index*, promulgated in 1559, was regarded as too severe in its strictures, and a revised and slightly moderated version appeared in 1564. The *Index* was continually updated over the centuries, with more than forty editions published between 1564 and its eventual suppression in 1966, making it the longest institutionalized censorship in Greater Western history. It was also, arguably, the least effective, since few of the condemned books ever went out of print. In fact, the *Index* represented a perfect shopping list for individuals who wanted to read materials officially denied them. True, 90 percent of the books ever placed on the list were dense theological treatises that non-Catholics or lay Catholics were unlikely ever to read in the first place. Even so, the 1564 *Index* singled out quite an impressive list of writers. It condemned the works of Pietro Aretino, John Calvin, Nicolaus Copernicus (the Polish astronomer who developed the heliocentric model of the universe, in which the sun, not Earth, is the fixed center), Desiderius Erasmus, Henry VIII of England, Martin Luther, Niccolò Machiavelli, François Rabelais, and William Tyndale (an early translator of the Bible into English). Also forbidden were the Qur'an and the Talmud. Later editions added the humanist *Essays* of Michel de Montaigne and the scientific writings of Johannes Kepler and Galileo Galilei.

Jesuit training emphasized all-round education, so that Society members would be prepared for any educational or missionary challenge thrown their way. Even today, the training of a Jesuit takes up to thirteen years. Although grounded in classical humanism, Jesuit education branched off into mathematics and astronomy. Several of the leading scholars of the age were Jesuits. Christoph Scheiner (1573–1650) was a German astronomer who discovered sunspots independently of Galileo; he also wrote one of the first treatises on the physiology of the human eye. Alexius Sylvius Polonus (1593–1653) was a Polish astronomer like Copernicus and specialized in the design of ever-more refined telescopes. Although primarily an engineer, he nevertheless used his instruments, mastery of mathematics, and Copernican theory to compose a new work on the design of the solar calendar.

Another influential Jesuit, Carlo Borromeo (1538–1584), was no scholar but dedicated his career to promoting a better-educated clergy. Coming from a wealthy aristocratic family (his mother was a Medici), he used his personal fortune and the large income from his position as archbishop of Milan to found numerous colleges and seminaries. He also established the Academy of the Vatican Nights, an informal symposium to keep church leaders informed of the newest learning.

WHAT ABOUT THE ORTHODOX EAST?

The 15th and 16th centuries were a time of neither renaissance nor reformation for the Orthodox world. The central fact of Orthodox life in this era was conquest by the Ottoman Turks, followed by efforts to adapt to Muslim rule. From about 1350 on, thousands of scholars, artists, soldiers, farmers, officials, and other refugees from Byzantium fled into western Europe. Apart from these scattered communities, the only part of the Orthodox world that remained uncontrolled by the Ottomans, once Constantinople fell in 1453, was Russia. The Turkish court eventually awarded its Orthodox subjects the status of a *millet* (Arabic for "nation"), which meant that the community governed its own internal affairs in accordance with its own laws and customs. But since Islamic law defined its subject communities by faith rather than ethnicity, the immediate impact of millet status was to strengthen the authority of the Orthodox Patriarch of Constantinople, who henceforth held sway over the previously autonomous Albanian, Arab, Bulgarian, Georgian, Greek, and Serbian Orthodox churches. All the traditional restrictions on subject Christians remained in place.

Ottoman policies toward its subject Christians were moderately tolerant. Forced conversions to Islam were forbidden by law but occasionally occurred; notably, individuals who did convert but then returned to Orthodoxy, or whose children returned to it, were customarily given three opportunities to recant their apostasy, after which they were killed (if male) or imprisoned (if female). The practice of *devshirme*—whereby Christian children were stolen from their families, raised as Muslims, and sent through the rigors of specialized military training to become Janissaries—continued unabated. Indeed, it accelerated through the 16th century. The Ottoman sultans relied on these slave-soldiers, who were under their direct authority, to provide a check on the ambitions of Turkish nobles. Hostilities between the Ottoman state and Europe, however, meant that Orthodox Christianity experienced none of the innovative influences of the Renaissance, Protestant Reformation, or Catholic Reformation. The ideas and values of Renaissance humanism—whether Christian or otherwise—made no inroads in the east; neither did the Protestant reformers show much interest in intellectual or religious exchange with the Orthodox. Martin Luther, fearing Turkish advances into central Europe, approved of a military campaign against the Ottomans but explicitly rejected the idea of a crusade. "Christian warfare," he insisted, was an oxymoron.

◆

It may have been an oxymoron, but it was about to become Europe's reality. The hopeful and confident humanism of the Renaissance gave way to one of the bitterest and most violent periods in Europe's history: the era of the Wars of Religion (ca. 1524–1648), which left millions dead across the continent.

The Reformation was, like the Renaissance, a movement with its eyes on the past. Only by returning to the pure values and practices of an earlier era could society set itself on the right path for development and growth. There was something to be said for the backward glance, but at the same time a number of startling discoveries were about to change everything in Greater Western life: new worlds, new civilizations, new political and economic alignments, new ideas about the cosmos, and new understandings of the fundamental structure of nature were about to challenge every assumption and institution of society. It is an irony of the age that the Greater West entered the 16th and 17th centuries with its eyes on the past as it raced headlong into the future.

WHO, WHAT, WHERE

Anabaptists
Catholic Reformation/
   Counter-Reformation
Christian humanism
Council of Trent
Erasmus

German Peasants'
   Revolt
humanism
indulgences
Jesuits
John Calvin

justification by faith
   alone
Martin Luther
Ninety-Five Theses
predestination
Protestant Reformation

SUGGESTED READINGS

Primary Sources

Boccaccio, Giovanni. *The Decameron.*

Calvin, John. *Institutes of Christian Religion.*

Cellini, Benvenuto. *Autobiography.*

Erasmus of Rotterdam. *Julius Excluded from Heaven.*

Erasmus of Rotterdam. *The Praise of Folly.*

Hutton, Ulrich von. *Letters of Obscure Men.*

Luther, Martin. *Address to the Christian Nobility of the German Nation.*

Luther, Martin. *The Freedom of a Christian.*

Luther, Martin. *Table Talk.*

Machiavelli, Niccolò. *Discourses on Livy.*

Machiavelli, Niccolò. *The Mandrake Root.*

Machiavelli, Niccolò. *The Prince.*

Rabelais, François. *Gargantua and Pantagruel.*

Vasari, Giorgio. *Lives of the Artists.*

Anthologies

Black, Robert, ed. *Renaissance Thought: A Reader* (2001).

Janz, Denis R., ed. *A Reformation Reader: Primary Texts with Introductions* (2008).

King, John N., ed. *Voices of the English Reformation: A Sourcebook* (2004).

Wiesner-Hanks, Merry. *The Renaissance and Reformation: A History in Documents* (2011).

Studies

Baylor, Michael G. *The German Reformation and the Peasants' War: A Brief History with Documents* (2012).

Benedict, Philip. *Christ's Churches Purely Reformed: A Social History of Calvinism* (2002).

Bolzoni, Lina. *The Gallery of Memory: Literary and Iconographic Models in the Age of the Printing Press* (2001).

Caffiero, Marina. *Forced Baptisms: Histories of Jews, Christians, and Converts in Papal Rome* (2011).

Diefendorf, Barbara B. *From Penitence to Charity: Pious Women and the Catholic Reformation in Paris* (2006).

Eisenstein, Elizabeth. *The Printing Revolution in Early Modern Europe* (2005).

King, Ross. *Machiavelli: Philosopher of Power* (2009).

Levi, Anthony. *Renaissance and Reformation: The Intellectual Genesis* (2004).

MacCulloch, Diarmaid. *The Reformation: A History* (2005).

Martines, Lauro. *Strong Words: Writing and Social Strain in the Italian Renaissance* (2001).

Mazzotta, Giuseppe. *Cosmopoiesis: The Renaissance Experiment* (2001).

McGrath, Alister E. *Reformation Thought: An Introduction* (2001).

Muslu, Cihan Yüksel. *The Ottomans and the Mamluks: Imperial Diplomacy and Warfare in the Islamic World* (2014).

Nauert, Charles G., Jr. *Humanism and the Culture of Renaissance Europe* (2006).

Oberman, Heiko A. *Luther: Man between God and the Devil* (2006).

O'Malley, John W. *Trent and All That: Renaming Catholicism in the Early Modern Era* (2000).

Ozment, Steven. *The Serpent and the Lamb: Cranach, Luther, and the Making of the Reformation* (2012).

Parks, Tim. *Medici Money: Banking, Metaphysics, and Art in Fifteenth-Century Florence* (2006).

Pettegree, Andrew. *The Book in the Renaissance* (2011).

Pettegree, Andrew. *Reformation and the Culture of Persuasion* (2005).

Randall, Michael. *The Gargantuan Polity: On the Individual and the Community in the French Renaissance* (2008).

Stjerna, Kirsi. *Women and the Reformation* (2008).

Taylor, Barry, and Alejandro Coroleu. *Humanism and Christian Letters in Early Modern Iberia, 1480–1630* (2010).

Wiesner-Hanks, Merry E. *Women and Gender in Early Modern Europe* (2008).

For additional resources, including maps, primary sources, visuals, web links, and quizzes, please go to www.oup.com/us/backman.

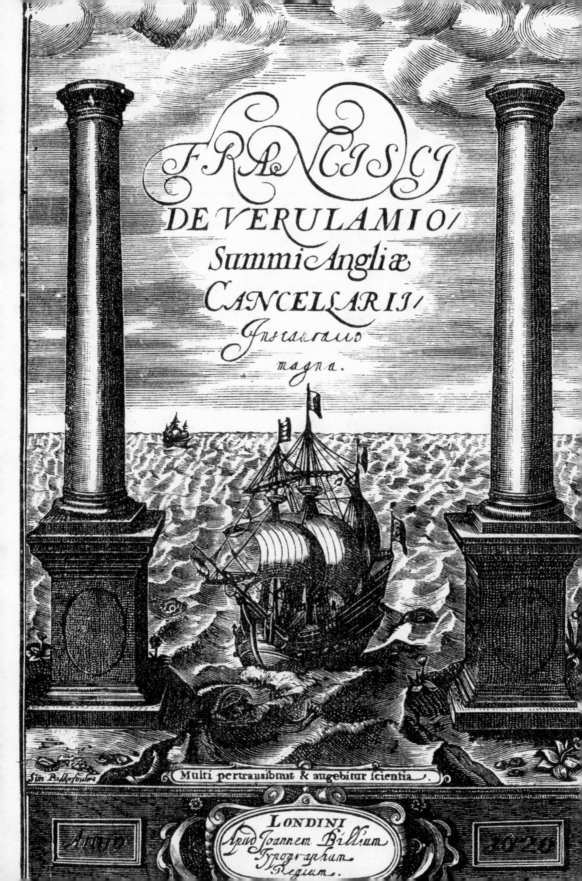

FRANCISCI

DE VERULAMIO,

Summi Angliæ

CANCELLARIJ,

Instauratio

magna.

Multi pertransibunt & augebitur scientia.

LONDINI
Apud Joannem Billium
Typographum
Regium

CHAPTER 13

Worlds Old and New

1450–1700

In the 13th century a Franciscan scholar from England named Roger Bacon (1214–1294) gleefully tore into everyone around him who thought of themselves as scientists. He could, and did, find fault in anyone. Phrases like "damned fools," "ignorant asses," "inept buffoons," and "miserable idiots" pepper his writings in his own colorful Latin. Science, he argued, had been for too long a prisoner to philosophers who never thought to test their abstractions against the evidence of their senses. When a renowned scholar like Albertus Magnus (ca. 1200–1280) came to lecture at the University of Paris and was received "like a second Aristotle," Bacon reacted bitterly: "Never before in the history of the world has there been committed a[n intellectual] crime as perverse as this."

Bacon did not oppose grand theories in themselves. Rather, he believed that the only valid way to reach them was through observation. "Experimental science is the Queen of All Sciences, the goal of all our speculation," he wrote in his *Opus Maius* (*Major*

THE AMERICAS IN 1600

ATLANTIC OCEAN

PACIFIC OCEAN

☐ Spanish
☐ Portuguese

The *Novum Organum* Francis Bacon was no scientist but an evangelist for science. By strict application of scientific methods, he believed, humanity could return to the state of perfect comprehension of and unity with the natural world that was lost with Adam and Eve's expulsion from Eden. The *Novum Organum* (*New Instrument*), published in 1620, laid out his vision for the method of attaining this true knowledge of the world. The frontispiece reprinted here shows a ship about to head out bravely into uncharted waters. The Latin inscription below quotes from the biblical book of Daniel: "Many will go, back and forth, and knowledge will be increased."

Work). But even that was not sufficient. One had to master all the sciences—including mathematics, optics, astronomy, botany, and physics—before one could even begin to theorize about any one of them. Bacon spent many years achieving just that mastery, as well as learning Greek and Hebrew (and possibly a smattering of Arabic), to reach the grand synthesis that he believed only he could achieve. In the end, however, struggles within the Franciscan order forced Bacon into house arrest and silence; he never had the chance to elaborate his grand Theory of Everything.

In the late 16th century Sir Francis Bacon (1561–1626) earned fame for his brilliance in law and philosophy, and he cultivated friendships among England's most wealthy and privileged people. Bacon (of no known relation to his medieval namesake) could, and did, flatter anyone. Bacon spent his last five years on the philosophical work that had always fascinated him. He planned a massive, comprehensive work to be called the *Great Instauration*—meaning the refounding of the entire Western intellectual tradition—but completed only a handful of discrete books that were to form parts of the whole. His *Novum Organum* (*New Instrument*) in 1620 reworked Aristotelian logic, whereas *The New Atlantis* (published in 1627, after the author's death) was a utopian fantasy. He envisioned, like Roger Bacon had done several centuries earlier, a grand masterwork, a complete synthesis of human intellectual understanding. His focus, however, was on the process of analysis rather than on the gathering of data or the testing of

CHAPTER TIMELINE

1480	1500	1520	1540	1560

- 1492 Columbus reaches the Americas
- 1494 Treaty of Tordesillas
- 1498 Vasco da Gama reaches India
- 1519–1521 Cortés's army conquers Aztec Empire
- 1519–1522 Magellan's fleet circumnavigates the globe
- 1531–1533 Pizarro's army conquers Inca Empire
- 1543 Copernicus, *On the Revolutions of the Heavenly Sphere*

hypotheses. Given facts A and B, what conclusions or assumptions can we validly draw from them—and how can we distinguish the valid from the invalid?

Both Bacons addressed the same problem, although from different angles: What are the intrinsic flaws in human thinking? What errors stand between us and Truth, and how can we overcome them? The world overwhelms us with data, impressions, facts, and observations, and our history overwhelms us with ideas, theories, opinions, and conjectures. We need a clear guide to dealing with all this input. How can we know that we are thinking properly?

The urgency of the question became all the more acute with the European discovery of the Americas in the late 15th century. How could all the holy books, the classical authors, the medieval theorists, and the brilliant minds of the Renaissance not have known about the existence of this "New World"—two entire continents filled with peoples, languages, religions, value systems, and traditions of which the Greater West was ignorant? If the best minds of the past four thousand years were of no help, then what would equip the people of the 16th and 17th centuries to come to grips with all of this new information? This shock to the system of Western thinking helped to spur a vibrant, even dizzying, new wave of scientific and philosophical advances known as the **Scientific Revolution** (roughly 1500–1750)—a period marked not only by a parade of new discoveries and ideas but also by intrinsic changes in the way of thinking about the physical universe that has since come to characterize Western views and values.

1600	1620	1640	1660	1680

- 1610 Galileo, *Starry Messenger*
- 1620 Francis Bacon, *New Instrument*
- 1632 Galileo, *Dialogue on the Two Chief World Systems*
- 1633 Galileo's trial by the Roman Inquisition
- 1637 Descartes, *Discourse on Method*
- 1660 Royal Society of London founded
- 1666 French Royal Academy of Science founded
- 1667 German Royal Academy of Science founded
- 1687 Newton, *Principia Mathematica*

The Scientific Revolution was not a rejection of tradition, unlike Renaissance humanism, but a new phase in its development. The astonishing discoveries of the age placed science at the center of intellectual life in a way that was unique to the West. Fields like mathematics, medicine, and astronomy had always played important roles in intellectual culture. Plato's Academy had expected everyone to master geometry before even beginning philosophical study. However, in the 16th and 17th centuries explorers and scientists did more than discover new continents, redraw the map of the world, place the sun at the center of the cosmos, discover the universal law of gravitation, and witness the Islamic retreat from science. They also came to define intellectual life and establish the standards by which it developed and was judged. The story from Bacon to Bacon helps to explain why.

EUROPEAN VOYAGES OF DISCOVERY

For more than four thousand years the entire known world had consisted of three continents: Europe, Africa, and Asia. From the start, the peoples of the Greater West had shown more restlessness and curiosity about the world than any other ancient culture. Phoenician travelers, beginning around 1200 BCE, had journeyed beyond the Straits of Gibraltar and into the Atlantic. The Greeks had circumnavigated the British Isles by 300 BCE, and by 100 CE the Romans had made contact with merchant-explorers from China. The latter ventured as far as the Euphrates River shortly after the time of Constantine the Great, around 360 CE, although much later the Ming dynasty closed China off from the outside world.[1] The first Christian missionaries had reached China well before the western Roman Empire fell in 476. Viking raiders had spread out through the Baltic, North, and Mediterranean seas and had reached a corner of North America by the 10th century. The Muslim Arabs, followed by the Persians and Turks, had carved out vast realms on all three continents and developed techniques to map the new territories. European stirrings in the Atlantic were thus only the latest phase in a centuries-long tradition of restlessness.

Portugal Takes the Lead

The Portuguese led the way. As early as 1415 their ships made contact with the coast of western Africa, down the expanse of what is today the country of Morocco. With the enthusiastic support of Prince Henry the Navigator (1394–1460), Portuguese fleets sailed next to the Azores and the Canary Islands. By 1445 they had reached the westernmost part of the continent, at today's neighboring states of Senegal and Gambia. In the 1460s they began to curve eastward

---

[1]   Under their great admiral Zheng He (1371–1435), Chinese fleets made it as far as the mouth of the Persian Gulf, to the Horn of Africa, and probably even up the Red Sea to Jiddah, not far from Mecca.

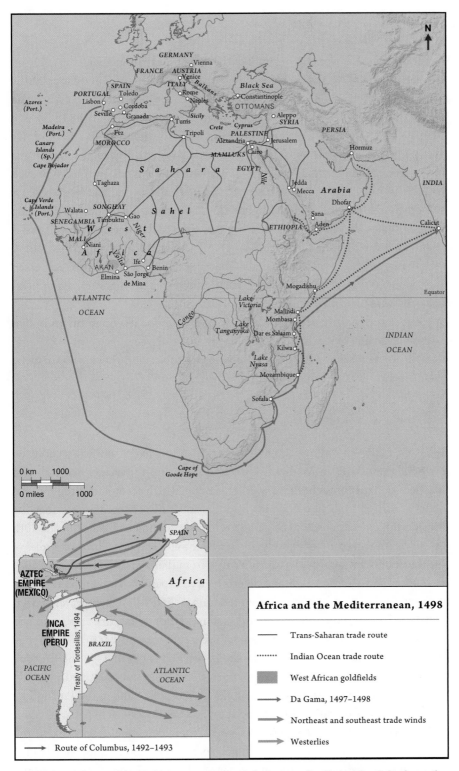

Africa and the Mediterranean, 1498

——	Trans-Saharan trade route
⋯⋯	Indian Ocean trade route
▨	West African goldfields
⟶	Da Gama, 1497–1498
⟶	Northeast and southeast trade winds
⟶	Westerlies
⟶	Route of Columbus, 1492–1493

MAP 13.1 Africa and the Mediterranean, 1498 Only six years after Christopher Columbus, sailing for Spain, reached the Americas, the Portuguese explorer Vasco da Gama made landfall in India.

under the massive overhanging bulk of the Saharan expanse. Their ships crossed the equator in 1474, and in 1488 they reached the Cape of Good Hope at the southern tip of Africa. Ten years later, in 1498, under the command of **Vasco da Gama** (ca. 1460–1524), the first European fleet made landfall in India (see Map 13.1). These were journeys of exploration and trade, not of conquest. Da Gama told the local ruler in Calicut, the center of the spice trade, that he was the ambassador of the king of Portugal—the ruler of many lands and a man of such wealth that no one in this part of the world could compare, and that for sixty years this king's predecessors had dispatched ships to explore the seas in the direction of India, where they had heard that Christian kings like themselves lived. To connect with these Christian monarchs was the sole aim of their explorations, not to seek luxury goods or precious metals—because the kings of Portugal possessed such tremendous wealth as to make them uninterested in whatever gold or silver or spices were to be found in India or any other place.

Da Gama meant hardly a word of this, of course, and it is doubtful his Indian host believed any of it. Christian missionary zeal and a genuine spirit of exploration for its own sake motivated those who put to sea and those who financed them. So, however, did an expectation of profit.

NEW CONTINENTS AND PROFITS

From the early 9th century sub-Saharan gold, spices, slaves, and ivory had been prized commodities in Mediterranean trade. Muslim merchants in Spain and Morocco had first brought these items to Europe, which accounts for the tremendous wealth of cities like Granada and Cordoba. (Tax records show that the Muslim inhabitants of Cordoba alone held six thousand black slaves in the 10th century.) These were luxury goods enjoyed by the elites. When Christian forces of the Reconquista drove the last Muslim rulers from Iberia in the 15th century, they took over control of this trade and determined to expand it. The commodities exchanged for these luxury items were predominantly textiles, metalwares, glazed pottery, glass, and paper. Not surprisingly, some of the coastal African peoples had embraced Islam in the intervening centuries, but this posed no bar to trade. Money mattered, not faith. When Vasco da Gama reached India in 1498, he mistook Hinduism for a quaint Eastern version of Christianity but identified precisely every spice and precious stone in the markets. Once in Calicut, the Portuguese quickly established trading posts along the whole southwestern Malabar Coast of India. Within twenty years they had spread their commercial network to the Malay Peninsula, the Indonesian archipelago, and the Moluccas (Spice Islands); within another two decades, they had reached China and Japan. Their first permanent trading post in China, at Macao, was established in 1555 (see Map 13.2).

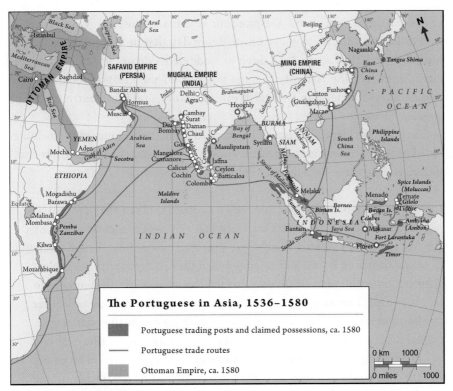

MAP 13.2   The Portuguese in Asia, 1536–1580   While the Spanish predominated in the New World, the Portuguese established themselves as the leading European commercial power in Asia in the 16th century.

Christopher Columbus's innovation in 1492 was to propose reaching Asia by sailing directly westward rather than circumnavigating Africa to the south. Although an Italian from Genoa, **Christopher Columbus** (1451–1506) sailed under the Spanish flag of Ferdinand and Isabella. Such international arrangements were common, so it is no wonder that just about every state ever associated with the first European to reach the Americas claims him as a native. To his fellow Italians he is Cristoforo Colombo, to the Spanish he is Cristóbal Colón, streets and squares in Barcelona commemorate Cristòfor Colom, and the Portuguese proudly recall Cristóvão Colombo.[2]

Christopher Columbus Discovers a "New World"

Every educated person in Europe and the Near East since the 12th century had known that the world was round. Columbus was unprepared for the size of the globe—thus the length of his historic journey, but not the fact of it. And then he ran into an unexpected roadblock, the Americas. Columbus never realized that the Caribbean islands he had landed at were in fact the outer islands

---

[2]   The English explorer John Cabot, who carried the Tudor flag as far as Newfoundland in 1497, was actually another Italian—Giovanni Caboto (1450–1508), from Venice.

of two vast new continents. Despite four voyages to the New World (that is, new to Europeans), he believed to his dying day that he had sailed to islands just off the coast of south Asia. Such misjudgments do not lessen his achievement, however. The Atlantic passage was one of the greatest technical and human-adventure feats in Greater Western history, and it had earth-changing consequences.

In his ship's log, Columbus duly recorded his first encounter with the indigenous people of the island that became known as *Hispaniola* (the "Spanish Island," today's Haiti and the Dominican Republic):

> When it became clear that they welcomed us, I saw that it would be easier to convert them to Our Holy Faith by peaceful means than by force, and so I offered them some simple gifts—red-dyed caps, necklaces of strung beads, and so on—which they received with great pleasure. So enthusiastic were they, in fact, that they began to swim out to our ships, carrying parrots, balls of cotton thread, spears, and other items to trade. . . . Still, they struck me as an exceptionally poor people, for all of them were naked—even the women, although I saw only one girl among them at the time. Every one of them I perceived to be young (that is, under the age of thirty), finely shaped and with handsome faces. . . . They appear to own no weapons and to have no knowledge of such, for when I showed them our swords they reached out and grabbed them by the blades, cutting themselves unexpectedly. . . . When I inquired, by pointing, about the scars visible on some of their bodies, they made me to understand, also by pointing, that people from another island had attacked them and tried to carry them off as slaves, but they resisted. . . . Overall they struck me as being clever, and I believe they would make good servants and could easily become Christian, since they have no religion of their own. They learned quickly to repeat the handful of words we taught them. If it please God, I intend to bring six of them home to Your Majesties, so that they might be taught to speak our language. Apart from the parrots, I saw no animals of any kind on the island.

Columbus's log entry reflects his disappointment in the poverty of the people. Expecting the vast riches of Asia's silk and spice trade, he found instead naked islanders—whom he mistakenly named "Indians"—with nothing but ready smiles and a number of parrots. On subsequent journeys he discovered more of the natural wealth available, and his enthusiasm recovered noticeably. In 1494 the monarchs of Spain and Portugal signed the Treaty of Tordesillas, which divided the lands of the newly expanded world between them: Spain laid claim to all the lands west of the meridian (north–south line) 1,300 miles west of the Cape Verde Islands, whereas Portugal held rights to all the new lands east of it. The treaty thus granted Portugal dominion over what became Brazil but left the rest of the New World to Spain; Portugal, in return, was spared Spanish competition in the Indian Ocean and South China Sea. Within a few years other adventurers had reached both the North American and the South American mainlands, and by 1507 at least one mapmaker—German cartographer Martin Waldseemüller (1470–1520)— began to appreciate that two entirely new continents had been found. On his revolutionary map, the *Universalis Cosmographia* ("World Map") of 1507, Waldseemüller named the new continents *America*, after the Italian cartographer Amerigo Vespucci (1454–1512), whose explorations and navigational charts he used in compiling his map.

The First Published Image of the New World
Christopher Columbus's first report to the Spanish kings of his discovery was published in Basel in early 1494; printed here is one of the illustrations that accompanied the Latin text. It shows Columbus arriving on the shore of "the island of Hispania" in a small landing craft. He offers a goblet as a peace offering to the inhabitants, who appear to be uniformly naked, male, and beardless, gathered at the shore to meet him.

News of Columbus's discovery spread quickly across Europe, and soon wave after wave of explorers and adventurers set sail. In 1513 the Spanish admiral Vasco Núñez de Balboa (1475–1519), standing atop a hill in what is today's nation of Panama, became the first European to see the Pacific Ocean. Only six years later Ferdinand Magellan (1480–1521) set out to circumnavigate the entire globe, an astonishing feat that took three years and claimed the lives of 262 of his initial crew of 280, including his own. Tales of the wealth available in the New World and in Asia set off a fiercely competitive wave of explorers, soldiers, and government representatives eager to stake out their claims (see Map 13.3).

Rise of the Atlantic Commercial Economies

Geographic location gave an immense advantage to the Atlantic seaboard nations of Europe: Portugal, Spain, France, the Low Countries, and England. The Mediterranean states, which had lived by maritime trade since 3000 BCE, were shut off from the New World bonanza since they could not pass the Straits of Gibraltar—which the Atlantic states (first Spain, and later England) had quickly sealed off like plugging a cork in a bottle. Left to trade with Asia only through the Ottoman-controlled land routes, they began a long and slow commercial decline. This resulted in a fundamental change in the structure of the European economy,

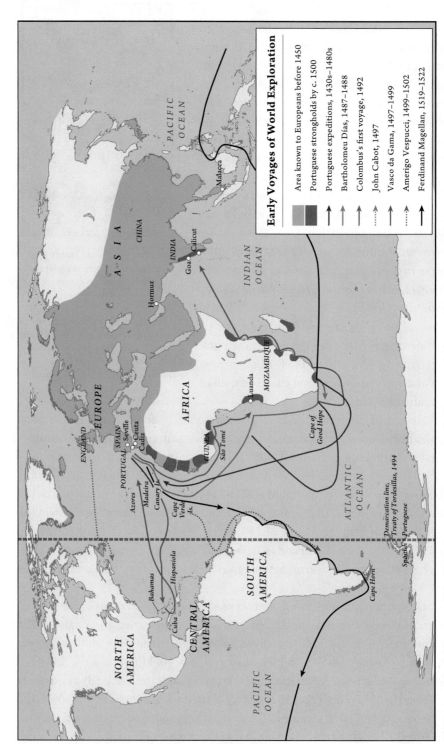

MAP 13.3   Early Voyages of World Exploration   In a remarkably short period of time, the Portuguese and Spanish went from exploring the eastern Atlantic to circumnavigating the globe.

and by 1600 economic dominance had shifted away from the Mediterranean. The Atlantic states entered the 17th century as the economic and political power-houses of Europe.

The sudden and massive influx of gold from the New World triggered the rise of the Atlantic commercial economies. This gold was seized chiefly from the Aztecs and Mayans of Central America and the Incas of what eventually became Peru and Bolivia. Credit for these seizures belongs above all to the bands of **conquistadores** ("conquerors") led by Hernán Cortés (1485–1547), who in 1519–1521 subdued the Aztecs, and Francisco Pizarro (1471–1541), who vanquished the Incas in 1531–1533. The conquerors' forces were astonishingly few in number: Cortés commanded an army of no more than five hundred conquistadores, and Pizarro had only about two hundred—although both men benefited from assistance by tribes hostile to the Aztec and Inca overlords. The Europeans' technological advantage is obvious: supplied with firearms, they could mow down the spear-carrying natives with relative ease. But their victory was made incalculably easier by an inadvertent biological warfare that preceded them on the scene.

The Conquest of Mexico   This painting, from the second half of the 17th century, illustrates the dramatic conquest of the Aztec capital of Tenochtitlán (today's Mexico City) by Hernán Cortés in 1519. The Aztec Empire had long been the most powerful (and violent) of the New World kingdoms. Cortés, shown astride his horse in full armor in the foreground, began his campaign with only a few hundred soldiers—although he picked up many native conscripts on his way to Tenochtitlán. By 1521 Cortés had conquered the once-great empire. With the addition of "New Spain" (Mexico) and Pizarro's conquest a decade later of the Peruvian highlands, the Spanish Empire became the largest in the world.

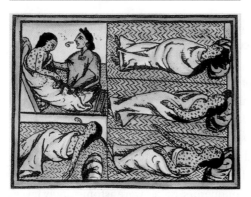

Smallpox Victims   The protracted isolation of the peoples of the Americas from the rest of the world made them vulnerable to a battery of diseases that European colonists brought with them: the breath of a Spaniard was said to be sufficient to kill. These 16th-century illustrations, drawn by a native Mexican artist, depict smallpox victims. In the upper-left panel a doctor attempts to treat his patient. Undoubtedly he failed.

CONQUEST AND EPIDEMICS

Separated by a vast ocean, the peoples of Europe and of the Americas had been exposed to different types of bacteria and viruses and had consequently developed different biological responses to them. The sailors who landed with Columbus on Hispaniola brought with them the viruses for smallpox and measles. Neither disease had ever existed before in the New World, so they ran unchecked with horrifying effect. On Hispaniola alone, the indigenous population, which an early Dominican missionary (Bartolomé de Las Casas, 1484–1566) had estimated to be 3 million strong in 1492, fell by 1538 to a mere five hundred: a loss greater than 99.99 percent. In the opposite direction, some Europeans contracted a form of syphilis in the New World that seems never to have been present before in Europe. Within a few years, 5 million Europeans had died of it. Yet the impact on the New World was far greater. Cortés was able to conquer Mexico by 1521 with only six hundred men at arms because 90 percent of the Aztecs had already been obliterated by smallpox by 1520.

A Franciscan missionary, Toribio de Benavente Motolinia (1484–1568), described how the natives "did not know how to treat the disease . . . and consequently died in whole piles, like bedbugs. In many places, in fact, entire households died all at once, and since it proved impossible to bury so great a number of corpses, our soldiers simply pulled down the houses over these people, letting their own homes serve as their tombs." Motolinia wrote that when Cortés led his men in triumph through the Aztec capital of Tenochtitlan the soldiers could traverse the entire city stepping only on the corpses of smallpox victims, without ever once setting foot on the ground. Pizarro found similar circumstances favoring him when he stormed through Peru and Bolivia. Even a century later, in far-off Massachusetts Bay, smallpox and measles erased nine-tenths of the Native American population between 1617 and 1619.

Since the late 20th century historians have used the term **Columbian Exchange** to describe the momentous interactions between the Old and New Worlds initiated by Columbus's landfall in the Americas.[3] From men to animals

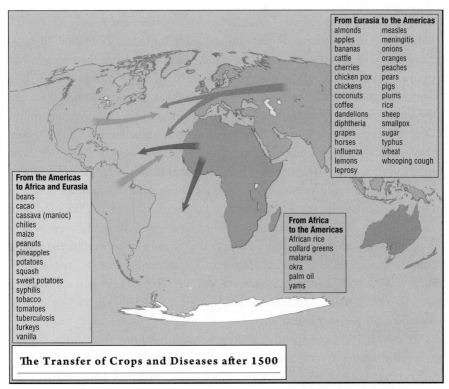

From Eurasia to the Americas

almonds	measles
apples	meningitis
bananas	onions
cattle	oranges
cherries	peaches
chicken pox	pears
chickens	pigs
coconuts	plums
coffee	rice
dandelions	sheep
diphtheria	smallpox
grapes	sugar
horses	typhus
influenza	wheat
lemons	whooping cough
leprosy	

From the Americas to Africa and Eurasia

beans
cacao
cassava (manioc)
chilies
maize
peanuts
pineapples
potatoes
squash
sweet potatoes
syphilis
tobacco
tomatoes
tuberculosis
turkeys
vanilla

From Africa to the Americas

African rice
collard greens
malaria
okra
palm oil
yams

The Transfer of Crops and Diseases after 1500

MAP 13.4   **The Transfer of Crops and Diseases after 1500**   The interchange of plants, animals, and microbes between the Old and New Worlds permanently altered demographic patterns, technologies, cultures, and cuisines on both sides of the Atlantic.

and from plants to microbes, the movement of life-forms across the Atlantic Ocean dramatically and permanently altered ecologies, societies, and cultures. Europeans introduced horses, chickens, cows, pigs, and goats to the New World (but also rats) and brought back to Europe minks, llamas, and turkeys. Within two centuries of 1492 they also brought apples, carrots, coffee, garlic, lettuce, oats, rye, and wheat to the Americas and sent the first avocados, blueberries, chili peppers, cocoa beans, cotton, potatoes, tobacco, tomatoes, and zucchini to Europe (see Map 13.4). (Tomatoes, however, were long believed to be poisonous and were valued only as a decorative species; there was no marinara sauce in Italy until the late 19th century.) Many of these exchanges were beneficial to both sides of the Atlantic. At the microbial level, however, a different story played out. Among European and African diseases transferred to the New World were not only smallpox and measles but also diphtheria, influenza, malaria, typhus, and yellow fever, among others.

The Columbian Exchange

---

3   Historian Alfred W. Crosby coined the phrase in his pioneering work, *The Columbian Exchange: Biological and Cultural Consequences of 1492* (1972).

European Exploitation

Such unintended suffering does not excuse the outright brutishness of the Europeans in the Americas. In sailing to Africa, India, and China, the Europeans had shown no interest in conquest and colonization since they were able to acquire what they wanted—nonperishable luxury goods—by simple trade. Their technological advantage, in military hardware, over the sub-Saharan Africans was as great as it was over the indigenous American peoples, but it did not prompt them to slaughter millions of Africans and seize their lands. Smallpox and other epidemic diseases changed everything, though, because they caused the Europeans to develop almost instantly a different attitude toward the New World: here lay two vast continents that were, in effect, uninhabited—or near enough to uninhabited to inspire the Europeans to finish the job. Moreover, the success of the Protestant Reformation accelerated European interest in the New World. Protestant leaders saw not only an opportunity for evangelization but also a means to finance their struggles back home. The coincidence of the discovery of the New World's gold and silver deposits, and the bubbling over of the Catholic–Protestant rift into outright war in the 1540s (discussed in chapter 14), was too great to be entirely coincidental.

Once they had seized control of the gold and silver mines, the Europeans set to the large-scale production of cash crops like cotton, sugar cane, and tobacco. These commodities fetched high prices, retained consistent demand, and traveled well across the long distance from New World to Old. The annihilation of the local populace presented a problem, however, since all three crops were exceptionally labor intensive in their production. Without a large infusion of people to work the land, producing these crops was out of the question. There were only two ways to put people on the land in the numbers needed: settlement and slavery.

THE COPERNICAN DRAMA

Science interested few people during the Renaissance; at best it formed a minor hobby for some. Like the classical Romans they emulated, Renaissance thinkers showed a keen interest in applied technology but spent little time on pure science, that is, the direct observation, investigation, and theoretical explanation of natural phenomena. One partial exception was the great artist Leonardo da Vinci (1452–1519), whose curiosity about the natural world and eye for observation inspired him to make intricate drawings of human anatomy, various forms of plant and animal life, and types of machines. The only other Renaissance figure who may qualify as a scientist was the Swiss physician Philip von Hohenheim, better known by his nickname of Paracelsus (1493–1541). His understanding and practice of medicine was thoroughly medieval, although he did some pioneering experimentation with various chemicals and minerals in the treatment of disease. His most significant discovery was the development of laudanum—a tincture of opium dissolved in alcohol that was used to treat a host of maladies until the early 20th century.

The rise of pure science—or the "new science"—began with developments in astronomy. Astronomy had formed a key component of Western science and *Origins in* philosophy from the beginning, going back to the ancient Greeks. The geocen- *Astronomy* tric model of the universe handed down for two thousand years posited a static Earth at the center, with the sun and other "moveable stars" (the planets) swirling about it in perfect circular orbits. The unmoving "fixed stars" comprised bright points on the ceiling of Creation. The universe was thus a single, finite, enclosed entity with the Earth—Nature's masterpiece—at its center. Christians, to the extent they thought about such things at all, saw no reason to challenge the geocentric model and indeed felt that it contributed to the Christian view of humanity as God's supreme creation. Science was religion's handmaiden. God created the universe, in fact, to provide humans with a home. To study the workings of the natural world, therefore, was to most Christians a way of praising God and

strengthening faith by deepening our appreciation of God's Creation. Throughout the Middle Ages, in fact, the church was the primary institution, and often the only one, promoting the study of science. When Western science revived in the 16th century, it did so once again hand in hand with Christian faith. It is a modern conceit that science advanced only when it divorced itself from religion; that divorce became finalized only in the 19th century. The Scientific Revolution therefore must be understood as an offshoot of religious history.

Flaws in the geocentric model were evident from the start. Even to the naked eye, the movement of the planets across the night sky is irregular: the transit of Venus (the appearance of Venus as a small black disk moving across the face of the sun caused when Venus passes between the Earth and the sun) is just one such irregularity. If the planets all move in ever-widening perfect concentric circles around a stationary Earth,

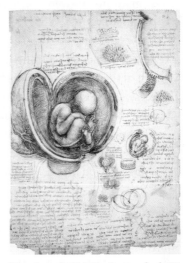

Drawing of a Fetus Leonardo da Vinci (1452–1519) performed as many as three dozen human dissections in his lifetime (he also dissected several cows and monkeys), which gave him unparalleled knowledge of the body. He prepared over two hundred detailed drawings for publication as a book on anatomy. As shown in this drawing of a fetus, he also wrote extensive notes. This image reveals as well da Vinci's use of "mirror writing," which he used not for any secret purpose but simply because he was left-handed and found it easier to write this way without smudging the page.

how could the orbits of Venus and the sun intersect in this way? Over the centuries astronomers had come up with scores of intricate arguments to explain away the inconsistencies of the geocentric model, but with each new refinement the system seemed less and less viable.

Copernicus's Theory of Heliocentrism

Sometime around 1510 the German Polish clergyman and astronomer **Nicolaus Copernicus** (Mikołaj Kopernik in Polish) began to develop a different model that resolved many of the irregularities. This **heliocentric** model posited that the sun was the fixed center, and the Earth was one of the planets in orbit around it. By 1514 he carefully circulated his findings among a handful of friends. They spent years gathering more precise observational data, and Copernicus continued to refine his hypothesis. His book, *On the Revolutions of the Heavenly Spheres*, was not published until 1543, the year of his death.

Copernicus had feared the book would set off a firestorm within the Catholic Church, but it did not. As early as 1536 a scientifically inclined cardinal, Nikolaus von Schönberg (1472–1537), had already written to him, encouraging his work:

> It was several years ago that I first heard of your skills, about which so many people were constantly speaking, and first developed such high regard for you.... What I learned was that you had not only mastered the knowledge of the ancient astronomers but had in fact created an entirely new cosmology according to which the Earth moves [in orbit] while the sun actually holds the most fundamental or central place in the universe.... At the risk of intruding upon your activities I want to urge you, with the utmost seriousness, to make these discoveries of yours known to scholars, and please to send me (as soon as is feasible) your writings on the workings of the universe, together with your data tables and anything else you may have that pertains to this important matter.

More criticism came from Protestant leaders, for whom the explicit teachings of scripture carried more weight. Luther himself is often said to have condemned "that damned fool Copernicus" for challenging the authority of scripture. (In reality, there is little evidence that Luther was fully aware of Copernicus's work.) Church condemnation did come, but not until some six decades later, when the debate had shifted, as we shall see, to Galileo's elaborations of the heliocentric theory and his claims for the scientific process that propounded it.

Copernicus had prepared for some resistance. In the preface to his book, he directly addressed the then-reigning pope, Paul III (r. 1534–1549). His book, he said, offered a simple hypothesis, an explanation of planetary movements that accommodated the available data far better than any permutation of the geocentric model. He closed with a dignified appeal to the church's concern for scholarly truth:

I have no doubt that our most skilled and talented mathematicians will concur with my findings, so long as they are willing to investigate, with all the honest seriousness that scholarship requires, the arguments I have set forth in this book in support of my theories. But still, in order that everyone, both the learned and the non-learned, may see that I hide from no man's judgment, I have decided to dedicate these findings of mine to Your Holiness, rather than to another, for even in this remote part of the world where I reside Your Holiness is regarded as preeminent in dignity for the position you hold, for your love of learning, and even for your interest in mathematics. . . . And if there should be any amateurs who (not letting their ignorance of mathematics stand in the way of a chance to pass judgment on such matters) presume to attack my theory because it contradicts some passage of Scripture that they misinterpret for their own purposes, I simply do not care; in fact, I dismiss their opinions as mere foolishness. . . . Mathematics is written for mathematicians. . . . I leave it to Your Holiness and all learned mathematicians to judge what I have written.

What follows, in other words, is a set of mathematical proofs subject only to the critical review of mathematicians. He makes no theological or even astronomical

Nicolaus Copernicus   This portrait of the great astronomer Nicolaus Copernicus (1473–1543) intentionally emphasizes his Catholic piety. Shown also is a page from his book *On the Revolution of the Heavenly Spheres* that illustrates the foundational discovery of the Scientific Revolution, Copernicus's heliocentric (sun-centered) model of the universe.

claims, but argues only that his model conforms to the available data more precisely than did earlier models.

Kepler's Laws of Planetary Motion

Word of Copernicus's work spread quickly around Europe, and a number of scholars elaborated on the heliocentric theory. The Danish astronomer Tycho Brahe (1546–1601), for example, devoted his career to making ever-more precise chartings of planetary movements and stellar positions. This improved data made possible the next major leap in astronomy, when Brahe's German pupil Johannes Kepler (1571–1630) formulated three famous principles that came to be known as *Kepler's laws of planetary motion*. These laws hold that the planets move in ellipses around the sun, that they move at non-uniform speeds, and that the velocity of each planet throughout its orbit is in direct proportion to its distance from the sun at any given moment. Kepler had fought a childhood battle with smallpox that had left him very nearsighted; unable to gather his own observational data, he used the mountain of astronomical tables and star charts left behind by his teacher. With these, he validated his model with a mathematical precision that few of his contemporaries could equal or even understand. Even Galileo initially ignored it.

GALILEO AND THE TRUTH OF NUMBERS

Galileo Galilei (1564–1642) was a genius in astronomy, mathematics, and physics, as famous in his day as Albert Einstein was in the 20th century. His achievements in any one of those fields alone would warrant his being remembered.[4] Trained in mathematics, which he later taught at the University of Padua, he learned astronomy largely on his own and with the use of his telescope. In *The Starry Messenger* (1610), the first report of his astronomical discoveries, he describes the most significant of them: the moons of Jupiter. The force of this discovery is often difficult for modern readers to appreciate. The geocentric model made no allowance for smaller bodies in orbit around the planets. Everything, in the classical view, orbited the Earth. Yet here was direct evidence against it.

The elaborate mathematical arguments of Copernicus and Kepler were easily ignored. By the astronomers' own admission, they were nothing more than conjectures, a way to make the numbers fall into neater computational alignment. Few people then alive even understood them. But Galileo's discovery was as solid and incontrovertible as the New World continents that Christopher Columbus had run into in 1492. Anyone with the telescope he developed—and Galileo himself sold them, as a business venture, on the side, as well as giving them to people whose patronage he sought—could look up in the sky and see Jupiter's moons

---

[4]   Galileo was a skilled tinkerer too, renowned for his redesign of the telescope (invented by Hans Lippershey, of the Netherlands) and of the geometric compass (used by surveyors and artillerymen).

for themselves. Galileo's findings were confirmed by none other than Christopher Clavius (1538–1612), the most prominent expert in mathematics and astronomy in the church, and the city of Rome gave Galileo a triumphant welcome in 1611.

Yet in 1633, only twenty-two years later, he was arrested and forced to recant. What had changed? Two factors principally, and Galileo shares in the blame for the first. In 1623 he published a treatise on comets in which he made a crucial mistake: he argued that comets were not physical objects but only optical illusions—tricks of refracted sunlight. Moreover, in putting forth this (wrong) hypothesis, he went out of his way (not unlike Roger Bacon) to insult astronomers who had asserted (correctly) that comets were in fact fiery solid bodies passing through the solar system far beyond the orbit of our moon. Several of those astronomers, however, were highly regarded clerics who taught at the church's college in Rome, and the papal court was in no mood to countenance such outright rudeness. Several years earlier, in 1616, the church had condemned the heliocentric model as contrary to scripture, and Galileo was given a friendly warning to refrain from promoting or teaching Copernicanism. He complied, for the most part, but the offensive passages in his new treatise on comets called for some sort of response. *Rising Tensions between Science and Religion*

If Galileo's first problem was scientific and political, his second concerned scripture. What happens when scientific conclusions and biblical statements are in conflict? In a letter to the Grand Duchess Christina, published in 1615, he argued that the Bible should be interpreted in a way that makes it compatible with scientific findings. Here he invited a debate that Copernicus and Kepler had studiously avoided. They had presented heliocentrism as a mathematical theory only. Although aware that it contradicted scripture, they offered no opinion about which form of truth was preferable. Galileo, however, brought the Copernican claims into direct open conflict with scripture—and he made it clear that in his mind the Bible had to accommodate science, not vice versa.

Science and religion in the Greater West had always known tension, but the strain was proof of their close relationship. Apart from Jewish and Muslim scholars, every European scientist of any note since the fall of the Roman Empire had been a sincere

Galileo Galilei by an Unknown Painter   Galileo was an accomplished musician (he played the lute) as well as a world-class astronomer, engineer, mathematician, and physicist. Never married, he had three children by his live-in companion, Marina Gamba (d. 1612), and was a caring, if distant, father. His daughter Viginia (1600–1634) became a nun, took the name Sister Maria Celeste, and consulted with her father on many of his researches. They are buried together in the Basilica di Santa Croce in Florence.

Christian, often at odds with the church but always identifying with it. Copernicus and Galileo were both devout Catholics, and Brahe and Kepler were pious Protestants. And every Jewish and Muslim scientist had been a devout, if sometimes unorthodox, believer. The first identifiable atheist—that is, one who expressly and openly denied the existence of any deity whatsoever—in Greater Western history was not a scientist at all but a German seminary dropout. Matthias Knutzen (1646–1675) published three pamphlets in 1674 denying "God, any Authority from On High, and all sects and their ministers." All that is needed to live a moral life, he wrote, is "to harm no one, live honestly, and give each person his due. . . . There is only this one life, after which there is neither any reward nor any punishment."

Scripture, Galileo implied, allows room to maneuver; science, however, does not. The church's position—and, to include the Protestants, the churches' position—was that two thousand years of tradition should not be overthrown because of some opaque mathematical formulas that relatively few people understood properly. The problem, essentially, came down to **epistemology**, or the study of the nature of knowledge itself. What exactly does it mean "to *know* something"? At what point can mere humans justifiably declare that a given statement is universally true?

INQUISITION AND INQUIRY

As we know from chapter 11, "Inquisition" is a historical term, a word denoting a specific phenomenon of the past. One could even call it a technical term, since it describes a precisely defined and regulated judicial process established by the Catholic Church in 1184. That process evolved over time, naturally, but even into the 19th century the word referred to a special type of investigation, conducted by ecclesiastical or secular authority, for the sake of public safety. But *Inquisition* is also a popular term, loosely used to describe almost any process or institution that one deems profoundly unfair.

The Inquisition of the early modern era differed significantly from its medieval forebear. Pope Lucius III (r. 1181–1185) had established the inquisition as a way of stopping the unjust execution of people for dissident religious beliefs. False beliefs within Christianity were a sin against the church but also a crime against the secular medieval state, and in the 12th and 13th centuries the aristocratic courts of Europe were quick to act against heretics—convicting them, killing them, and confiscating their property. The church took a dim view of heresy but championed the idea of intellectual free inquiry. Lucius's decree of 1184 helped to codify a strict, narrow definition of actionable heresy and brought state exercise of authority over heretics under the church's jurisdiction. As brutal and backward as the medieval inquisition is to modern sensibilities, it is

important to note that the number of people killed for dissident Christian beliefs across Europe actually declined—and sharply—after the inquisition's
establishment.

Nonetheless, ugly is ugly, and even without the use of physical torture (and
most medieval inquisitions never resorted to it) the threatening nature of the *Government*
inquiry was obvious and coercive. That ugliness grew in the early modern era *Takeover*
when the Inquisition was officially taken over as an institution of government. *of the*
In the 16th and 17th centuries the monarchical states in France, Portugal, and *Inquisition*
Spain assumed control of it—as did the lesser princes in Germany, Italy, and the
Low Countries—and used it to terrorize dissidents and control political opponents. Churchmen actively colluded in the process, certainly, but the notorious
Inquisition of the time was as much an indicator of the loss of church power as it
was an index of religious and intellectual intolerance.

Although some supported the idea, the Inquisition was not the weapon of
choice for dealing with the Protestant Reformation. The Protestants, after all, de- *Targets of*
clared their own separation from Rome and hence no longer came under the *Inquisition*
church's jurisdiction; later, as we saw in chapter 12, the policy of *cuius regio, eius
religio* ("the religion of the ruler determines the religion of the land") granted a
certain degree of toleration across the Catholic–Protestant divide. The Inquisition instead focused on two principal targets: false converts from Judaism and
Islam and advocates of the new science. The issue of false converts was a complex
one, arising from financial envy, racial prejudice, and unease about aristocratic
stature. The conversion of nonbelievers to Christianity had been a desire central
to Christian aspirations since the dawn of the religion, but fanatical worries arose
from the 15th century onward that many of Europe's converts were converts in
name only—people who publicly proclaimed their Christianity but privately retained their Jewish or Muslim practice. Such suspects were referred to as *crypto-
Jews* and *crypto-Muslims*.

The concern was not merely that they were religious frauds but that there was
something evil intrinsic to their makeup. Some element in their collective blood-
lines, it was feared, permanently tainted their Christianity and kept them from a
genuine and full commitment. That would have been bad enough for most of the
bigots of the time, but what made matters even worse was the upward social mo-
bility of the professional classes of the Renaissance and Reformation eras. Noble
families in economic decline often married wealthy, ambitious urbanites from
the rising merchant economy. For them, the danger of exposing their pure noble
blood to the supposedly inferior and possibly diseased elements in Jewish or
Muslim blood set off a clamor of concern. Crypto-Jews and crypto-Muslims, in
other words, were perceived as a threat to noble security and privilege as much as
a threat to faith.

Expulsion of the Moriscos from Spain   This painting by the 17th-century Spanish artist Pere Oromig depicts the expulsion of the Moriscos (suspected crypto-Muslims) from the coastal town of Vinaròs, in eastern Spain, in 1609. Moriscos comprised nearly one-third of the population of this part of Spain at the time.

The other major class of Inquisitorial victims, the proponents of the new science, are more difficult to generalize about. Their names have become *causes célèbres* over the centuries. Giordano Bruno (1548–1600), a Dominican friar, mathematician, and cosmologist, provides the most dramatic example. Bruno had little training in science but much amateur enthusiasm for it. Seizing eagerly on Copernican heliocentrism, he soon went further—without any good scientific basis for doing so. He argued that the universe is infinitely large, that the fixed stars were suns like ours with planets of their own in orbit around them, and that life on these planets is a likelihood. Thus he denied the special nature of human beings as part of God's Creation, which was tantamount to denying the special role of Christ as the universal savior. Bruno's admirers over time have given him too much credit: he spun out so many ideas about science that the chance of at least some of them turning out to be true was high. But although he was not a scientist in the sense that Galileo was, he too fell victim to the Inquisition. The court followed its usual tactic of delay, negotiation, and appeal; if Bruno would have only agreed to keep a low profile for a few years, he might well have been given his freedom. But he refused and was executed in a public square in Rome, with his ashes dumped into the Tiber River.

The Trial of Galileo   The most famous case of all is that of Galileo. Two inquiries into his science occurred, one in 1616 and another in 1633. The 1616 tribunal, led by

Cardinal Robert Bellarmine (1542–1621)—a Jesuit who, like most Jesuit astronomers, accepted Galileo's work up through *The Starry Messenger* (1610)—reiterated the church's partial condemnation of heliocentrism and, as we have seen, let Galileo go with a warning. Copernican theory could continue to be discussed and investigated, so long as it was presented only as a mathematical hypothesis instead of as incontrovertible truth. Sixteen years later, having won further fame with his discoveries in optics, physics, and the study of tides, as well as his mathematical theory of infinite sets, Galileo breached his 1616 agreement. In his *Dialogue on the Two Chief World Systems* (1632), he argued openly for the heliocentric model as the indisputable truth. The new treatise was written in the form of a dialogue between geocentric and heliocentric astronomers, and although Galileo was careful to make the heliocentrists capitulate at the end, he nevertheless made the old-style astronomers look foolish. Even worse, he named the spokesman for the traditionalists Simplicio ("Simpleton"). He should have known better. When Inquisitors petitioned to place Galileo on trial, an irritated Pope Urban VIII (r. 1623–1644) allowed them to proceed.

As Galileo learned, tone matters. The church had promoted scientific work for centuries and had a tradition of accepting ideas and discoveries not immediately reconcilable with doctrine. It understood that knowledge proceeds by probing, doubting, and testing. What matters is patience and humility. Galileo had sufficient patience but lacked humility when it came to his work. Other Catholic scientists of the era presented new findings every bit as jarring to traditional sensibilities as Galileo's but described them as discoveries in progress rather than indisputable truths. A German named Athanasius Kircher (1601–1680) was a pioneer of microbiology and linguistics.[5] An Italian physicist named Francesco Maria Grimaldi (1618–1663) made the first observations that led to the wave theory of light; he also compiled the first map of the lunar surface that described its geological features in detail. These men understood scientific research as a never-ending process, a slow groping toward truth, but one that can never declare final success. The infinite complexity of the universe precludes such hubris. But Galileo effectively altered the rules or at least claimed that the rules were alterable and that pure truth—final and complete—was attainable. His revolutionary breakthrough was not heliocentrism in itself but the argument that science justifies itself, ratifies itself. Biblical authority and intellectual tradition mean nothing in the face of empirical data and rigorous mathematical logic. The separation of science from religion, to Galileo, was not a divorce. It was an annulment.

---

[5]   Kircher was the first to describe microbes, and he correctly identified ancient Egyptian hieroglyphics with the Coptic language. He also wrote an entire encyclopedia of the Chinese language.

Hence the Inquisition's action against him arose from the complaint that Galileo had broken a contract with the church as much as from his scientific views. The formal judgment rendered by the tribunal reads as follows;

> Seeing that you, Galileo, . . . were denounced by this Holy Office in 1615 for asserting the truth of the false doctrine, maintained by some, that the sun is the unmoving center of the universe and that the Earth moves in orbit around it . . .
>
> And seeing that . . . it was agreed that if you refused to stop [proclaiming this theory as decided truth] this Holy Office could order you to abandon the teaching altogether . . . and that you could therefore be subject to imprisonment . . .
>
> And seeing that . . . your *Dialogue on the Two Chief World Systems* has recently been published . . . in which you try to give the impression that the matter is still undecided, calling it only "probable" . . . and that you confess that numerous passages of the book are written in such a way that a reader could in fact draw the conclusion that the arguments for [heliocentrism] are irrefutable . . .
>
> We conclude, proclaim, sentence, and pronounce that . . . you have made yourself strongly suspected of heresy.

The Trial of Galileo Galileo's endorsement of Copernican heliocentrism was not the reason for his trial and condemnation by the Roman Inquisition. The church itself, after all, had used the Copernican model when it reformed the calendar in 1582. Rather, at stake was Galileo's insistence that in any disagreement between scripture and science, science must win out; indeed, the assertions of scripture in such matters were simply irrelevant.

His punishment was house arrest and penance, and the Inquisition ordered his *Dialogue* to be burned. Galileo agreed and spent his last years in quiet work.[6] In 1638 he published his last major work, the *Discourses on Two New Sciences*, which treats problems of motion, acceleration, and mathematical theory. His trouble with the Inquisition was clearly related to, but not solely composed of, his belief in heliocentrism itself; rather, the immediate issue was his breaking of a sacred vow.

The more general and important issue, however, was in the debate about Truth itself. The case of Galileo and the Inquisition marks an important turning point in intellectual history—the rise of a belief in *quantification*. If the numbers in Theory A work more precisely and consistently than the numbers in Theory B, this belief asserts, then Theory A is for that reason alone accepted as true. But is that really the case? Numbers are powerful things, but they are not necessarily the surest (much less the only) route to Truth, and the Inquisition insisted on the point. Anyone who has ever argued that their scores on standardized exams do not reflect the reality of their knowledge and skills is holding to a position consonant with that of the Inquisition. Right or wrong, the Inquisition trusted God's Word more than it trusted mathematical formulas.

THE REVOLUTION BROADENS

It is unclear how much all of these discoveries and debates mattered outside the walls of academia and of the church. To a 17th-century peasant shoveling manure out of a cow stall, it probably did not matter whether that manure was at the fixed center of the universe or if it was in orbit around the sun; all he cared about was getting it out of the barn before the landlord came to punish him for not keeping up with his duties. But discoveries in other fields mattered a great deal at the time because of their immediate practical value. Increasingly, too, they mattered because of ethical tensions as older taboos declined, especially in regard to Islam.

In medicine, the English physician William Harvey (1578–1657) identified the circulation of blood in the human body via the intricate system of heart, veins, and arteries (see Table 13.1). The existence of internal organs and tissues came as no surprise, but physicians had never understood their individual functions or their working together as a system. Harvey's work opened the door to comprehending the human body as an integrated organism. In chemistry, the Anglo-Irish pioneer Robert Boyle (1627–1691), extrapolating from the atomic theory inherited from ancient Greece, described the molecular structure of compounds.

Advances in Medicine, Chemistry, Physics, and Biology

---

6   The legend that Galileo, at his verdict, muttered under his breath, "Even so, it [Earth] moves" is most likely false. The first instance of it appears in a fanciful Spanish painting after his death.

In physics he both determined the role of air in the propagation of sound and derived *Boyle's law,* which states that the volume and pressure of a gas at constant temperature vary inversely. These discoveries helped in deriving new chemicals and stabilizing air pumps. In biology the English natural scientist Robert Hooke (1635–1703) employed a compound microscope to discover the cellular structure of plants, which, when studied over time, gave hints of the actual process of growth. Organic life, Hooke was the first to assert, is an ongoing process of growth and decay according to natural principles. By analyzing fossils he came close to developing a full-blown theory of evolution almost two hundred years before Darwin.

TABLE 13.1   **Major Works of the Scientific Revolution, 1500–1700**

1543	*On the Revolutions of the Heavenly Spheres*	Nicolaus Copernicus (1473–1543)
1543	*On the Makeup of the Human Body*	Andreas Vesalius (1514–1564)
1600	*On the Magnet and Magnetic Bodies*	William Gilbert (1544–1603)
1609	*The New Astronomy or Celestial Physics*	Johannes Kepler (1571–1630)
1610	*The Starry Messenger*	Galileo Galilei (1564–1642)
1614	*The Wonderful Law of Logarithms*	John Napier (1550–1617)
1619	*The Harmonies of the World*	Johannes Kepler
1620	*New Instrument*	Sir Francis Bacon (1561–1626)
1628	*On the Motion of the Heart and the Blood*	William Harvey (1578–1657)
1632	*Dialogue on the Two Chief World Systems*	Galileo Galilei
1637	*Discourse on Method*	René Descartes (1596–1650)
1653	*On the Arithmetical Triangle*	Blaise Pascal (1623–1662)
1658	*The Spirit of Geometry*	
1660	*New Experiments Physico-Mechanical*	Robert Boyle (1627–1691)
1661	*The Skeptical Chymist*	
1665	*Micrographia*	Robert Hooke (1635–1703)
1687	*Principia Mathematica*	Sir Isaac Newton (1642–1727)

All this points to an important development. If Galileo had effectively removed God from the workings of the physical cosmos, the scientists who followed him began to discover the structures that took the place of Providence. However useful these discoveries might have proved, could they compensate for the loss of a divine purpose in life? When one takes away the idea that the universe functions, however mysteriously, according to a heavenly plan, then one risks the fear of a random, meaningless existence. The English poet and cleric John Donne (1572–1631) described this feeling of loss and confusion in "An

Anatomie of the World" (1611), written for an aristocratic patron on the anniversary of the death of his wife:

> And new philosophy calls all in doubt,
> The element of fire is quite put out,
> The sun is lost, and th'earth, and no man's wit
> Can well direct him where to look for it.
> And freely men confess that this world's spent,
> When in the planets and the firmament
> They seek so many new; they see that this
> Is crumbled out again to his atomies.
> 'Tis all in pieces, all coherence gone,
> All just supply, and all relation;
> Prince, subject, father, son, are things forgot,
> For every man alone thinks he hath got
> To be a phoenix, and that then can be
> None of that kind, of which he is, but he.
> This is the world's condition now.

The poem expresses above all the pain that follows a great personal loss. Yet it also captures the dread of a shapeless and unintelligible universe that was felt so

Sic Transit Gloria Mundi "Thus passes the glory of the world" is the cautionary message of this 1655 painting from Spain. A sleeping nobleman dreams of wealth, power, knowledge, art, beauty, and military prowess, while a skull joins the worldly objects on the table and an angel enters the dream, holding a banner that reminds the viewer that death is the end of all things.

widely at the time. "The world's condition now" seemed one of decay and doubt; ordered existence is so jumbled and out of joint that one does not even know "where to look for it."

It is a powerful poem that should be read whole. Not all scientific discoveries, it asserts, are advances, because they come at a cost. Take the discovery of the circulation of blood. This breakthrough occurred not simply because William Harvey happened to come along and figure it out. It became possible only with the dissection of human bodies—corpses, mostly, but not all.

THE ETHICAL COSTS OF SCIENCE

Deep cultural taboos against the desecration of the body had forbidden dissections for millennia. These taboos predate Christianity and even Judaism. The elaborate funeral rites of the Egyptians and Mesopotamians, with their careful cleansing and wrapping of the body, the incantation of prayers and hymns, the presentation of offerings, the ceremonial burial or burning of the remains under the guidance of priests—all these document a powerful impulse to treat the dead with decorum. At the end of Homer's *Iliad*, Achilles drags Hector's dead body behind his chariot as he circles Troy. For Achilles it is a moment of triumph; for the reader or listener, it is a moment of moral horror: How can the great Greek hero behave so monstrously? Does Achilles even deserve to be called a hero? To an ancient audience, the scene cast doubt on all that had gone before.

Changing Attitudes toward Human Dissection
William Harvey was able to make his great discovery because, by the 17th century, many Western states had come to believe that certain individuals *deserved* to have their bodies desecrated; it was a final supreme punishment for the evil and worthlessness of their lives. After Harvey's breakthrough, detailed knowledge of the operation of the internal organs followed quickly, but these advances required a new horror: the careful cutting open of people while they were still alive. Harvey himself participated in some of this. Victims of these procedures spent weeks, and sometimes months, in constant agony.[7]

Who were these miserable people? It varied from state to state, but in general the possibility of dissection after death awaited anyone convicted of murder, treason, or counterfeiting. Theft too opened the door to the cutting table, if the person one stole from was well connected. (Heretics and witches did not need to fear the dissector's knife; they were burned at the stake. Besides, it was assumed that they were unnatural and so would not contribute to the understanding of normal human physiology.) A hardness of heart toward certain sectors of society had to

---

7   Physicians would make strategically placed incisions, then peel away layers of skin and muscle, to observe, for example, the full process of digestion from stomach to bowel.

Two Views of Human Dissection   The great Dutch painter Rembrandt van Rijn (1606–1669) offers a dignified portrayal of the start of a lesson on human anatomy; at this time, religious and civil law permitted a handful of dissections of human cadavers to be performed, under strictly regulated conditions. By contrast, the later satirical drawing by the English artist William Hogarth (1697–1764), part of a series called "The Progress of Cruelty," shows a considerably more careless and cavalier approach, after British law permitted the dissection of those convicted of felonies. Hogarth undoubtedly exaggerates the horrible scene for effect. But partial dissections were in fact occasionally done on individuals who were, as in Hogarth's picture, still alive.

exist before Harvey could make his discovery. Many people felt a concern that scientific knowledge can come at too high a price, ethically speaking, for the benefits it brings.[8]

But the picture becomes cloudier the more we look at it. Dissections actually were fairly common in the Middle Ages in the Mediterranean regions of Europe and in the Middle East. In Muslim Spain a physician named Ibn Zuhr (1091–1161) performed dissections for research and several autopsies. He was in fact the first physician to deny that the human body was composed of four humors—although he found few people who believed him—and he invented the medical procedure now known as tracheotomy. A personal physician of the sultan Saladin himself, al-Baghdadi (1162–1231), anatomized the corpses of a famine that struck Egypt in 1200, where he had traveled to meet the great Jewish scholar Maimonides.

In Christian Europe decrees forbidding the dissection of human remains for the purpose of transporting them whole to a distant burial site appeared as early

---

[8]   Even today, people today seldom stop to wonder where the thousands of cadavers used each year in our medical schools come from. Individuals who donate their bodies to science make up only a fraction of the bodies used. The rest are the unclaimed remains of America's homeless population, donated by our county morgues. Practices vary from state to state in the United States. Illinois, for example, requires county medical examiners to keep unclaimed bodies for sixty days before releasing them to medical schools; Maryland requires a wait of only fourteen days. Medical examiners in New York, however, are allowed to release unclaimed cadavers within twenty-four hours.

as the 1160s, but these were not prohibitions of dissection generally. When in the Third Crusade (1189–1193) the German emperor Frederick Barbarossa (r. 1152–1190) drowned in a river in Anatolia, his troops, wanting to bury him in Jerusalem, tried to preserve his body in vinegar. The human body, it turns out, does not pickle well, and as Frederick decomposed, the crusaders buried his flesh, organs, and bones in three separate sites. By 1300, in fact, dissections for the teaching of anatomy were standard in the leading medical schools, such as the University of Montpellier. At the University of Bologna, another center for medical research and teaching, dissections were performed annually from 1315 on and were made available to the public. It was only in northern Europe that human dissections were both taboo and illegal, and those countries had a less developed scientific tradition. England forbade human dissections until the 16th century, and even after authorizing them on criminals, the law permitted a total of only ten per year throughout the kingdom.[9]

THE ISLAMIC RETREAT FROM SCIENCE

The ethical cost of science detached from religious faith may not have troubled the Muslim world in the same way as it did the Christian West. At least it seems that way, because science had largely disappeared from Muslim intellectual culture, displaced by legal and theological studies, historical writing, and poetry. From the 7th to the 11th centuries the Islamic world had excelled in every science—medicine, physics, astronomy, mathematics—on both the theoretical and the practical levels, leaving Latin Europe and the Orthodox East far behind. By 1200, however, the Latin West had taken the lead. Undoubtedly, the Mongols' wholesale destruction of the great Islamic libraries, observatories, and universities deserves a heavy share of the blame. But although books and laboratories may burn, their demise does not explain the death of a certain type of curiosity about the world. The simple fact is that, with a few exceptions, Islamic scholars and their patrons from the 14th century onward valued scientific knowledge less than they had done in earlier centuries. Throughout the Renaissance period in western Europe, much of the Islamic world was too engulfed in warfare and internal strife to continue supporting scientific academies and observatories. The arrival of the Ottomans and Mongols, the rise to power of the Safavids in Persia, and the political recalibrations all three caused instead inspired philosophical and historical pursuits in the effort to redefine the very nature of Islamic identity.

---

[9] The British Murder Act of 1752 finally allowed the bodies of executed murderers to be available for dissection. France, Germany, and the Low Countries allowed the anatomization of anyone convicted of gross felonies.

The popularity of Sufi mysticism remained problematic too. Their affinity for
Sufism set the Ottoman Turks at odds with the more staid Arab majority *Ibn Taymiyya's*
they governed. Urged on by heavyweight scholars like Ibn Taymiyya (1263– *Fundamentalist*
1328), Arab religious leaders in the early Ottoman centuries again placed *Movement*
the *umma* ("community") at the center of Sunni life. In this conservative view,
the traditions of the Qur'an, hadith, and sunnah were paramount, and all forms of
speculative theology and metaphysical innovation were denounced. Ibn Taymiyya's career, together with those of his acolytes, can in fact be thought of as a
small-scale Islamic analog to the Protestant Reformation:

- It demanded a strict return to the authority of early texts.
- It called for stripping away every aspect of religious life not
  specifically called for in those texts.
- It condemned as heretics all who disagreed with its followers
  or who used their ideas for other purposes.
- It was openly hostile to all forms of monastic life and to the
  cults of popular saints.
- It considered the earliest religious community (the Companions of the Prophet) the most perfect in its observance of confessional life.

All of these traits were shared by the Sunni and Protestant reformers.[10] Ibn
Taymiyya's party attacked Sufism as fundamentally un-Islamic, since it emphasized ecstatic union with God over strict observance of his laws. This conservative element in Islam, centered on the Great Mosque in Damascus, dominated
the curricula in the madrasas from the 14th through 16th centuries and kept the
schools' focus intently on the Qur'an, hadith, and sunnah. Their goal was to produce pious and obedient Muslims, not to advance learning. Memorization of the
traditional canon, not the pursuit of new knowledge, was the goal.

Another important reason why the Scientific Revolution posed a particular
problem for scientifically inclined Muslims was because of its overthrow of the *The*
classical Greek tradition. Islamic science had relied as heavily on Greek founda- *Decline of*
tions as medieval European science had done. A physical universe without any *Islamic*
rational ordering or, even worse, one that functioned entirely by its own internal *Science*
mechanisms independent of a divine will, ill suited Muslim habits of thought. The *and Its*
only scientific figure of real note in the Islamic world during this period was Taqi *Critics*
ad-Din (1526–1585), who was a highly skilled engineer rather than a true

---

[10] In modern times Taymiyya inspired Muhammad ibn Abd al-Wahhab (1703–1792), the founder of
      Wahhabism, the official doctrine of Saudi Arabia.

scientist. In 1577 he designed an astronomical observatory in Istanbul for the Ottoman ruler Murad III (r. 1574–1595), who wanted it to predict the success or failure of his political schemes. When Taqi ad-Din confidently predicted victory in Murad's planned offensive against Safavid Persia, only to have those predictions proven wrong when a new outbreak of bubonic plague hit the city once the campaign was begun, the sultan ordered the observatory torn down in 1580.

The decline of Islamic science did not go unnoticed. The great scholar Mustafa Katip Çelebi (1609–1657) bemoaned the shortcomings of his age:

> There are so many ignorant people . . . their minds as dead as rocks, paralyzed in thoughtless imitation of the ancients. Rejecting and belittling all new knowledge without even a pause to give it any consideration, they pass themselves off as learned men but really are just ignoramuses who know nothing about the world or the heavens. . . . The [Qur'anic] admonition—"Have they not contemplated the kingdom of Heaven and Earth?" [7.184]—means nothing at all to them, and they seem to think that to "contemplate the Earth and sky" means to stare at them like a cow.

He was not alone in his complaint. Even one of the Muslim emperors of Mughal India, Muhi ad-Din Muhammad Aurangzeb (r. 1658–1707), lamented the fall in intellectual stature of Islam. In a diatribe against one of his early tutors, he harshly condemned what passed for education in the Muslim world:

> And what were some of the things you taught me? You taught me that France was a small island whose greatest king had previously been the king of Portugal, then of Holland, and then of England! You taught me that the kings of France and of Spain are just like our own petty provincial princes! . . . God be praised! What impressive knowledge of geography and history you had! Wasn't it your duty to teach me about the ways of the world's nations—their exports, their military might, their methods of warfare, their customs and religions, their styles of government, their diplomatic aims? . . . Instead, all you thought I needed to know was Arabic grammar and law, as though I was a [religious] judge or jurist. . . . By the time my education was finished I knew nothing at all of any science or art, except how to toss off some obscure technical terms that no one really understands!

Throughout much of the Ottoman Empire, frustration at the increasingly arid curricula of the madrasas drove the more creative minds on to new schools known as *khanqas,* where the emphasis was on Sufi mysticism. Poetry, music, and metaphysical writing formed the core of this schooling, much of it powerfully imaginative and emotive. (Graduates from the *khanqas* frequently celebrated the completion of their studies by hurling the textbooks from their madrasa years into wells.) But science was still ignored. Memorization and transmission trumped exploration at every turn, leaving the European world unchallenged in its pursuit of scientific truth.

THINKING ABOUT TRUTH

Having severed its connection with the religious intellectual tradition, European science needed new standards. That included Standards of practice, criteria for determining the quality of evidence and argument, and principles for defining scientific truth. Without such agreement, scientific progress would be fitful at best, permanently hobbled at worst. Suppose one conducts an experiment several times and each time achieves the same result. At what point may one legitimately conclude that this result is *always* the result—the natural and inevitable result of that experiment? Five times? Five hundred times? Five thousand times? When does it cease to be a mere result and become a conclusion? When does a general conclusion become an accepted scientific theory, and when does it finally become—the Holy Grail of research—a law of nature? Starting with Galileo and those who supported him, science had sloughed off its ancient standards and criteria but had yet to agree on new ones to replace them. Even science, it turned out, needs a philosophy—or, as the new scientists put it, a method.

The 17th century was replete with efforts to establish this method, as new findings emerged from laboratories and lecture halls across Europe (see Map 13.5). Europe's monarchies gave enthusiastic support to scientific efforts. One of the first acts passed under England's King Charles II (r. 1660–1685) was to confirm the founding of the Royal Society of London for Improving Natural Knowledge (1660, commonly known as the Royal Society), the oldest scientific academy still in existence.[11] Six years later (1666) Louis XIV established the French Academy of Sciences (*Académie des Sciences*), and one year after that Germany's King Leopold I (r. 1658–1705) chartered the German Royal (now National) Academy of Science (*Akademie der Wissenschaften*). With such support behind them, scientists across Europe made startling advances. Two of the most significant figures in this effort were Sir Francis Bacon and René Descartes. They represented the essential halves of the **scientific method**: inductive reasoning

---

[11]   The Latin epigram to the coat of arms granted to the Royal Society reads *Nullius in verba*: "Take no one's word on anything."

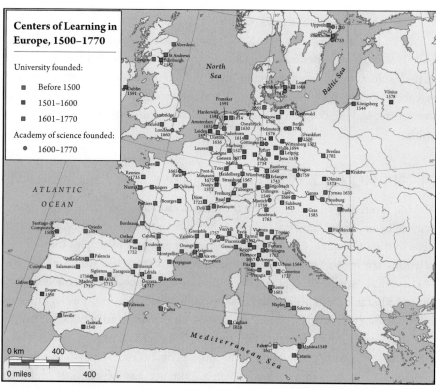

Centers of Learning in Europe, 1500–1770

University founded:

- ■ Before 1500
- ■ 1501–1600
- ■ 1601–1770

Academy of science founded:

- ● 1600–1770

MAP 13.5   Centers of Learning in Europe, 1500–1700   Europe's rulers invested heavily in scientific research in this period; the Islamic world's rulers did not. Thus came to an end the long-established lead held by the Muslims over Christian Europe in scientific sophistication.

through observation and experimental research and deductive reasoning from self-evident principles. Isaac Newton subsequently made their ideas the foundations for mathematically precise scientific laws.

Francis Bacon and the Promotion of the New Science

Sir **Francis Bacon** (1561–1626) we have already met. As the son of a career courtier, he grew up in high society, learned its manners, and became accustomed to its privileges. (His father, Sir Nicholas Bacon, had been the Lord Keeper of the Great Seal to Elizabeth I.) He worked as a lawyer and held a seat in Parliament. In 1589 he finally gained his first position in the royal administration and worked his way up, until, in the reign of James I (r. 1603–1625), he made it to the top of the ladder, serving as Lord Chancellor and—a last plum—in his father's old position as Keeper of the Great Seal. But Bacon had expensive tastes. Even with all his income, he built up enormous debts, which may or may not have led to his taking bribes. Scandals swirled around him for several years as enemies and creditors colluded to bring him down. In 1621 he finally fell from power in disgrace. Although he was allowed to keep his properties and aristocratic titles, he was barred from all political life and from most of privileged society.

A profoundly cautious man, except when it came to his spending habits, he advocated an uncompromising empirical and incremental approach to all knowledge, the gradual acquisition of discrete fact after fact, observation after observation, all of them subjected to repeated testing to ensure their accuracy, until one has finally assembled enough data to hazard a general hypothesis. Mankind is prone to drawing hasty assumptions, he argued, and the only antidote is the patient accumulation of tested and retested facts.

Francis Bacon   This 1617 portrait by Flemish painter Frans Pourbus shows Sir Francis Bacon (1561–1626) in all his finery, before his fall.

Roger Bacon, the medieval Franciscan (again, only intellectually related to Francis, as far as we know), had already identified four barriers to intellectual progress, errors so common as to be nearly universal:

> There are, in fact, four distinct impediments along the pathway to Truth—stumbling blocks, if you will, that get in the way of every man, no matter how learned he may be, and frustrate anyone who strives to reach the Truth. These impediments are: first, the precedents established by ill-equipped earlier authorities; second, long-established customs; third, the passionate sentiments of the ignorant masses; and fourth, our own habits of hiding our ignorance by the ostentatious display of what we think we do know.

Francis Bacon likewise identified four problems, which he called "illusions" (*idola* in Latin). Here he located the source of error in human nature, our own habits of thinking, the words we use, and tradition. Although the correlation is not exact, he clearly had the earlier Bacon in mind:

> There are four types of illusions that bedevil the human mind—illusions to which, in order to keep them distinct, I have attached particular names. These are the illusions of the tribe, illusions of the den, illusions of the marketplace, [and] finally illusions of the theater. . . .
>
> The *illusions of the tribe* are the fallacies inherent in human nature, . . . [above all] the human tendency to consider all things in relation to itself, whereas everything that we perceive via our senses and reason is actually just a reflection of ourselves, not of the universe. The human mind resembles nothing so much as a flawed mirror, and like such a mirror it imposes its own characteristics upon whatever it reflects, and distorts and disfigures it accordingly.

> The *illusions of the den* are the fallacies inherent in each individual. Every mind possesses—in addition to the fallacies common to all men everywhere—its own individual den or cavern whose qualities intercept and corrupt the light of Nature as it receives it. This may result from each person's individual and unique disposition, from his education, his interaction with others, or his reading. . . .
>
> There are also what I call the *illusions of the marketplace*, the illusions created by the daily interactions and conversations we have with each other—for we speak through language but words have been formed arbitrarily . . . and they throw everything into confusion. . . .
>
> Finally, the fallacies I call the *illusions of the theater*. By this term I mean those mistakes that creep into men's minds from the teachings of different philosophies and from erroneous arguments. We must regard every philosophical system yet designed or imagined as nothing more than a play that has been staged and performed—a charade, in other words.

He saw scientific thinking as the careful piling up of individual bricks of knowledge to create a solid edifice. But Bacon himself never did any actual science; a wealthy aristocrat and career administrator, he was accustomed to telling other people how to do their jobs. Descartes, on the other hand, practiced what he preached.

Descartes and the Quest for Truth

René Descartes (1596–1650) received a good Jesuit education as a youth, but when he left school in his native France he was, he wrote, "filled with so much doubt and false knowledge that I came to think that all my efforts to learn had done nothing but increase my ignorance." In November 1618 he met he met a gifted Dutch mathematician named Isaac Beeckman (1588–1637), and for entertainment they invented mathematical problems for each other. From this sort of play Descartes came to realize that geometric forms like lines and curves, when marked on a graph, could be described by algebraic formulas. Thus was born analytical geometry, a discovery that set the trajectory for Descartes's intellectual life. As he began to elaborate on his original finding in 1619, he all but disappeared for nine years—moving from city to city, from France to Italy to the Netherlands, never telling anyone his addresses (which he changed regularly anyway) and gradually selling off the properties he had inherited from his parents. "To live well, live in secret" became a favorite personal motto. He emerged from self-exile in 1628 in the Netherlands, where he remained for twenty years, although still moving frequently. He moved to Sweden in 1649 at the request of its queen, who appointed him her tutor, but he soon caught pneumonia and died in February 1650.

Descartes's greatest achievements were in mathematics and philosophy.[12] The invention of analytical geometry, apart from its inherent value, made possible the later discovery of calculus and mathematical analysis (differential equations and the like). His best-known work, however, remains the *Discourse on Method* (1637), which he wrote as an introduction to a volume of several scientific papers. In it he presents not only his own working method as a scientist but also a creed, a set of principles that guide one to true knowledge, a hybrid of science and philosophy.

In the *Discourse* he vows "never to accept something as true which I did not distinctly know for myself to be true." Rather than encourage skepticism and doubt, however, Descartes advocates passionately for certainty. Doubt is not a philosophy but merely a tool—and Descartes detested thinkers like Michel de Montaigne (1533–1592), the author of the famous *Essays*, who seemed to him to regard skepticism as the end point of human endeavor. For Descartes, doubt is the point at which one needs to start thinking the hardest. But what does "knowing" consist of? And what, precisely, is truth?

Descartes begins with a distrust of the senses. The data we gather about the world through our senses cannot be fully trusted for the simple reason that our sense perceptions are imperfect. Optical illusions are common; people often hear sounds or voices that are not actually present or fail to hear those that are. Individuals who have lost a limb frequently report feeling an itch on a part of their body that is no longer there. Knowledge based on sense data therefore can never be entirely trusted, since it depends on a flawed system of observation—a fact that undermines the very foundation of experimental science. One can try to validate one's data by performing an experiment numerous times and gathering the data with scrupulous repetitive care. Nonetheless, logically speaking there is no absolute certainty that an experiment that repeatedly renders a particular result after 5 million consecutive attempts may not suddenly give a different result on the 5-million-and-first.

True and absolute knowledge, if attainable at all, must therefore derive from a different source than empirical observation. For Descartes that source is logic. Logical thought is itself an absolute reality, or, as he famously put it, "I think, therefore I am" (*Cogito ergo sum*, in Latin). I can doubt everything I see, everything I hear, everything I touch, smell, or taste. I can even doubt whether I am alive. But even in the absence of all sense data, my thinking mind—all by itself—knows that I am doubting, knows that I am thinking about thinking, and therefore I know absolutely that I exist (see Figure 13.1).

---

12   Descartes also made numerous advances in optics, meteorology, physics, and even physiology. As a young man, he dissected cows.

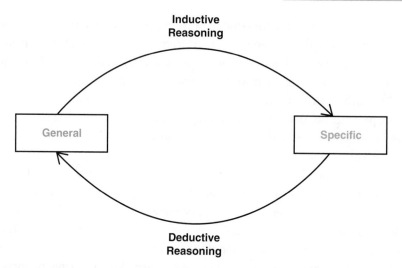

FIGURE 13.1   **Inductive versus Deductive Reasoning**

"Congratulations," one might say. "You exist. So what?" But Descartes's insight contains the germ of a revolution in scientific and philosophical thought. Absolute truth, he argues, is theoretical instead of physical, and the theoretical expression of physical reality is ultimately more real than any physical manifestation of it. Consider, for example, a circle. One can express the idea of a circle by drawing one on a piece of paper, but also by describing it in words: "A figure in two dimensions made up of all the points equidistant from a single central point." The description in words is one level of abstraction above the physical drawing on paper. But one can move to an even higher level of abstraction by describing a circle in algebraic notation, as a mathematical formula. This, to Descartes, is an absolute truth, because this formula will describe all circles, in every place and throughout all time. If scientific investigation seeks to understand the truth about circles, it must work at this abstract level. Only here can absolute truth exist and be understood.

Descartes described an entire universe guided by an immense, internally consistent, and utterly logical set of laws and formulas that the human mind can grasp—and this way of thinking has dominated Western scientific life ever since. Scientific research of every type—whether in physics, chemistry, microbiology, astronomy, medicine, or any other field—begins with an assumption that everything operates according to a set of natural laws. The goal of research is to peel back the visible covering of the universe and see the logically cohesive structure underneath. It may be a coherent structure of unimaginable complexity, but we do not doubt that it is there and that it makes rational sense.

John Donne had complained that the universe is "all in pieces, all coherence gone." Descartes was the first to argue convincingly that another type of system, based on fixed and unalterable natural laws, can take the place of biblical and classical authorities—and that humans can figure those laws out. Just as the human mind exists within but also beyond the body, the abstract laws of nature exist within and beyond the physical universe. They guide it, shape it, drive it, and ennoble it with purpose.

NEWTON'S MATHEMATICAL PRINCIPLES

The first person to deliver on Descartes's promise was Sir **Isaac Newton** (1642–1727), the greatest scientist in Western history before Albert Einstein (1879–1955). Born into an English farming family, from an early age he enjoyed tinkering with machines, a hobby he continued throughout his life.[13] He earned a bachelor's degree in 1664 from Cambridge University in classical studies, but by that time Newton had already started to teach himself mathematics and physics by reading the works of Descartes. When the plague swept through England, he withdrew to his family's rural home, where he began his work in optics and in the calculation of infinite series. The first resulted in his discovery that light can be broken into the spectrum of colors and has the properties of a wave, and the second resulted in his discoveries of integral and differential calculus. Within two years he had become the leading mathematician of his age and earned a prestigious professorship at Cambridge, where he remained for thirty years. He spent his last thirty years in London serving as master of the Royal Mint and president of the Royal Society.

Newton's greatest achievement was his *Philosophiae Naturalis Principia Mathematica* (*Mathematical Principles of Natural Philosophy*), published in 1687. It is not light reading. Newton was a moody, obsessive loner who loathed being disturbed in his work, especially by people who could not understand the complexity of his thinking—which was just about everyone. Only three hundred copies of the first edition of the *Principia* were printed, which was probably well more than the number of people capable of making sense of it. Newton insisted on having empirical data as the basis for his high-flying mathematical formulations, and hence the *Principia* skips from topic to topic, wherever there are sufficient data to begin computing. Nevertheless, the variety and number of topics Newton addresses add up to a comprehensive theory about the physical world.

Its fundamental and astonishing idea is the theory of universal gravitation. What prompted Newton's thinking was the question of why, if things like apples fall to the ground, the planets do not also fall to the Earth's surface. There is evidently nothing holding them in orbit in the sky. Physical theory had been *The Theory of Universal Gravitation*

---

13   Newton invented the reflecting telescope—one that uses a curved mirror rather than a second lens to focus captured beams of light.

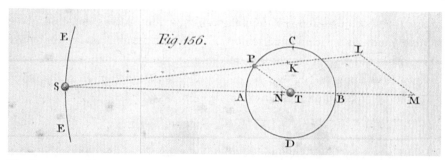

The Geometry of Gravity Sir Isaac Newton's *Principia Mathematica* (1687) was the closest thing the world had yet seen to a scientific Theory of Everything and dominated the field of physics until the start of the 20th century. This image (Figure 156) illustrates his thoughts on the gravitational interaction of three bodies: a central and fixed star, represented by the letter T, and two planets in orbit around it, P and S.

based for centuries on the belief that motion was an intrinsic quality of all matter. Water flows because that is what water does; the atoms that propel our bodies forward are in constant movement because movement is life itself. Death, in this view, is a cessation of natural movement. Newton argued instead that motion results from the interaction of objects, and he showed that the interaction can be calculated precisely by taking into account their mass, velocity, and direction of motion. In this way he developed the physical concept of force. But he then complicated matters by introducing another idea—what he called the "weight" (*gravitas* in Latin) or attraction that all physical objects feel toward one another whether they are in a static or dynamic state. Thus was born the idea of gravity.

In his descriptions of gravity, which he further showed to be determined in permanent ratios according to mass, distance, and force, he produced a comprehensive explanation for physical actions as simple as an apple's fall from a tree and as complex as the elliptical orbits of the planets in the solar system. Descartes had shown the logical necessity of a universal set of natural laws governing all matter. Now Newton provided the mathematical formulas that those laws consisted of. The universe was not only internally coherent according to a single, although undeniably massive, set of laws, but also those laws were knowable, calculable, and provable. When Newton died in 1727, he was given a hero's funeral and buried in the royal church of Westminster Abbey.

◆

The immediate impact of the Scientific Revolution was moderate, but it changed Greater Western culture profoundly. The universe became in the popular mind less of a divine and glorious mystery and more of a fascinating mechanism, with all that is good and bad in that transition. The new tenets included the belief in a rational explanation for everything we experience, the considered reliability of an idea that is based on quantifiable evidence, and the habit of privileging the demonstrably logical over the intuitive. All came increasingly to characterize much of European thought. Not coincidentally, European society, being open to the exploration of the world and the exploitation of its potentialities, became poised to emerge as a global power.

Not that sounds of alarm were not raised. When the Royal Society, England's premier institution for the promotion of science, was established in London, some warned that it was nothing short of the beginning of a Satanic apocalypse. One prominent Anglican clergyman, Robert South (1634–1716), denounced the members of the society in a sermon in 1667 as:

> the profane, atheistical, epicurean rabble . . . who have lived so much in the defiance of God . . . a company of lewd, shallow-brained huffs [blowhards] making atheism and contempt of religion the sole badge of wit, gallantry, and true discretion. . . . The truth is, the persons here reflected upon are of such a peculiar stamp of impiety, that they seem to be a set of fellows got together, and formed into a diabolical society, for the finding out new experiments in vice.

Developments in the Christian West and the Islamic West now sharply diverged. Europeans came increasingly to view the world as knowable, explorable, and understandable. In fact, it became something that they could dominate. At the same time, the Islamic world took a pronounced inward turn, eschewing science and exploration in favor of a reexamination of traditional values. Neither path was intrinsically right or wrong, but both resulted from conscious cultural choices and as the expressions of value. The consequences of those choices would be felt for centuries to come.

WHO, WHAT, WHERE

Christopher Columbus	Galileo Galilei	scientific method
Columbian Exchange	heliocentric	Scientific Revolution
conquistadores	Isaac Newton	Vasco da Gama
epistemology	Nicolaus Copernicus	
Francis Bacon	René Descartes	

SUGGESTED READINGS

Primary Sources

Bacon, Francis. *Novum Organum* (*New Instrument*).

Descartes, René. *Discourse on Method.*

Galilei, Galileo. *The Starry Messenger.*

Anthologies

Donnelly, John Patrick, ed. and trans. *Jesuit Writings of the Early Modern Period, 1540–1640* (2006).

Finocchiaro, Maurice A., ed. and trans. *The Essential Galileo Galilei* (2008).

Hellyer, Michael. *The Scientific Revolution: The Essential Readings* (2008).

Jacob, Margaret. *The Scientific Revolution: A Brief History with Documents* (2009).

Mayer, Thomas F. *The Trial of Galileo, 1612–1633* (2012).

Studies

Biagioli, Mario. *Galileo's Instruments of Credit: Telescopes, Images, Secrecy* (2007).

Bireley, Robert. *Religion and Politics in the Age of the Counterreformation: Emperor Ferdinand II, William Lamormaini, S. J., and the Formation of the Imperial Policy* (2011).

Blackwell, Richard J. *Behind the Scenes at Galileo's Trial* (2006).

Brooke, John, and Ian Maclean, eds. *Heterodoxy in Early Modern Science and Religion* (2006).

Crosby, Alfred W. *The Columbian Exchange: Biological and Cultural Consequences of 1492* (2003, orig. 1972).

Crosby, Alfred W. *Ecological Imperialism: The Biological Expansion of Europe, 900–1900* (2004, orig. 1986).

Dallal, Ahmad. *Islam, Science, and the Challenge of History* (2012).

Dear, Peter. *Revolutionizing the Sciences: European Knowledge and Its Ambitions, 1500–1700* (2009).

Evans, Robert J. W., and Alexander Marr. *Curiosity and Wonder from the Renaissance to the Enlightenment* (2006).

Feingold, Mordechai. *The Newtonian Moment: Isaac Newton and the Making of Modern Culture* (2004).

Gaukroger, Stephen. *The Collapse of Mechanism and the Rise of Sensibility: Science and the Shaping of Modernity, 1680–1760* (2011).

Gaukroger, Stephen. *The Emergence of a Scientific Culture: Science and the Shaping of Modernity, 1210–1685* (2006).

Gaukroger, Stephen. *Francis Bacon and the Transformation of Early-Modern Philosophy* (2001).

Godman, Peter. *The Saint as Censor: Robert Bellarmine between Inquisition and Index* (2000).

Henry, John. *Knowledge Is Power: How Magic, the Government, and an Apocalyptic Vision Inspired Francis Bacon to Create Modern Science* (2004).

Hessler, John W. *The Naming of America: Martin Waldseemüller's 1507 World Map and the Cosmographiae Introductio* (2008).

Hessler, John W. *A Renaissance Globemaker's Toolbox: Johannes Schöner and the Revolution in Modern Science, 1475–1550* (2013).

Jardine, Lisa. *Ingenious Pursuits: Building the Scientific Revolution* (2000).

Lindemann, Mary. *Medicine and Society in Early Modern Europe* (2010).

Mayer, Thomas F. *The Roman Inquisition: A Papal Bureaucracy and Its Laws in the Age of Galileo* (2013).

Park, Katharine. *Secrets of Women: Gender, Generation, and the Origins of Human Dissection* (2010).

Park, Katharine, and Lorraine Daston. *Early Modern Science* (2006).

Saliba, George. *Islamic Science and the Making of the European Renaissance* (2011).

Shapin, Steven, and Simon Schaffer. *Leviathan and the Air-Pump: Hobbes, Boyle, and the Experimental Life* (2011, orig. 1985).

Shea, William R., and Mariano Artigas. *Galileo in Rome: The Rise and Fall of a Troublesome Genius* (2003).

Spiller, Elizabeth. *Science, Reading, and Renaissance Literature: The Art of Making Knowledge, 1580–1670* (2004).

Tutino, Stefania. *Empire of Souls: Robert Bellarmine and the Christian Commonwealth* (2010).

For additional resources, including maps, primary sources, visuals, web links, and quizzes, please go to **www.oup.com/us/backman.**

The Wars of All Against All

1540–1648

The conflicts that divided Christianity were wars of words in Luther's and Calvin's time, but within a generation of their passing the words gave way to gunpowder. These wars were Europe's first in which mass armies and modern weaponry were the new norm, and the exponential increases in troop numbers and firepower resulted in carnage on a scale previously unimaginable. In 1066, Duke William of Normandy conquered all of England with an army of ten thousand soldiers; in 1632 nearly nine times that number of Protestant and Catholic

THE GREATER WEST, 1648

forces fought in a single battle at Alte Veste, near the German city of Nuremberg. Between 1540 and 1648 as many as 10 million soldiers and civilians were killed in religiously inspired wars from Britain to Bohemia and from Sweden to Serbia. The first blows landed in France and Holland, where civil dissension combined with religious difference and rivalry for New World riches to create a toxic brew of hatred. In England, by contrast, the ultimate adoption of Protestantism in fact signaled the end of an even longer civil war and the start of a golden age.

The Triumph of Death Painted around 1562 by Dutch master Peter Bruegel the Elder, this picture represents the horrors of the warfare then starting to reengulf western Europe—the Wars of Religion. The "Triumph of Death" motif dates to the 14th century, when the Black Death poured over the entire Greater West. Bruegel gave it new life in this savage depiction of hell on earth. "About suffering they were never wrong/the Old Masters," wrote Englishman W. H. Auden in his great poem, "Musée des Beaux Arts" (1938).

It took the Thirty Years' War in Germany (1618–1648), however, to embroil all of Christian Europe.

Although often referred to as the "Wars of Religion," the wars that wracked the Greater West in the 16th and 17th centuries enmeshed religious antagonisms with economic, social, and political conflict. A more accurate term might come from English philosopher Thomas Hobbes (1588–1679): "the war of all against all." The brief but bloody German Peasants' Revolt of 1524–1525 served as a prologue because it not only displayed the interaction of religious, economic, social, and political factors characteristic of the later conflicts but also spotlighted the enormous devastation wreaked on ordinary people during this period.

The war of all against all affected everyone from princes to peasants. It led to the toppling of Spain as the dominant European power and the rise of England and the Netherlands. It also included war within state boundaries, from the frenzied pursuit of "witches" to the increased persecution of Jews. The religious wars in Europe had their brutal analog in the Middle East as well, in the dynastic and territorial wars between the Ottoman Turks and the Safavid Persians, struggles with their own bitter elements of religious dissent and revolution. The most spectacular development in the Muslim world was the forced conversion of the Persians from Sunni to Shi'i Islam as a means of strengthening a distinct Iranian identity.

CHAPTER TIMELINE

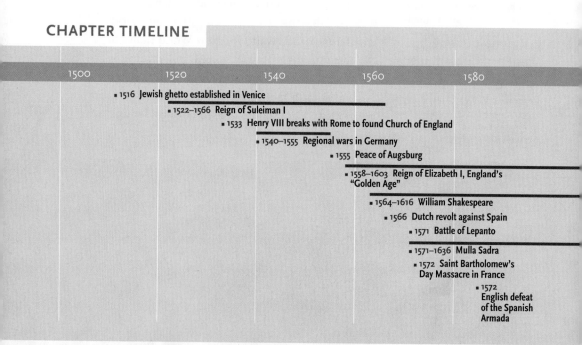

1500	1520	1540	1560	1580

- 1516 Jewish ghetto established in Venice
- 1522–1566 Reign of Suleiman I
- 1533 Henry VIII breaks with Rome to found Church of England
- 1540–1555 Regional wars in Germany
- 1555 Peace of Augsburg
- 1558–1603 Reign of Elizabeth I, England's "Golden Age"
- 1564–1616 William Shakespeare
- 1566 Dutch revolt against Spain
- 1571 Battle of Lepanto
- 1571–1636 Mulla Sadra
- 1572 Saint Bartholomew's Day Massacre in France
- 1572 English defeat of the Spanish Armada

Moreover, the Greater West's religious realignments took place within the context of increasing international competition and belligerence. So wrenching were the changes, greeds, and hatreds of the age that many of the fundamental values of civilization came into doubt—a crisis that led scholars, writers, and artists to reconsider what, if anything, they could still believe in.

FROM THE PEACE OF AUGSBURG TO THE EDICT OF NANTES: FRENCH WARS OF RELIGION

The Protestant movement was only seven years old when the German Peasants' Revolt erupted in 1524, but it had already progressed far enough to shred permanently any sense of Christian unity. Encouraged by Luther's open approval, the Protestant nobles had responded in force and crushed the rebellion ruthlessly. The experience sharpened more antagonisms than it resolved, however, and, as we saw in chapter 12, set the stage for battle with the Holy Roman Emperor Charles V (r. 1520–1566). The Catholic nobles in southern Germany—none of whom had stood up to support the peasants—feared the aroused might of their Protestant peers and looked to Charles to restore order.

But although they hoped for Protestantism's defeat, the Catholic princes were wary of Charles's ending up with more power in Germany as a result. When Charles finally began military action in the 1540s, support from the Catholic

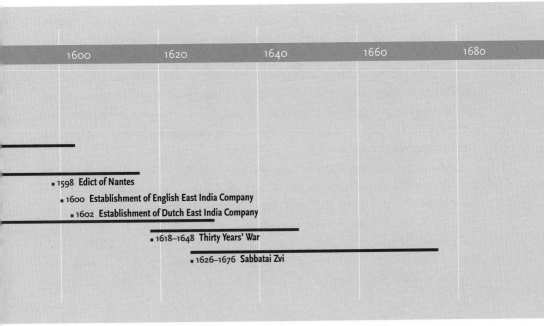

1600   1620   1640   1660   1680

- 1598 **Edict of Nantes**
- 1600 **Establishment of English East India Company**
- 1602 **Establishment of Dutch East India Company**
- 1618–1648 **Thirty Years' War**
- 1626–1676 **Sabbatai Zvi**

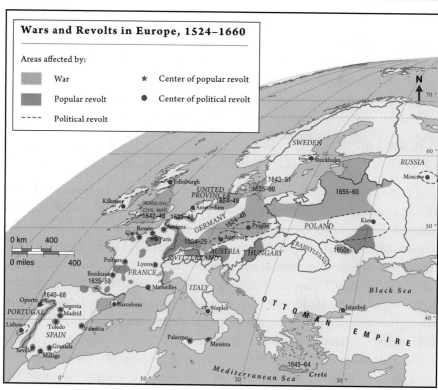

MAP 14.1   Wars and Revolts in Europe, 1524–1660   The 16th and 17th centuries in Europe saw a nearly constant series of violent clashes that were political, social, economic, and religious in nature.

princes was at best occasional and at worst verged on treason. For this reason, the war quickly degraded into an inconclusive series of advances and defeats. Finally, when it appeared certain that neither side could gain a clear victory, Charles and the Lutheran princes agreed to a compromise settlement. Known as the **Peace of Augsburg** (1555), it granted Lutheranism legal recognition and established the principle of *cuius regio, eius religio*—the religion of the ruler determines the religion of the land—with certain guarantees offered to ensure the rights of the religious minority.

Any hopes that the Augsburg compromise might serve as a model for other countries faded with the first test, when in 1562 France became embroiled in a religiously charged civil war that raged for more than three decades (see Map 14.1). The problem was that the Augsburg treaty had recognized the legal validity of Lutheranism but had not done so for Calvinism (since Calvin's version of Christianity had a negligible presence in Germany). And Calvin, who lived across the Swiss border, in Geneva, longed to secure legitimacy for his followers back in France, known as **Huguenots**.[1] By 1562 nearly one-fifth of the French population was Huguenot—primarily in the southern and eastern parts of the realm.

Calvin's chance came in 1562, when control of the French monarchy came up for grabs. The teenaged King Francis II had died in 1560 after only one year on the throne, leaving his even younger brother, Charles IX (r. 1560–1574), to succeed him. The question of the regency—that is, of someone appointed to run the government on Charles's behalf until he came of age—exposed political rivalries and religious antagonism as well. Each of the two leading noble families had ties to royalty, but one was Catholic and the other Huguenot. The Catholic faction was led by the duke of Guise, whereas the prince of Condé and Henri de Navarre led the Huguenots. The queen mother, Catherine de' Medici (d. 1589), a relation of the Florentine family who was closely aligned with the papacy, formed yet another faction of her own. Although essentially a court conflict among aristocratic rivals, the war quickly engulfed the whole population. The leaders of each faction appealed to the masses and turned a dispute over the *roi et loi* ("king and law") into a fight over *foi* ("faith"). Mob violence determined the course of the war almost as much as the actual armies did, because Catholics and Huguenots everywhere attacked each other. They ransacked each other's churches and plundered each other's shops and households. Clergy on both sides urged the fight onward.

The war's grimmest episode was the **Saint Bartholomew's Day Massacre**, a week-long orgy of violence that began as an assassination plot and turned into a mass riot (August 24–29, 1572). The Huguenot leaders had come to Paris to celebrate the wedding of Henri de Navarre, the Huguenot leader, to Marguerite de Valois, sister of the French king, Charles IX (r. 1560–1574). This marriage was intended to ease relations between Catholics and Protestants by uniting their causes in the royal family, but the attempt at a truce was undone by Catherine de' Medici, whose Catholic faction plotted to kill the Protestant leaders. News of the murders spurred mobs to action, and soon crowds in other cities had joined in. When the killing finally ended, thousands of Protestants lay dead, the victims of shooting, strangling, knifing, and drowning. In addition to Paris, massacres took place in Angers, Bordeaux, Bourges, Gaillac, La Charité, Lyons, Meaux, Orléans, Rouen, Saumur, Toulouse, and Troyes—all cities that had reverted to Catholic rule. The killings sparked Protestant fury, and the Huguenots redoubled their efforts to bring down the royal house, aided now by sympathetic

The Saint Bartholomew's Day Massacre

---

[1] The origin of this term is uncertain. In 16th-century French the slang word *eiguenot* (meaning "a confederate or ally") may have contributed to *Huguenot*, but it is possible that the word refers in some way to King Hugh Capet (*Hugues*, in French), the 10th-century monarch whom certain Protestant writers had described as a king noteworthy for his tolerance.

Saint Bartholomew Day's Massacre   On August 24, 1572, a plot to assassinate leaders of the Huguenot faction in Paris inspired a terrifying wave of mob violence by thousands of the city's Catholics against their Protestant neighbors. Some estimates put the number of Protestants killed in the riot as high as thirty thousand. The original target of the assassination plot, Gaspard de Coligny, the military leader of the Huguenots, can be seen hanging out of a window to the right. (He was only wounded, but was subsequently executed.) Catherine de' Medici is at the far back, center-left, emerging from the royal palace (the Louvre) and examining a pile of Protestant corpses. The only surviving work of French Huguenot painter François Dubois (1529–1584), this is the best-known depiction of the Saint Bartholomew Day's Massacre.

Protestants from Germany and the Netherlands. Catholic Spain responded in turn by sending its troops into southern France. France's civil war threatened to engulf all of Latin Europe.

Reign of Henri IV   The whole miserable struggle ended when the next French king, Henri III (r. 1574–1589), was murdered—ironically, by an unstable fanatic (Jacques Clément, disguised as a priest) who felt the king was insufficiently Catholic.[2] Soon afterward, Prince Henri de Navarre, married to Princess Marguerite, acceded to the throne. Although the Protestant champion, Henri made the cool calculation that France, being 80 percent Catholic, had to have a Catholic king. "Paris is worth a Mass," he reportedly declared, and then announced his conversion to Catholicism. It took several years to convince the Catholics of his earnestness and to mollify the disappointment of the Protestants. In the end, however, he won the

---

[2]   Jacques Clément was killed immediately by the king's bodyguards. When he learned of the regicide, Pope Sixtus V (r. 1585–1590)—also an unstable fanatic—praised Clément as a martyr and tried (unsuccessfully) to have him canonized. In his brief pontificate Sixtus ordered so many executions of criminals (including any priest who broke his vow of chastity) and political enemies that it was said there were more heads displayed on pikes in the city of Rome than there were melons on sale in the markets.

support of both and began a long reign that is widely regarded as one of the high points of French history—as Henri IV (r. 1589–1610). In 1598 he promulgated the **Edict of Nantes**, which guaranteed religious freedom, under certain restrictions, throughout the realm. This edict, together with the Peace of Augsburg, established a legal right to believe as one wished—but in both cases freedom of religion was technically imposed on the people by the king, rather than arising from a demand from the populace. In other words, religious freedom was a power of the monarch, not a right of the people. For a brief spell the Continent had achieved peace, but it had not attained tolerance nor even embraced the very idea of it.

STRIFE AND SETTLEMENT IN ENGLAND

Meanwhile, a different sort of religious settlement evolved in England. There a civil war known as the War of the Roses (1455–1485) had erupted soon after England's humiliating defeat by the French in the Hundred Years' War (1337–1453), as various factions fought to shift the blame for England's loss and to win the throne.[3] The War of the Roses never involved large numbers of commoners, but it decimated the English nobility. When it ended in 1485 a relatively minor aristocrat named Henry Tudor became king, largely by default. Ruling as Henry VII (r. 1485–1509), he understood that he could make no elaborate claims of distinguished lineage or heavenly favor—and he wisely did not attempt to do so. He governed modestly and frugally, making sure not to upset the delicate truce he had worked out with Parliament. Henry was quick to recognize the potential of the New World discoveries, however, and he invested heavily in developing England's meager maritime capability. It was Henry who commissioned the voyage in 1497 to North America of the explorer we met in chapter 13, John Cabot (Giovanni Caboto).

When his son Henry VIII (r. 1509–1547) came to the throne, the kingdom had begun its climb to wealth and power on the international stage. Portraits of Henry VIII convey an aura of swagger, of manly vitality and newfound wealth altogether absent from portraits of his cautious father. They differed not only in personality but also in royal self-regard. Henry VIII's portraits exude self-confidence and more than a touch of the gaudiness of the *nouveau riche*—for "newly rich" is precisely what the Tudor monarch was becoming. His marriage in 1509 to Catherine of Aragon, the daughter of the king of Spain and the widow of Henry's brother, was a corporate merger of the two leading Atlantic seaboard powers. It promised to secure England's new dominant position in Europe for generations to come.

---

3   The War of the Roses took its name from the white and red roses on the respective heraldic badges of the noble houses of York and Lancaster.

But then came the "King's Great Matter." Catherine, a pious, loving woman *Establishment* with a frail physique, had produced several sickly children, and only one—a *of the Church* daughter, Mary—had survived infancy. By 1527, after eighteen years of mar- *of England* riage, it seemed likely that Catherine would not produce the male heir Henry so desperately needed. Further, he had fallen in love with Anne Boleyn, a lady at court and a supporter of the Reformation. He decided to ask the pope to annul the marriage on the grounds that it had never been valid and, indeed, had violated divine law. [4] This move offended Rome (especially since the marriage had happened only by means of a special papal grant in the first place), the royal house of Spain (since their princess was being publicly humiliated), and the German emperor (since Charles V was Catherine's nephew and was already smarting from his losses to the Lutherans in his realm). Prior to this succession crisis Henry had shown no interest in the Protestant Reformation and had even published a treatise against Luther in 1521 that earned him the title of "Defender of the Faith" from a grateful Pope Leo X (r. 1513–1521). But the desire for a male heir and for Anne Boleyn trumped Henry's regard for Rome. After much dramatic although failed diplomacy, he decided in early 1533 to break with the Catholic Church and establish the **Church of England**, or Anglican Church. It was a Protestant church with the monarch as its supreme head.

In creating the Church of England, however, Henry did more than establish yet another form of Protestantism; he brought England directly into the turmoil raging across Europe. Yet another version of Christianity was arguably the last thing Western culture needed at the time. Worse, it set the two 16th-century powers leading the exploration of the New World and the new international economy at direct odds with one another. England and Spain, briefly united in Henry's marriage to Catherine and on the brink of becoming a joint superpower, instead remained bitter rivals through the rest of the century. Henry's action did result in an enormous increase in royal income, however. He ordered the suppression of every Catholic monastery in the realm and seized all their holdings—which may have amounted to one-fifth of the real estate in England and Wales. The Tudors used this wealth, along with their New World riches, to buy support in both houses of Parliament. Hence, too, the elaborately bejeweled and befurred portraits of the king.

At Henry's death in 1547, the throne passed briefly to his son Edward VI *Escalation* (r. 1547–1553). Only ten at his accession, Edward never emerged from the shadow *of Religious* of the regency council established for him. The steps made to eradicate Catholi- *Strife* cism were undone when Edward fell ill and died, and the throne passed, after some intrigue, to his elder half-sister, Mary (r. 1553–1558). Mary, as the daughter

---

4   Leviticus 20.21 condemns marriage with one's brother's widow and warns that such illicit unions "will be childless."

of the scorned Catherine of Aragon, was resolutely Catholic and determined to restore Catholicism. Her reign has entered popular memory as a nightmare of religious violence, earning her the nickname of "Bloody Mary." In reality, she was quite popular at first, especially with the many Catholics who still remained in the kingdom. Even many Protestants sympathized with her after her father's break with Rome. But her decision to marry Prince Philip of Spain in 1554 changed matters and dispelled any hopes that a peaceful religious settlement might be reached.

Henry VIII of England   Henry VIII (r. 1509–1547) commissioned German artist Hans Holbein the Younger to execute several portraits of the king. This one shows Henry in 1540, confident of his powers. It may have been a wedding gift for his fifth wife, Catherine Howard. Henry famously had six wives before he died. The first, Catherine of Aragon, had given him Mary (r. 1553–1558); the second, Anne Boleyn, produced another daughter, Elizabeth (r. 1558–1603); and the third, Jane Seymour, gave birth to his only son, Edward VI (r. 1547–1553). Wives four and five, Anne of Cleves and Catherine Howard, gave him nothing but misery, and number six, Catherine Parr, brought genuine affection and comfort to his last years.

A wave of political purges and religious persecutions marked Mary's last three years on the throne, with roughly three hundred Protestant leaders hunted down as enemies of the crown and killed. Their stories were told—with more love for sensational detail than for historical accuracy—by John Foxe (1516–1587) in his *Book of Martyrs*, first published in 1563 (with the melodramatic subtitle *Actes and Monuments of These Latter and Perillous Days, Touching Matters of the Church*). The work is enormous, longer even than the Bible. And for a while it had nearly as much authority over English Protestants; a decree in 1570 ordered that a copy of it be placed in every (Anglican) cathedral church in England.[5]

Mary died childless, and the crown passed to her half-sister, **Elizabeth I** (r. 1558–1603), during whose reign England reached the apogee of international power and prestige. At home, Elizabeth secured in 1563 a religious settlement that established the Anglican Church as the official faith, with the monarch as its supreme leader. This compromise, known as the Thirty-Nine Articles of Religion, was a hybrid of Catholic ritual and Protestant theology, and it eventually proved amenable to a majority of her subjects. Elizabeth's settlement placed

England's "Golden Age" under Elizabeth I

---

[5]   Until the start of the 19th century, the three most widely disseminated books in England and America were the Bible (Authorized Version); English writer and preacher John Bunyan's (1628–1688) *The Pilgrim's Progress*, a Christian allegory first published in 1678; and Foxe's *Book of Martyrs*.

Elizabeth I of England   The English artist George Gower (1540–1596) is believed to have painted this striking "Armada Portrait" of England's greatest queen. In her later years Elizabeth's royal outfits were even more lavish and outlandish than those of her father, Henry VIII, and in images like this one the effect was nearly iconic.

legal restrictions on Catholic holdouts, but she was even sterner with the more radical wings of the Protestant movement, especially the Puritans—strict Calvinists who opposed all vestiges of Catholic ritual in the Church of England and who began to see the New World as a more inviting place to live.

Elizabeth increased England's involvement in the new Atlantic economy, which brought her into direct conflict with Spain. She promoted the piracy campaigns of Sir Francis Drake (1540–1596) against the Spanish fleets returning from the New World, laden with gold and silver. She also underwrote further exploration of North America. Given the already tense relations between England and Spain, Elizabeth's actions were sure to cause further trouble—which came in 1588 when Philip II (r. 1554–1598) sent his famed Armada (Spanish for "fleet") of 130 massive warships to invade England. After trapping the Spanish in the English Channel, the smaller but lighter English fleet scattered the Armada by sending blazing fireships into its midst. More than half of the Spanish vessels were destroyed or put out of commission. Many ships were wrecked by storms as they tried to return to Spain by

THE SPANISH ARMADA

rounding the coasts of Scotland and Ireland. The defeat of their "Invincible Armada" shocked the Spanish, whereas Protestants throughout Europe rejoiced. After 1588 England's involvement in the hornets' nest of Continental politics would become only more intense.

The defeat of the Spanish Armada marked the high point of Elizabeth's popularity. Commonly regarded as England's Golden Age, the Elizabethan period *Elizabethan* was characterized by a heightened sense of national identity that victory over *Drama* Catholic Spain confirmed. The rapid growth in the popularity of staged plays confirmed this national pride, since plots taken from England's history proved especially popular with audiences. One of the earliest such plays was *The Famous Chronicle of King Edward I* (1592) by George Peele (1556–1596), which proved so popular that Christopher Marlowe (1564–1593) was inspired the following year to pen *Edward II*. Marlowe died soon after completing it, but his friend and rival William Shakespeare (1564–1616) carried on the tradition with a series of dramas focused on the line of kings that preceded the Tudor dynasty: Richard II, Henry IV, Henry V, Henry VI, and Richard III, among others. Shakespeare also penned comedies and tragedies—perhaps the greatest in each genre being *A Midsummer Night's Dream* (1595), *Twelfth Night* (1601), and *Measure for Measure* (1604) among the comedies and *Hamlet* (1601), *Othello* (1604), *Macbeth* (1605), and *King Lear* (1606) among the tragedies.[6]

DUTCH ASCENDANCY AND SPANISH ECLIPSE

Spain was also fighting at the time against the Netherlands, which had formed part of the Habsburg Empire. Smarting under Catholic rule, the staunchly *Revolt* Calvinist Dutch revolted against Philip II in 1566. They fought over religion, of *of the* course, but even more important was the money to be made in the New World. *Netherlands* The Dutch, who had involved themselves in overseas exploration from the start— many Dutch sailors and officers manned the early Portuguese voyages into the Indian Ocean and South China Sea—resented having to send a portion of their earnings to Madrid, and they therefore sued for independence. Formal recognition of an independent Netherlands had to wait until 1648, although the Dutch had achieved de facto freedom from Spain by 1581.

England was happy to see Spain lose to the Netherlands and so gave the Dutch whatever overt and covert assistance they could afford.[7] The benefits proved obvious. With Spanish naval might curtailed, England established its East India Company in 1600. The Dutch founded their own East India Company in

---

6   The precise chronology of Shakespeare's plays is uncertain and still hotly debated by scholars even after four hundred years of study. The dates assigned here are estimates.

7   The playwright Christopher Marlowe served briefly as a spy for Elizabeth in Holland.

1602, leaving the Netherlands and England as the two most prominent European trading nations in the Americas. Both were chartered joint-stock companies that enjoyed lucrative monopolies over specified commodities coming from specific locations; such companies were allowed to operate without much government control in the areas chartered to them. In North America, England built its first settlement in Virginia in 1607, and the Dutch colonized the southern portion of the island of Manhattan in 1612. Spain thus entered the 17th century in a state of severe economic decline, whereas England and the Netherlands succeeded it as rising powers.

THE THIRTY YEARS' WAR

Origins and Course of the War

Economic rivalries, political aspirations, and religious conflicts culminated in the last and bloodiest of the so-called Wars of Religion: the **Thirty Years' War** (1618–1648), which began as a conflict between Protestants and Catholics in Germany but ultimately involved nearly all European powers and desolated lands and peoples across central Europe. Since the death of Charles V in 1558, the Habsburg rulers had generally tried to achieve a peaceful accord with and between their various Protestant and Catholic subjects. Policies changed, however, during the political maneuverings that led to the reign of Ferdinand II (r. 1619–1637), an archly conservative Catholic who was determined to eradicate Protestantism within the Holy Roman Empire. Rebellions by his Protestant subjects in Bohemia set off a chain reaction, and soon full-scale war across Germany, Austria, and Bohemia began. The war dragged on for decades in part because the Atlantic states profited from it: so long as the Germans remained mired in civil strife, they could not interfere with or compete against the English, Dutch, French, and Spanish, who were busy plundering North and South America.

All of the fighting took place in German territories, but it involved nearly every state in the Greater West. Its effects were devastating: roughly one-fifth of the entire German population died. France and England each sent assistance to both sides of the conflict. When the Protestants were winning, they aided the Catholics, and when the Catholics were winning, they supported the Protestants. The Dutch assisted whichever side promised to help them maintain independence from Spain. Denmark entered the conflict with the aim of seizing northern German territory for itself. The king of Poland joined the fighting to defend the Catholic faith and to claim the throne of Sweden. The Swedes, for their part, fought to defend Protestantism—and to gain a military alliance with Orthodox Russia against Catholic Poland. International involvement became near universal when the Ottoman sultan Osman II (r. 1618–1622) invaded Catholic Poland with 400,000 infantry and later found himself being attacked by

The Horrors of War   In 1633 the French printmaker Jacques Callot (1592–1635) published his most famous series of prints—made in collaboration with his friend, French engraver Israel Henriet (1590–1661)—entitled "The Miseries and Misfortunes of War." Shown here is the seventh plate in that series (of seventeen), depicting soldiers ransacking a rural village during the Thirty Years' War. Scenes like this occurred across Europe during that conflict, which ended with 8 million dead.

Protestant forces coming out of Germany. By 1648, after more than 7 million military and civilian casualties, with still no clear victor in sight, the nations of Europe were exhausted—physically, economically, and morally—and agreed to a set to accords known as the **Peace of Westphalia** that finally put an end to the carnage.

As with the Hundred Years' War between England and France, the significance of the Thirty Years' War lay more in how it was fought than in the bleak *Mass* narrative of which side won which battle in any given year. This was the first war *Armies and* in which most of the fighting used modern weapons based on gunpowder. Armed *Modern* commoners now formed the overwhelming bulk of the armies, marching in formation, with lines of muskets flanked by cumbersome but mobile artillery. Under the command of cavalry officers still drawn from the upper classes, the armies were larger than any that had taken the field before. At the first battle of Nördlingen in 1643, for example, close to fifty thousand soldiers took part, and ten thousand lay dead on the field by battle's end. Only two years later a second battle was fought on the same site, with thirty thousand soldiers entering the fray and only twenty thousand coming out alive. Similar levels of slaughter took place at Khotyn in 1620, at Breitenfield in 1631, at Lützen in 1632, at Breda in 1634, at Jankau in 1635, and at Lens in 1648. Corpses rotted by the tens of thousands in fields all across central and eastern Europe.

Among the most vivid testimonies to the war's savagery is a remarkable novel by Hans Jakob Christoffel von Grimmelshausen (1621–1676). Kidnapped *Grimmelshausen's* by German Hessian soldiers when he was only ten, he was captured in *The Adventures of* battle and redrafted into military service by several armies until the war's *a Simpleton* end in 1648. His novel, *The Adventures of a Simpleton*, appeared in 1668 and tells of a young boy who, like von Grimmelshausen, is pressed into service and witnesses unspeakable horrors. An early scene sets the tone:

> At first I did not intend to force you, gentle reader, to accompany these soldiers to my father's homestead, for I know what evil things are about to happen there; but the nature of my story requires me to leave some record of the brutal acts performed, time and again, by those involved in the war here in our Germany.... After stabling their horses, the soldiers all set about their appointed tasks, the sum of which was the utter ruin and desolation of our farm. Some began to slaughter all of our animals and set them stewing or roasting, so that it appeared as though they were preparing a jolly feast; but others ransacked our house from top to bottom.... Whatever they did not want to cart away they tore to pieces. A few started to thrust their swords into the haystacks and bales of straw, to find any hidden sheep or swine they could add to the slaughter.... Our maid Ursula, shame to tell, was dragged into the stable and so roughed up that afterwards she refused to come out. Then they took one of our hired workmen and stretched him out flat upon the ground, and, prying his mouth open with a bit of old wood, they dumped a slop-bucket full of shit and piss down his throat. They called this a "Swedish cocktail."

After rounding up other farmers in the neighborhood, the soldiers began interrogating them:

> First they took the flints out of their pistols, jammed the farmers' thumbs into the opened space, and used the pistols as thumbscrews to torture them as they would witches. One poor fellow, even though he had confessed to no crime at all, they thrust into the oven, and lit it. They wrapped a rope around another fellow's head and twisted it with a piece of wood until blood gushed from his mouth, nose, and ears.... I cannot report much about what happened to the women, young girls, and maidservants of the district, for the soldiers prevented me from seeing it; but I remember hearing pitiful screams coming from each corner of our house.

Much of the novel's horror comes from Grimmelshausen's identification of the soldiers simply as *soldiers*. He often does not differentiate among Bavarians, Saxons, Austrians, Swedes, Dutch, French, Spaniards, Danes, Poles, Hungarians, Serbs, Lutherans, Calvinists, or Catholics. They are all the same: there are no meaningful sides to the conflict, and the war is its own repellent cause and justification. But the novel offers more than scenes of savagery. Simpleton runs away from the army and finds his way through a dizzying series of unpredictable adventures. He turns himself into a populist highwayman à la Robin Hood; he hides by impersonating a woman; he takes the place in high society of an aristocrat; he becomes a con artist and a religious pilgrim. He voyages to a fantastic underwater realm inhabited by mermen. In the end, he denounces the world as irredeemably corrupt and becomes a hermit. At turns hilarious and horrifying, the novel depicts a treacherous world without order. To search for simple human decency and the tiniest bit of stability in life is to seek the impossible.

Grimmelshausen wrote several other novels, each a sequel to his first, usually narrated by a minor character from *Simpleton*. The series recalls Geoffrey Chaucer's *Canterbury Tales* in its shifting kaleidoscope of experiences and views. The greatest German novel before Goethe, *Simpleton* has never been surpassed as a depiction of war as collective insanity. An additional aspect of that insanity consists of Simpleton's repeated encounters with a dreaded element of European life in the 16th and 17th centuries—witches.

ENEMIES WITHIN: THE HUNT FOR WITCHES

Popular belief in witchcraft had roots in pre-Christian classical, Germanic, and Celtic culture. Ancient and medieval attitudes toward witches differed from those of the early modern era, however. Earlier Europeans had held that some individuals are simply born with an intrinsic ability to summon supernatural forces at will, which they can use for good or ill. In contrast, people of the 16th and 17th centuries developed the belief that magical powers resulted from an explicit and conscious contract made between the witch (who could be male or female) and the devil, Satan. They believed witchcraft was intentional—a power that an individual chose to acquire—rather than an innate, although freakish, ability possessed from birth. And that made popular fear of it all the stronger, especially given the era's heavy emphasis on human weakness and sinfulness. If people could be so easily coaxed into a pact with Satan, then witchcraft could conceivably take over rhw world and bring about its ruin. A witch was not merely someone "possessed of powers" but someone actively engaged in evil, and the danger he or she represented required immediate action.

That action consisted of arrest, trial, torture, and execution on a scale that is difficult to comprehend. Campaigns against witches increased in number *Links between* markedly toward the end of the 15th century but became frenzied after *Persecution of* 1560, once Europe's religious disputes turned violent. From 1560 to 1670, *Witches and* nearly 200,000 people across Europe were accused of witchcraft and sub- *Wars of Religion* jected to judicial persecution or mob violence (see Figure 14.1). Roughly

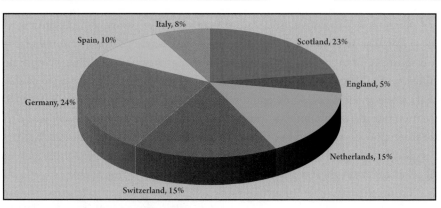

FIGURE 14.1   Witchcraft Trials, 1450–1750

one-quarter of them were executed. Those who confessed and repented—which required identifying other witches and agreeing to testify against them—were briefly imprisoned, frequently marked by a tattoo, fined, and released, to be socially shunned for the rest of their lives. And although there seems to be no substantial difference between the frequency of Protestant and Catholic prosecutions of witchcraft, it does appear that the Protestant–Catholic divide played a role: witchcraft mania struck most ferociously where Protestants and Catholics were most equal in number and hence locked in protracted conflict. Accusations of witchcraft seldom crossed confessional lines, however. Catholics and Protestants generally did not accuse the other group but instead members of their own denominations; in fact, they frequently shared information about supposed witches, seeing them as a threat to both groups. The witches who appeared in stage dramas like William Shakespeare's *Macbeth* were realistic characters to audiences, in addition to the symbolic role they played. Germany and Scotland had the most witchcraft trials per capita, but in the end, no country was immune to witchcraft mania.

Targeting Women   Neither was either sex: both men and women were believed capable of selling their souls to Satan. Nonetheless, at least three-quarters of those arrested for witchcraft, and nearly 90 percent of those executed for it, were women. (Ireland was the sole exception: roughly 90 percent of its prosecuted witches were male.) Popular assumptions about women's nature—as emotional, impulsive, passionate, demanding creatures—fueled the phenomenon. Women were regarded as generally weaker than men, but especially in regard to sex. Ideas about sexuality, derived from ancient Greek medicine, held that female lust, once aroused, was insatiable.[8] Only a demonic lover like Satan, it was assumed, could satisfy a

---

[8]   Many of the constraints placed on women—such as limiting their appearance in public or regulating their dress—were justified as protecting them from their own inability to control their passions.

woman's sexual longing—and that was precisely the appeal used by the devil to ensnare his victims. Men who became witches were generally assumed to have been enticed into it by women who had already given themselves over to satanic lust.

In this way, the witchcraft craze accords with the period's concern with sexuality in general. Ironically, the era's emphasis on early marriage was directly related to its fear of unchecked sexuality. It valued women as the "godly wives and mothers" responsible for their children's moral education, the dutiful subjects of their husbands, and the preservers of sacralized domestic life. A force as powerful and unpredictable as a woman's body needed to be firmly controlled—or else all hell, literally, could break loose.

Burning Witches This broadsheet from October 1555 announces the burning of convicted witches in the small village of Derneburg, in lower Saxony. In the background, someone is being beheaded, while flames engulf the interior of the building on the right. A child seems to have been flung to the ground in the doorway.

THE JEWS OF THE EAST AND WEST

The era was cruel to Jews as well. Late medieval hostility to Jews had resulted in a series of expulsion orders, first from England (1290), then from France (1306) and Germany (numerous times), and finally from Spain (1492) and Portugal (1497). Forced from one territory to the next, the Jews gradually concentrated in the Netherlands, Italy, North Africa, and the Ottoman Empire, where the Ashkenazic and Sephardic traditions of Judaism, introduced in chapter 10, once again confronted each other (see Map 14.2).

For the host countries, the sudden increase in the Jewish populations aggravated social tensions and led many to segregate the Jews into separate districts. Regulations like these had been common since the 12th century. The surge in Jewish numbers within those districts, however, frequently led to new legislation limiting the Jews' freedom to move and act within the larger community. Venice established the first modern **ghetto** in 1516, but other European cities were quick to follow. (The word *ghetto* likely derives from the Italian *borghetto*, meaning a "small borough" or "precinct.") Life in these communities was often difficult, since Jews from many backgrounds were thrust shoulder to shoulder within a larger social context of economic decline and Christian hostility. The economic

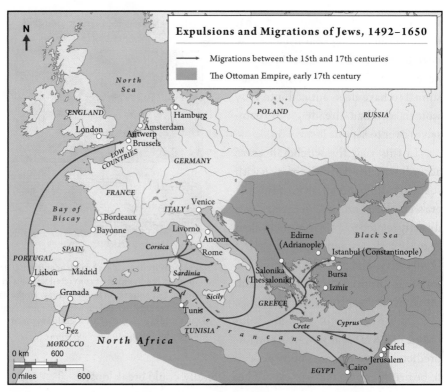

MAP 14.2   Expulsions and Migrations of Jews, 1492–1650   Exiled Jews fled in all directions, but considerable numbers favored moving northward into the Netherlands and eastward into the Ottoman Empire.

decline occurred largely because of the shift of economic power from the Mediterranean—where the Jews had taken refuge—to the Atlantic seaboard. Only those Jews who had migrated to the Netherlands moved into a society of economic growth.

In the Ottoman state, which, after 1515, included the Holy Land, Jewish refugees from Europe generally received a cordial welcome from the Ottoman rulers Bayezid II (r. 1481–1512) and Selim I (r. 1512–1520), who encouraged Jews to settle in the Holy Land.[9] Many Jews, on arriving, expressed surprise at the squalor into which the cities had fallen. An Italian refugee, Rabbi Obadiah of Bertinoro, sent a letter back to a friend in which he estimates there being "only about seventy [Jewish] households in all of Gaza," whereas in Hebron he found "only twenty households . . . half of them coming from Spain and just recently arrived."

---

[9]   Spanish Jews set up the first printing press in the Ottoman state. Two Sephardic Jews, Joseph Hamon (d. ca. 1540) and his son Moses Hamon (d. 1567), served for a total of thirty years as personal physicians to the sultans.

In Jerusalem itself he found "only seventy households left, all of them poverty-stricken and with no means of support.... Anyone who has food to last a year, or the means to procure it, is considered wealthy here."

Not surprisingly, as most Jews' social and economic lives grew shaky in the 16th and 17th centuries, many found solace in new messianic movements. *Messianic* In Italy, led by charismatic adventurers like Solomon Molcho (1500–1532) *Movements* and David Reubeni (1490–1541), and in the Ottoman Empire, inspired by rabbis Isaac Luria (1534–1572) and Hayyim Vital (1543–1620), thousands of Jews believed in the imminent arrival of the long-promised messiah. These four figures, and others like them, preached a message of intense spiritual and social reform to prepare for the restoration of David's kingdom (discussed in chapter 3). These movements involved a minority of the Jews, but they were popular enough to make the rulers of their host countries concerned about the potential for social unrest.

Reubeni was an especially enigmatic figure, known today primarily through his diary, published in 1895. A curly-haired and heavily bearded dwarf, he had a striking appearance. He probably came from the large Jewish community at Cranganore in India, but at some point he traveled to Khaybar, in today's Afghanistan. In 1522 he appeared in Sudan, speaking to crowds about a large Jewish kingdom in the east, supposedly ruled by his brother Joseph. For some reason, Reubeni also claimed to be a direct descendant of the Prophet Muhammad. His life's aim was to create a military alliance between European royalty and his supposed royal brother to open a two-front war on the Ottoman Empire. In 1524 he went to Rome, entering the city while riding a white horse, and was received by Pope Clement VII (r. 1523–1534). With Clement's recommendation in hand, he approached the Portuguese king João III (r. 1521–1557), the rulers of Milan and of Venice, and finally the Habsburg emperor Charles V, each of whom promised some form of aid. Reubeni's habit of complaining to these rulers about their treatment of native Jews, however, turned them against him. Sometime around 1531 he was arrested in Italy and sent to Spain, where he was tried by the Inquisition. No official record of his trial or execution survives, but a later chronicle records that in 1541 "a Jew from India who had come to Portugal" was put to death by the Inquisition at Llerana in southern Spain.

When Sabbatai Zvi (1626–1676) came along and preached his own version of messianic deliverance, he found an enormously receptive audience. He *The* was from Smyrna (modern Izmir, Turkey). **Kabbala**, a mystical interpretation *Sabbatean* of scripture developed by rabbis, had originated centuries before. In 1648, *Cult* however, in fulfillment of a kabbalistic prophecy, Zvi declared himself the messiah and ultimately moved to Istanbul, where he converted a Jewish scribe who promptly forged an ancient-looking revelation document from the patriarch Abraham.

> I, Abraham, confined for forty years to life in a cave, spent a long time in pondering when the miraculous time of deliverance might come, when suddenly, a heavenly voice cried out: "A son named Sabbatai will be born to Mordechai Zvi in the year 5386 [1626]. He, the great Messiah, will humble the Serpent and take his seat upon my throne."

Armed with this, Zvi preached to Jews throughout the Ottoman lands—Istanbul, Athens, Alexandria, Cairo, Gaza, Jerusalem, Aleppo—and gained followers everywhere. Jews as far away as Italy, France, Germany, and the Netherlands joined the movement. At least one entire community, at Avignon, made preparations to quit the city and move with all their belongings to Jerusalem, to join the anticipated new kingdom.

Zvi went so far as to issue a universal proclamation to all Jews:

A Messiah on His Throne   This page from a prayer book published in Amsterdam in 1666 shows Sabbatai Zvi (1626–1676) enthroned, with angels bringing him a heavenly crown. Note the lower image, which has him presiding over a table at which are gathered the representatives, presumably, of the Twelve Tribes of Israel. The Hebrew word in large print in the center of the image means the "restored harmony" expected to be provided by the messiah.

> Sabbatai Zvi, the first-born son of YHWH, and the Messiah and Redeemer of all the people of Israel, to all the sons of Israel, sends Peace. Since you have been thought worthy to behold the great Day of Fulfillment promised by YHWH through His prophets, all your sorrows and lamentations must end and be turned to celebrations, your fasts be turned into feasts, and your tears must cease. Rejoice, instead, with psalms and hymns! Let your days of sadness and despair become days of jubilation! For I have appeared!

As unlikely as it sounds, the proclamation generated enormous excitement throughout the international Jewish world. Zvi's portrait was printed in Jewish prayer books (frequently appearing next to images of King David). His initials were carved on synagogue walls and embroidered onto flags, and prayers for him were inserted into Jewish liturgies.

The speed of the Sabbatean cult's rise reflects the misery and difficulty of Jewish lives. Persecutions of the Jews grew in number and ferocity throughout the era, leading many to find hope only in a miraculous deliverance. Even a number of Christian groups welcomed the supposed messiah's arrival, although they were probably more excited by the idea of the Jews leaving Europe than they were about their liberation. But the Ottoman ruler Mehmed IV (r. 1648–1687) grew concerned about Zvi's popularity. Afraid that large numbers of Jews migrating to the Holy Land would push for its independence, he pressured Zvi to stop his activity. Zvi responded, on September 16, 1666, by suddenly announcing his conversion to Islam—for which Mehmed rewarded him with great wealth, a prominent position at court, and several new wives. To Jews everywhere, the blow was devastating, and the Sabbatean movement fell apart instantaneously.

Within Europe, most of the early leaders of Protestantism were surprised by the refusal of the Jews to convert to Christianity. For centuries, figures like *Escalating* Martin Luther believed, the Jews had bravely and correctly held out against the *Anti-* false teachings of the Catholics. "If I had been born a Jew," Luther wrote in *On Semitism* *Jesus Christ Having Been Born a Jew* (1523), "and if I had witnessed such idiots and buffoons [as the Catholics] trying to teach and administer Christian truth, I would as soon have turned myself into a pig as into a Christian." But surely, most reformers confidently felt, once the beautiful gospel truth was finally restored by the Protestants, the Jews would rush to accept it. Conversion would be their reward for enduring centuries of Catholic idiocy and persecution. "We will receive them with open arms, permit them to trade with us, to work with us, live among us, hear our Christian preaching, and witness our Christian way of life." When that failed to happen, the reaction was severe.

Luther himself penned many private letters to friends in which he railed against Jewish perfidy. He also expressed his wrath publicly in several viciously anti-Semitic tracts, the most notorious being *On the Jews and Their Lies* (1543):

> What ever shall Christians do with the damned, rejected Jews? We can hardly tolerate having them live among us as they do—for if we do, now that we know of their lies, hatred, and blasphemy, we will be complicit in their evil. We are powerless to convert them, but powerless too to put out the unquenchable fire of God's wrath, of which the prophets wrote. . . . Here is what I recommend. First, we ought to burn down their synagogues and schools, and bury underground whatever is immune to fire, so that no one ever again needs to see a single stone or cinder of them. . . . Their homes too should be set ablaze and destroyed. . . . Let all their prayer books and copies of the Talmud be taken from them, for it is by means of these that they propagate their idolatry, their lies, their foul cursing, and their blasphemies.

The tract goes on like this for more than a hundred pages. Luther may not have persuaded tolerant Christians to become otherwise—and it deserves pointing out that many Christians disagreed, in print, with Luther. Yet his uniquely authoritative position among Protestants probably encouraged and confirmed many anti-Semites in the bigotry they already had.

The early modern era, in sum, was marked by harsh religious tensions compounded by severe economic dislocations. Small wonder, then, that so many dispossessed Christians fled to the New World. Small wonder, too, that so many dispossessed Jews fled to the Old.

THE WANING OF THE SULTANATE

The Ottoman economy peaked under Suleiman I, who held the sultanate from 1520 to 1566. Suleiman, the contemporary of Charles V in Europe, is known in Europe as "Suleiman the Magnificent." In the Muslim world, he is called "Suleiman the Lawgiver" in recognition of his work codifying the great mass of legislation he inherited from his predecessors. He also made the imperial administration more efficient. As we saw in chapter 12, he was a successful warrior as well, extending Ottoman power to Hungary.

Economic Causes

With the growth of the Atlantic trade, however, the Ottoman economy gradually slowed and stagnated. Population increase both fueled the economy's peak under Suleiman and brought about the stagnation. When the economy was still expanding, immigration increased significantly. The arrival of the Jews formed only a part of this; a much greater factor was the influx of Muslims from Egypt and Syria and parts of Persia. Cities like Edirne, Trabzon, and Iznik grew by as much as 80 percent, while scores of cities grew by 40 to 50 percent. Rural villages increased in size and number by 30 to 40 percent over the 16th century. Much of this growth resulted from the flight of people from conflict zones between Ottoman and Safavid forces. Ultimately, overpopulation set in and was felt first in the countryside. Available farmland grew scarce, and local authorities responded by permitting the clearing of forests. Woodland, never abundant in much of the region, became even scarcer and contributed to a loss of commercial diversity.

Adding to the trouble was the influx of gold and silver from the New World, which led to spiraling inflation. In 1580, for example, it took 60 silver Turkish coins to equal 1 gold ducat (then the international standard currency of account), but only ten years later it required 120. By 1640 it took 250. Population growth and the concomitant increase in demand for goods and services also drove this "price revolution." The price of basic commodities like wheat increased by a factor of twenty between 1500 and 1600.

Istanbul This painting from 1537 shows a bird's-eye view of the Ottoman capital of Istanbul. The picture still follows the medieval tradition of orienting maps with east at the top; a modern viewer needs to turn his or her head sideways to the left. The Hippodrome and the former Church of Hagia Sophia (renamed the Ayasofya Mosque and renovated to include two minarets) are the two largest structures visible.

As in Christian Europe, economic misery made religious and ethnic tensions worse. Popular resentment of ethnic and religious foreigners, especially of the Sufis and Shi'a, increased. Street violence between factions forced local officials to take more direct and heavy-handed actions to keep the peace. But this required money. Over the 16th and 17th centuries, therefore, the power of the Ottoman sultanate waned. Provincial governors and urban or district commanders first demanded the right to collect their own taxes and then used the revenue to finance their new political muscle.

The sultan's loss of fiscal and political power escalated the conservative trend in religion. Madrasas across the Ottoman state declared their opposition to any sort of speculative thought. Preachers condemned public morals for straying from the early texts.[10] Even the natural sciences, which had been one of the   *Conservative Reaction*

---

[10]   Especially popular targets for preachers were the new enthusiasms for coffee and tobacco, brought over from the New World.

glories of Islam in the medieval period, came under attack. When Murad III (r. 1574–1595) had an astronomical observatory built in 1579, local preachers—mostly Arabs—condemned it as an offense against Allah to attempt to unravel the secrets of the act of creation. As we saw in chapter 13, the observatory was quickly torn down.

NEW CENTERS OF INTELLECTUAL AND CULTURAL LIFE

The creative centers of intellectual and cultural life thus moved from the Ottoman Empire to Safavid Egypt and Persia. Cairo emerged as the vital site for scientific work. It was also the home of Ibn Khaldun (1332–1406), whose great *Muqaddimah* (*Introduction to History*) posited a new philosophy of history, based on the interplay of group identity and materialism—or the pursuit of worldly goods.

Illuminationism   Safavid Persia, by contrast, became the center for metaphysics, the branch of philosophy that examines the nature of reality. Its great achievement was a philosophical program known as **illuminationism** (*al-hikmat al-ishraq*). Illuminationism derived from the attempt to harmonize Islamic doctrine with classical Greek thought and the mystical elements of Zoroastrianism and hence to give Sufism a measure of intellectual respectability within the larger Muslim world. Elements of illuminationism date to the 12th century, but the theory was given its fullest and most brilliant expression in the work of **Mulla Sadra** (1571–1640), the greatest Muslim philosopher of the modern era. Mulla Sadra's most important book, *Transcendent Wisdom Concerning the Four Journeys of the Intellect* (1638), maps out four stages in the route to spiritual and philosophical enlightenment. He dissects the cognitive processes that lead from the understanding of the physical world to a consideration of the essence of God and the nature of the relationship of humans to the Creator. Illumination is both a divine blessing and a technique of enlightenment, an aspect of spiritual discipline.

Illuminationism was in fact a common feature of Greater Western philosophical thinking of the age, although European and the Middle Eastern thinkers arrived at it by different trajectories. In western Europe it is expressed in the philosophies of Baruch Spinoza (1632–1677) and Gottfried Wilhelm von Leibniz (1646–1716). Spinoza, a heretical Jew expelled by his Amsterdam synagogue, was also a heretical illuminationist. He argued for a highly original form of pantheism (the identification of God with the universe and its phenomena) that asserted that God was nature itself (*natura naturans*, in his posthumously published masterpiece, the *Ethics*) and that every facet of and occurrence in nature is a necessary consequence of God's existence. But the identification of God and nature should not elicit an attitude of wonderment and awe from human beings. To Spinoza, human life has no divinely ordained purpose, and the occurrences of nature possess no supernatural meaning; they simply *are*. The rational study of nature leads to no spiritual revelation, only to a rational understanding of God's manifestation within nature—which, Spinoza insisted, is illumination enough for anyone.

The radical nature of Spinoza's views is evident from the writ of *herem* (a form of excommunication in Jewish law) issued by his synagogue. Its central portion reads,

> The leaders of this holy community, long familiar with the evil ideas and actions of Baruch de Spinoza, have tried repeatedly and by numerous stratagems to turn him from his evil ways; but we have failed to make him mend his wicked ways—in fact, we hear fresh reports every day about the abominable heresies he practices and teaches, and the monstrous deeds he continues to perform. . . . And [therefore] we have decided that the said Baruch de Spinoza should be excommunicated and expelled from the people of Israel. . . . [Wherefore], in accordance with the will of the Holy One (may He be ever blessed) and of this Holy Congregation, and in the presence of the holy scrolls of the Torah, with their 613 commandments, we hereby excommunicate, cast out, curse and damn Baruch de Spinoza with the same form of excommunication with which Joshua condemned Jericho, with the curse with which Elisha cursed the boys, and with all the curses which are written in the Book of the Law. Cursed be Baruch de Spinoza by day and cursed be he by night; cursed when he lies down and cursed when he rises up; cursed when he goes out and cursed when he comes in. The Lord will not spare him; His righteous anger and wrath will rage against this man, and bring upon him all the curses written in the Law. May the Lord blot out his name from under heaven, and condemn him to separation separate from all the tribes of Israel with all the curses of the covenant as they are contained the Law.

The rest of the writ is nearly as vehement.

In contrast to Spinoza, the German philosopher Leibniz saw divine emanation everywhere. He rejected pantheism in favor of an idea to which he gave the awkward name of *monadology*: all forms of natural life are composed of fundamental units he called "monads," which contain within themselves all the qualities of the life-form they make up. The concept is difficult to grasp—and Leibniz himself had difficulty in expressing it—but may be thought of, for

Spinoza   Baruch de Spinoza (1632–1677) was the greatest Jewish philosopher since Maimonides (1135–1204), although his ideas led to expulsion from his Amsterdam synagogue.

organic matter at least, as something akin to a particular life-form's unique genetic code. God himself, said Leibniz, is not present in nature, as Spinoza would have it, but his intent is present in the system of monads. The study of nature does not bring us, therefore, into God's presence, but it does illuminate for us the workings of His mind.

Mulla Sadra did not see God in creation like Spinoza; neither did he behold a divine intelligence in it like Leibniz. Rather, he saw a mystical unity in creation that parallels the unity of God Himself and draws the enlightened believer into a stronger desire for spiritual ascent, a return to the Oneness at the heart of all things. Sadra thus pulled together and harmonized Sufi mysticism, Shi'i doctrine, and Aristotelian rationalism:

> Philosophy is the process of perfecting the human soul by coming to a true understanding of things-as-they-are, which is achieved—when it is achieved at all—through rational demonstration rather than intuition or appeal to prior authority. By means of philosophy, we come to resemble our Creator, and this allows us to perceive and ascribe a rational order to His creation.

Most of Arab Islam during this period adhered to a staid and increasingly conservative form of Sunni Islam, eschewing scientific and metaphysical innovation in favor of rigid tradition. As early as the late 14th century Ibn Khaldun observed that most of the creative intellectual energy in the Islamic world came from non-Arabs. From the *Muqaddimah*:

> All the great grammarians have been Persian, . . . all the great legal scholars. . . . Only the Persians still write great books and dedicate themselves to preserving what is known. Thus, a saying attributed to the Prophet himself rings true: "If Knowledge was suspended from the highest ceiling in heaven, the Persians alone would get it." . . . All the intellectual arts, in fact, have long since been abandoned by the Arabs and become the sole preserve of the Persians.

The encouragement given to non-Arab Islamic and pre-Islamic traditions by the Ottomans thus stemmed from a sincere interest in promoting innovation and inquiry, but it also served a political purpose by providing a counterweight to the Arab-centric views holding sway from the Arabian peninsula through Palestine and Syria. It also provides another example of the interconnected nature of the cultural life of the Greater West.

WARS OF RELIGION: THE EASTERN FRONT

Christian Europe was not the only theater of conflict. Events in the Middle East, too, turned violent in the 16th and 17th centuries, thanks to a similarly toxic mixture of religious, economic, and ethnic enmity. Three large, multiethnic states dominated the Islamic world around 1500: the Ottoman Empire, the Mamluk Sultanate in Egypt and Syria, and Safavid Persia. Twenty years later only two remained, and they challenged each other for leadership of the Muslim world for the next two hundred years.

The Ottoman Turks and the Safavid Persians, heading up the Sunnis and Shi'a, respectively, were the standard-bearers of Islam. Ethnic Arabs held decidedly second-class status in both societies, and efforts to alter their position failed before the military might of the dominant regimes. Bayezid II (r. 1481–1512) and his son Selim I (r. 1512–1520) were anxious to continue the policy of aggressive Ottoman expansion and drove the Turkish army northward into the Black Sea, westward into the Balkans, southward toward Egypt, and eastward toward Persia. Bayezid even constructed a large naval fleet that defeated the Venetians in 1503 and left the Turks in command of the eastern Mediterranean sea-lanes. Bayezid had a more peaceful side to his personality, however, and took particular delight in managing the palace schools (sometimes even volunteering to examine students personally) and in fostering trade.

Selim—whose nickname Yavuz ("the Inflexible") describes his personality—began his reign with a near-paranoid fear of Persian designs on his realm and spent his first two years in power executing forty thousand suspected Safavid sympathizers in Anatolia. Non-Muslims fared better under these two than did non-Sunni Muslims. Nearly a quarter million Jews emigrated to the Ottoman realm after the European expulsions and settled in Anatolia and Palestine. Like many of their predecessors and courtiers, however, Bayezid and Selim practiced an eclectic form of Islam. It was formally Sunni but tinged with a passionate admiration for Sufism.

Just as tensions grew between the Ottomans and their Sunni Arab base, relations between the Ottomans and the Shi'i Safavids grew increasingly bitter. The Ottomans' economic stagnation worsened, whereas Safavid Persia not only carved out its own Islamic identity but also, as we have seen, challenged the very *Ottoman–Safavid Strife*

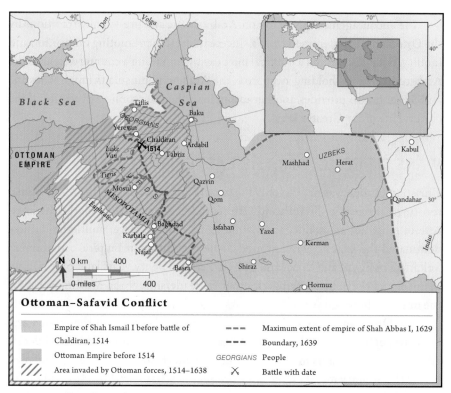

MAP 14.3 Ottoman–Safavid Conflict Struggles between the two great Islamic empires paralleled those among the states of Christian Europe in their virulent blend of political, religious, economic, and social factors.

notion that the center of Muslim civilization lay with the Arabs and Turks. The pulse of vital Islamic life, Persians insisted, had moved permanently eastward to Iran. The Persian shah (emperor) Ismail (r. 1501–1524), who believed himself divine, ordered the immediate conversion of all Sunnis in Iran to Shi'ism on penalty of death. And he made good on the threat by executing tens of thousands, confiscating their homes and goods, closing their mosques, and absconding with the funds for their schools. He also urged the Turkish people to overthrow the Ottomans. As a colorful warning to Bayezid II, Ismail had another political rival killed, the skin removed from his corpse and stitched around a life-size straw figure, and the "corpse" sent to Istanbul.[11]

Predictably, wars broke out between the two states and continued through the reign of Ismail's son and heir Tahmasp I (r. 1524–1576). Religious hatred intensified with each new reign (see Map 14.3). Ismail II (r. 1576–1577) played a

---

[11] Ismail kept his rival's skull—gold-plated and encrusted with jewels—and reportedly used it as a drinking cup.

role in Persia similar to that of England's Mary Tudor. He tried to force the realm to reconvert to Sunni Islam, but the purges and persecutions he ordered became so bloody that his closest supporters poisoned him after only two years on the throne. (Among other atrocities, he killed or blinded five of his brothers. Ismail died when someone put poison in his opium.) Occasional persecutions of Iran's Jewish and Christian communities broke out in the 16th century, but in the 17th religious relations improved significantly. In general, as the Shi'a became more firmly established and were less involved in strife with Sunni holdouts, they eased up on oppression of Jews and Christians. Moreover, many Jewish immigrants from farther west earned the shah's gratitude by introducing him to gunpowder and the casting of heavy artillery. The desire by rulers like Abbas the Great (r. 1588–1629) to increase Iran's export of silk textiles and Persian rugs also opened the way for Armenian Christians, long expert in the crafts, to thrive under Safavid rule.

Ottoman relations with Europe remained uneasy, especially with Habsburg Austria and Venice, their neighboring rivals for control of trade routes. The absence of a natural boundary between the Turkish and the Austrian realms kept mutual concerns for safety at a high level. And with the relative decline of Mediterranean trade compared with the Atlantic trade, control of the sea-lanes in and out of the Levant became all the more important. At the battle of Lepanto in 1571, an alliance of naval forces led by Venice and King Philip II of Spain defeated the Turkish fleet and decimated its corps of experienced officers. The so-called Long War (1593–1606) against Austria highlighted the need to modernize the Ottoman army with gunpowder weaponry, but resistance to Western technology among the Arab populace made this an unpopular development. *European Victories over the Ottomans*

Just as unpopular and destabilizing was the repeated phenomenon of women running the imperial government. The era of the 16th and 17th centuries in general—but especially the period from 1640 to 1670—is referred to as the **Sultanate of Women** (*kadınlar saltanatı* in Turkish; see Table 14.1). During the reigns of several weak sultans, such as Ibrahim I (r. 1640–1648), and several minorities, such as that under Mehmed IV (r. 1648–1687), the leading women of the imperial harem effectively controlled the government. Taking the title of "queen mother" (*valide sultan* in Turkish), these women ran the state, directed foreign policy, and oversaw the fiscal system. *Sultanate of Women*

What made matters worse, from the point of view of their disgruntled, mainly Arab, subjects, was the fact that most of these women were non-Muslim by birth, and their embrace of Islam was therefore suspect. (The Ottomans made a point of marrying as many Christian-born wives as possible, as a nod to their Christian subjects.) In the 16th century the most prominent sultanas were Nur-Banu and Safiye, who either ran or helped to run the Ottoman state in the years 1574–1583

TABLE 12.1   **Sultanate of Women**

Name	Years in power	Mother of	Wife of	Ethnicity
Ayşe Hafsa	1520–1534	Selim I	Suleiman I	Tatar
Nur-Banu	1574–1583	Selim II	Murad III	Venetian
Safiye	1595–1603	Murad III	Mehmed III	Venetian
Hatice	1617–1621	Ahmed I	Osman II	Serb
Kösem	1623–1648	Ahmed I	Murad IV and Ibrahim I	Greek
Turhan Hatice	1648–1683	Ibrahim I	Mehmed IV	Ukrainian

and 1595–1603, respectively. Both of Venetian descent, they restored relations with Venice after the battle of Lepanto and strengthened commercial ties between their empires. Two figures who especially stood out in the 17th century were Kösem, the Greek-born mother of Ibrahim, and her Turkish daughter-in-law Turhan Hatice, whose rivalry was as much personal as political and ended with Kösem's assassination in 1651.

ECONOMIC CHANGE IN AN ATLANTIC WORLD

After severe contraction in the late Middle Ages, Europe's population began to grow around 1500 and did so steadily for the next three hundred years, despite the carnage of the religious wars (see Figure 14.2). A gradual decline in outbreaks of plague accounts for much of this, but so does the tremendous improvement in the food supply. Famine has always been nature's principal method of population control. For the premodern world, steady growth in demographic numbers is a sure indicator of steady growth in the availability of food. Europe saw just such a steady growth from the 16th to 18th centuries, for two reasons. First, food exports to the Ottoman-controlled east declined. And second, as we saw in chapter 13, Europe was introduced to new crops from North and South America—the most important being corn (maize), beans, and potatoes. It is unlikely that these were brought back with the intention of introducing new foodstuffs. Rather, they were probably loaded on ships as victuals for those making the journey back to Europe. Most Europeans disdained corn (maize), which they thought inedible for humans; they prized it instead as

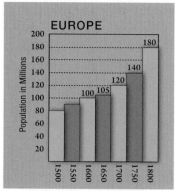

FIGURE 14.2   **Population Growth in Europe, 1500–1800**

animal fodder. Beans and potatoes, however, made radical changes in the European diet. By long-standing feudal custom, Europe's manors remained dedicated to grain production, but beans and potatoes quickly dominated the peasants' individual garden plots. Gradually, fields normally left fallow were also given over to the new crops, which helped replenish the soil. Their high yields made them popular, not as market crops but as staples of the peasants' own diets. By the 17th century peasant households were eating as many as two or three dozen potatoes a day—not the most satisfying of diets, but infinitely preferable to famine.

Increasing food supplies, however, could not halt the inflationary spiral of the "price revolution." Small landholders who could not keep up with their rents therefore risked sliding back in to debt bondage, and the manorial lords who lived off those rents faced severe potential drops in their own incomes as well. For many aristocrats, an answer to their trouble lay in the **enclosure movement**. By enclosing farmland—that is, by constructing a border of fences or thick hedgerows around it—landlords could evict their tenants, convert crop fields to meadows, and raise sheep or other herd animals instead. Their labor costs thus declined sharply, and the wool generated by their sheep was self-renewing. Moreover, the steady rise in human population meant a steadily growing demand for textiles. In this way landed nobles improved their incomes significantly, but at the expense of the evicted farmers. Lacking the funds to purchase new lands of their own, rural workers had difficulty supporting themselves.

Enclosure was not a new phenomenon, although it had been primarily a feature of British life rather than that of the Continent. Thomas More had described the consequences of land enclosure, albeit in satirical fashion, as early as 1516 in his *Utopia* (introduced in chapter 13):

> It's because of sheep. These animals, so naturally mild and so easy to tend, can now be said to have become uncontrollable devourers, consuming even the people themselves; they empty homes, devastate crop fields, and turn whole villages into ghost towns. Any place where sheep can be raised to produce fine and rich wool, the nobles, gentry, and even the abbots (those supposed "holy men"!), not content with their rents and yearly fees, and feeling that it is not enough to live in luxurious laziness and do no actual good in the world, but choosing instead to bring actual harm into it, enclose all the land for pasture and put an end to farming. They demolish homes and level villages. The churches they allow to remain, of course, but only so they can use them as sheepfolds. As though they did not waste enough [land] already on coverts and private parks, these fine people are now destroying every human dwelling and letting every scrap of usable farmland run wild. (Book 1)

Evicted farm families had few options. The younger men could enter the military or merchant marines, and the females could seek positions as domestic servants, but for many the solution lay in seeking new fortunes abroad. It was a difficult decision to travel thousands of miles from home, take up residence on a foreign continent, and begin the work of clearing the land afresh. But many chose to do so because of population rise and land hunger. The feverish religious hostilities of the time, too, provided ample reason to quit the Old World for the New.

◆

The 16th and 17th centuries, in sum, were not necessarily more religious or more filled with religious hatred than earlier periods in the history of the Greater West. However, religion became enmeshed in economic and ethnic rivalries on an unusually large scale and to a degree of fanaticism unlike anything that had existed before, with the possible exception of the medieval Crusades. Such antagonisms would not reach this fever pitch again until the 20th century.

WHO, WHAT, WHERE

Church of England	Huguenots	Peace of Westphalia
Edict of Nantes	illuminationism	Saint Bartholomew's
Elizabeth I	Kabbala	Day Massacre
enclosure movement	Mulla Sadra	Sultanate of Women
ghetto	Peace of Augsburg	Thirty Years' War

SUGGESTED READINGS

Primary Sources

Grimmelshausen, Hans Jakob Christoffel von. *The Adventures of a Simpleton.*

Mulla Sadra. *The Four Journeys of the Intellect.*

Anthologies

Diefendorf, Barbara B. *The Saint Bartholomew's Day Massacre: A Brief History with Documents* (2008).

Halperin, David J. *Sabbatai Zvi: Testimonies to a Fallen Messiah* (2007).

Kors, Alan Charles, and Edward Peters, eds. *Witchcraft in Europe, 400–1700: A Documentary History* (2000).

Pryor, Felix, comp. *Elizabeth I: Her Life in Letters* (2003).

Studies

Bonney, Richard. *The Thirty Years' War, 1618–1648* (2002).

Briggs, Robin. *Witches and Neighbors: The Social and Cultural Context of European Witchcraft* (1996).

Clark, Stuart. *Thinking with Demons: The Idea of Witchcraft in Early Modern Europe* (1999).

Dale, Stephen F. *The Muslim Empires of the Ottomans, Safavids, and Mughals* (2010).

Diefendorf, Barbara B. *Beneath the Cross: Catholics and Huguenots in Sixteenth-Century Paris* (1991).

Dursteler, Eric R. *Renegade Women: Gender, Identity, and Boundaries in the Early Modern Mediterranean* (2011).

Fairchilds, Cissie. *Women in Early Modern Europe, 1500–1700* (2007).

Goffman, Daniel. *The Ottoman Empire and Early Modern Europe* (2002).

Goldish, Matt. *The Sabbatean Prophets* (2004).

Greyerz, Kaspar von. *Religion and Culture in Early Modern Europe, 1500–1800* (2007).

Hartz, Glenn. *Leibniz's Final System: Monads, Matter, and Animals* (2006).

Holt, Mack P. *The French Wars of Religion, 1562–1629* (2005).

Israel, Jonathan I. *European Jewry in the Age of Mercantilism, 1550–1750* (1989).

Kamen, Henry. *Spain, 1469–1714: A Society of Conflict* (2005).

Kaplan, Benjamin J. *Divided by Faith: Religious Conflict and the Practice of Toleration in Early Modern Europe* (2007).

King, John N. *Foxe's Book of Martyrs and Early Modern Print Culture* (2006).

Kleinschmidt, Harald. *Charles V: The World Emperor* (2004).

MacHardy, Karin. *War, Religion, and Court Patronage in Habsburg Austria: The Social and Cultural Dimensions of Political Interaction, 1521–1622* (2003).

McCabe, Ina Baghdiantz. *A Global History of Consumption, 1500–1800* (2014).

Moris, Zailan. *Revelation, Intellectual Intuition, and Reason in the Philosophy of Mulla Sadra: An Analysis of the Al-Hikmah Al-'Arshiyyah* (2003).

Nadler, Steven. *Spinoza's Ethics: An Introduction* (2006).

Nadler, Steven. *Spinoza's Heresy: Immortality and the Jewish Mind* (2002).

Newman, Andrew J. *Safavid Iran: Rebirth of a Persian Empire* (2008).

O'Malley, John W. *Trent and All That: Renaming Catholicism in the Early Modern Era* (2000).

Parrott, David. *Richelieu's Army: War, Government, and Society in France, 1624–1642* (2001).

Peirce, Leslie. *Morality Tales: Law and Gender in the Ottoman Court of Aintab* (2003).

Pursell, Brennan C. *The Winter King: Frederick V of the Palatinate and the Coming of the Thirty Years' War* (2003).

Thomas, Hugh. *Rivers of Gold: The Rise of the Spanish Empire* (2004).

Van Zanden, Jan Luiten. *The Long Road to the Industrial Revolution: The European Economy in a Global Perspective, 1000–1800* (2009).

Wiesner-Hanks, Merry E. *Early Modern Europe, 1450–1789* (2006).

Wilson, Peter H. *The Thirty Years War: Europe's Tragedy* (2009).

For additional resources, including maps, primary sources, visuals, web links, and quizzes, please go to **www.oup.com/us/backman**.

CHAPTER 15

From Westphalia to Paris: Regimes Old and New

1648–1750

"Those who did not live in the 18th century before the [French] Revolution do not know life at its sweetest," declared the French career diplomat Charles de Talleyrand-Périgord (1754–1838). An egoist right to the tips of his aristocratic fingers, Talleyrand knew what he was talking about. The period of the Ancien Régime ("Old Regime"), from 1648 to 1789, was a time of unparalleled privilege and delight for the European upper aristocracy. The end of the Thirty Years' War in 1648 brought peace to once-warring states, freeing elites to concentrate instead on amassing wealth and power. Urban manufacturing and commerce had long since become the main engines of economic life, but the landed elite still enjoyed various rental incomes, judicial fees, annuities, ecclesiastical and governmental sinecures, and military

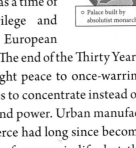

THE GREATER WEST IN THE AGE OF ABSOLUTISM

Peterhof
Potsdam
Schönbrunn
Versailles

o Palace built by absolutist monarch

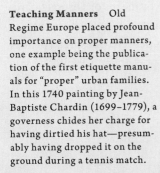

Teaching Manners Old Regime Europe placed profound importance on proper manners, one example being the publication of the first etiquette manuals for "proper" urban families. In this 1740 painting by Jean-Baptiste Chardin (1699–1779), a governess chides her charge for having dirtied his hat—presumably having dropped it on the ground during a tennis match.

revenues. That was more than enough for them to live in lavish comfort, especially given their most closely held privilege—exemption from paying taxes. A belief in absolute order spread throughout society, inspiring a demand for norms in the arts and even everyday life.

This was the Baroque Age, when fabulously ornate palaces, churches, summer residences, concert halls, libraries, museums, theaters, pleasure gardens, and private academies sprang up by the hundreds across Europe. Most were filled to bursting with paintings and sculptures and rang out with the music written to order by court composers and played by servant musicians—all for the enjoyment of the wealthy, powdered, perfumed, wigged, and brilliantly attired nobles. Their images, coats of arms, and marble-inscribed names bedecked everything in sight. The display sought not merely to impress but also to overwhelm the viewer with its expressive power. And that meant the power not of the architect, artist, or composer, but of the nobleman or woman whose authority and station made such glories possible. Europe's elites had always enjoyed their privileges, but never before on this scale.

The all-encompassing grandeur was designed to stun the people into a state of paralyzed awe. But such a display was possible only by means of a brutal hoarding of wealth. Few periods in Greater Western history ever saw a more intense concentration of power and wealth among the elites—or such widespread penury and suffering by the common people. The German poet Johann Wolfgang von

CHAPTER TIMELINE

1620	1640	1660	1680	1700

- 1642–1649 English Civil War
- 1643–1715 Peace of Westphalia
- 1648 Peace of Westphalia
- 1649 Charles I of England beheaded
- 1649–1660 Cromwell's rule in England
- 1651 Hobbes, Leviathan
- 1660 Monarchy restored in England
- 1670 Molière, *The Middle-Class Gentleman*
- 1675 Founding of Bedlam Asylum (England)
- 1683 Ottoman siege of Vienna repulsed
- 1688 England's Glorious Revolution
- 1689–1725 Reign of Peter the Great (Russia)
- 1701–1714 War of the Spanish Succession

Goethe (1749–1832) described Europe's peasant farmers as "caught between the land and the aristocracy as between an anvil and a hammer." Not a comforting image—especially when one realizes that Goethe did not make the observation out of sympathy for the commoners' plight but merely as a recognition of what was and needed to be.

Below this picture of serene Continental privilege, however, a different scene roiled. England suffered through a brutal civil war and Puritanical theocracy that ultimately gave way to an uneasy constitutional monarchy, whereas much of the Islamic world underwent another wave of religious reform that (true to the pattern) grew ever more conservative. As international trade grew and a new economic system came into being, Europe faced a new round of crises and war.

THE PEACE OF WESTPHALIA: 1648

By 1648 most of Continental Europe was exhausted by more than one hundred years of brutal religious warfare. Unable or unwilling to continue the carnage, all sides sued for peace. The **Peace of Westphalia** (1648) is an umbrella term for a collection of individual treaties that ended the hostilities. It rearranged political borders, created a framework of mutually agreed-on diplomatic principles, and established a network of recognized sovereign governments. More than one hundred delegations participated in the negotiations, which took seven years: sixteen

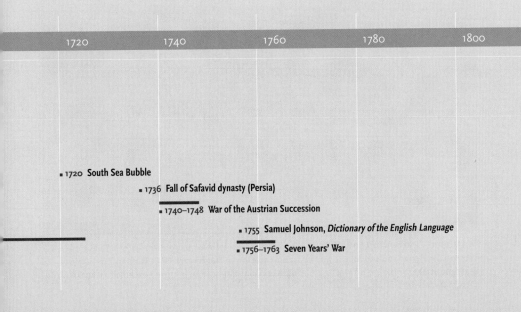

1720   1740   1760   1780   1800

- 1720 South Sea Bubble
- 1736 Fall of Safavid dynasty (Persia)
- 1740–1748 War of the Austrian Succession
- 1755 Samuel Johnson, *Dictionary of the English Language*
- 1756–1763 Seven Years' War

nations, sixty-six German imperial principalities, and twenty-seven nongovernmental interest groups (such as churches, corporations, and guilds). This was the first general diplomatic congress in European history, and it provided a model for subsequent international assemblies.

Quest for a Balance of Power   The peace dramatically revised the political map of Europe by splitting some states, joining others, carving out new independent entities, and moving many traditional boundaries (see Map 15.1). In so doing, it paid little attention to preserving ethnic domains. The goal instead was to produce a balance of

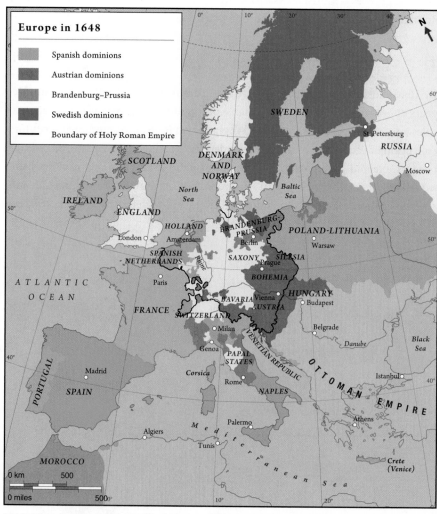

MAP 15.1   Europe in 1648   The balance of power sought by negotiators of the Peace of Westphalia depended especially on the fragmentation of the former Holy Roman Empire into multiple states, while maintaining a strong Austrian–Hungarian empire as a bulwark against the Ottoman rulers in Istanbul.

power between the states created by the Peace. If each new state was roughly equal in power to its neighbor, the thinking went, then wars would be less likely to break out between them. But to establish such a balance, the negotiators had to consider more than mere acreage; population density, economic and technological development, access to ports and rivers, and the availability of natural resources all had to be factored in. The resulting map created several new states (an independent Holland, Portugal, and Switzerland, for example) scattered among the larger territorial powers (Austria–Hungary, Bavaria, Brandenburg–Prussia, France, Poland–Lithuania, Spain, and Sweden). Moreover, countries now had a mechanism for creating alliances to check an ambitious neighbor. This eased tensions by allowing each state to control its own foreign policy in a meaningful way. Even small states like Switzerland or Holland had strategic strengths that made them valuable allies. Threatening to withdraw their support from an alliance could make even a large state like France or Spain reconsider its policies.

The Westphalia treaties also reaffirmed the principle of religious establishment—the idea that the ruler of each state could determine its offi- *Religious* cial religion (*cuius regio, eius religio*)—while guaranteeing the freedom of *Establishment* other faiths and denominations within certain prescribed limits. Strictly speaking, religious establishment meant more than a preference for any particular faith or denomination and was distinct from theocracy (government ruled by religious authority). Rather, it created a formal relationship between the state and the specific church. Religious establishment in the modern sense, in which the established church serves as an organ of the state, was a product of the Protestant Reformation: England established the (Anglican) Church of England in 1533, and the (Lutheran) Church of Sweden came into formal existence in 1536. Most of the states carved out by the Peace of Westphalia had in practice established churches, although few had the formal legal structures uniting church and state that England and Sweden did.

This sprawl of new or heavily revised territorial states left most monarchs without serious rivals for power. Where councils and parliaments had provided *The* a limited check on royal ambitions, few of these customs survived intact. The *Conditions* aristocracy remained wealthy, privileged, and secure in their control of the *for* agrarian countryside, but also unable to unite in opposition to royal aims. The *Absolutism* new states were professional bureaucracies—uninviting to most nobles, who found it more to their liking to remain in their baroque palaces and chateaux than to crowd into expensive cramped quarters in the busy capital cities. Moreover, individual rulers could now consolidate extensive, centralized authority over their common subjects, so long as they avoided using that power to threaten their neighbors. In other words, the alliances and guarantees that aimed to prevent a king from intimidating his neighbors actually helped him to tighten his grip on his own subjects. In this way the Peace helped to trigger the rise of royal **absolutism**, or a king's absolute power—not as a consciously deliberated policy, but rather as the unintended consequence of the quest for a balance of power.

THE ARGUMENT FOR TYRANNY

The argument for tyranny is a simple one, to its enthusiasts: it provides freedom. This may seem contrary to common sense, but the argument is sound. We define freedom by what we are free *from*. Many people, quite understandably, think of freedom as independence, as freedom from control. To others, however, true freedom consists of freedom from chaos. The restoration of order after a long period of anarchy can thrill people with a sense of regained liberty—the liberty of a reliable, well-regulated tranquility.

Restoration of Order

The argument is an old one. The Archaic and Classical Age Greeks celebrated their tyrants (*tyrannoi*, like Pisistratos) and wrote them into their constitutions as necessary correctives to democracy's occasional tendency to drive the cart into a ditch. The Roman Republic too allowed for constitutional dictatorship, a temporary although renewable grant of unlimited authority to revise the laws, reform government, and command the military. Julius Caesar had been a dictator—and a popular one until he appointed himself dictator for life, which made him effectively a king and all but assured his assassination. In times of crisis, as when an airplane is spinning out of control or a ship is foundering in a storm, the rights to individual self-expression and self-determination do not further the cause of rescue; there is no time to hold elections, seek consensus, and let everyone on board freely express their views about what to do. Instead, the argument goes, salvation requires a single firm hand on the controls and a single strong voice issuing commands to an obedient crowd. Tyrants can make mistakes, of course, but they at least have the potential of saving the ship or landing the plane. Noisy, messy democracy and respect for independence of thought and action in such a plight only guarantees a disaster.

The catastrophic wars of religion and civil wars before them, many now argued, were the result of liberalizing, mass-driven politics. Only a restoration of patriarchal society, headed by noble male authority, could save Europe from ruin. But this could not be done quietly or subtly. The aristocracy needed to parade its power, to boast of it, and to glorify it in everything it did. And the higher the aristocrat, the greater the need for spectacle. Kings, of course, needed to parade their glorious position more than anyone else. Privilege, in the age of absolutism, was not a consequence of power but the very essence of it. Jean Domat (1625–1696), a prominent French jurist and royal favorite, justified the ostentation:

> Law grants the sovereign many rights, one of which must be the right to public display of anything that gives evidence of the grandeur and majesty needed to express the authority and dignity of his high and wide-ranging office. . . . God Himself [after all] wants monarchs to augment the authority He has shared with them, in ways that promote the awed respect of the people, and this can be achieved only by the grandeur conveyed by the brilliance of their palaces.

The Peace of Westphalia did not institute absolute monarchy in any formal sense, but it did establish the conditions that made its rise likely. Some early indicators of royal dictatorship had emerged even before the Peace. In France the rapid concentration of power by the monarchy had begun under King Louis XIII (r. 1610–1643), whose chief minister—Armand-Jean du Plessis, Cardinal de Richelieu (1585–1642)— summed up the problems confronting the throne when he first came to power in 1624:

Cardinal de Richelieu

> The Protestants acted as though they shared the state with you, the nobles, as if they were your equals rather than your subjects, and the governors of the provinces as though they were monarchs of their own offices. These scenarios set a bad example, one so harmful to the kingdom that even Your most loyal courts were influenced by it and were driven—unreasonably—to

Richelieu Armand-Jean du Plessis, Cardinal de Richelieu (1585–1642), was the sickly younger son of a low-ranking noble family, who grew to become the most powerful figure in the kingdom of France after the king himself. Richelieu believed firmly in the necessity of an absolutist monarchy; only a strong central monarch, ably guided and determined to exert his authority energetically, could maintain civil order. Richelieu's rapid rise in the church and the French government went hand in hand. Consecrated a bishop in 1608, he became France's secretary of state in 1616; in 1622 he was made cardinal, and two years later he was Louis XIII's chief minister—a post he held until his death.

build up their authority to the detriment of Your own. Might I add that every individual seemed to measure his worth by the boldness of his presumption, ... each one deeming the privileges he held from You valuable only to the extent that they satisfied his greedy fantasies. ...

Sure in the knowledge of how much good a king can accomplish when he puts his power to proper use, I, in my confidence, dared to promise Your Majesty that You would soon regain control of Your state and that before much time elapsed Your wisdom and courage, together with God's blessing, would put the realm on a new path. I swore to Your Majesty that I would spare no effort and would use whatever power it pleased You to grant me to ruin the Protestants, to break the stiff-necked pride of the aristocracy, to return all Your subjects to Your dutiful service, and to restore Your name to the high position it deserves in foreign lands. (*Political Testament*, ch. 1)

Richelieu accomplished all this and more with a mix of careful negotiation and heavy-handed intimidation. He neutralized most of Louis XIII's foes thanks to his network of domestic and international spies, his ability to charm, his willingness to bribe, and above all his ruthless conviction that only an all-powerful throne could keep France safe and strong. Richelieu's passion for order and security was as evident in his personal life as in his public policies, and in this regard he represents most of the values of the Age of Absolutism.

THE SOCIAL CONTRACT

Thomas Hobbes

Richelieu's dedication to a supremely powerful monarchy was instinctive, but more than one philosopher of the time reached a similar position by rational thought. None of these thinkers directly created absolutism as a political force, but they helped explain the sentiments that gave rise to it. The philosopher most closely associated with the theory of absolutism is Thomas Hobbes (1588–1679). Hobbes was not England's first philosopher, nor even its first political philosopher; he was, however, the first to write philosophy in English. A contemporary of René Descartes, with whom he corresponded, and Sir Francis Bacon, whom we also met in chapter 13, Hobbes spent most of his adult life as a tutor and secretary to the 2nd and 3rd Earls of Devonshire (both named William Cavendish, 1591–1628 and 1617–1684), which left him ample time to take advantage of their magnificent library. He had broad interests that included history, law, mathematics, and physics, as well as philosophy. Forced to spend time in exile in Paris after the arrest and subsequent execution of King Charles I in 1649 because of his strong royalist views, Hobbes returned to

London in 1651 with the completed manuscript of his best-known work, *Leviathan.*

Although his own life was comfortable, Hobbes's philosophy owes much to the violence and misery of his age. He emphasizes the instincts for self-preservation and self-regard that are natural to all people. Our polite, civilized behavior toward one another is an acquired attribute, one that masks and hopefully controls our baser passions for food, wealth, power, pleasure, and status. The problem, he argues, lies in the finite nature of the things we desire. Seeking always to satisfy ourselves, we unavoidably live in a state of constant competition with one another. "The war of all against all," as he memorably put it, corrodes our civilized veneer and leads us into periodic anarchies like the one Europe suffered after 1500. Moreover, people are unequal in specific abilities—some being stronger, others faster or more cunning or more agile—but in the long run these differences balance each other out. The war of all against all therefore becomes a permanent state, with

> no place for industry, because the fruit thereof is uncertain; and consequently no culture of the earth; no navigation or use of the commodities that may be imported by sea; no commodious building; no instruments of moving and removing such things as require much force; no knowledge of the face of the Earth; no account of time; no arts; no letters; and which is worst of all, continual fear and danger of violent death; and the life of man [is] solitary, poor, nasty, brutish, and short.

It is a pessimistic view of life—but an understandable one, given the agonies Europe had experienced since the discovery of the New World, the Protestant Reformation, the Wars of Religion, civil wars, the Inquisition, and witchcraft mania.

Hobbes sees only one way out of the misery of the state of nature: limitless sovereign authority. Only by transferring our innate rights of self-determination to a governing authority entrusted with absolute power over the people can we hope to free ourselves from chaos. Interestingly, Hobbes does not much care whether the absolutist government is a monarchy, an oligarchy, or a democracy. All that matters is that the government, whatever its form, has unquestioned power to compel obedience. Unlimited and indivisible power to legislate, adjudicate, execute, and enforce, in a single sovereign entity, is the only way to live an ordered, peaceful, and prosperous life. Of course it also fails to prevent the abuse of that power, but Hobbes counters this charge with two assertions. First, no absolute tyranny can ever be worse than absolute chaos. And second, a people's total submission to the sovereign authority will temper any possible inclination that authority might have to abuse its power.

The Social Contract   Thomas Hobbes's *Leviathan* is the first work of political science in English. The Latin verse at the top of this title page of the first edition (1651) reads: "There is no power on earth like Him" (Job 42.25).

Leviathan is a difficult book to read. Its archaic English—all four hundred pages of it—defeats all but the most determined readers. (I have modernized its spelling and punctuation in the passages above.) But it deserves attention. A darker yet more substantial work than Machiavelli's *The Prince* (discussed in chapter 12), *Leviathan* elaborates what later became known as **social contract** theory. This theory holds that when people decide to live in community they enter a covenant with one another, compromising their individual free wills in return for the benefits of society. Government, which bears responsibility for preserving social stability, may therefore legitimately assert its will on the community whenever it deems it necessary to do so. Renunciation of personal liberty, in other words, is the price of peace, but the truest form of freedom, Hobbes insists, lies in that very renunciation.

Richelieu and Hobbes were not the only 17th-century figures to argue for absolutism, but they are the most interesting. Both men were brilliant, moody, and pessimistic about human nature, and each worked diligently to bring their ideas to fruition—Richelieu in deed, Hobbes on the page. Had they met, they might have recognized each other as kindred spirits despite their religious differences. For all his worldliness, Richelieu was a devout Catholic, and scholars still debate whether Hobbes was an atheist.[1]

Each also had humane pursuits. Richelieu collected classical manuscripts (later donated to the Sorbonne, of which he was the chief executive), founded the Academie Française (the premier literary society in France), patronized painters and sculptors, and ardently promoted theater. Hobbes dabbled in mathematics and physics, published his own translations of Thucydides and Homer, and wrote a vivid history of the English Civil War. Still, both men shared unsettling and ominous views about human nature and the hard realities of life. Their influence

---

[1]   Can one be committed to Christianity while endorsing secular absolutism? Hobbes says yes, but was he just trying to avoid inflaming the still-smoldering religious antagonisms of his age?

was profound, and the fears they articulated were shared by many—fears that allowed absolutism to take root and flourish. For a while on the Continent, it even enjoyed popular support.

No one was a greater enthusiast for the authority of monarchs than Jean Bodin (ca. 1529–1596), a modest cleric who studied philosophy and law, became *Jean Bodin* an advisor to kings Charles IX (r. 1560–1574) and Henri III (r. 1574–1589), and turned himself into France's first great political theorist. But Bodin has suffered too frequently from historians' characterization of him as a "divine-right absolutist," which is a misreading of his work. His most significant publication—one out of a whole shelf of books—was *Six Books on a Commonwealth* (*Les Six Livres de la République*), which appeared in 1576 when Bodin was at the height of his career. Throughout this work he carefully distinguishes between a state and a government. A state, to Bodin, is an organic community of people united by faith, values, and cultural inheritance, whereas a government is a human creation, a mechanism for meeting the needs of a community; just as there can be various forms or iterations of a state, there are likewise various forms of government. Bodin advocated a combination of monarchy and democracy, a government in which the sovereign monarch determines the shape of the government while securing the rights of all his subjects to have access to magistracies and other offices regardless of social class or economic status. The king alone determines the law, but all citizens participate equally in it. The king himself must remain unbound by the laws he creates (*legibus absolutus*—"not bound by the laws"), which for Bodin is the very definition of sovereignty. The sovereign monarch answers only to natural and divine laws—but he must indeed answer to them, and hence his power is not "absolute" in the sense historians usually, and inaccurately, attribute to Bodin.

ABSOLUTE POLITICS

The dominant dynasties, and the most representative, of the Old Regime were the Bourbons in France, the Hohenzollerns in Brandenburg–Prussia, the Habsburgs in Austria and (a separate branch of the family) in Spain, and the Romanovs in Russia. A web of intermarriages that in some cases went back generations or even centuries connected the royal families to one another. Even so, ties of affection were minimal and always gave way to politics. Standing armies became arms of the state as royal families undertook vast building projects to display their majestic authority.

Despite the supposed "balance of power" established at Westphalia, France was the dominant Continental state in every way. With somewhere between 15 *France* and 18 million people, France around 1648 had twice the population of Spain and

Another Siege of Vienna   In 1683 the Ottomans once more marched against the Habsburg Empire (their earlier efforts having been in 1529 and 1532). The Turks had an army of nearly 100,000 soldiers. The Habsburgs called on their Polish and Lithuanian allies to join in the defense and carried the day. In this painting by the Flemish artist Frans Geffels (1624–1694), the Turks have launched their assault on the city. The Poles and Lithuanians have not yet appeared on the scene. According to legend, as part of the celebration over the Habsburgs' ultimate defeat of the Turks, the Viennese bakers' guild created a new pastry: the croissant, which was designed to mock the Islamic crescent, visible on the Turks' flag above the tent on the left. The powerful Ottoman forces were symbolically reduced to puff pastries.

three times that of England. With its superior resources concentrated among the upper orders, all of whom lavished funds on the arts, French culture flowered. Young King **Louis XIV** (r. 1643–1715) set immediately to increase the size of his army in the hope of matching France's cultural clout with its military muscle.

Brandenberg–Prussia   Brandenburg–Prussia, by contrast, was a surviving remnant of the old Holy Roman Empire, steeped in tradition and pride but for the moment a poor, defenseless, war-shocked ruin (see Map 15.1). Much of the worst fighting of the Thirty Years' War had taken place here, leaving large stretches of the countryside desolate and many towns depopulated. Economic development came slowly, and most commercial, technological, and institutional innovations appeared here one or two generations after they had taken root in England, France, or Holland.

Austria   Habsburg Austria had a long genealogy going back to the Middle Ages, but the traumas of the 17th century had left much of its land depleted and demoralized. The Ottoman Turks advanced on Austria almost as soon as the Westphalia agreements were signed; by 1683 they had reached Vienna, which they besieged for two months before giving up.[2] (Forces from Poland, Russia, Venice, and the

---

[2]   The Turks used the ancient temple of the Parthenon in Athens as their main munitions storehouse. When Venetian artillery units took aim on it, the temple was blasted into the ruin it is today.

papacy joined the subsequent Austrian counteroffensive.) The Turkish defeat reenergized Austrian pride, an emotional swell that led to a sharp improvement in economic and social stability. This was the era, post 1683, of Austria's climb as a cultural capital, especially the cities of Salzburg and Vienna; the first Austrian composer of note, Heinrich Ignaz Franz Biber (1644–1704), almost single-handedly turned Salzburg into a pilgrimage site for music lovers.

The background to the Romanov dynasty lay in the decades of famines, civil wars, and foreign invasions known as the Time of Troubles (1584–1613). The most persistent invading force came from neighboring Poland–Lithuania, whose king tried to put a son on the Russian throne. In 1613 an army of nobles, townspeople, and peasants finally expelled the intruders and put on the throne a nobleman, Michael Romanov (r. 1613–1645), who established an enduring new dynasty. When **Peter I** (Peter the Great, r. 1689–1725) came to power in 1689 after a seven-year regency, he brought with him the style and techniques of autocratic rule that he had learned when traveling in the West. The Romanov dynasty would last more than three hundred years.

Russia

POLICE STATES

Autocracy is not conceptually difficult to grasp, since dictatorships follow a few set patterns of development. The regimes of the 17th and 18th centuries were above all police states. Raw military muscle and the willingness to use it both secured and expressed their power. The king's army in France mustered merely 20,000 soldiers in 1661; by 1700 it numbered 400,000. The Prussian army in the Thirty Years' War had consisted mostly of unreliable mercenaries, with the result that Swedish forces had ravaged the Prussian countryside almost at will. After 1648 the Prussian monarch began to assemble a professional standing army of his own. It began small: between 5,000 and 6,000 men. But by 1750 it had ballooned to 180,000. Control of the Austrian army was given to a professional military officer from France, Prince François-Eugène of Savoy (1663–1736), who oversaw its transformation from a ragtag mixture of old feudal forces and mercenaries into a national institution with modern methods of supply, training, and command. After only a few years' work, he had increased the size and quality of the Austrian forces to such an extent that they drove 100,000 Ottoman Turks eastward from Austrian lands by 1687, after which he turned the army around and expelled a French force advancing from the west. Austria thus entered the 18th century with a professionalized army of nearly 100,000 men.

Rise of Professional Armies

The transformation of the Russian military was even more dramatic. Long consisting of an informal conglomeration of semifeudalized noble cavalrymen known as *streltsi*, the army was disbanded and brutally purged of political rivals by Tsar Peter I in 1698. Peter was determined to bring Russia in line with Europe in terms of economic and political development and resolved to catch up with Europe by emulating it. He modeled his new army along French and Prussian lines, put his soldiers in Western-style uniforms, gave them Western weapons (muskets and artillery), and hired Western officers to train them.

These massive new armies drew from the lower orders of their respective societies for the rank and file; men from the urban and professional classes or the lower nobility dominated midlevel officer ranks. The highest ranks were still primarily the purview of the high nobility but tended to include only those for whom the military was a lifelong career. Only Prussia used a military draft; in every other country, volunteers served. And there was no shortage of volunteers. The king's army offered commoners three meals a day, regular wages, solid training, and the possibility of a pension after a certain number of years in service—things they had little or no chance of attaining on their own. These were "drum and bugle" armies, divided into companies that fought in formation using long, unbroken lines. Discipline was harsh and frequently brutal: beatings, fines, half-rations, and imprisonments were common. The penalty for breaking ranks was flogging. Executions were common too. In Austria, Prince François-Eugène often performed them himself on soldiers who failed to obey orders on the battlefield. Peter I once personally executed five soldiers accused of rebellion, after allowing others to prepare the way by torturing the men first.

Wars of Louis XIV   The Peace of Westphalia, however, was largely successful in maintaining a relatively stable Europe. Conflicts remained, a couple of them even large-scale matters, but Europe between 1648 and the start of the French Revolution in 1789 was a much more peaceful place than it had been in the 140 preceding years. Most of the wars of the era arose from Louis XIV's grandiose plans to create a greater France, or, more accurately, to secure a number of frontier regions that might buffer France from external attack: the War of Devolution (1667–1668), the Franco-Dutch War (1672–1678), the War of the League of Augsburg (1688–1697), and the War of the Spanish Succession (1701–1714). Louis came to regret his overreaching, although not until the end of his life. On his deathbed, Louis is reported to have advised his heir (his great-grandson Louis XV, r. 1715–1774), "I was too quick to start wars, and I kept them going out of vanity. . . . Be a peaceful ruler, and devote yourself above all to easing the suffering of your subjects."

The Cost of Security   Why then were such enormous armies created? With fewer foreign and civil wars to fight, what purpose did they serve? Monarchs put their soldiers to use policing their own populations. Soldiers marched the streets and plazas, stood in university lecture halls, observed church services, watched crowds entering and leaving theaters, patrolled the countryside, guarded government buildings, and monitored harbors. They guarded city gates, performed maneuvers in town squares, staffed prisons (one of the new inventions of the age), and inspected printing houses. Without such vast reserves of manpower, royal absolutism was unthinkable. Maintaining the military—paying salaries, providing weapons and uniforms, serving meals, offering housing, supporting pensioners—remained a central concern of every monarch of the 17th and 18th centuries. The costs even in peacetime were enormous; the occasional conflicts of the age drove the expenditures exponentially higher.

Old Regime monarchs also relied heavily on separate companies of royal commissioners and civil servants—called *intendants* in France and known collectively as the Directory in Prussia—who traveled through the provinces and inspected the handling of royal and administrative affairs. These commissioners held jurisdiction over all matters relating to public finance (whether collecting it or paying it out), public safety, and justice. They also formed part of the kings' extensive networks of intelligence gatherers. Drawn chiefly from the urban professional classes, commissioners served the king personally and did not hold public office, and hence they received their own salaries directly from the royal purse. They were expensive

Prussian Military Discipline   By 1750 the Prussian line infantry made full use of flintlock muskets and bayonets, as well as military drills, which involved the rotation of the front and rear lines after each salvo. "If my soldiers were to think, not one of them would remain in the army," Frederick II of Prussia (r. 1740–1786) is reputed to have said. This painting by Carl Röchling (1855–1920), a German artist known for his representation of historical military themes, shows Frederick's forces charging directly into the fire of the Austrians at the battle of Hohenfriedberg in 1745, which the Prussians won.

supervisors to maintain, since the kings not only paid their salaries but also equipped them with trappings appropriate to a representative of the king.

In Prussia, all government positions of high and middling rank were reserved for military personnel, which effectively excluded much of the traditional aristocracy from power. It also made the king's position all the more secure, since literally everyone who worked in his government received a salary directly from him. In return for their exclusion from government, the nobles received royal permission to reinstate serfdom (which had become largely obsolete by the end of the Middle Ages) on their estates.

SELF-INDULGENCE WITH A PURPOSE: THE EXAMPLE OF VERSAILLES

Expensive too were the grand building projects of the age. Palaces and churches decorated with baroque profusion arose by the score, year after year, as did lecture and concert halls, libraries and museums, scientific laboratories, and academies. Louis XIV, stung by rebellions and resistance in Paris, ordered construction of an immense palace complex at Versailles, 12 miles from the turbulent capital. Building began in the 1660s, but the project was so extensive that Louis and his court did not move from the Louvre to Versailles until 1682. And other rulers built their own imposing piles too.[3]

Versailles itself had been a small rural village of only a thousand inhabitants fifty years earlier. Louis's palace—known properly as the Château de Versailles—transformed the simple hunting lodge that had previously existed on the spot into a spectacularly vast edifice that housed the entire royal court. The château possessed well over a half-million square feet of floor space divided among seven hundred rooms, most of them magnificent. Thousands of paintings, drawings, sculptures, tapestries, and precious objects lined the walls and adorned every room. The effect on a first-time visitor is overwhelming—not so much for its genuine beauty as for the audacity of its grandeur.

Controlling the Nobles   Louis's decision to build a new home for his court was self-indulgent, but with a purpose. By creating a single space for the royal government and by demanding the constant attendance of France's aristocrats, Louis was able to keep an eye on the nobles and keep them under his sway. Louis never forgot that his reign had begun with an aristocratic rebellion against him. Called the **Fronde**, this rebellion (1648–1653) had not targeted Louis personally; the king was only ten years

---

[3]   Friedrich II of Prussia built the palace at Potsdam, just outside Berlin; Peter I of Russia built the vast Peterhof palace complex in the capital city he founded, St. Petersburg; the Habsburgs in Austria established the palace of Schönbrunn, just outside Vienna.

Versailles   As awe-inspiring as it is, this image still shows only one-third of the palace built by Louis XIV to house his court. It was the seat of government from 1682 to 1789. Meant to show-case French culture, everything that went into building the palace was manufactured in France. The cost was beyond calculation. Even the chamber pots were made of silver—some of which Louis had to have melted and cast as coinage to help pay for his War of the League of Augsburg (1688–1697).

old when the trouble began.[4] Instead, the Fronde was a reaction against the royal finance minister Cardinal Jules Mazarin (1602–1661), the successor to Cardinal Richelieu, who had imposed a tax on judicial officials and sought to curtail a number of aristocratic privileges. It took five years to quell the rebellion, and Louis resolved to keep a constant watch over the nobles by requiring their presence under his own ornate new roof. To make his job easier, he had the palace lined with secret passages, one-way mirrors, and peepholes, and he maintained a large private staff to spy on the goings-on in every room. The Duc de Saint-Simon (1675–1755), whose keen-eyed *Memoirs* provides an irreplaceable view of life at court, summarized the key role of Versailles as a means of controlling the nobles:

> [Louis] loved splendor, grandeur, and opulence in everything and inspired similar tastes in everyone in his court, even to the point

---

4   *Fronde* is the French word for a slingshot—a favorite weapon of the Paris rebels, who used them to shatter the upper windows of the royal buildings.

where the surest way to earn a royal favor—perhaps the honor of receiving a word from him—was to spend extravagantly on something like a horse and carriage.... There was a sly political purpose in this, for by making conspicuously expensive habits the fashion at court (even making them a sort of requirement for people of a certain rank) he forced the members of his court to live beyond their means, which inevitably brought them to depend on royal favors in order to maintain themselves. But this [habit of indebtedness] turned out to be a plague that gradually infected the entire country, for in no time at all it spread to Paris, then to the army, and finally to the provinces, and now a man of any social standing at all is judged solely by the costliness of his daily habits and the extravagance of his luxuries. Such foolhardiness—the result of vanity and ostentation—has brought vast worry in its wake and threatens to result in nothing short of a national disaster and utter collapse.

This was prescient: the story of the French economy in the 18th century is one of constant and compounded indebtedness, a fiscal rot of staggering proportions that ultimately brought down the entire regime. For the present, however, the spending continued at an astonishing pace.

Louis XIV of France   Louis ruled France for seventy-two years (r. 1643–1715), the longest reign in Western history. As the epitome of absolutist monarchy, he not only held sway over his kingdom but made France the leading state in Europe. This 1701 portrait by the French artist Hyacinthe Rigaud (1659–1743) shows the king at the height of his power. The curious draping of his royal robe is thought to be the result of royal vanity: Louis was widely reputed to be very proud of his shapely legs.

It is doubtful that Saint-Simon ever spoke so boldly to the king himself about the danger. A far braver man was François Fénelon (1651–1715), a Catholic priest appointed in 1689 as tutor to Louis XIV's grandson. As part of his teaching Fénelon composed a novel in 1694, *The Adventures of Telemachus*, which describes the travels and education of the son of the famed Greek king Odysseus. The novel mounts a stinging attack on the ideas of divine-right monarchy and absolutism. "Good kings are quite rare," it says at one point; "in fact, the majority of them are rather poor." It also denounces the pursuit of glory through war and the debilitating love of luxury. Fénelon's book became hugely popular across Europe and was translated into a half-dozen languages. Louis XIV hated it but recognized the good effect Fénelon's tutoring had on his grandson, a famously spoiled brat. Fénelon was brave enough to speak out in a 1694 letter to the king:

> Sire, for thirty years now Your ministers have broken every ancient law of this state, in order to increase Your power. They have infinitely increased both Your income and Your expenses, but in the process have impoverished all of France and have made Your name hated—all for the sake of the luxury of Your court. For the last twenty years these same ministers have turned France into an intolerable burden to her neighbors through bloody war. Wanting nothing but slaves, we now have no allies. And in the meantime, Your people are starving and rebellion is growing. You are thus left with only two choices: either to let the rebellion spread, or to resort to massacring the very people whom You have driven into desperation.

In 1696 Fénelon was appointed archbishop of Cambrai, but the following year was relieved of his position as tutor.

MERCANTILISM AND ABSOLUTISM

Supporting the absolutist regimes was a varied set of economic policies known collectively as **mercantilism**. For about 250 years, from roughly 1500 to 1750, this was the prevailing model for understanding and managing the economic life of northern Europe: England, France, and the Netherlands were the chief centers of mercantilist thinking, with Austria, Germany, Spain, and Sweden comprising a second tier. The Mediterranean economy also contained some mercantilist elements but was less dominated by them overall. Mercantilism, in general, defined economic wealth as tangible assets: the money in circulation, land and mineral resources, the available precious metals, the aggregate of physical goods that can be produced from nature's resources. Global wealth therefore is static. Since the Earth is not increasing in size, the amount of economically valuable material is fixed, and the aim of commerce is thus to maximize the amount of valuable assets in one's possession. The two most efficient means of doing so are to increase the amount of bullion in one's possession, either through mining precious metals or by appropriating the bullion of others, and to export more commercial goods than one imports. But either way, the world economy is a "zero-sum game"—meaning that one player's gain is equivalent to another player's loss. Wealth is thus a matter of distribution rather than creation.

Mercantilism in Theory

Mercantilism thus champions **protectionism**—the blocking of imports by tariff barriers, usually, and, if necessary, by law. The system, since it was based on the idea of artificially manipulating the distribution of

Mercantilism in Practice

wealth, also welcomed the awarding of monopolies by government (in return for sizable bribes and licensing fees), the fixing of prices and wages, the blocking of competition, and the imposition of high domestic taxes. In a world of finite wealth, the reasoning went, assets must be concentrated in a small number of hands. Only this could enable the grand expenditures such as those needed to defend the realm, administer the government, and maintain social order. Mercantilism, in other words, did not aim at the prosperity of an entire people, nor did it think that possible to achieve. Rather, its purpose was to concentrate wealth among as few individuals as possible. The absolutist regimes perfected their policies over the 17th and 18th centuries—and in the process drove their own subjects into the direst poverty. (It is worth pointing out, by way of illustration, that the economic policies of China in the late 20th and early 21st centuries likewise include many mercantilist elements.)

The classic statement in defense of mercantilism came from Thomas Mun (1571–1641), an English merchant and member of the board of directors of the English East India Company. He wrote *England's Treasure by Foreign Trade* in 1630, although it was not published until 1664. In it he argues, among other things, for the forced lowering of domestic wages. If the people of England cannot afford to purchase food, clothing, and other consumer goods, he points out, then the government will have larger amounts of those commodities available for export, which will bring more money into the royal purse.

Today we understand an economy to be an abstraction, an invisible system of interactions that more or less follows basic laws of the marketplace. In the early modern era, however, the idea of a system open to expansion or contraction was a foreign concept. Money, goods, land, and raw resources were things one could put in one's hand, feel the heft of, and know to be real. Producing, selling, and consuming goods are aspects of human agency, but the notion of "an economy" or "a market" as an autonomous thing that determines human action requires a conceptual leap, and few people in early modern Europe were capable of or interested in making such a leap. Merchants understood that a scarcity of goods—as when, for example, a drought results in decreased crop yields—meant that they could charge a higher price. However, they interpreted this not as a scientific "law of the market" but simply as a scenario they could exploit. When 16th-century Spain imported tons of gold bullion taken from the New World, the country expected to acquire enormous wealth. As we saw in chapter 14, what it got instead was an inflationary spiral unlike anything Europe had ever seen, the collapse of the currency, and the ruin of vast stretches of the peninsula. Compounding the problem, the Spanish rulers spent this money on a colossal scale—on palaces, museums, churches, artwork, and the army—rather than investing it in wealth-generating

Mercantilist Center   The town of Bristol was founded shortly before the Norman Conquest of 1066 and for a while was important chiefly as the launching place for English armies on their way to Ireland. The discovery of the New World raised its significance enormously, and by the 17th century Bristol was the second-largest and busiest port in the kingdom. Between 1600 and 1750 Bristol was the principal site from which English slave-traders shipped African slaves to the New World. This painting from around 1760 by an anonymous British artist shows the busy quay, where goods were loaded and unloaded.

industry.[5] But no one at the time, in Spain or elsewhere, would have agreed that there was any connection between the importation of New World precious metal and spiraling inflation. *That*, they would have insisted, makes as little sense as asserting that consumption of massive amounts of food could result in dramatic weight loss.

MERCANTILISM AND POVERTY

Mercantilism served two specific purposes. First, it generated impressive amounts of revenue for the leading merchants and financiers of the age, who benefited from monopolies, protectionist policies that banned foreign competition,

---

[5]   Spain did not fully recover as an economic power until the late 20th century.

and the relative decline of domestic markets—thanks to the poverty of the bulk of the population. With captive markets in overseas colonies, too, high prices could be demanded with impunity. Second, mercantilism produced enormous returns for the governments, which made money from bribes and monopoly licenses, high tariffs on imported goods, onerous taxation of the common people, and investment in the commercial activities of the leading mercantile firms. If mercantilism did not create prosperity for the nation, that was never its aim. All that mattered was the preservation of the state and the institutions it controlled.

Mercantilism had been at work in France and Spain since the 1530s, in England since the reign of Elizabeth I (r. 1558–1603), and in most of the rest of

Dutch Peasant Life   The Dutch painter Adriaen van Ostade (1610–1685) produced this 1647 etching of peasant life. The scene is less than idyllic but all the more realistic for that reason. Even in the Dutch Golden Age, most peasants lived hardscrabble lives.

Europe after 1648. Its effects were stark. In contrast to the baroque splendor of aristocratic palaces and ornate churches was the grinding poverty of the peasantry, village laborers, and local artisans and craftsmen. A French official's report on conditions among the rural populace of Normandy in 1651 paints a brutal picture:

> The most consistent food source here are the rats that the people hunt, so desperately hungry are they. They also eat plant roots that the farm animals will not touch. One can scarcely find words adequate to describing the horrors one sees everywhere. . . . This report, in fact, actually understates those horrors, rather than, as one might think, exaggerates them, for it describes only the tiniest fraction of the suffering in this district, suffering so dire that only those who have actually seen it can understand its scope. Hardly a single day passes in which at least two hundred people do not die. . . . I attest to having personally seen whole herds of people—men and women, that is, not cattle—wandering the fields between Rheims and Rethel, rooting in the dirt like pigs, and finding nothing edible, but only rotting fibers (and even these are only plentiful enough to feed half the herd), they collapse in exhaustion and have no strength left to continue searching for food. . . . The rest survive on a substitute for bread that does not deserve the name, made as it is from a mixture of chopped straw and dirt.

The question must be asked: Given such unspeakable suffering, why did people accept absolutist government—or at least not actively oppose it? The only answer is that things were even worse during the Wars of Religion. One can hardly exaggerate the bloody, murderous horror that plagued Europe before 1648.

DOMESTICATING DYNAMISM: REGULATING CULTURE

European culture, too, was subject to a form of absolutism, but not simply as an extension of royal power. The upper classes became obsessed with rule making and breaking. Rules of etiquette, standards of spelling and usage, norms for musical composition and visual art, academic curricula, domestic architecture, even the subtle social demands of fashion—all these multiplied under the pressure to conform. All came to express explicit standards of value, certainty, decorum, and taste. Such standards have existed in every age, but they have seldom dominated life as they did in Old Regime Europe.

The **baroque** style, which had emerged with the Catholic Counter-Reformation discussed in chapter 12, had emphasized dynamic energy and raw emotional power. Roughly half the paintings by Flemish artist Peter Paul Rubens

From the Baroque to Classicism

Ecstatic Divine Love   Gian Lorenzo Bernini (1598–1680) carved this ultimate statement of baroque sculptural style about 1650. St. Theresa of Avila was a Carmelite nun whose mystical revelations formed the backbone of her books of confessional and theological writings. Her best-known books are *The Way to Perfection, The Inner Castle,* and her absorbing autobiography. In this last book (actually the first one she wrote) she describes one of her visions, this one of a heavenly angel: "In his hand I saw a long spear of gold, from the point of which a small flame showed. It was as though he thrust it repeatedly into my heart, piercing my innermost parts; and whenever he pulled the spear out it was as though he drew my heart out as well, leaving me all on fire with love for God. The pain was so great it made me moan—and yet this great pain was so sweet that I wanted it never to end."

(1577–1640) glorify Catholic themes; most of the rest portray the magnificence of Europe's royals and high aristocrats. The great Spanish painter Diego Velázquez (1599–1660) likewise devoted roughly half of his output to portraits of the Spanish royal family, whereas the other half were split between Christian and classical themes.

In music, the baroque zenith was reached by the Italian father-son team of Alessandro (1660–1725) and Domenico Scarlatti (1685–1757), and Antonio Vivaldi (1678–1741). The Baroque Age in music experimented wildly with new forms of compositions, the most important being the cantata, oratorio, and opera—all of which combined vocal performance with instrumental accompaniment. One reason for the popularity of the cantata and oratorio was the fact that, by being largely musical settings of biblical verses, they could be played in Protestant and Catholic churches alike. Opera, in contrast, provided opportunities for a broader range of settings and themes; stories taken from classical literature were enduringly popular, but so too were operas drawn from contemporary drama and fiction. Most music lovers today rank Johann Sebastian Bach (1685–1750) as the greatest baroque composer. In his own time, however, this renowned German composer was considered just a good provincial musician, especially as an organist. A figure of *real* stature would have composed operas, which Bach refused to do.

Bach insisted that "all music should be for God" ("*Alle Musik soll für Gott sein*"). But as the baroque style spread across Europe, its focus shifted to glorifying the monarchies. What else stood between the people and Hobbesian chaos? The courts slowly replaced the dynamism of the baroque with the controlled

Camillus and the School of Falerii   This painting (ca. 1635) by the French master Nicolas
Poussin (1594–1655) re-creates a famous scene in the history of the Roman Republic. Camillus
was a great general who several times saved the early Republic from aggressors. In 396 BCE he
led an army against the enemy cities of Veii and Falerii and defeated them. According to tradition, a schoolteacher from Falerii offered to hand over all the students in his care to Camillus, as
slaves. Camillus instead ordered the schoolteacher to be executed as an example of the stern
justice that a ruler must sometimes perform—a message likely to be approved of by the French
court of Poussin's time.

formal tone of **classicism**. In the visual arts this was the age of Frenchmen Nicolas
Poussin (1594–1665) and Charles Le Brun (1619–1690); in theater, of Spanish
playwright Pedro Calderón de la Barca (1600–1681) and his French counterparts
Pierre Corneille (1606–1684) and Jean Racine (1639–1699); in literature, of
English writers John Milton (1608–1674) and John Dryden (1631–1700). The
strictures of formal classicism eased in the 18th century, but the insistence on
proper composition, content, and form continued.

The Absolutist Age also saw the first comprehensive dictionaries of the European languages. Bilingual dictionaries, the sort to help English speakers *Regulating*
learn French, or vice versa, had existed since the invention of the printing *Language:*
press. But dictionaries as normative reference works for native speakers and *The First*
writers were another matter altogether. Nearly two dozen hastily produced *Comprehensive*
English dictionaries had been published between 1550 and 1750 in a rush to *Dictionaries*
capitalize on the dramatic spread of literacy made possible by print. Only with

Samuel Johnson (1709–1784), however, was the extensive and definitive *Dictionary of the English Language* (1755) finally published.

Johnson's nine-year labor was a watershed event. A dictionary, after all, is a rulebook, one that asserts, for example, that the word *chair* is spelled C-H-A-I-R and in no other way—not chaar, chaire, chayr, chare, chaere, char, or any other phonetic estimation. Prior to the 17th century writers spelled words however they wished. As long as the reader understood what the writer was saying, what did it matter how individual words were spelled? (To date, for example, seven authentic signatures of William Shakespeare's have been found, and he spells his name differently each time.) A dictionary sets meanings and defines usage; it standardizes and regulates syntax. Johnson's *Dictionary* succeeded where earlier efforts had failed, and it remained authoritative until the publication of the complete *Oxford English Dictionary* in 1928. In France, a team of scholars produced the first installments of the *Dictionary of the French Academy* (*Dictionnaire de l'Académie Française*) in 1698, which did for the French language what Johnson did for English. The *Dictionary of the Academy "della Crusca"* (*Vocabolario degli Accademici della Crusca*) had appeared in Italy even earlier, in 1612, and the *Dictionary of the Spanish Language* (*Diccionario de la Lengua Española*) arrived in 1780.[6] The German language, by contrast, did not acquire a comparable dictionary until the Grimm brothers (of fairy-tale fame) published their *German Dictionary* (*Deutsches Wörterbuch*) in 1838.

THE CONTROL OF PRIVATE LIFE

Proper Manners

If language needed standardization and control, so much more did daily behavior. Norms of social behavior had long been determined by local custom. Books of etiquette date back to the Middle Ages, when treatises on "courtesie" were required reading for the higher nobility of the late 12th and 13th centuries. Generalized works of etiquette for the urban classes, however, became increasingly common in post-Westphalia Europe. Richard Brathwaite (1588–1673) published a trilogy of guides—*The English Gentleman, The English Gentlewoman*, and *Description of a Good Wife*—that established norms of behavior that lasted a hundred years; Boston schoolmaster Eleazar Moody's *The School of Good Manners* (1715) was an enormously popular guide for colonial parents who wanted to raise well-behaved children. In Italy, Baldassare Castiglione's *Il Libro del Cortegiano* (1528; in English as *The Book of the*

---

6   In Italian, *crusca* mean "bran." Hence the Academy of the Bran, metaphorically, was the institution that separated the bran (authentic and proper Italian words and usages) from the chaff (foreign words and corrupt usages).

Courtier in 1561) had established the norms for proper comportment in the Renaissance, but was overtaken in the 17th and 18th centuries by texts aimed at bourgeois society.

This is the society lampooned in the great comedy *The Middle-Class Gentleman* (*Le Bourgeois Gentilhomme*, 1670) by Molière (the pen name of Jean-Baptiste Poquelin, 1622–1673), whose very title is a part of the joke: a bourgeois commoner is attempting to behave with noble manners, as if one can become civilized by mimicking polite behavior! But a laughing matter in 1670 became serious business a generation later, as books on table etiquette, polite conversation, proper dress and comportment, and the rearing of well-behaved children grew in popularity. A French guide from 1729 helped explain the proper use of a new invention—the napkin[7]:

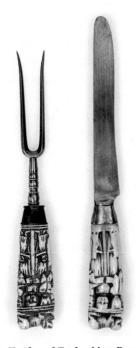

> When at table one ought always to use a napkin, plate, knife, spoon, and fork; in fact it is now considered to be utterly improper to be without any one of these.
>
> The proper thing is to wait until the highest-ranking dinner guest unfolds his napkin before unfolding one's own, but if everyone at table is a social equal, they should all unfold their napkins at the same time and without ceremony.
>
> It is poor manners to use the napkin to wipe one's face, and even poorer manners to wipe one's teeth; but the grossest behavior of all is to use the napkin to blow one's nose.

Table Knife and Fork   Most Europeans had traditionally used only knives and spoons at table. Forks, though known since Roman times, were used only as kitchen tools, if at all. Renaissance Italy reintroduced the use of table forks, although it is unclear whether this resulted from the desire to emulate the Romans or to limit one's exposure to disease—since people attending dinners commonly carried their own knives and forks with them in a box. As a rule, the farther north and west from Italy, the slower the adoption of the fork. In Germany and England especially, forks were long considered effeminate affectations, and the people of the American colonies did not embrace them until the late 18th century. The knife and fork shown here were made in Germany in the 17th century.

This text from 1729 signals change in its very title: *The Room: The Rules of Propriety and of*

---

[7]   Until the early 18th century, polite diners used the edges of the tablecloth to cover their laps and wipe their hands.

Christian Civility (La Salle: Les Règles de la Bienséance et de la Civilité Chrétienne). And as for bodily comportment,

> Decency and modesty demand that one keeps covered all the parts of the body, except the head and hands, when in society. Moreover, one should take every care never to touch with one's bare hand any part of the body that must remain properly covered; if one absolutely must do so, it must be done with the greatest discretion. A polite person simply must become accustomed to suffering small discomforts without twisting, rubbing, or scratching. . . .
>
> When one needs to urinate, one should always withdraw to a private place—for it is permissible to perform natural functions (and this is true even for children) so long as one does it where one is not seen. It is nevertheless altogether impolite to emit wind from one's body—either from below or above—even if it is done without any sound.

Contrast an English guide from 1619, written in verse:

> Let not your privy members be
> laid open to be viewed;
> it is most shameful and abhorr'd,
> detestable and rude.
> Retain not urine, nor the wind
> which do thy body vex;
> so [long as] it be done in secrecy,
> let that not thee perplex.

Guidebooks laid out rules for conversation, letter writing, dress, the issuing of invitations, and behavior at occasions such as weddings, funerals, balls, and theaters.

Regulation reigned in other areas of life too. In music, most of the major compositional forms moved toward formal definition: fugues and sonatas initially and eventually concertos and symphonies. Every opera had to have its text (libretto) approved by state censors before it could be staged to make sure the plot carried no subversive messages. Just as significantly, popular pressure gradually demanded further norms in opera—such as the strict separation of comedy (opera buffa) and tragic opera (opera seria), the use of plots from classical drama or from French neoclassical theater, and the use of the Italian language.[8]

---

[8]   Women were forbidden to take the stage in regular theater productions. Opera, however, offered them the chance to perform alongside men.

The Teatro San Carlo in Naples   Built in 1737, then rebuilt after a fire in 1816, this is the oldest continuously used opera house in Europe. The original upholstery was blue; the red was installed after the fire. Seen at the center here is the royal box, where members of the Bourbon dynasty sat. It was designed specifically for the staging of operas, with the auditorium built in a U-shape and tiered; an orchestra pit, so as not to overwhelm the singers; and all the backstage areas and equipment needed for any theatrical production. Opera houses were expensive, and most of those built in the 17th and 18th centuries resulted from the patronage of royals and high aristocrats. The tiered balconies were the reserve of the upper classes, with the seats of the main floor opened to non nobles. Thus opera, by its very popularity, helped to maintain the social system by embodying the privileged hierarchy while allowing the commoners to share in the delight made possible by aristocratic largesse.

Aspects of domestic, even private, life became subject to innovative strictures, too. Societies were brought up on the idea of maintaining order at all costs. For most urban dwellers, living quarters by long tradition had been single open-space rooms above the workshop, tavern, or storefront in which they worked. The activities of private life were conducted communally. Over the 17th and 18th centuries, however, domestic architecture took on interior walls, even among those with modest incomes. The activities of daily life—sleeping, cooking and eating, tending to hygiene, and socializing—were to be performed in discrete rooms. It is no accident that the word *privacy* was coined in the 17th century; before then, neither the word nor the concept existed.[9]

The Birth of Private Life

Even the human body became subject to a kind of control. Common people throughout the Middle Ages and Renaissance had worn simple garments that

---

9   Shakespeare seems to have been the first person who used the word "privacy." It appears in his comedy *The Merry Wives of Windsor* and in his narrative poem *Troilus and Cressida*, both published in 1602.

sheathed the body, whereas the 17th and 18th centuries saw the general introduction of underwear of various types. Henceforth, everyday dress for both men and women involved undergarments—not just to provide warmth but also to support and control the body's movement. Regulations like these were not imposed by government but arose naturally in a culture that valued order above everything else.

As standards of expected behavior rose, manners improved, and aesthetic values became defined and codified. In turn, attitudes toward those who failed to observe the new niceties grew harsher. Aristocratic culture had always prided itself on the chasm that separated it from the dirty masses, but a sense of cultural elitism began to emerge among bourgeois Europeans at this time as well. As a result, efforts spread to instill better behavior among the lower orders, some of them altruistic, others not. Centuries-old peasant entertainments like carnivals (rural festivals that usually preceded Lent, the Christian season of fasting and penitence in preparation for the Easter celebration of Christ's resurrection) were discouraged from the pulpit and judicial bench alike. English Puritan ministers railed against the evils of taverns, dances, country fairs, and popular folk songs. Protestant ministers in Germany struggled to stamp out rural irregularities in communal worship.

In the cities, the urban poor were no longer objects of pity and almsgiving but were denounced in sermons, speeches, broadsides, and newspapers (another invention of the age) as lazy, deceitful, uncouth, and potentially dangerous. New institutions arose to deal with them: poorhouses, hospitals, and reformatories. These institutions performed the valuable services of removing the unsightly destitute from polite society and then either rehabilitating them by teaching them a craft or effectively imprisoning them. In 1676 Louis XIV went so far as to order every city in France to build and maintain a hospital for warehousing the worst off of the urban poor.

In England, people whose behavior violated basic norms but who had not broken the law frequently ended up in Bedlam. Although the hospital dates back to the 13th century, in 1675 it became the first asylum for the mentally ill.[10] The idea caught on, and asylums soon dotted the whole European landscape. So too did prisons. Prior to the 18th century, jails or dungeons were simply holding areas for those waiting until judicial punishment (execution, lashing, maiming, or a simple fine) was carried out. But after 1700 state after state preferred to remove criminals from society altogether, and lengthy incarceration became the punishment of choice. Those whose presence offended polite society became isolated, institutionalized, and removed from the scene.

---

[10]   In 1725 Bedlam was divided into separate wings for those considered curable ("patients") and incurable ("lunatics").

ENGLAND'S SEPARATE PATH: THE RISE OF CONSTITUTIONAL MONARCHY

As we saw in chapter 14, England rose to the top tier of European nations in the second half of the 16th century. When Elizabeth I died in 1603, however, a constitutional crisis threatened to undo the internal stability of the realm and endangered England's position in the international economy. In response, the new Stuart dynasty asserted absolutist rule, but the effort ended in civil war. The causes of the English Civil War were similar to that of the Fronde in France: religious animosities, struggles for power among competing factions of aristocrats, and a fiscal system that could not keep pace with the increasing costs of government. But in England these conflicts led to the deposition and execution of a king, a radical experiment in representative government that quickly dissolved into autocratic rule and ultimatelyled to the establishment of a **constitutional monarchy** under conditions designed to safeguard Parliament's place in government, an arrangement that has endured to the present.

With the death of Elizabeth, who had never married, came the end of the Tudor dynasty. After some intrigue, the throne passed to James Stuart, the great-grandson of Henry VIII's sister. This marked the beginning of the trouble-plagued Stuart dynasty, which lasted, with interruptions, until 1714. Being Scottish, James I (r. 1603–1625) faced rude resistance from the start despite the legitimacy of his succession.[11] More than ethnic prejudice was at work in this, however, because James was a passionate advocate of royal absolutism. Before coming to power in England he had published a political treatise called *The True Law of Free Monarchies* (1598), in which he argued that since kingship existed "before any estates or ranks of men ... [and] before any parliaments were held or laws made," it is therefore unnatural for a king's power to be checked in any way. Indeed, kings hold their authority by divine right. The argument is as weak as James's stubbornness was strong, and the struggle to balance royal ambitions and parliamentary rights ultimately characterized the history of the entire Stuart dynasty.

The Reign of James I

James restated his position in a speech to the English Parliament in 1610:

> The state of monarchy is the supremest thing upon earth, for kings are not only God's lieutenants upon earth and sit upon God's throne, but even by God himself they are called gods. There be three principal [comparisons] that illustrate the state of monarchy: one taken out of the word of God, and the two other out of the grounds of policy and philosophy. In the Scriptures kings are called gods, and so their power after a certain

---

[11] James, who ruled as James VI in Scotland (r. 1567–1603), was the first to style himself the king of "Great Britain."

> relation compared to the Divine power. Kings are also compared to fa-
> thers of families; for a king is truly *parens patriae*, the politic father of his
> people. And lastly, kings are compared to the head of this microcosm of
> the body of man. . . . I conclude then this point touching the power of
> kings with this axiom of divinity, that as to dispute what God may do is
> blasphemy . . . so is it sedition in subjects to dispute what a king may do
> in the height of his power.

Colossally vain, James I also had a tremendous fear of assassination. His childhood in Scotland had been filled with political deceits, palace intrigues, kidnappings, and murder plots.[12] The horror of his early years made him distrustful of those around him, and once in power in Edinburgh and London he resolved that institutions like parliaments, courts, and churches were mere service organizations of the monarchy rather than sharers of power. Although he had been raised a Catholic, James found that Anglicanism suited his self-regard because it identified the king as undisputed head of the church. His greatest achievement was his support for a new English translation of the scriptures intended specifically for his newly adopted church—the so-called King James Bible, known officially as the Authorized Version.

The seldom-read dedication to the King James Bible provides a good example of absolutist ideology. It begins,

> Great and manifold were the blessings, most dread Sovereign, which
> Almighty God, the Father of all mercies, bestowed upon us the people of
> England, when first he sent Your Majesty's Royal Person to rule and
> reign over us. For whereas it was the expectation of many who wished
> not well unto our Sion, that, upon the setting of that bright Occidental
> [western] Star, Queen Elizabeth, of most happy memory some thick and
> palpable clouds of darkness would so have overshadowed this land, that
> men should have been in doubt which way they were to walk, and that it
> should hardly be known who was to direct the unsettled State; the
> appearance of Your Majesty, as of the Sun in his strength, instantly dis-
> pelled those supposed and surmised mists, and gave unto all that were
> well affected exceeding cause of comfort; especially when we beheld the
> Government established in Your Highness and Your hopeful Seed, by an
> undoubted Title; and this also accompanied with peace and tranquility
> at home and abroad.

---

[12]   In childhood, James had seen more than one family member cut down. He regularly wore a heavy dagger-proof tunic under his royal garments.

But among all our joys, there was no one that more filled our hearts than the blessed continuance of the preaching of God's sacred Word among us, which is that inestimable treasure which excelleth all the riches of earth; because the fruit thereof extendeth itself, not only to the time spent in this transitory world, but directeth and disposeth men unto that eternal happiness which is above in heaven.

Then not to suffer this to fall to the ground, but rather to take it up, and to continue it in that state wherein the famous Predecessor of Your Highness did leave it; nay, to go forward with the confidence and resolution of a man, in maintaining the truth of Christ, and propagating it far and near, is that which hath so bound and firmly knit the hearts of all Your Majesty's loyal and religious people unto You, that Your very name is precious among them: their eye doth behold You with comfort, and they bless You in their hearts, as that sanctified Person, who, under God, is the immediate author of their true happiness.

James fervently believed in mercantilism and followed its tenets to escape financial dependency on Parliament. Eager to increase English power in North America, he established the colonies at Jamestown (1607) and Plymouth (1620), in what would eventually become the states of Virginia and Massachusetts. He also tried, although unsuccessfully, to arrange a marriage between his son Charles and a Spanish princess. He awarded many monopolies and collected enormous licensing fees, which raised opposition from the gentry, but he compensated them by creating (and selling to the highest bidders, most of whom came from the gentry—wealthy commoners who had acquired landed estates, partially in an attempt to simulate the life of the aristocracy) an unprecedented number of new noble titles. James granted more than two thousand knighthoods, but the "baronetcy" was his signature invention: he happily bestowed this honor on anyone who would pay his asking

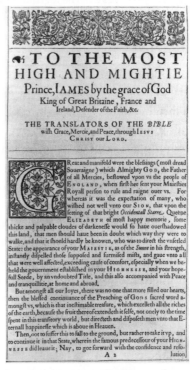

Divine Writ James I's greatest achievement was his support for a new English translation of the scriptures intended specifically for his newly adopted church— the so-called King James Bible, known officially as the Authorized Version.

price of ten thousand pounds. Many purchasers came forward. When James first came to the English throne in 1603 the House of Lords had fifty-nine members; when he died in 1625 the House had more than twice that number.

Civil War   When James's son Charles I (r. 1625–1649) became king, opposition to the Stuarts had grown to the point that Parliament openly demanded constitutional reforms. Charles had inherited his father's vanity and stubbornness, however, in addition to his titles, and had no intention of compromising royal prerogatives. Unfortunately for him, he also inherited England's involvement in the Thirty Years' War. Meeting commitments to numerous parties in that struggle placed ever-greater pressure on royal finances, but Parliament passed a Petition for Right (1628) that denied the crown additional taxes and restricted the king's judicial authority. The following year Charles summoned a new Parliament, immediately arrested nine of its leaders, and dissolved the assembly; no new Parliament met for eleven years, during which time Charles bullied new fees and levies from the provinces. By 1640 king and country were wholly estranged. When Charles, once more strapped for cash, did finally summon Parliament again later that year, the legislators prepared a "Grand Remonstrance"—a lengthy list of formal complaints about royal abuses of authority.[13] Charles's troops eventually stormed the Parliament but were resisted. England's Civil War (1642–1649) had begun.

The parliamentary forces were disorganized at first but soon came under the leadership of Oliver Cromwell (1599–1658), a strict Puritan in religion and a member of the gentry by social status. Without much military experience, he nevertheless rose quickly through the officer ranks. He was one of the three or four most powerful figures on the scene when the army defeated Charles in battle and took him prisoner in 1645. Few people wanted to abolish the monarchy altogether, and most hoped to force the king to some sort of compromise. When news came that Charles was in secret negotiations with Royalist sympathizers to launch a Scottish invasion of England, however, patience was at an end. Parliament placed Charles on trial for treason in 1648, and when the tribunal returned a guilty verdict, Cromwell was one of the signatories to the king's death warrant. Charles was publicly beheaded on January 30, 1649, the first time in history that a reigning king had been legally deposed and executed by his own government.

---

[13]   On the advice of the Anglican archbishop of Canterbury, William Laud (1573–1645), Charles tried to force the autonomous Protestant Church of Scotland into the mold of the Church of England—and got a Scottish invasion of England for his trouble. He needed funds for a defensive campaign; hence the new Parliament.

But the people who had opposed the monarchy soon found that, having removed the head of the state, they could not agree on a replacement. Dissension broke out almost immediately; after several tense weeks, Cromwell took over the government by general acclamation. Parliament declared England a Commonwealth, an English translation of the Latin *res publica*, and in 1653 Cromwell himself took the title of Lord Protector. But this radical experiment in representative government quickly dissolved into a thinly disguised Puritanical theocracy. New restrictions on Catholics (whom Cromwell hated) were instituted; the Anglican Book of Common Prayer was condemned. Cromwell's government forced the closing of theaters (places renowned for their encouragement of immoral lifestyles, in the Puritans' judgment). On the other hand, he invited the Jews to return to England (they had been expelled in 1290 by King Edward I), in the hopes that their return would trigger the onset of the end of the world, as he believed was predicted in biblical prophecy.

Repression and Restoration

Cromwell intended that his son should succeed him, but his death in 1658 only revived the prospect of civil war. With no one of Cromwell's energy and forcefulness to hold the kingdom together and with hostility between religious denominations so stirred up, fears arose that civil war was imminent. In 1660 a newly elected Parliament invited Charles I's exiled son, who had taken refuge in France and Holland, to return to England and restore the monarchy, as the only means to pacify and stabilize the realm. Charles II (r. 1660–1685), who has come down in English history as the "merry king" but in truth was as intelligent as carefree, agreed to certain limits on royal power and took the throne amid a general sense of celebration. After over a decade of government by dour Puritans, the people welcomed Charles's love of pleasure and laughter and his reopening of the theater houses closed under Cromwell.

But the party was short-lived. An outbreak of bubonic plague in 1665 and the Great Fire of London in 1666 destroyed much of the city and took tens of thousands of lives. Charles quickly adopted a more serious approach to his duties, although he never managed to keep his living expenses within the budget the Parliament had set for him. In 1672 he attempted to force through a royal declaration that removed all legal penalties from the practice of Roman Catholicism, but backed down when Parliament resisted. Doubts about Charles's own religious loyalty filled the rest of his years on the throne, fueled by his marriage to a Portuguese princess, Catarina de Bragança, who was unpopular with the English on account of her Catholicism and her lasting inability to learn English.

Charles had no legitimate heir, since his wife's pregnancies had all ended in miscarriages and stillbirths. On his death in 1685 the crown passed to Charles's brother James II (r. 1685–1688), who was openly Roman Catholic and determined

The Glorious Revolution

to introduce absolutism.[14] James's short reign was filled with dissension, since the Parliament refused to remove the legal strictures that limited Catholic rights. Even more worrisome was the new king's desire for a much larger standing royal army. England had traditionally never kept soldiers in uniform and on the public payroll during peacetime. James's proposal, moreover, appeared too much in line with the actions of the post-Westphalian monarchs across Europe and stirred the Parliament into dramatic action.

In 1688 a group of leading members of Parliament invited the Protestant ruler of Holland, Prince William of Orange, husband of James II's daughter Mary, to invade their realm and depose James, on the condition that they accept a bill of rights guaranteeing Parliament's full partnership in a constitutional government. William and Mary agreed. James initially thought he could defeat his daughter and son-in-law but soon realized otherwise, and so he fled the scene. He was soon captured by William's men, who, with William's consent, allowed him to escape to France—where he lived out his days in the court of Louis XIV. Since the coup proceeded without significant violence (James's soldiers deserted him en masse), it is known as England's **Glorious Revolution**. Without shedding a drop of blood, England had staged a successful revolution, brought down an unpopular monarch, and brought to power a popular royal couple dedicated to Protestantism and constitutional rule.

OTTOMAN ABSOLUTISM

Political developments farther east mirrored Continental Europe's trajectory into absolutist government; both the Ottoman and the Safavid empires increased the centralization of their administrations in the 16th and 17th centuries. Language and culture distinguished them as much as did political regimes. The Ottomans controlled the Arabic-speaking nations, and the Safavids governed the Persian speakers. Important religious distinctions existed as well, with Sunni Islam dominating among the Arab peoples and Shi'i Islam practiced by the bulk of Persian speakers. Although overwhelmingly Muslim, neither of these states was religiously monolithic because large Christian and Jewish populations continued to reside in them.

Measures to Maintain Power

Ottoman military encroachments on Europe had continued well into the 17th century, and, as we have seen, at least three times (1529, 1532, and 1683) their armies had advanced as far as Vienna. After 1683 the Turks were put on the

---

[14]   Charles II was received in the Roman Catholic Church on his deathbed. James II had formally converted to Catholicism while growing up on the Continent during Cromwell's rule.

defensive for the first time in their history, a position exacerbated by the ascendancy of European merchant fleets in the Indian Ocean (see Map 15.2). Since they had previously lost control of the eastern Mediterranean at the battle of Lepanto in 1571 (discussed in chapter 14), the new setbacks occasioned two new developments for the Turks. First, they gradually relinquished control over the farthest provinces of their empire—Morocco and Algiers, along the North African coast (called the Berber, or Barbary, Coast by Europeans), which henceforth became independent states.[15] Second, the Ottomans delegated more power to provincial governors, with a system of tax farming that assigned local fiscal control to leading families. These steps were not, however, a complete capitulation of authority. Turkish autocracy had always differed from European absolutism in a fundamental way. Since the 15th century the monopoly of power was held by the dynastic house of Osman rather than by any specific individual. The sultan in Istanbul, as leader of the royal family, held primacy of place over his relatives, but power was rightfully held by every representative of Osman's line. The empire's system of government was therefore an oligarchical absolutism, but was no less absolutist for that.

Like that of its Western contemporaries, Ottoman absolutism was based on military might. The most important component of the army was the large corps of Janissaries (introduced in chapter 11). These "new soldiers" (the literal meaning of the Turkish word *yeniçeri*) were formed of Christian children from the Balkans and the Caucasus who, under the practice of *devşirme,* were stolen from their families, forcibly converted to Islam, and pushed into military service— just as had been the practice centuries before with the Mamluk slave-soldiers. They were sworn to celibacy during their years in the army, granted pensions and the right to marry on retirement, and accorded exceptionally high social status. By the 17th century civil government was largely dominated by former Janissaries. At that time too the traditional practice of *devşirme* was abolished, as ethnically Turkish families sought to place their own children in the corps in hopes of social and political advancement. Given the relative decrease in their military activity after 1683, the Janissaries were increasingly used (again like their European counterparts) as domestic police forces. In this role they

---

[15]   To resist Spanish dominance in the western Mediterranean, these new states encouraged the "Barbary pirates" to attack ships on either side of the Strait of Gibraltar. More than money, the Barbary pirates sailed in search of Christians they could abduct and enslave. Men were taken as galley slaves; women and girls, after forced conversions to Islam, were sold as slaves to restock wealthy figures' harems; and the boys, similarly Islamized, were destined chiefly for military service. By 1700 more than a million men, women, and children had been captured and enslaved.

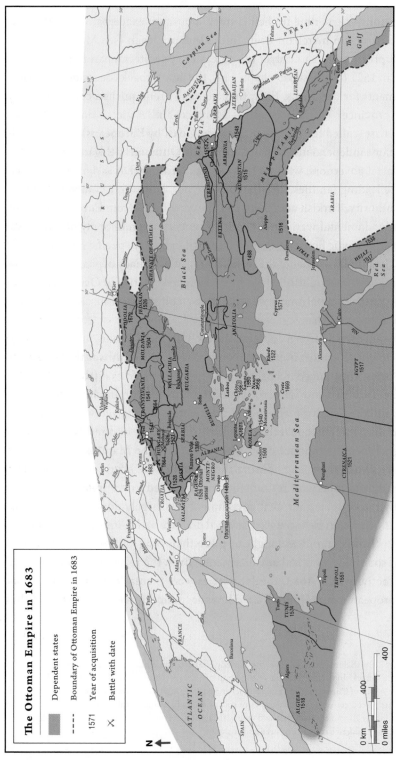

MAP 15.2   The Ottoman Empire in 1683   In early modern times the Ottomans developed one of the world's most extensive and lasting empires. What held the hugely diverse Ottoman Empire together was its flexible bureaucratic structure, which frequently rewarded faithful conquered subjects and allowed loose tributary arrangements at the fringes.

maintained order, quelled revolts, and represented the ever-watchful eye of the sultan and his family.

PERSIAN ABSOLUTISM

As we know from chapter 14, the Safavid dynasty in Persia had been established in 1501, with Shi'ism proclaimed the state religion. The Safavids had emerged from a heterodox Sufi order and regarded themselves as either the earthly representatives of the Shi'i hidden imam or the hidden imam himself. Given their religious origins, they were not likely to recognize any checks on their power—an analog to European notions of divine-right monarchy. To be prudent, from their capital at Isfahan (roughly 100 miles south of today's Iranian capital of Tehran), they complemented the religious basis of their claims to absolute authority by relying on the unwavering support of a large and potent army. Most of their army was composed of regular infantry units that served only as needed. More significant for maintaining the regime was a unique network of militant units known collectively as the *Qizilbash* (meaning "crimson" or "red-headed"). These companies—identifiable by the distinctive red-topped headpieces they wore (and from which they take their name)—regarded the Safavid ruler as divine. So great was their zeal that the Qizilbash customarily went into battle without any type of defensive armor. They were convinced that Allah and their Safavid lord's blessing would protect them from harm.[16]

Under the greatest Safavid shah, Abbas I (r. 1587–1629), the Persians recaptured Baghdad and established commercial ties with both the British and the Dutch East India Companies. Baghdad had never fully recovered from the devastation wreaked on it by the Mongols and may have held as few as fifty thousand people. An elaborate irrigation network had made the river valleys fertile since Sumerian times. Now that too lay in ruins, and most of Iraq had become a patchwork of scrubby pastoral zones loosely but violently controlled by rival tribes. But Baghdad itself still mattered as a forward defensive position against a renewed Ottoman offensive. Friendly ties with the East India Companies were vital, since conflicts over control of the sea-lanes had shifted commercial routes away from the Persian Gulf and toward the Red Sea, on the other side of the Arabian peninsula. The shift threatened to cost the Iranians considerable revenue.

Like the European monarchs, the shahs centralized their nation's wealth as much as they did its political power, and they spent as lavishly on themselves as

---

[16] The Qizilbash still exist as a distinct religious community in Afghanistan, Azerbaijan, Iran, and Pakistan. The third president of modern-day Pakistan, Agha Yahya Khan (1969–1971), was Qizilbash.

did Louis XIV. Magnificent palaces, pleasure gardens, libraries, astronomical observatories, and public adornments filled the cities. They built mosques and madrasas by the dozen and restored older centers of worship that had been damaged during the Mongol and Tatar years. In Iraq the holy shrines in the cities of Karbala and Najaf—dear to the Shi'a—were rebuilt and again became important sites of

Isfahan Isfahan, in central Iran, was the capital of Safavid Persia from 1598 to 1736. Located on a high plain just east of the Zagros Mountains, its steep elevation—comparable to that of Denver, in the United States—makes for chilly winters and hot summers. Shown in this image is the Shah Mosque, built in 1611 and considered one of the great masterpieces of Persian architecture. The large square behind it (the Naqsh-e Jahan Square) was built to serve a purpose similar to that of the Château de Versailles—that is, it housed all the Safavid rulers' leading nobles and ministers of state, keeping them all in his direct sight. The mosque itself comes off the square at a unique angle, so that the towering entrance arch (called an *iwan*) and the central dome can both be seen from everywhere in the square. Visible to the right of the great dome is a smaller, lower dome that marks the "winter mosque"—a smaller, warmer site for use during the cold winters.

pilgrimage. Abbas II (r. 1642–1666) extended his realm northward into Afghanistan, taking the strategic city of Kandahar from the Mughal Empire in India, and ruled over a thriving and peaceable realm.

But the later Safavids gave in to the pleasures of their lavish lifestyle and spent more time enjoying themselves than governing, which led to the dynasty's downfall in 1736. Decades of turmoil ensued until, in 1796, a new Persian dynasty took over—the Qajar—which held absolute power over Iran until 1925. The founder of the new dynasty, Mohammad Khan Qajar (r. 1794–1797), had been castrated as a young boy by a rival for leadership of the Qajar tribe, an experience that likely contributed to his predilection for extreme cruelty and violence.[17] Mohammad was killed himself in 1797 by household servants whom he had ordered to be executed; after his assassination the Qajar shahs focused resolutely on maintaining their political power and the wealth that made it possible.

Rise of the Qajar Dynasty

Yet they also distanced themselves from the theocratic ideology of the Safavids. Religious and legal authority thus devolved from the court-appointed officials (*qadis*) of earlier times to the caste of scholars in shari'a law produced by the madrasas. In the case of Shi'i Islam, these were predominately clerics who held the title of **mullah** ("guardian"—a position roughly analogous to a Jewish rabbi). Leadership of the mullahs fell to a higher office still, the **ayatollah** ("sign from God," literally). By 1800, Iran had evolved into a dual absolutist state: political and military might was monopolized by the secular state under the autocratic control of the shah, whereas religious authority remained the preserve of an elite corps of mullahs led by their clerical superiors, the ayatollahs.

INTERNATIONAL TRADE IN A MERCANTILIST AGE

Absolutist Europe and constitutional England formed the center of a vast network of international trade (see Map 15.3). It proved a hybrid of commercial, colonial, mercantilist, and capitalist practices. It also turned on new markets, sustained by slavery and domestic labor.

Starting with Sweden in 1664, Europe's leading countries created royal or national banks that quickly developed systems of credit to finance manufacturing, commerce, and development. Strict mercantilism demanded the use of

---

[17] Mohammad once ordered the blinding of twenty thousand men in a city that resisted his authority. He also had the Georgian city of Tbilisi burned to the ground and its entire Christian population put to death in 1795.

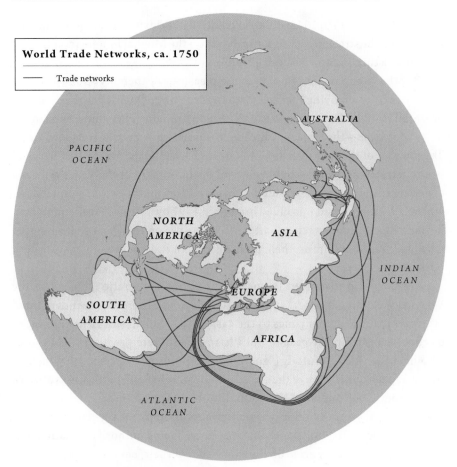

MAP 15.3   World Trade Networks, ca. 1750   One of the most significant developments of the modern period was the permanent linking of the world's regions through trade networks.

precious-metal coins, and aristocratic Europe's demand for Asian luxury goods never abated. Hence there was a continuous drainage of gold and silver from the West, which led to the introduction of paper money. Released from dependence on actual bullion, the new national banks dramatically increased loans, bonds, and other opportunities to invest. Credit now became available "on account," as promises to repay. National stock exchanges soon followed. Joint-stock companies like the British East India Company, the Dutch East India Company, and the South Sea Company benefited from the influx of investments. Their charters granted them monopolies on certain manufactures and trades, which allowed many to build impressive long-term returns. But investment opportunities were limited to those with excess capital, or wealth to

National Banks and Investment Opportunities

invest, which was still a small percentage of the population. Mercantilist practices kept most laborers' wages at rock-bottom levels, and price controls and domestic taxes kept most skilled draftsmen from setting aside investment capital. As a result, most of the benefits of the international economy went to a small number of investors.

Investment was a new concept. The idea behind it—that capital itself, not people, can *do work*—is an abstraction that few fully understood. In purchasing stock, one is not buying a good or service, but rather the right to share in the profit generated by the future production and sale of those goods or services. Moreover, it takes money to produce goods and services, which usually means borrowing. In purchasing stock, one is also purchasing a share of a company's debt. Elaborate legal and financial arrangements can equally beguile and confuse those entering the investment market. The combination led frequently to speculative schemes, or "bubbles," that ruined thousands of investors.

The most famous crash was the South Sea Bubble of 1720. The South Sea Company had been formed in London in 1711 to trade with the Spanish colonies *South Sea* in North America. To finance its activities, the company purchased England's *Bubble* national debt (then some 50 million pounds, a substantial amount) in return for the right to exchange government bonds for shares in the company. Bondholders who despaired of the government's ability to redeem its bonds were thrilled by the possibility of New World riches and rushed to invest in the company. Soon a wave of speculation drove share prices to unprecedented heights, and the company encouraged the buying frenzy. It announced ever-more spectacular ventures that it intended to undertake, like the manufacture of a (nonexistent) machine that could remove salt from seawater—not to mention an ultrasecret "undertaking of great profit in due time to be revealed." Shares rose from 150 pounds each to more than 1,000 pounds before the inevitable crash came and investors were wiped out.

THE SLAVE TRADE AND DOMESTIC SUBJUGATION

Far more reliable investments than shares in the South Sea Company were New World agriculture and the slave trade that enabled it. Until the 19th century, when settlers moved westward across the Great Plains, the New World did not produce food for export. Crops like potatoes, beans, and corn (maize) had already been introduced into European farming and consequently were not shipped across the Atlantic.

But sugar cane, cotton, and tobacco did not grow well in Europe. Being non- *Height of* perishable, they could also be transported overseas to generate enormous profits, *the Slave Trade* but they were labor-intensive crops. The need for slaves thus grew, as did the demand for the crops they produced. Throughout the 18th century between 75,000 and 100,000 African slaves were shipped across the Atlantic annually, until the slave trade was finally abolished (by France in 1793, England in 1807). Exact accounting is impossible, but somewhere around 12 million sub-Saharan Africans were brought to the New World in chains. The greatest number of them went to the Caribbean islands, where they perished in horrifying numbers while working the sugarcane fields. Roughly a half-million were sent to what eventually became the American South (see Map 15.4).

The profits generated by slave-produced New World agriculture were enormous. England's colonial profits rose from 10 million pounds to 40 million pounds between 1700 and 1776. France saw its revenues increase from 15 million to 250 million *livres* in the same period. But the profits of the era were not distributed throughout society; they went to the highest social strata. Domestically, the rural economy was a ruin. As much as 20 percent of the European population lived in abject poverty.

Alcoholism and Disease The introduction of maize and potatoes alleviated famine in Europe, but also raised a new danger—alcoholism. Crops no longer needed for food could be converted into distilled spirits, which provided the poor with an escape from the dreariness and hardship of their lives. Before, liquor distillation had primarily been a secret of monasteries. By now, however, the Protestant Reformation had advanced the knowledge of distillation across Europe. Gin became the hard liquor of choice among the poor, since it was so plentiful and cheap. By 1740, in England, gin production was nearly six times the nation's beer production—and all of it was drunk locally. The city of London alone had more than six thousand gin shops, which sold cheap gin in bottles with rounded bottoms (to encourage buyers to drain the entire bottle, lest they risk a spill on setting it down). When the government in 1736 tried to reduce consumption by imposing a heavy tax on gin, crowds took to the street by the thousands until they won a repeal of the tax.[18]

Those poor not killed off by drink often succumbed to disease, since the physical conditions in which the poor lived were appalling. In the district of Brittany, in northwestern France, dysentery killed 100,000 people in a single year (1779). Until about 1750, only one-half of all European children born lived to the age of ten, and only one-half of the females who made it to their tenth birthday

---

[18] As liquor became a favorite item for governments to tax, people operated their private stills at night, so that the smoke produced would not be seen. That is why homemade liquor is known as *moonshine*. This usage of the word first appeared in 1782 in a London magazine.

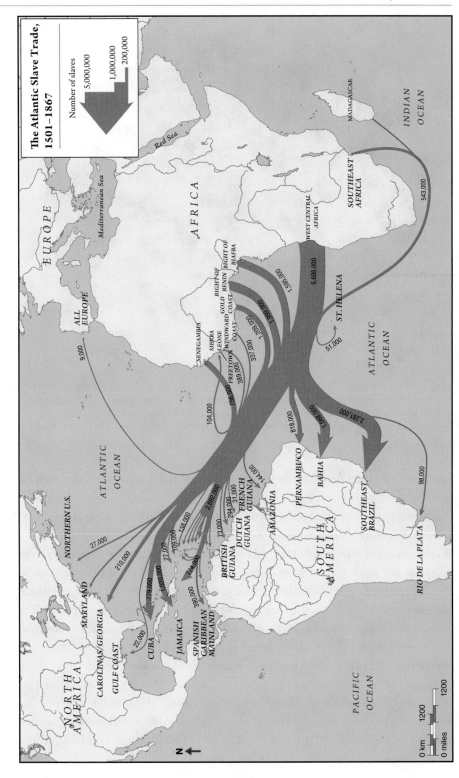

The Atlantic Slave Trade, 1501–1867

Number of slaves
5,000,000
1,000,000
200,000

MAP 15.4　The Atlantic Slave Trade　The Atlantic slave trade connected European ports to African slave-trading outposts and to plantations in the Caribbean, South America, and North America. The European countries bordering the Atlantic Ocean benefited most from this trade.

Cottage Industry   In this example of cottage industry, an Irish family beats flax in order to expose the fibers contained within; once cracked open, the flax fibers are then soaked in water, removed, and spun by hand into linen thread.

survived until their fortieth. Pregnancy and childbirth were a death sentence for most of them.

Cottage Industry

Rural women became wage earners through the **putting-out system** of textile manufacture, which became increasingly widespread in the 18th century. Also known as **cottage industry**, this system transferred cloth production from towns to the countryside. Women had woven cloth for their families for centuries, but in the late Middle Ages textile production had shifted to cities, where it came under the control of guilds that regulated production and set prices. The putting-out system returned the center of cloth making to the rural economy, as new merchants sought to avoid the urban guilds and improve profits. These entrepreneurs typically purchased bulk quantities of raw wool and cotton, which they distributed throughout rural districts, often following routes claimed by competing entrepreneurs. Then they retraced their steps, collecting the finished cloth from women and taking it to urban markets. Rural families needed this work desperately. Wages remained low, but by assigning tasks like carding or spinning to their children, countrywomen were able to produce more finished cloth. Once redeemed, it often made the difference between life and death.[19]

THE RETURN OF UNCERTAINTY

Given the miseries of the age, the passivity of the people in the face of the excesses of absolutist society is striking. Even the most dramatic political action, like England's civil war and revolution, was undertaken by bourgeois and aristocratic factions. The underclass had seldom known prosperity and independence—and so had grown not to expect them. Disruptions could still spark them into action, as rebellions like the German Peasants' Revolt of 1524–1525 showed. Yet as long as absolutism kept the peace, as it generally did between 1648 and 1700, peasants complained of their lot but seldom rose up against it.

The reappearance of warfare after 1700 added just the uncertainty, insecurity, and violence needed to trigger mass unrest. First came the War of the Spanish Succession (1701–1714). When King Charles II, the last Habsburg king of Spain, died without an heir in 1700, France's Louis XIV and Austria's Leopold I—each of whom was married to a sister of Charles—greedily eyed the Spanish crown and its enormous overseas empire. Charles's will had named an heir to the throne: the grandson of his sister, the closest male relative available. But Louis hoped to win the crown for himself before the young man, Philip V, took power. Louis consequently invaded Spain; he also invaded the Spanish Netherlands, which brought him into a parallel war with England. The English army at this time was led by a career soldier named John Churchill, who defeated Louis's forces and brought the islands of Gibraltar and Menorca, plus France's New World territories of Newfoundland and Hudson's Bay, into England's possession.[20] *War of the Spanish Succession*

A subsequent conflict was the War of the Austrian Succession (1740–1748), which arose when ambitious outsiders challenged Maria Theresa's succession to the throne because Salic law precluded royal inheritance by a woman. Several countries joined in this fray, less to advance claims of their own than to do anything they could to weaken the Habsburg family in general. *War of the Austrian Succession*

But the largest and most devastating conflict of the age was the **Seven Years' War** (1756–1763), which pitted Great Britain, Brandenburg–Prussia, and some smaller German principalities against an alliance of Austria, France, Russia, Saxony, and Sweden (see Map 15.5). This last war arose, in general, in response to the changes made to the Westphalian "balance of power" by the earlier two *The Seven Years' War*

---

[19]   Cloth was the leading commodity in this system, but not the only one. Leatherwork, soap and candle making, and even metalwork formed part of the cottage economy too.

[20]   His achievement resulted in his being created the 1st Duke of Marlborough, which raised the Churchills to the status of one of England's greatest noble families.

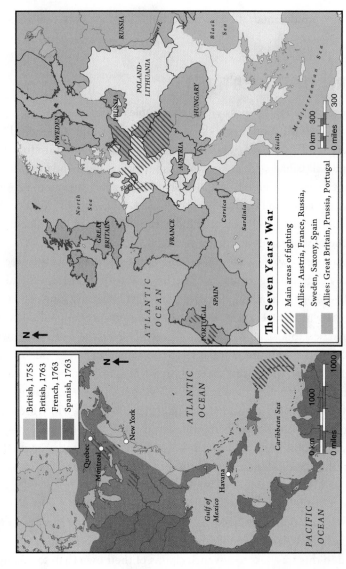

MAP 15.5   The Seven Years' War   In what historians often term the first worldwide war, the French and British fought each other in Europe, the West Indies, North America, and India. Skirmishing in North America helped to start the war, which became more general when Austria, France, and Russia allied to check Prussian influence in central Europe. The treaty between Austria and Prussia restored the status quo in Europe, but the changes overseas were much more dramatic. Britain gained control over Canada and India and was now the dominant naval power.

conflicts. England claimed that France was in illegal possession of numerous territories in North America and took preemptive action by seizing several of the disputed lands and a large number of French merchant vessels. Fast-militarizing Prussia, meanwhile, resented Austrian–Hungarian power in eastern Europe and provoked hostilities by forming an alliance with England. At this point, other kingdoms got involved, joining or forming new coalitions to try to maintain (or, in the case of Russia, to disrupt) the "balance of power" on the Continent. The result was seven years of Continent-wide war (1756–1763).

Together, these wars produced horrendous casualties. The Seven Years' War alone resulted in more than a million deaths. Cannon-fed sieges of cities and organized campaigns of arson marked the conflicts. Roused by the vast ruin of the countryside, the disruption of trade, the wasted expenditure, and the callous abuse of the peasantry, popular voices began to rise up and to demand change. Bread riots, calls for peace, and complaints over endless governmental deficits arose across Europe. Demonstrations against the treatment of the many by the very, very few erupted from Ireland to Austria and from Sicily to Sweden. The Treaty of Paris (1763) ended the immediate conflict by a complex formula of land reallocations, but few realms felt secure.

Surely something could be done to restore order. As the century progressed, new voices arose, voices dedicated to the idea that change was possible, necessary, and within reach. The world was a dark place that needed new light and hope.

WHO, WHAT, WHERE

absolutism	Fronde	protectionism
ayatollah	Glorious Revolution	putting-out system
baroque	Louis XIV	Seven Years' War
classicism	mercantilism	social contract
constitutional	mullah	
monarchy	Peace of Westphalia	
cottage industry	Peter I	

SUGGESTED READINGS

Primary Sources

Bodin, Jean. *Six Books on a Commonwealth.*

Fénelon, François. *The Adventures of Telemachus.*

Hobbes, Thomas. *Leviathan.*

Molière. *The Middle-Class Gentleman.*

Richelieu. *Political Testament.*

Saint-Simon. *Memoirs.*

Tocqueville, Alexis de. *The Ancien Régime and the French Revolution.*

Anthologies

Beik, William. *Louis XIV and Absolutism: A Brief Study with Documents* (2000).

Gregg, Stephen H., ed. *Empire and Identity: An Eighteenth-Century Sourcebook* (2005).

Helfferich, Tryntje, ed. and trans. *The Thirty Years War: A Documentary History* (2009).

Wilson, Peter H., comp. *The Thirty Years War: A Sourcebook* (2010).

Studies

Anderson, Fred. *Crucible of War: The Seven Years' War and the Fate of Empire in British North America, 1754–1766* (2000).

Beik, William. *A Social and Cultural History of Early Modern France* (2009).

Bennett, Martyn. *Oliver Cromwell* (2006).

Bergin, Joseph. *Church, Society, and Religious Change in France, 1580–1730* (2009).

Brewer, John. *The Pleasures of the Imagination: English Culture in the 18th Century* (2013).

Brewer, John. *The Sinews of Power: War, Money, and the English State, 1688–1783* (2014).

Casale, Giancarlo. *The Ottoman Age of Exploration* (2010).

Clark, Christopher. *Iron Kingdom: The Rise and Downfall of Prussia, 1600–1947* (2006).

Cracraft, James. *The Revolution of Peter the Great* (2006).

Dale, Stephen F. *The Muslim Empires of the Ottomans, Safavids, and Mughals* (2010).

Fowler, William M., Jr. *Empires at War: The Seven Years' War and the Struggle for North America, 1754–1763* (2005).

Harris, Tim. *Revolution: The Great Crisis of the British Monarchy, 1685–1720* (2006).

Hufton, Owlen. *Europe: Privilege and Protest, 1730–1788* (2001).

Hughes, Lindsey. *Russia in the Age of Peter the Great* (2000).

Ingrao, Charles. *The Habsburg Monarchy, 1618–1815* (2000).

Jones, Colin. *The Great Nation: France from Louis XV to Napoleon, 1715–99* (2003).

Levi, Anthony. *Louis XIV* (2004).

Linebaugh, Peter. *The London Hanged: Crime and Civil Society in the Eighteenth Century* (2006).

Martinich, A. P. *Hobbes* (2005).

Matthee, Rudolph P. *The Politics of Trade in Safavid Iran: Silk for Silver, 1600–1730* (2006).

Newman, Andrew J. *Safavid Iran: Rebirth of a Persian Empire* (2008).

Ormrod, David. *The Rise of Commercial Empires: England and the Netherlands in the Age of Mercantilism, 1650–1770* (2003).

Prak, Maarten. *The Dutch Republic in the Seventeenth Century: The Golden Age* (2005).

Quataert, Donald. *The Ottoman Empire, 1700–1822* (2000).

Rowlands, Guy. *The Dynastic State and the Army under Louis XIV: Royal Service and Private Interest, 1661–1701* (2002).

Smith, Jay M. *Nobility Reimagined: The Patriotic Nation in Eighteenth-Century France* (2005).

Streusand, Douglas E. *Islamic Gunpowder Empires: Ottomans, Safavids, and Mughals* (2010).

Szabo, Franz A. J. *The Seven Years' War in Europe, 1756–1763* (2007).

Wheatcroft, Andrew. *The Enemy at the Gate: Habsburgs, Ottomans, and the Battle for Europe* (2009).

Whisenhunt, William B., and Peter Stearns. *Catherine the Great: Enlightened Empress of Russia* (2006).

Zagorin, Perez. *Hobbes and the Law of Nature* (2009).

For additional resources, including maps, primary sources, visuals, web links, and quizzes, please go to **www.oup.com/us/backman**.

Reference Maps

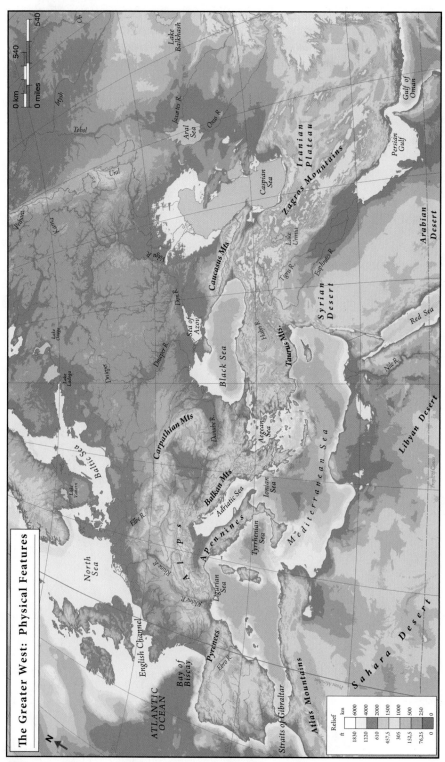

The Greater West: Physical Features

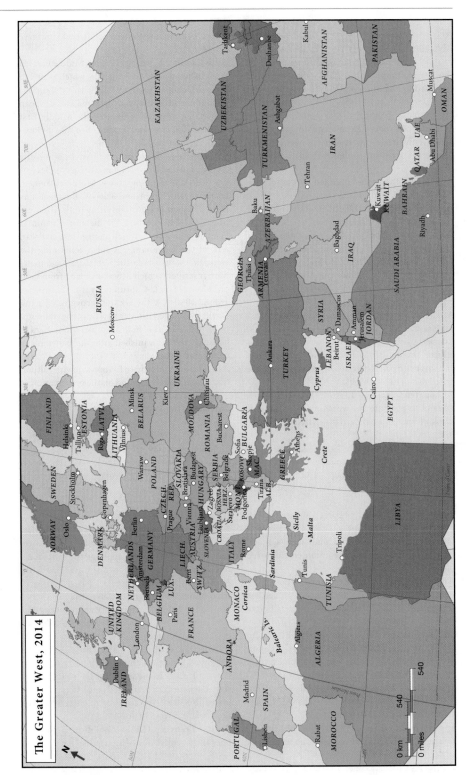

The Greater West, 2014

Glossary

A

Abbasids   Dynasty of Islamic caliphs who came to power in 750 and remained formal heads of the Islamic Empire until 1258, when they were unseated by the Mongols. Moved Islamic capital from Damascus to Baghdad.

absolutism   Political theory granting limitless authority to a sovereign ruler, holding that a sovereign entrusted with absolute power will best protect the sovereign's subjects from disorder and chaos.

Academy   The school founded by the philosopher Plato in Athens in 385 BCE.

Act of Union   (1800) Parliamentary legislation that united Great Britain and Ireland.

Acts of Toleration   Throughout the 17th and 18th centuries, laws promulgated to offer full or partial constitutional rights to Jews.

aestheticism   The belief, popular in the late 19th century, that art and artists have no obligation other than to strive for beauty.

Afrikaners   The descendants of the first Dutch settlers of South Africa; formerly known as the Boers; the language they speak is called Afrikaans.

Ahura Mazda   The One Lord or eternal God, worshipped by Zoroastrians, who believe he is the creator of all living things.

Akhenaten   (r. 1352–1336 BCE) Pharaoh whose attempt to promote the worship of the sun god, Aten, ultimately weakened his dynasty's position in Egypt.

Alexander the Great   (356–323 BCE) The Macedonian king whose conquest of the Persian Empire led to the greatly increased cultural interactions of Greece and the Middle East in the Hellenistic Age.

Anabaptists   Apocalyptic sect of Swiss exiles who rejected infant baptism, called for a second baptism in adulthood, and embraced a literal reading of scripture and the imminent approach of Christ's Second Coming.

Ancien Régime   **(Old Regime)** The French aristocracy from 1648 to 1789, seen as a golden age (for those privileged enough to enjoy it) before the French Revolution.

anti-Semitism   Term coined in 1881 to describe the vicious hatred toward and persecution of Jews, both officially and unofficially, that emerged across Europe in the 19th century.

apartheid   Official policy of racial segregation instituted in South Africa by the Afrikaner-dominated National Party in 1948.

appeasement   In the 1930s, the granting of political and territorial concessions to Hitler's Germany by many Western countries to preserve peace.

Arab Revolt   Uprising (1916) of Middle Eastern Arab tribes against Turkish rule, which aimed to replace Ottoman imperial rule with autonomous Arab countries but instead furthered the European imperialist project by dividing the Middle East between England and France. See also **Sykes–Picot Agreement**.

Arab Spring   Wave of rebellions in ethnically Arab countries, beginning in Tunisia in December 2010 and rippling across Morocco, Yemen, Iraq, Bahrain, Egypt, and Kuwait. The rebellions turned violent in Libya, resulting in the eventual overthrow and death of the dictator Muammar Qaddafi, and in Syria, which plunged into civil war.

Ark of the Covenant   A chest containing the stone tables on which the Ten Commandments were inscribed, which Moses received from God on Mount Sinai. Captured by the Philistines around 1050 BCE, the ark was recovered by King David (r. ca. 1005–965 BCE), whose son Solomon (r. ca. 965–928 BCE) built a temple in Jerusalem to house it. The ark vanished after the Babylonians conquered Jerusalem in 586 BCE.

Ashkenazim   Northern European Jewish cultural tradition uniquely focused on the preservation of Talmudic tradition.

atheism   The rejection, or absence, of religious belief.

Augustus   Original title of the Roman emperors; given first to Octavius.

Avesta   The holy book of the Zoroastrians.

ayatollah   Arabic, "sign from God"; the supreme clerical authority in Iran.

B

Ba'ath Party   Founded in 1947 by Arab Christian writer Michel Aflaq as the political representation of secular **pan-Arabism**, applying socialist ideals of state-sponsored care for the masses (from the Arab word for "renaissance").

baby boom   Demographic bubble in the United States (1946–1964) when postwar prosperity and the return of soldiers from combat resulted in an elevated birth rate.

Babylonian Captivity   After the Chaldaeans destroyed Jerusalem and the Temple in 587 BCE, they took many of the surviving Jews back east as slaves, where they remained until they were released in 538 BCE by the Persian emperor Cyrus the Great (r. 576–530 BCE).

Bacon, Francis   (1561–1626) British philosopher and scientist who—by arguing that thinkers should amass many observations and then draw general conclusions based on these data—pioneered the scientific method and inductive reasoning.

Baghdad   The capital and largest city of modern Iraq, in the center of the country on the Tigris River. Founded in the 8th century, it became a large and powerful city whose greatness is reflected in the *Arabian Nights*.

Balfour Declaration   Agreement (1917) that announced Britain's support for a national Jewish homeland in Palestine.

Baroque Age   Concurrent with the **Ancien Régime**, an era in Europe of extraordinary artistic accomplishment in the service of the tremendously wealthy and privileged aristocratic class.

Bastille   A royal fortress and prison in Paris. In June 1789, a Revolutionary crowd attacked the Bastille to show support for the newly created National Assembly. The fall of the Bastille was the first instance of the people's role in Revolutionary change in France.

Battle of Britain   The World War II air campaign waged by the German Air Force (Luftwaffe) against the United Kingdom during the summer and autumn of 1940. The failure of Nazi Germany to achieve its objective of destroying Britain's air defenses is considered by historians its first major defeat and a crucial turning point in the war.

Battle of Midway   A crucial naval battle in the Pacific theater of World War II; between June 4 and 7, 1942, six months after Japan's attack on Pearl Harbor, the U.S. Navy decisively defeated an attacking fleet of the Imperial Japanese Navy.

Battle of Waterloo   The last battle lost by Napoleon; it took place near Brussels on June 18, 1815, and led to the deposed emperor's final exile.

Bayle, Pierre   (1647–1706) French **philosophe** best known for his seminal work, the *Historical and Critical Dictionary*, published beginning in 1697.

Berlin airlift   The 1948 transport of vital supplies to West Berlin by air, primarily under U.S. auspices, in response to a blockade of the city that had been instituted by the Soviet Union to force the Allies to abandon West Berlin.

Big Science   A term used by scientists and historians to describe a series of changes in science that occurred in industrial nations during and after World War II as scientific progress increasingly came to rely on large-scale projects usually funded by national governments or groups of governments.

bin Laden, Osama   (1957–2011) Leader of the militant Islamic group al-Qaeda, which executed terrorist plots, including the September 11, 2001, attacks on the United States, to end the presence of U.S. forces in his home country, Saudi Arabia.

bishop   A high-ranking Christian cleric, in modern churches usually in charge of a diocese and in some churches regarded as having received the highest ordination in unbroken succession from the **twelve apostles**.

von Bismarck, Otto   (1815–1898) Leading Prussian politician and German prime minister who waged war to create a united German Empire, which was established in 1871.

Black Death   Successive outbreaks of bubonic plague, beginning in 1347, that killed up to a third of European and Muslim populations over the course of the 14th century.

Blitzkrieg   Nazi strategy of "lightning war" that used rapid motorized firepower to overwhelm an enemy before it could mount a defense.

Boer War   Conflict (1899–1902) between British and **Afrikaners** (formerly known as "Boers") in South Africa, with terrible casualties on both sides.

Bolsheviks   Political party led by Vladimir Lenin in the Russian (Bolshevik) Revolution that overthrew the Russian government in 1917, establishing a form of Communism that maintained power in the Soviet Union until 1991. A variation on classical Marxism, requiring the systematic use of violence, the establishment of a supposedly temporary dictatorship by party members to effect the overthrow of pre-revolutionary practices, and the violent exportation of revolution to other countries.

Boniface VIII   (r. 1294–1303) The pope whose clash with King Philip IV of France left the papacy considerably weakened.

Book of the Dead   An anthology of prayers, poems, and similar texts collected during the Egyptian Middle Kingdom (2035–1640 BCE). Placed in the coffin, the Book of the Dead was believed to allow the deceased to enter paradise.

bourgeoisie   The prosperous and primarily urban middle class of Enlightenment Europe.

Boxer Rebellion   Violent attempt (1898–1901) by Chinese peasants, motivated by millennial Buddhist beliefs, to purge Westerners and Western influence from China.

Bronze Age   The period between 4000 and 1500 BCE characterized by the ability of ancient Near East inhabitants to smelt copper (and its alloy, bronze, which combines copper with tin) for weapons, farm implements, and tools.

C

Caesar, Julius (100–44 BCE) The Roman general who conquered the Gauls, invaded Britain, and expanded Rome's territory in Anatolia. He became the dictator of Rome in 46 BCE. His assassination led to the rise of his grandnephew and adopted son, Gaius Octavius Caesar, who ruled the empire as Caesar Augustus.

Cairo Declaration on Human Rights Adopted in 1990 by the Organization of the Islamic Conference to replace the earlier (and secular) **Universal Declaration of Human Rights** with a specifically Islamic conceptualization.

caliph Successor to the Prophet Muhammad as political and religious leader of the Islamic world. Meaning "deputy" in the literal sense, in common usage it was roughly comparable to the English word "emperor."

Calvin, John (1509–1564) French-born theologian and reformer whose radical form of Protestantism, known as Calvinism, was adopted in many Swiss cities, notably Geneva.

capitalism The modern economic system characterized by an entrepreneurial class of property owners who employ others and produce something (or provide services) for a market to make a profit.

capitulations Trade agreements between the Ottoman Empire and European nations that by the 19th century overwhelmingly favored European interests.

Carolingian Renaissance A cultural and intellectual flowering that took place around the court of **Charlemagne** in the late 8th and early 9th centuries.

Carolingians Ambitious Frankish dynasty that overthrew the **Merovingians**, defended western Christendom against Muslim invaders, and united France.

Catholic Reformation General reform of Catholic life initiated by the **Council of Trent** (1546–1563). Also known as the "Counter-Reformation."

di Cavour, Camillo (1810–1861) Prime minister of Piedmont-Sardinia and founder of the Italian Liberal Party; he played a key role in the movement for Italian unification under the Piedmontese king, Victor Emmanuel II.

censor A powerful office in the Roman Republic, whose duties were to maintain the census, to administer the state's finances for public works, and to preserve public morals.

Charlemagne (r. 767–814) The Carolingian king whose conquests vastly expanded the Frankish kingdom. In 800, he was crowned emperor by the pope in Rome, establishing a precedent that would have wide-ranging consequences for western Europe's relationship with the eastern Roman Empire in Byzantium and for the relationship between the papacy and secular rulers.

Charles Martel (r. 718–741) The Frankish ruler who began the series of military campaigns that established the Franks as the undisputed masters of all Gaul; grandfather of Charlemagne, Charles Martel ("the Hammer") laid the groundwork for the rise of the Carolingian dynasty.

Chartist movement Labor movement begun by the London Working Men's Association in 1838.

chivalry In 12th-century Europe, an ethic that embraced ideal knightly behavior: comportment, noble demeanor, learning, and piety.

Christian democracy Western European ideological hybrid of social conservatism and economic liberalism.

Christian humanism Anticlerical movement of the northern Renaissance that emphasized the simple reading of scripture (especially the New Testament), the singing of hymns, and communal prayer.

Church of England Protestant church founded by King Henry VIII of England when he broke with the Catholic Church in 1533. Also known as the Anglican Church; the monarchy is its supreme head.

Ciompi Rebellion Popular uprising in Italy in 1378.

city-state A form of political organization that incorporates a single city with its surrounding countryside and villages.

civilization A way of life based in cities with dense populations organized as political states, large buildings constructed for communal activities, the production of food, diverse economies, a sense of local identity, and some knowledge of writing.

classicism Artistic movement that replaced the flourishes of the Baroque with a more controlled and formal sensibility.

Cleisthenes (ca. 570–508 BCE) Statesman regarded as the founder of Athenian democracy, serving as chief archon (highest magistrate) of Athens (ca. 525–524 BCE). He successfully allied himself with the popular Assembly against the nobles and imposed democratic reform. Perhaps his most important innovation was the basing of individual political responsibility on citizenship of a place rather than on membership in a clan.

Cold War Term coined by American financier and presidential advisor Bernard Baruch to describe the relationship (1947–1991) between the Soviet bloc and Western nations allied with the United States; each side possessed nuclear weapons, yet neither side dared to either use those weapons or disarm.

College of Cardinals Created by Pope Nicholas II (r. 1059–1061) and given sole power to elect the next pope.

Columbian Exchange The widespread exchange of peoples, plants, animals, diseases, goods, and culture between the African and Eurasian landmass and the region that encompasses the Americas, Australia, and the Pacific islands, precipitated by the 1492 voyage of **Christopher Columbus**.

Columbus, Christopher (1451–1506) A Genoese sailor who persuaded King Ferdinand and Queen Isabella of Spain to fund his expedition across the Atlantic, with the purpose of discovering a new trade route to Asia. His miscalculations landed him and his crew in the Bahamas and the island of Hispaniola in 1492.

comfort women Euphemism used in imperial Japan for the quarter-million Chinese, Filipino, and other women captured and forced into sexual slavery in World War II.

command economies Economies that aim to provide the highest possible yield for whoever holds the raw materials and captive markets.

Communism Socialist movement that advocates the destruction of capitalism and the development of a new, classless society of freedom.

The Communist Manifesto Book by Karl Marx and Friedrich Engels (1848) that presents a Marxist view of history as class struggle.

Concert of Europe The body of diplomatic agreements designed primarily by Austrian minister Klemens von Metternich between 1814 and 1848 and supported by other European powers until the start of World War I in 1914. Its goal was to maintain a balance of power on the Continent and to prevent destabilizing social and political change in Europe.

Concordat of Worms The agreement between pope and emperor in 1122 that ended the investiture conflict and established the independence of the papacy.

Conference of Berlin International conference (1884–1885) of European nations that set the standards by which any European country could claim an African territory over another European rival, touching off the "Scramble for Africa."

Congress of Vienna Conference of European diplomats convened from 1814 to 1815 to redraw boundaries and work toward peace after decades of conflict.

conquistadores The 16th-century Spanish forces who subdued South and Central America.

conservatism Political approach that values tradition and stability above the individual.

Constantine the Great (r. 312–337) The first emperor of Rome to convert to Christianity, Constantine founded a new imperial capital, **Constantinople**, in 324.

Constantinople Founded by the emperor Constantine on the site of a maritime settlement known as Byzantium, Constantinople became the new capital of the Roman Empire in 324 and continued to be the seat of imperial power after its capture by the Ottoman Turks in 1453. It is now known as Istanbul.

constitutionalism A system of government in which rulers share power with parliaments made up of elected representatives.

consul In the Roman Republic, the executive office in charge of the government.

Continental System Economic system, implemented by Napoleon, with two key aims: to create an integrated Continental economy and to bring about the collapse of Britain through the imposition of a strict trade embargo.

Copernicus, Nicolaus (1473–1543) Polish astronomer who advanced the theory that the Earth moved around the sun.

cottage industry The transfer of textile production from urban industry, where it was controlled by guilds, to rural producers, particularly women. Also known as the "putting-out system."

Council of Trent Ecumenical council convened from 1546 to 1563 to address the challenges of Protestantism by clarifying the teachings and practices of the Catholic Church.

Counter-Reformation See **Catholic Reformation**.

covenant The special promise God made to the Jews, symbolized by Moses's leading of the Hebrews out of bondage in Egypt and into the Promised Land; in return, the Jews agreed to live by the Torah.

Crimean War Rooted in the longstanding desire of Russia to increase its influence over the Ottoman Empire, the immediate cause of the war (1853–1856) had to do with Russian claims to protective oversight over Orthodox Christians in the Ottoman Empire, but more strategic goals were at stake. The war pitted France and Britain, who were allied with the Ottomans, against Russia. Although Russia accepted unfavorable terms at a conference in Paris in 1856 that ended the conflict, both sides performed ineptly, a fact that became widely known because the war was the first conflict to be covered by journalists and photographers.

Cuban Missile Crisis Standoff between the Soviet Union and the United States in 1962, when Soviet leader Nikita Khrushchev built military bases in Cuba equipped with nuclear missiles. After two weeks of intense negotiations, Khrushchev withdrew the missiles.

cult of domesticity Cultural view in the 19th century that idealized women's role in the home, discouraging them from seeking work or other opportunities outside of their domestic duties.

cuneiform Technique of writing developed in Mesopotamia whereby wedge-shaped marks were impressed in clay tablets.

curiales The class of urban elites in ancient Rome who, although they were unsalaried, were responsible for municipal government and tax collection; obliged to make up any shortfalls in civic finance from their own personal wealth, they were entitled to retain a portion of the tax revenues they collected for personal use.

Customs Union The free-trade zone established by Prussia in the early 19th century; an important early step in German unification. Also known as *Zollverein* (German for "Customs Union").

Cynicism In philosophy, the school of thought that originated in ancient Greece and believes virtue to be the only good and self-control to be the only means of achieving virtue.

Cyrus the Great (ca. 585–529 BCE). Founder of the Persian Empire.

D

Dark Ages The period in western Europe from the 4th to the 8th centuries, so named because of the chaos that reigned after the fall of the western Roman Empire and the endless depredations of various barbarian invasions. See also **Late Antiquity**.

David (r. ca. 1005–965 BCE) Hebrew king who pushed the borders of the Israelite kingdom to their greatest extent and established Jerusalem as the capital city.

Declaration of the Rights of Man and Citizen The preamble to the French constitution drafted in August 1789; it established the sovereignty of the nation and equal rights for citizens.

decolonization European withdrawal during the 20th century from its former colonies.

deism Enlightenment-era belief in a single and possibly benevolent God who created the cosmos—but who plays no active role in it. As a result, a dual policy of religious freedom and of freedom from religious intolerance is essential to human progress.

Delian League A military alliance formed in 478 BCE (Athens assumed control a year later) among all the Greek poleis, dedicated to maintaining a strong defense—particularly against Persia.

democracy In its original incarnation in ancient Greece, this form of government allowed a class of propertied male citizens to participate in the governance of their polis (city-state) but excluded women, slaves, and citizens without property from the political process.

Descartes, René (1596–1650) French philosopher and mathematician who emphasized the use of deductive reasoning.

détente A "loosening" of tensions between two nations. Used especially to describe efforts to improve diplomatic ties between the United States and the Soviet Union in the 1970s and 1980s. Ironically, *détente* is also a colloquial French term for the trigger of a gun.

dhimmi Legal status of Jewish and Christian populations living under Muslim rule; officially granted freedom of religion, Jews and Christians had to accept certain restrictions on their communal practice and pay a poll tax (*jizya*) in return for Islamic protection. Restrictions included bans on any public expression of faith and curtailment of the ability to build or repair synagogues and churches.

dialectical materialism In Marxist theory, the idea that history is driven forward by materialist concerns; to Lenin, this led inevitably to confrontation between the proletariat and the bourgeoisie.

Diaspora The "exile" or "scattering" of the Hebrews after the Assyrians brutally conquered the Kingdom of Israel in 721 BCE and the Chaldaeans (or Neo-Babylonians) conquered Judah in 587 BCE.

Diderot, Denis (1713–1784) French **philosophe** who was the guiding force behind the publication of the first encyclopedia. The *Encyclopedia* showed how reason could be applied to nearly all realms of thought and aimed to be a compendium of all human knowledge.

Diet The medieval German parliament.

Diocletian (r. 284–305) Roman emperor who established the **tetrarchy** (rule by four) and initiated the **Great Persecution**, a time when many Christians became martyrs for their faith.

Documentary Hypothesis The belief of many modern biblical scholars that the Torah was compiled from four original sources: "J," by the Yahwist (ca. 950 BCE); "E," by the Elohist (ca. 750 BCE); "D," by the Deuteronomist (ca. 650 BCE); and "P," by the Priestly Author (ca. 550 BCE).

Dominicans   Mendicant order focused on education that established schools across Europe.

E

Edict of Milan   Issued by the Roman emperor Constantine in 313 CE, it legalized Christianity and guaranteed religious freedom for all faiths within the empire.

Edict of Nantes   Decree by Henri IV in 1598 that guaranteed religious freedom, with certain restrictions, throughout France.

Elizabeth I   (r. 1558–1603) English queen who oversaw the return of the Protestant Church of England and, in 1588, the successful defense of the realm against the Spanish Armada.

empire   A centralized political entity consolidated through the conquest and colonization of other regions and peoples to benefit the ruler and his homeland.

enclosure movement   Trend of aristocratic landowners toward evicting small farmers (by enclosing formerly open fields with stone walls or hedges) and instead using those fields for the more profitable grazing of livestock, especially sheep.

English Peasants' Revolt   Popular uprising in England in 1381.

En-Heduanna   (ca. 2285–2250 BCE) Daughter of King Sargon of Akkad and the poet who is the world's first author known by name.

Enlightenment   Term coined in the second half of the 18th century to describe an array of intellectual and cultural activities of the 1700s distinguished by a worldview informed by rational values and scientific inquiry.

Epic of Gilgamesh   One of the earliest known works of literature, originating in Sumer but first recorded by Babylonian scribes; relates the adventures of the semimythical Sumerian king Gilgamesh as he battles gods and monsters in pursuit of enlightenment.

Epicureanism   Philosophy based on the work of the Greek philosopher Epicurus (341—270 BCE) that promotes a life free of pain and fear as the way to happiness.

epistemology   The philosophical inquiry into the nature of knowledge (and, by extension, learning).

equestrians   In ancient Rome, an upper class ranking immediately below senators.

Erasmus, Desiderius (ca. 1469–1536) Dutch-born scholar, social commentator, and Christian humanist whose new translation of the Bible influenced the theology of Martin Luther.

Essenes   An ascetic and eschatological sect within Second Temple Judaism.

Estates General   French parliament, established by the Capetian kings. Reestablished in 1789 (after having last met in 1614) at the behest of the French aristocracy. The three estates were the nobles, the clergy, and the common people.

Etruscans   A literate and prosperous people who associated with the **Latins** and profoundly influenced the emerging religious and moral culture of Rome.

European Union   United group of independent European nations established in 1993 to provide a process for coordinating policies formed at the level of member states.

evangelicalism   Protestant style of worship developed in the Protestant Church that emphasizes the work of the Holy Spirit in the world and the centrality of biblical truth while retaining more of the traditional elements of Protestant denominations.

existentialism   Rationalist philosophy associated with Jean-Paul Sartre whose key tenet, "existence precedes essence," demands that we take action and make something of the world, or at least of our lives in it.

F

Fascism   The belief that force, directly applied to achieve a specific end, is the best form of government, exemplified by the dictatorships of Adolf Hitler (r. 1934–1945) and Benito Mussolini (r. 1922–1945).

fatwa   An Islamic legal pronouncement.

feminist movement   A series of movements from the 19th century through the present day that aim to reform policies and practices that oppress the rights and well-being of women.

Fertile Crescent   The region of the Middle East roughly framed by the Mediterranean to the west, the Arabian peninsula to the south, and the Tarsus and Zagros mountains to the north and east. The Tigris and Euphrates rivers flow through the center of this region, whose rich soils and abundant water gave rise to early agriculture. The Fertile Crescent connected central Asian and eastern Mediterranean economies.

feudal bonds   The relationship between lord and vassal, whereby the lord granted dominion over property to the vassal in exchange for the vassal's pledge of service to the lord.

Final Solution   Nazi program of systematic deportation and murder of Jews throughout Germany and all German-occupied territories during World War II.

Five-Year Plans   Soviet effort launched under Joseph Stalin in 1928 to replace the market with a state-owned and state-managed economy to promote rapid economic development over a five-year period and thereby catch and overtake the leading capitalist countries.

flying shuttle   Invented by Englishman John Kay in 1733, this device sped up the process of weaving.

Fourteen Points   Woodrow Wilson's proposal, presented to the Paris Peace Conference (1919), for rebuilding Europe in the aftermath of World War I; ultimately rejected because of French and British concerns.

Franciscans   Mendicant order established by Saint Francis of Assisi (1181–1226) dedicated to preaching and service to the urban poor.

Franco, Francisco   (1892–1975) Right-wing general who in 1936 successfully overthrew the democratic republic in Spain and instituted a repressive dictatorship.

freemasonry   Secret society that claimed its origins lay in medieval trade guilds; its members, wealthy bourgeoisie and noblemen alike, met in private clubs (or "lodges") to conduct business.

Fronde   Rebellion (1648–1653) of French aristocrats against the tax policies of Cardinal Mazarin during the regency for the underage King Louis XIV.

fundamentalism   American Protestant style of worship that insists on the presence of a fundamental Truth in every scriptural passage and urges personal and societal reform before the approach of Armageddon; from the 1980s, fundamentalism has had considerable influence on American politics, particularly the Republican Party.

G

Galilei, Galileo   (1564–1642) Italian physicist and inventor; the implications of his ideas raised the ire of the Catholic Church, and he was forced to retract most of his findings.

da Gama, Vasco   (ca. 1460s–1524) A Portuguese explorer and the first European to reach India by sea (1497–1499), linking Europe and Asia for the first time by ocean route.

Gandhi, Mohandas (Mahatma)   (1869–1948) Indian leader who advocated nonviolent noncooperation to protest colonial rule and helped win home rule for India in 1947.

Garibaldi, Giuseppe   (1807–1882) Italian revolutionary leader who led the fight to free Sicily and Naples from the Habsburg Empire; the lands were then peacefully annexed by Sardinia to produce a unified Italy.

general theory of relativity   Einstein's theory (1915) describing gravity's relationship to **space-time**.

German Peasants' Revolt   A widespread popular rebellion in the German-speaking areas of central Europe from 1524 to 1525.

ghettos   In early modern and modern Europe, segregated communities of Jews in cities.

Girondists   One of several factions during the French Revolution; a relatively moderate group, they championed a constitutional monarchy until they were driven from power by the more radical **Jacobins**.

glasnost   "Openness," literally, in Russian. Specifically, the policy in the Soviet Union under Premier Mikhail Gorbachev to relax the traditional censorship of Soviet television, radio, and print media and to permit greater freedom of speech.

Glorious Revolution   Coup in 1688 that deposed the Catholic king James II of England and replaced him with the popular Protestant ruler of Holland, William of Orange (who was married to James II's daughter, Mary).

gold standard   Monetary system, initially introduced in the West by Britain in 1821 and abandoned by most countries in the aftermath of the Great Depression, that pegs a currency to the price of gold.

Good Friday Accord   Treaty signed in 1998 that ended eighty years of terrorist conflict in Northern Ireland.

Great Depression   (1929–1936) Global economic depression that began with the crash of the New York Stock Exchange on October 29, 1929, resulting in massive unemployment and economic crises worldwide.

Great Fear   The term used by historians to describe the French rural panic of 1789, which led to peasant attacks on aristocrats or on seigneurial records of peasants' dues.

Great Persecution   The violent program initiated by the Roman emperor Diocletian in 303 to make Christians convert to traditional religion or risk confiscation of their property and even death.

Great Purge   Brutal efforts, beginning with show trials in 1936, by Josef Stalin (r. 1931–1953) to eliminate anyone he considered an enemy of the Soviet Union.

Great Pyramids The ancient Egyptian pyramids located at Giza, on the outskirts of modern Cairo.

Great Schism The papal dispute of 1378–1417 when the church had competing popes. Also known as the "Great Western Schism," to distinguish it from the longstanding rupture between the Greek East and Latin West.

Gregorian Reform The papal movement for church reform associated with Gregory VII (r. 1073–1085). Its ideals included ending three practices: the purchase of church offices, clerical marriage, and **lay investiture**.

guilds Artisanal and commercial trade associations that set prices, quality standards, methods and volume of production, and wages paid to workers. Guilds also assigned market shares to individual artisans or merchants.

gulag Network of Soviet Russian prison camps used to incarcerate political dissidents and enemies. Begun under Vladimir Lenin and greatly expanded under Joseph Stalin, the gulag accounted for the deaths of roughly a million prisoners annually from the 1930s to the 1980s.

H

hadith The written record of the actions and non-Qur'anic teachings of the Prophet Muhammad. The two most significant collections are those by al-Bukhari (d. 870) and al-Muslim (d. 875).

hajj The pilgrimage of Muslims to Mecca, held annually. All able-bodied Muslims are expected to undertake the hajj at least once in their lives.

Hamas Conservative religious–political Palestinian group (and offshoot of the **Muslim Brotherhood**) equally devoted to charitable campaigns and social work among the Palestinians and to a terrorist war on Israel.

Hammurabi (r. ca. 1792–1750 BCE) Ruler of Babylon who issued a collection of laws that constitutes the world's oldest surviving law code.

Hasidim Adherents to a revivalist movement in Judaism, started in the mid-18th century in the Polish–Lithuanian Commonwealth by the Ba'al Shem Tov (d. 1760). Using highly emotive language and physical expression, Hasidic Judaism challenged the rather staid formalism of synagogue worship.

Haskalah Hebrew term for "enlightenment."

Hatshepsut (r. ca. 1479–1458 BCE) New Kingdom Egyptian pharaoh who launched several successful military campaigns and extended trade and diplomacy. She was an ambitious builder who probably constructed the first tomb in the Valley of the Kings. Although she never pretended to be a man, she was routinely portrayed with a masculine figure and a ceremonial beard.

heliocentrism First articulated by Copernicus, the observation that the Earth is one of several planets that orbit around a stationary sun.

helot Slave owned by the city-state of ancient Sparta. Comprising roughly 75 percent of the Spartan population, helots performed virtually all the labor, leaving the Spartans themselves free to perform military and civic service.

hieroglyphs System of writing used in ancient Egypt, especially in official records.

hijab The "covering" of women required in Islamic society. Varies widely from country to country, depending on ethnicity, denomination, and, to some extent, class. Least extensive covering is a simple headscarf; most extensive is the full-length burqa.

Hijrah The migration, or exodus, of Prophet Muhammad and his company of the faithful from Mecca to Medina in 622 CE. Marks Year 1 in the Islamic calendar (1 AH).

Hippocratic oath An oath historically taken by physicians, it is one of the most widely known of Greek medical texts. Scholars widely believe that Hippocrates (ca. 460–378 BCE), often called the father of Western medicine, wrote the oath.

historical materialism In Marxist theory, the process by which economic concerns propel historical change.

Hitler, Adolf (1889–1945) The author of *Mein Kampf* ("My Struggle") and leader of the Nazis who became chancellor of Germany in 1933. Hitler and his Nazi regime started World War II and orchestrated the **Holocaust**.

Holocaust The systematic murder of some 6 million Jews by the Nazis during World War II in an attempt to exterminate European Jewry.

Homer (8th century BCE) Greece's first and most famous author, who composed *The Iliad* and *The Odyssey*.

honestiores The Roman senatorial and equestrian classes, municipal officials, and army veterans, and their status entitling them to immunity from torture, lesser criminal fines, and, in capital crimes, exemption from crucifixion.

hoplites Ancient Greek infantrymen serving in a phalanx; name derives from Greek word (*hoplos*) for the smallish, circular shields they carried.

hubris Arrogant self-pride, the deadliest of moral sins to the ancient Greeks; specifically, the delusional belief that one is in control of one's own fate. Frequently used as a plot device to trigger the dire events in Greek tragedy.

Huguenots The Calvinists in 16th-century France, led by Henri de Navarre.

humanism A literary and linguistic movement cultivated particularly during the Renaissance (ca. 1350–1600) and founded on reviving classical Latin and Greek texts, styles, and values.

humiliores Everyone in the Roman Empire apart from the honestiores and the slaves (the latter, in terms of the law, were counted as property rather than people). The humiliores were expected to obey the law, pay their taxes, participate in public religious rites, and hold to the ethical duties of family care and public service.

Hundred Years' War From 1337 to 1453 CE, the war fought between England and France, beginning when England's king Edward III (r. 1327–1377) laid claim to the French throne; France (led, at one point, by the young girl Joan of Arc) eventually won.

Hyksos ascendancy The Second Intermediate Period (1640–1570 BCE) of the Middle Kingdom, so named because of the revolt of foreign laborers against the Egyptian government.

I

Ideal Forms In Plato's philosophy, the concept of a perfect and ultimate reality, of which our own perceived reality is but a flawed and flimsy reflection. Because we have a dualistic nature composed of an eternal soul temporarily housed in a flawed and mortal body, we can apprehend and aspire to that perfection.

ideologies Coherent sets of beliefs about the way the social and political order should be organized.

illuminationism Twelfth-century Persian philosophical program that attempts to harmonize Sufism, Shi'ism, and rational philosophy.

imam In Sunni Islam, a community leader who recites Qur'anic verses during prayer services. In Shi'i Islam, a charismatic spiritual leader, a successor and descendant of the Prophet Muhammad through the line of Fatima and Ali.

imperator Title assumed by Augustus and all subsequent rulers of Rome; often translated as "emperor," but in the Republic referred to a triumphant military general.

imperialism European (and, later, American) dominance of non-Western cultures for the exploitation of natural resources as well as political gain. See also **informal imperialism** and **new imperialism**.

Indo-European A horde of nomadic and herding nations, loosely related by their dialects of the language family, who began to migrate from their homeland near the Black Sea toward western Europe, the Aegean, and Anatolia from about 2000 BCE. Other groups migrated eastward.

indulgences Donations to the Catholic Church as a means of satisfying the requirements for the forgiveness of sin.

Industrial Revolution The burgeoning 19th-century economy driven by mechanization, factories, an investment in infrastructure, and a growing workforce.

informal imperialism The use of indirect means to control an area. Indirect means can be a military presence but is usually centered on economic control. Trading and loans are two essential parts of economic-centered informal imperialism.

inquisition Campaign by the Catholic Church to identify and correct heresy; heretics who would not admit their errors were punished, in some instances brutally.

Intifada "Uprising." Organized mass protests of Palestinians against Israeli occupation of the West Bank and Gaza (1987–1993). The Second Intifada lasted from 2000 to 2005.

Ionian League An alliance (ca. 750 BCE) of several Greek coastal cities in Anatolia organized by the vibrant and prosperous city of Miletus.

Iron Curtain Military and ideological barrier dividing the Soviet bloc from western Europe between the end of World War II and the dissolution of the Soviet Union.

Israel In antiquity, one of two Hebrew kingdoms (937–721 BCE), this one in the north of Palestine with Shechem as its capital. See also **Judah**.

J

Jacobins Radical party that seized power from the **Girondists** during the French Revolution. Resolutely antimonarchist, the Jacobins executed King Louis XVI and his family in 1793, outlawed Christianity, and sought to create a classless society based on radical principles.

Jacquerie Popular uprising in France (1358).

al-Jahiliyya Term (literally "Age of Ignorance" or "Age of Barbarism") used by Arab historians to describe the era between the death of Jesus and the birth of Muhammad.

Janissaries Elite military caste in the Ottoman Empire, 14th–19th centuries. The ranks of Janissaries were filled with Christian children, either orphaned or kidnapped from their parents, who were then converted and given a special, highly disciplined military upbringing.

Jesuits Ecclesiastical order, founded by Saint Ignacio de Loyola in 1540, particularly devoted to education and missionary work.

Jesus of Nazareth (ca. 4 BCE–30 CE) A Jewish preacher and teacher who was arrested for seditious political activity, tried, and crucified by the Romans. After his execution, his followers claimed that he had been resurrected from the dead and taken up into heaven. They began to teach that Jesus had been the divine representative of God, the messiah foretold by ancient Hebrew prophets, and that he had suffered for the sins of humanity and would return to judge all the world's inhabitants at the end of time.

jihad "Struggle," literally. Refers to any conscious, intentional, and persistent effort to advance the cause of Islam in the world. The term has a broad range of meanings, from something as innocuous as a personal vow to live a more committed Islamic life to a determination to wage religious war against the perceived enemies of God.

Joan of Arc (1412–1431) A French peasant girl whose conviction that God had sent her to save France in fact helped France win the **Hundred Years' War.**

John the Baptist (late 1st century BCE–ca. 35 CE) An itinerant preacher and a major religious figure in Christianity, he is described in the Bible as following the unique practice of baptism for the forgiveness of sins. Most scholars agree that John baptized Jesus.

Judah One of two Hebrew kingdoms (937–721 BCE), this one in the south of Palestine and centered on Jerusalem. See also **Israel**.

judges As described in the Bible, the leaders of each of the twelve tribes of Hebrews who moved into Palestine around 1200 BCE, after being delivered from Egypt.

Junkers Landed aristocracy in Brandenburg–Prussia in the 17th–18th centuries. In popular usage the term came in the 19th century to designate all types of conservative, wealthy elites.

justification by faith alone Luther's understanding that one attains salvation not through the purchasing of **indulgences** or other outward acts but simply by having faith in Christ.

Justinian I Sixth-century emperor of the eastern Roman (Byzantine) Empire, famous for waging costly wars to reunite the empire.

K

Ka'ba The holiest shrine of Islam. Temple in Mecca housing the stone believed to mark the site of Abraham's altar to Allah. Originally a pagan shrine dedicated to all the deities of the pre-Islamic Arab tribes. Site of the **hajj**.

Kabbala A mystical interpretation of scripture developed by rabbis that became newly popular in the 17th century in part via the influence of Sabbatai Zvi (1626–1676).

kalam "Theology." Unsystematic effort to provide rational explanation of basic religious mysteries in early Islam on the nature of the Qur'an and the attributes of Allah.

khan The hereditary leader of a given tribe of Mongols.

Khan, Genghis (Chinggis) (r. 1206–1227) Founder and Great Khan (emperor) of the Mongol Empire, which became the largest contiguous empire in history under his successors.

Korean War A war (1950–1953) between North and South Korea, in which a UN force led by the United States fought for the south and China fought for the north, which was also assisted by the Soviet Union. The war, which ended in stalemate, arose from the division of Korea at the end of World War II and from the global tensions of the Cold War that developed immediately afterward.

Kristallnacht "Crystal Night," literally; the "Night of Broken Glass," poetically. The organized Nazi attacks on Jewish businesses, synagogues, and homes throughout Germany on November 9, 1938. Widely regarded as the turning point from Nazi anti-Semitic discrimination to blatant pursuit of genocide.

kulak "Fist," literally. Term popularized by Lenin and Stalin to designate relatively wealthy peasant freeholders who opposed the Communist regime in early-20th-century Russia.

Kulturkampf Otto von Bismarck's "cultural war" against Catholicism in Germany.

Kyoto Protocol International agreement, adopted in 1997, to combat global warming by reducing greenhouse gas emissions. The United States is not among the almost two hundred nations that have since signed and ratified the protocol.

L

laissez-faire "Leave it alone" (French), literally. Term used to identify the economic doctrine of allowing markets to self-regulate, without government interference. First articulated by Adam Smith in *The Wealth of Nations* (1776).

Late Antiquity Term ancient historians use for the **Dark Ages**.

Lateran Agreement Agreement (1929) between Mussolini and Pope Pius XI that recognized the Vatican as a sovereign state in exchange for the Catholic Church's support of Mussolini's Fascist regime.

latifundia Slave-worked plantations in ancient Rome, especially during the Republic.

Latins Name of the original settlers of the region of Latium.

lay investiture The installation of clerics into their offices by lay rulers.

League of Augsburg Alliance forged by Holy Roman Emperor Leopold I in 1686 for defense against French expansionism; members included England, the Low Countries, Sweden, and several German principalities as well as the Holy Roman Empire.

League of Nations Woodrow Wilson's proposed international body that would arbitrate disputes, oversee demilitarization, and provide for collective security.

Lebensraum "Living space," literally. The conviction that the territorial losses forced on Germany by the Treaty of Versailles (1919) had denied the German people sufficient space in which to live and thrive. Under the Nazis, it evolved into the policy of demanding the unification of all German-inhabited lands.

legate Commander of a legion selected by the Roman emperor from members of the Senate. In smaller provinces, the legate also served as the provincial governor.

Lenin, Vladimir (1870–1924) Leader of the Bolshevik Revolution in Russia (1917) and the first leader of the Soviet Union.

liberalism Political view calling for civil liberties, equality under the law, the right to vote, and a free-market economy.

libertarian Political stance that supports small and highly limited government and opposes almost all forms of taxation.

Linear A Script used by Minoan culture on ancient Crete. Its underlying language has not been identified, and hence the script has not been deciphered.

Linear B Syllabic script used by ancient Mycenaeans in Crete. Its underlying language is an early dialect of Greek, and the script was deciphered by 1953.

Locke, John (1632–1704) English philosopher and political theorist known for his contributions to **liberalism**. Locke had great faith in human reason and believed that just societies were those that infringed least on the natural rights and freedoms of individuals.

Logos "Word," literally. Neoplatonic term for the spirit of wisdom that lies at the center of creation, from which emanate the **Ideal Forms** and all the elements of the cosmos. Term adopted by early Christians (see Gospel of John) to refer to Christ as the "Word of God" made flesh.

lord In the feudal system, the figure who could grant vassals dominion over manors.

Louis XIV (r. 1643–1715) Called the "Sun King," he is famous for his success at strengthening the institutions of the French absolutist state.

Louis XVI (r. 1774–1792) French king who was tried for treason during the French Revolution; he was executed on January 21, 1793.

lugal Old Sumerian title of city-state kings in Mesopotamia.

Luther, Martin (1483–1546) A German monk who started the Protestant Reformation in 1517 by challenging the practices and doctrines of the Catholic Church and advocating salvation through faith alone.

Lyceum School founded by the philosopher Aristotle in Athens in 335 BCE.

M

ma'at Concept of cosmic order in ancient Egypt in which everything is in perfect balance; includes the notions of meaning, justice, and truth, although in a passive sense, asking people not to upset divine harmony by attempting to alter the political and religious order.

madrasa Islamic religious school attached, administratively and often physically, to a mosque. Study focuses on memorization of the Qur'an, with subsequent forays into Islamic law and literature.

magi Zoroastrian priests.

Maginot Line Barricade of artillery casements, machine-gun pillboxes, tank formations, barbed wire, minefields, and concrete bunkers built by France along its border with Germany.

Magna Carta Agreement in 1215 between the king of England and English lords establishing certain constraints on royal power.

Mahdi Messianic figure expected by Shi'i Muslims; believed to be the return of the "Hidden Imam" who has gone into seclusion until the end of time.

mamluk A slave-soldier in the medieval Islamic world.

mandates Semi-independent states created in the Middle East by the League of Nations after World War I, dividing territories of the former Ottoman Empire between Britain and France.

Manhattan Project Secret American program to develop an atomic bomb, begun in 1939 under the scientific direction of J. Robert Oppenheimer.

manors In a feudal system, collective farms under the authority of lords.

market Term coined by economist Adam Smith (1776) to describe commerce as a rational pattern of human behavior.

Marshall Plan American plan to rebuild western Europe after World War II by providing cash, credit, raw materials, and technical assistance to jump-start industrial production.

martyr Greek for "witness," the term for someone who dies for his or her religious beliefs.

Marx, Karl (1818–1883) German philosopher and economist who believed that a revolution of the working classes would overthrow the capitalist order and create a classless society. Author of *Das Kapital* and, with Friedrich Engels, *The Communist Manifesto*.

mawali Non-Arab Muslim converts in the Islamic Empire.

Mehmed II (r. 1444–1446) The sultan under whom the Ottoman Turks conquered Constantinople in 1453.

Mehmet Ali Pasha (r. 1805–1848) Pro-Western dynastic leader of Egypt who built a powerful Egyptian military force, professionalized the government along Western lines, and developed both industry and education.

mendicant orders Groups (such as the Dominicans and the Franciscans) dedicated to assisting the clergy in the performance of their evangelical mission.

Menes (r. ca. 31st century BCE) Ancient Egyptian ruler credited with the unification of Egypt. Also known as "Narmer."

Mensheviks Faction of the Russian Revolution that was generally more moderate than Lenin's Bolshevik faction and was ultimately defeated by the **Bolsheviks** in 1917.

mercantilism The economic policy of **absolutism**, defining economic wealth as tangible assets and promoting protectionism with the aim of concentrating wealth among as few individuals as possible.

Merovingians Warrior dynasty who ruled as kings of the Franks from ca. 500 to the ascent of the **Carolingians** (ca. 754).

messiah In the Jewish tradition, an earthly savior who would bring justice and create a safe, unified state for the Jews.

von Metternich, Klemens (1773–1859) Austrian prince who took the lead in devising the post-Napoleonic settlement arranged by the Congress of Vienna (1814–1815).

modernism 1. To the Catholic Church in the early 20th century, a deplorable trend toward intellectual novelty that trivialized scriptural truth and claimed "that there is nothing divine in sacred tradition [of the church]." 2. Highly diverse cultural movement (roughly 1860–1950) that simultaneously rejects previous attitudes about how artists should work and resists the contemporary impersonality of mass-produced culture.

monasticism In the rapidly Christianizing world, the movement to reject normal family and social life, along with the concern for wealth, status, and power, in favor of a harsh life of solitude and spiritual discipline in communities of other monks.

Mongols Diverse group of nomadic Asian tribes that, through a series of brutal conquests in China, Russia, and the Muslim world, covered at its height in 1279 nearly one-quarter of the Earth's land surface.

monotheism The belief in a single, supreme deity.

Montesquieu (1689–1755) An Enlightenment thinker and writer whose most influential work was *The Spirit of Laws*, in which he analyzed the structures that shape law and characterized governments according to three types: republics, monarchies, and despotisms.

Montessori, Maria (1870–1952) An Italian physician and educator best known for the philosophy of education that bears her name. Montessori education emphasizes independence, freedom within limits, and respect for a child's natural psychological, physical, and social development.

Muhammad (ca. 570–632) The prophet of Islam. He united a community of believers around his religious tenets, above all that there was one God whose words had been revealed to him. Later, written down, these revelations became the Qur'an.

Muhammad Ali Pasha (r. 1805–1848) An Ottoman Albanian commander in the Ottoman army who became leader of Egypt with the Ottomans' initial approval. Although not a modern nationalist, he is often cited as the founder of modern Egypt because of the dramatic reforms in the military, economic, and cultural spheres that he instituted.

Muhammad ibn Saud (r. 1744–1765) Founder of the first Saudi state and the Saud dynasty.

mullah A Persian word used primarily in non-Arabic speaking Shi'i Muslim countries (e.g., Iran, Afghanistan, Pakistan) to designate a low-level cleric. It is a term of respect rather than a designation of office. With a literal meaning of "guardian" or "caretaker," it carries a colloquial sense analogous to the English word *reverend*, stripped of any ecclesial meaning. Used primarily by Shi'i Muslims and throughout Pakistan and India by both Sunnis and Shi'a.

Mulla Sadra   The greatest Muslim philosopher of the modern era; his most important book is *The Four Journeys of the Intellect* (1638).

Muslim Brotherhood   Religious–political group founded in Egypt in 1928 that, after years of repression by Egypt's military and secular regime, assumed power following elections in 2011.

Mussolini, Benito   (r. 1922–1945) The Italian founder of the Fascist Party who, after the March on Rome in 1922, became dictator of Italy; allied himself with Hitler and the Nazis during World War II.

mystery religions   Religious worship that provided initiation into secret knowledge and divine protection, including hope for a better afterlife.

N

al-Nahda   Arabic, "awakening" or "renaissance"; 19th-century Islamic intellectual and cultural movement centered in Egypt that advocated the integration of Islamic and European culture.

Napoleon Bonaparte   (1769–1821) The French general who became First Consul in 1799 and emperor (Napoleon I) in 1804; he dominated European affairs for nearly two decades while leading France against a series of coalitions in the so-called Napoleonic Wars. One of the greatest commanders in history, his campaigns are studied at military schools worldwide; his lasting legal achievement, the **Napoleonic Code**, has been adapted by dozens of nations. After losing the battle of Waterloo in 1815, he was exiled to the island of St. Helena.

Napoleonic Code   Systematic law code established by Napoleon that (among other principals) emphasized individuals' rights to property and standardized the legal structures for contracts, leases, and establishing stock corporations.

Narmer   See **Menes**.

National Assembly   In France, the governing body that succeeded the Estates General in 1789 during the French Revolution. It was composed of, and defined by, the delegates of the Third Estate.

nationalism   A collective consciousness or awareness that the members of an individual nation-group share a depth of feelings, values, and attitudes toward the world.

National Society of Women's Suffrage   The first national group in the United Kingdom to campaign for women's right to vote. Formed in 1867, the organization helped lay the foundations of the women's suffrage movement.

Nazism   The political movement in Germany led by Adolf Hitler, which advocated a violent anti-Semitic, anti-Marxist, pan-German ideology.

Neoplatonism   Spiritual philosophy derived from Plato that influenced both late Roman paganism and early Christian theologians.

New Deal   American economic initiatives launched by President Franklin Delano Roosevelt to help the nation recover from the Great Depression by increasing government spending to employ men and women, provide price supports for farmers, offer unemployment insurance and retirement benefits, and create welfare programs.

New Economic Policy   The policy adopted in 1921 by the **Bolsheviks** after they abandoned War Communism. Under the NEP, the state still controlled all major industries and financial concerns, although individuals could own private property, trade freely within limits, and farm their own land for their own benefit. Fixed taxes replaced grain requisition. The policy successfully helped Soviet agriculture recover from civil war.

New Historians   Young Jewish scholars and journalists, mostly born in Israel, whose archival research and writing has led to a more complex and less idealistic understanding of Zionism and the founding of Israel.

new imperialism   A period of colonial expansion—and its accompanying ideologies—by the European powers, the United States, and the empire of Japan during the late 19th and early 20th centuries.

New Testament   Canon of twenty-seven works written after the death of Christ by or about various apostles.

Newton, Isaac   (1642–1727) One of the foremost scientists of all time, Newton was an English mathematician and physicist; he is especially noted for his development of calculus, work on the properties of light, and theory of gravitation.

New Woman   The subject of innumerable journalistic and literary works in Europe, America, and parts of the Islamic world; a woman who, from the 1880s on, thanks to tremendous economic, cultural, and political shifts, was free to travel, get an education, and have a career.

Nicene Creed   Statement of fundamental Christian beliefs issued by an ecumenical council convened by the Roman emperor Constantine in 323–325.

nihilism   Philosophical position of extreme skepticism that holds existence to be random, even meaningless.

Ninety-Five Theses   A list, published by **Martin Luther** in 1517, of assertions condemning the theology of **indulgences**.

North Atlantic Treaty Organization (NATO) Defensive alliance created by the United States in 1949 to protect western Europe.

Nuremberg Trials   Trials of Nazi leaders for war crimes before an international tribunal of judges and prosecutors from the Allied countries, held in 1945–1946 in Nuremberg, Germany.

O

Olympian deities   The numerous gods, worshipped by the ancient Greeks, whose passions and exploits are recounted in Greek mythology.

Operation Barbarossa   The codename for Hitler's invasion of the Soviet Union in 1941.

Organization of Petroleum Exporting Countries (OPEC)   Group of twelve oil-exporting countries that strongly influences both the production and the pricing of oil. A 1973 boycott by OPEC drove gas prices to record levels, disrupting the American economy.

Ottoman Turks   Dynasty founded by Osman (r. 1281–1324) that established a powerful state from the Balkans to Mesopotamia to North Africa.

P

pacifism   In the aftermath of World War I, a term used to describe any principled and total rejection of violence as a means of resolving disputes.

Pale of Settlement   Region of Russian Empire where Jews were allowed to live (they were generally not allowed to live anywhere else in Russia), and the site of devastating pogroms in the late 19th century.

Palestinian Liberation Organization (PLO) Political organization of Palestinian Arabs created in 1964 in opposition to the existence of the Jewish state of Israel.

pan-Arabism   Ideology promoting the unification of all Arabs, particularly in opposition to Western imperialism. See also **Ba'ath Party**.

Panhellenism   The "all-Greek" culture that allowed ancient Greek colonies to maintain a connection to their homeland and to each other through their shared language and heritage.

Pankhurst, Emmeline   (1858–1928) Organizer of a militant branch of the British suffrage movement, working actively for women's right to vote.

pan-Slavism   Populist approach of Tsar Alexander III (r. 1881–1894) that resulted in vicious persecution of Russian Jews, who were portrayed as exploiters of the common Russian people.

Pantheon   A temple built by the emperor Hadrian (r. 117–138 CE) in Rome and dedicated to the whole roster of major deities within the empire.

parlements   Ancient French aristocratic-led system of legal courts reestablished during the regency of Louis XV as a way to extend aristocratic privileges; Louis XV tried to overturn the parlements when he came of age.

parliament   A representative body having supreme legislative powers within a state or multinational organization.

pater familias   In the Roman Republic, the head (always male) of a household. The pater familias had complete authority over the familia and was the sole possessor of its property.

patrician   In ancient Rome, a member of a noble family or class.

patrilinear   Describes a social system in Mesopotamia and elsewhere, in which only men can inherit property.

Pax Romana   The "Roman Peace," a period of general peace and prosperity in the Roman Empire from Augustus (d. 14 CE) to Marcus Aurelius (d. 180 CE).

Peace of Augsburg   Compromise settlement (1555) between Charles V and Lutheran princes that granted Lutheranism legal recognition. With this policy, the religion of the local ruler determined the state religion of the principality, with certain guarantees offered for the rights of the religious minority.

Peace of Paris   The series of peace treaties (1919–1920) that provided the settlement of World War I. The Treaty of Versailles with Germany was the centerpiece of the Peace of Paris.

Peace of Westphalia   A collection of treaties (1648) negotiated by the first general diplomatic congress in Western history. Involving more than one hundred delegations, it brought a century of European conflict to a close.

Peloponnesian War   (431–404 BCE) Prolonged war between Athens, which sought to dominate all of Greece, and Sparta, one of the last holdouts against Athenian supremacy. An epidemic of typhus in 429 BCE weakened Athens, while the Spartans' alliance with Persia allowed them to challenge and defeat the Athenian navy.

Pentecostalism   American Protestant style of worship that is charismatic, even anti-intellectual, in its emphasis on a mystical union with God manifested by the ability to speak in tongues and perform miraculous healings.

perestroika   Collective term for the economic policies of Mikhail Gorbachev in the Soviet Union that allowed for the limited introduction of free-market mechanisms. "Restructuring," literally.

Pericles   (ca. 495–429 BCE) Athens's political leader during Greece's Golden Age.

Peter I   (r. 1689–1725) Russian tsar who undertook the Westernization of Russia and built a new capital city named after himself, St. Petersburg.

phalanx   A fighting unit of Greek foot soldiers: eight horizontal lines of ten to twenty men each, who stood shoulder to shoulder and moved as a single unit.

pharaoh   A term (meaning "household") that became the title borne by the rulers of ancient Egypt. The pharaoh was regarded as the divine representative of the gods and the embodiment of Egypt itself.

Pharisees   One of three "philosophical sects" into which Judean society was divided. Unlike other Jews, they held a belief in the immortality of the soul and the resurrection of the dead; they also anticipated the arrival of a messiah.

Philippine–American War   Armed conflict (1899–1902) between the United States and Filipino revolutionaries that arose from the struggle of the First Philippine Republic to secure independence from the United States following the latter's acquisition of the Philippines from Spain after the **Spanish–American War**.

philosophes   French for "philosophers"; public intellectuals of the Enlightenment, applied to all regardless of their homeland.

plebeians   The class of free landowning Roman citizens, represented in the government of the Roman Republic by the Plebeian Council.

plutocracy   From the Greek terms for "wealth" (*ploutos*) and "power" (*kratos*), a society or system ruled and dominated by the small minority of the richest citizens.

pogroms   Beginning in 1881, vicious attacks from 1648 on against entire Jewish communities in the **Pale of Settlement**.

polis   The ancient Greek city-state (plural form *poleis*).

pope   Bishop of Rome and leader of the worldwide Catholic Church. The power of the Roman bishop is largely derived from his role as the traditional successor to St. Peter, to whom, according to the Bible, Jesus gave the keys of Heaven, naming him the "rock" on which the church would be built.

Prague Spring   Reforms initiated in 1968 Communist Czechoslovakia by moderate leader Alexander Dubček, who described it as "socialism with a human face"; the reforms were squashed by a Soviet military intervention in August 1968.

predestination   The doctrine of **John Calvin** that God preordained salvation or damnation for each person before Creation; those chosen for salvation were considered the "elect."

Princeps   Title taken by the emperor Octavian, meaning "first in honor" (because his name appeared first on the censor's list of Roman citizens).

proletariat   A term popularized by Marx to describe the working classes. A revolution of the proletariat, Marx believed, would bring about the end of capitalism and the birth of a classless society.

protectionism   The blocking of imports by tariff barriers or other legal means to promote the interests of a domestic mercantilist economy.

Protestant Reformation   Movement initiated by Martin Luther that sought to re-create what he believed to be Christian belief and practice as they had existed in the apostolic church.

psychoanalysis   Technique associated with Sigmund Freud (1856–1939) that seeks to understand the unconscious mind.

Punic Wars   Three wars Rome fought with Carthage between 264 and 146 BCE, resulting in Roman dominance of the entire western Mediterranean basin.

putting-out system   See **cottage industry**.

Pythagoreans   Group of philosophers named after Pythagoras (570–495 BCE), who had developed the famous theorem about right triangles. They sought to identify rational order and laws governing the natural world; hence their focus on mathematics.

Q

qadi   Islamic religious judge.

al-Qaeda   "The Base," literally. Islamic terrorist organization created in the late 1980s by former rebels against the Soviet Army in Afghanistan. Led by Osama bin Laden until his death in 2011.

quantum theory   New theory of physics proposed by Max Planck (1858–1947) suggesting that both light and matter exist as waves and as particles.

Qur'an   The holy book of Islam, revealed to the Prophet Muhammad.

R

rabbi   An honorific Hebrew word meaning "my master." Rabbis were originally teachers of Jewish Law. During the Babylonian Captivity, far from their ruined Temple, many Jews turned to their rabbis for religious guidance. Rabbis became leaders of the exiled Jews and during this time refined the laws governing Jewish life.

Ramses II (r. ca. 1279–1213 BCE) Also known as Ramses the Great, he is often regarded as the most powerful and celebrated pharaoh of the Egyptian Empire. In addition to building cities, temples, and monuments, he led several military expeditions eastward, reasserting Egyptian control over Canaan, and also southward, into Nubia.

Rape of Nanjing Atrocities perpetrated by invading Japanese soldiers in the Chinese capital of Nanjing in December 1937–January 1938. Hundreds of thousands of Chinese civilians were brutally murdered.

rationalism The essential characteristic of Greek thought, from Mycenaean times to the earliest known philosophers of Miletus (Thales, Anaximander, and Anaximenes); attempts to explain the natural world through observation rather than through mythology.

Realpolitik Politics based on strategic and tactical realities instead of idealism.

Reconquista "Reconquest," in Spanish. Refers to the long struggle (985–1492) between Christian and Muslim warlord-princes for control of the Iberian Peninsula.

redistributive taxation Taxation that is intended to spread incomes more fairly among people by taxing rich people more and poor people less.

Reichstag Name of the lower parliamentary chamber in the German imperial government, 1871–1945.

Reign of Terror Brutal period of the French Revolution (1792) during which, at the direction of Robespierre, tens of thousands of French citizens believed to be opposed in any way to the Revolution were executed.

relativity In physics, the concept that every vantage point in the universe, whether moving or stationary, is as valid as every other vantage point; as a cultural metaphor, the new and possibly frightening idea that there are no fixed points, no absolute time, and no absolute space.

Renaissance Literally "rebirth" (French); an era of tremendous cultural achievement as artists, scholars, and philosophers rediscovered the works of classical Greece and Rome and applied those ideas and aesthetics to contemporary arts, humanism, and modern statecraft.

res publica Latin term for "republic" or "commonwealth"; a form of government based on a system of checks and balances that emerged in Rome in 509 BCE.

Rhodes, Cecil (1853–1902) A British businessman, mining magnate, and politician in South Africa. An ardent believer in British colonialism, Rhodes was the founder of the southern African territory of Rhodesia (modern Zimbabwe), which was named after him in 1895.

Risorgimento "Resurgence," literally; the name given to the 19th-century movement for Italian national reunification.

Robespierre, Maximilien (1758–1794) A French lawyer and politician who, as leader of the Committee of Public Safety, laid out the principles of a "republic of virtue" and of the Terror, a period of French Revolutionary violence marked by mass executions of "enemies of the Revolution." His arrest and execution in July 1794 brought an end to the Terror.

Romanticism Cultural and artistic movement in opposition to industrialization, preferring emotion and instinct over structural order and rational thought.

Rousseau, Jean-Jacques (1712–1778) One of the most important **philosophes**, he argued that only a government based on a social contract among the citizens could make people truly moral and free.

Rule of Saint Benedict A communal handbook written by Saint Benedict of Nursia (480–547) to guide the monastery he had established; its focus on the physical and intellectual as well as spiritual well-being of monks led to its being widely adopted by monastic communities across medieval Europe.

Rumi (1207–1273) Sufi poet whose work championed Islam without disparaging other faiths.

Russo-Japanese War In this armed conflict (1904–1905), Japanese and Russian expansion collided in Mongolia and Manchuria. Russia was humiliated after the Japanese navy sank its fleet, which helped provoke a revolt in Russia and led to an American-brokered peace treaty.

S

Sadducees One of three "philosophical sects" into which Judean society was divided; a party of aristocrats who were reputedly strict upholders of Temple ritual, dedicated to the literal reading of scripture and the rejection of the oral Torah.

Saint Bartholomew's Day Massacre Riot (August 23–29, 1572) between Catholics and Protestant Huguenots that began in Paris and spread across France, resulting in the deaths of thousands.

salons In urban, Enlightenment-era society, regular gatherings, often hosted by wealthy or aristocratic women in their own homes, to which **philosophes**, artists, and other cultural figures were invited to discuss ideas.

sans-culottes "Those without breeches," literally. Colloquial reference to political Revolutionary militants in Paris drawn from the lower orders.

Sappho (ca. 620–550 BCE) The most famous woman lyric poet of Ancient Greece, Sappho was revered as the "Tenth Muse" and emulated by many male poets. "Lesbian" is derived from Lesbos, her native island.

Sargon I (r. 2334–2279 BCE) The Akkadian ruler who consolidated power in Mesopotamia.

Schlieffen Plan Military strategy created by German chief of general staff Alfred Graf von Schlieffen in 1905 that called for German forces to circumvent French defenses by striking swiftly through Belgium and Luxembourg; this was exactly how Germany proceeded at the start of World War I nine years later.

scholasticism Method of research and teaching in medieval universities, characterized by the application of Aristotelian logic and the attempt to harmonize all knowledge.

scientific management Management theory that increases the productivity of labor by breaking down manufacturing into small, distinct steps.

scientific method The combination of experimental observation and mathematical deduction used to determine the laws of nature; first developed in the 17th century, it became the secular standard of truth.

Scientific Revolution From 1500 to 1700, a cultural, philosophical, and intellectual shift from a view of the universe as divinely created to a concept of the natural world as a system that could be understood through study and observation.

Second Industrial Revolution Continuation of the earlier Industrial Revolution, but with a focus instead on producing capital goods (goods, such as steel and chemicals, used to produce other goods).

Second Vatican Council Convened by Pope John XXIII (r. 1958–1963) as part of the effort to modernize the church's teachings and governance.

second-wave feminism Women's movement in the 1960s and 1970s that focused on sexual health, access to abortion and contraception, equal rights in the workplace, childcare services, gender roles in society, and portrayals of women in popular culture. (The "first wave" of feminism had focused almost exclusively on women's suffrage.)

secularism The declining power of religious beliefs and institutions and the subsequent decline in religious practice.

Sephardim Jewish people centered around the Mediterranean, where they remained in constant contact with Arab, Greek, and Latin cultural developments.

Septuagint A Greek translation of the Hebrew Bible created by a group of seventy-two scholars who convened in Alexandria around 260 BCE (the name is derived from the Greek word for "seventy"). It includes several books later excluded from the Jewish canon.

serfs Dependent farmers who performed labor on manors in exchange for the security and primitive justice provided by the landlord.

Seven Years' War A worldwide series of battles (1756–1763) between Austria, France, Russia, and Sweden on the one side and Prussia and Great Britain on the other.

Sha'arawi, Huda'i (1879–1947) Pioneering Egyptian feminist leader, nationalist, and founder of the Egyptian Feminist Union.

shah Persian term for "emperor."

shari'a Islamic religious law.

Shi'a Muslims who believe that political and religious legitimacy can pass only to members of the Prophet Muhammad's hereditary line.

simony Paying money or presenting gifts in return for ecclesiastical office, a widespread abuse in the Roman Catholic Church in the post-Carolingian era that inspired the Gregorian Reform.

Six-Day War Military action (June 5–10, 1967) initiated by Israel against Egypt, Jordan, and Syria; Israel seized the Gaza Strip, the Golan Heights along the Israeli border with Syria, the Sinai Peninsula, and the entire West Bank, including the eastern part of the then-divided city of Jerusalem. After the stunning defeat of Arab allies, much of Arab popular resentment turned toward the United States.

Skepticism In ancient Greece, the philosophical school based on the fundamental idea that nothing can be known for certain: our senses are easily fooled, and reason follows too easily our desires.

Smith, Adam (1723–1790) Scottish economist and liberal philosopher who proposed that competition between self-interested individuals led naturally to a healthy economy. He became famous for his influential book *The Wealth of Nations* (1776).

Social Catholicism   Nineteenth-century European Catholic movement founded on the idea that the challenge to Christian society under industrialism was structural rather than personal.

social contract   Articulated in Thomas Hobbes's *Leviathan* (1651), the theory that when people decide to live in community they enter a covenant with each other, compromising their individual free wills in return for the benefits of society. Government, which bears responsibility for preserving social stability, may therefore legitimately assert its will on the community whenever it deems it necessary to do so.

social Darwinism   Misuse of Darwin's theory of evolution by natural selection to morally justify imperialism as a healthy competition among societies.

socialism   A social and political ideology, originating in the early 19th century, that advocated the reorganization of society to overcome the new tensions created by industrialization and restore social harmony through communities based on cooperation.

Socratic method   The Athenian philosopher Socrates's method of teaching through conversation, in which he asked probing questions to make his listeners examine their assumptions.

Solomon   (according to tradition, r. ca. 970– 931 BCE) A king of Israel and son of **David**; the Hebrew Bible credits Solomon as the builder of the First Temple in Jerusalem.

Solon   (d. 559 BCE) Athenian political reformer whose changes promoted early democracy.

Song of Songs   Biblical book, also known as the Song of Solomon, consisting of a poetic dialogue between a bride and bridegroom. Centuries of scholars have interpreted the Song of Songs as an allegory of the covenant between God and his people.

Sophists   In Greece in the 5th century BCE, a group of thinkers who traveled from city to city teaching rhetoric and philosophy.

South Sea Bubble   Economic crash (1720) sparked when the South Sea Company, an English company formed to trade with Spanish colonies in the New World, encouraged investors to speculate wildly on its supposed ventures but then could not make good on its unrealistic promises.

space-time   Einstein's concept of time and space as elastic and therefore understood as different facets of a single dimension.

Spanish–American War   War (1898) between the United States and Spain in Cuba, Puerto Rico, and the Philippines. It ended with a treaty in which the United States took over the Philippines, Guam, and Puerto Rico; Cuba won partial independence.

Spanish Civil War   Internal conflict (1936– 1939) between conservative and liberal forces in Spain that drew anti-Fascist support from around the world. The conservatives, under the Fascist dictator Francisco Franco (r. 1936– 1975), won.

special theory of relativity   Einstein's theory (1905) that maintains that all measurements of space and time are relative; the basis of the idea that nothing can go faster than the speed of light.

spinning jenny   Invention of Englishman James Hargreaves (ca. 1720–1774) that revolutionized the British textile industry by allowing a worker to spin much more thread than was possible on a hand spinner.

Stalin, Joseph   (1879–1953) Soviet leader who, with considerable backing, formed a brutal dictatorship in the 1930s and forcefully converted the country into an industrial power.

Stöcker, Helene   (1869–1943) German feminist, pacifist, and sexual reformer. In 1905 she helped found the League for the Protection of Mothers.

Stoicism   Philosophy most famously described and taught by Seneca (4 BCE–65 CE) and Epictetus (55–135 CE) that conformed to Roman morals through an emphasis on duty, forbearance, self-discipline, and concern for others.

suffrage   The right to vote.

suffragettes   European activists for women's rights who, in contrast with **suffragists**, favored confrontation, aggressive action, and, whenever they thought it necessary, even violence to change society.

suffragists   Activists for women's rights who, in contrast with **suffragettes**, worked peaceably and within the legal system for women's rights.

Sufism   A mystical, esoteric approach to Islam that flourished in the Ottoman Empire.

sultan   "Commander," literally. Term for chief military officer in the Turkish Empire. Under the Ottomans, the word came to represent the head of state.

Sultanate of Women   Period (1640s and 1650s) of the Ottoman Empire when leading members of the imperial harem effectively controlled the state, directed foreign policy, and oversaw the fiscal system.

summa   A "summary," or an encyclopedic effort to organize all thought on a given topic; a popular genre among the scholastic writers of the 13th and 14th centuries, representing the conviction that a rational order underlies all of human life.

sunnah   The collected sayings and actions of the Prophet Muhammad, used to establish Islamic legal precedents.

Sunni   Muslims who regard selection by the community as the sole legitimate means to leadership of the Islamic world.

supermen   Term used by Friedrich Nietzsche (1844–1900) to describe cultural, political, and intellectual figures with a will to power.

Sykes–Picot Agreement   Pact between England and France (1916) that took advantage of the **Arab Revolt** to divide the dominions of the Middle East between the two nations.

Syllabus of Errors   Sixty-five teachings Pope Pius X decreed irredeemably anti-Catholic in two 1907 encyclicals.

symposia   All-male drinking parties in ancient Greece where philosophical ideas were discussed.

syncretism   The merging of religious doctrines.

T

Talmud   Codification of rabbinical law and commentary that became central to Jewish life starting in the Middle Ages. Two dominant forms exist: the Babylonian Talmud, compiled around 500 CE, and the Palestinian Talmud (also known as the Jerusalem Talmud), compiled around 400 CE. Reference to the "Talmud" usually means the Babylonian Talmud.

Tamerlane   (r. ca. 1370–1405) A Turkish-Mongol conqueror and the founder of the Timurid dynasty in Central Asia, Tamerlane is considered the last of the great nomadic conquerors of the Eurasian steppe; his empire set the stage for the rise of the more structured and lasting gunpowder empires in the 16th and 17th centuries. Also known as "Timur."

Tanakh   A common name for the canonical Hebrew Bible—an acronym based on the letters T (for Torah, meaning "Instructions"), N (for Nevi'im, or "Prophets"), and K (for Ketuvim, or "Writings"). Traditionally believed to have been assembled by the "Men of the Great Assembly" around 450 BCE, modern scholars believe the compilation occurred later, between 200 BCE and 200 CE.

Tanzimat   (Turkish, "reorganization"); a 19th-century movement by the Ottoman government to promote economic development and the integration of the empire's non-Muslims and non-Turks into civil society.

telos   According to Aristotle, the intrinsic purpose or necessary role in the cosmic drama of every existing thing.

Tennis Court Oath   Oath taken by representatives of the Third Estate in June 1789, in which they pledged to form a **National Assembly** and write a constitution limiting the powers of the king.

tetrarchy   Under Diocletian, a new system whereby the Roman Empire was formally divided into two halves, with a separate emperor (*augustus*, in Latin) for each. Each half was further divided in half again, and each augustus therefore had a subordinate vice emperor, or *caesar*.

themes   New system of organizing the army under Byzantine emperor Heraclius in the 7th century that redistributed land to military officers and soldiers.

theory of evolution by natural selection   As explained by Charles Darwin in his 1859 book *On the Origin of Species by Means of Natural Selection*, the process by which the superabundance of offspring produced by all living beings results in their competition for resources; over time, that competition favors traits in offspring that provide an advantage over their rivals.

Thermidorian Reaction   The violent backlash against the rule of **Robespierre** that dismantled the Terror.

Third Estate   The branch of the French legislative body made up of elected representatives of the common people, including the bourgeoisie and wage earners. See also **Estates General**.

third-wave feminism   A movement beginning in the early 1990s and continuing to the present, it arose partially as a response to the perceived failures of and backlash against **second-wave feminism**. Unlike the determined positions of second-wave feminists, third-wave feminists emphasize the diversity of female experience and multiple avenues to female empowerment.

Thirty Years' War   Conflict that began in 1618 between Protestants and Catholics in Germany and gradually enveloped most of Europe, ending in 1648 after massive losses of life and property.

Tokyo Trials   Trials (1946–1948) of Japanese officials for war crimes before an international tribunal of judges and prosecutors from the Allied countries.

Torah   The first five books of the **Tanakh**, attributed to Moses.

totalitarianism   A system of government that controls all aspects of society, using fear and intimidation to maintain power.

Treaty of Rome   Treaty agreed to by western European leaders in 1957 that established the European Economic Community to help postwar recovery and counterbalance American economic power.

Treaty of Verdun   The treaty that, in 843, split the Carolingian Empire into three parts; its borders roughly outline modern western European states.

Treaty of Versailles   Controversial agreements that formally ended World War I on June 28, 1919; ruinous concessions demanded from a defeated Germany were a contributing factor in the run-up to World War II.

trireme   Ancient Greek warship with three tiers of oarsmen and a bronze-tipped battering ram on the prow.

twelve apostles   According to the Bible, the primary disciples of **Jesus**, who became the primary teachers of his gospel message.

Twelve Tables   The first written law code of the Roman Republic, ca. 450 BCE.

tyrant   A person in a Greek polis who took power temporarily to bring about dramatic reform in a politically deadlocked state. In terms of social class, the tyrants were aristocrats but were allied with the masses.

U

'ulama   Arab for "brotherhood" or "community," a central focus of Sunni life.

Umayyads   Name of the ruling dynasty in the Islamic Empire, 661–750. Governing the empire from their new capital at Damascus, the Umayyads were overthrown in 750 by the **Abbasids**, who transferred the capital to the newly built Baghdad.

ummah   The community of Muslim believers.

uniformitarianism   Scottish geologist James Hutton's theory that geological change consists of the slow accumulation of smaller changes—and these changes continue to happen in the present.

United Nations (UN)   Organization of member nations established in 1945, including a permanently standing International Court of Justice and International Criminal Court.

Universal Declaration of Human Rights   The first statement of global rights in history, drafted and promoted by American First Lady Eleanor Roosevelt and approved on December 10, 1948, by most members of the United Nations (Saudi Arabia, South Africa, and the Soviet Union abstained).

urbanism   The growth of towns and cities resulting from the movement of people from rural to urban areas; this trend was encouraged by the development of factories and railroads.

V

vassal   In a feudal system, a free man who pledges to serve a lord in exchange for dominion over a manor or manors bestowed by the lord.

vizier   Regional administrator under the Abbasid dynasty and later under the Ottomans. From the word meaning "burden sharer."

Voltaire   (1694–1778) The pen name of François-Marie Arouet, leading **philosophe** and one of the most influential writers of the Enlightenment.

W

Wahhabism   Conservative reform movement within Sunni Islam, taking its name from the 18th-century figure Muhammad ibn Abd al-Wahhab. The movement stresses returning to strict reliance on the Qur'an and hadith, purging Islam of non-Arabic traditions, and restoring ethnic Arabs to leadership in international Islam. The official sect in Saudi Arabia in the 20th and 21st centuries.

War of the Roses   English civil war for the throne (1455–1485) fought between the noble houses of York and Lancaster.

welfare states   In post–World War II Western Europe, societies in which the central government, funded by heavy taxation, provided all essential social services.

Wergild   Old Germanic term—"man money," literally—for the compensation owed by an offender to his victim, according to custom.

will to power   Term used by German philosopher Friedrich Nietzsche (1844–1900) to describe the passionate striving to make meaning and leave a mark on the world.

Women's International League for Peace and Freedom   Pacifist group founded in 1915 that campaigned for equal rights for all citizens, economic justice, and greater understanding and empathy between peoples.

Women's Social and Political Union   Militant organization founded in 1903 that campaigned for women's suffrage in Great Britain. It was led by **Emmeline Pankhurst** and is best known for hunger strikes, for breaking windows in prominent buildings, and for arson of unoccupied houses and churches.

World Trade Organization   Intergovernmental organization seeking to liberalize trade between nations.

Y

YHWH   The term for "God" used by the Yahwist author of the Torah (see **Documentary Hypothesis**), represented in English-language Bibles by the all-capitals word LORD.

Young Turks   Modernizing faction in Turkey that promoted pan-ethnic Islamic nationalism, overthrowing the sultan Abdul Hamid II in 1909 and replacing him with his half-brother Mehmed V (r. 1909–1918).

Z

ziggurats Step-pyramid temples of ancient Mesopotamia, believed to be the dwelling places of the gods.

Zionism From Hebrew *Tsiyon*, the name for the central portion of Jerusalem, but by extension referring to all of Israel/Palestine. Movement by Jews (especially from eastern Europe) to establish a Jewish state in the Holy Land as a refuge from European persecution beginning in the 19th century.

Zollverein See **Customs Union**.

Zoroastrianism Monotheistic religion founded by Zoroaster in Persia ca. 1300 BCE. In its emphasis on moral behavior, personal salvation, and the eventual victory of Good in a cosmic battle with Evil, Zoroastrianism is considered by many a precursor of Judaism (and, by extension, Christianity).

Credits

CHAPTER 1: pg. xxxviii: De Agostini Picture Library/G. Dagli Orti/Bridgeman Images; pg. xl: © jaroslava V/Shutterstock; pg. 2: Copyright © The Trustees of the British Museum; pg. 6: Çatalhöyük Research Project; pg. 15: North-eastern facade of the ziggurat, c.2100 BC (photo)/Ur, Iraq/© World Religions Photo Library/Bridgeman Images; pg.16: Erich Lessing/Art Resource, NY; pg.19: © The Trustees of the British Museum/Art Resource, NY; pg. 25: Werner Forman/ Art Resource, NY; pg. 26: Erich Lessing/Art Resource, NY; pg. 29: © AGF Srl/Alamy; pg. 32: De Agostini Picture Library/C. Sappa/Bridgeman Images

CHAPTER 2: pg. 36: HIP/Art Resource, NY; pg. 39: Erich Lessing/Art Resource, NY; pg. 46: © Trustees of the British Museum; pg. 48: Gianni Dagli Orti/The Art Archive at Art Resource, NY; pg. 50: © DeA Picture Library/Art Resource, NY; pg. 52: Erich Lessing/Art Resource, NY; pg. 57: Drawn by Boudier, from a photograph by Beato; pg. 58: National Museum of Iran, Tehran, Iran/ Bridgeman Images; pg. 62: Erich Lessing/Art Resource, NY; pg. 64: Gianni Dagli Orti/The Art Archive at Art Resource, NY; pg. 66: © Tim Page/ CORBIS

CHAPTER 3: pg. 70: Courtesy of the Library of Congress; pg. 75: © Rafael Ben-Ari/Alamy; pg. 82: Private Collection/The Stapleton Collection/ Bridgeman Images; pg. 84: Erich Lessing/Art Resource, NY; pg. 85: Ruth and Naomi, Copping, Harold (1863-1932)/Private Collection/© Look and Learn/Bridgeman Images; pg. 94: Art Resource, NY; pg. 95: Erich Lessing/Art Resource, NY

CHAPTER 4: pg. 98: Marie Mauzy/Art Resource, NY; pg. 103: © Rob Rayworth/Alamy; pg. 104: Album/Art Resource, NY; pg. 105: © Kat Kallou/ Alamy; pg. 108: Erich Lessing/Art Resource, NY; pg. 112: Gianni Dagli Orti/The Art Archive at Art Resource, NY; pg. 112: Image copyright © The Metropolitan Museum of Art. Image source: Art Resource, NY; pg. 116: Greek, Archaic, about 540 B.C.E. Place of manufacture: Greece, Laconia, Sparta. Bronze. H. 12.8 cm (5 1/16 in). Museum of Fine Arts, Boston; Museum purchase with funds donated by contributions, 85-515. Photograph © 2015 Museum of Fine Arts, Boston; pg. 122: Image courtesy of the Ohio Statehouse Photo Archive; pg. 126: Album/Art Resource, NY

CHAPTER 5: pg. 128: Victoria & Albert Museum, London, UK/Ancient Art and Architecture Collection Ltd./Bridgeman Images; pg.132: © Paul Liebhardt/Alamy; pg. 133: © The Trustees of the British Museum/Art Resource, NY; pg. 135: bpk, Berlin/Staatliche Antikensammlung/Hermann Buresch/Art Resource, NY; pg. 137: Erich Lessing/Art Resource, NY; pg. 139: © Balage Balogh/ Art Resource, NY; pg. 150: Image copyright © The Metropolitan Museum of Art. Image source: Art Resource, NY; pg. 152: © Vanni Archive/ Art Resource, NY; pg. 154: Scala/Art Resource, NY; pg. 154: Erich Lessing/Art Resource, NY; pg. 158: Erich Lessing/Art Resource, NY; pg. 162: The Art Archive at Art Resource, NY; pg. 163: Alinari/Art Resource, NY

CHAPTER 6: pg. 170: © Jon Arnold Images Ltd/ Alamy; pg. 176: Scala/Art Resource, NY; pg. 180: © Araldo de Luca/CORBIS; pg. 184: © Vanni Archive/ Art Resource, NY; pg. 188: De Agostini Picture Library/A. Dagli Orti/Bridgeman Images; pg. 195: Alinari/Art Resource, NY; pg. 198: Ancient Art and Architecture Collection Ltd.; pg. 201: Erich Lessing/Art Resource, NY; pg. 204: © Roger Wood/CORBIS

CHAPTER 7: pg. 208: Erich Lessing/Art Resource, NY; pg. 212: Scala/Ministero per i Beni e le Attività culturali/Art Resource, NY; pg. 214: Cincinnati Art Museum, Ohio, USA/Gift of Mr. and Mrs. Fletcher E. Nyce/Bridgeman Images; pg. 222: Steps leading up to the Huldah Gates (photo)/Jerusalem, Israel/Photo © Zev Radovan/ Bridgeman Images; pg. 226: Scala/Art Resource, NY; pg. 232: Erich Lessing/Art Resource, NY; pg. 234: Erich Lessing/Art Resource, NY; pg. 235: © Corbis

CHAPTER 8: pg. 240: Museo Arqueologico Nacional, Madrid, Spain/Bridgeman Images; pg. 243: Scala/Art Resource, NY; pg. 245: Courtesy of the Oriental Institute of the University of Chicago; pg. 248: Courtesy of the Kekelidze Institute of Manuscripts, Tbilisi, Georgia; pg. 250: Mondadori Portfolio/Electa/Giuseppe Schiavinotto/Bridgeman Images; pg. 256: Bridgeman-Giraudon/Art Resource, NY; pg. 256: © Vanni Archive/ Art Resource, NY; pg. 267: Erich Lessing/ Art Resource, NY; pg. 268: © Werner Forman/ Corbis; pg. 272: © British Library Board/Robana/ Art Resource, NY

CHAPTER 9: pg. 276: age fotostock/SuperStock; pg. 281: © STOCKFOLIO®/Alamy; pg. 284: © The Trustees of the Chester Beatty Library, Dublin/ Bridgeman Images; pg. 288: © Silvija Seres; pg. 289: © Kazuyoshi Nomachi/Corbis; pg. 292:

Scala/Art Resource, NY; pg. 298: Iman Zahdah Chah Zaid Mosque, Isfahan, Iran/Index/Bridgeman Images; pg. 302: BN, Arabe 5847, fol 5v

CHAPTER 10: pg. 308: Bridgeman-Giraudon/Art Resource, NY; pg. 317: Bibliotheque Nationale, Paris, France/Bridgeman Images; pg. 319: Alfredo Dagli Orti/The Art Archive at Art Resource, NY; pg. 327: Textile/Universal History Archive/UIG/Bridgeman Images; pg. 330: Photononstop/SuperStock; pg. 334: bpk, Berlin/ Dietmar Katz/Art Resource, NY; pg. 339: Erich Lessing/Art Resource, NY; pg. 342: Art Resource, NY; pg. 347: Erich Lessing/Art Resource, NY

CHAPTER 11: pg. 352: © DeA Picture Library/ Art Resource, NY; pg. 359: Erich Lessing/Art Resource, NY; pg. 362: Erich Lessing/Art Resource, NY; pg. 363: Archive Timothy McCarthy/Art Resource, NY; pg. 368: © JTB MEDIA CREATION, Inc./Alamy; pg. 370: Album/Art Resource, NY; pg. 374: © RMN-Grand Palais/Art Resource, NY; pg. 377: Snark/Art Resource, NY; pg. 380: Scala/White Images/Art Resource, NY; pg. 384: Image copyright © The Metropolitan Museum of Art. Image source: Art Resource, NY; pg. 384: National Palace Museum, Beijing; pg. 387: The John Work Garrett Library, The Sheridan Libraries, The Johns Hopkins University; pg. 390: Werner Forman Archive/Museum of Islamic Art, Cairo. HIP/Art Resource, NY; pg. 395: Erich Lessing/Art Resource, NY

CHAPTER 12: pg. 398: Erich Lessing/Art Resource, NY; pg. 403: Santa Maria Novella, Florence, Italy/Bridgeman Images; pg. 405: © National Gallery, London/Art Resource, NY; pg. 408: Scala/Art Resource, NY; pg. 410: The Granger Collection, NYC—All rights reserved.; pg. 414: public domain; pg. 416: Scala/Art Resource, NY; pg. 419: Scala/Art Resource, NY; pg. 420: Deutsches Historisches Museum, Berlin, Germany/© DHM/ Bridgeman Images; pg. 421: © amphotos/Alamy; pg. 425: Photo: Albertina, Vienna, from Geisberg, Der deutsche Holzschnitt in der ersten Halfte des 16. Jahrhundert, Munchen 1923-1930; 30. Lieferung, Nr. 1243."; pg. 427: The Pierpont Morgan Library/ Art Resource, NY; pg. 432: © Sergej Borzov-Fotolia. com; pg. 434: National Portrait Gallery, London; pg. 438: Courtesy of the Library of Congress; pg. 442: Scala/Ministero per i Beni e le Attività culturali/Art Resource, NY; pg. 442: © RMN-Grand

Palais/Art Resource, NY; pg. 443: Courtesy José Luís Fernández-Castañeda, S.J., parish priest of the Church of San Pedro, Lima, and Administrator of the Jesuit Order in Peru.

CHAPTER 13: pg. 448: Private Collection/ © Look and Learn/Bridgeman Images; pg. 457: Snark/Art Resource, NY; pg. 459: Library of Congress, Rare Book and Special Collections Division; pg. 460: Peter Newark American Pictures; pg. 463: public domain; pg. 465: Erich Lessing/Art Resource, NY; pg. 465: Courtesy of the Library of Congress; pg. 467: Erich Lessing/Art Resource, NY; pg. 470: Caja de Ahorros de Valencia, Valencia, Spain/Index/Bridgeman Images; pg. 472: Erich Lessing/Art Resource, NY; pg. 475: Erich Lessing/ Art Resource, NY; pg. 477: Scala/Art Resource, NY; pg. 477: Bridgeman-Giraudon/Art Resource, NY; pg. 483: bpk, Berlin/National Portrait Gallery /Jochen Remmer/Art Resource, NY; pg. 488: Private Collection/Bridgeman Images

CHAPTER 14: pg. 492: Scala/Art Resource, NY; pg. 498: Scala/White Images/Art Resource, NY; pg. 501: Palazzo Barberini, Rome, Italy/Bridgeman Images; pg. 502: Woburn Abbey, Bedfordshire, UK/Bridgeman Images; pg. 505: Deutsches Historisches Museum, Berlin, Germany/© DHM/ Bridgeman Images; pg. 509: The Granger Collection, NYC—All rights reserved.; pg. 512: public domain ; pg. 515: Gianni Dagli Orti/The Art Archive at Art Resource, NY; pg. 518: Erich Lessing/ Art Resource, NY

CHAPTER 15: pg. 526: National Trust Photo Library/Art Resource, NY; pg. 533: © RMN-Grand Palais/Art Resource, NY; pg. 536: © British Library Board/Robana/Art Resource, NY; pg. 538: Gianni Dagli Orti/The Art Archive at Art Resource, NY; pg. 541: akg-images; pg. 543: © Chad Ehlers/ Alamy; pg. 544: Erich Lessing/Art Resource, NY; pg. 547: © Bristol Museum and Art Gallery, UK/ Bridgeman Images; pg. 548: © liszt collection/ Alamy; pg. 550: Nimatallah/Art Resource, NY; pg. 551: Norton Simon Collection, Pasadena, CA, USA/Bridgeman Images; pg. 553: © Photo: Bayerisches Nationalmuseum München, Bastian Krack. Fork: Inv. No. 36/37; Knife: Inv. No. 36/38; pg. 555: © Danita Delimont/Alamy; pg. 559: The Pierpont Morgan Library/Art Resource, NY; pg. 566: © Roger Wood/CORBIS; pg. 572: Eileen Tweedy/The Art Archive at Art Resource, NY

Index

Page numbers in *italics* indicate a map, table, or figure on the designated page.